W9-DHV-578

Silver Burdett Ginn
Mathematics

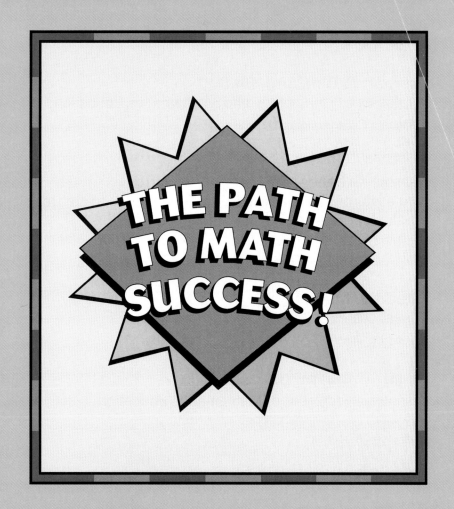

THE PATH TO MATH SUCCESS!

Silver Burdett Ginn
Parsippany, NJ

Atlanta, GA • Deerfield, IL • Irving, TX • Needham, MA • Upland, CA

Program Authors

Francis (Skip) Fennell, Ph.D.
Professor of Education and Chair, Education Department

Western Maryland College
Westminster, Maryland

Joan Ferrini-Mundy, Ph.D.
Professor of Mathematics

University of New Hampshire
Durham, New Hampshire

Herbert P. Ginsburg, Ph.D.
Professor of Psychology and Mathematics Education

Teachers College, Columbia University
New York, New York

Carole Greenes, Ed.D.
Professor of Mathematics Education and Associate Dean,
 School of Education

Boston University
Boston, Massachusetts

Stuart J. Murphy
Visual Learning Specialist

Evanston, Illinois

William Tate, Ph.D.
Associate Professor of Mathematics Education

University of Wisconsin-Madison
Madison, Wisconsin

Acknowledgements appear on page 546, which constitutes an extension of this copyright page.

©1999 Silver Burdett Ginn Inc. All rights reserved. Printed in the United States of America. This publication, or parts thereof, may not be reproduced in any form by photographic, electronic, mechanical, or any other method, for any use, including information storage and retrieval, without written permission from the publisher.

2 3 4 5 6 7 8 9 10 WC 07 06 05 04 03 02 01 00 99

Silver Burdett Ginn
A Division of Simon & Schuster
299 Jefferson Road, P.O. Box 480
Parsippany, NJ 07054-0480

Grade Level Authors

Mary Behr Altieri, M.S.
Mathematics Teacher
1993 Presidential Awardee
Lakeland Central School District
Shrub Oak, New York

Jennie Bennett, Ed.D.
Instructional Mathematics Supervisor
Houston Independent School District
Houston, Texas

Charles Calhoun, Ph.D.
Associate Professor of Elementary
  Education Mathematics
University of Alabama at Birmingham
Birmingham, Alabama

Lucille Croom, Ph.D.
Professor of Mathematics
Hunter College of the City University
  of New York
New York, New York

Robert A. Laing, Ph.D.
Professor of Mathematics Education
Western Michigan University
Kalamazoo, Michigan

Kay B. Sammons, M.S.
Supervisor of Elementary Mathematics
Howard County Public Schools
Ellicott City, Maryland

Marian Small, Ed.D.
Professor of Mathematics Education
University of New Brunswick
Fredericton, New Brunswick, Canada

Contributing Authors

Stephen Krulik, Ed.D.
Professor of Mathematics Education
Temple University
Philadelphia, Pennsylvania

Donna J. Long
Mathematics/Title 1 Coordinator
Metropolitan School District of
  Wayne Township
Indianapolis, Indiana

Jesse A. Rudnick, Ed.D.
Professor Emeritus of Mathematics
  Education
Temple University
Philadelphia, Pennsylvania

Clementine Sherman
Director, USI Math and Science
Dade County Public Schools
Miami, Florida

Bruce R. Vogeli, Ph.D.
Clifford Brewster Upton Professor of
  Mathematics
Teachers College, Columbia University
New York, New York

Contents

Chapter 1: All About Whole Numbers and Decimals

Multiplying and Dividing Whole Numbers and Decimals

Number Theory and Fractions

Chapter Theme: Travel

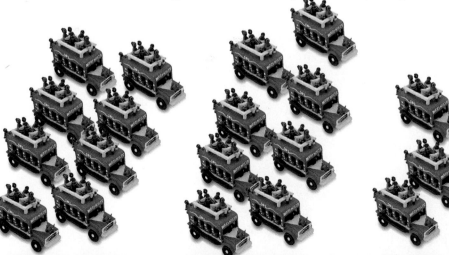

Chapter 5

Adding and Subtracting Fractions

Chapter 6

Multiplying and Dividing Fractions

Chapter Theme: Business
Real Facts: Donation Goals for United Negro College Fund 224
Real People: Donna Carter-Butler, Fund Raiser 224

Chapter 7

Measurement

32 USA

Centennial Olympic Games

Chapter Theme: Sports

Chapter 8
Ratio, Proportion, and Probability

Chapter Theme: Hobbies

Chapter 9 — Understanding and Using Percent

Chapter Theme: Shopping

Chapter 10

Geometry

Chapter Theme: Amusement Parks
Real Facts: Geometric Shapes Used in Computer Designs 384
Real People: Evelyn O'Shea, Virtual Reality Designer 384

Chapter 11

Perimeter, Area, and Volume

Chapter Theme: Field Day
Real Facts: Measurements of Miniature Golf Course Hole 432
Real People: Al Tirrell, Miniature Golf Course Designer 432

Integers and Equations

Chapter Theme: Fascinating Facts
Real Facts: Effects of Volcanic Eruptions 470
Real People: Christina Heliker, Volcanologist 470

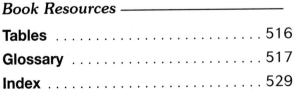

Becoming a Better Test Taker 539

Chapter 1

All About Whole Numbers and Decimals

Chapter Theme: OUR EARTH

Real-World Math

.....................Real Facts.....................

Every year, volunteers pick up garbage along miles of shoreline throughout the United States. The volunteers in this photograph are cleaning a beach in Texas.

In 1997, about 50,000 Californians took part in their annual Coastal Cleanup Day. They picked up about 500,000 lb of garbage and about 48,000 lb of recyclables! The table shows some of the more than 20 counties that participated.

California Coastal Cleanup Day 1997			
County	Volunteers	Trash (lb)	Recyclables (lb)
Del Norte	1,291	3,650	235
Mendocino	94	319	221
Sonoma	366	1,499	494
San Diego	6,000	15,000	7,000
Los Angeles	13,625	16,358	4,447

• How could you use place value to list the counties in order of pounds of trash collected?

• How would you graph the number of pounds of trash and recyclables collected?

.....................Real People.....................

Meet Ashley Bryan. He is a writer and artist who creates works of art from things he finds on the beach at Little Cranberry Island, Maine.

Using recycled objects to create art helps the environment and makes the world more beautiful!

Growing and Growing

Understanding place value can help you understand large numbers, such as those used by geographers.

Learning About It

The global environment includes the air, land, and water essential to all living things. Billions of people share these natural resources, and the number of people grows daily.

A place-value chart can help you to read the number on the population clock shown.

Period	BILLIONS			MILLIONS			THOUSANDS			ONES		
Place Value	hundred billions	ten billions	billions	hundred millions	ten millions	millions	hundred thousands	ten thousands	thousands	hundreds	tens	ones
		5,	8	2	4,	3	7	9,	5	1	9	

Word Bank

standard form
expanded form

The value of each digit in a number depends on its place. The first 5 in 5,824,379,519 is in the billions place. The value of the 5 is 5 × 1,000,000,000, or 5,000,000,000.

THERE'S ALWAYS A WAY!

Whole numbers can be expressed in many ways.

- **Standard form** 13,823,407,000
  Use commas to separate the number into periods.

- **Short word form** 13 billion, 823 million, 407 thousand.
  Write the number in each period followed by the period name (except for ones).

- **Expanded form** 10,000,000,000 + 3,000,000,000 + 800,000,000 + 20,000,000 + 3,000,000 + 400,000 + 7,000
  Show the value of each nonzero digit.

Think and Discuss What does the zero in 12,980,899,984 tell you? Why do you need this zero?

Try It Out

Write the value of the underlined digit in short word form.

1. 1,9<u>8</u>4,654 **2.** 7<u>1</u>,901,665 **3.** 12,144,7<u>6</u>4,984 **4.** 1<u>5</u>6,397,002

Practice

Write the value of the underlined digit in short word form.

5. 5,0<u>4</u>0,123 **6.** 91,01<u>4</u>,477 **7.** 10,4<u>5</u>6,789,000 **8.** 7,214,<u>9</u>62

9. 1,0<u>1</u>0,443 **10.** 325,<u>7</u>17 **11.** <u>2</u>1,455,390,200 **12.** 35,4<u>2</u>7,096

Write each number in short word form.

13. 45,237 **14.** 150,490 **15.** 6,540,004

16. 1,780,330, 040 **17.** 22,400,400,000 **18.** 1,500,000,243

Write each number in standard form.

19. 75 million, 420 thousand, 29 **20.** 4 billion, 305 million, 241 thousand

21. 14 billion, 10 thousand, 200 **22.** 9 billion, 9 million, 9 thousand, 9

23. Write each number in Exercises 19–22 in expanded form.

Problem Solving

Use the bar graph at the right to solve Problems 24–26.

24. Which region had a population in the billions in 1995?

25. How many regions are expected to have populations greater than one billion by 2010? Name the regions.

26. **Create Your Own** Make up a question that can be answered by using the graph. Then trade questions with a partner and solve.

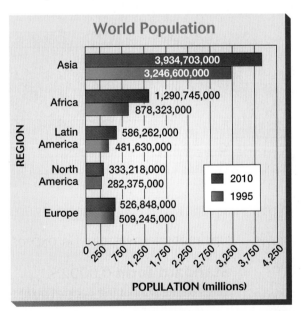

World Population

Region	2010	1995
Asia	3,934,703,000	3,246,600,000
Africa	1,290,745,000	878,323,000
Latin America	586,262,000	481,630,000
North America	333,218,000	282,375,000
Europe	526,848,000	509,245,000

POPULATION (millions)
0 250 750 1,250 1,750 2,250 2,750 3,250 3,750 4,250

INTERNET ACTIVITY
www.sbgmath.com

Review and Remember

Compute.

27. 15 − 8 **28.** 9 × 7 **29.** 16 + 7 **30.** 56 ÷ 8 **31.** 11 × 9

32. 6 × 4 **33.** 22 − 4 **34.** 36 ÷ 9 **35.** 26 + 9 **36.** 8 × 8

For Extra Practice, see Set A, page 38.

3

Up in the Air

How small is small? A chart of decimal place values can help you to understand decimals.

Industrial Pollution

Highway Dust

Asbestos

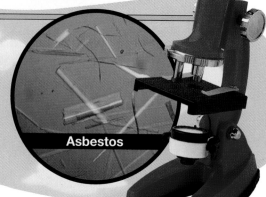

Learning About It

Many activities release particles, such as those shown in the pictures, into the air. Scientists search for ways to remove these particles to make our air safe to breathe.

What is the meaning of 0.00025? 0.005? You can extend the place-value chart used in Lesson 1 to help you read and write decimal numbers.

▲ Science Connection
The magnified photographs show particles ranging in diameter from 0.00025 mm to 0.005 mm. Particles this small can remain floating in air for several years.

		ONES		DECIMALS					
hundreds	tens	ones	tenths	hundredths	thousandths	ten-thousandths	hundred-thousandths	millionths	
		0 .	0	0	0	2	5		← **Read:** 25 hundred-thousandths
		0 .	0	0	5				← **Read:** 5 thousandths

THERE'S ALWAYS A WAY!

Decimal numbers can be expressed in many ways.

● **Standard form** 0.00025
Zeros to the right of the decimal point serve as placeholders.

● **Short word form** 25 hundred-thousandths
Write the number followed by the name of the last decimal place.

● **Expanded form** 0.0002 + 0.00005
Show the value of each nonzero digit.

Think and Discuss Look at these two numbers, 5,005 and 5.005. What do the two numbers have in common? How are the numbers different?

Try It Out

Write the value of the underlined digit in short word form.

1. 0.6̲2   **2.** 4.2̲35   **3.** 144.008̲   **4.** 1,506̲.0101   **5.** 23.0010̲3

6. Write each number in Exercises 1–5 in expanded form.

Write each number in standard form.

7. 5 hundredths   **8.** 45 thousandths   **9.** 7 and 9 hundred-thousandths

Practice

Write the value of the underlined digit in short word form.

10. 0.06̲2   **11.** 8.06̲2   **12.** 2.0000̲2   **13.** 2̲2.222   **14.** 5.000̲5

15. Write each number in Exercises 10–14 in expanded form.

Write each number in short word form.

16. 0.5   **17.** 0.005   **18.** 0.25   **19.** 0.00008   **20.** 10.005

21. 1.05   **22.** 0.105   **23.** 25.52   **24.** 105.0005   **25.** 0.0234

Write each number in standard form.

26. 7 ten-thousandths   **27.** 17 hundredths   **28.** 45 thousandths   **29.** 2 and 5 tenths

Problem Solving

30. Science Connection Pollen grains, which can cause allergic reactions in some people, range in size from 25 thousandths of a millimeter to 5 hundredths of a millimeter. Write these numbers in standard form.

31. Ordinary dust is made up of particles less than 0.0625 mm. Write this number in short word form.

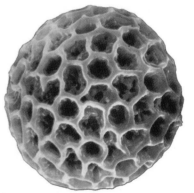
▲ Pollen grain magnified 100 times

Review and Remember

Using Algebra Find the value of n.

32. $12 - n = 7$ **33.** $6 + n = 14$ **34.** $54 \div n = 9$ **35.** $7 \times n = 42$

36. $15 + n = 28$ **37.** $49 \div n = 7$ **38.** $6 \times n = 48$ **39.** $16 - n = 7$

For Extra Practice, see Set B, page 38.

Come to Order

You can use place value to compare and order whole numbers and decimals.

Learning About It

Many countries establish national parks to protect wilderness areas and the wildlife the areas support. Which of the parks shown in the pictures is the largest?

To find out, compare the sizes of the parks. When dealing with more than two numbers, compare the numbers two at a time. Start at the left and compare digits in the same place-value position.

Yellowstone National Park
2,219,791 acres

$$3 > 2 \begin{cases} 2,219,791 \\ 3,584,000 \\ 113,370 \end{cases} 3 > 0$$

Serengeti is the largest park shown.

More Examples

A. Which decimal is greater, 0.357 or 0.359?

Start at the left and compare digits in the same place.

0 . 3 5 **7**
0 . 3 5 **9**   9 > 7

same

0.359 > 0.357

B. Which decimal is less, 2.34 or 2.3?

Start at the left and compare digits in the same place. Annex zeros where necessary.

2 . 3 **4**
2 . 3 **0**   0 < 4

same

2.3 < 2.34

C. Which decimal is the greatest, 1.4357, 1.3475, or 1.4375?

Compare two numbers at a time, starting at the left.

1 . **4** 3 5 7
1 . **3** 4 7 5   4 > 3

same

1.4357 > 1.3475

1 . 4 3 **5** 7
1 . 4 3 **7** 5   7 > 5

same

1.4375 > 1.4357

1.4375 is greatest.

Serengeti National Park
3,584,000 acres

Braulio Carrillo National Park
113,370 acres

Connecting Ideas

Once you have compared the numbers in a list, you can arrange them in order, from greatest to least or least to greatest.

INTERNET ACTIVITY
www.sbgmath.com

Order the parks from greatest to least.

Start at the left and compare digits in the same place.

2,219,791
3,584,000 ← greatest
113,370

Now compare the two remaining numbers.

2,219,791 ← greater

113,370

3,584,000 > 2,219,791 > 113,370
Serengeti > Yellowstone > Braulio Carrillo

More Examples

A. Order the decimals from least to greatest. Start at the left and compare digits in the same place.

0.347
0.349
0.336 ← least
‿
same

0.347 ← less
0.349
same

0.336 < 0.347 < 0.349

B. Order the decimals from least to greatest. Annex zeros where necessary.

2.71
2.60 ← less
2.65
‿
same

2.71
2.65 ← less
‿
same

2.6 < 2.65 < 2.71

Think and Discuss Name two numbers between 5.7 and 5.8.

Try It Out

Compare. Use >, <, or = for each ●.

1. 15,674 ● 15,900   **2.** 104,671 ● 99,548   **3.** 18,499 ● 8,500

4. 0.34 ● 3.4   **5.** 0.7 ● 0.71   **6.** 1 ● 0.99

Write two numbers that are found between the numbers in each pair.

7. 4.8 and 4.89   **8.** 9 and 9.5   **9.** 54.8 and 54.9

Practice

Compare. Use >, <, or = for each ●.

10. 4.85 ● 4.84   **11.** 3,642 ● 3,652   **12.** 9.760 ● 9.76

13. 0.38 ● 1.38   **14.** 947 ● 9,470   **15.** 6.35 ● 6.357

Write the numbers in each set in order from least to greatest.

16. 2,590; 2,677; 4,500; 999   **17.** 16,488; 15,900; 10,003; 9,000

18. 3,000,000; 99,000; 210,876   **19.** 97; 76,098; 50.897; 500; 1,447

20. 0.56; 0.021; 0.003; 0.9   **21.** 2; 0.15; 1.5; 2.7; 0.03; 17

Write three numbers that are found between the numbers in each pair.

22. 1 and 2   **23.** 3,490 and 3,500

24. 0.17 and 0.2   **25.** 76 and 76.1

26. 9,598 and 10,000   **27.** 0.003 and 0.004

28. Create Your Own Create a six-digit whole number that can be increased by interchanging any two digits in the number.

29. Analyze What are the largest and the smallest four-digit numbers you can write using only the digits 0, 1, 2, and 3? Use each digit only once. Include decimals.

Social Studies Connection ➤
President Theodore Roosevelt (left) and John Muir are shown in Yosemite National Park. The two men worked together to establish national parks and protect forests.

Problem Solving

Use the graph about Yellowstone National Park to solve Problems 30–32.

30. Compare the attendance for July with that for August. Which is greater?

31. **Predict** If you were asked to predict which two months would have the fewest visitors to the park in a typical year, which months would you select? Explain.

32. **What If?** Suppose the September attendance doubled. Would the order of attendance from greatest to least change? Explain.

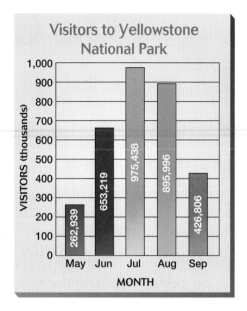

Visitors to Yellowstone National Park

Review and Remember

Complete each exercise.

33. 9×7 **34.** 9×70 **35.** $63 \div 7$ **36.** $630 \div 70$ **37.** $130 - 50$

Critical Thinking Corner

Visual Thinking

Babylonian Numbers

The early Babylonians used a simple grouping system to name numbers less than 60. The symbols they used are shown at the right. Study Examples A and B.

A.  $= 4 \times 10 - 2 = 38$

B.  $= 2 \times 10 + 5 = 25$

Name the numbers shown by the Babylonian symbols.

1.    **2.**    **3.**

Write each number, using Babylonian symbols.

4. 18   **5.** 59   **6.** 23   **7.** 35

For Extra Practice, see Set C, page 38.

Using Algebra

Do the Cancan

You can use variables to represent numbers in an equation or an expression.

Learning About It

Lynda has invented a machine for a science project. Her machine will separate tin cans from mixed trash and deposit them in a box.

The table shows what happens when four of Lynda's classmates use the machine.

Work with a partner.

Step 1 Find the combined weight of the cans and box after Winona's trash is separated. How did you find this weight?

Step 2 Let *w* represent the weight of the cans. Write a rule using *w* to find the combined weight of the cans and the box.

Your rule uses *w* as a variable. A **variable** is a letter used to represent an unknown.

Step 3 Test your rule by substituting the following values for the weight of the cans. Compare your results with the data in the table above.

$w = 5$ lb $w = 8$ lb $w = 10$ lb

Word Bank

variable
equation

Name	Weight of the Cans (in pounds)	Weight of the Cans and the Box (in pounds)
Joe	5	8
Paul	8	11
Sally	10	13
Winona	7	▪

Step 4 When Shirley used the machine, the combined weight of the cans and the box was 19 pounds. What was the weight of the cans? To find out, you can write an equation using the rule you wrote in Step 2. An **equation** is a number sentence with an equal sign.

Weight of the Cans		Weight of the Box		Combined Weight
w	$+$	3	$=$	19

$?\ + 3 = 19$ (What plus 3 equals 19?)

$16 + 3 = 19$

$w = 16$

The weight of the cans was 16 pounds.

Step 5 Find the value of each variable. Then check your work by replacing the variable with your answer and solving the equation.

a. $x + 2 = 5$ **b.** $p - 2 = 8$ **c.** $9 + n = 27$ **d.** $14 - y = 6$

Think and Discuss Use the pattern in the table to write a rule using the variable x.

2	15	6	x
7	20	11	■

Practice

Find the value for each expression.

1. $x + 5$ for $x = 3$ **2.** $y - 4$ for $y = 10$ **3.** $15 - b$ for $b = 14$ **4.** $p + 8$ for $p = 13$

Complete the pattern in the table. Then write a rule for finding the second entry using the variable x.

5.

1st Entry	2	6	10	8	14
2nd Entry	5	9	13	11	■

6.

1st Entry	8	12	5	20	29
2nd Entry	4	8	1	16	■

Using Mental Math Find the value of each variable. Then check your work.

7. $x + 4 = 7$ **8.** $p - 7 = 13$ **9.** $6 + n = 18$ **10.** $10 - y = 4$

11. Create Your Own Write a rule. Then make a table like those in Exercises 5 and 6. Have your partner figure out the rule for your table.

Developing Skills for
Problem Solving

First read for understanding and then focus on determining whether data is exact or estimated.

READ FOR UNDERSTANDING

Students at Cranberry Middle School took part in a project to reduce home energy usage. About half of the 983 students involved in the project reported some success. Of these successful students, 205 use oil to heat their homes. The rest use electricity, gas, or solar energy.

1 How many students were involved in the project?

2 How many of the homes where energy usage was reduced use oil?

3 About what fraction of the 983 students reported some success?

THINK AND DISCUSS

MATH FOCUS

Exact or Estimated Data Exact data represents an amount that has been counted. Estimated data represents an amount that has been rounded or that cannot be rounded or measured.

Reread the paragraph at the top of the page.

4 Is 983 the exact number of students who participated in the project or is it an estimate? How do you know?

5 About half the students involved in the project reported some success. Does this statement give you an exact number or an estimate? Explain your reasoning.

6 Suppose 495 students reported some success. How many of these students' homes used electricity, gas, or solar energy? Is your answer exact or is it an estimate? Explain.

Show What You Learned

Use the information below the ad to answer each question. Give a reason for your choice.

Anna used the ad at the right to show how a compact fluorescent bulb can save energy. She explained that a regular 60-watt bulb lasts only about 715 hours and that this 20-watt bulb uses less energy.

Save Energy and Money with COMPACT FLUORESCENT BULBS

Compared with other electric bulbs, these new bulbs

- use about $\frac{1}{4}$ as much energy!
- last about 10 times longer than a regular 60-watt bulb!

Buy now and get a rebate of $5 per bulb!

Limit: 4 bulbs

20 watts

1 Which of these is an estimate?
- **a.** the amount of the rebate
- **b.** the amount of energy saved over the life of the bulb
- **c.** the wattage of the compact fluorescent bulb

2 Based on the information in the paragraph and in the ad, how long should one of the new bulbs last?
- **a.** about 7,000 hours
- **b.** exactly 7,000 hours
- **c.** about 71,000 hours

3 Which number would you estimate?
- **a.** the amount of energy you expect a household to save
- **b.** the rebate given for 3 bulbs
- **c.** both **a** and **b**

Richard's family bought the car described in the ad for $17,659.99. The old car got less than 20 miles per gallon. The new car gets over 30 miles per gallon.

4 Which of these is an exact number?
- **a.** the cost of the new car
- **b.** the gas mileage of the old car
- **c.** the gas mileage of the new car

WALRATH MOTORS

Announces the arrival of our new economy sedan.

Guaranteed best mileage in its class!

Come in for a test drive today!

SUPREME

5 How many miles can the new car travel on 10 gallons of gas?
- **a.** less than 100 miles
- **b.** about 200 miles
- **c.** over 300 miles

6 **Explain** How would you calculate the amount of gas that will be used by the new car in 4 years? Would your answer be an estimate or an exact answer?

A Helping Hand

Properties of addition can help you compute mentally.

Learning About It

Many steps are being taken to save animals threatened by changes in their environment. According to the table, how many species of birds, fish, and reptiles are endangered in the United States? Properties of addition and mental math strategies can help you compute this information in your head.

Animals at Risk	
Animal Group	**Number Endangered**
Mammals	55
Birds	76
Reptiles	14
Amphibians	14
Fish	68
Clams	51

Commutative Property	Associative Property	Identity Property
The order in which numbers are added does not affect the sum. $8 + 12 = 12 + 8$	The way in which addends are grouped does not affect the sum. $7 + (11 + 5) = (7 + 11) + 5$	The sum of any number and zero is that number. $45 + 0 = 45$

One strategy is to look for compatible numbers.

$$76 + 68 + 14 = 76 + 14 + 68 \longleftarrow \text{Commutative Property}$$

Compatible numbers are easy $\longrightarrow = (76 + 14) + 68 \longleftarrow$ Associative Property
to compute mentally.
$$= \quad 90 \quad + 68 = 158$$

There are 158 endangered species of birds, fish, and reptiles.

Break-apart and compensation are other strategies that are useful for computing mentally.

$128 + 64$
$128 + (60 + 4) \longleftarrow$ "Break apart" a number to give you easier numbers to work with.
$(128 + 60) + 4 \longleftarrow$ Associative Property
$\quad 188 \quad + 4 = 192$

With compensation, you change one number to a multiple of ten or to a whole number and adjust the other number.

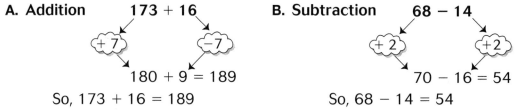

A. Addition $173 + 16$

$(+7)$ (-7)

$180 + 9 = 189$

So, $173 + 16 = 189$

B. Subtraction $68 - 14$

$(+2)$ $(+2)$

$70 - 16 = 54$

So, $68 - 14 = 54$

Think and Discuss How could you use mental math to compute $5.5 + 1.4$?

Try It Out

Use compatible numbers to compute mentally.

1. $28 + 75 + 32$ **2.** $14 + 16 + 92$ **3.** $0.9 + 6.2 + 7.1$ **4.** $0.45 + 0.55 + 65$

Use break-apart to compute mentally.

5. $260 - 47$ **6.** $325 + 225$ **7.** $45 - 27$ **8.** $197 + 183$

Use compensation to compute mentally.

9. $88 + 64$ **10.** $52 + 91$ **11.** $117 + 62$ **12.** $4.6 + 1.3$

13. $73 - 37$ **14.** $306 - 98$ **15.** $124 - 79$ **16.** $15 - 8.89$

Practice

For each exercise, choose a strategy and compute mentally.

17. $28 + 75$ **18.** $80 + 27$ **19.** $157 + 75$ **20.** $223 + 25$

21. $78 + 4.7$ **22.** $27 + 81 + 13$ **23.** $2.7 + 1.3$ **24.** $98 - 13$

25. $73 + 37$ **26.** $61 - 34$ **27.** $324 - 98$ **28.** $683 - 79$

29. $113 + 35 + 65$ **30.** $483 - 299$ **31.** $196 - 89$ **32.** $198 + 498$

Problem Solving

Compute mentally, using information from the table on page 14.

33. How many more species of birds are endangered than fish?

34. Analyze How many more species of birds and reptiles are endangered than mammals and amphibians?

Review and Remember

Find the value of n.

35. $13 + n = 17$ **36.** $n - 11 = 22$

37. $n + 99 = 101$ **38.** $75 - n = 25$

39. $n + 15 = 30$ **40.** $12 - n = 7$

▲ **Kid Connection**
Vicky Mendez, a 12-year-old student in Guatemala, helps to tag an endangered quetzal.

INTERNET ACTIVITY
www.sbgmath.com

✓ Checkpoint

Understanding Whole Numbers and Decimals

Write the value of each underlined digit in short word form.
(pages 2–3)

1. 53<u>1</u>,490   **2.** 2<u>4</u>,852,656   **3.** 34,563,<u>5</u>47   **4.** <u>4</u>,904

5. 53,87<u>5</u>   **6.** 23,<u>4</u>05,900   **7.** 466,<u>8</u>00   **8.** 750,003,00<u>3</u>

Write each number in standard form and in expanded form. (pages 2–3)

9. 34 billion, 800 thousand, 34   **10.** 600 million, 304 thousand, 22

Write the value of the underlined digit in short word form. (pages 4–5)

11. 34.46<u>7</u>   **12.** 563.88<u>4</u>84   **13.** 0.<u>4</u>07   **14.** 1.4<u>8</u>853

15. 6.0<u>5</u>6   **16.** 0.006<u>3</u>   **17.** 90.<u>7</u>85   **18.** <u>3</u>.00048

Write each number in standard form and in expanded form. (pages 4–5)

19. 34 hundredths   **20.** 62 and 45 thousandths   **21.** 6 and 9 hundred-thousandths

Compare. Write >, <, or = for each ⬤. (pages 6–9)

22. 46,988 ⬤ 46,989   **23.** 58.07 ⬤ 58.070   **24.** 0.81 ⬤ 0.817

25. 9.784 ⬤ 9.783   **26.** 89,438 ⬤ 89,458   **27.** 48.963 ⬤ 47.963

Write two numbers between the numbers in each pair. (pages 6–9)

28. 6.3 and 6.4   **29.** 45 and 45.6   **30.** 27.39 and 28

Write the numbers in order from least to greatest. (pages 6–9)

31. 537; 535; 549; 550   **32.** 7,654; 6,982; 5,697

33. 0.34; 0.78; 0.57; 0.38   **34.** 2.845; 2.859; 2.823

What do you think?

How can a digit, such as 8, have different values in different numbers?

Use compatible numbers, compensation, or break-apart to compute mentally. (pages 14–15)

35. 68 + 22 + 79   **36.** 536 − 508   **37.** 637 + 405

Problem Solving

Use the graph to solve Problems 38 and 39.

38. Name the continents that had populations in the billions in 1900.

39. List the continents, in order, from least to greatest population for 1980.

40. Analyze Show how you can use a combination of break-apart and compatible numbers to mentally add 64 and 36.

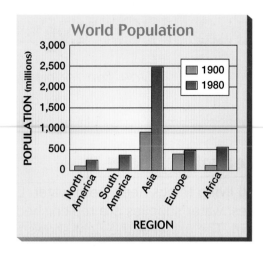

World Population

Journal Idea

What real-world information can be expressed in very large numbers? in very small numbers?

Critical Thinking Corner

Visual Thinking

The Abacus

The abacus is the earliest mechanical computing device ever used. The classic Chinese abacus, as shown at the right, has two decks. Beads are considered counted when moved towards the center beam.

The number shown on the abacus at the right is 87,654,321.

Name the number that is shown on each abacus.

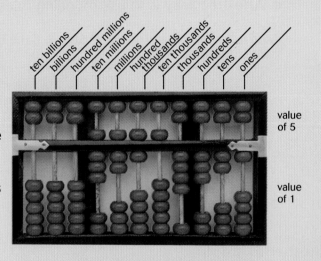

1.

2.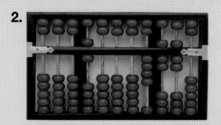

Raindrops Keep Falling

*You can round whole numbers and decimals to
get an approximate value.*

Learning About It

All living things need fresh water. Earth's
freshwater supplies are replenished by
rain. The graph at the right shows the
average yearly rainfall for five states. On
the average how much rainfall, to the
nearest tenth of an inch, falls in Texas?

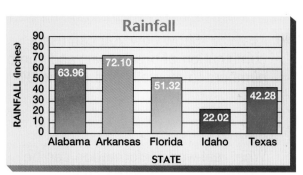

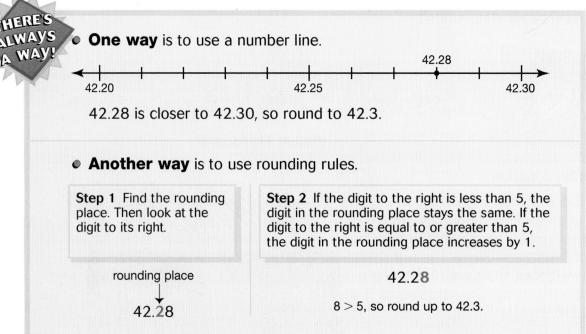

THERE'S ALWAYS A WAY!

● **One way** is to use a number line.

42.28 is closer to 42.30, so round to 42.3.

● **Another way** is to use rounding rules.

Step 1 Find the rounding place. Then look at the digit to its right.

Step 2 If the digit to the right is less than 5, the digit in the rounding place stays the same. If the digit to the right is equal to or greater than 5, the digit in the rounding place increases by 1.

rounding place
↓
42.28

42.2**8**

8 > 5, so round up to 42.3.

An average of about 42.3 inches of rain falls in Texas.

Another Example

Round 1,639 to hundreds.

Find the rounding place. ⟶ 1,**6**39

3 < 5, so the rounding place stays the same. ⟶ 1,600

Think and Discuss When rounding whole numbers, why
is it necessary to replace all digits to the right of the
rounding place with zeros?

Try It Out

Round 2,593.6781 to the nearest place named.

1. nearest hundred

2. nearest thousandth

3. nearest tenth

4. nearest one

5. nearest thousand

6. nearest hundredth

Practice

Round each number to the place underlined.

7. 4̲99.95

8. 17̲.3

9. 0.0̲9

10. 45̲.59

11. 12̲3.106

12. 2̲7.003

13. 198̲.789

14. 1.14̲6

15. 196.0̲51

16. 2̲2.01

17. 4̲89.1

18. 1,1̲99

19. 0.05̲61

20. 1.89̲7

21. 0.1̲32

22. 1.99̲9

23. 23.100̲7

24. 0.12̲59

25. 8.1̲798

26. 7̲.6000

27. 1̲55.76

28. 109̲.29

29. 1,59̲9.6

30. 9̲99.5

Problem Solving

Use the graph on page 18 to solve Problems 31–33.

31. What is the average rainfall for Florida, rounded to the nearest ten inches?

32. How much rain falls, to the nearest tenth of an inch, in Arkansas and Texas combined?

33. **Analyze** How would you find out how much more rain falls, to the nearest inch, in Arkansas and Idaho combined than falls in Alabama?

34. **Explain** Look back at Problem 33. Describe how you found the solution.

▲ **Science Connection**
A rain gauge is used to measure rainfall.

Review and Remember

Using Algebra Compare. Write >, <, or = in the ●.

35. $2 + 5 - 7$ ● 0

36. $23 + 4$ ● $15 + 10$

37. $3 + 7 + 8$ ● $20 - 2$

38. $5 + 9$ ● $6 - 3$

39. $20 + 20$ ● $10 + 10$

40. $17 - 6 + 6$ ● $12 + 5$

41. 19 ● $20 + 6$

42. 14 ● $20 - 10 + 4$

43. $6 + 4 + 9$ ● $24 + 6 - 10$

For Extra Practice, see Set E, page 39.

Not Exactly!

*Rounding and front-end estimation
are two ways to estimate a sum or difference.*

Learning About It

One of the cleanest ways to generate electricity
is to use the energy of moving water. About
$\frac{1}{10}$ of the electrical power generated in the
United States comes from hydroelectric plants.
The pictures show some of the tallest
hydroelectric dams in the world.

> **Hoover Dam
> United States
> 725 feet**

> **Aswan High Dam
> Egypt
> 364 feet**

> **Grand Dixence Dam
> Switzerland
> 935 feet**

Hoover Dam

Grand Dixence Dam

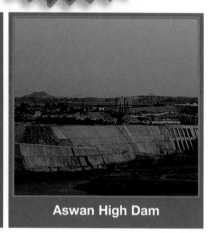

Aswan High Dam

Estimate how much taller Hoover Dam is than the
Aswan High Dam.

You can use rounding to estimate a sum or difference.

Step 1 Round each number to the greatest place of the least number.	**Step 2** Subtract.
$\begin{array}{r} 725 \\ -364 \\ \end{array}$ rounds to $\begin{array}{r} 700 \\ -400 \\ \end{array}$	$\begin{array}{r} 700 \\ -400 \\ \hline 300 \text{ feet} \\ \end{array}$

Hoover Dam is about 300 feet higher than the
Aswan High Dam.

To get a more precise estimate, round each number
to the nearest ten and subtract.

More Examples

A. Estimate to the nearest whole number.

4.76	rounds to	5
0.47	rounds to	0
+ 2.25	rounds to	+ 2
		7

B. Estimate to the nearest tenth.

4.76	rounds to	4.8
0.47	rounds to	0.5
+ 2.25	rounds to	+ 2.3
		7.6

Connecting Ideas

Rounding is just one way to estimate sums and differences. You can also estimate by using front-end estimation.

Estimate: 3,146 + 2,902 + 510 + 2,495

Step 1 Add the front digits that have the same place value.

```
    3,146
    2,902
      510
  + 2,495
    7,000  ←——  rough
                estimate
```

Step 2 For greater precision, adjust the estimate by using the digits to the right of the front digits.

```
    3,146 ⎫
    2,902 ⎬ about 1,000
      510 ⎫
  + 2,495 ⎭ about 1,000
    7,000 + 2,000 = 9,000    adjusted
                             estimate
```

Think and Discuss Describe an everyday situation in which you would estimate a sum or a difference. Explain why you would use estimation.

Try It Out

Estimate each sum by rounding.

	1.	2.	3.	4.
	5,274	35.2	30.090	0.235
	+ 4,315	+ 8.7	+ 5.00	+ 0.365

Estimate each sum, using front-end estimation. Then give an adjusted estimate.

	5.	6.	7.	8.
	883	679	2,528	4,640
	+ 919	+ 810	+ 4,072	+ 1,397

	9.	10.	11.	12.
	6.21	5.79	3.20	16.5
	1.34	0.91	4.23	6.1
	+ 0.76	+ 1.15	+ 2.37	+ 21.7

Practice

Estimate each sum or difference by rounding.

13.   25,684
          − 9,240

14.   5,385
          − 2,196

15.   49,396
          − 17,210

16. $256.25
          − $ 58.75

17.   8.906
          − 1.500

18.   0.987
          − 0.192

19.   384.12
          − 59.60

20.   0.541
          − 0.194

21.   1,458
           2,387
          + 525

22.   339
            17
          + 450

23.   6,129
            371
             49
          + 588

24.   0.159
           0.150
           0.509
          + 1.723

**Estimate each sum using front-end estimation.
Then give an adjusted estimate.**

25.   844
           397
          + 460

26.   184
           202
          + 525

27.   1,475
           3,689
          + 4,003

28.   3,394
           7,006
          + 2,609

29. $10.73
            2.25
          + 3.98

30.   0.005
           1.849
          + 0.156

31.   16.50
           20.37
            9.13
          + 7.07

32.   1.987
           0.50
           3.10
          + 1.78

Using Algebra **Find the value of each variable.**

33. $869 + 421 = 421 + y$

34. $(37 + 18) + n = 37 + (18 + 12)$

35. $1,839,472 + b = 1,839,472$

36. $367 + 18 = 370 + x$

37. $75 + (19 + 25) = 75 + (k + 19)$

38. $32 − 17 = 30 − p$

39. $h + (12 + 9) = (8 + 12) + 9$

40. $536 + 78 = (530 + 70) + m$

41. $(15 + w) + 15 = 30 + 9$

▲ **Social Studies Connection**
These centuries-old statues of Ramses II had to be dismantled and moved before the Aswan High Dam could be built.

Problem Solving

Use the graph at the right to solve Problems 42–44.

42. Estimate how much taller New Melones Dam is than Hungry Horse.

43. Estimate the total combined height of Grand Coulee, Oroville, and Hoover dams.

44. **Analyze** About how much greater is the combined height of the Oroville and Hungry Horse dams than the combined height of the Hoover and Grand Coulee dams?

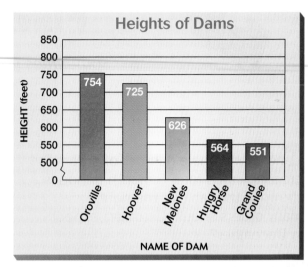

Heights of Dams

Oroville: 754
Hoover: 725
New Melones: 626
Hungry Horse: 564
Grand Coulee: 551

HEIGHT (feet) — NAME OF DAM

45. **Journal Idea** Describe two real-life situations that require an exact answer and two real-life situations in which only an estimate is needed.

The table at the right shows the amount of electricity, in kilowatts, generated by five hydroelectric plants in the United States. Use the information in the table to solve Problems 46–48.

46. Estimate the number of kilowatts of electricity generated by the plants at the Oroville and Hoover dams.

47. Estimate the number of kilowatts generated by the two plants generating the smallest number of kilowatts.

Plant Name	Number of Kilowatts
Oroville	2,500,000,000
Hoover	1,500,000
New Melones	300,000
Hungry Horse	428,000
Grand Coulee	6,500,000

48. Use front-end estimation with adjustment to find the approximate number of kilowatts generated at all five plants.

Review and Remember

Name each plane figure.

49.

50.

51.

52.

For Extra Practice, see Set F, page 40.

Problem Solving
Find a Pattern

Sometimes you can solve a problem by finding a pattern.

The approximate number of orders for greeting cards for a 6-month period is shown in the table at the right. How many orders should CardMart expect in December?

Greeting Card Orders per Month						
June	July	Aug.	Sept.	Oct.	Nov.	Dec.
200	250	350	500	700	950	?

UNDERSTAND

need to find?

find the number of orders ...December.

solve the problem?

the increase in the number ... month to month. Then **find a pattern** and predict the number of orders for December.

SOLVE

By looking at the table, you see that the number of orders increases by 50 more than the increase for the previous month. So the increase from November to December should be 250 + 50, or 300.

Greeting Card Orders per Month						
June	July	Aug.	Sept.	Oct.	Nov.	Dec.
200	250	350	500	700	950	1,250

+50 +100 +150 +200 +250 +300

Nov. + increase = Dec.

950 + 300 = 1,250

CardMart should expect 1,250 orders in December.

LOOK BACK

How can you check the answer?

Using the Strategy

Find a pattern to solve each problem. Use the design below for Problems 1–2.

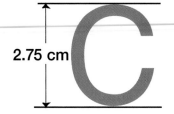 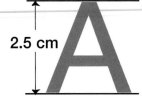 

2.75 cm   2.5 cm   2.25 cm

1 The design for CardMart's new logo is being created, as shown in the drawing. How high do you think the next letter will be?

2 **You Decide** Finish CardMart's logo by continuing this pattern or by creating your own pattern for the letters in the rest of the name.

3 Greeting cards are arranged in a window display with 1 card in the first row, 3 in the second row, 6 in the third row, and 10 in the fourth row. If the pattern continues, how many cards are in the seventh row?

4 **Analyze** Patrice designed a card with the pattern shown below on the front of the card. If the pattern continues, what letter is in the 54th position? Explain how you got your answer.
GOODLUCKGOODLUCKGOODLUCK

Mixed Strategy Review

Try these or other strategies to solve each problem. Tell which strategy you used.

Problem Solving Strategies

- Find a Pattern
- Draw a Diagram
- Make a Table
- Work Backwards
- Guess and Check
- Make an Organized List

5 Erin needs ten 1-meter pieces of ribbon to hang in the window display at CardMart. How many cuts will she need to make in a 10-meter length of ribbon?

6 CardMart's sales were about $10,000 in 1994, $11,000 in 1995, $13,000 in 1996, and $16,000 in 1997. If this pattern continues, what will sales be in the year 2001?

7 A customer receives $4.76 in change after buying a box of greeting cards for $15.75, a roll of ribbon for $2.99, and a box of writing paper for $11.50. How much money had the customer given the clerk?

8 **Explain** Display cases in CardMart hold either 30 or 40 boxes of cards. There are 5 cases holding a total of 170 boxes. How many 40-box display cases are there? Tell how you solved the problem.

Waste Not... Recycle!

The key to adding whole numbers and decimals is to keep your place-value columns lined up properly.

Learning About It

On average, each person in America throws away more than three pounds of solid trash daily. At this rate, a typical sixth-grade class throws away more than 15 tons a year!

Materials thrown away by a typical sixth-grade class each year.

Glass
2,520 pounds

Paper Goods
12,600 pounds

Metals
2,835 pounds

Plastics
2,835 pounds

Other Materials
10,710 pounds

Many materials, such as paper goods and metals, can be recycled. Use the picture above to find how many pounds of paper goods and metals might be discarded by your class each year.

$$12,600 + 2,835$$

Estimate first: $13,000 + 3,000 = 16,000$

THERE'S ALWAYS A WAY!

- **One way** is to use paper and pencil.

$$
\begin{array}{r}
12,600 \\
+\ 2,835 \\
\hline
15,435
\end{array}
$$

- **Another way** is to use a calculator.

Press: 1 2 6 0 0 +
2 8 3 5 =

Display: 15435

About 15,435 pounds of paper goods and metals are discarded each year.

Connecting Ideas

When adding whole numbers, addends are arranged so that place values are aligned properly. When adding decimals, you do this by aligning the decimal points.

$$1.8 + 250.03 + 16.196$$

Estimate first by rounding to the nearest whole number.

$$2 + 250 + 16 = 268$$

Then find the exact sum.

Remember to align the decimal points.

```
    1.800
  250.030
+  16.196
  268.026
```

Zeros can be placed to the right of the decimal point as placeholders.

Compare the computed sum to the estimate. The sum 268.026 is close to the estimate, 268.

Fine Arts Connection ◣
Another way to recycle trash is to turn it into art. *Memory Bottle with Thermometer and Watch* is on display at the National Museum of American Art, in Washington D.C.

More Examples

A. $5,250 + $64 + $186

```
   $5,250
       64
+     186
   $5,500
```

B. 4.253 + 10.03 + 0.015

```
    4.253
   10.030
+   0.015
   14.298
```

Think and Discuss Explain why aligning the digits like this would give an incorrect answer.

```
   500.000
+ 1500.00
```

Try It Out

Estimate first. Then find the exact sum.

1. 1 + 0.678 + 0.55 + 15

2. 43 + 0.15 + 1.2 + 155

3.
```
  $123.00
    17.50
+  100.16
```

4.
```
    15.70
   186.59
+    3.00
```

5.
```
  $9,576.00
       3.89
+    339.50
```

6.
```
     0.176
     5.000
+  445.300
```

7.
```
   $45.54
     3.02
+  127.34
```

8.
```
    0.378
    9.000
+  10.002
```

9.
```
   12,375
      450
+   1,055
```

10.
```
   17.680
    0.009
+  23.001
```

27

Practice

Estimate. Then use a calculator to add.

11.	$234.50	**12.**	13,005	**13.**	5.67	**14.**	17.0
	+ 187.95		+ 8,472		+ 38.09		+ 3.7

15.	17,205	**16.**	4.007	**17.**	0.010	**18.**	$125.08
	13,040		0.123		17.506		0.75
	+ 235		+ 12.654		+ 12.494		+ 15.17

19. 1,498 + 16 + 1.5 + 0.09

20. 0.999 + 16.7 + 0.98 + 1

21. $15.30 + $0.75 + $20 + $0.05

22. 22 + 1,009 + 0.5 + 9 + 0.007

Choose a Method Use mental math, paper and pencil, or
a calculator to find the sum. Tell which method you used.

23.	$2,509	**24.**	34.07	**25.**	0.004	**26.**	16.7890
	1,670		7.60		3.800		4.3500
	+ 990		+ 2.00		+ 0.530		+ 0.0009

27.	$175.75	**28.**	10.004	**29.**	0.4002	**30.**	21,425.00
	325.00		5.808		19.2004		12,009.95
	+ 0.55		+ 11.238		+ 106.0240		+ 20.55

31. 1.95 + 235.14 + 0.82 + 125.00

32. 10,005 + 0.435 + 24.65 + 9

33. $705.26 + 12.24 + 0.50 + 32.00

34. 0.418 + 4.018 + 40.18 + 401.8

35. 148 + 17 + 5.004

36. 189.72 + 15.7 + 20 + 0.04

37. 3.09 + 42.7 + 81

38. 214.19 + 37 + 1.08 + 77.214

39. Analyze Refer to the picture on page 26. What
information do you need to determine the total
weight of the different kinds of trash described
in the photo?

▼ The buildings and structures
in these pictures are all
made from recycled
materials.

28

Problem Solving

The table below shows the recyclable materials collected by three sixth-grade classes. Use it to answer Problems 40–43.

Clean-Up Week			
Material	Mr. Perry's Class	Mrs. Hanson's Class	Ms. Shao's Class
Paper	161 lb	102.5 lb	187.75 lb
Metal and Plastic	78.5 lb	53 lb	92.8 lb
Glass	57.6 lb	77.4 lb	48.7 lb

40. What was the total weight of the materials collected by Ms. Shao's class?

41. Analyze How would you find out which class collected the most recyclables by weight?

42. What If? Suppose your class collected more glass during clean-up week than Ms. Shao's class and less glass then Mr. Hanson's class. How many pounds could your class have collected? Explain.

Review and Remember

Using Algebra Find and complete each pattern.

43. 4, 8, 12, ▆, ▆   **44.** 3, 6, 12, ▆, ▆   **45.** 5, 9, 14, ▆, ▆   **46.** 7, 14, 28, ▆, ▆

Money $ense

More or Less

Who has more money, Juan or Ari? How can the two boys exchange coins or bills so that each has the same amount?

You're Getting Warmer

As in addition, aligning place values is important in subtraction.

Learning About It

Many scientists believe that the average temperature of the earth's surface is increasing. This change, called global warming, is the result of carbon dioxide gas (CO_2) being released into the atmosphere.

One way to reduce the CO_2 released is to develop engines that get better mileage, or miles per gallon of fuel burned.

How much more CO_2 is released by the car that gets 26 miles per gallon of gasoline than one that gets 45 miles per gallon?

To find out, you have to subtract.

▲ **Science Connection** The figures show how much CO_2 is released into the air over the average life of two different cars (about 100,000 miles).

THERE'S ALWAYS A WAY!

● **One way** is to use paper and pencil.

$$
\begin{array}{r}
\overset{7\ 15}{78,\cancel{5}80} \\
-51,860 \\
\hline
26,720
\end{array}
$$
Regroup to subtract.

● **Another way** is to use a calculator.

Press: (7)(8)(5)(8)(0)(−)
(5)(1)(8)(6)(0)(=)

Display: 26720

The car that gets 26 miles per gallon releases 26,720 more pounds of CO_2 into the air.

More Examples

A.
$$
\begin{array}{r}
\overset{6\ 18\ \ 7\ 13}{\cancel{7}\cancel{8},\cancel{8}\cancel{3}9} \\
-\ 9,256 \\
\hline
69,583
\end{array}
$$

B.
$$
\begin{array}{r}
\overset{8\ 12\ 17\ 14}{9,\cancel{3}\cancel{8}\cancel{4}} \\
-\ 8,795 \\
\hline
589
\end{array}
$$

C.
$$
\begin{array}{r}
\overset{0\ 13}{79,8\cancel{1}\cancel{3}} \\
-\ 68,007 \\
\hline
11,806
\end{array}
$$

Connecting Ideas

You can use the regrouping skills you learned for subtracting whole numbers to subtract decimals. When subtracting decimals, you must remember to align the decimal points.

Subtract: 7.84 − 6.56

Step 1 Line up the decimal points.	Step 2 Subtract hundredths. Regroup if necessary.	Step 3 Subtract tenths. Regroup if necessary.	Step 4 Subtract whole numbers. Place the decimal point.
$$\begin{array}{r} 7.84 \\ -\ 6.56 \\ \hline \end{array}$$	$$\begin{array}{r} {}^{7\,14} \\ 7.8\!\!\!/4 \\ -\ 6.56 \\ \hline 8 \end{array}$$	$$\begin{array}{r} {}^{7} \\ 7.\!\!\!/84 \\ -\ 6.56 \\ \hline 28 \end{array}$$	$$\begin{array}{r} 7.84 \\ -\ 6.56 \\ \hline 1.28 \end{array}$$

Sometimes you need to use zeros to hold places. Look at the More Examples.

More Examples

A. 76 − 21.5

$$\begin{array}{r} {}^{5\,10} \\ 76.\!\!\!/0 \\ -\ 21.5 \\ \hline 54.5 \end{array}$$

B. 3.45 − 1.7

$$\begin{array}{r} {}^{2\,14} \\ 3.\!\!\!/45 \\ -\ 1.70 \\ \hline 1.75 \end{array}$$

Think and Discuss You use a calculator to subtract 58.86 from 78.58 and get an answer of 1,972. How can you tell that the answer is not correct? Explain what went wrong.

▲ **Science Connection**
Scientists study satellite images of Earth's surface for evidence of global warming.

Try It Out

Estimate. Then subtract to find the exact difference.

1. $\begin{array}{r} 158{,}200 \\ -\ 119{,}678 \\ \hline \end{array}$	**2.** $\begin{array}{r} 100{,}000 \\ -\ 49{,}696 \\ \hline \end{array}$	**3.** $\begin{array}{r} 17{,}487 \\ -\ 544 \\ \hline \end{array}$	**4.** $\begin{array}{r} \$15.60 \\ -\ 8.90 \\ \hline \end{array}$
5. $\begin{array}{r} 12.069 \\ -\ 3.070 \\ \hline \end{array}$	**6.** $\begin{array}{r} 24.60 \\ -\ 0.45 \\ \hline \end{array}$	**7.** $\begin{array}{r} \$55.99 \\ -\ 9.45 \\ \hline \end{array}$	**8.** $\begin{array}{r} \$148.68 \\ -\ 9.70 \\ \hline \end{array}$

9. 129 − 5.063

10. 5.678 − 1

11. 5.3 − 2.27

12. 29.3 − 17

13. $15 − $5.40

14. 1,450 − 1,275

15. 333 − 0.05

16. 10.5 − 7

Practice

 Estimate. Then use a calculator to subtract.

17. 12,300
  − 9,438

18. $458.19
  − 378.46

19. 8,000
  − 3,478

20. 5,047
  − 339

21. 850.00
  − 225.76

22. 77.145
  − 22.000

23. 87.43
  − 0.76

24. $4.55
  − 3.20

25. 16.40
  − 15.93

26. 0.999
  − 0.300

27. 6.000
  − 5.683

28. 12.23
  − 9.00

29. 14 − 0.55

30. 288.55 − 72

31. 33.1 − 7

32. 8 − 0.55

33. $4.78 − $3.25

34. 1,500 − 700

35. 45 − 0.22

36. 4.7 − 0.92

Choose a Method Use paper and pencil, mental math, or a calculator to subtract. Tell which method you used.

37. 120,000
  − 8,000

38. 15,987
  − 955

39. 659.00
  − 5.44

40. 17.60
  − 15.98

41. $499.75
  − 76.55

42. 7,955.03
  − 7.90

43. 0.9000
  − 0.3333

44. 2,367.0
  − 999.7

45. $25.78
  − 2.07

46. 7,456
  − 4,356

47. 56.010
  − 23.843

48. 244.600
  − 234.477

49. 7 − 1.55

50. 5,000 − 0.46

51. 0.9 − 0.62

52. 27.304 − 9

53. 4.41 − 1.44

54. 6.874 − 5.875

55. 8.006 − 6

56. $24.80 − $2.48

57. Explain Describe the regrouping and subtraction you have to do in Exercise 51.

58. 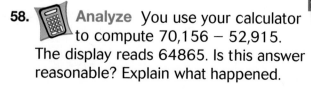 **Analyze** You use your calculator to compute 70,156 − 52,915. The display reads 64865. Is this answer reasonable? Explain what happened.

▲ **Science Connection** Using electric cars reduces the amount of CO_2 released into the air.

Problem Solving

The bar graph shows how the area covered by tropical rain forests in the Americas changed over a ten-year period. Use the graph to answer Problems 59–62.

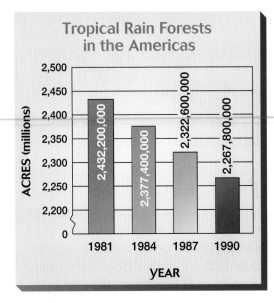

Tropical Rain Forests in the Americas

ACRES (millions)

- 1981: 2,432,200,000
- 1984: 2,377,400,000
- 1987: 2,322,600,000
- 1990: 2,267,800,000

YEAR

59. How many acres of rain forest were destroyed between 1981 and 1987?

60. How many more acres of trees were there in 1984 than in 1990?

61. How many acres of trees are being destroyed every three years?

62. Journal Idea Describe the trend in the area covered by rain forests and tell what you think will happen over the next ten years.

▲ **Science Connection** The trees and other plants of the rain forests remove CO_2 from the air and replace it with oxygen. Destruction of the rain forests may result in a dramatic increase in CO_2 levels in the atmosphere.

Review and Remember

Using Algebra Compare. Write $>$, $<$, or $=$ for the ●.

63. 4×3 ● 6×2

64. 3×5 ● 2×8

65. 9×4 ● 6×6

66. 8×6 ● 4×10

67. 5×8 ● 20×2

68. 11×5 ● 12×4

69. 6×6 ● 7×5

70. 5×9 ● 9×5

71. 9×2 ● 4×5

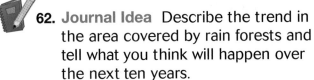

Time for Technology

Surfing the Net

Science Web Sites

You can use the Internet to find information about **science** and **rain forests**.

Explore the interactive games and information on this site to learn more about rain forests.

www.eduweb.com/amazon.html

Follow links to other sites on science, ecology, and ecosystems. Share your findings with the class or record your findings in your journal.

Problem Solving
Using Data From Graphs

Information from graphs can help you solve problems.

The graph shows about how much solid trash is produced in Raetown monthly. Most food waste and yard waste can be composted and used to enrich the soil. About how many pounds of the trash collected in 2 months could be composted?

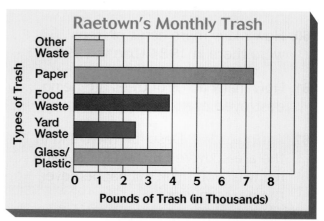

Raetown's Monthly Trash

Types of Trash: Other Waste, Paper, Food Waste, Yard Waste, Glass/Plastic

Pounds of Trash (in Thousands): 0 1 2 3 4 5 6 7 8

 UNDERSTAND

What do you need to know?

You need to know the approximate number of pounds of food waste and yard waste produced each month.

 PLAN

How can you solve the problem?

Estimate the amount shown by each bar. You can add 4 thousand and 2.5 thousand to find about how many pounds of food waste and yard waste are produced in one month. Double this amount to find an estimated number of pounds for 2 months.

▲ Can old, worn-out sneakers be useful? Look at the pictures on page 35 to find out.

 SOLVE

4.0 thousand	6.5 thousand
+ 2.5 thousand	+ 6.5 thousand
6.5 thousand	13.0 thousand, or 13,000

About 13,000 pounds of trash could be composted in two months.

 LOOK BACK

What If? Suppose you wanted to use a closer estimate for the number of pounds of food waste in one month. What number would you choose?

Show What You Learned

Use the bar graph on page 34 to solve Problems 1–3.

1 **Using Estimation** About how many pounds of paper are thrown out in 3 months?

2 What material makes up the greatest part of the solid trash in Raetown per month? Does this material make up more than or less than half the town's trash?

3 **Explain** Alethia estimated that the combined weight of glass, plastic, and paper thrown out in Raetown in 1 year is more than 100,000 pounds. Explain how she may have arrived at this estimate.

A conveyer belt carries old sneakers into a grinder.

The double bar graph below shows what happens to the solid trash produced by two local towns in one year. Use the graph to solve Problems 4–7.

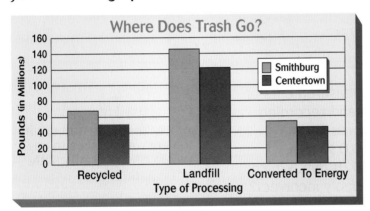

Where Does Trash Go?

Pounds (in Millions) — Type of Processing

Legend: Smithburg, Centertown

Recycled, Landfill, Converted To Energy

Bales of ground-up sneakers are awaiting shipment.

4 In 1 year, about how many more pounds of trash are produced by the people of Smithburg than by the people of Centertown?

5 **Analyze** In 1 year, the town of Greenfield recycles about half as much trash as does Smithburg. Greenfield takes twice as much trash to the landfill as does Centertown, and converts 50 million pounds of trash to energy. About how many pounds of trash do the people of Greenfield produce per year?

6 In 2 years, about how many more pounds of trash is recycled in Smithburg than Centertown?

7 **Create Your Own** Write a problem related to the graph that requires subtraction to find the answer.

This basketball court was made from ground-up sneakers.

Problem Solving

★ ★ ★ ★ ★ **Preparing for Tests**

Practice What You Learned

Choose the correct letter for each answer.

1 For the last four Saturdays, the numbers of customers that came to Randy's store were 17, 20, 23, and 18. For the last four Sundays, the numbers were 9, 8, 7, and 11. What is a reasonable number of customers Randy might expect next weekend?

- **A.** 10
- **B.** 20
- **C.** 30
- **D.** 40
- **E.** 50

Tip

Make a Table to organize the information in this problem.

2 A scientist is making precise measurements of the diameters of pollen grains and recording those measurements. Her records show measurements of 0.061 mm, 0.037 mm, 0.042 mm, 0.813 mm, and 0.028 mm. Which of these measurements is probably incorrect?

- **A.** 0.813 millimeters
- **B.** 0.061 millimeters
- **C.** 0.042 millimeters
- **D.** 0.037 millimeters
- **E.** 0.028 millimeters

Tip

Look at the five numbers in the answer choices to see which one is significantly different.

3 Eve spends $625 per month on rent and $240 for food. Her gas bill for September was $97.34; her electric bill for the same month was $49.46. Which is the best estimate for Eve's monthly rent and utilities expenses?

- **A.** Less than $650
- **B.** $650
- **C.** $700
- **D.** $750
- **E.** More than $800

Tip

Start by rounding the rent and the gas and electric bills to the nearest ten dollars.

4 Niko needs 30 cm of ribbon and 30 cm of velcro for a crafts project. Which of these is the length of ribbon that Niko needs?
(1 m = 100 cm)

A. 0.6 meters
B. 0.3 meters
C. 0.03 meters
D. 0.003 meters
E. Not Here

5 The graph below shows the results of a voter survey.

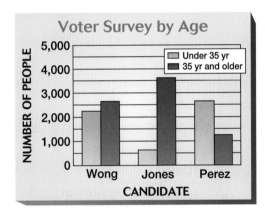

Voter Survey by Age

Based on this graph, who is likely to win the election?

A. Wong
B. Jones
C. Perez
D. Jones or Perez
E. Not Here

6 George is organizing 147 tapes and 128 CDs. He puts no more than 25 tapes in each box. Which is the best estimate for the number of boxes he needs for the tapes?

A. Less than 5
B. Between 5 and 10
C. Between 10 and 20
D. Between 20 and 25
E. More than 25

7 Sid has a garden that is 26 m by 34 m. The garden has a fence around it. Between the garden and the fence, there is a path 1.5 m wide. What is a reasonable length for the fence?

A. It is less than 50 meters.
B. It is exactly 63 meters.
C. It is about 100 meters.
D. It is exactly 120 meters.
E. It is more than 120 meters.

8 Hal stacks boxes for a window display. He puts 8 boxes in the bottom row, 7 in the next row, 6 in the third row up, and so on. There is 1 box in the top row. How many boxes are in the display?

A. 35
B. 46
C. 56
D. 64
E. Not Here

9 Paula's car gets about 35 miles to a gallon of gasoline. Which of these is reasonable for the amount of gas Paula needs for a 350-mile car trip?

A. Less than 5 gallons
B. Exactly 10 gallons
C. About 10 gallons
D. Exactly 100 gallons
E. About 100 gallons

10 Tom is twice as old as Julie. Sharon's age equals the sum of Tom's age and Julie's age. Which expression can be used to find Sharon's age, if J equals Julie's age?

A. $J + 2$
B. $J \times 2$
C. $(J \times 2) + J$
D. $(J + 2) \times J$
E. $(J + 2) + (J \times 2)$

 **Checkpoint**

Adding and Subtracting Whole Numbers and Decimals

Vocabulary

Fill in the blank with the correct word.

1. The number 12,650,254 is written in ___?___ .

2. A ___?___ is a letter used to represent an unknown.

3. A number written as 10,000 + 5,000 + 900 + 80 + 3 is in ___?___ .

4. An ___?___ is a number sentence with an equal sign.

Word Bank

equation
expanded form
standard form
variable

Concepts and Skills

Round each number to the place underlined. (pages 18–19)

5. 32.0<u>0</u>8   6. 0.<u>5</u>83   7. 1<u>7</u>3.95   8. 1,6<u>0</u>9.05   9. 4,2<u>9</u>9.14

Estimate each sum or difference by rounding. (pages 20–23)

10.	11.	12.	13.	14.
2,734	19,087	0.748	0.974	5,179
+ 5,873	− 9,883	+ 8.526	− 0.872	+ 391

Estimate each sum, using front-end estimation. Then give an adjusted estimate. (pages 20–23)

15.	16.	17.	18.	19.
437	2.054	$127.42	5.265	0.586
925	8.964	421.07	8.974	0.421
+ 873	+ 5.372	+ 31.50	9.608	0.973
			+ 4.519	+ 0.989

Estimate. Then add to find the exact sum. (pages 26–29)

20. $15.43 + $19.88 + $20.50   21. 2.076 + 0.0753 + 8.0083 + 2.4

22. 0.99 + 21.7 + 0.96 + 4   23. 35 + 2,004 + 0.3 + 6 + 14.047

Estimate. Then subtract to find the exact difference. (pages 30–33)

24. 23.8 − 4.75   25. 2.19 − 0.8142   26. 0.87 − 0.195

27. $12 − $3.87   28. 5,000 − 3,068   29. 250.18 − 124.78

Problem Solving

The table at the right shows the average yearly rainfall in five places. Use the table to solve Problems 30–35.

Wettest U.S. Places	
Place	**Rainfall (inches)**
Quillayute, Washington	104.50
Astoria, Oregon	69.60
Blue Canyon, California	67.87
Mobile, Alabama	64.64
Tallahassee, Florida	64.59

30. Estimate the amount of rain that falls in Astoria and Blue Canyon.

31. Estimate the total amount of rain that falls in all 5 places. Then find an adjusted estimate.

32. How much more rain falls in Quillayute than in Tallahassee?

33. Which two places have a difference of 3.23 inches in yearly rainfall?

34. Estimate the difference in rainfall between Mobile and Tallahassee. What do you notice?

35. Analyze How does the combined yearly rainfall of the two wettest places compare with the combined yearly rainfall of the other three places?

What do you think?

When adding and subtracting decimals, why is it important that the decimals be aligned?

Journal Idea

Make a list of important data facts that are usually rounded.

You Decide

Activity

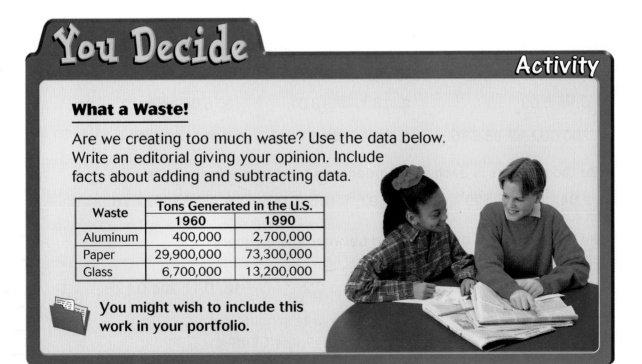

What a Waste!

Are we creating too much waste? Use the data below. Write an editorial giving your opinion. Include facts about adding and subtracting data.

Waste	Tons Generated in the U.S.	
	1960	**1990**
Aluminum	400,000	2,700,000
Paper	29,900,000	73,300,000
Glass	6,700,000	13,200,000

You might wish to include this work in your portfolio.

Extra Practice

Set A (pages 2–3)

Write the value of the underlined digit.

1. 7,2̲05,837
2. 48,91̲2,003
3. 940,062̲,028,000

Write each number in short word form.

4. 24,030
5. 807,028
6. 92,000,381,012

Write each number in standard form.

7. 56 million, 25 thousand, 18
8. 9 billion, 23 thousand, 8

Set B (pages 4–5)

Write the value of the underlined digit.

1. 0.05̲2
2. 5.004̲2
3. 8.0000̲7
4. 11.121̲2

Write each number in short word form.

5. 0.3
6. 0.73
7. 9.000009
8. 4.672

Write each number in standard form.

9. 6 tenths
10. 12 and 17 thousandths
11. 3 and 106 hundred-thousandths

Set C (pages 6–9)

Compare. Use >, <, or = for each ⬤.

1. 6 ⬤ 6.03
2. 18.1 ⬤ 18.01
3. 6.062 ⬤ 6.2
4. 200,002 ⬤ 88,385
5. 6.113 ⬤ 6.1125
6. 0.30058 ⬤ 0.31

Write the numbers in each set in order from least to greatest.

7. 7,842; 987; 7,699
8. 5.97; 5.135; 5.099
9. 23.936; 24.76; 24.8

Write three numbers that are found between the numbers in each pair.

10. 11 and 12
11. 0.15 and 0.2
12. 0.11 and 0.12

13. Analyze Use the digits 0, 1, and 2 to write six different three-digit numbers, including decimals, in order from least to greatest.

Extra Practice

Set D (pages 14–15)

Use compatible numbers to compute mentally.

1. 54 + 19 + 26   **2.** 33 + 11 + 27   **3.** 19 + 15 + 25   **4.** 19 + 37 + 41

Use break-apart to compute mentally.

5. 184 + 57   **6.** 55 − 37   **7.** 535 + 230   **8.** 680 − 56

Use compensation to compute mentally.

9. 54 + 43   **10.** 623 + 85   **11.** 42 − 15   **12.** 89 − 67

For each exercise choose a strategy and compute mentally.

13. 39 + 56   **14.** 22 + 15 + 58   **15.** 68 − 49   **16.** 47 + 65

17. 363 + 48   **18.** 48 − 35   **19.** 143 − 45   **20.** 14 + 23 + 47

Compute mentally, using information from the graph.

21. How much heavier is a gorilla than a baboon?

22. A gorilla and an orangutan step on a scale together. What does the scale read?

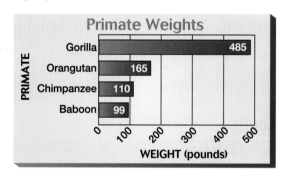

Set E (pages 18–19)

Round each number to the place underlined.

1. 5.0<u>3</u>2   **2.** 9.07<u>2</u>5   **3.** 12.1<u>1</u>91   **4.** <u>8</u>.099

5. 0.3<u>4</u>82   **6.** 52<u>0</u>.97   **7.** 84.0<u>0</u>81   **8.** 9.2<u>6</u>35

Use the chart at the right for Exercises 9 and 10.

9. What is the area of Tongass National Forest to the nearest million acres?

10. Estimate the combined area of Tonto and Boise national forests.

U.S. National Forests	
Name	Area (acres)
Tongass	16,791,874
Chugach	5,404,414
Toiyabe	3,212,229
Tonto	2,874,593
Boise	2,647,740

Extra Practice

Set F (pages 20–23)

Estimate each sum or difference by rounding.

1.	37,543 + 9,824	2.	3,842 − 2,356	3.	83,908 + 88,643	4.	$314.09 − 123.55

Estimate each sum, using front-end estimation. Then give an adjusted estimate.

5.	543 275 + 906	6.	1,826 2,473 + 3,860	7.	3.002 2.908 + 5.899	8.	0.384 2.183 + 5.902

Compare. Use >, <, or = for ⬤.

9. 8.09 + 1.91 ⬤ 8 + 2   10. 22 − 19.23 ⬤ 22.23 − 19

Set G (pages 26–29)

Estimate. Then add to find the exact sum.

1.	14.08 + 2.76	2.	$14.98 + 7.19	3.	$473.07 + 0.98	4.	83.019 + 9.800

Add.

5.	$473.07 0.98 + 8.31	6.	8.093 9.480 + 3.008	7.	$3,785.23 978.23 + 800.00	8.	118.921 97.900 + 19.890

9. 5.94 + 7.2 + 6.273 + 0.9   10. 18.003 + 0.9871 + 4.86 + 9.98

Set H (pages 30–33)

Estimate. Then subtract to find the exact difference.

1.	5,800 − 735	2.	320.58 − 19.88	3.	$263.27 − 108.92	4.	725.85 − 6.99

5.	57,020 − 9,584	6.	$7.93 − 4.89	7.	58.86 − 0.97	8.	28.64 − 0.57

Chapter Test

Round 248.37096 to the place named.

1. tenths   **2.** ones   **3.** ten-thousandths

Write each in standard form.

4. 7 and 24 ten-thousandths   **5.** 27 billion, 70 thousand, 512

Compare. Use >, <, or = for ●.

6. 5.083 ● 5.83   **7.** 0.075 ● 0.08

Use mental math to add or subtract.

8. $87 + 29 + 13$ **9.** $167 - 125$ **10.** $243 + 98$

Estimate each sum or difference.

11.	15,450	**12.**	7.038	**13.**	0.235
	3,857		− 2.960		0.541
	+ 9,285				+ 0.296

Estimate. Then add or subtract.

14.	95,374	**15.**	18.057	**16.**	$13.87	**17.**	4,643
	+ 16,285		− 9.365		25.08		− 851
					+ 9.78		

18. $11 − $8.49   **19.** $3.2 + 5.85 + 7.489 + 7.98$ **20.** $24.601 - 12.9083$

Use mental math to find the value of each variable.

21. $x + 5 = 12$ **22.** $p - 8 = 9$ **23.** $7 + n = 19$

Solve.

24. If Bobbie swims 2 days and takes a day off, and then he runs for 3 days and takes a day off, what will he do on the fifteenth day?

25. During a snowstorm, Clifton got 36.25 inches of snow and Central Valley got 29.9 inches of snow. How much more snow fell in Clifton?

 Self-Check

Look back at Exercises 21–23. Did you input the value of the variable to check your answer?

Performance Assessment

Show What You Know About Whole Numbers and Decimals

1 Study these numbers. Then answer each question.

432,950   432,949   442,950   342,950   5.04   5.401   5.4

a. Write the greatest <u>whole</u> number using as many names as you can.

b. Round the least <u>whole</u> number to the thousands place.

c. Write the word name for the least number.

d. Order all the numbers from least to greatest.

Self-Check Did you remember to include all the numbers when ordering the numbers?

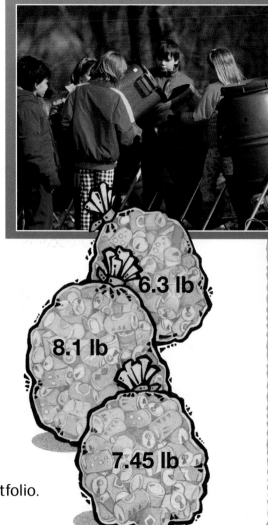

2 The Science Club set a goal to collect 50 lb of aluminum cans for recycling. The club took three trash bags filled with aluminum cans to the recycling center to be weighed. The bags held 6.3 lb, 8.1 lb, and 7.45 lb of cans.

a. What is the total weight of the aluminum cans?

b. How many more pounds of aluminum do they need to collect?

c. Using the information above, about how many trash bags will they need to collect the 50 pounds of cans? Explain.

Self-Check For Question 2b, did you remember that the club has a goal to collect 50 pounds of aluminum cans?

6.3 lb

8.1 lb

7.45 lb

For Your Portfolio

You might wish to include this work in your portfolio.

Extension

Roman Numerals and the Decimal System

The ancient Romans developed a number system based on addition and subtraction. They used the following letters as symbols to name numbers.

M	D	C	L	X	V	I
1,000	500	100	50	10	5	1

Roman numerals are read from left to right. To find the decimal value of a Roman numeral, use the following rules:

Addition	Subtraction
Add if the value of the symbols, from left to right, stays the same or decreases. LXXVI = 76	Subtract if the value of the symbols, from left to right, increases. XCIV = 94

Use what you know about the decimal system and Roman numerals to answer Exercises 1–4.

1. Is the order of the symbols important in each system? If so, how is it important?

2. Write the current year in each system.

3. Social Studies Connection This panel from a building in Washington, D.C., shows the year that Georgia became a state. What year was that?

4. Research another numeration system and present your findings to the class.

5. What are some advantages and disadvantages of each system?

Write the Roman numerals in decimal form.

6. DCVII   7. CXLV   8. DCCIII   9. MMCDXLIV

Write the following decimal numerals in Roman form.

10. 3,367   11. 2,021   12. 736   13. 269

Cumulative Review

Choose the correct letter for each answer.

Number Concepts	Operations

Number Concepts

1. Which numbers are in the correct order from *least* to *greatest*?

   A. 68.9, 68.03, 67.91, 67.85
   B. 68.03, 67.91, 67.85, 68.9
   C. 67.85, 67.91, 68.03, 68.9
   D. 67.85, 67.91, 68.9, 68.03

2. In Big Bend National Park, Texas, the Rio Grande Village Nature Trail is $1\frac{1}{4}$ miles long; the Santa Elena Canyon Trail, $1\frac{3}{4}$ miles long; and the Boquillas Canyon Access Trail, $1\frac{1}{2}$ miles long. Which list below shows the trail lengths in correct order from *greatest* to *least*?

   A. $1\frac{1}{4}$ mi, $1\frac{3}{4}$ mi, $1\frac{1}{2}$ mi
   B. $1\frac{3}{4}$ mi, $1\frac{1}{2}$ mi, $1\frac{1}{4}$ mi
   C. $1\frac{1}{4}$ mi, $1\frac{1}{2}$ mi, $1\frac{3}{4}$ mi
   D. $1\frac{1}{2}$ mi, $1\frac{1}{4}$ mi, $1\frac{3}{4}$ mi

3. What is 12.46 rounded to the nearest *tenth*?

   A. 10
   B. 12.4
   C. 12.5
   D. 12.6

4. Which is the least common multiple of 4 and 10?

   A. 2   **C.** 20
   B. 8   **D.** 40

Operations

5. $21.214 - 19.95 =$

   A. 192.19   **C.** 1.264
   B. 41.164   **D.** 0.264

6. Sam has $\frac{3}{8}$ cup of oil. He adds $\frac{1}{4}$ cup of oil and $\frac{1}{3}$ cup of water to a cake mix. How much liquid does he add to the cake mix?

   A. $\frac{1}{12}$ c

   B. $\frac{1}{7}$ c

   C. $\frac{2}{7}$ c

   D. $\frac{7}{12}$ c

7. There are 16 tracks in a railroad yard. There are 32 trains with a total of 672 train cars parked on the tracks. Which is the best estimate of the number of cars on each train if there is an equal number of cars per train?

   A. 10   **C.** 30
   B. 20   **D.** 33

8. Which number is the product of 327 and 24?

   A. 1,962
   B. 7,748
   C. 7,828
   D. 7,848
   E. Not Here

Geometry and Spatial Reasoning	Measurement

9. Which best describes the two pentagons?

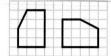

A. The pentagons are not similar.
B. The pentagons are congruent.
C. The pentagons are both symmetrical.
D. The pentagons are regular polygons.
E. The pentagons are reflections of each other.

---

10. A three-dimensional figure has 6 faces that are all squares. This figure is a—

A. Cube
B. Cylinder
C. Pyramid
D. Triangular prism

---

11. Which figure has more than 1 line of symmetry?

---

12. Which side is parallel to side *AB* in the hexagon *ABCDEF*?

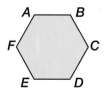

A. Side *AF*   C. Side *CD*
B. Side *BC*   D. Side *DE*

---

13. Samantha's baby sister is 54 weeks old, and her younger brother is 3 years old. How many *days* old is Samantha's sister?

A. 948 days
B. 417 days
C. 378 days
D. 358 days

---

14. Frank is building a shelf for his 24 books. The average thickness of a book is 1.5 inches. Which is the least number of *feet* long the shelf needs to be to hold all of his books?

A. 3 ft
B. 9 ft
C. 16 ft
D. 36 ft
E. Not Here

---

15. When Fred had a cold, he drank a gallon and a half of orange juice in 2 days. How many *ounces* did he drink in 2 days? (1 gal = 64 oz)

A. 96 oz
B. 48 oz
C. 64 oz
D. 32 oz

---

16. Colin wants to glue some shells on a square piece of cardboard to form a border. The *perimeter* of the square is 48 inches. If each shell takes up a 3-inch by 3-inch section, how many shells does he need?

A. 45
B. 36
C. 16
D. 12

Chapter 2
Multiplying and Dividing Whole Numbers and Decimals

Chapter Theme: MUSEUMS

Real-World Math

....................Real Facts....................

Dioramas bring history alive! Builders of historical dioramas portray scenes accurately by keeping the relative sizes of people, horses, and other objects proportional. Before building a diorama, the designer plans the size of the area within which he or she will work.

Possible Diorama Measurements			
Diorama	Width	Length	Area of Floor
1	22 in.	30 in.	
2	12 in.	24 in.	
3	6 ft	7 ft	

- Copy and complete the table to find the area of each diorama's **floor**. How did you find the floor area of the first diorama?

- Suppose you have a table with an area of 3 square feet to display a diorama. Will any of the dioramas listed fit on the table? Explain.

..............Real People....................

Meet Nancy Nagel. She designs and builds dioramas that depict historical scenes. In the photograph, she is painting figures for a Civil War diorama. An elaborate diorama like this may take years to complete.

Out of Order

Using Algebra

The order in which you perform operations can affect the answer.

Learning About It

Suppose your class is going to the museum. As you get ready, you have to perform some tasks in a particular order. For example, you put on your socks before putting on your shoes. Similarly, when calculating with more than one operation, you need to follow the order of operations.

Calculate **17 − (3 + 1) ÷ 2**.

- Compute all values in parentheses first.

$$17 - \underbrace{(3 + 1)}_{\downarrow} \div 2$$
$$17 - \quad 4 \div 2$$

- Next, multiply and divide from left to right.

$$17 - \underbrace{4 \div 2}_{\downarrow}$$
$$17 - \quad 2$$

- Finally, add and subtract from left to right.

$$\underbrace{17 - 2}_{\downarrow}$$
$$15$$

More Examples

A. $4 + \underbrace{6 \times 5}$
$$4 + 30 = 34$$

B. $12 - \underbrace{72 \div 8} + 3$
$$\underbrace{12 - 9} + 3$$
$$3 + 3 = 6$$

Think and Discuss Where should you put parentheses to make 36 ÷ 9 − 3 = 6 a true statement?

Try It Out

Tell which operation to perform first. Then use order of operations to evaluate each expression.

1. $3 + 9 \div 3$ **2.** $8 - 5 + 9$ **3.** $7 \times (3 + 1)$ **4.** $14 - 3 \times 2 + 7$

5. $10 - 6 \div 2$ **6.** $24 \div (8 + 4)$ **7.** $2 \times (4 - 3) \times 5$ **8.** $6 + 7 - 4 \div 2 \times 3 - 5$

Practice

Use order of operations to evaluate each expression.

9. $7 + 3 \times 6$ **10.** $(2 + 3) \times 9$ **11.** $15 - 96 \div 12$ **12.** $12 \times 2 - 12$

13. $16 \div (4 \times 2)$ **14.** $6 - 3 \times 2 + 4$ **15.** $63 \div 7 - 6$ **16.** $3 + (4 \times 6) - 7$

17. $(10 - 6) \div 2$ **18.** $8 \times 6 \div 3$ **19.** $6 + 24 \div 3$ **20.** $12 + (5 + 7) \div 2$

Use parentheses to make each statement true.

21. $24 \div 8 - 2 = 4$ **22.** $4 + 6 \times 2 = 20$ **23.** $4 + 10 \div 2 = 7$

24. $7 \times 6 + 2 = 56$ **25.** $2 + 3 \times 4 = 20$ **26.** $9 \times 3 - 1 \div 6 = 3$

Problem Solving

Use order of operations to solve Problems 27–29.

27. On a class trip, Zachary visited 3 museums and 1 monument. Museum tickets were $2.50 each. The monument ticket was $2.00. How much did Zachary spend for tickets?

28. Ted sold homemade cookies for his class trip. He made 2 dozen oatmeal cookies and 3 dozen peanut butter cookies. He gave away 8 cookies and sold the rest. How many cookies did Ted sell?

29. **You Decide** You have $14 to spend on exhibits at a museum. The rock exhibit costs $5.50, the space exhibit costs $4.75, the plant exhibit costs $3.25, and the dinosaur exhibit costs $3.75. Which exhibits would you choose to see?

Review and Remember

Write the value of the underlined digit.

30. 246,913   **31.** 62.98   **32.** 361.024   **33.** 639

34. 2,136.4   **35.** 0.4169   **36.** 1,200,561   **37.** 8.956

For Extra Practice, see Set A, page 92.

Mapping the Floors

Using strategies and multiplication properties can help you compute mentally.

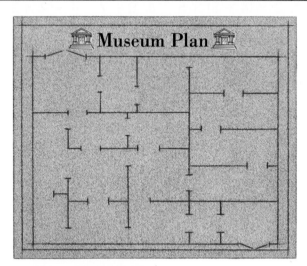

Museum Plan

Learning About It

The top three floors of the museum that you are visiting have identical layouts. The floor plan above shows the number of exhibit areas on each floor. How many exhibit areas are there in all?

Properties of multiplication and mental math strategies can help you compute mentally.

One strategy is the break-apart strategy.

$3 \times 17 = 3 \times (10 + 7)$ ◄──── "Break apart" a number to give you easier numbers with which to work.

$\quad = (3 \times 10) + (3 \times 7)$ ◄

$\quad = \quad 30 \quad + 21 = 51$ ──── distributive property

There are 51 exhibit areas in all.

Compatible numbers is another strategy for computing mentally.

$2 \times (38 \times 5) = 2 \times (5 \times 38)$ ◄──── commutative property

$\quad = (2 \times 5) \times 38$ ◄──── associative property

$\quad = \quad 10 \quad \times \quad 38 = 380$

Think and Discuss What property can you use to find the product of $53 \times 86 \times 892 \times 0 \times 876$ mentally?

Multiplication Properties

Commutative Property
The order in which numbers are multiplied does not affect the product.

$$5 \times 20 = 20 \times 5$$

Associative Property
The way in which factors are grouped does not affect the product.

$$3 \times (2 \times 5) = (3 \times 2) \times 5$$

Identity Property
The product of one and any number is that number.

$$45 \times 1 = 45$$

Property of Zero
The product of zero and any number is zero.

$$9,999 \times 0 = 0$$

Distributive Property
Multiplying a factor by a group of addends yields the same result as multiplying that factor by each addend and then adding the products.

$$6 \times (5 + 4) = (6 \times 5) + (6 \times 4)$$

Try It Out

Use multiplication properties and mental math to simplify each expression.

1. 4×23 **2.** 13×5 **3.** $(5 \times 8) \times 2$ **4.** $3 \times (7 \times 3)$

Practice

Use multiplication properties and mental math to simplify each expression.

5. 3×18 **6.** 6×31 **7.** 3×47 **8.** $2 \times (5 \times 56)$

9. $5 \times 12 \times 1$ **10.** $6 \times 7 \times 2$ **11.** $1 \times (9 \times 7)$ **12.** $16 \times 8 \times 0$

Write a number sentence to give an example of each property.

13. Identity **14.** Distributive **15.** Commutative **16.** Zero **17.** Associative

Find the missing value. Name the property you use.

18. $13 \times n = 0$ **19.** $8 \times (2 + n) = (8 \times 2) + (8 \times 7)$ **20.** $24 \times n = 9 \times 24$

21. $54 \times n = 54$ **22.** $3(5 + 3) = (3 \times 5) + (3 \times n)$ **23.** $n \times 12 = 12 \times 48$

24. $36 \times n = 0$ **25.** $4 \times (6 \times 7) = (4 \times n) \times 7$ **26.** $(34 \times n) \times 7 = 34 \times (2 \times 7)$

Problem Solving

27. Jill gave 3 tours. Each tour made visits to 3 exhibit areas on the first floor and 2 exhibit areas on the second floor. Write an expression, using multiplication, to show how many areas she visited.

28. **Explain** Dixie toured 2 exhibit areas on each of 3 floors. Babette toured 3 exhibit areas on each of 2 floors. Who toured more areas? How do you know?

29. **Journal Idea** Tasha visited all the exhibit areas on one floor and 4 exhibit areas on each of the other 2 floors. Jon told her that she would visit 21 exhibits altogether, but Tasha said she would visit 25 exhibits. How do you know who is correct? Explain your reasoning.

The Bruce Museum in Greenwich, Connecticut, has a miniature doll house collection on display.

Review and Remember

Evaluate.

30. 5×12 **31.** $28 \div 4$ **32.** $42 + 39$ **33.** $29 - 18$ **34.** $63 \div 7$

For Extra Practice, see Set B, page 92.

Using Algebra

Pay What You Can

You can use variables to represent numbers when solving problems.

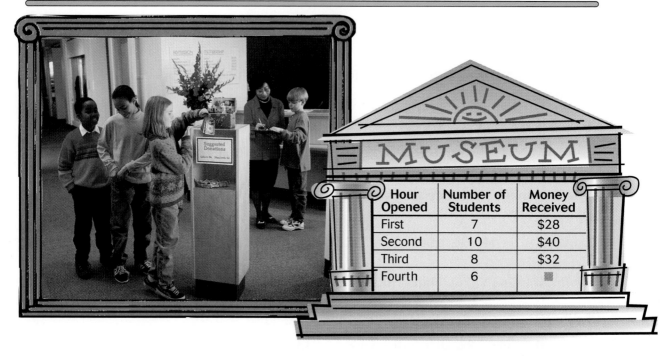

Hour Opened	Number of Students	Money Received
First	7	$28
Second	10	$40
Third	8	$32
Fourth	6	▨

Learning About It

Students who visit the craft museum give a donation. The table above shows how much the museum received each hour.

Work with a partner.

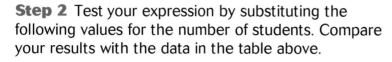

Step 1 Let *s* represent the number of students who visit the museum each hour. Write an expression using the variable *s* to show how much the museum receives each hour in donations from students.

Step 2 Test your expression by substituting the following values for the number of students. Compare your results with the data in the table above.

$$s = 7 \qquad s = 10 \qquad s = 8$$

Step 3 Use your expression to find out how much money the museum received during the fourth hour.

Step 4 During the fifth hour that the museum was open, students gave $36 in donations. How many students entered the museum during the fifth hour?

Step 5 Use mental math to help you find the value of each variable. Then check your work by placing the value back into the equation.

a. $8 \times a = 64$ **b.** $36 \div b = 4$ **c.** $5 \times k = 50$ **d.** $70 \div y = 10$

Think and Discuss Use the pattern in the table at the right to write an expression using the variable d.

7	9	3	d
42	54	18	■

Practice

Find the value of each expression.

1. $3 \times p$ for $p = 10$ **2.** $56 \div s$ for $s = 7$ **3.** $a \times 4$ for $a = 8$

4. $63 \div m$ for $m = 9$ **5.** $6 \times t$ for $t = 8$ **6.** $100 \div d$ for $d = 4$

Write a rule to find the next number in the table.

7.

2	6	18	54	z
4	12	36	108	■

8.

3	9	27	81	z
1	3	9	27	■

Use mental math to help you find the value of each variable. Then check your work by placing the value back into the equation.

9. $7 \times f = 21$ **10.** $6 = 36 \div w$ **11.** $54 \div j = 9$ **12.** $32 = 4 \times k$

13. Create Your Own Make up a rule and a table like those in Exercises 7 and 8. Have your partner figure out the rule and write it using the variable z.

Money $ense

A Collective Purchase

Amy, Kim, and Anthony are buying one or two posters and some other items for their exhibit in the science fair at school. Amy has $3.50, Kim has $4.40, and Anthony has $3.05. If the three students combine their money, what items can they buy?

TYRANNOSAURUS

THE NATURE MUSEUM

POSTERS $3.50
MODELS
    LARGE $4.98
    SMALL $2.98
SHELLS
    LARGE $1.50
    SMALL $0.85

Chip Off the Old Block

Patterns in our number system can help you to multiply.

Learning About It

At the Computer Museum in Boston, learning about computers is fun. Some computer chips may be small enough to fit through the eye of a needle. If a computer chip measured 5 mm, what would the size of the chip be in a model 10 times the actual size? 100 times? 1,000 times?

Patterns of 10 can help you find products mentally.

$5 \times 1 \quad = 5$
$5 \times 10 \quad = 50$
$5 \times 100 \quad = 500$
$5 \times 1,000 = 5,000$

5 mm

10 times actual size

50 mm

More Examples

A. $6 \times 5 \quad = 30$
$6 \times 50 \quad = 300$
$6 \times 500 \quad = 3,000$
$6 \times 5,000 = 30,000$

B. $9 \times 2 \quad = 18$
$9 \times 20 \quad = 180$
$90 \times 20 \quad = 1,800$
$90 \times 200 = 18,000$

C. $3.46 \times 1 \quad = 3.46$
$3.46 \times 10 \quad = 3\ 4.6 \quad = 34.6$
$3.46 \times 100 \quad = 3\ 46. \quad = 346$
$3.46 \times 1,000 = 3\ 460. = 3,460$

D. $0.91 \times 1 \quad = 0.91$
$9.1 \times 10 \quad = 91. \quad = 91$
$91 \times 100 \quad = 9100. \quad = 9,100$
$910 \times 1,000 = 910000. = 910,000$

Think and Discuss Describe the movement of the decimal point when you multiply by multiples of ten.

Try It Out

Find each product mentally.

1. 6×10
6×100
$6 \times 1,000$

2. 8×50
8×500
$8 \times 5,000$

3. 9×60
9×600
$9 \times 6,000$

4. 30×30
300×300
$3,000 \times 3,000$

5. 5.8×1
5.8×10
5.8×100

6. 1.2×10
12×100
$120 \times 1,000$

Practice

Mental Math Use patterns to find each product.

7. 5 × 10   **8.** 7 × 100   **9.** 1.14 × 10   **10.** 0.7 × 10

11. 16 × 1,000   **12.** 30.5 × 100   **13.** 40 × 60   **14.** 50 × 20

15. 17.165 × 10   **16.** 0.2 × 100   **17.** 32 × 100   **18.** 70 × 300

19. 4.3 × 1,000   **20.** 0.007 × 10   **21.** 300 × 400   **22.** 314.02 × 1,000

Compare. Use <, >, or = for each ●.

23. 30 × 60 ● 18 × 10   **24.** 50 × 600 ● 30 × 100

25. 200 × 60 ● 12 × 1,000   **26.** 20 × 5,000 ● 200 × 500

Use patterns of multiples of 10 to find the missing number.

27. 83.7 × n = 8,370   **28.** 1.002 × n = 1,002   **29.** 0.0007 × n = 0.07

30. 13.44 × n = 134.4   **31.** 1.7 × n = 1,700   **32.** 0.06 × n = 0.6

Problem Solving

33. A real computer keyboard measures 1.5 feet. If the length of a model keyboard is increased 30 times, how long will it be?

34. A real computer screen is 17 inches high. How high will the screen on the model computer be if it is increased 20 times?

35. **What If?** Suppose one side of a real computer chip measures 13 mm. How long would one side of a chip be on the model computer?

Science Connection
The Computer Museum in Boston created a model whose parts are 20–50 times those of a desktop computer.

Review and Remember

Compare. Use <, >, or = for each ●.

36. 0.87 ● 0.89   **37.** 587 ● 5,870   **38.** 2.063 ● 2.043

39. 0.19 ● 0.190   **40.** 28,609 ● 28,143   **41.** 567.25 ● 560.25

42. 45.010 ● 45.01   **43.** 6,723 ● 7,812   **44.** 7,342 ● 734

Big and Bigger!

You can use what you know about multiplication properties and multiples of ten to multiply large numbers.

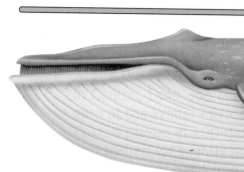

Learning About It

The African elephant, the largest land animal, has been known to weigh as much as 26,328 pounds. The blue whale can weigh as much as 15 African elephants. How much does a blue whale weigh?

$$26{,}328 \times 15 = n$$

Estimate first: $\quad 25{,}000 \times 20 = 500{,}000$

Then multiply to find the exact answer.

Science Connection
Models of the largest animals in the world are on display in the American Museum of Natural History, in New York City.

INTERNET ACTIVITY
www.sbgmath.com

THERE'S ALWAYS A WAY!

• **One way** is to use paper and pencil.

Step 1 Multiply by the ones.	**Step 2** Multiply by the tens.	**Step 3** Add the partial products.
26,328 × 15 131640	26,328 × 15 131640 263280	26,328 × 15 131640 263280 394,920

• **Another way** is to use a calculator.

Press: 2 6 3 2 8 × 1 5 =

Display: *394920*

A blue whale can weigh 394,920 pounds.

More Examples

A.
```
     5,224
   ×  205
    26 120  ←——  5 × 5,224
 1 044 800  ←—— 200 × 5,224
 1,070,920
```

B.
```
      7,390
    ×  571
      7 390  ←——    1 × 7,390
    517 300  ←——   70 × 7,390
  3 695 000  ←——  500 × 7,390
  4,219,690
```

Think and Discuss When multiplying a number by 3,005, how many partial products will you have? How do you know?

Try It Out

Choose a Method Use paper and pencil or a calculator to find each product. Tell which method you use.

1.
```
   27
 × 16
```
2.
```
   209
 ×  36
```
3.
```
   399
 × 705
```
4.
```
  1,650
 ×  463
```
5.
```
  2,007
 ×  290
```

Practice

Choose a Method Use paper and pencil or a calculator to find each product. Tell which method you use.

6.
```
   37
 × 95
```
7.
```
   90
 × 12
```
8.
```
   417
 ×  26
```
9.
```
   120
 ×  48
```
10.
```
   600
 ×  57
```

11.
```
   562
 ×  93
```
12.
```
   387
 × 205
```
13.
```
   504
 × 380
```
14.
```
  1,053
 ×  406
```
15.
```
  2,890
 ×  999
```

Problem Solving

16. Each day 2,400 people visit the elephant exhibit. The museum is open 360 days each year. How many visitors come to the exhibit in a year?

17. **Analyze** Last summer, the museum had a special "Moving Dinosaurs" show. The show was presented ten times a day for 127 days, and 405 people attended each presentation. How many people saw the show?

▲ **Science Connection**
Model of *Tyrannosaurus rex* from the "Moving Dinosaurs" show

Review and Remember

Find the sum or difference.

18. $11.22 + $0.28

19. $0.75 − $0.68

20. $9.47 + $3.14 + $0.89

21. $14.41 − $13.31

22. $124.87 − $77.32

23. $15.91 + $22.29

For Extra Practice, see Set E, page 93.

The Ants Go Marching

You can use grid paper to show the multiplication of two decimals.

Actual size: 0.5 in.

?

Learning About It

The Insect Museum in Washington, D.C., has one of the largest ant farms in the country. The ants at the right are shown magnified $2\frac{1}{2}$ times. The smaller ant is 0.2 times as long as the larger one. How long is the smaller ant?

Work with a partner. Find **0.2 × 0.5**.

Step 1 Use grid paper to model the problem.

What You Need

For each pair:
  grid paper
  blue marker

Mark off a 10 × 10 square grid.	To show the size of the larger ant, use a blue marker to color 0.5 of the grid.	To show the size of the smaller ant, mark 0.2 of the blue area in pencil.

What part of the entire square grid is blue and marked in pencil? How long is the smaller ant?

0.2 × 0.5 in. = 0.1 in.

Step 2 Make a chart like the one below. Record your work in the chart as shown.

Use 10 × 10 grids to find the product of each pair of factors listed in the chart. Record your results in your chart.

Expression	Boxes Shaded with Marker and Pencil	Product
0.2 × 0.5	10	0.10 or 0.1
0.3 × 0.5		
0.1 × 0.8		
0.3 × 0.4		

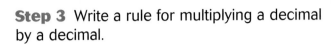

Step 3 Write a rule for multiplying a decimal by a decimal.

Think and Discuss Work with your partner to model 2 × 0.5, using a 10 × 10 grid.

Practice

Match each number sentence with the correct model.

1. 0.3 × 0.2 = 0.06   **2.** 0.6 × 2 = 1.2   **3.** 0.5 × 0.4 = 0.2

a.   b. 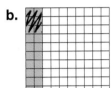   c.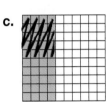

Model each multiplication, using a grid or grids.

4. 0.2 × 0.6   **5.** 0.4 × 2   **6.** 0.1 × 2.5   **7.** 0.6 × 0.6

8. 0.3 × 0.7   **9.** 2 × 0.8   **10.** 0.6 × 0.4   **11.** 1.5 × 0.2

 Use a calculator to find each product for Exercises 12–15. Describe how the decimal point moves in each set of expressions.

12. 0.2 × 4   **13.** 0.3 × 5   **14.** 0.25 × 4   **15.** 2.3 × 12
    0.2 × 0.4   0.3 × 0.5   0.25 × 0.4   2.3 × 1.2
    0.2 × 0.04   0.3 × 0.05   0.25 × 0.04   2.3 × 0.12

16. What If? Suppose an ant is 4 times the length of the actual ant on page 58. How long would it be?

17. Create Your Own Write an expression that shows the multiplication of a decimal by a decimal. Have your partner find the product by using a grid.

 18. Journal Idea If a whole number is multiplied by a decimal less than 1, will the product be greater or less than the whole number? Explain your thinking.

▲ **Science Connection** An ant farm consists of thousands of ants working together to provide food, build shelter, care for the young, and protect the colony from enemies.

Up, Up, and Aweigh

The key to multiplying decimals is locating the decimal point in the product.

> Mars' gravity is 0.38 that of Earth's gravity.

Learning About It

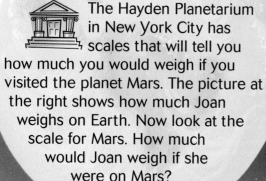

The Hayden Planetarium in New York City has scales that will tell you how much you would weigh if you visited the planet Mars. The picture at the right shows how much Joan weighs on Earth. Now look at the scale for Mars. How much would Joan weigh if she were on Mars?

86 lb   **?**

THERE'S ALWAYS A WAY!

● **One way** is to use paper and pencil.

Step 1 Multiply as with whole numbers.

$$
\begin{array}{r}
0.38 \\
\times\ \ 86 \\
\hline
228 \\
+3040 \\
\hline
3268
\end{array}
$$

Step 2 Use what you know about patterns to place the decimal point in the product.

$$
\begin{array}{r}
0.38 \quad \longleftarrow 2\ \text{decimal places} \\
\times\ \ 86 \\
\hline
228 \\
+3040 \\
\hline
32.68 \quad \longleftarrow 2\ \text{decimal places}
\end{array}
$$

● **Another way** is to use a calculator.

Press: ⓪ ⦿ ③ ⑧ ✕ ⑧ ⑥ ⑤

Display: *32.68*

Joan would weigh 32.68 lb on Mars.

Neptune's gravity is 1.08 that of Earth's gravity.

Connecting Ideas

Multiplying two decimals is almost like multiplying a whole number by a decimal.

Suppose Lisa weighs 94.2 lb on Earth. If Lisa's weight on Neptune is 1.08 times her weight on Earth, how much would she weigh on Neptune?

```
     1.08  ←——— 2 decimal places
  ×  94.2  ←——— + 1 decimal place
    ─────
      216
     4320
  +97200
  ───────
  101.736  ←——— 3 decimal places
```

Count the number of decimal places in **both** factors to determine how many decimal places are in the product.

More Examples

A.
```
     $3.16
  ×    7.5
  ───────
     1580
  +22120
  ───────
  $23.700 = $23.70
```

B.
```
    0.206
  × 0.14
  ──────
    824
  + 2060
  ──────
  0.02884
```

Use zeros as placeholders if necessary.

Think and Discuss If you paid $3.99 per lb, how much money would you pay for 2.1 lb of meat?

Try It Out

Multiply.

1. 2 × 0.4

2. 6 × 0.07

3. 9 × 5.7

4. 23 × 4.2

5. 5.76 × 4.08

6. 0.08 × 0.007

7. 0.62 × 0.038

8. 3.16 × 15.7

9.
```
    6.21
  × 0.03
```

10.
```
    42.7
  ×   21
```

11.
```
   2.637
  × 4.36
```

12.
```
    5.03
  × 0.07
```

13.
```
    13.4
  ×   17
```

14.
```
    52.7
  ×  3.9
```

15.
```
    0.026
  × 0.005
```

16.
```
    525
  × 0.6
```

17.
```
    6.28
  × 0.41
```

18.
```
    3.98
  ×  2.4
```

19.
```
    0.431
  × 0.202
```

20.
```
    0.399
  ×   0.4
```

▲ **Science Connection** In space, astronauts experience weightlessness.

Practice

Put the decimal point in the correct place in each product.

21.   0.261
       × 0.032
       ‾‾‾‾‾‾‾
        8352

22.   54.3
        × 2.1
       ‾‾‾‾‾‾‾
        11403

23.   92.51
        ×   3
       ‾‾‾‾‾‾‾
        27753

24.   0.651
        × 0.02
       ‾‾‾‾‾‾‾
        1302

25.   1.521
        × 0.032
       ‾‾‾‾‾‾‾
        48672

Multiply.

26. 3.5
        × 8

27. 0.27
        × 15

28. 8.9
        × 52

29. 3.5
        × 40

30. 0.84
        × 91

31.   3.8
        × 0.42

32.   0.29
        × 24.3

33.   3.54
        × 0.8

34. 16.3
        × 5.7

35.   20.3
        × 2.05

36.   0.8
        × 0.5

37. 0.06
        × 0.7

38. 0.23
        × 0.5

39. 0.001
        ×   9.7

40.   0.09
        × 0.32

Choose a Method Use mental math, paper and pencil, or a calculator to multiply. Tell which method you use.

41. $16.00
        ×   2.5

42. $3.50
        ×0.75

43. $20.75
        ×   3

44. $18
        × 5.5

45. $0.50
        × 60

46. 165
        × 3.9

47. 15.29
        ×   8.4

48. 0.003
        × 0.07

49. 0.076
        ×   25

50. $16.55
        ×   3.9

Problem Solving

Look at the diagram of the solar system at the right to solve Problems 51–52.

51. Science Connection The distance from Saturn to the sun is 9.54 times that of Earth to the sun. How far is Saturn from the sun?

52. The distance from Jupiter to the sun is 13.43 times that of Mercury to the sun. How far is Jupiter from the sun?

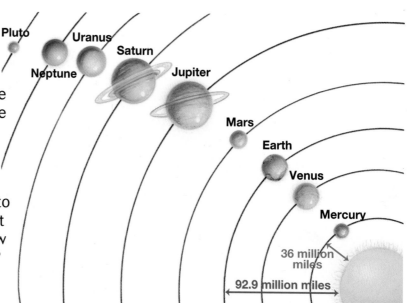

Pluto Uranus Saturn Neptune Jupiter Mars Earth Venus Mercury

36 million miles

92.9 million miles

Use the table at the right to solve Problems 53–56.

53. How much would Paul weigh on Saturn if he weighs 77.4 lb on Earth?

54. If your dog Pluto weighs 55.6 lb on Earth, how much would he weigh on Pluto?

55. **Analyze** Katherine and Seth each weigh 72 lb on Earth. If Katherine goes to Venus and Seth goes to Neptune, will they still weigh the same? How do you know?

56. **Analyze** On Earth, Leslie weighs 80 lb and Jason weighs 75 lb. Leslie goes to Neptune and Jason goes to Saturn. Whose weight is greater now? How much greater?

Surface Gravity on Each Planet	
Mercury	0.38
Venus	0.90
Earth	1.00
Mars	0.38
Jupiter	2.64
Saturn	1.13
Uranus	1.07
Neptune	1.08
Pluto	0.029

Review and Remember

Using Algebra Use mental math to find the missing number.

57. $5 + n = 10$

58. $n + 3 = 9$

59. $12 + n = 15$

60. $23 + n = 29$

61. $n - 7 = 4$

62. $20 - n = 11$

63. $16 - n = 9$

64. $n + 75 = 100$

65. $n + 14 = 20$

66. $39 - n = 19$

67. $66 + n = 88$

68. $n - 100 = 400$

Critical Thinking Corner

Number Sense

Placing the Decimal Point

Without multiplying a–d, answer Questions 1–4.

a. 3.24
$\times 71.2$

b. 32.4
$\times 7.12$

c. 3.24
$\times 7.12$

d. 32.4
$\times 71.2$

1. Which two examples have equal products?

2. Which example has the greatest product?

3. Which example has the least product?

4. How many times greater is the greatest product than the least?

Checkpoint

Multiplying Whole Numbers and Decimals

Using Algebra **Use order of operations to evaluate each expression.** (pages 46–47)

1. $3 + 2 \times 5$ **2.** $(3 + 7) \times 6$ **3.** $18 \div (5 + 1)$ **4.** $5 - 4 \div 2$

5. $9 \times (13 - 3)$ **6.** $(4 + 12) \div 4$ **7.** $7 - 2 \times 3 + 8$ **8.** $1 + (5 + 7) \times 2$

Write a number sentence to give an example of each property. (pages 48–49)

9. Commutative **10.** Identity **11.** Associative **12.** Zero **13.** Distributive

Using Algebra **Find the missing number. Name the property you used.** (pages 48–49)

14. $22 \times 16 = n \times 22$ **15.** $4 \times (10 + 9) = (4 \times n) + (4 \times 9)$ **16.** $46 \times n = 46$

17. $n \times 19 = 0$ **18.** $4 \times (7 \times 10) = (4 \times n) \times 10$ **19.** $n \times 12 = 12 \times 3$

Find each product. (pages 52–53)

20. 2×10 **21.** 5×300 **22.** 15×20 **23.** 12.5×600

24. 3.42×100 **25.** 0.6×300 **26.** 30×400 **27.** $213.2 \times 1,000$

Estimate each product. (pages 54–55)

28. 19×9 **29.** 22×11 **30.** 54×19 **31.** 109×77

32. $\begin{array}{r} 104 \\ \times\ 83 \\ \hline \end{array}$ **33.** $\begin{array}{r} 477 \\ \times\ 136 \\ \hline \end{array}$ **34.** $\begin{array}{r} 558 \\ \times\ 326 \\ \hline \end{array}$ **35.** $\begin{array}{r} 692 \\ \times\ 452 \\ \hline \end{array}$

Estimate first. Then find the exact product. (pages 56–57)

36. 18×48 **37.** 36×67 **38.** 54×21 **39.** 87×76

40. $\begin{array}{r} 112 \\ \times\ 43 \\ \hline \end{array}$ **41.** $\begin{array}{r} 225 \\ \times\ 67 \\ \hline \end{array}$ **42.** $\begin{array}{r} 458 \\ \times\ 82 \\ \hline \end{array}$ **43.** $\begin{array}{r} 627 \\ \times\ 124 \\ \hline \end{array}$

44. $\begin{array}{r} 474 \\ \times\ 205 \\ \hline \end{array}$ **45.** $\begin{array}{r} 703 \\ \times\ 126 \\ \hline \end{array}$ **46.** $\begin{array}{r} 1,279 \\ \times\ 111 \\ \hline \end{array}$ **47.** $\begin{array}{r} 2,638 \\ \times\ 389 \\ \hline \end{array}$

Find each product. (pages 60–63)

48. 2.63×7

49. 4.8×23

50. 0.79×100

51.
$$\begin{array}{r} 9.3 \\ \times\ 6.3 \\ \hline \end{array}$$

52.
$$\begin{array}{r} 12.56 \\ \times\ \ 3.4 \\ \hline \end{array}$$

53.
$$\begin{array}{r} 0.08 \\ \times\ \ 27 \\ \hline \end{array}$$

54.
$$\begin{array}{r} 25.5 \\ \times\ \ 6.3 \\ \hline \end{array}$$

55.
$$\begin{array}{r} 18.48 \\ \times\ 12.3 \\ \hline \end{array}$$

56.
$$\begin{array}{r} 0.006 \\ \times\ 21.8 \\ \hline \end{array}$$

What do you think?

How do the break-apart strategy and the distributive property help you multiply?

Problem Solving

57. Jamie is making a model computer. If an actual computer monitor is 12 inches tall, how tall will Jamie's model be if it is 10 times as large? How tall would it be if it was 100 times as large?

58. Science Connection If Terence were on Mars, he would weigh 0.38 as much as he weighs on Earth. Terence weighs 87 lb on Earth. How much would he weigh on Mars?

59. The Natural History Museum was open 360 days last year and had 1,475 visitors each day. How many people visited the Natural History Museum last year?

60. In the 1980 football season, Terry Bradshaw attempted twice as many passes as he completed. If he completed 218 passes, how many attempts did he make?

Journal Idea

In your own words, write the rule for each of the following multiplication properties.

a. commutative

b. associative

c. distributive

Critical Thinking Corner

Number Sense

Total Cost

Elizabeth bought 6 model elephants at the museum gift shop. Each elephant cost $3.90. She gave the salesperson $18.54. The salesperson told Elizabeth that she still owed $4.86.

What went wrong?

Developing Skills for
Problem Solving

*First read for understanding and then
focus on interpreting remainders.*

READ FOR UNDERSTANDING

A group of eleven sixth-grade students
wanted to visit the museum's special exhibit
on optical illusions. After reading the sign,
Mary said, "We have to go in groups of 4.
I don't think we can all get in."

Salita said, "We can all get into the exhibit
if we can get five more people to join us." Ed
said, "We don't need as many as five people."

MUSEUM EXHIBIT
Optical Illusions
Groups of 4 only

1 How many sixth-graders are there?

2 How are people admitted to the exhibit?

THINK AND DISCUSS

Interpreting Remainders When using
division to solve a problem, a remainder can
affect the solution. How you interpret the
remainder depends on what is being divided
and why.

Reread the paragraph at the top of the page.

3 Is Mary's statement true? Explain.

4 How many students may not be able to visit the exhibit?

5 What was the reasoning behind Salita's statement?
Behind Ed's statement?

6 What is the least number of students that must join the
group in order for all the students to get into the
exhibit? Explain.

7 How was being able to interpret the remainder correctly
useful in solving this problem?

Show What You Learned

Answer each question. Give a reason for your choice.

Ms. Hartley's class wants to view the Virtual Reality Show. There are 26 students, and Ms. Hartley wants one parent to accompany each group of 4 students. She will go with any remaining students.

VIRTUAL REALITY SHOW

2 Shows Daily

1 Which calculation will help you find the number of parents Ms. Hartley needs?

a. $26 \div 5$

b. $26 \div 4$

c. $26 \div 1$

2 Look back at Problem 1. What does the remainder represent?

a. The number of groups

b. The number of parents needed

c. The number of students in Ms. Hartley's group

3 **Explain** Write a division sentence to find the number of groups that will view the show. What do you do with the remainder in the quotient?

Boats are lined up at the dock, waiting to take Mr. Ramos, 37 students, and some parents for a ride around the museum's lake. Each boat holds 6 people. There are enough parents for Mr. Ramos to assign one parent and 5 students to each boat. Mr. Ramos joins the remaining students in another boat.

4 Which calculation is most useful for finding the number of boats needed?

a.
$$\begin{array}{r} 4 \text{ R1} \\ 9\overline{)37} \\ -36 \\ \hline 1 \end{array}$$

b.
$$\begin{array}{r} 6 \text{ R1} \\ 6\overline{)37} \\ -36 \\ \hline 1 \end{array}$$

c.
$$\begin{array}{r} 7 \text{ R2} \\ 5\overline{)37} \\ -35 \\ \hline 2 \end{array}$$

5 What part of the calculation in Problem 4 tells you how many parents are present?

a. The divisor

b. The quotient

c. The remainder

6 **Explain** What part of the calculation tells you how many students were in the boat with Mr. Ramos?

Mental Math: Dividing by Multiples of Ten

Riches of the Earth

Patterns in our number system can help you to divide mentally.

Learning About It

The Geology Museum in Wisconsin has many minerals on exhibit. The crystal pictured here is enlarged 10 times. What is its actual length?

Patterns of ten can help you find quotients mentally.

$$95 \div 1 = 95$$
$$95 \div 10 = 9.5$$
$$95 \div 100 = 0.95$$
$$95 \div 1{,}000 = 0.095$$

← 95 mm →

actual size

10 times enlargement

The actual length is 9.5 millimeters.

More Examples

A. $600 \div 6 = 100$
$600 \div 60 = 10$
$600 \div 600 = 1$
$600 \div 6{,}000 = 0.1$

B. $48.4 \div 2 = 24.2$
$48.4 \div 20 = 2.42$
$48.4 \div 200 = 0.242$
$48.4 \div 2{,}000 = 0.0242$

> For each zero in the divisor that is a multiple of ten, move the decimal point one place to the left.

Think and Discuss How is dividing by a multiple of ten similar to multiplying by a multiple of ten? How is it different?

Try It Out

Use patterns to help you find each quotient mentally.

1. $20 \div 10$
$20 \div 100$
$20 \div 1{,}000$

2. $814 \div 100$
$814 \div 1{,}000$
$814 \div 10{,}000$

3. $1{,}700 \div 170$
$1{,}700 \div 1{,}700$
$1{,}700 \div 17{,}000$

4. $6{,}000 \div 10$
$600 \div 100$
$60 \div 1{,}000$

5. $4.5 \div 1$
$4.5 \div 10$
$4.5 \div 100$

6. $95.8 \div 1$
$95.8 \div 10$
$95.8 \div 100$

7. $2{,}500 \div 25$
$2{,}500 \div 250$
$2{,}500 \div 2{,}500$

8. $10{,}000 \div 10$
$1{,}000 \div 100$
$100 \div 1{,}000$

Practice

Find each quotient.

9. $5 \div 10$ **10.** $4.6 \div 100$ **11.** $316 \div 100$ **12.** $4.9 \div 10$

13. $0.7 \div 1{,}000$ **14.** $0.17 \div 10$ **15.** $27 \div 100$ **16.** $9.247 \div 1000$

17. $4{,}116 \div 10$ **18.** $9 \div 100$ **19.** $0.3 \div 10$ **20.** $301 \div 100$

21. $3 \div 1{,}000$ **22.** $0.07 \div 10$ **23.** $4.19 \div 100$ **24.** $2{,}467 \div 1000$

Compare. Use <, >, or = for each ●.

25. $20 \div 10 \; ● \; 60 \div 30$ **26.** $100 \div 25 \; ● \; 90 \div 30$

27. $300 \div 30 \; ● \; 100 \div 50$ **28.** $1{,}000 \div 200 \; ● \; 5{,}000 \div 100$

Solve for n.

29. $4 \div n = 0.4$ **30.** $7.7 \div n = 0.077$ **31.** $0.5 \div n = 0.005$

32. $197 \div n = 1.97$ **33.** $2.06 \div n = 0.00206$ **34.** $1{,}000 \div n = 100$

35. $2.27 \div n = 0.0227$ **36.** $6 \div n = 0.006$ **37.** $40 \div n = 4$

38. $0.1 \div n = 0.01$ **39.** $398 \div n = 0.398$ **40.** $654 \div n = 6.54$

Problem Solving

41. For art class, you make a clay model of a cubic crystal. The model is a cube with edges 24 mm long. If your model is 4,000 times as large as an actual crystal, how long are the edges of the actual crystal?

42. A sample of gold ore weighing 2,800 grams is on exhibit in the museum. The sample contains 5.6 grams of pure gold. The sample is how many times as heavy as the gold it contains?

▲ This chunk of gold ore consists of rock mixed with pure gold.

Review and Remember

Estimate each sum or difference by rounding.

43. $\begin{array}{r} 6{,}234 \\ +\ 2{,}395 \\ \hline \end{array}$ **44.** $\begin{array}{r} 45.3 \\ -\ 7.6 \\ \hline \end{array}$ **45.** $\begin{array}{r} 20.090 \\ -\ 4.001 \\ \hline \end{array}$ **46.** $\begin{array}{r} 0.013 \\ +\ 0.475 \\ \hline \end{array}$

Baskets Galore

You can estimate quotients by using compatible numbers.

Learning About It

In daily life, many division problems require only an estimate of the quotient. For example, at any given time, the Southwest Museum has 12,880 baskets on exhibit. If each display has 13 baskets, about how many displays are there?

You can estimate the number of displays by changing the numbers to make them compatible for mental division.

12,880 ÷ 13

⬇

13,000 ÷ 13 = 1,000

> Remember, compatible numbers are easy to work with mentally.

The Southwest Museum has about 1,000 displays.

Fine Arts Connection The Southwest Museum of Native Cultures of the Americas has one of the largest basketry collections in the United States with approximately 13,000 baskets.

More Examples

A. 584 ÷ 32
⬇   ⬇
600 ÷ 30 = 20

584 ÷ 32 is about 20

B. 34,604 ÷ 57
⬇   ⬇
36,000 ÷ 60 = 600

34,604 ÷ 57 is about 600

Think and Discuss What compatible numbers would you use to estimate 41,289 ÷ 600? Explain your answer.

Try It Out

Write compatible numbers for each exercise.

1. 1,354 ÷ 12   **2.** 2,378 ÷ 74   **3.** 19,263 ÷ 89   **4.** 126,591 ÷ 13

5. 5,465 ÷ 14   **6.** 11,639 ÷ 36   **7.** 34,983 ÷ 53   **8.** 264,898 ÷ 16

9. 420 ÷ 22   **10.** 8,390 ÷ 118   **11.** 17,900 ÷ 895   **12.** 251,127 ÷ 497

Practice

Write compatible numbers for each exercise.

13. 542 ÷ 62

14. 856 ÷ 84

15. 1,621 ÷ 52

16. 2,851 ÷ 29

17. 3,175 ÷ 58

18. $370 ÷ 42

19. 1,408 ÷ 33

20. 6,325 ÷ 28

Estimate the quotient.

21. 4,579 ÷ 94

22. 6,253 ÷ 73

23. 23,968 ÷ 24

24. 78,043 ÷ 25

25. 2,469 ÷ 25

26. 92,167 ÷ 87

27. 3,625 ÷ 9

28. 64,751 ÷ 6,500

29. 2,378 ÷ 7

30. 3,567 ÷ 14

31. 11,362 ÷ 12

32. 20,263 ÷ 9

33. 56,783 ÷ 82

34. 83,478 ÷ 5

35. 126,000 ÷ 7

36. 162,325 ÷ 42

37. Explain Why would it be easier to use rounding to estimate the quotient of 642 ÷ 72?

Problem Solving

38. The pottery collection has 9,420 clay pots. If there are 9 exhibits, approximately how many pots are in each exhibit?

39. Mental Math A sweetgrass basket weaver made 2,400 baskets in 6 months. About how many baskets did she weave per month?

40. The school's estimate of the cost of the field trip for 34 students is $600. Estimate the cost per student. Why would a student want to estimate his or her cost before the field trip?

41. Mr. Williams gives 35 tours of the museum each week. How many tours would he give if he worked 49 weeks of the year?

▲ Ceremonial Navajo jar, entitled *Buffalo People*

Review and Remember

Using Algebra **Find the rule. Complete each table.**

42.

Input	Output
9	3
21	■
■	6
■	10

43.

Input	Output
5	60
12	■
■	120
■	240

44.

Input	Output
360	9
800	■
■	60
1,640	■

Problem Solving
Guess and Check

Sometimes using the guess and check strategy can help you solve a problem.

The sales receipt at the right shows how much Kenesha paid for two items she bought at the science museum gift shop. The spaceship model cost twice as much as the Milky Way Galaxy poster. How much did she pay for each item?

SPACESHIP MODEL

MILKY WAY GALAXY POSTER

TOTAL $22.50

UNDERSTAND

What do you need to find?

You need to find the price of each item.

PLAN

How can you solve the problem?

You can **guess and check** to solve the problem. Guess the price of the poster. Double your guess for the price of the model. Check by finding the sum. If necessary, adjust your guesses. Continue to guess and check until the sum of your guesses is exactly $22.50.

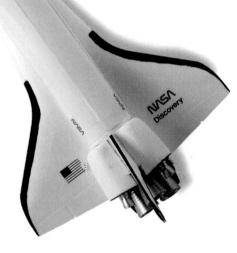

SOLVE

Guess $7.00 for the poster and $14.00 for the model. Check by adding. $7.00 + $14.00 = $21.00

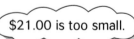
$21.00 is too small.

Guess $7.50 for the poster and $15.00 for the model. Check by adding. $7.50 + $15.00 = $22.50

She paid $7.50 for the poster and $15.00 for the model.

LOOK BACK

What If? Suppose the total cost for the 2 items was $27.00. What would Kenesha have paid for each item?

Using the Strategy

Try using guess and check to solve Problems 1–4.

Large Conch Shells
$1.50 each

Small Conch Shells
$0.50 each

1 Thomas paid $7.00 for 8 conch shells. Small shells cost $0.50 each. Large shells cost $1.50 each. How many of each size did he buy?

2 A video titled *The Explorer's Guide to the Oceans* is 35 minutes longer than *The Explorer's Guide to Rivers*. The combined running time of the videos is 2 hours 11 minutes. How long is each video?

3 Karyn paid $27.00 for two books. The hardcover book cost three times as much as the paperback book. How much did each book cost?

4 Ryan bought 27 gemstones. He bought twice as many pieces of amethyst as he did quartz, and 3 times as many pieces of garnet as he did amethyst. How many pieces of each gemstone did he buy?

Mixed Strategy Review

Try these or other strategies to solve each problem. Tell which strategy you used.

THERE'S ALWAYS A WAY!

Problem Solving Strategies

- Find a Pattern
- Work Backwards
- Use Logical Reasoning
- Write an Equation
- Make a Table
- Solve a Simpler Problem

5 **Analyze** Josie gave 12 gemstones from her collection to Andy. She then received 15 gemstones from Lisa and gave 24 to Sophia. She now has 62 gemstones. How many gemstones did she have originally?

6 **Explain** Lauren received $0.55 in change after buying 3 large postcards at a cost of $0.75 each and 4 small postcards at a cost of $0.55 each. How much money did she give the clerk?

7 In the jewelry case, a necklace is displayed to the left of a bracelet and next to a ring. A watch is displayed to the right of the necklace but to the left of the bracelet. List the pieces of jewelry in order, from left to right, as they appear in the case.

8 In a display case, six rocks are arranged according to weight. The lightest rock weighs 3.4 oz, and the next rock weighs 4.5 oz. If the samples increase in weight by the same amount, what are the weights of the remaining rocks in the display?

Snake in the Grass

You can find exact answers to division problems by using division facts and your understanding of place value.

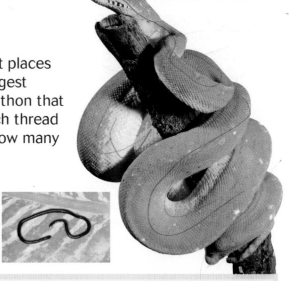

Learning About It

Zoos are like living museums. They are great places to learn about animals. For example, the longest snake at one county zoo is an Indonesian python that measures 377 inches. The shortest is a 4-inch thread snake from the West Indies. The python is how many times as long as the thread snake?

$$377 \div 4 = n$$

Estimate first: $360 \div 4 = 90$

Then divide to find the exact answer.

THERE'S ALWAYS A WAY!

● **One way** is to use the long form of division.

Step 1 Use your estimate to help you place the first digit in the quotient. Divide the tens.	**Step 2** Divide the ones.	**Step 3** Multiply to check.
$$\begin{array}{r} 9 \\ 4\overline{)377} \\ -36 \\ \hline 1 \end{array}$$ • Divide • Multiply • Subtract • Compare $\quad 1 < 4$	$$\begin{array}{r} 94\text{ R1} \\ 4\overline{)377} \\ -36\downarrow \\ \hline 17 \\ -16 \\ \hline 1 \end{array}$$ • Bring Down • Divide • Multiply • Subtract • Compare • Write the remainder in the quotient.	$$\begin{array}{r} 94 \\ \times\ 4 \\ \hline 376 \\ +\ 1 \\ \hline 377 \end{array}$$

● **Another way** is to use the short form of division.

Step 1 Divide the tens.	**Step 2** Divide the ones.
$$\begin{array}{r} 9 \\ 4\overline{)37^17} \end{array}$$ $4 \times 9 = 36$ $37 - 36 = 1$	$$\begin{array}{r} 94\text{ R1} \\ 4\overline{)37^17} \end{array}$$ $4 \times 4 = 16$ $17 - 16 = 1$

The python is a little more than 94 times as long as the thread snake. The answer is close to the estimate of 90.

Think and Discuss How does estimating first help you find the first digit in the quotient?

Try It Out

Divide. Check your answer by multiplying.

1. 3)59
2. 7)98
3. 5)39
4. 9)86
5. 9)108
6. 4)113
7. 6)495
8. 8)729
9. 3)4,167
10. 7)3,961
11. 2)5,211
12. 5)6,135

Practice

Find each quotient.

13. 2)299
14. 4)600
15. 6)365
16. 5)512
17. 9)3,456
18. 7)7,004
19. 8)6,400
20. 9)15,813
21. 2)13,765
22. 3)33,200
23. 4)14,063
24. 5)13,307

Using Algebra Use mental math to find the value for *n* that makes each equation true.

25. $35 \div n = 5$
26. $44 \div n = 4$
27. $72 \div n = 8$
28. $8 \times n = 808$
29. $4 \times n = 416$
30. $6 \times n = 2,400$

Problem Solving

31. **Science Connection** The king cobra can measure up to 219 inches long. The prairie ringneck measures 9 inches. The cobra is how many times as long as the ringneck?

32. **Science Connection** The heaviest snake is the anaconda. It can weigh as much as 487 pounds. If the garter snake weighs 3 pounds, how many times as heavy is the anaconda?

33. The zoo is open on Saturdays from 9 A.M.–8 P.M. The snake house is a popular attraction and has 144 visitors each hour. How many people visit the snake house on Saturday?

34. A snake is 4 times as old as another snake. In 16 years the older snake will be twice the age of the younger snake. How old is the younger snake now? What strategy did you use to find out?

INTERNET ACTIVITY
www.sbgmath.com

Review and Remember

Round each number to the underlined place.

35. 18.904
36. 4,490
37. 81.29
38. 0.876
38. 1,999
40. 26,406

Those Bones

Dividing by two-digit divisors is like dividing by one-digit divisors. Estimating can help you place digits in the quotients correctly.

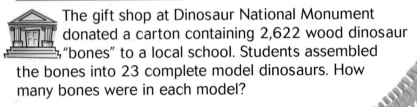

Learning About It

The gift shop at Dinosaur National Monument donated a carton containing 2,622 wood dinosaur "bones" to a local school. Students assembled the bones into 23 complete model dinosaurs. How many bones were in each model?

$$2,622 \div 23 = n$$

Estimate first: $\quad 2,400 \div 24 = 100$

Then divide to find an exact answer.

Step 1 Use your estimate to help you place the first digit in the quotient. Divide the hundreds.	**Step 2** Divide the tens.	**Step 3** Divide the ones.

$$\begin{array}{r} 1 \\ 23\overline{)2,622} \\ -23 \\ \hline 3 \end{array}$$
• Divide
• Multiply
• Subtract
• Compare
  $3 < 23$

$$\begin{array}{r} 11 \\ 23\overline{)2,622} \\ -23\downarrow \\ \hline 32 \\ -23 \\ \hline 9 \end{array}$$
• Bring Down
• Divide
• Multiply
• Subtract
• Compare
  $9 < 23$

$$\begin{array}{r} 114 \\ 23\overline{)2,622} \\ -23 \\ \hline 32 \\ -23\downarrow \\ \hline 92 \\ -92 \\ \hline 0 \end{array}$$
• Bring Down
• Divide
• Multiply
• Subtract
• Compare
• Write the remainder, if any, in the quotient.

Each complete model will have 114 bones.

More Examples

A.
$$\begin{array}{r} 108 \text{ R2} \\ 27\overline{)2,918} \\ -27\downarrow \\ \hline 21 \\ -0\downarrow \\ \hline 218 \\ -216 \\ \hline 2 \end{array}$$

Since 21 < 27, put a 0 in the quotient.

B.
$$\begin{array}{r} 41 \text{ R7} \\ 50\overline{)2,057} \\ -2\,00\downarrow \\ \hline 57 \\ -50 \\ \hline 7 \end{array}$$

Think and Discuss Look at $300 \div 34$. What is the first digit in the quotient? Explain your thinking.

Try It Out

Tell whether the first digit in the quotient is in the correct place. If it is not, put it in the correct place.

1. $\frac{2}{15\overline{)316}}$

2. $\frac{7}{91\overline{)657}}$

3. $\frac{1}{56\overline{)5,932}}$

4. $\frac{5}{62\overline{)36,743}}$

Divide. Check your answer by multiplying.

5. $31\overline{)238}$

6. $49\overline{)397}$

7. $15\overline{)453}$

8. $10\overline{)4,020}$

▲ Wall of bones at Dinosaur National Monument

Practice

Divide.

9. $13\overline{)455}$ **10.** $65\overline{)288}$ **11.** $49\overline{)453}$ **12.** $26\overline{)182}$

13. $38\overline{)3,914}$ **14.** $74\overline{)8,889}$ **15.** $80\overline{)1,604}$ **16.** $32\overline{)2,759}$

17. $77\overline{)8,037}$ **18.** $27\overline{)34,999}$ **19.** $15\overline{)39,670}$ **20.** $36\overline{)20,044}$

21. $16\overline{)35,744}$ **22.** $99\overline{)40,095}$ **23.** $37\overline{)39,072}$ **24.** $56\overline{)59,421}$

Problem Solving

25. There are 4,623 dinosaurs in 23 displays around the country. How many dinosaurs are in each display, if each display has the same number of dinosaurs?

26. There are 37 cases filled with dinosaur teeth. If each case displays 1,240 dinosaur teeth, how many dinosaur teeth are being displayed?

Review and Remember

Add or subtract.

27.
$$\begin{array}{r} 3,671 \\ -\ 245 \\ \hline \end{array}$$

28.
$$\begin{array}{r} 27,985 \\ +\ \ \ 497 \\ \hline \end{array}$$

29.
$$\begin{array}{r} 30,002 \\ -\ \ \ 202 \\ \hline \end{array}$$

30.
$$\begin{array}{r} 621,405 \\ +\ 23,597 \\ \hline \end{array}$$

31.
$$\begin{array}{r} 0.853 \\ +\ 0.753 \\ \hline \end{array}$$

32.
$$\begin{array}{r} 3.618 \\ +\ 0.721 \\ \hline \end{array}$$

33.
$$\begin{array}{r} 62.9 \\ -\ 4.385 \\ \hline \end{array}$$

34.
$$\begin{array}{r} 692.85 \\ -\ 46.917 \\ \hline \end{array}$$

At the Gift Shop

You can apply what you know about dividing whole numbers to dividing a decimal by a whole number.

Learning About It

In the museum gift shop, you and four friends buy three posters, a puzzle, and a model rocket. If you share the cost of the items equally, how much should each of you pay?

$$\$26.30 \div 5 = n$$

Estimate first: $\$30.00 \div 5 = \$6.00$

Then divide to find an exact answer.

$26.30

Step 1 Place a decimal point in the quotient directly over the decimal point in the dividend.	**Step 2** Divide as with whole numbers. Use your estimate to help you place the first digit.	**Step 3** Check by multiplying.
5)$26.30	$5.26 5)$26.30 − 25 1 3 − 1 0 30 − 30 0	$5.26 × 5 $26.30

Each person should pay $5.26. This is close to the estimate of $6.00.

More Examples

A.
```
    0.85
 9)7.65
  − 7 2
    45
   − 45
     0
```

> When the quotient is less than 1, put a zero in the ones place.

B.
```
    0.032
 6)0.192
   − 18
     12
    − 12
      0
```

> Since $1 < 6$, put a zero in the tenths place of the quotient as a placeholder.

Connecting Ideas

You have learned how to place the zeros in a quotient when needed. Sometimes it is also necessary to place zeros in the dividend.

$$37 \div 4 = n$$

Estimate first: $40 \div 4 = 10$

Then divide $37 \div 4$ to get an exact answer.

Step 1 Place a decimal point in the quotient. Then divide.	**Step 2** Place a zero in the tenths place. Then divide.	**Step 3** Place a zero in the hundredths place. Then divide.
``` 9. 4)37. − 36 1 ```	``` 9.2 4)37.0 − 36 1 0 − 8 2 ```	``` 9.25 4)37.00 − 36 1 0 − 8 20 − 20 0 ```

More Examples

A.
```
    0.2075
 24)4.9800
   − 4 8
     180
    −168
     120
    − 120
       0
```

B.
```
     0.02
 12)0.24
   − 24
     0
```

> Place zeros in the quotient as needed.

Think and Discuss Why do you put the decimal point after the 37 and not before it in Step 1?

Try It Out

Estimate the quotient. Then divide.

1. $4.2 \div 7$ 2. $31.6 \div 8$ 3. $\$12.20 \div 5$ 4. $62.3 \div 7$

5. $\$18.24 \div 3$ 6. $\$17.10 \div 9$ 7. $\$32.40 \div 12$ 8. $\$4.73 \div 11$

Tell whether the first digit in the quotient is in the correct place. If it is not, put it in the correct place.

9. $3\overline{)28.29}$ quotient 9 10. $8\overline{)2.96}$ quotient 0.3 11. $4\overline{)28.4}$ quotient 6 12. $65\overline{)383.5}$ quotient $.5$

13. $63\overline{)12.6}$ quotient 2 14. $6\overline{)18.78}$ quotient $.3$ 15. $6\overline{)494.4}$ quotient 8 16. $9\overline{)6.6669}$ quotient 0.7

Practice

Estimate the quotient. Then divide.

17. $3\overline{)\$18.24}$ 18. $9\overline{)\$17.10}$ 19. $12\overline{)\$35.40}$ 20. $11\overline{)\$4.73}$

21. $7\overline{)20.062}$ 22. $13\overline{)9.10}$ 23. $11\overline{)1.309}$ 24. $4\overline{)0.412}$

25. $17\overline{)8.551}$ 26. $6\overline{)0.384}$ 27. $20\overline{)85.70}$ 28. $39\overline{)469.56}$

Check each exercise by multiplying. Indicate whether the exercise is correct or incorrect.

29. $2.7 \div 9 = 0.3$ 30. $41.4 \div 6 = 6.8$ 31. $6.03 \div 9 = 0.67$

32. $43.8 \div 6 = 0.72$ 33. $2.37 \div 3 = 7.9$ 34. $124.63 \div 11 = 11.33$

35. $62.7 \div 3 = 20.9$ 36. $97.5 \div 12 = 8.120$ 37. $0.248 \div 2 = 0.124$

38. $6\overline{)0.054}$ quotient 0.009 39. $13\overline{)3.003}$ quotient 2.31 40. $9\overline{)100.62}$ quotient 1.18

Divide.

41. $3\overline{)28.53}$ 42. $8\overline{)4.88}$ 43. $9\overline{)6.669}$ 44. $12\overline{)1.08}$

45. $\$37.20 \div 60$ 46. $\$0.96 \div 32$ 47. $\$96.81 \div 21$ 48. $\$28.86 \div 26$

49. $22.05 \div 70$ 50. $30.736 \div 8$ 51. $175.95 \div 207$ 52. $234.96 \div 132$

53. $32.7 \div 5$ 54. $1.61 \div 4$ 55. $211.4 \div 7$ 56. $3.672 \div 18$

57. $11\overline{)23.1}$ 58. $19\overline{)38.76}$ 59. $8\overline{)0.128}$ 60. $22\overline{)6.842}$

Problem Solving

61. Seventeen students each bought two posters in the museum gift shop. The total cost was $168.30. How much did each student spend?

62. Analyze If each student in Problem 61 paid with a $20 bill, how much change should each receive?

63. In one room of the museum, a wall that is 35.52 feet long is divided into 24 equal sections. How long is each section?

64. Analyze On a typical weekend at the museum gift store, sales total $1,367.08. Sales for the rest of the week typically total $2,542.60. How much more money does the gift shop take in on a Saturday or Sunday than it does on a weekday?

Review and Remember

Round each number to the underlined place.

65. 4̲8   **66.** 1̲91   **67.** 6̲49   **68.** 3.4̲9   **69.** 3̲,601   **70.** 41̲.88

71. 2.96̲1   **72.** 3,9̲61   **73.** 4̲3,916   **74.** 0.63̲14   **75.** 56̲.56   **76.** 437.9̲1

Time for Technology

Using a Calculator

Patterns in Numbers

You can read 6^2 as "six squared" or "six to the second power." To find 6^2 you multiply 6×6.

Find the value of the expressions below. Look for patterns to help you.

1.
$6 - 5 =$
$6^2 - 5^2 =$
$56^2 - 55^2 =$
$556^2 - 555^2 =$

2.
$7 - 4 =$
$7^2 - 4^2 =$
$57^2 - 54^2 =$
$557^2 - 554^2 =$

3.
$8 - 3 =$
$8^2 - 3^2 =$
$58^2 - 53^2 =$
$558^2 - 553^2 =$

4. Continue the pattern for the expression $9 - 2 = 7$.

For Extra Practice, see Set K, page 95.

Grouping It

You can use a number line to show division of two decimals.

Learning About It

When you divide whole numbers, you want to find equal groups. For example, when you divide 6 by 3, you want to find how many equal groups of 3 you can make from 6.

You can show this on a number line.

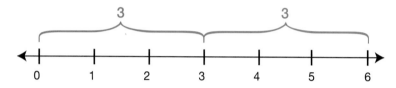

When you divide 6 by 3, you get 2 equal groups.

$$6 \div 3 = 2$$

This method can also be used for dividing decimals.

Work with a partner. Find $1.8 \div 0.3$.

Step 1 Copy the number line below on a piece of grid paper. Let each square = 0.1 unit.

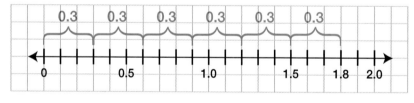

> How many groups of 0.3 can you make from 1.8?

$$1.8 \div 0.3 = 6$$

Step 2 Make a chart like the one below. Working with your partner, use the number line to help you divide the decimals shown.

Division example	How many equal groups?	Division sentence
1.8 ÷ 0.3	6	1.8 ÷ 0.3 = 6
0.8 ÷ 0.4		
1.4 ÷ 0.2		
0.9 ÷ 0.3		
1.6 ÷ 0.8		

What You Need

For each pair:
   grid paper

Step 3 Suppose you wanted to use this method to divide by hundredths. You would need a number line like the one shown below.

Find $0.8 \div 0.05$.

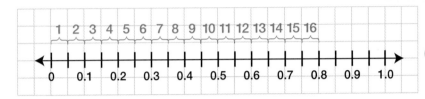

How many groups of 0.05 can be made from 0.8?

You can make 16 groups of 0.05 from 0.8.

So, $0.8 \div 0.05 = 16$

Think and Discuss How could you use multiplication to check your solution to Step 3?

Practice

Draw number lines to find each quotient.

1. $1.8 \div 0.3$ **2.** $1.6 \div 0.4$ **3.** $0.6 \div 0.02$

4. Find each quotient.

   a. $0.4 \div 2$ **b.** $0.4 \div 0.2$ **c.** $0.4 \div 0.02$

5. Generalize Look back at Exercise 4. What happens to the quotients as the divisors get smaller and smaller?

6. Find each quotient.

   a. $4 \div 2$ **b.** $0.4 \div 2$ **c.** $0.04 \div 2$

7. Generalize Look back at Exercise 6. What happens to the quotients as the dividends get smaller and smaller?

8. The side section of horizontal stripes on King Tut's mask is about 16.2 cm long. Each horizontal stripe in that section is about 0.9 cm thick. How many horizontal stripes are in that section?

9. Create Your Own Create two exercises that involve dividing a decimal by a decimal. Your partner should create number lines to find the quotients. Change roles and repeat the exercise.

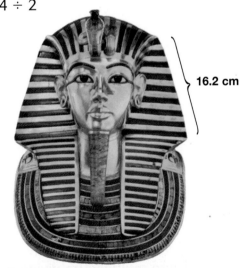

16.2 cm

▲ **Social Studies Connection**
King Tutankhamen's gold death mask

Dividing a Decimal by a Decimal

An Art Reduction

You can use what you know about dividing decimals by whole numbers to divide decimals by decimals.

Learning About It

You have received an art poster from a pen pal in Mexico. The poster is a copy of a painting by Diego Rivera, one of Mexico's most famous artists. The area of the poster is 1.65 square feet (1.65 ft^2). The original painting is how many times as large as the poster?

To find out, divide 13.2 by 1.65.

P E A S A N T S

By **DIEGO RIVERA**

Fine Arts Connection ➤
Peasants, by Diego Rivera. The painting covers an area of about 13.2 ft^2.

Step 1 Think of a multiple of 10 that will make the divisor a whole number.	Step 2 Multiply the dividend and the divisor by the same multiple of 10.	Step 3 Place the decimal point in the quotient and divide.
$1.65 \times 100 = 165$ $1.65 \overline{)13.2}$	$165. \overline{)1320.}$	$\begin{array}{r} 8. \\ 165 \overline{)1320.} \\ -1320 \\ \hline 0 \end{array}$

The original is 8 times as large as the poster.

More Examples

A.
$$\begin{array}{r} 6\,5. \\ 82 \overline{)5330.} \\ -492 \\ \hline 410 \\ -410 \\ \hline 0 \end{array}$$

Multiply the divisor and the dividend by 10. Place the decimal point in the quotient.

B.
$$\begin{array}{r} 3.8 \\ 045 \overline{)171.0} \\ -135 \\ \hline 360 \\ -360 \\ \hline 0 \end{array}$$

Multiply the divisor and the dividend by 100. Place the decimal point in the quotient. Add zeros to continue dividing.

Think and Discuss When dividing decimals, why is it necessary to multiply the dividend by the same multiple of 10 that you used to multiply the divisor?

Try It Out

Find each quotient.

1. $0.9\overline{)6.39}$ **2.** $2.5\overline{)12.75}$ **3.** $4.5\overline{)10.755}$ **4.** $0.42\overline{)4.788}$

5. $1.75\overline{)35}$ **6.** $2.8\overline{)14}$ **7.** $0.07\overline{)0.49}$ **8.** $0.31\overline{)1.24}$

Practice

Tell what multiple of ten you would use to make the divisor a whole number.

9. $16.48 \div 0.04$ **10.** $2.31 \div 1.1$ **11.** $0.50 \div 0.025$ **12.** $91 \div 0.13$

13. $24 \div 0.004$ **14.** $5.1 \div 1.7$ **15.** $75.6 \div 1.8$ **16.** $0.10 \div 0.0002$

Find each quotient.

17. $3.4\overline{)12.92}$ **18.** $0.8\overline{)26.08}$ **19.** $4.5\overline{)22.5}$ **20.** $0.03\overline{)0.228}$

21. $1.08\overline{)3.456}$ **22.** $1.9\overline{)5.738}$ **23.** $0.004\overline{)6.8}$ **24.** $0.013\overline{)0.52}$

25. $0.07\overline{)1.33}$ **26.** $0.007\overline{)0.868}$ **27.** $9.5\overline{)2.299}$ **28.** $0.06\overline{)0.576}$

29. $1.7\overline{)3.995}$ **30.** $0.81\overline{)3,402}$ **31.** $0.65\overline{)20.8}$ **32.** $5.7\overline{)3.534}$

Problem Solving

33. You want to cover a rectangular bulletin board with rectangular art posters. The area of the bulletin board is 49.2 ft². If each poster has an area of 3.075 ft², how many posters will you need?

34. Analyze You need 12 art boards, which cost $1.35 each. You have $11.50. How many art boards can you buy?

35. Chris spent half of her money on a poster. Then she spent half of what she had left for a small figurine. She bought lunch for $5.00. When she got home she had $2.50 left. How much did she have to start with? What strategy did you use to find out?

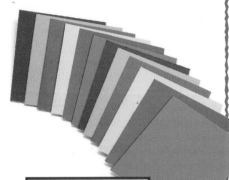

Art Boards
$1.35 each

Review and Remember

Evaluate.

36. $1.04 + 16.5 + 0.44$ **37.** $7.15 - 6.05$ **38.** 5×20 **39.** $0.024 + 1.408$

40. $2.434 - 1.545$ **41.** $44.56 - 23.567$ **42.** 46×3 **43.** 911×214

Rock It

The rounding techniques used for whole numbers can be used to round to any decimal place.

Learning About It

The Rock and Mineral Museum bought 95 rock samples for $35 from a retailer in Brazil. How much did one rock sample cost?

To find out, divide the total cost by the number of rock samples.

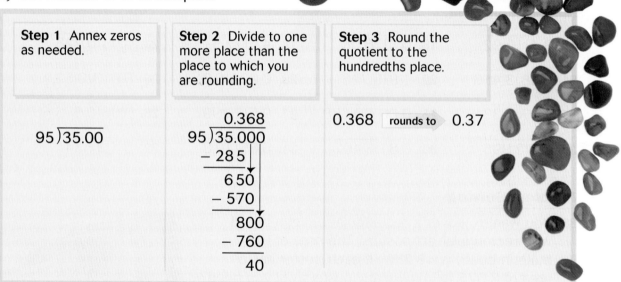

Step 1 Annex zeros as needed.	**Step 2** Divide to one more place than the place to which you are rounding.	**Step 3** Round the quotient to the hundredths place.
$$95\overline{)35.00}$$	$$\begin{array}{r} 0.368 \\ 95\overline{)35.000} \\ -285 \\ \hline 650 \\ -570 \\ \hline 800 \\ -760 \\ \hline 40 \end{array}$$	0.368 **rounds to** 0.37

One rock sample costs $0.37.

More Examples

A. Round the quotient to the nearest tenth.
10.8 ÷ 5.2

$$\begin{array}{r} 2.07 \\ 52.\overline{)108.00} \\ -104 \\ \hline 400 \\ -364 \\ \hline 36 \end{array}$$

Divide to the hundredths. Round 2.07 to 2.1

 B. Find 6,025 ÷ 436 on your calculator. Round the quotient to the nearest hundredth.

Display:  13.818807   Look at the thousandths place.

Since 8 > 5, the rounded quotient is 13.82.

Think and Discuss To what place do you divide if you want to round to the nearest whole number? Explain.

Try It Out

Divide. Round the quotient to the place named.

1. 149 ÷ 7
tenths

2. 35 ÷ 4.8
hundredths

3. 0.75 ÷ 0.8
thousandths

4. $20.79 ÷ 15
ones

Practice

Divide. Round the quotient to the place named.

5. 5,287 ÷ 52
tenths

6. $80 ÷ 45
ones

7. 20.83 ÷ 7.3
hundredths

8. 200 ÷ 0.3
thousandths

9. $10.45 ÷ 20
hundredths

10. 9 ÷ 70
thousandths

11. 50 ÷ 6.7
ones

12. 5.6 ÷ 59
tenths

Divide. Round the quotient to the nearest hundredth.

13. $15.38 ÷ 9

14. $300 ÷ 8

15. $759 ÷ 1.7

16. $2,000 ÷ 528

17. 4.5)63.49

18. 0.98)12,785

19. 7.8)3,999

20. 0.65)568.55

Problem Solving

Use the graph at the right for Problems 21–24.

21. What is the cost of one garnet sample?

22. How much more does one amber sample cost than one amethyst sample?

23. **You Decide** You want to buy 2 dozen gemstones. If you have $100, what can you buy?

24. **Analyze** You bought 1 amethyst sample, 3 amber samples, 2 garnet samples, and 5 malachite samples. About how much change do you receive from $50?

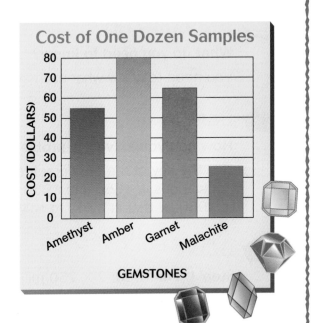

Cost of One Dozen Samples

INTERNET ACTIVITY
www.sbgmath.com

Review and Remember

Using Algebra Compare. Use <, >, or = to fill in the ⬤.

25. 4 × 3 + 2 ⬤ 7 × 2

26. (3 + 7) × 5 ⬤ 6 × 8

27. 3 × 5 × 2 ⬤ 20 + 5

28. 9 − 6 + 3 ⬤ 2 × 5 − 4

For Extra Practice, see Set M, page 96.

Problem Solving
Using a Pictograph

You can interpret pictographs to solve problems.

World Population

1995	👤👤👤👤👤👤👤👤👤👤👤👤👤👤👤👤👤👤👤👤
1950	👤👤👤👤👤👤👤👤👤👤
1900	👤👤👤👤👤👤
1850	👤👤👤👤👤
1750	👤👤👤
1650	👤👤

👤 = 250 Million People

The world population in 1950 was how many times as great as it was in 1650?

 ### UNDERSTAND

What do you need to know?

You need to know what each symbol represents.

 ### PLAN

How can you solve the problem?

Use the key of the pictograph and multiply to find the populations in 1650 and 1950. Then divide the population in 1950 by that in 1650 to solve the problem.

 ### SOLVE

Step 1 For 1650: 2 × 250 million = 500 million people
For 1950: 10 × 250 million = 2,500 million people

Step 2 Use mental math to find 2,500 million ÷ 500 million.
Use smaller numbers and think: 25 ÷ 5 = 5.
So 2,500,000,000 ÷ 500,000,000 = 5

The population in 1950 was 5 times as great as in 1650.

 ### LOOK BACK

How else could you use the pictograph to solve the problem?

Show What You Learned

Use the pictograph on page 88 to solve Problems 1–4.

1 Between which years did the world population double? triple?

2 About how many more people were alive in 1950 than in 1750?

3 *Predict* What will be the world population in the year 2000? Give reasons to support your answer.

4 *Analyze* By about how many more people did the population increase between 1950 and 1995 than it increased between 1900 and 1950?

Use the pictograph below to solve Problems 5–8.

2015: Projected Populations of 6 Cities

City	Population
Tokyo, Japan	👤👤👤👤👤👤👤👤👤
São Paolo, Brazil	👤👤👤👤👤👤
Bombay, India	👤👤👤👤👤👤👤👤
Beijing, China	👤👤👤👤👤👤
Jakarta, Indonesia	👤👤👤👤👤👤
Buenos Aires, Argentina	👤👤👤

👤 = 3 Million People

5 Which cities are expected to have populations greater than 22,000,000 people by the year 2015?

6 *Explain* The projected population in Los Angeles in 2015 is 14,300,000 people. How would you show this data in the pictograph?

7 Answer *true* or *false*.

   a. By the year 2015, Tokyo is projected to have more than twice the population of Buenos Aires.

   b. By the year 2015, the population of Jakarta is projected to be about 9 million people less than that of Bombay.

   c. The projected populations of Jakarta and São Paulo are about the same.

8 *Create Your Own* Use the pictograph to create a problem of your own. Share it with a partner.

Checkpoint

Dividing Whole Numbers and Decimals

Vocabulary

Match each definition to the correct property.

1. The product of zero and any number is zero.

2. The order in which numbers are multiplied does not affect the product.

3. The way in which factors are grouped does not affect the product.

4. The product of one and any number is that number.

Word Bank

Associative Property
Commutative Property
Distributive Property
Identity Property
Property of Zero

Concepts and Skills

Use mental math to find the quotients. (pages 68–69)

5. $7.8 \div 10$

6. $9.4 \div 100$

7. $87 \div 1,000$

8. $2.6 \div 100$

9. $9.72 \div 100$

10. $0.8 \div 100$

11. $3.25 \div 1,000$

12. $95 \div 100$

Write compatible numbers for each quotient.
Then estimate the quotient. (pages 70–71)

13. $527 \div 54$

14. $4,381 \div 71$

15. $48,197 \div 49$

16. $22,222 \div 73$

Estimate the quotient. Then divide to find an exact answer. (pages 74–81)

17. $5\overline{)9,020}$

18. $3\overline{)8,713}$

19. $9\overline{)24,562}$

20. $38\overline{)4,928}$

21. $84\overline{)7,487}$

22. $73\overline{)25,863}$

23. $12\overline{)9.6}$

24. $25\overline{)3.75}$

25. $30\overline{)\$18.90}$

26. $42\overline{)18.9}$

27. $19\overline{)45.6}$

28. $78\overline{)238.68}$

Find each quotient. (pages 84–85)

29. $0.8\overline{)19.6}$

30. $7.5\overline{)326.25}$

31. $6.3\overline{)577.08}$

32. $0.84\overline{)0.4872}$

Divide. Round the quotient to the place named.

(pages 86–87)

33. $19\overline{)37}$ hundredths

34. $62\overline{)6.5}$ thousandths

35. $0.36\overline{)0.71}$ ones

36. $5.4\overline{)0.94}$ tenths

Problem Solving

Use the table at the right to solve Problems 37–40.

37. A tiger's weight is about how many times as great as a cheetah's weight?

38. A bobcat is how many times as heavy as a domestic cat?

39. **Explain** Would seven average cheetahs be heavier than two tigers?

40. A tiger is how many times as heavy as a domestic cat?

Journal Idea

Explain how you would check a division example with a rounded quotient.

What do you think?

Is it more difficult to estimate quotients with decimals or quotients with whole numbers?

Feline Weights

Feline	Pounds
Tiger	420
Jaguar	239
Cheetah	120
Bobcat	24
Domestic cat	12

You Decide

Activity

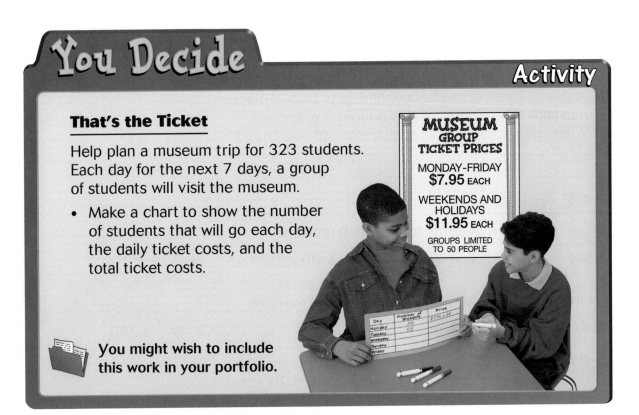

That's the Ticket

Help plan a museum trip for 323 students. Each day for the next 7 days, a group of students will visit the museum.

- Make a chart to show the number of students that will go each day, the daily ticket costs, and the total ticket costs.

You might wish to include this work in your portfolio.

MUSEUM GROUP TICKET PRICES

MONDAY–FRIDAY
$7.95 EACH

WEEKENDS AND HOLIDAYS
$11.95 EACH

GROUPS LIMITED TO 50 PEOPLE

Extra Practice

Set A (pages 46–47)

Using Algebra Evaluate each expression.

1. $5 + 4 \times 2$ **2.** $10 \div 2 \times 10$ **3.** $(50 + 6) \div 8$ **4.** $7 + (4 \times 7) \div 5$

5. $3 \times 8 - 24$ **6.** $91 \div (16 - 3)$ **7.** $(18 + 7) \times (11 - 7)$ **8.** $(4 \times 8) \div 16 + 8$

9. Three groups of 9 students each were admitted to the gemstone exhibit. Then 2 more students were allowed to join each group. How many students were admitted to the gemstone exhibit?

Set B (pages 48–49)

Use multiplication properties and mental math to evaluate the expressions.

1. 8×24 **2.** 7×52 **3.** 4×19 **4.** 9×35

5. $7 \times 10 \times 2$ **6.** $4 \times 8 \times 3$ **7.** $2 \times (5 \times 7)$ **8.** $15 \times 4 \times 0$

Using Algebra Find the value of each n. Name the property used.

9. $15 \times 8 = n \times 15$ **10.** $(8 \times n) \times 3 = 8 \times (2 \times 3)$ **11.** $52 \times n = 0$

12. $9 \times n = 5 \times 9$ **13.** $2 \times (4+5) = (2 \times 4) + (2 \times n)$ **14.** $8 \times n = 8$

15. Explain Three students bought 4 gifts each at the museum shop. Four students bought 3 gifts each. Which group bought more gifts. How do you know?

Set C (pages 52–53)

Mental Math Use patterns to find each product.

1. 0.4×10 **2.** 9×100 **3.** 30×90 **4.** 2.22×100

Use multiples of 10 to find the value of each variable.

5. $44.8 \times n = 448$ **6.** $9.19 \times a = 919$ **7.** $4.2 \times r = 4{,}200$

8. A museum shop sold a model of an ant that was 20 times as large as a real ant. If the real ant is 20 mm long, how long is the model?

Extra Practice

Set D   (pages 54–55)

Choose the best estimate.

1. 57×19 **a.** 1,500   **b.** 1,200   **c.** 600

2. 423×2.9 **a.** 1,200   **b.** 800   **c.** 1,500

Estimate the product.

3. 7×28 **4.** 9×7.1 **5.** 56×5.05 **6.** 83×79

7. 52.9×593 **8.** 6.4×821 **9.** 85×412 **10.** 912×779

Set E   (pages 56–57)

Choose a Method Use mental math, paper and pencil, or a calculator to find the product. Tell which method you use.

1. $\begin{array}{r} 52 \\ \times 43 \\ \hline \end{array}$ **2.** $\begin{array}{r} 138 \\ \times 28 \\ \hline \end{array}$ **3.** $\begin{array}{r} 419 \\ \times 509 \\ \hline \end{array}$ **4.** $\begin{array}{r} 5{,}238 \\ \times 447 \\ \hline \end{array}$

5. The museum theater shows a film about dinosaurs 360 days a year. If 750 people watch the film every day, how many people watch the film every year?

Set F   (pages 60–63)

Place the decimal point in the answer.

1. $\begin{array}{r} 9.92 \\ \times 0.53 \\ \hline 52576 \end{array}$ **2.** $\begin{array}{r} 82.7 \\ \times 3.8 \\ \hline 31426 \end{array}$ **3.** $\begin{array}{r} 47.52 \\ \times 18 \\ \hline 85536 \end{array}$ **4.** $\begin{array}{r} 0.328 \\ \times 0.08 \\ \hline 2624 \end{array}$ **5.** $\begin{array}{r} 4.23 \\ \times 5.9 \\ \hline 24957 \end{array}$

Multiply.

6. $\begin{array}{r} 6.4 \\ \times 7 \\ \hline \end{array}$ **7.** $\begin{array}{r} 0.95 \\ \times 0.8 \\ \hline \end{array}$ **8.** $\begin{array}{r} 5.7 \\ \times 20 \\ \hline \end{array}$ **9.** $\begin{array}{r} 3.6 \\ \times 4.8 \\ \hline \end{array}$ **10.** $\begin{array}{r} 37.5 \\ \times 9.5 \\ \hline \end{array}$

11. Science Connection The diameter of Saturn is about 9.45 times as great as the diameter of Earth. If Earth's diameter is 7,926 miles, what is Saturn's diameter?

Extra Practice

Set G (pages 68–69)

Find the quotient.

1. $97 \div 100$ 2. $82 \div 1{,}000$ 3. $8.9 \div 100$ 4. $5.18 \div 100$

5. $98 \div 10$ 6. $5 \div 1{,}000$ 7. $0.5 \div 100$ 8. $73 \div 1{,}000$

Using Algebra   **Find the missing variable.**

9. $14 \div n = 0.14$ 10. $0.9 \div n = 0.009$ 11. $8.37 \div n = 0.837$

12. A chart in the museum said that about 10,500 troy ounces of gold are mined in the U.S. every year. This was a misprint. Someone had divided the correct number by 1,000. What is the correct number?

Set H (pages 70–71)

Write compatible numbers for each exercise.

1. $863 \div 84$ 2. $1{,}394 \div 47$ 3. $36{,}502 \div 72$ 4. $93{,}420 \div 96$

Estimate the quotient. Multiply to determine if your estimate is too high or low.

5. $2{,}594 \div 8$ 6. $30{,}562 \div 3$ 7. $14{,}982 \div 15$ 8. $273{,}275 \div 29$

9. The admission to a museum for 84 students is $264.15. About how much does one student pay?

Set I (pages 74–75)

Divide.

1. $3\overline{)523}$ 2. $8\overline{)910}$ 3. $6\overline{)473}$ 4. $4\overline{)2{,}808}$

5. $5\overline{)4{,}805}$ 6. $6\overline{)23{,}418}$ 7. $7\overline{)10{,}552}$ 8. $8\overline{)17{,}823}$

Using Algebra   **Find the value of n that makes the equation true.**

9. $56 \div n = 8$ 10. $612 \div n = 6$ 11. $3{,}500 \div n = 500$

12. **Science Connection** A royal python is about 35 feet long. A diamondback rattlesnake is about 9 feet long. The python is about how many times as long as the diamondback?

Extra Practice

Set J (pages 76–77)

Divide.

1. $32\overline{)518}$

2. $63\overline{)297}$

3. $59\overline{)299}$

4. $25\overline{)472}$

5. $37\overline{)2,387}$

6. $58\overline{)9,105}$

7. $29\overline{)4,352}$

8. $46\overline{)8,008}$

9. $82\overline{)73,258}$

10. $91\overline{)83,100}$

11. $46\overline{)23,254}$

12. $74\overline{)91,188}$

13. $42\overline{)47,223}$

14. $37\overline{)26,053}$

15. $84\overline{)41,334}$

16. $52\overline{)48,118}$

17. The *Seismosaurus* weighed about 80 tons. *Diplodocus* weighed only 12 tons. About how many times as heavy was *Seismosaurus* than *Diplodocus*?

Set K (pages 78–81)

Estimate the quotient. Then divide.

1. $5\overline{)3.5}$

2. $7\overline{)21.7}$

3. $3\overline{)12.9}$

4. $6\overline{)\$5.46}$

5. $9\overline{)4.59}$

6. $12\overline{)\$20.40}$

7. $21\overline{)44.1}$

8. $11\overline{)3.08}$

9. $64.8 \div 8$

10. $7.50 \div 0.15$

11. $9.1 \div 7$

12. $88 \div 2.2$

13. $1.89 \div 0.9$

14. $323.2 \div 1.6$

15. $2.84 \div 40$

16. $38.19 \div 1.9$

Divide until the remainder is zero.

17. $5\overline{)2.95}$

18. $6\overline{)3.24}$

19. $15\overline{)1.35}$

20. $22\overline{)0.44}$

21. $1.7\overline{)10.2}$

22. $23\overline{)96.6}$

23. $0.42\overline{)7.14}$

24. $88\overline{)2.2}$

25. $1.8 \div 36$

26. $6.25 \div 250$

27. $11.7 \div 1.3$

28. $1.53 \div 0.9$

29. $\$25.20 \div 40$

30. $\$24.94 \div 43$

31. $\$54.60 \div 65$

32. $\$40.47 \div 57$

33. $7778.4 \div 168$

34. $283.21 \div 223$

35. $4970.4 \div 152$

36. $30,555 \div 210$

37. On one weekend, the gift shop in the museum sold 84 model dinosaurs for $662.76. If all the models were the same price, how much did each one cost?

38. Look back at Problem 37. Could you buy 7 dinosaurs with $50? How much money do you need?

Extra Practice

Set L   (pages 84–85)

Find the quotient.

1. $0.5\overline{)2.55}$ 2. $0.03\overline{)0.711}$ 3. $0.09\overline{)1.323}$ 4. $0.56\overline{)53.2}$

5. $0.4\overline{)19.2}$ 6. $0.25\overline{)52.5}$ 7. $0.16\overline{)8.32}$ 8. $4.7\overline{)1,739}$

9. $0.83\overline{)118.69}$ 10. $2.9\overline{)21.17}$ 11. $0.007\overline{)3.57}$ 12. $0.64\overline{)5,508.8}$

13. $0.64 \div 1.6$ 14. $32.13 \div 21$ 15. $18.7 \div 11$ 16. $5.10 \div 0.17$

17. Sixty-two posters totally cover one wall of the museum gift shop. The area of the wall is 155 ft². If the posters are all the same size, what is the area of each poster?

18. Look back at Problem 17. Could 110 of the same posters fit on a wall that has an area of 240 ft²? Explain.

Set M   (pages 86–87)

Divide. Round the quotient to the place named.

1. $3\overline{)18.2}$ 2. $7\overline{)9.18}$ 3. $0.11\overline{)2.37}$ 4. $16\overline{)3}$
   tenths   hundredths   thousandths   thousandths

5. $52 \div 4.8$ 6. $23 \div 12.5$ 7. $72 \div 59.9$ 8. $1.2 \div 4.14$
   tenths   ones   tenths   hundredths

Divide. Round to the nearest whole number.

9. $5.4\overline{)23.85}$ 10. $25\overline{)2.08}$ 11. $0.4\overline{)9.87}$ 12. $41\overline{)178.90}$

13. $1.3\overline{)107.05}$ 14. $0.07\overline{)15.23}$ 15. $19\overline{)500.44}$ 16. $0.3\overline{)21.37}$

17. $0.52 \div 32$ 18. $17.28 \div 4.1$ 19. $3.06 \div 0.09$ 20. $6.95 \div 2.44$

21. $85 \div 1.7$ 22. $81.00 \div 4.5$ 23. $21.21 \div 30$ 24. $1.04 \div 0.13$

25. You bought 30 gemstones from the gift shop for $171. If each gemstone was the same price, how much did each cost?

26. Look back at Problem 25. Suppose you sold each gemstone for $8.99. How much money would you make?

Chapter Test

Match the problem with the solution.

1. $5 + 5 \times 4$ a. 40

2. $(5 + 5) \times 4$ b. 45

3. $5 \times (5 + 4)$ c. 25

Find the product or quotient.

4. 27.3×100 5. $0.47 \times 1,000$

6. $8.27 \div 10$ 7. $0.8 \div 100$

Estimate the product or quotient.

8. 8×7.9 9. 53×69

10. $489 \div 49$ 11. $8,099 \div 81$

Find the value of the variable. Name the property used.

12. $9 \times n = 5 \times 9$

13. $5 \times (n + 3) = (5 \times 6) + (5 \times 3)$

Find the value of n that makes the equation true.

14. $63 \div n = 9$

15. $5 \times n = 330$

Multiply.

16. $\begin{array}{r} 235 \\ \times\ 46 \\ \hline \end{array}$ 17. $\begin{array}{r} 3.74 \\ \times\ 86.3 \\ \hline \end{array}$ 18. $\begin{array}{r} 9.63 \\ \times\ 0.08 \\ \hline \end{array}$ 19. $\begin{array}{r} 0.787 \\ \times\ 0.021 \\ \hline \end{array}$

Find the quotient. Divide until the remainder is zero.

20. $8 \overline{)4.32}$ 21. $0.84 \overline{)8.148}$

Divide. Round the quotient to the place named.

22. $8.7 \overline{)9.318}$ 23. $44 \overline{)\$93.59}$
   thousandths   hundredths

Solve.

24. The museum gift shop sold 57 posters for $561.45. How much did one poster cost?

25. A 35-pound package is on one end of a balance scale. You have 4 weights—1 lb; 3 lb; 9 lb; and 27 lb—to balance the scale. How would you balance the scale?

 Self-Check Look back at Exercises 20–21. Did you multiply to check your answer?

Performance Assessment

Show What You Know About Whole Numbers and Decimals

Work with a partner.

What You Need

2 number cubes

1 Place the numbers below on two number cubes. Then roll each number cube.

Cube 1	Cube 2
4.15	24
0.2	6
0.09	30
3.6	5
3.08	2
1.2	3

a. Find the product of the numbers that appear face up on each cube.

b. With any two numbers you roll, could you ever get a product greater than 125? Explain.

c. Look at the numbers that appear face up on each cube. Divide the whole number by the decimal. Round the quotient to the nearest tenth.

d. With any two numbers you roll, could you get a quotient less than 1? Explain.

Self-Check Did you remember that a product is found by multiplying?

2 Your age is the number of years you have lived. Have you lived a million minutes? Explain how you know.

Self-Check Did you remember that a year is 365 days?

For Your Portfolio

You might wish to include this work in your portfolio.

Extension

Scientific Notation

Scientists believe that the last dinosaurs became extinct about 65,000,000 years ago. Dinosaur extinction is just one of many significant events that have occurred in Earth's history. When dating events in geologic time, scientists frequently use scientific notation instead of writing the whole number, because the numbers are so large.

A number in scientific notation is the product of two factors. The first factor is a number from 1 to 10. The second factor is a power of 10 in exponent form.

For example, $65,000,000 = 6.5 \times 10,000,000 = 6.5 \times 10^7$

Copy the table below. Write each number, using scientific notation.

Geologic Time		
Event	Number of Years Ago	Number of Years Ago in Scientific Notation
Earth forms.	4,500,000,000	**1.**
Bacteria and algae appear on Earth.	3,500,000,000	**2.**
Dinosaurs first appear on Earth.	230,000,000	**3.**
Dinosaurs become extinct.	65,000,000	6.5×10^7
Modern forms of mammals, birds, and sea life appear on Earth.	5,000,000	**4.**
The last ice age ends.	11,000	**5.**
Mt. Vesuvius erupts and destroys Pompeii.	1,900	**6.**
The dodo bird becomes extinct.	300	**7.**
Mount St. Helens erupts.	20	**8.**
You were born.	?	**9.**

Write each number in standard form.
Then write it using scientific notation.

10. one billion three hundred million

11. four hundred fifty million

12. five hundred thirty-three thousand

13. eight hundred fifty-six

Cumulative Review

★ ★ ★ ★ ★ **Preparing for Tests**

Choose the correct letter for each answer.

Number Concepts	Operations

Number Concepts

1. What is the prime factorization of the number 24?

   A. $2 \times 2 \times 12$
   B. $2 \times 2 \times 3$
   C. $2 \times 2 \times 4$
   D. $2 \times 2 \times 2 \times 3$

2. Which number sentence is true?

   A. $\frac{5}{6} > \frac{7}{8}$

   B. $\frac{5}{10} > \frac{3}{8}$

   C. $\frac{2}{5} > \frac{2}{3}$

   D. $\frac{3}{10} = \frac{4}{8}$

3. What is the greatest common factor of 15 and 30?

   A. 60
   B. 30
   C. 15
   D. 5

4. Jane is making a scrapbook of fall leaves she collected. Her scrapbook has 8 pages. She has 6 orange leaves, 10 red leaves, and 8 yellow leaves. What fraction of her leaves are yellow?

   A. $\frac{1}{3}$

   B. $\frac{4}{8}$

   C. $\frac{3}{4}$

   D. $\frac{8}{10}$

Operations

5. Michele made 3 trips to deliver pizzas. She delivered 3 pizzas to the first floor and 4 pizzas to the second floor each trip. How many pizzas did she deliver?

   A. 9
   B. 12
   C. 21
   D. 36

6. A dinosaur was about 40 feet tall. If the average adult human male is about 6 feet tall, which is a reasonable number for how many men would have to stand on each other's shoulders to match the height of the dinosaur?

   A. 6
   B. 7
   C. 9
   D. 13

7. A certain Bengal tiger weighs 558 pounds. The average house cat weighs about 8 pounds. The tiger is how many times as heavy as the cat?

   A. About 40   **C.** About 60
   B. About 50   **D.** About 70

8. What is the sum of 567.3 and 4.04?

   A. 571.34   **C.** 575.44
   B. 575.04   **D.** 607.7

Patterns, Relationships, and Algebraic Thinking	Geometry and Spatial Reasoning

Patterns, Relationships, and Algebraic Thinking

9. A shop has a scale that subtracts 2 ounces from each order of nuts, N, sold by the ounce to cover bag weight. Which equation shows the actual weight of a bag, B, with the nuts in it?

A. $N + 2 = B$ **C.** $B + N = 2$
B. $N - 2 = B$ **D.** $N \times 2 = B$

10. Paul walks in a walk-a-thon each year. For every 2 kilometers he walks, Paul raises \$14 for charity. What is the ratio of number of kilometers walked to number of dollars raised?

A. $\frac{7}{1}$ **C.** $\frac{3}{14}$

B. $\frac{2}{3}$ **D.** $\frac{1}{7}$

11. The table shows the relationship between Input and Output. Which equation can be used to solve for ■?

Input	Output
4	32
7	56
11	88
15	■

A. $15 \times 8 = $ ■   **C.** $11 \times 15 = $ ■
B. $15 + 8 = $ ■   **D.** $15 \div 8 = $ ■

12. A pool is 75 meters long. If a swimmer can swim about 10 laps in 7 minutes, how many laps would she be able to swim in 28 minutes?

A. 24   **C.** 40
B. 28   **D.** 42

Geometry and Spatial Reasoning

13. The radius of a circle is shown. Which method would you use to find the *diameter* of the circle?

A. Divide the radius in half.
B. Multiply the radius by 2.
C. Square the radius.
D. Add 2 to the radius.

14. What kind of angle is a 120° angle?

A. Right
B. Acute
C. Straight
D. Obtuse

15. Which of the following sets of angles would form a right triangle?

A. 45°, 45°, 90°
B. 40°, 60°, 80°
C. 20°, 40°, 120°
D. 30°, 50°, 100°

16. Which of the following illustrates a translation of the letter **L**?

A.   **C.**

B.   **D.**

Chapter 3 Using Data and Statistics

Chapter Theme: ENTERTAINMENT

REAL-WORLD Math

·················· **Real Facts** ··················

One way television networks know the popularity of their shows is by the number of letters received from viewers. Networks use this data to decide what shows should be canceled and what shows can be featured in prime time. The line graph below shows the trend in the number of letters received during a four-month period in 1997 for two shows on the Nickelodeon channel.

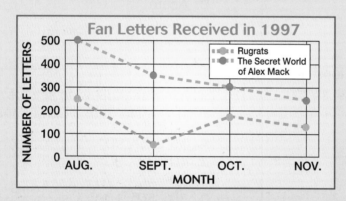

- Describe the trends in fan letters for the two shows during the months shown.

- What would you estimate is the average number of letters received monthly by *Rugrats* during this period?

···················· **Real People** ····················

Meet Sakeena Irish, a researcher for Nickelodeon. She keeps track of letters and phone calls made to Nickelodeon about the company's shows, such as the Kids' Choice Awards shown at the right. Sakeena provides valuable data that can be used to rate the popularity of the shows and help programmers make decisions.

EXPLORE: Collecting and Organizing Data

Can You Palm It?

You can collect data, organize it, and display it.

Learning About It

Can you palm a basketball? Many basketball players can hold a basketball with one hand because of their large hand spans. How large is your hand span? You can use a ruler to find out.

Work with a group.

Step 1 Measure, to the nearest $\frac{1}{2}$ inch, the hand span of each person in your group.

Step 2 Record your data in a chart like the one shown below.

What You Need

For each group:
  inch rulers

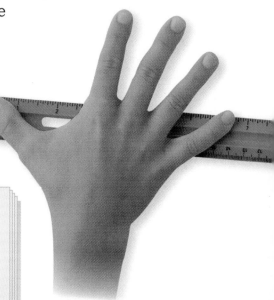

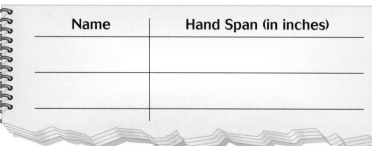

Name	Hand Span (in inches)

Step 3 Collect and record the same data for the class.

Step 4 Record the values from your chart on a line plot like the one shown below.

Name	Hand Span (in inches)
Phyllis	$6\frac{1}{2}$
Sherry	$6\frac{1}{2}$
Donna	7
Jane	7
Joe	6

```
        X           X
X       X           X
+-------+-----------+-->
6      6 1/2        7
```

Math Note

A line plot helps to organize data and show where the data clusters.

Think and Discuss How is a line plot like a bar graph?

Practice

1. What is the greatest hand span in your class? What is the least?

2. What is the most common hand span length?

3. **What If?** Suppose you measured the hand spans of another sixth grade class. Would you expect the most common hand span to be the same as that of your class? Why or why not?

4. **Explain** Which would be a better estimate of a typical sixth grader's hand span, the most common hand span of a large group of sixth graders or of a small group?

5. **Predict** Do you expect a tall person to have a greater hand span than a short person? How would you test your conclusions?

6. Basketball player Shaquille O'Neal is about 7 ft tall. How do you think his hand span compares to that of Michael Jordan?

Did You Know?

Michael Jordan is 6 ft 6 in. tall and his hand span is about $10\frac{1}{2}$ in. How much bigger is his hand span than yours?

Dancing Around !

You can describe data using the mean, median, mode, and range.

Learning About It

Many dancers belong to dance troupes that may perform several times a year. The table at right shows the number of performances given by a dance troupe over a period of seven years. The numbers below are from the table and are arranged in order from least to greatest.

Word Bank

range
mean
median
mode

Performances Each Year	
Year	Performances
1990	100
1991	100
1992	95
1993	103
1994	97
1995	98
1996	100

◀ **Fine Arts Connection** The Alvin Ailey American Dance Theater is a dance troupe that specializes in modern and African American dance.

The **range** can tell you if the data is spread far apart or clustered. To find the range, subtract the least number from the greatest number in a set of data. $103 - 95 = 8$ The range is 8.

| 95 | 97 | 98 | 100 | 100 | 100 | 103 |

The **mean** is the sum of all the data divided by the number of data.
$100 + 100 + 95 + 103 + 97 + 98 + 100 = 693$
$693 \div 7 = 99$
The mean is 99.

The **median** is the middle number or the average of the two middle numbers when the data is arranged in order.
The median is 100.

The **mode** is the number or numbers that occur most often in a set of data. Sometimes there is no mode or more than one mode. 100 occurs most often.

Think and Discuss Mean, median, and mode are used to describe data. Based on the mean, median, and mode of the data above, would you expect this dance troupe to be giving more or fewer than 90 performances next year?

Try It Out

Find the mean, median, mode, and range for each set of data.

1. 12, 14, 22, 16, 18

2. 3, 3, 3, 4, 5, 5, 5, 12

Practice

Find the mean, median, mode, and range for each set of data.

3. 15, 8 ,10, 15, 20, 10

4. 6.9, 7.4, 6.9, 5.2, 8.7, 6.9

5. 80, 60, 50, 30, 70, 10

6. 50, 62, 47, 75

Use the data set 2, 5, 3, 5, 5 to answer Exercises 7–9. Write *true* or *false* as your answer.

7. The mean is less than the median.

8. The median is 3.

9. The mode equals the median.

Problem Solving

10. You went to AileyCamp for 6 weeks. The first week you danced for 30 minutes. Each week you danced 5 minutes more than the week before. What was the average number of minutes you danced per week?

11. **You Decide** After camp you plan to practice an average of 3 hours a day for 5 days. You practiced 2 hours one day and 5 hours another day. Decide how many hours you need to practice the rest of the 5 days to average 3 hours a day.

12. In a dance class of 20 students there were 4 more boys than girls. How many boys were in the class? What strategy did you use to find out?

▲ Kid Connection
AileyCamp is a summer day-camp program designed to develop and improve self-discipline, listening, self-esteem, critical thinking, problem solving, and cooperative learning in young people through dance.

Review and Remember

Compare. Write <, > or = for each ●.

13. 58.32 ● 5.832   **14.** 0.698 ● 0.436   **15.** 382 ● 0.382   **16.** 14.6 ● 1.46

For Extra Practice, see Set A, page 132.

Radio Rules !

Bar graphs help you compare sets of data.

Learning About It

You just got home from school. What is the first thing you do to relax after your hard day? Many people would say turn on the radio. Listening to the radio is a popular form of entertainment.

Radio station WSBG took a music survey of 200 sixth graders from the U.S. and Mexico. The table on the right shows the results of the survey.

Favorite Music

Type of Music	U.S.	Mexico	Total
Country	10	8	18
Dance	36	38	74
Jazz	5	4	9
Rap	19	26	45
Rock	30	24	54

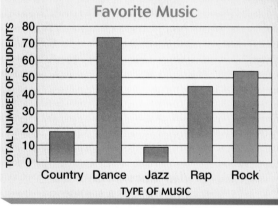

A **bar graph** compares data.

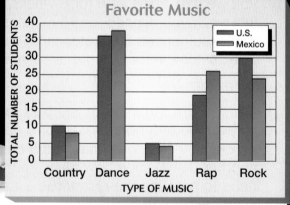

A **double bar graph** compares two sets of data.

Use the graphs above to answer the questions.

- What is the most popular type of music?

- How many more students from the U.S. than students from Mexico like rock music?

- For which type of music do the U.S. and Mexican students have the biggest difference in taste?

Word Bank

bar graph

double bar graph

Connecting Ideas

Now that you know how a bar graph presents data, you can make bar graphs.

Fred surveyed his friends to find out how much time they spent listening to music in the morning and in the evening. The table on the right shows the results of Fred's survey.

Follow the steps below to make a double bar graph to show the information from the survey.

Radio Listening Time

Person	Morning (in minutes)	Evening (in minutes)
Sue	20	10
Phyllis	30	5
Salita	15	20
Martin	30	40
Moe	30	60
Sherry	20	15

Step 1 Choose a title.

Step 2 Choose a scale and mark equal intervals. For this data, the vertical scale should begin at 0 and end at 60.

Step 3 Label the horizontal axis *People* and the vertical axis *Minutes*.

Step 4 Draw a bar for each item.

Step 5 Make a key to show what each bar represents.

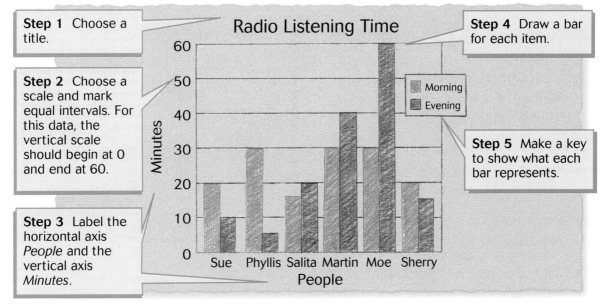

Think and Discuss How would the graph look if the scale was changed to 20-minute intervals? 5-minute intervals?

Try It Out

For Exercises 1–3, use the graph above.

1. For how many more minutes did Moe listen in the morning than Sherry?

2. **Explain** How can you find the range in minutes for evening listeners by using the graph?

3. How many people spend more time listening to evening radio than morning radio?

4. Use the table on the right to make a double bar graph.

Morning Radio Listeners

Class	Yes	No
Mr. Brown	20	10
Ms. Reichman	24	6
Mr. Ashton	15	7
Ms. Devito	18	5
Ms. Brendel	16	12

Practice

For Exercises 5–7, use the bar graph at right.

5. Which artist or group has the most albums? Which has the least?

6. How many more albums has Gloria Estefan made than Luis Miguel?

7. What is the mean number of albums produced by these artists?

Latin American Recording Artists

ARTIST: Luis Miguel, Gloria Estefan, Barrio Boyzz

ALBUMS: 0 1 2 3 4 5 6 7 8

Source: SCHWANN SPECTRUM, 1996

For Exercises 8–10, use the double bar graph at right.

8. For which type of music did the number of stations decline from 1994 to 1995?

9. In 1995, about how many more Spanish or ethnic radio stations were there than Top 40 stations?

10. Which type of music showed the greatest growth from 1994 to 1995?

Radio Stations in the U.S.

1994
1995

NUMBER OF RADIO STATIONS: 0 100 200 300 400 500 600 700 800 900

TYPE OF MUSIC: Spanish/Ethnic, Urban Black, Top 40, Rock

Source: M. Street Corporation, 1995

11. Make a double bar graph for the data in the table below.

Instruments of Latino Bands

Instrument	Mariachi Band	Mambo Band
Requinto	2	3
Guitarrón	2	1
Trumpet	3	4
Guitar	4	3
Violin	3	0
Conga	0	2

12. Create Your Own Write three questions about the graph you made for Exercise 11. Then have a classmate answer them.

Fine Arts Connection ➤
Latin American music has its roots in African, Native American, and European music.

Problem Solving

A pictograph uses symbols to display data.
Use the pictograph to answer Problems 13–14.

Music Video Watchers per School

West Windsor	🚶🚶🚶🚶🚶
Washington	🚶🚶🚶🚶🚶🚶
Franklin	🚶🚶🚶
Lafayette	🚶🚶🚶🚶🚶🚶🚶🚶

🚶 = 100 Students

13. What does each 🚶 represent? How would you represent 50 students? 1,000 students?

14. How many more students watched music videos at Washington School than at West Windsor School?

15. Use the table on the right to make a pictograph. Follow the guidelines below.

   a. Label the axes.

   b. Choose a symbol and its value. Draw symbols to show the data.

   c. Title the graph. Then make a key.

Music Video Watchers

Grade	Number of Students
4	14
5	18
6	24
7	20
8	22

Review and Remember

Choose a Method Use pencil and paper or a calculator to complete Exercises 16–21. Tell which method you used.

16. $0.48 + 0.36$

17. $9.81 \div 3$

18. $4.821 - 0.036$

19. $0.008 + 0.643$

20. 38.2×4.6

21. $1.48 - 0.697$

Time for Technology

Using the Math Processor™ CD-ROM

Using the Graphing Tool

• Open a spreadsheet. Input the data from the Music Video Watchers table above.

• Link the spreadsheet to a pictograph.

• Click on the top of one bar in the graph. Select an item from the catalog and click on it to see a pictograph.

• Link the spreadsheet to a bar graph. In cell B7 of the spreadsheet, enter SUM(B2:B6).

• Link the spreadsheet to a circle graph.

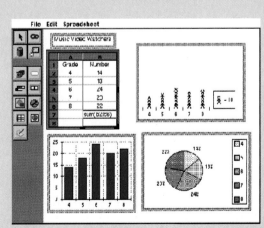

Developing Skills for
Problem Solving

*First read for understanding and then
focus on interpreting line graphs without numbers.*

READ FOR UNDERSTANDING

*S*unny Day's Fan Club was first started by a few people who enjoyed her country music. Today she has many fans throughout the world. The line graph at the right shows how membership in her fan club has changed over time.

① What type of graph is shown?

② What are the labels for each axis?

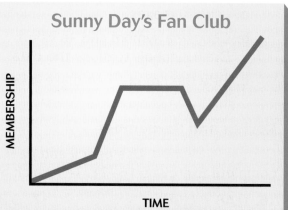

Sunny Day's Fan Club

MEMBERSHIP

TIME

THINK AND DISCUSS

MATH FOCUS

Understanding Line Graphs   A line graph shows change over time. How a line slants and how steeply it slants are visual clues to interpreting the graph.

Study the graph at the top of the page.

③ How does the graph show an increase of members?

④ Which part of the graph shows that membership remained the same for a time?

⑤ Did membership grow steadily? Explain.

⑥ Describe how you can gather information from a graph even when there are no numbers on it.

Show What You Learned

Answer each question. Give a reason for each choice.

When Sunny Day first started, her music was recorded on cassette tapes. Today she records on tapes and compact discs (CDs). The graph shows the sales of her tapes and CDs.

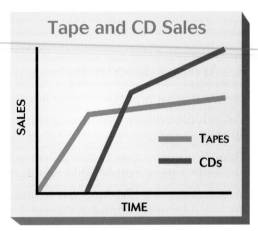

Tape and CD Sales

SALES

TAPES
CDs

TIME

1 How do the sales compare?

   a. Sunny Day now sells the same number of tapes and CDs.

   b. Sunny Day now sells more CDs than tapes.

   c. Sunny Day now sells more tapes than CDs.

2 When did the increase in Sunny Day's tape sales begin to slow down?

   a. Before she started making CDs

   b. About the time she started making CDs

   c. After she started making CDs

3 Which statement is incorrect?

   a. The number of CD sales is increasing faster than the number of tape sales.

   b. Both tapes and CDs are still being purchased.

   c. Only CDs are still being purchased.

The graph below shows how the music levels, or volume, varied during Sunny Day's last concert.

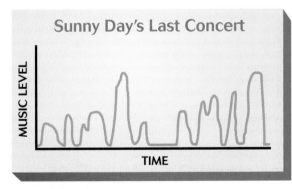

Sunny Day's Last Concert

MUSIC LEVEL

TIME

4 What does the graph indicate about the music levels of the songs that Sunny Day played at the concert?

5 What indicates that there was an intermission?

6 **Explain** How does the graph show that the songs varied in length?

Media Mania!

Line graphs help you analyze data that changes over time.

Learning About It

How has the number of television sets in American homes changed over the years? A **line graph** can be used to show change over time. You can make a line graph using the data in the table to see how the number of TVs changes over time.

Follow these steps to make a line graph.

TVs in the Home	
Years	**TVs (in millions)**
1988	168
1989	176
1990	193
1991	193
1992	192
1993	201
1994	211

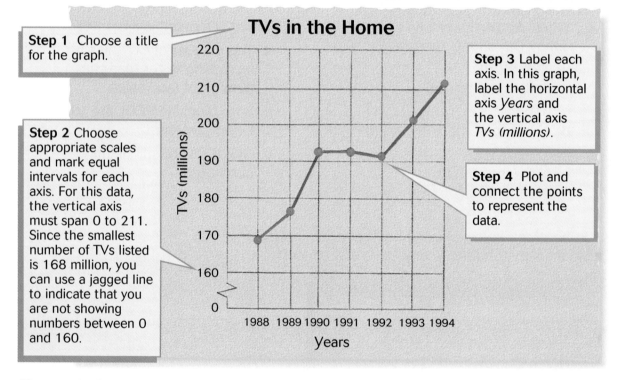

Step 1 Choose a title for the graph.

Step 2 Choose appropriate scales and mark equal intervals for each axis. For this data, the vertical axis must span 0 to 211. Since the smallest number of TVs listed is 168 million, you can use a jagged line to indicate that you are not showing numbers between 0 and 160.

Step 3 Label each axis. In this graph, label the horizontal axis *Years* and the vertical axis *TVs (millions)*.

Step 4 Plot and connect the points to represent the data.

The graph shows an increase over the years in the number of TVs. Use the graph to answer these questions.

- What does an interval on the vertical axis represent?
- Did the number of TVs increase every year? How does the graph support your answer?
- Between which two consecutive years did the greatest change occur?
- What is your prediction for the number of TVs in 2000? Explain.

Word Bank

line graph
double line graph

Connecting Ideas

Creating a double line graph is similar to making a single line graph. When you make a double line graph, you plot two sets of data on the same axes.

The **double line graph** below shows the same data for TVs as shown on page 112. It also shows data for VCRs.

TVs and VCRs in the Home

Years	TVs (in millions)	VCRs (in millions)
1988	168	51
1989	176	58
1990	193	63
1991	193	67
1992	192	69
1993	201	72
1994	211	78

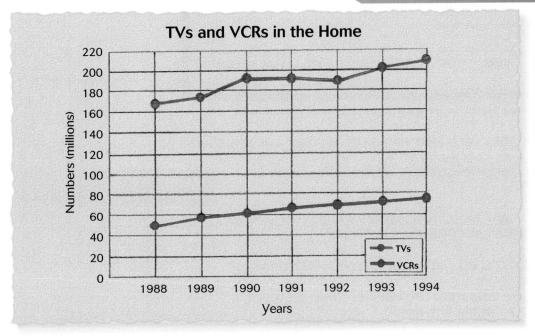

Think and Discuss The table and the graph show the same data. What comparisons are easier to make using the table? What comparisons are easier to make using the graph?

Try It Out

Use the graph above to answer Exercises 1–3.

1. How much did the number of VCRs increase from 1988 to 1990?

2. From 1988 to 1994, which increased more, the number of TVs or the number of VCRs?

3. How does the graph support your answer to Exercise 2?

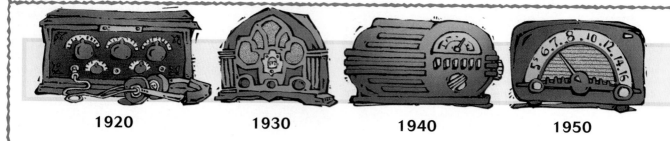

1920   1930   1940   1950

Practice

For Exercises 4–7, use the line graph below.

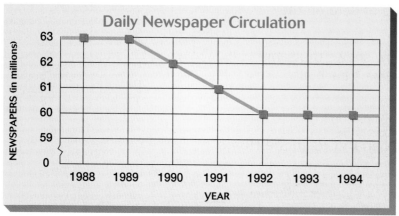

Source: Editor and Publisher, Co. , Editor and Publisher International Yearbook Annual, 1994

4. What does each interval on the vertical axis represent?

5. How many newspapers were in circulation in 1989?

6. How many more newspapers were in circulation in 1988 than in 1994?

7. What trend do you observe from 1992 onward?

★**8.** Use the data from the table at the right to make a double line graph.

Marie's TV and Radio Time (in hours)		
Week	TV	Radio
1	20	3
2	17	9
3	12	14
4	8	18
5	5	26

Use the graph you made to complete Exercises 9–13.

9. What scale and interval did you choose for the vertical axis? Explain your choice.

10. What trends does your graph show? Describe how it shows them.

11. Between which two consecutive weeks did the TV time decrease the most? least?

12. What If? Suppose Marie listened to the radio 3 hours less each week. How would your graph change?

13. Explain What other graphs could you make?

1960   1970   1980   1990

Problem Solving

Use the graph at the right to estimate answers to Problems 14–16.

14. How many AM radio stations were there in 1990?

15. How many FM radio stations were there in 1990?

16. Predict How many more AM stations than FM stations will there be in 2000?

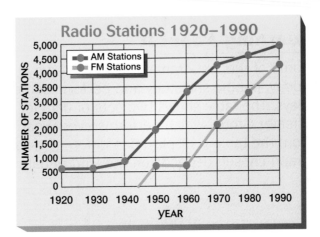

17. Create Your Own Collect data on the time you spend listening to AM and FM radio stations during one week. Record your data in a chart and then create a line graph. What trends does your graph show?

Review and Remember

Using Algebra Write the rule and complete each pattern.

18. 4, 12, 36, 108, ____, ____, ____

19. 1.2, 2.4, 4.8, 9.6, ____, ____, ____

20. 8, 4, 2, 1, ____, ____, ____

21. 2, 5, 11, 23, ____, ____, ____

Money $ense

And the Total Is?

The table below shows the attendance figures for the school play. How much money was made over the 5 days?

Day	Adult Tickets	Student Tickets
Wed.	95	105
Thurs.	90	100
Fri.	100	95
Sat.	90	100
Sun.	105	85

For Extra Practice, see Set C, page 133.

Comedies and Dramas

Now that you know how to read and make graphs,
you can choose which type of graph to use for a set of data.

Learning About It

Some of the first dramas were created by the early Greeks. Today, people still study and perform some of these popular plays. The table shows two sets of data for the Harbold Theater Group, which performs every year. Different data from the table is displayed in different graphs. The type of graph chosen depends on the kind of data shown.

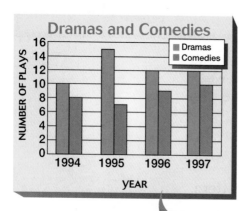

Dramas and Comedies

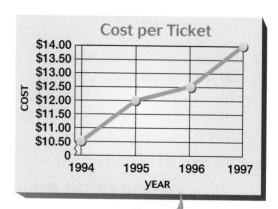

Cost per Ticket

Harbold Theater Group

Year	Number of Dramas	Number of Comedies	Attendance	Cost per Ticket
1994	10	8	6,500	$10.50
1995	15	7	4,000	$12.00
1996	12	9	5,500	$12.50
1997	12	10	8,000	$14.00

Attendance

1994	🚹🚹🚹🚹🚹🚹🚹🚹🚹🚹🚹🚹🚹
1995	🚹🚹🚹🚹🚹🚹🚹🚹
1996	🚹🚹🚹🚹🚹🚹🚹🚹🚹🚹🚹
1997	🚹🚹🚹🚹🚹🚹🚹🚹🚹🚹🚹🚹🚹🚹🚹🚹

🚹 = 500 People

Think and Discuss Look carefully at each graph. What kind of data does each graph display? Explain why each graph is a reasonable choice for displaying the data.

Try It Out

For Exercises 1 and 2, look at the graphs on page 116.

1. Which other type of graph could you use to show attendance?

2. Which other type of graph would make it easy to compare the cost of tickets from year to year?

Practice

For Exercises 3 and 4, decide on the best graph for the data given. Then make the graph.

3.

The Salvo Comedy Show		
Year	Number of Rehearsals	Number of Shows
1993	180	60
1994	160	80
1995	120	110
1996	140	95
1997	90	130

4.

Top Grossing Comedies	
Movies	Gross in Millions
Home Alone	$286
Ghostbusters	$219
Mrs. Doubtfire	$219
Aladdin	$217

Source: Variety, Feb. 20-26, 1995

5. **Explain** Look at Exercise 4. What graph would not be appropriate?

Problem Solving

6. Use the data in the table below to make a bar graph, a pictograph, and a double bar graph.

The Devito Drama Club			
Year	Adult Actors	Child Actors	Total Ticket Sales
1995	30	8	$2,400.00
1996	24	12	$4,000.00
1997	44	14	$6,800.00

7. **Describe** Which information from the table did you use to make your graphs? Why did you choose what you did?

▼ Kid Connection
Macaulay Culkin was 11 when the movie *Home Alone* came out, in 1990. *Home Alone* and *Home Alone 2* grossed over $875 million worldwide.

Review and Remember

Write the value of the digit 3 in each number.

8. 0.388   **9.** 43.28   **10.** 0.0063   **11.** 36

For Extra Practice, see Set D, page 133.

Checkpoint

Statistics, Bar Graphs, and Line Graphs

Match each word with its definition. (pages 104–115)

1. A graph that shows change over time

2. The middle number in ordered data

3. The sum of a set of data divided by the number in the set

4. A graph that shows a comparison of data

5. The number or numbers that occur most often in a set of data

Word Bank

bar graph
line graph
mean
median
mode

For Exercises 6–9, use the table. (pages 104–105)

6. What is the mean?

7. What is the median?

8. What is the mode?

9. What is the range?

Test Scores			
Person	**Score**	**Person**	**Score**
Shelly	83	Lisa	78
Mark	78	Marty	92
Sahara	92	Sally	78
Duncan	73	Dani	84

For Exercises 10–12, use the double bar graph. (pages 106–109)

10. What color is liked most?

11. How many more students like red than dislike red?

12. What colors had the smallest range between the number of students liking and disliking them?

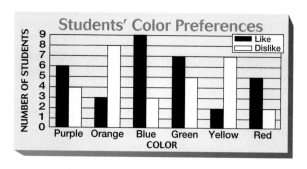

For Exercises 13–15, use the double line graph. (pages 112–115)

13. In which city is the average daily temperature rising?

14. Which week had the greatest difference in temperature between the cities?

15. During which two weeks in Orlando was the temperature the same?

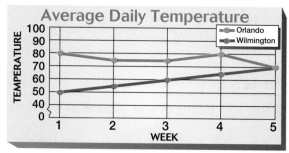

For Exercises 16 and 17, choose the best graph to make for each table. (pages 116–117)

16.

Students and Activities				
Grade	5th	6th	7th	8th
Band	5	7	9	13
Choir	7	7	10	12

17.

Water Depth (ft)		
Week	Lake A	Lake B
1	47	40
2	47	46
3	47	49
4	48	49
5	48	50

Problem Solving

Use the data from the graphs you made in Exercises 16 and 17 to solve Problems 18–20.

18. Which grade has the same number of students in the band and choir?

19. What is the mean, median and mode for the water depth in Lake B?

20. In which grade was there the greatest difference between the number of band members and the number of choir members?

Journal Idea

Choose a graph. Name the steps for making that graph. How do the steps change from one type of graph to another?

What do you think?

Which type of graph best shows how data changes over time?

Critical Thinking Corner

Visual Thinking

Investigating Scattergrams

A scattergram shows you whether a relationship exists between two sets of data. When the points of a scattergram show a trend or pattern, a relationship may exist between the sets of data.

Half-Mile Run

1. What relationship, if any, is there between the weeks of training and the athlete's time?

2. Explain How is the training affecting the athlete's performance?

3. Predict What might the athlete's time be after 10 weeks of training?

Problem Solving
Make a Graph

Making an appropriate graph can help you solve problems.

The Somerset School is having its annual music festival. The table at the right shows the attendance for last year's festival. The planners want to schedule the number of workers needed throughout the day based on last year's attendance. Last year, the number of workers increased as the number of people attending increased. During what part of the day should the planners schedule the greatest number of workers?

Attendance Last Year	
Time	**Total Attendance**
9 A.M.	104
10 A.M.	345
11 A.M.	359
12 NOON	339
1 P.M.	137
2 P.M.	373
3 P.M.	405
4 P.M.	488
5 P.M.	534
6 P.M.	545
7 P.M.	568
8 P.M.	561
9 P.M.	555

 UNDERSTAND

What do you need to find?

You need to find the times of the day that attendance is the greatest.

 PLAN

How can you solve the problem?

To better understand the information in the table, you can **make an appropriate graph**. Since a line graph is used to show change over time, you should make a line graph to analyze how the attendance changed throughout the day.

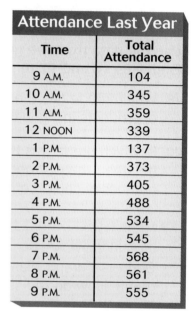

SOLVE

You can conclude from the graph that the greatest number of workers will be needed between 4 P.M. and 9 P.M.

 LOOK BACK

When would you have most of the workers take lunch? Why?

Using the Strategy

Make a graph to show the prices of concert tickets.
Then use your graph to answer Problems 1–2.

1 During which year was there the greatest difference in ticket price between Section A and Section B? How can you tell?

2 Which section had the greater increase in ticket prices from 1993 to 1997?

Make a graph to show the sales of concert CDs.
Then use your graph to answer Problems 3–4.

3 Based on CD sales, in which year might concert attendance have dropped?

4 Based on your graph, can you predict the number of CDs that might be sold at the next concert? Why or why not?

Concert Ticket Prices (in dollars)		
Year	Section A	Section B
1993	15	24
1994	18	31
1995	22	37
1996	27	46
1997	30	54

Concert CD Sales	
Year	Sales
1993	151
1994	178
1995	197
1996	140
1997	210

Mixed Strategy Review

Try these or other strategies to solve each problem.
Tell which strategy you used.

Problem Solving Strategies

- Guess and Check
- Draw a Diagram
- Find a Pattern
- Work Backwards
- Make a Table
- Write an Equation

5 Ann bought 8 tickets for $210. Adult tickets cost $30 each. Student tickets cost $20 each. How many of each kind of ticket did she buy?

6 Cindy spent a total of $6.50 buying souvenirs. She spent $2.50 on a magnet, $3.25 on a mug, and the rest of the money on postcards. How much did she spend on postcards?

7 Using Algebra During the first hour of the festival, Rick sold 7 hot dogs. He sold 15 during the second hour, 23 during the third hour, and 31 during the fourth hour. At this rate, how many hot dogs will he sell in the seventh hour?

8 Analyze Bill bought 15 souvenir mugs. He bought 3 more small mugs than large mugs. How many of each size mug did he buy?

An Olympic Opening

Making a stem-and-leaf plot is another way to organize and display data.

Learning About It

If you watched the 1996 Summer Olympic Games in Atlanta, you helped make history! About 209 million people watched the Olympics, which was one of the most watched events in television history. Below are the average points scored by the teams in the basketball tournament.

Word Bank

stem-and-leaf plot

Average Olympic Basketball Scores

ANGOLA 56	ARGENTINA 70	AUSTRALIA 98	BRAZIL 92	CHINA 72	CROATIA 85
GREECE 80	LITHUANIA 85	PUERTO RICO 89	S. KOREA 81	USA 104	YUGOSLAVIA 96

One way to display the data is to make a stem-and-leaf plot. A **stem-and-leaf plot** shows where data clusters. Follow the steps below to make a stem-and-leaf plot.

Step 1 Title the stem-and-leaf plot.

Step 2 Write the tens digits from the data in order from least to greatest. Write a 10 for numbers from 100 to 109.

Step 3 Next to each tens digit, write the ones digit for each number in the data in order from least to greatest.

Step 4 Write an example that shows what the stem-and-leaf represents. For example, 5 is the tens digit and 6 is the ones digit.

Average Olympic Basketball Scores

Stem	Leaves
5	6
6	
7	0 2
8	0 1 5 5 9
9	2 6 8
10	4

5|6 means 56 points

Think and Discuss Within what range of points did most teams score per game?

Try It Out

The stem-and-leaf plot on the right shows the number of medals won by the top twelve nations. Use it for Exercises 1 and 2.

1. Write a list of the data displayed in the plot.

2. Find the range, median, and mode for the data.

Make a stem-and-leaf plot for the following data. Find the range, median, and mode.

3. 14, 7, 23, 35, 42, 42, 46, 45, 18, 28, 40, 33

1994 Winter Olympics Medals Won

Stem	Leaves
0	556699
1	33
2	0346

Key: 1|3 means 13 medals

Practice

Use the data in the table at the right to make a stem-and-leaf plot. Answer Exercises 4 and 5.

4. Find the mean, median, and mode.

5. **Explain** How can you use the stem-and-leaf plot to find the range?

6. **Analyze** Name and make another graph that represents the data well.

1992 Summer Olympics Gold Medals Awarded

Unified Team	45
United States	37
Germany	33
China	16
Cuba	14
Spain	13
South Korea	12
Hungary	11
France	8
Australia	7

Problem Solving

Use the stem-and-leaf plot on the right to solve Problems 7–9.

7. Where does the data in the stem-and-leaf plot seem to cluster?

8. About how many more medals were won by the team with the most medals compared to the team with the least?

9. **Explain** If you added 68 to the plot, which would change the most, the mean, median, mode, or range? the least?

Track Medals Won

Stem	Leaves
1	77889
2	26
3	1
4	1238899
5	011

Key: 4|7 means 47 medals

INTERNET ACTIVITY
www.sbgmath.com

Review and Remember

Round each decimal to the nearest thousandth.

10. 4.3863   11. 538.6491   12. 0.00386   13. 0.4937   14. 7.7316

Going to the Circus

Frequency tables and histograms can help you organize your data.

Learning About It

Everything you love about the circus is about to begin! Circuses put on many shows each year. The typical season lasts 7 months. In many circuses, whole families perform together in certain acts.

> **Word Bank**
>
> **frequency table**
> **histogram**

The ages of 30 performers in a small circus are listed below.

8, 11, 20, 36, 49, 56, 24, 7, 32, 53,
31, 42, 8, 61, 27, 13, 14, 38, 50, 16,
9, 61, 24, 37, 7, 26, 31, 29, 68, 39

How many performers are from 10 to 19 years of age ?

Making a **frequency table** is one way to organize large quantities of data.

Follow the steps below to make a frequency table.

Ages of Circus Performers		
Intervals	Tally Marks	Frequency
0–9	卌	5
10–19	IIII	4
20–29	卌 I	6
30–39	卌 II	7
40–49	II	2
50–59	III	3

Step 1 Arrange the data into equal intervals.

Step 2 Record the frequency for each interval using tally marks.

Step 3 Count the tally marks and record the frequency.

Four performers are from 10 to 19 years old.

Connecting Ideas

You can make a graph to display the information in a frequency table. This graph is called a histogram.

A **histogram** is a graph that uses bars to display a set of data that has been organized into frequencies within equal intervals.

Follow the steps below to make a histogram.

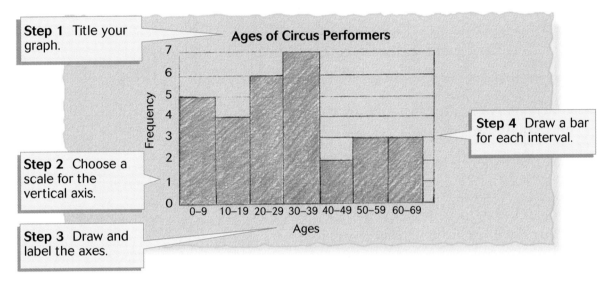

Step 1 Title your graph.

Step 2 Choose a scale for the vertical axis.

Step 3 Draw and label the axes.

Step 4 Draw a bar for each interval.

Think and Discuss What are the advantages and disadvantages of organizing your data in a frequency table or histogram?

Try It Out

Use the histogram above to answer Exercises 1 and 2.

1. How many circus performers are less than 10 years old?

2. Which age group has the most circus performers?

Make a frequency table and a histogram for the data sets below.

3. Number of minutes per performance: 2, 4, 3, 5, 8, 2, 3, 4, 1, 7, 10, 11, 6, 4, 1, 2, 7, 3, 11, 4

4. Ages of the clowns: 17, 33, 42, 48, 55, 57, 18, 28, 24, 43, 51, 48, 19

5. Look at Exercise 3. What other graph can be made with this information?

Practice

6. Use the frequency table below to make a histogram.

Robert Brothers Circus Minutes for Each Act		
Intervals (minutes)	Tally Marks	Frequency
0–2	II	2
3–5	JHT II	7
6–8	JHT II	7
9–11	II	2
12–14	II	2

7. Which intervals in the histogram you made had the greatest frequency?

8. Make a frequency table and a histogram for the data.
6, 8, 14, 13, 7, 11, 4, 5, 3, 8, 2, 10, 8, 9, 4, 7, 3, 4, 4

9. Look at the histogram that you made for Exercise 8. What interval had the greatest frequency?

Problem Solving

Use the histogram below to solve Problems 10–12.

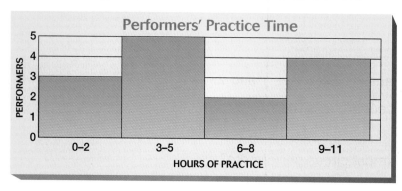

10. Explain How can you use the histogram to find frequencies?

11. How many performers practiced between 0 and 2 hours each day?

12. How many more performers practiced between 3 and 5 hours than practiced 2 hours or less every day?

13. Analyze How might a circus owner use a histogram or frequency table of monthly performances to plan next year's shows?

14. Journal Idea Explain how histograms and bar graphs are alike.

15. Describe a set of data that is best displayed by a histogram.

Review and Remember

Using Algebra Solve each equation to find n.

16. $n \times 3 = 9$

17. $2 + n = 5$

18. $18 - n = 12$

19. $n \div 7 = 3$

20. $n \times 4 = 32$

21. $n + 13 = 20$

22. $58 + n = 60$

23. $n \div 10 = 5$

24. $70 - n = 50$

25. $n \times 9 = 90$

26. $n - 2 = 3$

27. $8 \div n = 2$

Critical Thinking Corner

Visual Thinking

Circle Graphs

At what age do you think dancers start learning dance? The table shows the ages of 100 dancers when they started dancing. You can represent the information in the table by using a circle graph.

When Dancers Dance	
Starting Age	Number of Dancers
0–4	3
5–9	65
10–14	21
15–18	6
19+	5

When Dancers Dance

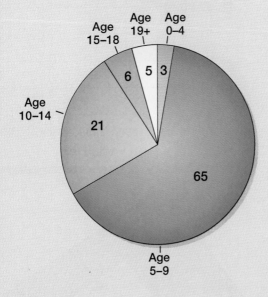

1. How many students started dance lessons between the ages of 10 and 14?

2. Which age group had the smallest number of students?

3. At what ages did more than half of the students start dance lessons?

4. How many more people started dance lessons between the ages of 5 and 9 than between the ages of 10 and 18?

For Extra Practice, see Set F, page 134.

Problem Solving
Using Graphs to Persuade

*The scale on a graph can influence the way
you interpret data.*

Videoland wants to raise their video rental prices to $3.75. Before the owners do this, they want to convince their customers that the price increase is small. Which of the graphs shown might convince you that the price increase is small?

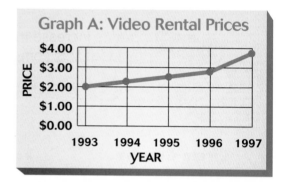

Graph A: Video Rental Prices

 UNDERSTAND

What do you need to know?

You need to know why the graphs look so different even though they show identical data.

 PLAN

How can you solve the problem?

Compare the data displayed on the graphs. Then interpret the graphs by looking at the scales on both graphs.

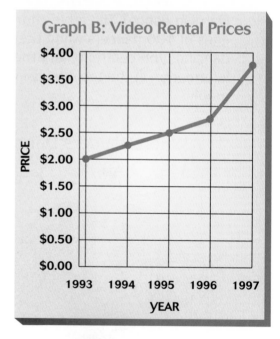

Graph B: Video Rental Prices

 SOLVE

The same data is displayed on each graph. The scale on Graph A has $1 intervals, so the price increase appears smaller. The scale on Graph B has $0.50 intervals, so the price increase appears greater. Since the price increase *looks* smaller on Graph A, Videoland would probably use Graph A.

 LOOK BACK

How can graphs be used to persuade people's thinking?

Show What You Learned

Use Graphs C and D to solve Problems 1–6.

Videoland, which rents and sells videos, is trying to persuade people to invest in the company by showing how profitable the company is.

① Study the graphs at the right. Describe what each graph shows.

② Based on Graph C, how much did Videoland's profits increase from 1994 to 1996? How does this compare with data shown on Graph D?

③ Compare the vertical scales on Graphs C and D. How are they alike? How are they different?

④ How does your interpretation change as you view the graphs?

⑤ Which graph might Videoland use to persuade potential shareholders of tremendous profit? Explain.

⑥ Al said that if you change the horizontal scale on Graph D enough, Graph D could look more like Graph C. Is he correct? Explain how you can find out.

⑦ **Explain** Explain how changing intervals on the scale of a graph influences how data is displayed and interpreted.

⑧ **Generalize** You can change the scale on a line graph to persuade. Can you also change the scale on a bar graph to persuade?

⑨ **Create Your Own** Make graphs to persuade your teacher that you spend a lot of time doing your homework compared to the time you spend watching television.

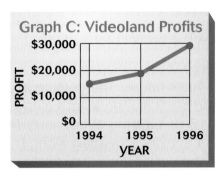

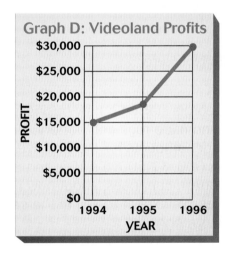

Problem Solving

★ ★ ★ ★ ★ **Preparing for Tests**

Practice What You Learned

Choose the correct letter for each answer.

1 There is an L-shaped walkway along two sides of Tim's house. The outside length along one side is 10 m. The length along the other side is 18 m. Starting at one end, Tim is putting fence posts 1 m apart along the outside edge of the walk. How many posts does he need?

A. 31
B. 30
C. 29
D. 28
E. Not Here

Tip

Draw a Diagram to help you solve this problem. Remember to label your diagram.

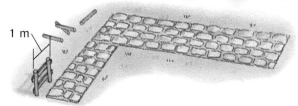

1 m

2 Georgia started a new business selling handmade rugs and pottery. Here are her total order amounts for the first five months: $1,750; $2,000; $2,500; $3,250; and $4,250. If this pattern continues, about how much should Georgia expect to sell in the *seventh* month?

A. $5,500
B. $5,750
C. $6,500
D. $7,000
E. $8,725

Tip

Using the *Find a Pattern* strategy can help you solve this problem.

3 At a fun park, one ride has small cars that hold 4 people and large cars that hold 6 people. If 32 students ride at the same time, which combination of cars can they fill so that there are no empty seats?

A. 2 small cars, 5 large cars
B. 3 small cars, 3 large cars
C. 4 small cars, 3 large cars
D. 5 small cars, 2 large cars
E. Not Here

Tip

Try the answer choices to see if any of them fit the situation.

4 A box has a volume of about 2,400 cubic inches. It measures 8 inches long by 10 inches wide. Which is a reasonable estimate for the height?

A. Less than 3 feet
B. About 10 feet
C. About 20 feet
D. About 30 feet
E. More than 100 feet

5 Movie tickets are $5 for children and $7.50 for adults. Which number sentence shows the cost, C, of tickets for 2 adults and 4 children?

A. $C = (2 + 4) \times (\$5 + \$7.50)$
B. $C = (2 \times \$5) + (4 \times \$7.50)$
C. $C = (4 \times \$5) + (2 \times \$7.50)$
D. $C = (2 \times 4) + (5 \times \$7.50)$
E. Not Here

6 For a science experiment, Ike made a line graph showing the change in height of a plant over 4 weeks. He used the horizontal scale to show time. Which of these is reasonable for the shape of Ike's line graph?

A. It slopes down from left to right.
B. It is a horizontal line.
C. It slopes up, then down.
D. It slopes down, then up.
E. Not Here

7 Julia and her sister bought 2 tents for $579 each and 2 sleeping bags for $59 each. Which is a reasonable estimate of Julia's share of the purchases?

A. Less than $500
B. Between $500 and $600
C. Between $600 and $700
D. Between $700 and $800
E. More than $800

8 The graph shows the results of a magazine survey.

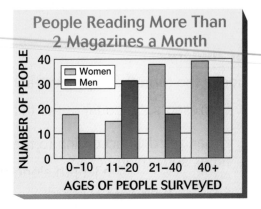

In which age group do about twice as many women as men read more than 2 magazines a month?

A. People younger than 21
B. Ages 0–10
C. Ages 11–20
D. Ages 21–40
E. People older than 40

9 Mel makes $34,000 a year. He can afford to spend about $\frac{1}{4}$ of his monthly income for rent. Which of these is reasonable for how much Mel can spend for rent?

A. About $600
B. Between $600 and $650
C. Between $650 and $750
D. Between $7,000 and $8,000
E. About $8,000

10 Jake has scores of 85, 80, 85, and 90 on 4 tests. If Jake takes 1 more test, which of these test scores will give him a mean score of 86 for all 5 tests?

A. 70
B. 75
C. 80
D. 85
E. 90

Checkpoint

Stem-and-Leaf Plots and Histograms

Vocabulary

Choose the term that best fits each description.

1. Represents the count of the tally marks.

2. Organizes data according to the number of times something occurs.

3. Shows where data clusters.

4. Uses bars to show the frequencies of data organized into equal intervals.

Word Bank

frequency table
histogram
stem-and-leaf plot
tally chart

Concepts and Skills

Use the stem-and-leaf plot at the right to complete Exercises 5–7. (pages 122–123)

5. List the data displayed in the plot.

6. Find the median and mode of the data.

7. Find the range of the data.

8. The data below shows the number of minutes that Ms. Lee's students spent at the library in one week. Make a stem-and-leaf plot for the data.
7, 8, 9, 15, 10, 12, 28, 29, 34, 36, 31, 28, 27, 11, 17, 34, 35, 8, 19, 16, 22, 29, 18

Number of CDs Owned	
Stem	Leaves
1	003
2	56
4	147
6	358
9	13

Use the histogram to complete Exercises 9–11.
(pages 124–127)

9. How many people saw 2–3 movies per week?

10. How many more people saw 2–3 movies than 6–7 movies?

11. Between which two consecutive intervals is there the greatest difference in the number of people?

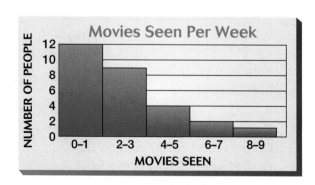

Problem Solving

12. When making a stem-and-leaf plot, must the data be in order before you create the plot?

13. How is a stem-and-leaf plot similar to a histogram? How are they different?

14. Use the frequency table at the right to make a histogram.

15. Look at the histogram you made for Exercise 14. How would your histogram change if you added the interval 19–21 with a frequency of 3? What trends do you observe from this histogram?

What do you think?

How do you know which graph to make for certain data?

Number of Videos Owned

Interval	Tally Marks	Frequency
10–12	ⅢⅢ IIII	9
13–15	ⅢⅢ II	7
16–18	III	3

Journal Idea

What are some advantages and disadvantages of using graphs to display data? Give some examples.

You Decide

Activity

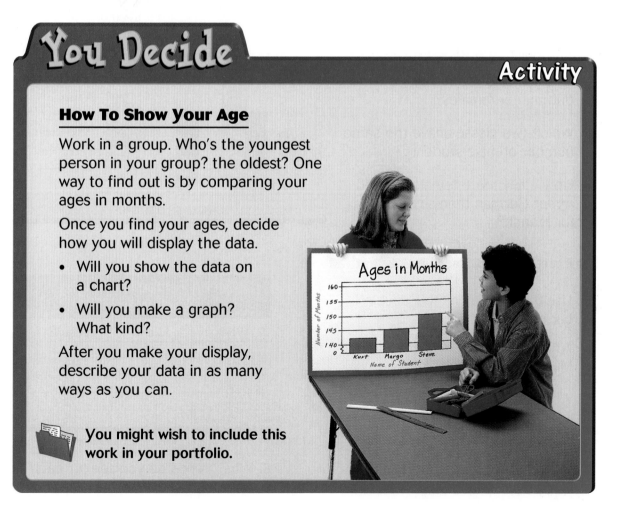

How To Show Your Age

Work in a group. Who's the youngest person in your group? the oldest? One way to find out is by comparing your ages in months.

Once you find your ages, decide how you will display the data.

- Will you show the data on a chart?

- Will you make a graph? What kind?

After you make your display, describe your data in as many ways as you can.

You might wish to include this work in your portfolio.

Extra Practice

Set A (pages 104–105)

Find the mean, median, mode, and range.

1. 14, 7, 5, 3, 7, 6
2. 8, 6, 13, 16, 13, 4
3. 16.3, 7.8, 5.9, 6, 12, 6
4. 3, 5, 7.4, 3.1, 5, 2.7, 11.6
5. 13.6, 22.3, 13.4, 7.2, 3.8, 7.2
6. 1.34, 2.5, 4, 2.52, 0.34, 4

Solve.

7. Rich and Jerry walked 4 miles for 4 days. Then they walked 2 miles for 4 days. What was the average number of miles they walked per day in 8 days?

8. Art listened to an average of 6 hours of radio per day for 5 days. If he listened to 3 hours of radio for 2 days, how many hours could he have listened the other 3 days?

Set B (pages 106–109)

Use the bar graph for Exercises 1–3.

1. In which class do males outnumber females?

2. Which two classes have the same number of male students?

3. How many more females signed up for German than signed up for French?

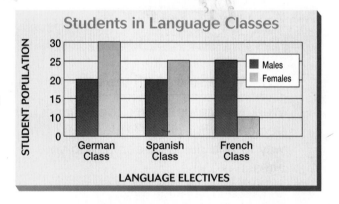

For Exercises 4–8, use the data in the table.

4. Use the data to create a double bar graph.

5. What was the mean temperature in Miami during Week 1?

6. Which week had the greatest difference in temperature between Miami and Boston?

Mean Temperature (°F) Each Week		
Week	Miami	Boston
1	85	72
2	83	68
3	87	70
4	84	72
5	92	65

7. Find the range, median, and mode for the temperature in Miami and Boston.

8. What trends do you see for each city? Explain.

Extra Practice

Set C (pages 112–115)

Use the line graph on the right for Exercises 1–3.

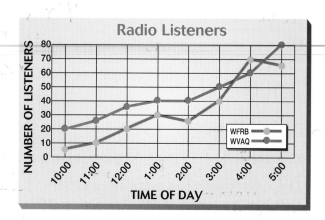

1. Which station has the most listeners at 4:00?

2. How many more people listen to WFRB at 3:00 than at 2:00?

3. How does the number of listeners change between 1:00 and 2:00 for the station WVAQ?

4. Use the data in the table below to create a double line graph.

CD and Cassette Sales

Day	CDs Sold	Cassettes Sold
1	35	30
2	46	25
3	49	33
4	58	40
5	72	55

Set D (pages 116–117)

Use the following tables for Exercises 1–3.

The Number of Concerts Seen

Year	Concerts
1994	2
1995	6
1996	8
1997	9
1998	12

Amusement Parks

Amusement Park	Liked	Disliked
Waterworld	12	6
Cartoon Island	8	10
Castle Land	14	4
Bear Country	6	12
Sun and Fun	10	8

1. Make a graph for each set of data above.

2. In which year were the most concerts seen?

3. Which park was disliked the most? least?

Extra Practice

Set E (pages 122–123)

Use the stem-and-leaf plot on the right for Exercises 1 and 2.

1. List the data.

2. Find the mean, median, and mode of the data.

Use the following data for Exercises 3 and 4.

The data shows the number of children's videos that a store rented each day over a 20–day period.

10, 37, 21, 16, 28, 35, 41, 12, 26, 10,
25, 39, 42, 16, 27, 38, 17, 22, 18, 11

3. Create a stem and leaf plot for the data.

4. Where does most of the data cluster in the stem and leaf plot?

Number of Books Read

Stem	Leaves
2	0 3 7
3	0 7
5	2 3
7	8
8	1 5 6

Set F (pages 124–127)

Use the histogram on the right for Exercises 1–4.

1. How many people rent more than 3 videos each week?

2. How many more people rent 0-1 videos than 8-9 videos each week?

3. What trend do you notice? How many people do you think would rent more than 9 videos?

4. Between which two consecutive intervals was there the greatest decrease in the number of people?

5. Make a histogram using the data in the table at the right.

6. What conclusions can you draw from your histogram?

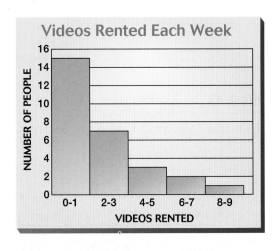

Hours of Television Viewed Each Day

Hours	Frequency
0-1	5
2-3	6
4-5	8
6-7	13
8-9	7

Chapter Test

Use the bar graph to answer Questions 1–4.

1. What subject is liked by the same number of boys and girls?

2. Based on the graph how many students were surveyed altogether?

3. How many more boys than girls like reading?

4. What subject was disliked the most by boys?

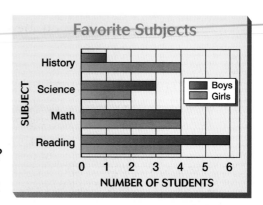

Use the table on the right to answer Questions 5–6.

5. Make a double line graph.

6. When does Station A play more songs than Station B?

Number of Songs Played		
Time	Station A	Station B
1st hour	16	18
2nd hour	14	17
3rd hour	17	13
4th hour	19	24

Use the stem-and-leaf plot on the right for Questions 7–10.

7. What does 1 | 2 mean?

8. How many numbers are between 20 and 30?

9. Does 0 | 8 mean the same thing as 8 | 0? Explain.

10. Which stem has four numbers? List them.

Library Books Borrowed	
Stem	Leaves
0	6 8 8
1	2 4 5 8 9
2	3 6 6 6 7 7 9
3	1 2 5 9

Key: 1|2 = 12 books

Fred had the following test scores: 100, 97, 86, 70, 85, 90. Use his scores to find each measure in Questions 11–14.

11. Mean   12. Median   13. Mode   14. Range

15. What kind of graph helps compare data over time? What kind of graph helps compare different quantities?

Self-Check

How are certain graphs easier to make than others? Does this depend on your data? Explain your answer.

Performance Assessment

Show What You Know About Data and Statistics

1 The table below shows the attendance at the science fiction movie *Battle Star* for the past 7 weeks.

Week	Battle Star Attendance	
	18 years old or under	19 years old or over
1	200	500
2	150	420
3	285	400
4	285	400
5	450	380
6	480	380
7	490	350

a. Choose an appropriate graph to organize and display the data.

b. Make the graph.

c. Draw conclusions about the information the graph displays.

Self-Check Did you notice that the range is from 150 people to 500 people?

2 Look at the line graph on the right.

a. What kind of information does the graph present?

b. What does each interval on the vertical scale represent?

c. What will the graph look like if the intervals on the vertical scale are 0.5 inch? 0.1 inch?

Self-Check Do you understand how changing the interval changes the appearance of the graph?

Normal Precipitation
Washington, D.C.

 For Your Portfolio

You might wish to include this work in your portfolio.

Extension

Box-and-Whisker Plots

Box-and-whisker plots are used to emphasize the median and the extremes of a set of data. Follow the steps below to make a box-and-whisker plot using the temperature data in the table.

Step 1 Order the data from least to greatest. Find and mark the median to divide the data into two parts.

60, 60, 61, 62, 63, 65, 65, 67, 68, 70, 70, 72, 72, 75, 75, 75, 75, 75, 76, 78, 78, 80, 83, 83, 85, 85, 90, 90, 92, 96, 97

INTERNET ACTIVITY
www.sbgmath.com

Step 2 Divide the data into four quartiles by finding the median of each of the two parts.

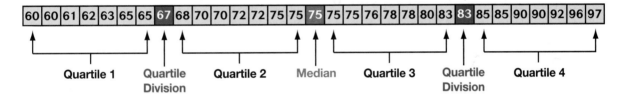

Step 3 Draw the part of the number line needed to display the data. Mark the number line with the **quartile** measures you have found.

Step 4 Draw a **box** around the second and third quartiles. Mark the median of the data with a line through the box.

Step 5 Draw a segment from the box to the least value and a segment from the box to the greatest value. These are the **whiskers**.

1. Make a box-and-whisker plot for the data below.
   80, 85, 110, 100, 96, 124, 89, 104, 106, 117, 85, 117, 94, 106, 89, 117, 100, 96, 117, 106, 110

Using Math in Science

*Collect data to investigate the surface tension of water and **make a histogram** of your observations.*

Water Strength

You have invented a new game. Your game challenges players to see who can get the greatest number of water drops to fit on the surface of a penny before the water runs off. How many drops can you fit?

What You Need

For each group:
  penny
  container of water
  dropper
  paper towel
  liquid detergent
  graph paper

Explore

Step 1 Make a chart like the one below with enough rows for 10 trials.

Trial Number	Predicted Number of Drops	Actual Number of Drops
1		
2		
3		

Step 2 Predict the number of drops of water you can add to a penny's surface before the water runs off. Record your prediction in the chart.

Step 3 Use the dropper to place one drop of water on a penny. *Carefully* add a second drop of water. This drop joins with the first drop to form a mound of water. The water particles, attracted to each other, form a "skin" known as surface tension. Surface tension causes the water droplet to form a ball.

Step 4 Continue adding drops to the penny, one at a time, until the water overflows. Keep track of the number of drops you add. Record the total number in the chart under "Actual Number of Drops" for Trial 1.

Step 5 Dry the penny with a paper towel. Wipe up any water that overflowed.

Step 6 Repeat Steps 2–4 nine more times. Record your predictions and results in the correct rows.

Step 7 Use the data in your chart to make a histogram of your results. At the right is a sample histogram. Use this as a model for making a histogram using your data. Remember to title your histogram.

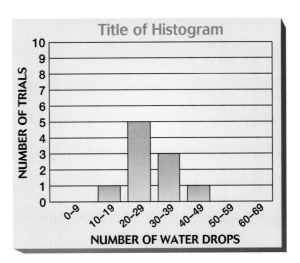

Title of Histogram

Step 8 Repeat the activity. This time, dip the penny in liquid detergent before each trial. Note the shape of the water on the surface of the penny.

Analyze

1. How did your results compare with your predictions?

2. What was the range of drops you could fit on the dry penny?

3. What was the range of drops you could fit on the penny dipped in detergent?

4. How does a detergent affect the surface tension of water?

For Your Portfolio

Write about what you discovered. Explain how you used a histogram to help organize and understand your data. Tell if the results of your experiment surprised you. Explain why or why not.

Explore Further!

Predict Would you be able to fit fewer or more drops on the surface of a dime? A quarter? Design an experiment to test your prediction.

Cumulative Review

★ ★ ★ ★ ★ Preparing for Tests

Choose the correct letter for each answer.

Operations	Probability and Statistics

Operations

1. Sal read 2 more books than 4 times the number of books Taylor read. If Taylor read 6 books, how many books did Sal read?

   A. 48   **C.** 24
   B. 26   **D.** 12

2. What is the sum of 11.99, 112.35, and 0.062?

   A. 232.807   **C.** 124.960
   B. 130.540   **D.** 124.402

3. Paul bought 50 sheets of stationery at $0.30 a sheet and 50 matching envelopes at $0.45 per envelope. How much did the stationery and envelopes cost, excluding tax?

   A. $15.00   **C.** $37.50
   B. $22.50   **D.** $50.00

4. Kate and Ian hiked $1\frac{1}{3}$ mi before stopping for lunch. After lunch they hiked another $1\frac{1}{6}$ mi before stopping to rest. Then they hiked $1\frac{1}{3}$ mi before setting up camp. How far did they hike?

   A. $3\frac{1}{6}$ miles

   B. $3\frac{1}{2}$ miles

   C. $3\frac{2}{3}$ miles

   D. $3\frac{5}{6}$ miles

   E. Not Here

Probability and Statistics

5. Fran's math grades are: 98, 85, 88, 85, 92, 93, 82, 85, and 93. What was Fran's *median* score?

   A. 98   **C.** 88
   B. 92   **D.** 85

6. What is the range of this data?

   32.6, 34.9, 31.7, 38.8, 40.9, 30.3

   A. 10.6   **C.** 7.1
   B. 9.2   **D.** 2.3

Use the data below for Questions 7 and 8.

Student Sport Survey		
Favorite Sport	**Number**	**Percent**
1. Baseball	15	30%
2. Basketball	18	36%
3. Football	10	20%
4. Soccer	7	14%

7. The numbers in the circle graphs below refer to the numbers of the sports listed in Column 1. Which graph best represents the data?

   A.   **C.**

   B.   **D.**

8. How many more students chose football or soccer than chose baseball?

   A. 17   **C.** 8
   B. 12   **D.** 2

Geometry and Spatial Reasoning	Patterns, Relationships, and Algebraic Thinking

Geometry and Spatial Reasoning

9. Which quadrilateral always has 4 right angles?

A. Rectangle
B. Rhombus
C. Trapezoid
D. Parallelogram

10. A circle has a circumference of about 108 cm and a diameter of 36 cm. What is its *radius*?

A. 6 cm
B. 9 cm
C. 18 cm
D. 54 cm

11. If △*STU* is congruent to △*JKL*, then–

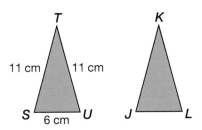

A. side *JL* measures 11 cm.
B. side *KL* measures 11 cm.
C. side *TU* and *JL* are congruent.
D. side *JK* measures 6 cm.

12. Which of the following illustrates a reflection of the letter **E**?

A.    C.

B. 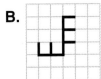   D.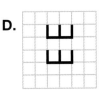

Patterns, Relationships, and Algebraic Thinking

13. When Sam kept track of the number of books he read each month, he found a pattern. How many books did he read in June?

Jan.	Feb.	Mar.	Apr.	May	June
5	7	10	14	19	▨

A. 23   C. 25
B. 24   D. 26

14. Roy ran for 1 hour at 10 miles per hour and then ran for 2 hours at 3 miles per hour. Which number sentence could be used to find *M*, the total number of miles that Roy ran?

A. $M = (10 + 3) + (1 + 2)$
B. $M = (10 \times 1) + (3 \times 2)$
C. $M = (10 + 1) \times (3 + 2)$
D. $M = (10 + 3) \times 3$

Use the grid for Questions 15–16.

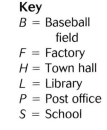

Key
B = Baseball field
F = Factory
H = Town hall
L = Library
P = Post office
S = School

15. Which town landmark is located at (5, 3)?

A. Post office   C. School
B. Baseball field   D. Town hall

16. Which ordered pair best names the location of the factory?

A. (6, 2)   C. (1, 6)
B. (3, 5)   D. (2, 6)

Chapter 4

Number Theory and Fractions

Chapter Theme: TRAVEL

.........Real Facts.........

If you like to hike, check out the Appalachian Trail! This continuous footpath stretches more than 2,100 miles through 14 states from Maine to Georgia. Nearly two-thirds of our population live within a day's drive of the trail. The hikers in the picture at the right are on a part of the trail in North Carolina.

The Appalachian Trail consists of many segments that each have their own names. The table below lists four trail segments in Georgia.

Appalachian Trail in Georgia	
Trail Name	Length in Miles
Springer Mountain to Woody Gap	20.0
Woody Gap to Neels Gap	11.5
Neels Gap to Hogpen Gap	6.8
Hogpen Gap to Unicoi Gap	14.2

• If you walked all but 1 of the trails listed, what fraction of the trails listed would you have walked?

• Suppose you walked from Springer Mountain to Woody Gap. About what fraction of the total length of listed trails would you have walked?

.........Real People.........

Meet Robert Siegler, a forest supervisor in North Carolina. He teaches visitors to the Holmes Educational State Forest about good forest management. They learn how to care for trees, water, wildlife, and soil.

Any Way You Cut It

Fractions can be used to describe parts of a whole.

Learning About It

Sourdough bread is a specialty in many San Francisco bakeries. Look at the two loaves of sourdough bread shown below. Suppose you were given two sections of the loaf on the top and your friend was given four sections of the one on the bottom. Did you each receive the same amount of bread?

You can use fraction strips to compare fractions and to find fractions that are equal in value.

Work with a partner.

Word Bank

equivalent fractions

What You Need

For each pair:
fraction strips

1		
$\frac{1}{3}$	$\frac{1}{3}$	
$\frac{1}{6}$ $\frac{1}{6}$	$\frac{1}{6}$ $\frac{1}{6}$	

Step 1 Compare $\frac{2}{3}$ and $\frac{4}{6}$.

- Place two $\frac{1}{3}$ strips under one whole strip.
- Find out how many $\frac{1}{6}$ pieces fit exactly under $\frac{2}{3}$.

As the model shows, you and your friend received the same amount of sourdough bread.

$\frac{2}{3}$ and $\frac{4}{6}$ are **equivalent fractions**.

What other like fraction strips fit exactly under $\frac{2}{3}$?

What other fraction is equivalent to $\frac{2}{3}$?

Step 2 Record your work in a chart like the one below. Use fraction strips to find equivalent fractions for each fraction listed in the chart.

Fraction	Equivalent Fractions
$\frac{2}{3}$	$\frac{4}{6}$
$\frac{5}{10}$	
$\frac{3}{12}$	
$\frac{6}{8}$	
$\frac{4}{4}$	

Think and Discuss Find the next three equivalent fractions below. Write a rule to describe the pattern.

$\frac{1}{4}, \frac{2}{8}, \frac{3}{12}, \blacksquare, \blacksquare, \blacksquare$

Practice

Write the missing number to make equivalent fractions.

1. $\frac{1}{3} = \frac{\blacksquare}{6}$

2. $\frac{9}{12} = \frac{\blacksquare}{4}$

3. **Create Your Own** Use like fraction pieces to model a fraction. Have your partner use fraction strips to find one or more equivalent fractions.

Using Algebra Use a pattern to find the next three equivalent fractions. Write a rule to describe each pattern.

4. $\frac{2}{5}, \frac{4}{10}, \frac{6}{15}, \blacksquare, \blacksquare, \blacksquare$

5. $\frac{6}{18}, \frac{5}{15}, \frac{4}{12}, \blacksquare, \blacksquare, \blacksquare$

6. $\frac{3}{12}, \frac{4}{16}, \frac{5}{20}, \blacksquare, \blacksquare, \blacksquare$

7. $\frac{21}{35}, \frac{18}{30}, \frac{15}{25}, \blacksquare, \blacksquare, \blacksquare$

The cable cars found in San Francisco are among the most popular attractions of the city. ➤

INTERNET ACTIVITY

www.sbgmath.com

Even Steven

Two different fractions can be equal in value.

Learning About It

You are visiting the Alamo, perhaps the most famous landmark in Texas. You and a friend each buy 12 stamps and 12 picture postcards there. The next day, you mail 4 of your 12 cards, and your friend mails $\frac{1}{3}$ of her cards. Do you and your friend mail the same number of cards?

Is $\frac{1}{3}$ equal to $\frac{4}{12}$? How can you find out?

12 stamps total   4 stamps

THERE'S ALWAYS A WAY!

- **One way** is to use fraction strips. One whole strip equals 1 set of 12 cards.

$$\frac{1}{3} = \frac{4}{12}$$

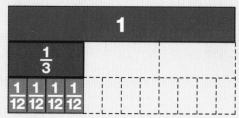

- **Another way** is to use pencil and paper.

  Multiply or divide the numerator and denominator by the same number.

  Multiply $3 \times \blacksquare = 12$

  $$\frac{1}{3} = \frac{1 \times 4}{3 \times 4} = \frac{4}{12}$$

  Divide $12 \div \blacksquare = 3$

  $$\frac{4}{12} = \frac{4 \div 4}{12 \div 4} = \frac{1}{3}$$

  Remember $\frac{4}{4} = 1$

Since $\frac{1}{3}$ equals $\frac{4}{12}$, you and your friend mailed the same number of cards; $\frac{1}{3}$ and $\frac{4}{12}$ are equivalent fractions.

Think and Discuss What property do you use to make a fraction equivalent to $\frac{1}{2}$?

Social Studies Connection ➤
In 1836 the Alamo was the scene of a fierce battle between a group of Texans and a much larger Mexican force.

SAN ANTONIO

Try It Out

Using Algebra **Find each missing numerator or denominator.**

1. $\frac{3}{10} = \frac{\blacksquare}{30}$

2. $\frac{4}{7} = \frac{16}{\blacksquare}$

3. $\frac{\blacksquare}{9} = \frac{1}{3}$

4. $\frac{3}{\blacksquare} = \frac{6}{8}$

5. $\frac{9}{18} = \frac{\blacksquare}{2}$

Practice

Using Algebra **Write each missing number to make an equivalent fraction.**

6. $\frac{3 \times \blacksquare}{5 \times \blacksquare} = \frac{12}{20}$

7. $\frac{4 \times \blacksquare}{7 \times \blacksquare} = \frac{12}{21}$

8. $\frac{6 \div \blacksquare}{8 \div \blacksquare} = \frac{3}{4}$

9. $\frac{9 \div \blacksquare}{27 \div \blacksquare} = \frac{1}{3}$

Using Algebra **Find each missing numerator or denominator.**

10. $\frac{4}{5} = \frac{\blacksquare}{15}$

11. $\frac{14}{16} = \frac{\blacksquare}{8}$

12. $\frac{3}{\blacksquare} = \frac{12}{28}$

13. $\frac{2}{6} = \frac{\blacksquare}{3}$

14. $\frac{\blacksquare}{16} = \frac{3}{4}$

15. $\frac{3}{4} = \frac{6}{\blacksquare}$

16. $\frac{14}{42} = \frac{\blacksquare}{3}$

17. $\frac{5}{\blacksquare} = \frac{15}{27}$

18. $\frac{\blacksquare}{13} = \frac{3}{39}$

19. $\frac{9}{30} = \frac{3}{\blacksquare}$

20. **Analyze** Place 3, 6, 9, and 18 in the boxes to make a true statement. $\frac{\blacksquare}{\blacksquare} = \frac{\blacksquare}{\blacksquare}$

Problem Solving

21. **Explain** You and your friend each take 36 photographs. Nine of yours were taken at night. One third of your friend's photographs were taken at night. Did you each take the same number of photographs at night?

22. **What If?** Suppose you divide 36 pictures equally between two albums. If you put $\frac{1}{2}$ of the pictures in one album and 18 pictures in the other, how can you be sure you divided them equally?

Review and Remember

Use a calculator to find the mean of each set of data.

23. 4, 6, 7, 8, 8

24. 21, 41, 51, 60

25. 225, 567, 879

26. 12.4, 10.34

For Extra Practice, see Set A, page 178. 145

Equal Shares

Divisibility rules can help you decide if you can divide evenly by a number.

Learning About It

Picture yourself on the beach at Sanibel Island, Florida, which is famous for its beautiful seashells. If you and two friends collect 144 shells, can you divide them equally?

> **Word Bank**
>
> **divisible**

To find out, you need to know if 144 is divisible by 3. **Divisible** means "having no remainder after division." You can find out if 144 is divisible by 3 without dividing. A number is divisible by 3 if the sum of the digits is divisible by 3.

Step 1 Find the sum of the digits.	**Step 2** Divide the sum by 3.
$1 + 4 + 4 = 9$	$9 \div 3 = 3$ no remainder

144 is divisible by 3. You and your friends can divide the shells equally.

Divisibility rules help you find out if a number is divisible.

Divisibility Rules
A number is divisible by
2 if the last digit is 0, 2, 4, 6, or 8.
3 if the sum of the digits is divisible by 3.
4 if the number formed by the last two digits is divisible by 4.
5 if the last digit is 5 or 0.
6 if the number is divisible by both 2 and 3.
9 if the sum of the digits is divisible by 9.
10 if the last digit is 0.

Think and Discuss What is the greatest four-digit number that is divisible by 3?

Try It Out

Which lettered number is divisible by each given number?
Write the letter of the correct answer.

1. divisible by 5
- **a.** 2,234
- **b.** 36,140
- **c.** 9,223

2. divisible by 4
- **a.** 54,635
- **b.** 7,593
- **c.** 31,836

3. divisible by 6
- **a.** 1,115
- **b.** 6,135
- **c.** 2,526

4. divisible by 9
- **a.** 27,723
- **b.** 6,543
- **c.** 72,817

5. 1,032 is divisible by 6. Is it divisible by 4? by 5?
How do you know?

Practice

Tell if each number is divisible by 2, 3, 4, 5, 6, 9, 10 , or none of these.

6. 213   **7.** 550   **8.** 1,032   **9.** 3,742   **10.** 5,310

11. 111,000   **12.** 17,985   **13.** 47,388   **14.** 9,999   **15.** 41,112

Replace ■ with a digit that makes each number divisible by 4.

16. 41■   **17.** 52■   **18.** 10,00■   **19.** 2■2   **20.** 85■28

21. Find a number divisible by 6 that is between
1,000 and 1,200.

Problem Solving

22. You Decide The nature center
is creating an exhibit of 356
shells. Decide how many display
cases to use if an equal number
of shells must be in each case.

23. Analyze You want to make
some jewelry, using 17 shells.
Each piece of jewelry uses
either 3 or 4 shells. How can
you use all the shells?

Review and Remember

Complete the following exercises.

24. 12.3 + 1.23 + 123   **25.** 2.64 − 2.6   **26.** 33.5 × 3.2

27. 9 + (6 − 3)   **28.** 27 ÷ (5 + 4)   **29.** 111 × (9 − 8)

For Extra Practice, see Set B, page 178.

Developing Skills for
Problem Solving

First read for understanding and then focus on whether the solution to a problem is reasonable.

READ FOR UNDERSTANDING

*S*ome riverboat cruises offer tickets with and without lunch. Today, 60 of the 180 passengers bought tickets that include lunch. Each lunch table can seat up to 6 people. On most cruises, half the passengers eat in groups of 2 and half eat in groups of 4.

1 How many passengers are on the cruise?

2 How many passengers have lunch tickets?

3 How many passengers can sit at a table?

▲ **Social Studies Connection**
A riverboat cruises the Mississippi River near New Orleans.

THINK AND DISCUSS

MATH FOCUS

Reasonable Answers   When you solve a problem, you should always check to make sure that your answer is reasonable. You can use your estimate or look back at the information in the problem to see if the answer makes sense.

4 Is it reasonable to say that 60 tables are needed? Why or why not?

5 The captain has instructed the crew to set up 25 tables for the lunch crowd. Is this a reasonable number of tables? Explain.

6 Why is it important to check to see if an answer is reasonable?

Show What You Learned

Answer each question. Give a reason for your choice.

During a 14-day cruise, each of the cruise ship's 275 passengers will sit at the captain's table for at least one meal. The table seats a total of 10 people, including the captain. Three meals are served each day.

1 Which of the following shows how to find the number of passengers that can eat with the captain in one day?

a. Multiply the number of passengers by 14.

b. Multiply the number of passengers at the table at any one meal by 3.

c. Multiply the number of passengers at the table at any one meal by 14.

2 Is it reasonable to say that the maximum number of people who can dine with the captain during the cruise is 378 people?

a. No, because $275 \times 3 = 825$

b. Yes, because $14 \times 10 \times 3 = 420$

c. Yes, because $14 \times 9 \times 3 = 378$

3 Is it reasonable to say that some passengers will have the chance to eat a meal with the captain more than once?

a. Yes, because the number of passengers that can eat with the captain is greater than 275.

b. Yes, because there will be 28 meals in 14 days.

c. Both **a** and **b**

The passengers on a whale-watching cruise lined the railings to look for whales. Half of the 90 passengers were on the middle deck. One third of the remaining passengers watched from the upper deck. The rest watched from the lower deck.

4 Which fact in the problem makes it reasonable to say that the middle deck has 45 passengers?

a. Half the passengers are on the middle deck.

b. One third of the remaining passengers are on the upper deck.

c. The rest are on the lower deck.

5 Is it reasonable to say that there were 45 people on the middle deck, 15 on the upper deck, and 30 on the lower deck?

a. Yes, because $45 + 15 + 30 = 90$

b. Yes, because $45 = 15 + 30$

c. Both **a** and **b**

6 **Explain** A crew member stated that there were 3 times as many passengers on the lower deck than were on the upper deck. Was his statement reasonable? Explain.

You Call Three...

You can use an exponent to show a number being used as a factor.

Learning About It

You call three friends and invite them to your house to look at your collection of seashells. Each friend calls three friends and invites them to come along. Then each of those friends invites three friends.

You can draw a picture to show how many people were invited.

Word Bank

exponent
base
power

3

3×3

3×3×3

You can use an **exponent** to tell how many times a number is used as a factor.

The number is called the **base**. The exponent is called the **power** of the base. For example, three to the third power is written 3^3.

$$\underbrace{3 \times 3 \times 3}_{\text{factors}} = 3^{3} \overset{\text{exponent}}{\underset{\text{base}}{}}$$

More Examples

A. Evaluate 4^3.

$$4^3 = \underbrace{4 \times 4 \times 4}_{\text{3 factors}} = 64$$

B. Evaluate 0.2^2.

$$0.2^2 = 0.2 \times 0.2 = 0.04$$

Remember your rule for multiplying decimals.

> ◀ **Math Note**
>
> You can read 3^3 as "three cubed" or "three to the third power." To find 3^3, multiply $3 \times 3 \times 3$.

Think and Discuss   What is the value of 4^1? How do you know?

Try It Out

Use exponents to write each expression.

1. $2 \times 2 \times 2$ 2. 5×5 3. $4 \times 4 \times 4 \times 4$ 4. $9 \times 9 \times 9 \times 9 \times 9$

Write each number as a product of factors and then evaluate.

5. 7^2 6. 6^6 7. 4^5 8. 5^4 9. 4^4 10. 3^3

Practice

Write each product as an exponent and evaluate.

11. 8×8 12. $11 \times 11 \times 11$ 13. $4 \times 4 \times 4 \times 4$ 14. $7 \times 7 \times 7 \times 7 \times 7$

15. 64×64 16. $5 \times 5 \times 5$ 17. $22 \times 22 \times 22$ 18. $3 \times 3 \times 3 \times 3 \times 3 \times 3$

Evaluate.

19. 2^3 20. 3^2 21. 4^3 22. 8^2 23. 2^5 24. 2^7

25. 0.3^2 26. 15^2 27. 20^3 28. 3^4 29. 1^{12} 30. 12^1

Using Mental Math Evaluate.

31. $2^3 + 2$ 32. $10^2 - 10$ 33. $7^2 + 7^1$ 34. $30^2 + 10^2$ 35. $3^3 - 2$

Problem Solving

36. You are going to show pictures of your trip after school. You invite 2 friends after first period. They each invite 2 friends after second period. This goes on until classes end after eighth period. How many friends are invited altogether? What strategy did you use to solve this problem?

37. **Journal Idea** Anita says that there are 4^3 eggs in a dozen. Sean says that there are 3^4 eggs in a dozen. Is either person correct? Explain your reasoning.

Review and Remember

Find each measure for the following data set: 31, 34, 23, 34, 67, 47, 79.

38. range   39. mean   40. median   41. mode

For Extra Practice, see Set C, page 178.

Prime Time

Every whole number greater than 1 is either prime or composite.

Learning About It

If you traveled to Colombia, you might bring home examples of native folk art like the models shown here. Suppose you had 19 models like these. Could you share them equally with any number of friends? To help you find out, use the divisibility rules on page 146.

Word Bank

prime number
composite number
prime factorization

According to the divisibility rules, 19 is not divisible by 2, 3, 4, 5, 6, 9, or 10. It is also not divisible by 7 or 8. Since 19 is only divisible by itself and 1, 19 is a prime number.

Prime Number   **19**

A **prime number** is a whole number greater than 1 with exactly two factors, itself and 1.

$$19 = 19 \times 1$$

factors: 19, 1

Composite Number   **20**

A **composite number** is a whole number greater than 1 with more than two factors. For example, 20 is a composite number with six factors.

$$20 = \begin{array}{l} 20 \times 1 \\ 10 \times 2 \\ 5 \times 4 \end{array}$$

factors: 1, 2, 4, 5, 10, 20

Connecting Ideas

You have seen that whole numbers greater than 1 are either prime or composite. Each composite number can be written as a product of prime numbers.

You can make a factor tree to find the **prime factorization** of a composite number, such as 40.

Choose any two factors of 40.

Continue writing factors until all the factors are prime.

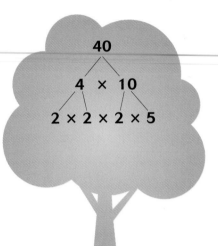

The prime factorization for 40 is $2 \times 2 \times 2 \times 5$, or $2^3 \times 5$.

Think and Discuss Will the prime factorization of 40 change if you start the tree with 5×8? Explain.

Try It Out

Tell if each number is prime or composite.

1. 15   **2.** 37   **3.** 50   **4.** 51   **5.** 23

Complete each factor tree for 24.

6.
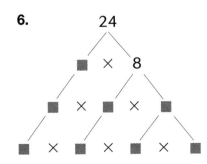

7.
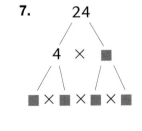

8.
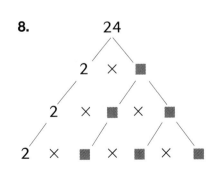

Write the prime factorization of each number.

9. 12   **10.** 27   **11.** 32   **12.** 36   **13.** 60

COLOMBIA

◄ **Social Studies Connection**
Outdoor markets are a common sight in many Latin American countries. People go there to buy fresh food, clothing, flowers, and household goods.

Practice

Tell if each number is prime or composite.

14. 39   **15.** 19   **16.** 31   **17.** 35   **18.** 43

19. 29   **20.** 21   **21.** 42   **22.** 47   **23.** 321

Using Algebra Tell whether the prime factorization of each given number is correct. If incorrect, write the correct prime factorizations.

24. $18 = 2 \times 9$ **25.** $50 = 5^2 \times 2$ **26.** $20 = 2^3 \times 5$

27. $24 = 2^3 \times 3$ **28.** $42 = 2 \times 3 \times 5$ **29.** $98 = 2^2 \times 7$

30. $16 = 4^2$ **31.** $100 = 2 \times 100$ **32.** $120 = 2 \times 3^2 \times 5$

Using Algebra Use exponents to write the prime factorization of each number.

33. 64   **34.** 48   **35.** 76   **36.** 81   **37.** 90

38. 141   **39.** 56   **40.** 100   **41.** 96   **42.** 40

43. 124   **44.** 125   **45.** 400   **46.** 144   **47.** 2,500

Using Algebra Match the prime factorization in Column A with the number it represents in Column B. Use a calculator.

Column A	Column B
48. $2^5 \times 3^2$	**a.** 360
49. $2^3 \times 3^2 \times 5$	**b.** 1,350
50. $3^4 \times 5 \times 7^2$	**c.** 288
51. $2 \times 3^3 \times 5^2$	**d.** 4,500
52. $2^2 \times 3^2 \times 5^3$	**e.** 19,845

Problem Solving

Use the graph to solve each problem.

53. Rachel wants to give all her model cars away. To how many friends can she give an equal number of two or more cars?

54. Which two people cannot share two or more of their cars equally among any number of friends? Explain.

55. How many model cars would Cynthia have to add to her collection to be able to divide her collection equally among herself and three friends?

56. **Analyze** Two of the people combined their collections of model cars. They then divided the combined collection into ten equal groups of cars. Who were the two people? How many cars were in each equal group?

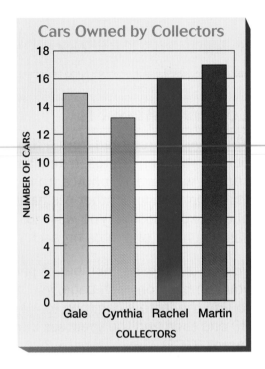

Cars Owned by Collectors

Review and Remember

Complete the following exercises.

57. $1.038 + 0.46$ **58.** $98.4 - 4.3$ **59.** 16.2×8.4 **60.** $18.27 \div 6$

61. $0.281 - 0.007$ **62.** $2.81 + 0.194$ **63.** $9.9 \div 2.2$ **64.** 2.2×0.18

Critical Thinking Corner

Number Sense

Triangular and Square Numbers

The numbers 3, 6, and 10 are *triangular numbers*. They can be arranged in triangles as shown below.

The numbers 4, 9, and 16 are *square numbers*. They can be arranged in squares as shown below.

1   3   6   10

1   4   9   16

1. Draw the next arrangement for each pattern and write the number.

2. **Using Algebra** What is the pattern in each number sequence?

For Extra Practice, see Set D, page 179.

Picture This

You can use what you know about prime numbers to find the greatest common factor.

Learning About It

You have just returned from a trip and are putting vacation photos in an album. One section will have 12 photos from Philadelphia, and another will have 30 photos from Boston. You want to have the same number of photos on each page.

To find the greatest number of photos you can have on each page, you need to find the factors common to 12 and 30 and then find the **greatest common factor (GCF)**.

Word Bank

greatest common factor
simplest form

THERE'S ALWAYS A WAY!

● **One way** is to list the factors of each number.

Step 1 Find the factors of 12 and 30.

Step 2 List the factors from least to greatest. Circle the common factors. Find the greatest common factor.

12: 1 × 12; 2 × 6; 3 × 4
30: 1 × 30; 2 × 15; 3 × 10; 5 × 6

12: ①, ②, ③, 4, **⑥**, 12
30: ①, ②, ③, 5, **⑥**, 10, 15, 30

The GCF is 6.

● **Another way** is to use prime factorization.

Step 1 Factor each number into primes.

Step 2 Find the common prime factors and multiply.

```
    12              30
   2 × 6          15 × 2
  2 × 3 × 2      5 × 3 × 2
```

$12 = 2 \times ②\times③$
$30 = 5 \times ②\times③$
The GCF is 2 × 3, or 6.

You can place 6 photos on each page.

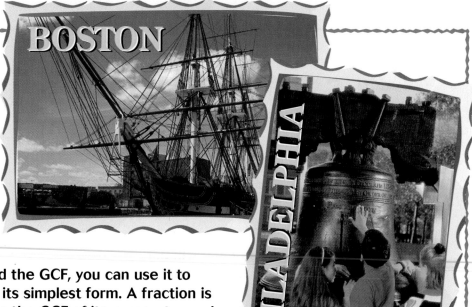

BOSTON

PHILADELPHIA

Social Studies Connection
Boston and Philadelphia have many historical places to see. Philadelphia was our nation's capital from 1790 to 1800. ➤

Connecting Ideas

Now that you can find the GCF, you can use it to express a fraction in its simplest form. A fraction is in simplest form when the GCF of its numerator and denominator is 1.

You put 42 photos in your album. A friend said that 12 photos from Philadelphia make up $\frac{2}{7}$ of all the photos. Was your friend correct?

To find out, write $\frac{12}{42}$ in **simplest form**.

Step 1 Find the greatest common factor of the numerator and the denominator.	**Step 2** Divide the numerator and denominator by the greatest common factor.
$\frac{12}{42} = \frac{2 \times \boxed{2} \times \boxed{3}}{7 \times \boxed{2} \times \boxed{3}}$ GCF = $2 \times 3 = 6$ 6 is the greatest common factor.	$\frac{12 \div 6}{42 \div 6} = \frac{2}{7}$

The 12 photos of Philadelphia are $\frac{2}{7}$ of all the photos.

Think and Discuss $\frac{18}{30}$ and $\frac{6}{10}$ are equivalent fractions. Is $\frac{6}{10}$ in simplest form? Explain.

Try It Out

Find the greatest common factor (GCF).

1. 6, 15   **2.** 21, 49   **3.** 18, 42   **4.** 30, 50

5. 16, 24   **6.** 20, 45   **7.** 11, 44   **8.** 6, 70, 78

Write each fraction in simplest form.

9. $\frac{12}{22}$ **10.** $\frac{14}{28}$ **11.** $\frac{24}{40}$ **12.** $\frac{38}{46}$ **13.** $\frac{24}{54}$

14. Explain The greatest common factor of two numbers is 12. One of the numbers is 24. Could the other number be 40?

Practice

Find the greatest common factor.

15. 10, 16   **16.** 36, 48   **17.** 32, 80   **18.** 24, 56

19. 20, 25   **20.** 32, 24   **21.** 45, 63   **22.** 90, 105

23. 84, 120   **24.** 300, 144   **25.** 16, 32, 48 **26.** 45, 36, 63

Choose the simplest form of each fraction.

27. $\frac{16}{24}$

    a. $\frac{3}{7}$ **b.** $\frac{2}{3}$

    c. $\frac{4}{6}$ **d.** $\frac{1}{2}$

28. $\frac{18}{30}$

    a. $\frac{3}{5}$ **b.** $\frac{3}{4}$

    c. $\frac{9}{15}$ **d.** $\frac{9}{10}$

29. $\frac{45}{60}$

    a. $\frac{5}{12}$ **b.** $\frac{2}{3}$

    c. $\frac{3}{4}$ **d.** $\frac{2}{5}$

Write each fraction in simplest form.

30. $\frac{9}{12}$ **31.** $\frac{14}{18}$ **32.** $\frac{36}{44}$ **33.** $\frac{24}{34}$ **34.** $\frac{40}{45}$ **35.** $\frac{27}{64}$

36. $\frac{25}{25}$ **37.** $\frac{18}{30}$ **38.** $\frac{49}{49}$ **39.** $\frac{100}{200}$ **40.** $\frac{12}{26}$ **41.** $\frac{10}{45}$

42. $\frac{16}{20}$ **43.** $\frac{25}{40}$ **44.** $\frac{70}{100}$ **45.** $\frac{66}{99}$ **46.** $\frac{49}{63}$ **47.** $\frac{33}{99}$

Find the fraction in each set that is in simplest form.

48. $\frac{2}{5}, \frac{3}{9}, \frac{4}{12}$ **49.** $\frac{2}{8}, \frac{18}{27}, \frac{7}{18}$ **50.** $\frac{3}{27}, \frac{1}{9}, \frac{5}{10}$ **51.** $\frac{4}{16}, \frac{3}{3}, \frac{7}{9}$

52. $\frac{3}{4}, \frac{5}{15}, \frac{12}{36}$ **53.** $\frac{3}{6}, \frac{13}{34}, \frac{30}{50}$ **54.** $\frac{2}{8}, \frac{3}{5}, \frac{9}{90}, \frac{36}{36}$ **55.** $\frac{5}{25}, \frac{6}{48}, \frac{7}{49}, \frac{1}{1}$

Use the Venn diagram for Exercises 56 and 57.

56. The Venn diagram shows the prime factors of 24 and 36. What is the prime factorization of each number?

57. What does the shaded area show?

58. **Create Your Own** Choose two even numbers and draw a Venn diagram to show their prime factors.

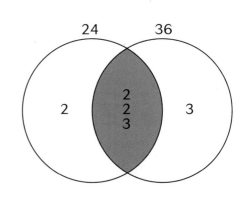

Problem Solving

59. Explain The 60 pictures in your album include 12 from Boston. Is it true that $\frac{1}{6}$ of them are from Boston?

60. In your friend's album, $\frac{1}{5}$ of the 75 pictures are from Philadelphia. How many pictures are from Philadelphia?

61. You separate some of your pictures into three groups, showing 16 from Philadelphia, 12 from Boston, and 20 that you took of your friends. You want to display them in an album with the same number of pictures on each page. What is the greatest number of pictures you can have on a page?

Review and Remember

Use the graph at the right to answer Exercises 62–64.

62. What is the average daily temperature in Philadelphia in August?

63. What is the average daily temperature in Boston in September?

64. Journal Idea Write a short paragraph comparing the temperatures in Boston and Philadelphia in the summer.

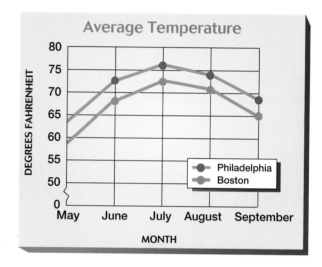

Average Temperature

DEGREES FAHRENHEIT

80
75
70
65
60
55
50
0

May   June   July   August   September

MONTH

Philadelphia
Boston

Money $ense

Pick a Plan

You and a friend have a chance to work on a cruise ship doing a variety of jobs. You will work 4 hours a day for 5 days.

To be paid you can choose between **Plan A** and **Plan B**. Your friend chooses Plan A. Which payment plan would you choose and why?

SKIPPER CRUISE LINES

$.01 FOR THE FIRST HOUR

Hourly pay doubles each hour for the next 19 hours

PLAN A

GIANT BOAT CRUISES

$10.00 PER HOUR ON DAY ONE

Hourly pay doubles each day for the next four days

PLAN B

Number Theory and Fractions

Using Algebra **Find the missing numbers.** (pages 144–145)

1. $\frac{3}{7} = \frac{\blacksquare}{28}$

2. $\frac{9}{\blacksquare} = \frac{45}{50}$

3. $\frac{\blacksquare}{8} = \frac{3}{4}$

4. $\frac{24}{36} = \frac{\blacksquare}{6}$

5. $\frac{12}{\blacksquare} = \frac{6}{20}$

Using Algebra **Write the missing number to make an equivalent fraction.** (pages 144–145)

6. $\frac{1 \times \blacksquare}{2 \times \blacksquare} = \frac{4}{8}$

7. $\frac{15 \div \blacksquare}{25 \div \blacksquare} = \frac{3}{5}$

8. $\frac{2 \times \blacksquare}{5 \times \blacksquare} = \frac{4}{10}$

9. $\frac{34 \div \blacksquare}{51 \div \blacksquare} = \frac{2}{3}$

Tell if each number is divisible by 2, 3, 4, 5, 6, 9, 10, or none of these. (pages 146–149)

10. 372

11. 585

12. 1,488

13. 2,970

14. 14,756

Write the product as an exponent and evaluate. (pages 150–151)

15. $7 \times 7 \times 7 \times 7$

16. $4 \times 4 \times 4 \times 4 \times 4$

17. $11 \times 11 \times 11$

18. $5 \times 5 \times 5 \times 5$

Using Algebra **Evaluate.** (pages 150–151)

19. 1^6

20. 3^5

21. 7^2

22. 4^4

23. 10^5

24. 20^1

25. 0.3^3

26. 0.9^2

27. 0.24^1

28. 0.6^4

Using Algebra **Tell if the number is prime or composite. If the number is composite, write the prime factorization using exponents.** (pages 152–155)

29. 14

30. 51

31. 61

32. 72

33. 97

34. 36

35. 78

36. 176

37. 120

38. 210

39. 131

40. 256

41. 495

42. 79

43. 720

Find the greatest common factor (GCF). (pages 156–159)

44. 15, 36

45. 32, 48

46. 16, 24, 72

47. 36, 40, 56

Write each fraction in simplest form. (pages 156–159)

48. $\frac{18}{24}$

49. $\frac{16}{36}$

50. $\frac{22}{24}$

51. $\frac{16}{100}$

52. $\frac{48}{114}$

Problem Solving

53. You want to give your friend the same number of pictures that you keep for yourself. You give your friend 9 pictures and take $\frac{1}{3}$ for yourself. If there are 27 pictures altogether, do you each have the same number of pictures?

54. You call to invite two friends to a party. They each call two friends and those friends each call two friends. How many people were called during the third round?

55. Of the 54 pictures in your album, 6 are from Philadelphia. What fractional part of your pictures are from Philadelphia?

What do you think?

Is it easier to find the greatest common factor by using prime factorization or by listing all the factors? Explain.

Journal Idea

Use the divisibility rules to show that all prime numbers greater than 2 are odd.

Critical Thinking Corner

Logical Thinking

Sum It Up

In 1742 Christian Goldbach, a German mathematician, made an interesting prediction, which became known as Goldbach's conjecture. A conjecture is a prediction based on educated guesswork. Goldbach conjectured that "every even number greater than 2 can be written as the sum of two prime numbers." To this day, Goldbach's conjecture has not been proven.

$24 = 17 + 7$

Investigate Goldbach's Conjecture

Using Algebra Work with a partner.

1. Make a list of the even numbers less than 30. Start with 4.

2. Show each number as the sum of two prime numbers. For example: $4 = 2 + 2$

3. Which even numbers, less than 30, can be written as sums of two prime numbers?

4. Which even numbers, less than 30, can be written as sums in more than one way?

Problem Solving
Use Logical Reasoning

You can use logical reasoning to solve problems.

Read the newspaper ad. Then use the clues to find the missing phone-number digits.

 UNDERSTAND

What do you need to find?

You need to find values for *a*, *b*, *c*, and *d* in the phone number.

 PLAN

How can you solve the problem?

You can **use logical reasoning** and a table to organize the information.

 SOLVE

Make a table. As you read the clues, cross out digits that you know are incorrect and circle a digit when you know it is the only correct answer.

- **Clue 1**: Doesn't help yet.
- **Clue 2**: Circle 7 and cross off all other digits for *a*. Use CLUE 1: cross off 7 for *b*, *c*, and *d*.
- **Clue 3**: Cross off numbers that are not prime for *b* and *d*. Cross off numbers that *are* prime for *c*.
- **Clue 4**: Circle 0 and cross off all other digits for *c*.
- **Clue 5**: Circle 5 and cross off all other digits for *d*. Cross off 5 for *b*.
- **Clue 6**: Circle 2 and cross off 3 for *b*. The telephone number is 555-7205.

 LOOK BACK

Check that all the digits satisfy each clue.

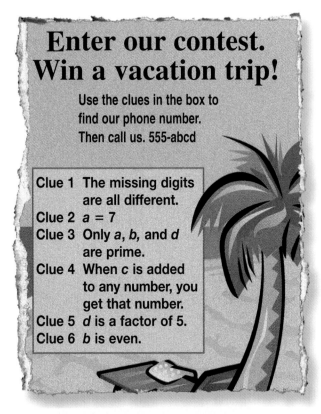

Enter our contest. Win a vacation trip!

Use the clues in the box to find our phone number. Then call us. 555-abcd

Clue 1	The missing digits are all different.
Clue 2	*a* = 7
Clue 3	Only *a*, *b*, and *d* are prime.
Clue 4	When *c* is added to any number, you get that number.
Clue 5	*d* is a factor of 5.
Clue 6	*b* is even.

a	b	c	d
0̶	0̶	⓪	0̶
1̶	1̶	1̶	1̶
2̶	②	2̶	2̶
3̶	3̶	3̶	3̶
4̶	4̶	4̶	4̶
5̶	5̶	5̶	⑤
6̶	6̶	6̶	6̶
⑦	7̶	7̶	7̶
8̶	8̶	8̶	8̶
9̶	9̶	9̶	9̶

Using the Strategy

Try using logical reasoning to find the missing digits of each telephone number for Problems 1–3.

1 123-*efgh*
Clue 1: *e*, *f*, *g*, and *h* are different.
Clue 2: Only *f* and *h* are prime.
Clue 3: Only *e* and *f* are even.
Clue 4: *e* is a multiple of 3.
Clue 5: *g* is a factor of every number.
Clue 6: The sum of *e*, *f*, *g*, and *h* is 12.

2 555-*abcd*
Clue 1: *a*, *b*, *c*, and *d* are different.
Clue 2: *d* is the only odd number.
Clue 3: *a* is the only prime number.
Clue 4: $d = 3^2$
Clue 5: $c < 8$
Clue 6: $c - b = a$

3 800-*jkmn*
Clue 1: *j*, *k*, *m*, and *n* are different.
Clue 2: Only *m*, and *n* are prime.
Clue 3: Only *j*, *m*, and *n* are odd.
Clue 4: $n = 5$
Clue 5: $m < n$
Clue 6: $j \times j = 1$
Clue 7: The sum of $k + k$ is 0.

Mixed Strategy Review

Try these or other strategies to solve each problem.
Tell which strategy you used.

THERE'S ALWAYS A WAY!

Problem Solving Strategies

- *Draw a Diagram*
- *Guess and Check*
- *Find a Pattern*
- *Use Simulation*

The table at the right shows students' class trip choices. Use the table for Problem 4.

4 The town has school buses in 3 different sizes. Some can seat 30 students, some can seat 40, and some can seat 48. Which of these buses can be used for all the trips assuming there are no empty seats?

Trip	Number of Students
Mountain Train Ride	150
Harbor Cruise	210
Parks and Museum	90
Historic Tour of the City	240

5 The mountain train reaches a speed of 5.4 miles per hour (mph) after traveling 2 miles, 6.8 mph after 4 miles, and 8.2 mph after 6 miles. If the speed continues to increase at this rate, how fast will the train be traveling when it has gone 20 miles?

6 You want to walk around the city. Starting at the first monument, you walk 4 blocks north, 5 blocks east, 2 blocks south, and finally 4 blocks west. How can you return to your starting point, using the shortest route along the city blocks?

Mix It Up

A fraction with a numerator larger than the denominator can be written as a mixed number.

Learning About It

How would you like to be able to step outside and pick a fresh orange? Many families in Florida have orange trees right in their back yard.

To share 2 oranges equally among 8 people, you would cut each orange into 4 quarters, or 4 equal pieces.

Any whole number can be written as a fraction. $2 = \frac{8}{4}$

Word Bank

mixed number
improper fraction

This picture shows two whole oranges and one quarter of an orange, or $2\frac{1}{4}$ oranges.

$2\frac{1}{4}$ is a **mixed number**.

To write a mixed number as a fraction, write the whole number as a fraction. Then combine the fractions.

$$2\frac{1}{4} = \frac{8}{4} + \frac{1}{4} = \frac{8+1}{4} = \frac{9}{4}$$

This picture shows nine quarter oranges or $\frac{9}{4}$ oranges.

$\frac{9}{4}$ is an **improper fraction**.

To write an improper fraction as a mixed number, divide the numerator by the denominator. Simplify if possible.

$$\frac{9}{4} = 4\overline{)9}\,^{2\frac{1}{4}}$$

Think and Discuss When does an improper fraction become a whole number?

Try It Out

Write each improper fraction as a mixed number or as a whole number.

1. $\frac{7}{3}$ 2. $\frac{22}{3}$ 3. $\frac{35}{18}$ 4. $\frac{36}{6}$ 5. $\frac{47}{2}$ 6. $\frac{78}{13}$

Write each mixed number as an improper fraction.

7. $2\frac{1}{2}$ 8. $3\frac{2}{3}$ 9. $4\frac{9}{10}$ 10. $7\frac{7}{10}$ 11. $6\frac{5}{8}$ 12. $11\frac{1}{9}$

◄ **Health and Fitness Connection**

Oranges are a good source of vitamin C. They were first grown in Asia about 4,000 years ago.

INTERNET ACTIVITY

www.sbgmath.com

Practice

Write the improper fraction and the mixed number for each picture.

13.   **14.** 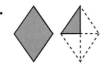   **15.**

Write each improper fraction as a mixed number or as a whole number.

16. $\frac{22}{7}$ **17.** $\frac{19}{3}$ **18.** $\frac{64}{8}$ **19.** $\frac{21}{4}$ **20.** $\frac{48}{7}$ **21.** $\frac{63}{2}$ **22.** $\frac{53}{10}$ **23.** $\frac{87}{4}$

Write each mixed number as an improper fraction.

24. $2\frac{1}{3}$ **25.** $6\frac{5}{6}$ **26.** $3\frac{2}{9}$ **27.** $7\frac{3}{8}$ **28.** $5\frac{2}{3}$ **29.** $9\frac{4}{7}$ **30.** $10\frac{3}{5}$

Problem Solving

31. Analyze You have an improper fraction with a denominator of 20. If the fraction is equal to $3\frac{1}{5}$, what is the fraction?

32. You cut oranges into thirds to share with your friends. You give away all 36 pieces. How many oranges did you cut?

Review and Remember

Estimate. Then use a calculator to find the quotient.

33. $765 \div 9$ **34.** $880 \div 22$ **35.** $1,035 \div 45$ **36.** $78.2 \div 0.46$ **37.** $565.4 \div 2.2$

On the Right Track

You can use prime factorization to find the least common multiple.

Learning About It

After visiting the Lionel Trains Visitor's Center in Michigan, you and some friends set up a large two-track system—a 10-second track and a 6-second track—like the one shown. If both trains leave the station at the same time, how much time will pass before they are at the station at the same time again?

To find out, you need to find the **least common multiple (LCM)** of 10 and 6.

Word Bank

least common
    multiple (LCM)
multiples
least common
    denominator (LCD)

THERE'S ALWAYS A WAY!

- **One way** is to list some **multiples** of each number.
  Multiples of 10: 10, 20, **30**,…
  Multiples of 6: 6, 12, 18, 24, **30**,…
  The least common multiple of 10 and 6 is 30.

- **Another way** is to use prime factorization.

  Step 1 Factor each number into primes.

  $$
  \begin{array}{cc}
  10 & 6 \\
  /\,\backslash & /\,\backslash \\
  2 \times 5 & 2 \times 3
  \end{array}
  $$

  Step 2 Use the prime factorizations to write the smallest product containing 10 and 6.

  $10 = 2 \times 5$ Write each prime factorization, aligning common factors.

  $6 = 2 \quad \times 3$

  $2 \times 5 \times 3 = 30$ Write the product as shown, using each common factor once.

The LCM of 10 and 6 is 30.

After 30 seconds, the trains will both be at the station again.

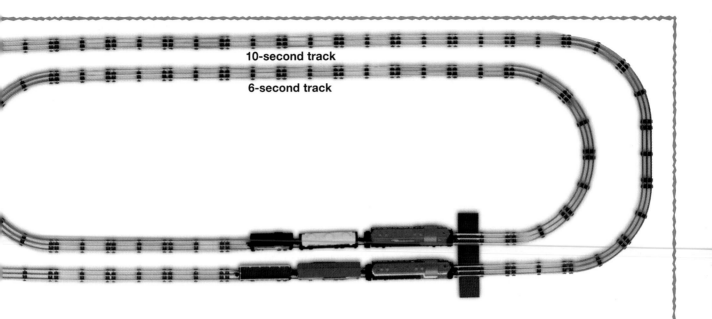

10-second track

6-second track

Another Example

Find the least common multiple of 12, 16, and 21.

$$12 = 2 \times 2 \times 3$$
$$16 = 2 \times 2 \quad\quad \times 2 \times 2$$
$$21 = \quad\quad\quad 3 \quad\quad\quad\quad \times 7$$
$$2 \times 2 \times 3 \times 2 \times 2 \times 7 = 336. \text{ This is the LCM.}$$

Connecting Ideas

You can use your ability to determine the least common multiple to find the least common denominator (LCD) of two fractions. Using the LCD will help you compare unlike fractions.

Use the **least common denominator** to rewrite $\frac{3}{4}$ and $\frac{5}{6}$ as like fractions.

Step 1 Find the LCM of the denominators. You can use prime factorization.	**Step 2** Write equivalent fractions, using the LCM as the least common denominator.

$\frac{3}{4}$ $\quad 4 = 2 \times 2$

$\frac{5}{6}$ $\quad 6 = 2 \times \quad\quad 3$

$\quad\quad\quad 2 \times 2 \times 3 = 12$ LCM

$\frac{3}{4} = \frac{3 \times 3}{4 \times 3} = \frac{9}{12}$ $\quad$ Think $\quad 4 \times \blacksquare = 12$

$\frac{5}{6} = \frac{5 \times 2}{6 \times 2} = \frac{10}{12}$ $\quad$ Think $\quad 6 \times \blacksquare = 12$

Think and Discuss Does the least common multiple of 4 and 6 contain both 4 and 6 as factors? Explain.

Try It Out

Find the least common multiple for each set of numbers.

1. 5, 6   **2.** 3, 7   **3.** 3, 9   **4.** 4, 14   **5.** 4, 6, 8

Use the LCD to write each pair as like fractions.

6. $\frac{5}{6}, \frac{5}{20}$ **7.** $\frac{6}{10}, \frac{4}{30}$ **8.** $\frac{7}{6}, \frac{8}{10}$ **9.** $\frac{8}{9}, \frac{4}{12}$ **10.** $\frac{4}{3}, \frac{5}{8}, \frac{7}{9}$

11. Discuss Find the product of the GCF and the LCM of 10 and 6. Find the product of the GCF and the LCM of 4 and 6. What do you notice?

Practice

Write the first four multiples for each number.

12. 5   **13.** 8   **14.** 11   **15.** 14   **16.** 60

Find the least common multiple for each set of numbers.

17. 2, 3   **18.** 2, 7   **19.** 3, 5   **20.** 4, 7   **21.** 4, 9

22. 5, 12   **23.** 4, 12   **24.** 7, 21   **25.** 3, 14   **26.** 16, 6

27. 5, 14   **28.** 6, 14   **29.** 1, 4, 40   **30.** 13, 26, 2   **31.** 9, 12, 18

Use the LCD to write each pair as like fractions.

32. $\frac{2}{3}, \frac{2}{5}$ **33.** $\frac{1}{8}, \frac{5}{40}$ **34.** $\frac{2}{9}, \frac{4}{30}$ **35.** $\frac{7}{6}, \frac{12}{8}$ **36.** $\frac{10}{12}, \frac{20}{60}$

37. $\frac{2}{24}, \frac{36}{48}$ **38.** $\frac{4}{6}, \frac{25}{24}$ **39.** $\frac{2}{8}, \frac{2}{4}, \frac{1}{3}$ **40.** $\frac{7}{8}, \frac{1}{6}, \frac{2}{8}$ **41.** $\frac{6}{18}, \frac{2}{36}, \frac{10}{9}$

◄ The Lionel Trains Visitor's Center is located in Chesterfield, Michigan. It has ten running trains on a 14' × 40' layout.

Problem Solving

42. One model train travels around a loop every 5 minutes. The other travels on another loop every 4 minutes. If they begin at the same point at the same time, how much time will pass before they meet at that point again?

43. **Analyze** One train leaves the station for Chatham every 15 minutes. Another leaves for Summit every 20 minutes. If service to both towns starts at 9:15 A.M., when will the trains leave the station again at the same time?

44. Suppose the Lionel Trains Visitor's Center gives a discount coupon to every tenth visitor. Every twelfth visitor gets a free bumper sticker. Which will be the first visitor to receive both?

45. Tom walks his dog in a park every other day. Alice jogs in the park every fourth day. They both arrive at the park entrance at 8 A.M. If they meet there on Monday, on what day will they meet there again?

46. Lenny, Mark, and Liza are going to jog along 3 different trails in the park. To complete one circuit, Lenny takes 6 min., Mark takes 12 min., and Liza takes 9 min. If they start at the same place and the same time, how long will it be before they are together again at the starting point?

Review and Remember

Using Algebra Find each missing number.

47. $\frac{3}{6} = \frac{\blacksquare}{30}$

48. $\frac{7}{\blacksquare} = \frac{42}{60}$

49. $\frac{1}{3} = \frac{9}{\blacksquare}$

50. $\frac{18}{27} = \frac{\blacksquare}{3}$

51. $\frac{1}{6} = \frac{7}{\blacksquare}$

52. $\frac{2}{7} = \frac{\blacksquare}{42}$

53. $\frac{8}{\blacksquare} = \frac{2}{5}$

54. $\frac{2}{3} = \frac{\blacksquare}{33}$

Time for Technology

Using the Math Processor™ CD-ROM

Using Number Spaces

You can use number spaces to help solve equations. Find the missing number in Exercise 47 above using cross multiplication.

- Open and link two number spaces [⊡].

- In one space, key: 3 * 30 / 6. In the other space, click [=]. Repeat the steps above for Exercises 48–54.

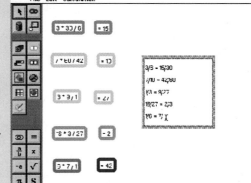

Trail Riders

Before you can compare unlike fractions, you have to rewrite them with a common denominator.

KEY

🚲 Bike Trails

········ $\frac{7}{8}$ mi

‒ ‒ ‒ $\frac{4}{5}$ mi

Learning About It

You and a friend are biking in Pocahontas State Park in Virginia. You follow the red trail and your friend follows the blue trail. Who rides farther?

To find out, compare $\frac{7}{8}$ and $\frac{4}{5}$.

THERE'S ALWAYS A WAY!

• **One way** is to compare fraction strips.

$\frac{1}{8}$	$\frac{1}{8}$	$\frac{1}{8}$	$\frac{1}{8}$	$\frac{1}{8}$	$\frac{1}{8}$	$\frac{1}{8}$

$\frac{1}{5}$	$\frac{1}{5}$	$\frac{1}{5}$	$\frac{1}{5}$

$\frac{7}{8} > \frac{4}{5}$

• **Another way** is to rename the fractions so they have the same denominator and compare.

Step 1 Find the LCD.	**Step 2** Write equivalent fractions, using the LCD.	**Step 3** Compare the fractions.
The LCM of 8 and 5 is 40.	$\frac{7}{8} = \frac{7 \times 5}{8 \times 5} = \frac{35}{40}$	$\frac{35}{40} > \frac{32}{40}$
The LCD of $\frac{7}{8}$ and $\frac{4}{5}$ is 40.	$\frac{4}{5} = \frac{4 \times 8}{5 \times 8} = \frac{32}{40}$	So $\frac{7}{8} > \frac{4}{5}$

You do—the red trail is longer.

More Examples

A. Compare $7\frac{12}{15}$ and $7\frac{5}{6}$.
The whole numbers are equal.
Compare the fractions.
The LCM of 15 and 6 is 30.

$\frac{12}{15} = \frac{24}{30}$ $\frac{5}{6} = \frac{25}{30}$

$\frac{24}{30} < \frac{25}{30}$, so $7\frac{12}{15} < 7\frac{5}{6}$

B. Arrange $\frac{3}{4}$, $\frac{7}{8}$, and $\frac{5}{6}$ in order from least to greatest.

The LCM of 4, 8, and 6 is 24.

$\frac{3}{4} = \frac{18}{24}$ $\frac{7}{8} = \frac{21}{24}$ $\frac{5}{6} = \frac{20}{24}$

$\frac{18}{24} < \frac{20}{24} < \frac{21}{24}$, so $\frac{3}{4} < \frac{5}{6} < \frac{7}{8}$

Think and Discuss Compare $\frac{1}{3}$ and $\frac{1}{4}$. Compare $\frac{1}{3}$ and $\frac{1}{2}$. Write a rule for comparing unlike fractions with the same numerator.

Virginia

Try It Out

Write the fractions by using the LCD, and then compare. Write <, >, or = for each .

1. $\frac{1}{2}$ ● $\frac{1}{3}$

2. $\frac{1}{8}$ ● $\frac{3}{24}$

3. $1\frac{2}{3}$ ● $1\frac{3}{4}$

▲ **Social Studies Connection**
Pocahontas State Park is named after the daughter of an American Indian chief. She was a friend of the early English settlers in Jamestown, Virginia.

Arrange in order from least to greatest.

4. $\frac{3}{7}, \frac{1}{3}, \frac{1}{5}$

5. $1\frac{1}{4}, 1\frac{2}{7}, \frac{7}{8}$

6. $2\frac{3}{5}, 2\frac{5}{8}, 2\frac{1}{4}$

7. $3\frac{11}{12}, 3\frac{5}{6}, 3\frac{9}{10}$

Practice

Write the LCD for each set of fractions.

8. $\frac{5}{9}, \frac{5}{6}$

9. $\frac{7}{10}, \frac{2}{7}$

10. $\frac{3}{10}, \frac{8}{15}$

11. $\frac{3}{4}, \frac{1}{6}$

12. $\frac{5}{6}, \frac{7}{8}$

Compare. Write <, >, or = for each ●.

13. $\frac{3}{4}$ ● $\frac{1}{4}$

14. $\frac{7}{9}$ ● $\frac{2}{3}$

15. $\frac{4}{5}$ ● $\frac{3}{4}$

16. $\frac{5}{8}$ ● $\frac{10}{16}$

17. $\frac{5}{8}$ ● $\frac{5}{12}$

18. $\frac{5}{4}$ ● $\frac{7}{5}$

19. $\frac{7}{10}$ ● $\frac{4}{9}$

20. $\frac{7}{6}$ ● $\frac{9}{6}$

Arrange in order from least to greatest.

21. $\frac{1}{3}, \frac{5}{9}, \frac{1}{6}$

22. $\frac{3}{5}, \frac{1}{2}, \frac{11}{10}$

23. $\frac{2}{3}, \frac{4}{5}, \frac{1}{2}$

24. $2\frac{4}{12}, 3\frac{1}{2}, \frac{3}{7}, \frac{4}{8}$

Problem Solving

25. In June, $1\frac{3}{4}$ in. of rain fell. In July, $1\frac{7}{8}$ in. fell, and in August, $1\frac{5}{6}$ in. fell. Which month had the most rain? the least?

26. You hiked $3\frac{11}{12}$ miles, canoed $3\frac{9}{10}$ miles, and rode your bike $3\frac{5}{6}$ miles. During which activity did you travel the greatest distance? the shortest?

Review and Remember

Complete the following exercises.

27. 0.2×3.3

28. $9.1 \div 0.13$

29. $10.2 - 0.6$

30. $4.72 + 3.28$

Problem Solving
Using Fractions and Decimals

Understanding fractions and decimals can help you solve problems.

The drawing at the right shows the floor plan of the Visitor's Center gift shop. The new manager is planning to rearrange the displays. She plans to use $\frac{1}{4}$ of the total space for postcards, $\frac{1}{3}$ for T-shirts, $\frac{1}{4}$ for hats, and $\frac{1}{6}$ for posters. Which display spaces will change and how?

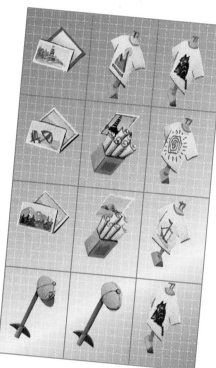

▲ Current Floor Plan

 UNDERSTAND

What do you need to know?

You need to know what fraction of the space is currently being used for each item and what fraction of the space each item will be given.

 PLAN

How can you solve the problem?

You can **make a table** to organize your information. Show the current display space, the planned space, and the comparison between the two.

 SOLVE

- The current space for T-shirts is greater than the planned space, so the space for T-shirts will decrease.

- The current space for hats is less than the planned space, so the space for hats will increase.

- The spaces for postcards and for posters will stay the same.

Item	Current Space	Planned Space	Comparison
Postcards	$\frac{1}{4}$	$\frac{1}{4}$	$\frac{1}{4} = \frac{1}{4}$
T-shirts	$\frac{5}{12}$	$\frac{1}{3}$	$\frac{5}{12} > \frac{1}{3}$
Hats	$\frac{1}{6}$	$\frac{1}{4}$	$\frac{1}{6} < \frac{1}{4}$
Posters	$\frac{1}{6}$	$\frac{1}{6}$	$\frac{1}{6} = \frac{1}{6}$

 LOOK BACK

How was understanding fractions useful in interpreting the floor plan diagram?

Show What You Learned

Use the prices shown for Problems 1–4.

1 What could you buy for exactly $20?

2 You have $50. Can you buy 4 hats and 5 posters? Explain.

3 You buy 2 T-shirts and pay with $40. How many hats can you buy with the change?

4 Create Your Own Write a problem using these prices so that the answer to your problem is $6.75.

T-Shirts
$15.75
each

Postcards
25¢
each

Hats
$4.75
each

Posters
$6.95
each

Use the tourist brochure for Problems 5–8.

Crystal Falls Park

Cape Ernie Visitor's Center

Castle Rock Lighthouse

22.75 miles

22.3 miles

22.9 miles

22.5 miles

Boathouse Restaurant

White Sands Beach

5 Which tourist attraction is closer to the Cape Ernie Visitor's Center — Crystal Falls Park or Castle Rock Lighthouse? How much closer is it?

6 You leave Castle Rock Lighthouse, pass the visitor's center, and continue on to the Boathouse Restaurant. Then you return to the visitor's center. How far do you travel?

7 Explain The odometer in your car shows that you have traveled 22.5 miles since leaving the visitor's center. Could you be at Crystal Falls Park? How do you know?

8 What If? Suppose the odometer shows that you have traveled 22.50 miles since leaving the visitor's center. Could you be at White Sands Beach? Why or why not?

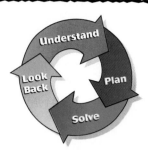

Problem Solving

Practice What You Learned

Choose the correct letter for each answer.

1 A magazine reporter found that of 350 readers, 2 out of 7 wanted more articles on sports. How many of these readers do **NOT** want more articles on sports?

A. 50
B. 100
C. 140
D. 250
E. Not Here

Tip

Look at the facts that are given. Make sure your answer makes sense compared to those facts.

MORE SPORTS   OK AS IS

---

2 Irma works more than 1 hour, but less than 4 hours, a day 5 days a week at an after-school job. She earns $5.25 per hour. Which of these is a reasonable amount for Irma to expect to earn in 1 month?

A. $75
B. $100
C. $300
D. $800
E. $1,000

Tip

Make a Table using 1, 2, 3, and 4 hours each day.

---

3 Angela used her computer to send an e-mail message to each of 3 friends. Each of them sent the message to 2 people. Then each of those people sent the message to 4 more people. How many people altogether read Angela's message?

A. 9
B. 12
C. 24
D. 48
E. Not Here

Tip

Use one of the strategies to solve this problem.
• *Find a Pattern*
• *Draw a Diagram*
• *Use Logical Reasoning*

4 Volunteers in a soup kitchen serve about 370 meals a month. If the kitchen is open for lunch and dinner every day, what is a good estimate for the number of meals served each year?

A. Less than 3,000
B. Between 3,000 and 3,500
C. Between 3,500 and 4,500
D. Between 5,000 and 6,000
E. More than 8,000

5 A plane flies 789 miles in about 3 hours. Which is the best estimate of how far it can fly in 5 hours?

A. Less than 800 miles
B. Between 800 and 1,000 miles
C. Between 1,000 and 2,000 miles
D. About 3,000 miles
E. More than 3,000 miles

6 Which is the best interpretation of the information shown on this graph?

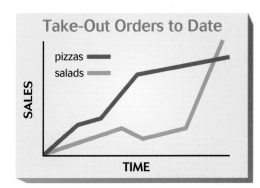

A. At present, salad sales are greater than pizza sales.
B. Pizza sales are increasing, and salad sales are decreasing.
C. Both pizzas and salads are decreasing.
D. At present, more pizzas are sold than salads.
E. Pizzas are selling faster than salads.

7 A survey showed that 72 people owned videotape players. This was more than $\frac{1}{3}$ of the people in the survey. Of the people surveyed, $\frac{1}{8}$ owned CD players. Which of these is a reasonable number of people in the survey?

A. 24   **D.** 225
B. 25   **E.** 250
C. 200

8 A diagonal is a line segment that connects 2 vertices of a polygon and is not a side. Diane made a design by drawing the rest of the diagonals on a pentagon like this one. What shape was her design?

A. Star
B. Triangle
C. Circle
D. The letter *A*
E. Not Here

9 Ann has $1.70 in her pocket. She has only dimes and quarters. Which number sentence could represent *T*, the total value of the coins?

A. $T = (2 \times 0.10) + (2 \times 0.25)$
B. $T = (2 \times 0.10) + (6 \times 0.25)$
C. $T = (6 \times 0.10) + (6 \times 0.25)$
D. $T = (8 \times 0.10) + (8 \times 0.25)$
E. $T = (2 + 0.10) \times (8 + 0.25)$

10 A restaurant cuts pizzas into 8 equal slices. One night they sold 50 slices of pizza. How many pizzas did they cut?

A. 6
B. 7
C. 48
D. 50
E. Not Here

Downhill Racer

You can write a decimal as a fraction or a fraction as a decimal.

Learning About It

Swoosh, swoosh, swoosh. Picture yourself and a friend, skiing at Sun Valley, Idaho. Look at the map of the slopes. Suppose you take the blue trail and your friend takes the red trail. Who will ski farther?

To help you compare 0.7 and $\frac{3}{4}$, write $\frac{3}{4}$ as a decimal.

To write a fraction as a decimal, divide the numerator by the denominator.

$$\frac{3}{4} = 4\overline{)3.00}^{\,0.75}$$

Since 0.75 is greater than 0.7, your friend will ski farther.

To write a decimal as a fraction, you can use what you know about place value.

$$0.6 = \frac{6}{10} = \frac{3}{5}$$

KEY

— 0.7 mi

— $\frac{3}{4}$ mi

More Examples

A. Write $3\frac{4}{5}$ as a decimal.

$$\frac{4}{5} = 5\overline{)4.0}^{\,0.8}$$

$$3\frac{4}{5} = 3 + 0.8 = 3.8$$

B. Write $\frac{1}{3}$ as a decimal.

$$3\overline{)1.00}^{\,0.33}$$
$$\underline{-9}\quad\text{The remainder is always 1.}$$
$$10\quad\text{The decimal repeats.}$$

$$\frac{1}{3} = 0.\overline{3}\quad\text{The bar means the digit repeats.}$$

Think and Discuss How are $\frac{5}{10}$ and 0.5 the same? How are they different?

Try It Out

Write each fraction as a decimal and each decimal as a fraction in simplest form.

1. $\frac{2}{5}$

2. $\frac{3}{8}$

3. $\frac{2}{3}$

4. $3\frac{1}{8}$

5. $4\frac{3}{20}$

6. 0.4

7. 0.08

8. 0.12

9. 0.55

10. 0.87

Practice

Write each fraction as a decimal and each decimal as a fraction in simplest form. Choose a method. Use paper and pencil or a calculator.

11. $\frac{1}{2}$

12. 0.44

13. $\frac{1}{5}$

14. 0.35

15. 5.65

16. $\frac{3}{50}$

17. 0.43

18. 0.08

19. $\frac{3}{10}$

20. $3\frac{1}{3}$

21. $\frac{1}{20}$

22. 0.09

23. 0.15

24. 0.025

25. $\frac{4}{5}$

Problem Solving

When you left home for Sun Valley, the odometer in the car showed 456.2 miles.

26. On the first day of your trip, you traveled $287\frac{7}{10}$ miles. What did the odometer show at the end of the day?

27. By the end of the second day, you were 500 miles from home. How many miles did you travel on the second day?

28. When you arrived at Sun Valley, you had traveled a total of $895\frac{1}{2}$ miles. What did the odometer show at the end of the trip?

IDAHO

Review and Remember

Compare. Write >, <, or = in the ●.

29. 0.386 ● 0.387

30. 1.23 ● 2.16

31. 0.4321 ● 0.4312

32. 1.46 ● 1.46

For Extra Practice, see Set I, page 180.

Checkpoint

Fractions and Mixed Numbers

Vocabulary

Write the missing word that completes each sentence.

1. A ___?___ is a whole number greater than one with exactly two factors, itself and one.

2. You can use an ___?___ to tell how many times a number is used as a factor.

3. You can make a factor tree to find the ___?___ of a composite number.

Word Bank

base
composite number
exponent
prime factorization
prime number

Concepts and Skills

Write each mixed number as an improper fraction. Write each improper fraction as a mixed number. (pages 164–169)

4. $4\frac{1}{3}$

5. $\frac{100}{4}$

6. $\frac{44}{12}$

7. $\frac{31}{8}$

8. $5\frac{7}{8}$

9. $6\frac{2}{5}$

Find the least common multiple for each set of numbers. (pages 166–169)

10. 6, 9

11. 1, 6

12. 2, 6, 7

13. 2, 3, 7

14. 4, 5, 8

Use the least common denominator to write like fractions. (pages 166–169)

15. $\frac{2}{9}, \frac{1}{4}$

16. $\frac{9}{2}, \frac{10}{7}$

17. $\frac{4}{5}, \frac{5}{8}$

18. $\frac{4}{9}, \frac{1}{6}, \frac{5}{12}$

19. $\frac{3}{5}, \frac{1}{6}, \frac{2}{3}$

In Exercises 20–23, write <, >, or = for each ⬤. In Exercises 24–27, arrange in order from least to greatest. (pages 170–171)

20. $\frac{2}{7}$ ⬤ $\frac{1}{3}$

21. $\frac{5}{8}$ ⬤ $\frac{3}{5}$

22. $\frac{5}{9}$ ⬤ $\frac{4}{7}$

23. $\frac{8}{9}$ ⬤ $\frac{7}{8}$

24. $\frac{5}{7}, \frac{3}{8}, \frac{1}{2}$

25. $\frac{4}{9}, \frac{1}{3}, \frac{5}{6}$

26. $\frac{2}{5}, \frac{1}{2}, \frac{4}{9}$

27. $5\frac{3}{4}, 5\frac{11}{16}, 6$

Write each fraction as a decimal and each decimal as a fraction in simplest form. (pages 174–175)

28. 0.55

29. $\frac{16}{25}$

30. 0.125

31. $\frac{5}{100}$

Problem Solving

32. From 9 A.M. to 10 A.M., a bus tour leaves Waldo Station for Monroe every 4 minutes. Another tour leaves the same station for Litchfield every 6 minutes. During that hour, how many times do the two tours leave the station at the same time?

33. During the week, $\frac{3}{8}$ of the passengers go to Monroe and $\frac{2}{5}$ go to Litchfield. Where do more passengers go, Monroe or Litchfield?

34. The distance from Waldo Station to Litchfield is $8\frac{1}{2}$ mi. The distance from Waldo Station to Monroe is 8.6 mi. Which town is farther from Waldo Station?

35. Liberty Bus Lines operates tours numbered 19, 39, 41, 51, 73, 93, 211, and 288. Only tours with prime numbers leave from Waldo Station. Which tours do <u>not</u> leave from Waldo Station?

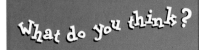

What do you think?

Can the value of a proper fraction ever be greater than that of an improper fraction? Explain.

Journal Idea

Explain the steps you would follow to compare 2.8 and $2\frac{7}{8}$.

You Decide

Activity

The Company You Keep

Decide on 4 companies you would like to own. Make a chart showing the opening price, closing price, and the change in price in dollars and cents (to the nearest cent).

Company	Open	Close
Fast Track RR	22 1/8	22 3/4
HiFly Airways	44 7/8	46 1/4
Blue Cab Inc.	19 3/4	19 7/8
City Line Bus Co.	37	41 1/8
Leisure Boats Inc.	76 1/2	77 3/8

You might wish to include this work in your portfolio.

Extra Practice

Set A (pages 144–145)

Using Algebra Write the missing number.

1. $\dfrac{4}{5} \times \dfrac{\blacksquare}{\blacksquare} = \dfrac{16}{20}$

2. $\dfrac{7}{8} \times \dfrac{\blacksquare}{\blacksquare} = \dfrac{21}{24}$

3. $\dfrac{12}{16} \div \dfrac{\blacksquare}{\blacksquare} = \dfrac{3}{4}$

Using Algebra Find the missing numerator or denominator.

4. $\dfrac{2}{5} = \dfrac{\blacksquare}{20}$

5. $\dfrac{5}{15} = \dfrac{1}{\blacksquare}$

6. $\dfrac{4}{10} = \dfrac{12}{\blacksquare}$

7. $\dfrac{21}{28} = \dfrac{3}{\blacksquare}$

8. Sarah has 25 postcards to mail. Of these, $\dfrac{1}{5}$ need stamps. If Sarah has 6 stamps, does she have enough?

Set B (pages 146–147)

Tell if each number is divisible by 2, 3, 4, 5, 6, 9, 10, or none of these.

1. 378

2. 2,205

3. 121

4. 44,100

Find the missing digit to make each number divisible by 9.

5. 3 ▧ 4

6. ▧ , 225

7. 77, ▧ 77

8. 40, 22 ▧

9. 3 ▧ , 555

10. If there are 120 band members, can they line up in equal rows of 6 or in equal rows of 9?

11. Look back at problem 10. Suppose 11 people are ill and cannot participate. Can the band march in equal rows? Explain your answer.

Set C (pages 150–151)

Using Algebra Write the product, using an exponent. Then evaluate.

1. 5×5

2. $10 \times 10 \times 10$

3. $2 \times 2 \times 2 \times 2$

4. $1 \times 1 \times 1 \times 1 \times 1 \times 1$

Using Algebra Evaluate.

5. 2^9

6. 5^5

7. 3^5

8. 12^3

9. 0^9

10. Every half hour a microbe splits and becomes two microbes. How many microbes will there be in three hours?

Extra Practice

Set D (pages 152–155)

Tell if each number is prime or composite.

1. 27   **2.** 77   **3.** 53   **4.** 38   **5.** 91

Write the prime factorization of each number. Use exponents.

6. 45   **7.** 84   **8.** 200   **9.** 150   **10.** 58

11. A collection of glassware is displayed in a museum. If there are 107 pieces, can an equal number be put in 2 or more cases?

Set E (pages 156–159)

Find the greatest common factor.

1. 5, 10   **2.** 15, 35   **3.** 12, 20   **4.** 14, 28, 49

Write each fraction in simplest form.

5. $\dfrac{8}{10}$ **6.** $\dfrac{21}{28}$ **7.** $\dfrac{11}{22}$ **8.** $\dfrac{26}{32}$ **9.** $\dfrac{18}{63}$

10. Twenty-five tourists had their pictures taken by a photographer. Twenty tourists bought pictures. Is it true that $\dfrac{4}{5}$ of the tourists bought pictures?

Set F (pages 164–165)

Write each improper fraction as a mixed number.

1. $\dfrac{23}{4}$ **2.** $\dfrac{9}{7}$ **3.** $\dfrac{12}{5}$ **4.** $\dfrac{18}{3}$ **5.** $\dfrac{25}{4}$

Write each mixed number as an improper fraction.

6. $5\dfrac{3}{4}$ **7.** $6\dfrac{1}{2}$ **8.** $2\dfrac{3}{5}$ **9.** $2\dfrac{4}{9}$ **10.** $3\dfrac{5}{8}$

11. You have 5 oranges cut into thirds. How many friends could be given 2 pieces each if you save 1 piece for yourself?

Extra Practice

Set G (pages 166–169)

Find the least common multiple for each set of numbers.

1. 5, 9
2. 9, 10
3. 6, 20
4. 2, 4, 6
5. 3, 6, 8

Use the least common denominator to write like fractions.

6. $\frac{3}{4}, \frac{2}{3}$
7. $\frac{7}{8}, \frac{3}{5}$
8. $\frac{3}{7}, \frac{2}{3}$

9. It takes Connie 5 minutes to swim one lap in the pool. It takes Joan 6 minutes. If they start together, after how many minutes will they both be at their starting point?

Set H (pages 170–171)

Write the LCD for each set of fractions.

1. $\frac{3}{5}, \frac{1}{6}$
2. $\frac{9}{10}, \frac{3}{8}$
3. $\frac{5}{7}, \frac{3}{4}$
4. $2\frac{4}{9}, 1\frac{2}{3}$

Compare. Write <, >, or = for each ●.

5. $\frac{5}{8}$ ● $\frac{4}{5}$
6. $\frac{3}{7}$ ● $\frac{6}{14}$
7. $\frac{2}{3}$ ● $\frac{3}{6}$
8. $\frac{7}{8}$ ● $\frac{3}{4}$

Arrange in order from least to greatest.

9. $\frac{2}{3}, \frac{3}{4}, \frac{5}{8}$
10. $2\frac{1}{5}, 1\frac{3}{4}, 1\frac{9}{10}$
11. $4\frac{3}{4}, 4\frac{1}{2}, 4\frac{1}{4}$

12. Luke and Justin went on a bike tour for their vacation. Luke carried $12\frac{3}{8}$ lb of supplies. Justin carried $12\frac{5}{16}$ lb. Who carried more supplies?

Set I (pages 174–175)

Write each fraction as a decimal.

1. $\frac{3}{4}$
2. $\frac{27}{100}$
3. $\frac{6}{25}$
4. $7\frac{11}{20}$
5. $4\frac{3}{10}$

Write each decimal as a fraction in simplest form.

6. 0.4
7. 0.48
8. 0.01
9. 0.64
10. 0.875

11. Gina skied 2.8 miles in 5 minutes. Ronnie skied $2\frac{7}{8}$ miles in the same time. Who skied faster?

Chapter Test

Write the prime factorization of each number.
Use exponents.

1. 180   **2.** 175   **3.** 91   **4.** 53

Find the greatest common factor and least common
multiple of each set of numbers.

5. 6, 9   **6.** 8,12   **7.** 7, 21   **8.** 10, 15, 20

Write each improper fraction as a mixed number and each
mixed number as an improper fraction.

9. $\frac{19}{10}$ **10.** $2\frac{7}{8}$ **11.** $\frac{15}{7}$ **12.** $5\frac{4}{9}$

Use the least common denominator to write like fractions.

13. $\frac{3}{5}, \frac{3}{4}$ **14.** $\frac{5}{6}, \frac{3}{8}, \frac{2}{3}$ **15.** $\frac{1}{2}, \frac{2}{3}, \frac{5}{9}$ **16.** $\frac{2}{3}, \frac{3}{7}$

Write each fraction as a decimal and each decimal as a
fraction in simplest form.

17. $\frac{18}{20}$ **18.** $\frac{2}{25}$ **19.** 0.88   **20.** $\frac{6}{15}$ **21.** 0.125

Arrange in order from least to greatest.

22. $\frac{7}{8}, \frac{5}{6}, \frac{3}{4}$ **23.** $3\frac{3}{10}, 3\frac{2}{5}, 3\frac{1}{4}$ **24.** 3.716, 31.67, 3.617

Solve.

25. At the opening of a new campsite, every third
visitor wins a free cap. Every fifth visitor wins a
T-shirt. Every tenth visitor wins a poster. Which
visitors win all three prizes?

 Self-Check

Look back at questions 1–4. Explain how the rules
of divisibility helped you find the answers.

Performance Assessment

Show What You Know About Number Theory

1 Study these numbers.

> 42   15   21   36   11   25

a. Classify each number as prime or composite.

b. Which pair of numbers has the largest GCF?

c. Which number is a multiple of 9? How do you know?

d. Which number has a prime factorization of more than three factors?

Self-Check Did you remember what factors and multiples are?

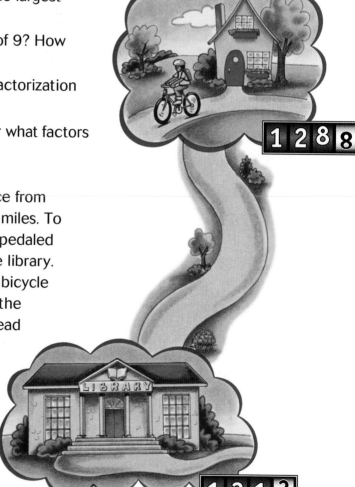

2 Robert was told that the distance from his home to the library was $3\frac{1}{2}$ miles. To find out if this was true, Robert pedaled his bicycle from his home to the library. At the beginning of the trip, his bicycle odometer read 128.8 miles. By the time he reached the library, it read 131.3 miles.

a. Was the information Robert was told correct?

b. If Robert pedaled from his home to the library, and back again, how many miles would he pedal altogether?

Self-Check Did you remember to check your computations?

For Your Portfolio

You might wish to include this work in your portfolio.

Extension

Repeating Decimals

Sometimes a decimal number has a repeating pattern
that never ends.

Study each example below.

A. $\frac{2}{3}$

$$
\begin{array}{r}
0.66 \\
3\overline{)2.00} \\
-18 \\
\hline
20 \\
-18 \\
\hline
2
\end{array}
$$
← The remainder repeats.

$\frac{2}{3} = 0.\overline{6}$ ← The bar shows that the digit 6 repeats.

B. $\frac{8}{11}$

$$
\begin{array}{r}
0.7272 \\
11\overline{)8.0000} \\
-77 \\
\hline
30 \\
-22 \\
\hline
80 \\
-77 \\
\hline
30 \\
-22 \\
\hline
8
\end{array}
$$

$\frac{8}{11} = 0.\overline{72}$

C. $\frac{5}{12}$

$$
\begin{array}{r}
0.4166 \\
12\overline{)5.0000} \\
-48 \\
\hline
20 \\
-12 \\
\hline
80 \\
-72 \\
\hline
80 \\
-72 \\
\hline
8
\end{array}
$$

$\frac{5}{12} = 0.41\overline{6}$

Copy the chart below. Use your calculator to find each decimal.

Fraction	$\frac{1}{9}$	$\frac{2}{9}$	$\frac{3}{9}$	$\frac{4}{9}$	$\frac{5}{9}$	$\frac{6}{9}$	$\frac{7}{9}$	$\frac{8}{9}$	$\frac{9}{9}$	$\frac{10}{9}$
Decimal	$0.\overline{1}$									

1. Describe Describe the decimal pattern for ninths.

2. Analyze Compare the decimal form for $\frac{3}{9}$ and for $\frac{1}{3}$.

Copy the chart below. Use your calculator to find each decimal.

Fraction	$\frac{1}{11}$	$\frac{2}{11}$	$\frac{3}{11}$	$\frac{4}{11}$	$\frac{5}{11}$	$\frac{6}{11}$	$\frac{7}{11}$	$\frac{8}{11}$	$\frac{9}{11}$	$\frac{10}{11}$
Decimal	$0.\overline{09}$									

3. Describe Describe the decimal pattern for elevenths.

4. Write $3\frac{5}{11}$ as a decimal.

5. On the calculator, compare $\frac{5}{22}$ and $5 \times \frac{1}{22}$.

Cumulative Review

Choose the correct letter for each answer.

Number Concepts	Patterns, Relationships, and Algebraic Thinking

1. Which fraction is equivalent to $\frac{9}{12}$?

A. $\frac{2}{3}$ **C.** $\frac{7}{10}$

B. $\frac{4}{6}$ **D.** $\frac{6}{8}$

---

2. Mark wants to arrange the drill bits in his toolbox by diameter in groups from *least* to *greatest*. He has $\frac{1}{4}$-inch, $\frac{1}{8}$-inch, and $\frac{1}{2}$-inch bits. Which list shows the order in which he should put them?

A. $\frac{1}{8}, \frac{1}{4}, \frac{1}{2}$ **C.** $\frac{1}{4}, \frac{1}{8}, \frac{1}{2}$

B. $\frac{1}{2}, \frac{1}{8}, \frac{1}{4}$ **D.** $\frac{1}{2}, \frac{1}{4}, \frac{1}{8}$

---

3. Which expression shows 18 as a product of prime factors?

A. 2×9

B. 3×6

C. $2 \times 3 \times 3$

D. 1×18

---

4. As of November 1997, the Austin Public Library collection included 1,549,667 books, records, audio cassettes, and videotapes. What is this number rounded to the nearest thousand?

A. 2,000,000
B. 1,550,000
C. 1,549,000
D. 1,540,000

5. Which number is missing from this pattern?

$10 \times 1 = 10$
$10 \times 10 = 100$
$10 \times 100 = 1,000$
$10 \times \underline{\quad} = 10,000$

A. 1,000   **C.** 100,000
B. 10,000   **D.** 1,000,000

---

6. There are 20 students in Mr. Lee's class. If the ratio of girls to boys is exactly 3 to 2, how many boys and girls are in the class?

A. 8 girls and 16 boys
B. 12 girls and 8 boys
C. 8 girls and 12 boys
D. 16 girls and 14 boys

---

7. Jack estimates that he passes by the same corner an average of 12 times a week. Which number sentence should you use to find out how many times Jack passes that corner in a year?

A. $365 \div 12 = x$
B. $12 \times (52 + 7) = x$
C. $52 \times 12 = x$
D. $52 \times (12 \times 7) = x$

---

8. If $\frac{75}{y} = \frac{3}{4}$, then $y =$

A. 25   **C.** 75
B. 50   **D.** 100

Probability and Statistics	Geometry and Spatial Reasoning

Probability and Statistics

9. A bag contains 4 blue, 12 red, 1 green, and 5 yellow counters. Linda picks out 1 counter 20 times, replacing it each time. Which color did Linda probably pick out the **greatest** number of times?

   A. Blue   **C.** Red
   B. Green   **D.** Yellow

10. A number cube is labelled 1, 1, 2, 3, 3, 4. What is the probability that the number 2 will **NOT** land face up when the cube is tossed?

   A. 0   **C.** $\frac{1}{2}$

   B. $\frac{1}{6}$ **D.** $\frac{5}{6}$

Use the graph for Questions 11 and 12.

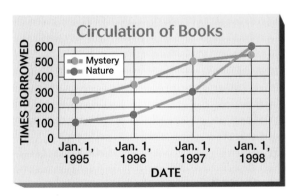

11. About how many more nature books than mystery books had been borrowed by January 1, 1998?

   A. 200   **C.** 100
   B. 150   **D.** 50

12. On Jan. 1 of what year had 500 mystery books been borrowed?

   A. 1995   **C.** 1997
   B. 1996   **D.** 1998

Geometry and Spatial Reasoning

13. Which angle in this figure is an acute angle?

   A. 1
   B. 2
   C. 3
   D. 4

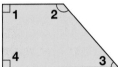

14. If triangle *ABC* is an equilateral triangle, what is the measure of angle *A*?

   A. 90°
   B. 60°
   C. 50°
   D. 45°

15. Which of the following represents a pair of perpendicular lines?

   A.   **C.**

   B.   **D.**

16. Which polygon is similar but not congruent to the figure shown at the right?

   A.   **C.**

   B.   **D.**

Chapter 5

Adding and Subtracting Fractions

Chapter Theme: PLANTS

REAL-WORLD Math

..............Real Facts..................

Square-foot gardening is popular with urban gardeners because many crops can be grown in a small area. Gardens are based on 12-inch squares. The diagram below shows how a gardener might place plants in a 1-foot by 4-foot space. For example, 1 broccoli plant requires 1 square foot.

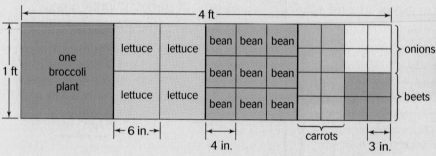

- What fraction of the garden does the broccoli plant occupy?
- What fraction of a square foot is planted with carrots?
- How could you use fractions to find the part of the garden that is not planted with beans?

..............Real People..................

Meet Lorka Muñoz, an urban gardener. She helps people plant community gardens that provide healthful, inexpensive food, and flowers for bouquets. The volunteers on the right are working in a community garden in San Rafael, California.

Sprouting Fractions

A science experiment with seeds can help you understand how to add and subtract fractions with like denominators.

Learning About It

As part of a science experiment, students planted seeds in a seed tray divided into 8 sections, as shown. What fraction of the tray was planted with radish or bean seeds?

To find out, add $\frac{3}{8} + \frac{1}{8}$.

$$\frac{3}{8} \qquad \frac{1}{8}$$

THERE'S ALWAYS A WAY!

- **One way** is to use fraction strips.

- **Another way** is to use paper and pencil.

Step 1 Add the numerators. Use the common denominator.

Step 2 Simplify if possible.

$$\frac{3}{8} + \frac{1}{8} = \frac{4}{8} \qquad\qquad \frac{3}{8} + \frac{1}{8} = \frac{4}{8} = \frac{1}{2}$$

One half of the tray was planted with radish or bean seeds.

How much more of the tray was planted with radish seeds or bean seeds than with corn seeds?

To find out, subtract $\frac{4}{8} - \frac{2}{8}$.

Step 1 Subtract the numerators. Use the common denominator.

Step 2 Simplify if possible.

$$\frac{4}{8} - \frac{2}{8} = \frac{2}{8} \qquad\qquad \frac{4}{8} - \frac{2}{8} = \frac{2}{8} = \frac{1}{4}$$

One-fourth more of the tray was planted with radish or bean seeds.

Think and Discuss How is adding fractions with like denominators similar to subtracting fractions with like denominators?

Try It Out

Add or subtract. Write each answer in simplest form.

1. $\dfrac{11}{15} - \dfrac{4}{15}$

2. $\dfrac{1}{8} + \dfrac{3}{8}$

3. $\dfrac{7}{8} - \dfrac{5}{8}$

4. $\dfrac{7}{12} - \dfrac{3}{12}$

5. $\dfrac{8}{9} - \dfrac{2}{9}$

6. $\dfrac{5}{6} - \dfrac{1}{6}$

7. $\dfrac{9}{10} + \dfrac{7}{10}$

8. $\dfrac{2}{5} + \dfrac{3}{5}$

9. $\dfrac{1}{9} + \dfrac{4}{9} - \dfrac{3}{9}$

10. $\dfrac{11}{12} + \dfrac{5}{12} + \dfrac{3}{12}$

11. **Describe** Write two fractions with like denominators whose sum is greater than 1.

Practice

Add or subtract. Write each answer in simplest form.

12. $\dfrac{7}{11} + \dfrac{2}{11}$

13. $\dfrac{3}{5} - \dfrac{2}{5}$

14. $\dfrac{7}{9} + \dfrac{1}{9}$

15. $\dfrac{5}{8} + \dfrac{1}{8}$

16. $\dfrac{7}{15} - \dfrac{1}{15}$

17. $\dfrac{7}{8} - \dfrac{3}{8}$

18. $\dfrac{3}{8} + \dfrac{5}{8}$

19. $\dfrac{11}{12} - \dfrac{5}{12}$

20. $\dfrac{9}{10} + \dfrac{7}{10}$

21. $\dfrac{9}{12} - \dfrac{5}{12}$

22. $\dfrac{5}{6} + \dfrac{5}{6}$

23. $\dfrac{11}{16} - \dfrac{3}{16}$

24. $\dfrac{7}{12} + \dfrac{2}{12}$

25. $\dfrac{7}{8} - \dfrac{3}{8}$

26. $\dfrac{11}{16} + \dfrac{9}{16}$

27. $\dfrac{19}{20} - \dfrac{11}{20}$

28. $\dfrac{3}{5} + \dfrac{4}{5} - \dfrac{2}{5}$

29. $\dfrac{5}{9} + \dfrac{7}{9} - \dfrac{3}{9}$

30. $\dfrac{11}{21} - \dfrac{5}{21} + \dfrac{7}{21}$

31. $\dfrac{7}{8} + \dfrac{5}{8} - \dfrac{1}{8}$

Problem Solving

32. The tray at the right has 12 sections. Mark uses $\dfrac{1}{12}$ of a tray, and Jenny uses $\dfrac{7}{12}$ of the same tray. What fraction of the tray did they use altogether?

33. Jack and Sue planted seeds in a large seed tray. Jack used $\dfrac{7}{16}$ of the tray, and Sue used $\dfrac{5}{16}$ of the same tray. What part of the tray was left unplanted?

Review and Remember

Simplify.

34. $6\dfrac{6}{9}$

35. $8\dfrac{4}{12}$

36. $1\dfrac{9}{7}$

37. $7\dfrac{15}{10}$

38. $4\dfrac{8}{8}$

For Extra Practice, see Set A, page 218.

Using What You Grow

You can use what you know about adding and subtracting fractions with like denominators when you add and subtract mixed numbers.

Learning About It

$9\frac{3}{8}$ lb $7\frac{7}{8}$ lb

Carmen, Jessie, and Sean went to the market to buy vegetables. They bought tomatoes and onions to make salsa for a fiesta. How much did the vegetables weigh altogether?

To find out, add $9\frac{3}{8} + 7\frac{7}{8}$.

Step 1 Add the fractions.	**Step 2** Add the whole numbers.	**Step 3** Simplify the sum.
$9\frac{3}{8}$ $+7\frac{7}{8}$ $\frac{10}{8}$	$9\frac{3}{8}$ $+7\frac{7}{8}$ $16\frac{10}{8}$	$9\frac{3}{8}$ $+7\frac{7}{8}$ $16\frac{10}{8} = 16 + 1\frac{2}{8} = 17\frac{2}{8} = 17\frac{1}{4}$

The vegetables weigh $17\frac{1}{4}$ lb.

More Examples

A. Add the whole numbers. $\nearrow 3\frac{3}{8} \searrow$ Add the fractions.

$+6\frac{5}{8}$

$9\frac{8}{8} = 9 + 1 = 10$

Simplify the sum.

B. Add the whole numbers. $\nearrow 12\frac{5}{9} \searrow$ Add the fractions.

$\frac{8}{9}$

$+\ 9\frac{2}{9}$

$21\frac{15}{9} = 21 + 1\frac{6}{9} = 22\frac{6}{9} = 22\frac{2}{3}$

Simplify the sum.

Connecting Ideas

When you added, you sometimes had to rename a fraction to simplify the sum. When you subtract, you may need to rename a fraction before you can subtract.

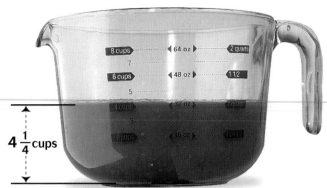

Carmen will use $2\frac{3}{4}$ cups of the tomatoes to make salsa. How many cups of tomatoes will be left?

$4\frac{1}{4}$ cups

To find out, subtract $4\frac{1}{4} - 2\frac{3}{4}$.

Step 1 You need to rename before you subtract because $\frac{1}{4} < \frac{3}{4}$.	**Step 2** Subtract the fractions and then the whole numbers. Simplify if necessary.
$4\frac{1}{4} = 3\frac{4}{4} + \frac{1}{4} = \quad 3\frac{5}{4}$ $- 2\frac{3}{4} \qquad\qquad -2\frac{3}{4}$	$3\frac{5}{4}$ $-2\frac{3}{4}$ $\overline{1\frac{2}{4} = 1\frac{1}{2}}$

There will be $1\frac{1}{2}$ cups of tomatoes left.

More Examples

A. $\quad 10\frac{3}{5}$
$\quad\underline{-\quad 6}$
$\qquad 4\frac{3}{5}$

B. $\quad 11\frac{7}{8}$
$\quad\underline{-\quad 4\frac{3}{8}}$
$\qquad 7\frac{4}{8} = 7\frac{1}{2}$

C. $\quad 9 \;= 8\frac{5}{5}$
$\quad\underline{-\, 2\frac{3}{5} = 2\frac{3}{5}}$
$\qquad\quad 6\frac{2}{5}$

D. $\quad 7\frac{1}{8} = 6\frac{9}{8}$
$\quad\underline{-\, 3\frac{3}{8} = 3\frac{3}{8}}$
$\qquad\quad 3\frac{6}{8} = 3\frac{3}{4}$

Think and Discuss How would you rename 10 to subtract $10 - 3\frac{5}{8}$?

Try It Out

Add or subtract. Write each answer in simplest form.

1. $\quad 4$
$\quad\underline{+5\frac{6}{7}}$

2. $10\frac{2}{7}$
$\underline{-\ 8}$

3. $\quad 3\frac{7}{8}$
$\quad\underline{+\, 7\frac{5}{8}}$

4. $\quad 8\frac{3}{5}$
$\quad\underline{+\, 6\frac{2}{5}}$

5. $\quad 13\frac{11}{12}$
$\quad\underline{-\ 9\frac{5}{12}}$

6. $3 + 8\frac{5}{6} + 2\frac{1}{6}$

7. $7\frac{7}{10} - 2\frac{9}{10}$

8. $8\frac{1}{4} + 7\frac{3}{4} + 1\frac{3}{4}$

9. $7 \ -\frac{3}{8}$

Practice

Choose a Method Add or subtract, using models, mental math, or paper and pencil. Write each answer in simplest form.

10. $4\frac{1}{6}$
    $+ 1\frac{4}{6}$

11. $2\frac{1}{3}$
    $+ 4\frac{2}{3}$

12. $5\frac{4}{10}$
    $- 4\frac{1}{10}$

13. $10\frac{1}{2}$
    $- 6$

14. $6\frac{5}{12}$
    $- 2\frac{1}{12}$

15. $9\frac{11}{12}$
    $+ 9\frac{3}{12}$

16. $3\frac{4}{5}$
    $- 2\frac{3}{5}$

17. $6\frac{5}{8}$
    $- 3$

18. $6\frac{1}{4}$
    $+ 8\frac{3}{4}$

19. $17\frac{3}{8}$
    $- 6\frac{2}{8}$

20. $7\frac{1}{3}$
    $- 3\frac{2}{3}$

21. $21\frac{7}{9}$
    $+ 13$

22. 10
    $- 7\frac{5}{6}$

23. $15\frac{7}{8}$
    $+ 4\frac{5}{8}$

24. $12\frac{7}{12}$
    $+ 7\frac{7}{12}$

25. $4\frac{1}{3} - 2\frac{2}{3}$

26. $8\frac{6}{8} + 4\frac{7}{8}$

27. $3\frac{6}{7} + 1\frac{5}{7}$

28. $6 - 4\frac{3}{4}$

Problem Solving

Use the recipe at the right to solve each problem.

29. Jessie has chopped $\frac{3}{4}$ cup of bell pepper. How much more bell pepper does she need to chop?

30. **You Decide** Sean is looking for two ingredients that when combined total 5 cups or more. Which ones might he choose?

31. **Explain** Can the ingredients for the salsa recipe be mixed together in a bowl that holds 7 cups?

32. Carmen added $1\frac{1}{8}$ cups of water. How much more did the recipe call for?

Spicy Salsa

$4\frac{1}{4}$ cups fresh diced tomatoes

$\frac{3}{4}$ cup diced onion

$1\frac{1}{4}$ cups chopped bell pepper

$1\frac{3}{4}$ cups water

4 chili peppers

1 tsp. oregano

2 tsp. olive oil

In Mexico, salsa is commonly eaten with practically every dish from scrambled eggs to meat and poultry. ➤

INTERNET ACTIVITY
www.sbgmath.com

Use the prices above to solve each problem. Remember, all mixed numbers can be written as decimals, and money is always rounded up to the next cent.

33. Jill bought $2\frac{1}{2}$ lb of onions and 5 lb of tomatoes. How much did she spend?

34. Salita bought $2\frac{1}{2}$ lb of bell peppers, $4\frac{1}{4}$ lb of tomatoes, and $3\frac{3}{4}$ lb of onions. How much did she spend?

35. Adena bought $4\frac{3}{4}$ lb of onions and 5 lb of tomatoes. How much change did she get from a $10 bill?

36. What If? If Adena added 3 more pounds of tomatoes to her shopping order would she still get change from $10?

Review and Remember

Using Algebra Find each missing number.

37. $\frac{5}{8} = \frac{\blacksquare}{24}$

38. $\frac{3}{\blacksquare} = \frac{9}{24}$

39. $\frac{1}{3} = \frac{\blacksquare}{18}$

40. $\frac{4}{10} = \frac{20}{\blacksquare}$

41. $\frac{10}{25} = \frac{2}{\blacksquare}$

42. $\frac{3}{7} = \frac{\blacksquare}{21}$

43. $\frac{\blacksquare}{14} = \frac{1}{2}$

44. $\frac{40}{\blacksquare} = \frac{5}{8}$

 Money $ense

Veggies Anyone?

 Using the recipe shown here, how much will it cost to prepare a vegetable salad for 18 people?

Hint You cannot buy fractional parts of a vegetable, such as a head of lettuce.

Vegetable Salad	
Serves 6	
zucchini	$\frac{3}{4}$ lb
tomato	$1\frac{1}{2}$ lb
broccoli	$\frac{3}{4}$ lb
corn	4 ears
lettuce	$1\frac{1}{2}$ heads

★ **Specials** ★

ZUCCHINI	TOMATOES	BROCCOLI
$.69 lb	$1.20 lb	$.80 lb

CORN	LETTUCE
$1.70 6 EARS	$.89 HEAD

For Extra Practice, see Set B, page 218.

Behold a Bonsai !

You know how to round whole numbers to estimate. You can also use rounding for fractions.

Learning About It

Bonsai trees originated in China about 1,000 years ago. About how much taller is the sneaker than the tree?

Estimate: $5\frac{15}{16} - 4\frac{5}{8}$.

You can round each number to estimate.

Use the number line to help you to round.

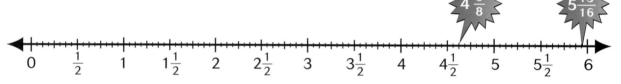

Step 1 Look at the number line above.	**Step 2** Round each number.	**Step 3** Now subtract.
$5\frac{15}{16}$ is close to **6**. $4\frac{5}{8}$ is close to $4\frac{1}{2}$.	$5\frac{15}{16} - 4\frac{5}{8}$ $6 \quad - 4\frac{1}{2}$	$6 - 4\frac{1}{2} = 1\frac{1}{2}$

The sneaker is about $1\frac{1}{2}$ inches taller than the bonsai tree.

More Examples

A. $2\frac{1}{4}$ rounds to 2
   $+\,3\frac{6}{7}$ rounds to $+\,4$
   —————————————
   6

B. $3\frac{3}{4}$ rounds to 4
   $1\frac{5}{8}$ rounds to $1\frac{1}{2}$
   $+\,2\frac{3}{8}$ rounds to $+\,2\frac{1}{2}$
   ——————————————————
   $7\frac{2}{2} = 7 + 1 = 8$

Think and Discuss   The sum of two mixed numbers is about 6. One of the numbers is $2\frac{7}{8}$. What could the other number be? How do you know?

Try It Out

Round each number.

1. $\frac{6}{7}$

2. $\frac{5}{8}$

3. $\frac{1}{12}$

4. $5\frac{3}{18}$

5. $1\frac{7}{9}$

Estimate each sum or difference.

6. $\frac{2}{3} + \frac{3}{4}$

7. $1\frac{7}{8} + 2\frac{1}{4}$

8. $4\frac{1}{10} - 2\frac{11}{12}$

9. $3\frac{9}{10} - 1\frac{1}{3}$

10. $2\frac{5}{6} - 1\frac{5}{12}$

Practice

Estimate each sum or difference.

11. $1\frac{7}{8} + 10\frac{3}{4}$

12. $14\frac{1}{2} + 2\frac{1}{8}$

13. $8\frac{1}{3} - 3\frac{11}{12}$

14. $20 - \frac{7}{8}$

15. $2\frac{5}{6} - \frac{1}{4}$

16. $5\frac{2}{3} + 7\frac{9}{10}$

17. $\frac{5}{8} + 9\frac{1}{10}$

18. $18\frac{3}{8} - 5\frac{4}{5}$

19. $4\frac{7}{8} + 19\frac{2}{7}$

20. $1\frac{9}{10} + \frac{1}{6}$

21. $16\frac{7}{16} - 3\frac{4}{5}$

22. $5\frac{4}{5} + 6\frac{1}{12}$

Problem Solving

23. Look at the diagram. Estimate the total height of the three bonsai trees whose heights are given.

24. If Amanda is $62\frac{1}{2}$ inches tall, about how tall is the fourth tree?

25. **Analyze** Amanda paid $24.00 for pots for her trees. Round pots cost $4.00 each and square pots cost $6.00. How many of each did she buy?

Review and Remember

Estimate first. Then use a calculator to find each answer.

26. 48.2×3.56

27. $69.52 \div 1.1$

28. 41.8×7.6

29. $44.3848 \div 8.72$

30. $5\overline{)401.5}$

31. $17\overline{)95.2}$

Science Connection ▶
The height of fully grown bonsai trees varies from 2 inches to 24 inches.

$20\frac{5}{8}''$

$62\frac{1}{2}''$

$15\frac{7}{8}''$

$13\frac{7}{16}''$

Developing Skills for
Problem Solving

First read for understanding and then focus on steps to a solution.

READE FOR UNDERSTANDING

*E*ighty students and some adults went on a 3-day camping and hiking trip. Each adult was responsible for five students. Each student had to pay $100 to go on the trip.

1 How many students went on the trip?

2 How many students was each adult responsible for?

THINK AND DISCUSS

Multistep Problems Sometimes you need to find the answer to one or more questions before you can find the solution to a problem.

Reread the first paragraph on the page.

3 How many adults went on the trip? Explain how you know.

4 How many people went on the camping trip? What steps are needed to solve this problem?

Show What You Learned

Answer each question. Give a reason for your choice.

The pictures at the right show the departure time for the campers as well as the time they spent at lunch and rest stops. The total driving time was $7\frac{1}{2}$ hours.

① What steps do you need to follow to find when the bus will reach the campsite?

    a. Add the total number of hours driving, resting, and eating to the departure time.

    b. Add the number of stops the bus made to the departure time.

    c. Add the total number of hours driving and subtract the time spent on eating and resting. Add this total to the departure time.

② Which statement best describes the time that the bus arrived at the campsite?

    a. 3:30 P.M., because they left at 8:00 A.M. and drove for $7\frac{1}{2}$ hours

    b. 12:00 noon, because they left at 8:00 A.M. and made 4 stops

    c. 6:30 P.M., because they left at 8:00 A.M., made 3 hours' worth of stops and traveled for $7\frac{1}{2}$ hours

Adults carried large backpacks that weighed $21\frac{5}{8}$ pounds each. The students carried smaller backpacks, which were $8\frac{1}{2}$ pounds lighter than those carried by the adults. Each person also carried a canteen weighing $1\frac{1}{4}$ pounds.

③ Which of these questions do you need to answer before you can find how much weight each student carried?

    a. How much did a small backpack weigh?

    b. How much more did a large backpack weigh than a small backpack?

    c. How many students went on the hike?

④ **Explain** How much weight did each student carry? Explain the steps needed to find out.

DEPARTURE

REST STOP $\frac{5}{6}$ h

LUNCH STOP $1\frac{1}{3}$ h

REST STOP $\frac{5}{6}$ h

ARRIVAL

Checkpoint

Like Denominators

Add or subtract. Write each answer in simplest form. (pages 186–187)

1. $\dfrac{3}{5}$
$+\dfrac{1}{5}$

2. $\dfrac{7}{9}$
$-\dfrac{2}{9}$

3. $\dfrac{1}{8}$
$+\dfrac{3}{8}$

4. $\dfrac{7}{10}$
$-\dfrac{3}{10}$

5. $\dfrac{5}{12}$
$+\dfrac{4}{12}$

6. $\dfrac{6}{7} + \dfrac{5}{7}$

7. $\dfrac{7}{8} - \dfrac{3}{8}$

8. $\dfrac{11}{16} + \dfrac{5}{16}$

9. $\dfrac{9}{10} - \dfrac{1}{10}$

10. $\dfrac{7}{8} + \dfrac{5}{8} + \dfrac{3}{8}$

Add or subtract. Write each answer in simplest form. (pages 188–191)

11. $4\dfrac{3}{7}$
$+2\dfrac{2}{7}$

12. $5\dfrac{7}{8}$
$-2\dfrac{1}{8}$

13. 9
$-4\dfrac{5}{9}$

14. $1\dfrac{3}{4}$
$-\dfrac{3}{4}$

15. $6\dfrac{5}{12}$
$+4\dfrac{7}{12}$

16. $5\dfrac{11}{12}$
$-3\dfrac{5}{12}$

17. 11
$-7\dfrac{7}{10}$

18. $5\dfrac{7}{8}$
$+4\dfrac{7}{8}$

19. $11\dfrac{4}{5}$
$+9\dfrac{1}{5}$

20. $7\dfrac{1}{9}$
$-6\dfrac{8}{9}$

Estimate first. Then find the exact answer. (pages 192–193)

21. $6\dfrac{4}{7} + 3\dfrac{2}{7}$

22. $9\dfrac{1}{12} - 7\dfrac{5}{12}$

23. $5\dfrac{9}{11} + 1\dfrac{3}{11}$

24. $9\dfrac{1}{10} - 8\dfrac{9}{10}$

Mixed Practice

Add or subtract. Write each answer in simplest form.

25. $3\dfrac{5}{6}$
$-2\dfrac{1}{6}$

26. $\dfrac{3}{11}$
$+\dfrac{7}{11}$

27. $5\dfrac{3}{4}$
$-2\dfrac{1}{4}$

28. $6\dfrac{7}{15}$
$-\dfrac{3}{15}$

29. $3\dfrac{3}{5}$
$+2\dfrac{4}{5}$

30. 10
$-1\dfrac{5}{7}$

31. $6\dfrac{4}{9} - \dfrac{7}{9}$

32. $\dfrac{9}{16} - \dfrac{5}{16}$

33. $5\dfrac{1}{3} - 2\dfrac{2}{3}$

What do you think?

If you are subtracting mixed numbers, when do you need to rename one of them?

Problem Solving

34. The Girl Scouts of Central Middle School did a project on the growth of plants. They recorded the growth of a bean seed over a 3-week period. The seed sprouted and grew $\frac{3}{16}$ inch, $1\frac{1}{16}$ inches, and $\frac{5}{16}$ inch. How tall was the bean sprout after 3 weeks?

35. A diner served 32 people lunch. Fifteen customers had the soup-and-salad special. Twenty customers had soup, and 25 had salad. How many had neither soup nor salad? What strategy did you use?

Journal Idea

List and explain the steps needed to add or subtract mixed numbers with like denominators.

Critical Thinking Corner
Number Sense

Egyptian Unit Fractions

In the Rhind papyrus, the Egyptians used unit fractions and sums of different unit fractions to show many other fractions. A unit fraction is a fraction with a numerator of 1, such as $\frac{1}{2}$ or $\frac{1}{3}$.

▲ **Social Studies Connection**
The Rhind papyrus was written in Egypt thousands of years ago.

To show $\frac{3}{10}$, they might write

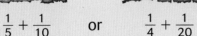

$\frac{1}{5} + \frac{1}{10}$ or $\frac{1}{4} + \frac{1}{20}$

Think: $\frac{3}{10} = \frac{2}{10} + \frac{1}{10} = \frac{1}{5} + \frac{1}{10}$

Think: $\frac{3}{10} = \frac{6}{20} = \frac{5}{20} + \frac{1}{20} = \frac{1}{4} + \frac{1}{20}$

To represent $\frac{7}{12}$, the Egyptians might have written

$\frac{1}{4} + \frac{1}{3}$

What other way can you think of to represent $\frac{7}{12}$, using only unit fractions?

Choose your own nonunit fraction. Show the fraction as the sum of different unit fractions in as many ways as you can.

Line Them Up

*Sometimes you have to work with fractions
that have unlike denominators.*

Learning About It

You can use fraction strips to explore how to add
and subtract fractions with unlike denominators.

Work with a group.

Step 1 Use fraction strips to add.
Try $\frac{1}{2} + \frac{2}{3}$.

Place one $\frac{1}{2}$ strip and two
$\frac{1}{3}$ strips under the whole strip
on the table. Then look for like
fraction strips that fit exactly
underneath the whole strip.

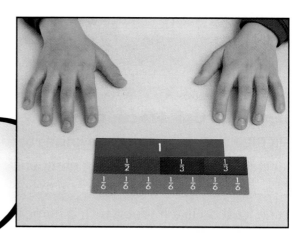

What You Need

*For each group:
fraction strips*

Step 2 Use fraction strips to find the sum of each
pair of fractions listed. Copy this chart and record
your work. Discuss with your group what to do.

First Fraction	Second Fraction	Sum
$\frac{1}{2}$	$\frac{2}{3}$	$\frac{1}{2} + \frac{2}{3} = \frac{7}{6} = 1\frac{1}{6}$
$\frac{2}{5}$	$\frac{3}{10}$	
$\frac{7}{12}$	$\frac{2}{3}$	
$\frac{1}{4}$	$\frac{7}{8}$	

Step 3 Now use fraction strips to subtract.

Try $\frac{1}{2} - \frac{1}{3}$.

Think: $\frac{1}{3} + \bigcirc = \frac{1}{2}$

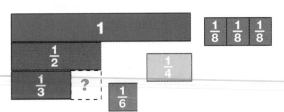

Look for a piece that fits.

Step 4 Record your work in a chart like the one below. Use strips to find each difference. Discuss with your group what to do.

First Fraction	Second Fraction	Difference
$\frac{1}{2}$	$\frac{1}{3}$	$\frac{1}{2} - \frac{1}{3} = \frac{1}{6}$
$\frac{4}{5}$	$\frac{3}{10}$	
$\frac{11}{12}$	$\frac{1}{4}$	
$\frac{3}{4}$	$\frac{2}{3}$	

Think and Discuss Look back at $\frac{1}{2} - \frac{1}{3} = \frac{1}{6}$. How are 2 and 3 related to 6?

Practice

Use fraction strips to help you add or subtract.

1. $\frac{3}{4}$
   $+ \frac{1}{2}$

   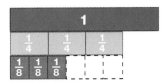

2. $\frac{3}{4}$
   $- \frac{3}{8}$

3. Write an addition problem or a subtraction problem that uses fractions with unlike denominators. Have your group solve it, using fraction strips.

4. **Explain** When you subtract proper fractions, is the answer always less than 1?

5. **Journal Idea** Describe how adding fractions with like denominators is different from adding fractions with unlike denominators.

From Here to There

*Before you can add or subtract fractions with
unlike denominators, you have to rename them.*

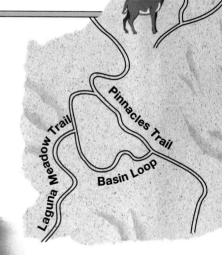

Learning About It

A favorite hiking spot in Texas is in the Chisos Mountains.
The Chisos Mountains are part of Big Bend National Park
in Texas.

Look at the map at the right showing the Lost Mine Trail.
The directions below describe the route Susan followed.
How far did she walk to see ocotillo plants?

From Kibbe Spring

1. Walk $\frac{1}{2}$ mile southeast
to see century plants.

2. Walk $\frac{1}{3}$ mile more to
see ocotillo plants.

To find out, add $\frac{1}{2} + \frac{1}{3}$.

THERE'S ALWAYS A WAY!

● **One way** is to use fraction strips to model the problem.

$$\begin{array}{r} \frac{1}{3} \\ + \frac{1}{2} \\ \hline \frac{5}{6} \end{array}$$

1		
$\frac{1}{3}$	$\frac{1}{2}$	
$\frac{1}{6}$ $\frac{1}{6}$	$\frac{1}{6}$ $\frac{1}{6}$	$\frac{1}{6}$

● **Another way** is to use paper and pencil to solve the problem.

Step 1 Find the least common denominator (LCD).	**Step 2** Write the equivalent fractions.	**Step 3** Add. Simplify if possible.
$\begin{array}{r} \frac{1}{3} \\ + \frac{1}{2} \end{array}$ The LCD is **6**.	$\begin{array}{r} \frac{1 \times 2}{3 \times 2} = \frac{2}{6} \\ + \frac{1 \times 3}{2 \times 3} = + \frac{3}{6} \end{array}$	$\begin{array}{r} \frac{2}{6} \\ + \frac{3}{6} \\ \hline \frac{5}{6} \end{array}$

Susan walked $\frac{5}{6}$ mile.

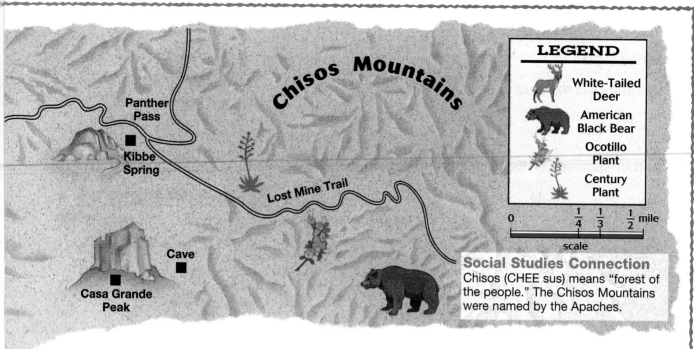

LEGEND

White-Tailed Deer

American Black Bear

Ocotillo Plant

Century Plant

Social Studies Connection
Chisos (CHEE sus) means "forest of the people." The Chisos Mountains were named by the Apaches.

Connecting Ideas

Finding the LCD helped you add fractions with unlike denominators. You will also have to find the LCD when you subtract fractions with unlike denominators.

Sam and Joe started at Kibbe Spring and visited different attractions. Sam walked $\frac{3}{4}$ mile. Joe walked $\frac{1}{3}$ mile. How much farther did Sam walk than Joe?

To find out, subtract $\frac{3}{4} - \frac{1}{3}$.

Step 1 Find the least common denominator (LCD).	**Step 2** Write the equivalent fractions.	**Step 3** Subtract. Simplify if possible.
$\frac{3}{4}$ $-\frac{1}{3}$ The LCD is 12.	$\dfrac{3\times 3}{4\times 3} = \dfrac{9}{12}$ $-\dfrac{1\times 4}{3\times 4} = -\dfrac{4}{12}$	$\dfrac{9}{12}$ $-\dfrac{4}{12}$ $\dfrac{5}{12}$

Sam walked $\frac{5}{12}$ mile farther than Joe.

Think and Discuss What if you used 24 as the common denominator to find $\frac{3}{4} - \frac{1}{3}$? Would the result be the same?

Try It Out

Use the LCD to rename each fraction. Then add or subtract. Use fraction strips if you wish.

1. $\frac{1}{5} + \frac{1}{2}$ **2.** $\frac{5}{12} - \frac{1}{4}$ **3.** $\frac{5}{6} + \frac{1}{4}$ **4.** $\frac{3}{4} - \frac{1}{3}$ **5.** $\frac{2}{3} + \frac{1}{6}$

The Great Plant-Food Experiment

When adding or subtracting mixed numbers, you may need to rename.

Learning About It

Students at an agricultural school planted two rows of corn. The first row of corn was given an experimental plant food. The second row of corn was not given any plant food. The graph shows growth over a five-week period. How many inches did the experimental plants grow during weeks 4 and 5?

To find out add $8\frac{2}{3} + 10\frac{3}{4}$.

Estimate first: $8\frac{1}{2} + 11 = 19\frac{1}{2}$

To find the exact answer, add $8\frac{2}{3} + 10\frac{3}{4}$.

Step 1 Write equivalent fractions, using the LCD.	**Step 2** Add. Then simplify the sum.
$8\frac{2}{3} = 8\frac{8}{12}$ $+10\frac{3}{4} = +10\frac{9}{12}$	$8\frac{8}{12}$ $+10\frac{9}{12}$ $18\frac{17}{12} = 18 + 1\frac{5}{12} = 19\frac{5}{12}$

The plants grew $19\frac{5}{12}$ inches.

The answer is reasonable because it is close to the estimate of $19\frac{1}{2}$ inches.

More Examples

A. $6\frac{9}{10} = 6\frac{18}{20}$

$4\frac{3}{4} = 4\frac{15}{20}$

$+2\frac{2}{5} = 2\frac{8}{20}$

$12\frac{41}{20} = 14\frac{1}{20}$

B. $6\frac{1}{4} + 1\frac{1}{4} + 2\frac{1}{2} =$

$6\frac{1}{4} + 1\frac{1}{4} + 2\frac{2}{4} =$

$6\frac{1}{4} + 3\frac{3}{4} = 9\frac{4}{4} = 10$

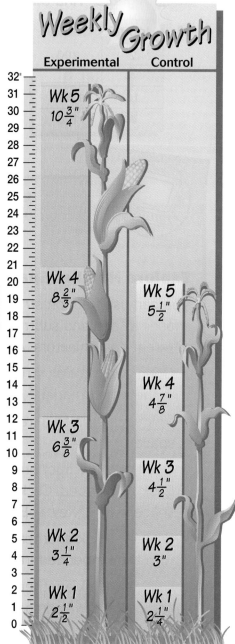

Weekly Growth

Experimental | Control

32"
31
30 — Wk 5 $10\frac{3}{4}$"
29
28
27
26
25
24
23
22
21
20 — Wk 4 $8\frac{2}{3}$" | Wk 5 $5\frac{1}{2}$"
19
18
17
16
15
14 | Wk 4 $4\frac{7}{8}$"
13
12 — Wk 3 $6\frac{3}{8}$"
11
10
9 | Wk 3 $4\frac{1}{2}$"
8
7
6
5 — Wk 2 $3\frac{1}{4}$" | Wk 2 3"
4
3
2 — Wk 1 $2\frac{1}{2}$" | Wk 1 $2\frac{1}{4}$"
1
0

NUMBER OF INCHES

Connecting Ideas

When you added mixed numbers, you worked with the fractions first. Do the same when you subtract mixed numbers.

A second plant-food experiment was carried out on pea plants. The double line graph shows the results of the experiment. How much taller were the experimental plants at the end of two weeks?

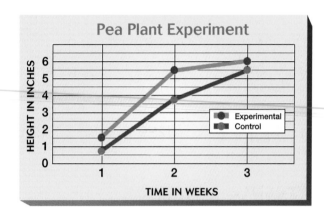

To find out, subtract $5\frac{1}{2} - 3\frac{3}{4}$.

Step 1 Write equivalent fractions, using the LCD. Try to subtract.	**Step 2** Rename if you cannot subtract.	**Step 3** Subtract. Simplify if possible.
$5\frac{1}{2} = 5\frac{2}{4}$ $-3\frac{3}{4} = -3\frac{3}{4}$	Rename $5\frac{2}{4}$. $5\frac{2}{4} = 4 + \frac{4}{4} + \frac{2}{4} = 4\frac{6}{4}$	$4\frac{6}{4}$ $-3\frac{3}{4}$ $1\frac{3}{4}$

The experimental plants were $1\frac{3}{4}$ inches taller.

More Examples

A.
$$5\frac{5}{6} = 5\frac{20}{24}$$
$$-2\frac{1}{8} = -2\frac{3}{24}$$
$$3\frac{17}{24}$$

B.
$$40\frac{1}{7} = 40\frac{3}{21} = 39\frac{24}{21}$$
$$-15\frac{2}{3} = -15\frac{14}{21} = -15\frac{14}{21}$$
$$24\frac{10}{21}$$

Think and Discuss Look back at Example B. Explain why you need to rename $40\frac{3}{21}$ before subtracting $15\frac{14}{21}$.

Try It Out

Estimate first. Then add or subtract. Write each answer in simplest form. Check that your answer is reasonable.

1. $9\frac{1}{4}$
    $+ 2\frac{1}{3}$

2. $6\frac{3}{5}$
    $+ 4\frac{2}{3}$

3. $12\frac{5}{8}$
    $+ 9\frac{1}{4}$

4. $4\frac{5}{6}$
    $+ 5\frac{5}{8}$

5. $5\frac{1}{6}$
    $+ 3\frac{5}{9}$

Add or subtract. Write each answer in simplest form.

6. $12\frac{7}{8}$
$-\ 6\frac{3}{4}$

7. $5\frac{1}{2}$
$-\ 3\frac{1}{3}$

8. $24\frac{15}{16}$
$-\ 21\frac{5}{8}$

9. $5\frac{5}{8}$
$-\ 2\frac{3}{4}$

10. $9\frac{3}{5}$
$-\ 4\frac{2}{3}$

11. $4\frac{7}{8} + 1\frac{1}{4}$

12. $9\frac{1}{10} + 3\frac{1}{5}$

13. $11\frac{3}{5} - 6\frac{9}{10}$

14. $14\frac{1}{4} - 13\frac{7}{10}$

Practice

Add or subtract. Write each answer in simplest form.

15. $2\frac{5}{16}$
$+\ 1\frac{1}{4}$

16. $3\frac{5}{6}$
$-\ 1\frac{1}{3}$

17. $9\frac{1}{2}$
$+\ 4\frac{7}{8}$

18. $6\frac{2}{3}$
$+\ 4\frac{3}{5}$

19. $5\frac{1}{2}$
$+\ 2\frac{3}{10}$

20. $12\frac{9}{13}$
$+\ 8\frac{15}{26}$

21. $8\frac{2}{9}$
$+\ 3\frac{1}{6}$

22. $3\frac{5}{12}$
$-\ 2\frac{7}{9}$

23. $12\frac{3}{8}$
$-\ 3\frac{7}{10}$

24. $6\frac{1}{7}$
$-\ 4\frac{2}{3}$

25. $3\frac{5}{6} + 8\frac{1}{2}$

26. $7\frac{1}{5} - 7\frac{3}{15}$

27. $3\frac{3}{4} + 5\frac{1}{3}$

28. $7\frac{3}{5} - 2\frac{1}{2}$

29. $2\frac{1}{8} + 5\frac{3}{20}$

30. $1\frac{2}{9} - \frac{3}{4}$

31. $9\frac{3}{18} - 7\frac{11}{12}$

32. $9\frac{3}{5} + 6\frac{7}{10}$

33. $\left(3\frac{1}{6} + 1\frac{2}{3}\right) - 2\frac{5}{6}$

34. $\frac{7}{12} + 2\frac{1}{6} + 5\frac{2}{3}$

35. $6\frac{3}{4} + 2\frac{5}{8} + 1\frac{1}{6}$

36. Journal Idea When you are subtracting a mixed number in simplest form from a whole number, can you have a whole number as a solution? Explain why or why not.

43
$-\ 26\frac{1}{5}$
$?$

Using Mental Math Use properties to find each answer.

37. $7\frac{1}{5} + 2\frac{2}{3} + 3\frac{4}{5}$

38. $4\frac{3}{8} + 3\frac{1}{8} + 2\frac{1}{2}$

39. $9\frac{3}{4} + 10 + \frac{1}{4}$

40. $4\frac{1}{2} + 1\frac{1}{4} + 2\frac{1}{4}$

41. $4\frac{8}{9} + 6\frac{1}{5} + 2\frac{4}{5}$

42. $7\frac{3}{8} + 6\frac{1}{8} + 2\frac{2}{8}$

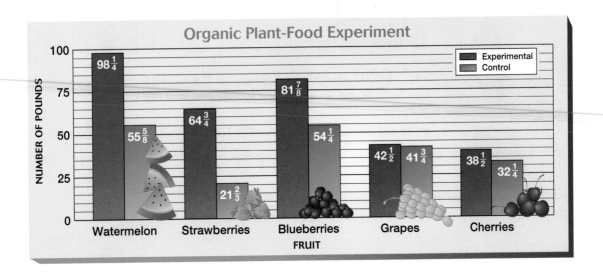

Organic Plant-Food Experiment

NUMBER OF POUNDS

100 — 75 — 50 — 25 — 0

Legend: ■ Experimental ■ Control

- Watermelon: $98\frac{1}{4}$, $55\frac{5}{8}$
- Strawberries: $64\frac{3}{4}$, $21\frac{2}{3}$
- Blueberries: $81\frac{7}{8}$, $54\frac{1}{4}$
- Grapes: $42\frac{1}{2}$, $41\frac{3}{4}$
- Cherries: $38\frac{1}{2}$, $32\frac{1}{4}$

FRUIT

Problem Solving

The bar graph above shows the effectiveness of the organic plant food on various crops. Use the bar graph above to solve each problem.

43. How many pounds of watermelons, strawberries, and blueberries were produced by plants that received the plant food?

44. You Decide Marcin wants to buy two kinds of fruit that each yield more than 40 lb but less than 95 lb. Which fruit could he buy?

45. Which fruit showed the smallest difference in weight between plants that received the food and those that did not? How great was the difference?

46. Using Estimation Find the difference in the total weight of the fruits that received the plant food and the weight of those that did not.

47. Create Your Own Use the bar graph above to write a problem requiring addition and a problem requiring subtraction.

48. Analyze The weight of two fruits that did not receive plant food is about 60 pounds. What are the two fruits?

Review and Remember

Write the value of the digit 5 in each number.

49. 0.09685

50. 0.38257

51. 705,969,431

52. 8,765,309

53. 754,000

54. 3,543,103.6

Find the mean, median, mode, and range for each set of data.

55. 7, 8, 6, 5, 4, 3

56. 4.2, 4.6, 4.6, 4.2

57. 40, 60, 90, 30

58. 14, 14, 16, 18, 20

59. 590, 593, 598, 591

60. 74, 76, 78, 74

For Extra Practice, see Set E, page 219.

Problem Solving
Work Backwards

You can work backwards to solve some problems.

If Kim gave the cashier $10.00 and received $1.80 in change, how many pounds of tomatoes did Kim buy?

 UNDERSTAND

What do you need to know?

You need to know how much Kim spent on tomatoes.

 PLAN

How can you solve the problem?

You can **work backwards**, starting with the change Kim received from a $10 bill. Use this information and information from the receipt to the right to determine how much she spent on tomatoes. Then you can find how many pounds of tomatoes she bought.

RECEIPT
10 ears of corn at 5 for $1.00
1 qt of berries at $2.00 per qt
? Tomatoes at $1.20 per lb

 SOLVE

Money given		Change		Money spent
$10.00	−	$1.80	=	$8.20

Money spent		Cost of 10 ears of corn		Cost of 1 qt of berries		Cost of tomatoes
$8.20	−	$2.00	−	$2.00	=	$4.20

Cost of tomatoes		Cost per pound		Amount of tomatoes
$4.20	÷	$1.20	=	3.5 lb

Kim bought $3\frac{1}{2}$ lb of tomatoes.

 LOOK BACK

How can you check the answer? Explain.

Using the Strategy

Use the prices on the right to solve Problems 1–3.

1. Jamie bought 5 ears of corn, 2 quarts of berries, and some tomatoes. If she received $2 in change from a $10 bill, how many pounds of tomatoes did she buy?

2. Joe bought $4\frac{1}{2}$ lb of tomatoes, some broccoli, and 10 ears of corn. If he spent $9.60, how many pounds of broccoli did he buy?

3. Sue bought $5\frac{1}{2}$ lb of tomatoes, a quart of berries, and an 8-lb watermelon. She said the watermelon cost $1.25. If she received $0.65 in change from a $10 bill, was she correct about the price of the watermelon? Explain how you know.

Berries $2.00 per qt.

Corn 5 for $1.00

Broccoli 80¢ per lb

Tomatoes $1.20 per lb

Mixed Strategy Review

Try these or other strategies to sove each problem.
Tell which strategy you used.

THERE'S ALWAYS A WAY!

Problem Solving Strategies

- Find a Pattern
- Guess and Check
- Work Backwards
- Make a Table
- Write an Equation
- Use Logical Reasoning

4. Carla spent $8 for tomatoes and broccoli. She bought the same number of pounds of each. How much of each did she buy?

5. Chris bought 3 lb of tomatoes. He gave the cashier $10. How much change should he receive?

6. Look at the ads at the right. Chad bought $8\frac{1}{2}$ lb of apples and some grapes. He spent $9.05. How many pounds of grapes did he buy?

7. Pat bicycled $1\frac{1}{2}$ miles on Monday. On Tuesday she rode $\frac{1}{4}$ mile more than she did on Monday. For the next three days she rode $\frac{1}{4}$ mile more than she did each previous day. How many miles had she traveled after 5 days?

Grapes 75¢ per lb

Apples 80¢ per lb

Putting It All Together

*Sometimes one method of adding or subtracting
fractions or mixed numbers works better than another.*

Learning About It

You can use fraction strips, pencil and paper, or mental math to add or subtract fractions and mixed numbers. Sometimes one way works better than another.

THERE'S ALWAYS A WAY!

● **One way** is to use fraction strips to add or subtract.

$$\begin{aligned} &\frac{2}{3} \\ +\ &\frac{1}{6} \\ \hline &\frac{5}{6} \end{aligned}$$

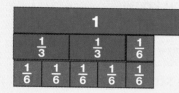

● **Another way** is to use paper and pencil.

$$8\frac{3}{4} = 8\frac{9}{12} = 7 + \frac{12}{12} + \frac{9}{12} = 7\frac{21}{12}$$
$$-4\frac{5}{6} = -4\frac{10}{12} \qquad\qquad\qquad = -4\frac{10}{12}$$
$$\overline{\qquad\qquad\qquad\qquad\qquad\qquad\qquad 3\frac{11}{12}}$$

● **Another way** is to add mentally.

$$\frac{3}{5} + 1\frac{4}{5} + \frac{2}{5} = 1\frac{4}{5} + \frac{3}{5} + \frac{2}{5} = 1\frac{4}{5} + 1 = 2\frac{4}{5}$$

Think and Discuss How do you choose which method to use for adding or subtracting fractions?

Try It Out

Add or subtract. Write each answer in simplest form.

1. $21\frac{2}{3} + 21\frac{9}{10}$ **2.** $\frac{1}{4} + \frac{3}{8}$ **3.** $\frac{1}{2} - \frac{1}{10}$ **4.** $\frac{7}{8} - \frac{9}{32}$

5. $16\frac{1}{2} - 9\frac{9}{11}$ **6.** $1\frac{3}{7} + \frac{4}{7}$ **7.** $4\frac{2}{3} - 3\frac{1}{2}$ **8.** $\frac{4}{6} - \frac{3}{18}$

Practice

Add or subtract. Write each answer in simplest form.

9. $\frac{8}{9} + \frac{4}{5}$

10. $\frac{1}{9} + \frac{1}{6} + \frac{1}{3}$

11. $7\frac{3}{10} - 5\frac{7}{10}$

12. $13\frac{2}{3} + 11\frac{3}{4}$

13. $2\frac{1}{2} + 3\frac{4}{7}$

14. $1\frac{4}{9} - \frac{1}{3}$

15. $\frac{4}{11} - \frac{3}{22}$

16. $7\frac{3}{4} + 4\frac{2}{6}$

17. $1\frac{3}{8} + \frac{5}{8}$

18. $\frac{5}{6} + 6\frac{2}{3} - 2\frac{1}{6}$

19. $\frac{3}{16} + 4\frac{5}{8} - \frac{3}{4}$

20. $6\frac{1}{2} + 3\frac{3}{4} - 2\frac{1}{8}$

Problem Solving

Use data from the map to solve Problems 21–24.

The map shows four hiking trails. The length of each hiking trail is shown in miles.

21. How much shorter is trail A than trail B?

22. If you hiked trail D in the morning and trail C in the afternoon, how far would you hike?

23. Which trail is the longest? shortest? How much longer is the longest trail than the shortest?

24. What is the total length of trails A, B, and C?

25. Analyze During a camping trip, Karyn hiked $2\frac{1}{4}$ mi in the morning and $3\frac{1}{2}$ mi in the afternoon on Saturday, the last day of the trip. If she had hiked a total of $17\frac{1}{2}$ mi during the trip, how far had she hiked before Saturday?

26. Karyn enjoys reading nature books. Half of her books are about birds. One fourth are about wildflowers and the remaining 2 are about wildlife. How many nature books does she have? What strategy did you use to solve the problem?

Review and Remember

Estimate first. Then find the answer.

27. $5.37 + 4.63$

28. 5.25×1.9

29. $63.49 \div 7$

30. 86.4×4.8

31. $1.95 - 0.37$

32. $1.96 - 0.039$

33. $0.0039 + 0.602$

34. $404.6 \div 5$

Using Algebra A Barrel of Cactus!

You know how to solve equations with whole numbers. You can also solve them with fractions.

Learning About It

This miniature barrel cactus grows in Mexico. One day the bloom was $\frac{1}{2}$ in. tall. Then it grew to a height of $\frac{3}{4}$ in. How much did it grow to reach the new height?

You can write an equation to describe the problem.

$$\frac{1}{2} + x = \frac{3}{4}$$

Solve the equation to find x.

THERE'S ALWAYS A WAY!

• **One way** is to use fraction strips.

$$\frac{1}{2} + x = \frac{3}{4}$$

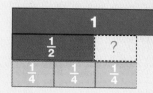

$$x = \frac{1}{4}$$

• **Another way** is to use mental math.

$$\frac{1}{2} + x = \frac{3}{4}$$

$\frac{1}{2}$ plus (what number) equals $\frac{3}{4}$?

$$\frac{1}{2} + \bigcirc? = \frac{3}{4}$$

$$\frac{1}{2} + \frac{1}{4} = \frac{3}{4}$$

$$x = \frac{1}{4}$$

The cactus bloom grew $\frac{1}{4}$ inch.

More Examples

A.
$$x - \frac{3}{10} = \frac{7}{10}$$
$$\bigcirc? - \frac{3}{10} = \frac{7}{10}$$
$$1 - \frac{3}{10} = \frac{7}{10}$$
$$x = 1$$

B.
$$4\frac{2}{3} - x = 2\frac{2}{3}$$
$$4\frac{2}{3} - \bigcirc? = 2\frac{2}{3}$$
$$4\frac{2}{3} - 2 = 2\frac{2}{3}$$
$$x = 2$$

C.
$$x - 2 = 3\frac{3}{8}$$
$$\bigcirc? - 2 = 3\frac{3}{8}$$
$$5\frac{3}{8} - 2 = 3\frac{3}{8}$$
$$x = 5\frac{3}{8}$$

Think and Discuss Is there another way to solve the cactus problem? Explain.

Try It Out

Solve each equation to find x.

1. $x + \frac{3}{5} = 1$ **2.** $\frac{7}{9} = x + \frac{4}{9}$ **3.** $x - \frac{5}{6} = \frac{1}{6}$ **4.** $x + 2 = 3\frac{1}{4}$

Practice

Solve each equation to find x.

5. $x + \frac{5}{6} = 4$ **6.** $10 = x + 1\frac{1}{2}$ **7.** $x - \frac{2}{3} = 1\frac{1}{3}$ **8.** $x + \frac{5}{8} = 6$

9. $x - 6\frac{1}{4} = 3$ **10.** $x - 5 = 8\frac{1}{6}$ **11.** $12\frac{2}{5} = x - \frac{1}{5}$ **12.** $x + 2\frac{1}{2} = 7\frac{3}{4}$

Problem Solving

Write an equation to describe each problem. Then solve.

13. At the end of the school year, Aaron's height was $62\frac{1}{2}$ in. During the school year, he had grown $2\frac{1}{2}$ in. What was his height at the beginning of the school year?

14. Jack cut $8\frac{3}{16}$ feet off the beanstalk. The beanstalk is now $1\frac{12}{16}$ feet tall. How high was the beanstalk before it was cut?

Review and Remember

Round to the nearest tenth.

15. 4.386   **16.** 0.0119   **17.** 75.69   **18.** 451.96   **19.** 19.958

Critical Thinking Corner

Number Sense

Fraction Subtraction

It takes about $\frac{1}{2}$ hour for a Venus' flytrap to close fully. How long does it take to complete the third stage?

▼ Flytrap fully closed

Stage 1
$\frac{1}{5}$ second

Stage 2
$\frac{2}{5}$ second

Stage 3
❓

Problem Solving
Using Fractions and Mixed Numbers

Some problems involve fractions and mixed numbers.

Tammy decided to make a birdhouse from a scrap of plywood. After cutting out pieces A–F shown, will Tammy have enough plywood left for piece G if it is $6\frac{7}{8}$" high and $5\frac{1}{4}$" wide?

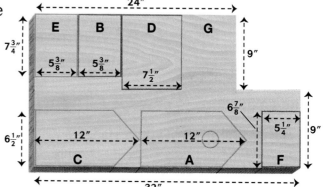

UNDERSTAND

What do you need to find?

You need to find the size of the remaining plywood after the other pieces have been cut.

PLAN

How can you solve the problem?

You can compare the dimensions of the remaining plywood with the dimensions of piece G.

SOLVE

What do you need to find?

You can see that the remaining piece of plywood is high enough ($9" > 6\frac{7}{8}$"). To see if it is wide enough, follow these steps.

Step 1 Add.	**Step 2** Subtract.	**Step 3** Compare.
$5\frac{3}{8} + 5\frac{3}{8} + 7\frac{1}{2} = 18\frac{1}{4}$	$24 - 18\frac{1}{4} = 5\frac{3}{4}$	$5\frac{3}{4} > 5\frac{1}{4}$

Since the width and height of the remaining piece are greater than the piece needed, Tammy will have enough plywood for piece G.

LOOK BACK

How can you check your answer?

Show What You Learned

Use the diagram on page 214 to solve Problems 1–3.

1. Margaret has a board that is $\frac{1}{2}$ foot by 1 foot. Does she have enough to make piece A? If not, what other piece, if any, can she cut from it?

2. **Explain** Mark has two plywood boards that are 15 inches by 20 inches. Can he cut pieces A, G, and C from one board?

3. Paul has a board that is 20 inches by 7 inches. He wants to cut out a B piece and an E piece from it. Draw a picture of the leftover board and label the dimensions.

4. Shirley has $10.00 to buy seeds for the bird feeder. Small bags cost $1.75 each, and larger bags cost $2.75 each. If she buys 3 large bags, does she have enough money left to buy any small bags? If so, how many?

5. **Create Your Own** Use the diagram on page 214 to write a problem that would involve adding and subtracting fractions or mixed numbers. Explain how you would solve your problem.

Science Connection Different birds are ➤ attracted to different birdhouses because of their size, location, and shape. Wrens will nest in a birdhouse similar to this one.

Time for Technology

Using a Calculator

Adding Fractions

The key sequence below shows how to add $5\frac{3}{4}$ and $2\frac{1}{3}$ on a calculator.

Press: (5) (Unit) (3) (/) (4) (+) (2) (Unit) (1) (/) (3) (=) (Ab/c)

Display: (8ᴜ 1/12)

Use the calculator to add or subtract.

1. $5\frac{1}{4} + 3\frac{3}{8}$ 2. $7\frac{5}{6} + 2\frac{1}{9}$ 3. $11\frac{1}{5} - 2\frac{4}{7}$

Problem Solving

★ ★ ★ ★ ★ **Preparing for Tests**

Practice What You Learned

Choose the correct letter for each answer.

1 Every 8 seconds a warning signal on a buoy in a harbor bongs twice. Another signal bongs once every 12 seconds. How often do the two signals bong at the same time?

A. Every 12 seconds
B. Every 24 seconds
C. Every 48 seconds
D. Every 72 seconds
E. Not Here

Tip

Use the *Draw a Diagram* strategy for this problem.

---

2 Tina's age, t, is $1\frac{1}{2}$ times Mark's age, m. Which expression shows the sum of their ages?

A. $\frac{3}{2}m$

B. $\frac{2}{3}m$

C. $m + \frac{3}{2}m$

D. $t + \frac{1}{2}t$

E. $t + \frac{3}{2}t$

Tip

The equation $t = \frac{3}{2}m$ shows Tina's age in terms of Mark's age.

---

3 In one 5-day period, Sam practiced the clarinet $1\frac{1}{4}$ hours, 2 hours, $2\frac{3}{4}$ hours, $\frac{3}{4}$ hours, and $1\frac{1}{2}$ hours, What was the total number of hours that Sam spent practicing the clarinet during that period?

A. $6\frac{1}{4}$ h

B. $7\frac{1}{2}$ h

C. $8\frac{1}{4}$ h

D. $8\frac{1}{2}$ h

E. $9\frac{1}{4}$ h

Tip

Estimation can help you eliminate answer choices in this problem.

4 Jo's shop had weekly sales of 100, 80, 110, 90, 120, and 100 large baskets. If the sales pattern for large baskets continues, about how many will Jo sell next week?

A. About 90 baskets
B. About 110 baskets
C. About 130 baskets
D. About 150 baskets
E. About 170 baskets

5 Irma had $72. She bought 2 tote bags for $18.79 each and an umbrella for $5.73. She gave the clerk $60. How much change did she get?

A. $16.69
B. $25.48
C. $28.69
D. $43.31
E. Not Here

6 Karla bought $2\frac{1}{8}$ lb of oranges, $3\frac{3}{4}$ lb of grapes, $5\frac{1}{2}$ lb of potatoes, and $1\frac{3}{4}$ lb of nuts. Which is the best estimate of the number of pounds of *oranges and grapes* she bought?

A. 13 lb
B. 12 lb
C. 11 lb
D. 6 lb
E. 4 lb

7 Gina has scores of 85, 95, and 80 on three math tests. Which score will give her an average *greater than* 85 for four math tests?

A. 65
B. 70
C. 75
D. 80
E. Not Here

8 Nick bought $3\frac{1}{4}$ yard of fabric. He used 18 in. for a pillow. Which of these is reasonable for the amount of fabric Nick has left?

A. About 60 in.
B. About 100 in.
C. About 110 in.
D. About 120 in.
E. About 130 in.

Use this graph for Problems 9 and 10.

It shows the money two people earned each month for seven months.

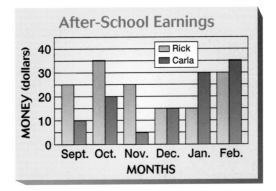

9 Based on the graph, which is true?

A. Both people earned less in October than in September.
B. Both people earned less in December than in January.
C. Both people earned more in December than in November.
D. Both people earned more in February than in January.
E. Both people earned more in November than in October.

10 Which is the best estimate of the amount of money both people earned *after* December 31?

A. Less than $100
B. Between $100 and $150
C. Between $150 and $175
D. Between $175 and $200
E. More than $200

Checkpoint
Unlike Denominators

Vocabulary

Write the missing word that completes each sentence.

When adding or subtracting fractions with unlike denominators you need to first find the __1.__ . Then you __2.__ to make __3.__ . Once you have found the sum or difference you need to __4.__ the answer if possible.

Word Bank

equivalent fractions
least common
  denominator
multiply
simplify

Concepts and Skills

Add or subtract the fractions. Write each answer in simplest form. (pages 200–203)

5. $\dfrac{3}{2}$
   $-\dfrac{1}{4}$

6. $\dfrac{3}{4}$
   $-\dfrac{3}{8}$

7. $\dfrac{5}{13}$
   $-\dfrac{1}{26}$

8. $\dfrac{4}{5}$
   $+\dfrac{2}{15}$

9. $\dfrac{5}{6}$
   $+\dfrac{1}{3}$

10. $\dfrac{4}{9} + \dfrac{1}{18}$

11. $\dfrac{9}{16} - \dfrac{1}{8}$

12. $\dfrac{12}{20} + \dfrac{4}{5}$

13. $\dfrac{1}{3} + \dfrac{1}{6}$

14. $\dfrac{3}{8} - \dfrac{1}{4}$

Add or subtract the mixed numbers. Write each answer in simplest form. (pages 204–207)

15. $2\dfrac{4}{6}$
   $-1\dfrac{2}{8}$

16. $4\dfrac{7}{10}$
   $-\dfrac{3}{12}$

17. $5\dfrac{2}{9}$
   $+7\dfrac{5}{6}$

18. $3\dfrac{8}{10}$
   $-1\dfrac{2}{5}$

19. 12
   $-7\dfrac{1}{3}$

20. $12\dfrac{5}{6} - 7$

21. $15\dfrac{5}{6} - 4\dfrac{2}{3}$

22. $12\dfrac{3}{8} + 7$

23. $12\dfrac{7}{12} - 3\dfrac{5}{6}$

Add or subtract. Write each answer in simplest form.
(pages 210–211)

24. $\dfrac{3}{4}$
   $+\dfrac{1}{2}$

25. $3\dfrac{9}{10}$
   $+4\dfrac{4}{6}$

26. $9\dfrac{5}{10}$
   $-4\dfrac{1}{5}$

27. $4\dfrac{2}{7}$
   $-3\dfrac{1}{14}$

Using Algebra   Solve each equation. (pages 212–213)

28. $x + \dfrac{1}{4} = 1\dfrac{1}{2}$

29. $x - \dfrac{1}{2} = 2$

30. $x - \dfrac{3}{4} = 2\dfrac{1}{8}$

31. $x + \dfrac{1}{8} = 4\dfrac{5}{8}$

Problem Solving

32. When Amy left for vacation, her marigolds were $1\frac{3}{8}$ in. tall. When she returned, they were $2\frac{11}{12}$ in. tall. How many inches did Amy's marigolds grow while she was away?

33. Erin needs $2\frac{1}{8}$ cups of blueberries for her muffins. If she uses a total of $3\frac{7}{8}$ berries in the muffin recipe, how many cups of raspberries did she use?

34. Trail A is $5\frac{1}{8}$ miles. Trails B and C are each $2\frac{1}{3}$ miles. Trail D is $2\frac{1}{2}$ miles longer than Trail A. Estimate the total length of the trails.

35. **What If?** Suppose Trails B and C are each $2\frac{1}{2}$ miles long. Would the estimated total change? Explain why or why not.

What do you think?

How can you use what you know about fractions to add and subtract mixed numbers?

Journal Idea

When do you need to rename a mixed number before subtracting? Give an example.

You Decide

Activity

Let's Go For a Walk

Here's a great way to get in shape.

- Start out walking no more than 6 miles per week.

- Plan a walking program. Limit your walk to less than 1 mile for each of the first 3 days and no more than $1\frac{3}{4}$ miles for each of the last 4 days.

- Decide exactly how far you will walk each day so that you walk 6 miles per week.

- Make a chart to show your plan.

Walking Program	
Day	Distance
1	$\frac{1}{4}$ mi
2	$\frac{1}{4}$ mi
3	$\frac{1}{2}$ mi
4	$\frac{3}{4}$ mi
5	1 mi
6	$1\frac{1}{4}$ mi
7	$1\frac{1}{2}$ mi

You might wish to include this work in your portfolio.

Extra Practice

Set A (pages 186–187)

Add or subtract. Write each answer in simplest form.

1. $\dfrac{3}{14}$
$+\dfrac{5}{14}$

2. $\dfrac{15}{16}$
$-\dfrac{3}{16}$

3. $\dfrac{9}{13}$
$+\dfrac{11}{13}$

4. $\dfrac{7}{9}$
$+\dfrac{1}{9}$

5. $\dfrac{3}{5}$
$-\dfrac{2}{5}$

6. $\dfrac{7}{8} - \dfrac{3}{8}$

7. $\dfrac{19}{20} - \dfrac{11}{20}$

8. $\dfrac{5}{9} + \left(\dfrac{7}{9} - \dfrac{3}{9}\right)$

9. $\dfrac{1}{5} + \left(\dfrac{4}{5} - \dfrac{2}{5}\right)$

10. Andrea and Rick planted seeds in a tray. Andrea used $\dfrac{7}{16}$ of the tray and Rick used $\dfrac{5}{16}$ of the tray. What fraction of the tray did they use altogether?

11. Rosemary has a plant that was $\dfrac{3}{8}$ in. tall. The next week it was $\dfrac{7}{8}$ in. tall. How many inches did it grow in 1 week?

Set B (pages 188–191)

Add or subtract. Write each answer in simplest form.

1. $15\dfrac{1}{10}$
$+ 3\dfrac{3}{10}$

2. $4\dfrac{13}{15}$
$- 2\dfrac{1}{15}$

3. $3\dfrac{2}{3}$
$+ 7\dfrac{1}{3}$

4. $6\dfrac{3}{5}$
$- 4\dfrac{2}{5}$

5. $6\dfrac{11}{12}$
$- 3\dfrac{1}{12}$

6. $7\dfrac{3}{8} - 1\dfrac{1}{8}$

7. $6\dfrac{11}{12} - 4\dfrac{7}{12}$

8. $8\dfrac{1}{4} + 2\dfrac{1}{4}$

9. $16\dfrac{2}{3} - 4\dfrac{1}{3}$

10. Colleen has a mixing bowl that holds 7 cups. She puts in $2\dfrac{1}{4}$ cups of carrots and $\dfrac{3}{4}$ cup of onion. How many more cups of vegetables can the bowl hold?

11. Mike used $2\dfrac{1}{4}$ cups of peppers, $4\dfrac{3}{4}$ cups of tomatoes, and 3 cups of onions for salsa. How many cups of ingredients did he use altogether?

Set C (pages 192–193)

Estimate each sum or difference.

1. $1\dfrac{7}{8} + 2\dfrac{13}{14}$

2. $4\dfrac{1}{2} + 4\dfrac{5}{8}$

3. $18\dfrac{1}{9} - 2\dfrac{11}{12}$

4. $26 - 5\dfrac{7}{8}$

5. $2\dfrac{3}{6} + 4\dfrac{1}{5}$

6. $3\dfrac{5}{8} - 2\dfrac{1}{6}$

7. $15\dfrac{2}{3} + 1\dfrac{9}{10}$

8. $2\dfrac{2}{3} + 5\dfrac{1}{10}$

9. $7\dfrac{7}{8} + 4\dfrac{4}{5}$

10. $10\dfrac{11}{12} - \dfrac{9}{10}$

11. $6\dfrac{1}{2} + 11\dfrac{11}{12}$

12. $7\dfrac{5}{6} - 2\dfrac{1}{4}$

13. $6\dfrac{1}{8} + 8\dfrac{7}{8}$

14. $5\dfrac{14}{15} - 1\dfrac{3}{10}$

15. $9\dfrac{1}{10} + 3\dfrac{4}{5}$

Extra Practice

Set D (pages 200–203)

Add or subtract. Write each answer in simplest form.

1. $\dfrac{1}{6}$ $-\dfrac{1}{8}$

2. $\dfrac{7}{4}$ $-\dfrac{2}{3}$

3. $\dfrac{3}{8}$ $+\dfrac{1}{5}$

4. $\dfrac{2}{3}$ $+\dfrac{1}{9}$

5. $\dfrac{9}{10}$ $-\dfrac{3}{4}$

6. $\dfrac{5}{6} - \dfrac{1}{3}$

7. $\dfrac{1}{2} + \dfrac{1}{8}$

8. $\dfrac{17}{20} - \dfrac{3}{10}$

9. $\dfrac{11}{12} + \dfrac{5}{6}$

10. Karyn walked $\dfrac{5}{8}$ of a mile. Moe walked $\dfrac{1}{4}$ of a mile. What fraction of a mile did they walk altogether?

11. Jeff biked $\dfrac{1}{2}$ of a mile. Fred biked $\dfrac{11}{12}$ of a mile. How many more miles did Fred bike than Jeff?

Set E (pages 204–207)

Add or subtract. Write each answer in simplest form.

1. $3\dfrac{3}{5}$ $+5\dfrac{3}{4}$

2. $6\dfrac{3}{9}$ $-1\dfrac{1}{6}$

3. $8\dfrac{7}{12}$ $-3\dfrac{1}{4}$

4. $2\dfrac{1}{2}$ $+5\dfrac{1}{4}$

5. $7\dfrac{3}{5}$ $+5\dfrac{2}{3}$

6. $5\dfrac{7}{8}$ $-3\dfrac{3}{4}$

7. $2\dfrac{1}{2}$ $+1\dfrac{1}{3}$

8. $6\dfrac{3}{4}$ $+2\dfrac{3}{8}$

9. $13\dfrac{11}{12}$ $-8\dfrac{2}{3}$

10. $5\dfrac{1}{4}$ $-1\dfrac{1}{6}$

11. $8\dfrac{1}{2} + 2\dfrac{2}{3}$

12. $4\dfrac{1}{8} + 3\dfrac{5}{6}$

13. $6\dfrac{1}{2} - 3\dfrac{7}{8}$

14. $7\dfrac{2}{3} - 3\dfrac{4}{5}$

15. Heather's marigolds were $2\dfrac{3}{8}$ inches tall at the end of May. When they were full grown, the marigolds were $7\dfrac{9}{12}$ inches tall. How many inches did they grow after May?

16. Brian has $\dfrac{1}{8}$ cup of rhubarb, $\dfrac{1}{2}$ cup of apples, and $2\dfrac{1}{8}$ cups of cherries. He needs $4\dfrac{1}{4}$ cups of fruit. Does he have enough fruit? Explain how you know.

17. Robert has bales of hay in his barn. He used $3\dfrac{3}{4}$ bales of hay in the morning and $2\dfrac{1}{2}$ bales in the afternoon. If he used 1 more bale in the evening, how many bales did he use altogether?

18. Lynda mows lawns to make money. It took her 10 hours to mow 4 lawns. She spent $2\dfrac{3}{4}$ hours on each of two lawns and $1\dfrac{1}{2}$ hours mowing the third lawn. How many hours did she spend on the fourth lawn?

Extra Practice

Set F (pages 210–211)

Add or subtract. Write each answer in simplest form.

1. $\dfrac{3}{4}$
$+\dfrac{5}{16}$

2. $4\dfrac{5}{6}$
$-1\dfrac{3}{10}$

3. $2\dfrac{1}{26}$
$+4\dfrac{11}{13}$

4. $9\dfrac{7}{8}$
$+\dfrac{1}{9}$

5. $3\dfrac{1}{5}$
$-\dfrac{2}{15}$

6. $6\dfrac{7}{12}$
$-3\dfrac{2}{4}$

7. $7\dfrac{5}{8}$
$+3\dfrac{1}{4}$

8. $2\dfrac{3}{4}$
$+6\dfrac{1}{8}$

9. $2\dfrac{2}{5}$
$-\dfrac{2}{7}$

10. $6\dfrac{7}{15}$
$-\dfrac{1}{45}$

11. $4\dfrac{3}{8} - \dfrac{1}{12}$

12. $4\dfrac{11}{12} - 2\dfrac{7}{9}$

13. $10\dfrac{1}{4} + 5\dfrac{1}{5}$

14. $16\dfrac{2}{3} - 7\dfrac{1}{6}$

15. Tung wants to make scallion pancakes. He mixed $4\dfrac{5}{6}$ cups of scallions, $6\dfrac{1}{2}$ cups of flour, and $1\dfrac{1}{3}$ cups of vegetable oil. What size bowl will he need?

16. Jenny ran 10 miles in 4 days. She ran $3\dfrac{3}{4}$ miles on the first day and $2\dfrac{1}{2}$ miles on the second and third days. How many miles did she run on the fourth day?

17. Tom bought $5\dfrac{1}{2}$ pounds of tomatoes, $2\dfrac{3}{4}$ pounds of peppers, and $1\dfrac{1}{8}$ pounds of onions. How many pounds of vegetables did he buy?

18. Linda ran $5\dfrac{1}{6}$ miles the first week, $3\dfrac{1}{3}$ miles the second week, and $4\dfrac{3}{4}$ miles the third week. If she ran a total of 20 miles in 4 weeks, how many miles did she run the fourth week?

Set G (pages 212–213)

Using Algebra Solve each equation. Check your solution.

1. $x + \dfrac{1}{3} = 4\dfrac{1}{3}$

2. $9\dfrac{1}{2} = x + 1\dfrac{1}{2}$

3. $x + \dfrac{2}{3} = 1\dfrac{2}{3}$

4. $x + \dfrac{5}{8} = 6\dfrac{5}{8}$

5. $x - 6 = 3\dfrac{1}{4}$

6. $x + 5 = 8\dfrac{1}{5}$

7. $12\dfrac{1}{5} = x - \dfrac{1}{5}$

8. $x + 2 = 7\dfrac{1}{2}$

9. $x + 9 = 9\dfrac{3}{4}$

10. $6\dfrac{1}{3} = x + 5\dfrac{1}{3}$

11. $x - 3 = 4\dfrac{1}{5}$

12. $x + \dfrac{1}{2} = 8$

Using Algebra Write an equation. Then solve.

13. After a plant grew $\dfrac{1}{2}$ inch, it measured $6\dfrac{1}{2}$ in. tall. What was the height before it grew $\dfrac{1}{2}$ inch?

14. A seedling was $\dfrac{1}{4}$ inch tall. It grew 2 inches. How tall was the seedling then?

Chapter Test

Complete each sentence.

1. A fraction that cannot be reduced is already ___?___ .

2. ___?___ fractions name the same number.

3. To add $\frac{1}{8}$ and $\frac{1}{6}$, you need to find the ___?___ .

4. A mixed number is a whole number with a ___?___ .

5. Before you can add or subtract fractions with unlike denominators, you have to ___?___ them.

6. ___?___ fractions have numerators greater than their denominators.

Choose the best estimate.

7. $9\frac{7}{8} + \frac{27}{50}$

   a. $1\frac{1}{2}$ **b.** 10 **c.** 9

8. $3\frac{17}{20} + 5\frac{1}{8}$

   a. 8 **b.** $8\frac{1}{2}$ **c.** 9

9. $14\frac{5}{8} - 13\frac{7}{8}$

   a. $\frac{1}{2}$ **b.** $1\frac{1}{4}$ **c.** 0

Add or subtract. Write each answer in simplest form.

10. $\begin{array}{r} \frac{11}{12} \\ -\ \frac{7}{12} \\ \hline \end{array}$

11. $\begin{array}{r} 6\frac{3}{10} \\ +\ 7\frac{3}{4} \\ \hline \end{array}$

12. $\begin{array}{r} 6 \\ +\ 9\frac{3}{5} \\ \hline \end{array}$

13. $\begin{array}{r} \frac{2}{3} \\ -\ \frac{2}{5} \\ \hline \end{array}$

14. $\begin{array}{r} 7\frac{3}{10} \\ +\ 4\frac{1}{2} \\ \hline \end{array}$

15. $\left(5 - 2\frac{3}{8}\right) + \frac{1}{5}$

16. $\left(13\frac{2}{3} - 1\frac{1}{6}\right) - \frac{2}{9}$

17. $\left(4\frac{2}{3} + 1\frac{1}{7}\right) - 3$

18. $5\frac{7}{9} + 4\frac{3}{4} + 3\frac{5}{6}$

Solve.

19. Susan is weaving a rug. She completed $\frac{1}{2}$ of it in a week. She completed $\frac{1}{3}$ more of the rug in the second week. How much of the rug is left to do?

20. On a two-day hike Denise walked $4\frac{2}{5}$ miles and $3\frac{7}{10}$ miles. Tommy walked $3\frac{1}{2}$ miles and $4\frac{1}{4}$ miles. Who walked farther? How much farther?

 Self–Check

Look back at the problems above. Which were easiest? hardest? Why?

Performance Assessment

Show What You Know About Fractions

① Work with a partner. Copy and complete the grid below. To complete the addition fraction grid, follow the row rule and the column rule below. Begin with $\frac{3}{5}$ in row 4 column 2.

What You Need

$\frac{1}{2}$ inch grid paper

Row rule: Add $\frac{3}{10}$

Example: $\frac{3}{5} + \frac{3}{10} = \frac{9}{10}$

Column rule: Add $\frac{1}{5}$

Example: $\frac{3}{5} + \frac{1}{5} = \frac{4}{5}$

Addition Fraction Grids

	$\frac{4}{5}$			
	$\frac{3}{5}$	$\frac{9}{10}$		

How did you find the fractions for the shaded boxes?

Self-Check Did you remember to simplify all the fractions?

② Margaret is planting marigolds around her rectangular garden. The garden measures $12\frac{1}{2}$ feet by $16\frac{3}{4}$ feet.

  a. Find the distance around her garden.

  b. The seedlings were $3\frac{1}{2}$ inches tall when they were planted. Three weeks later they were about $5\frac{3}{8}$ inches tall. Write a problem that could be solved using the information.

Self-Check Did you remember that the garden has 4 sides?

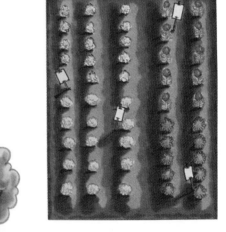

 For Your Portfolio

You might wish to include this work in your portfolio.

Extension

Take a Closer Look

Is there always a fraction between any two fractions? Look at several pairs of fractions to find out.

1 Is there a fraction between $\frac{1}{3}$ and $\frac{2}{3}$?

To find out, look at the line segment from 0 to 1. Divide this segment into smaller pieces. Divide the segment into sixths.

What fraction is between $\frac{1}{3}$ and $\frac{2}{3}$?

2 Is there a fraction between $\frac{2}{6}$ and $\frac{3}{6}$? How would you find out? Could you divide the line segment into smaller pieces again? What denominator would you use?

3 Name the fraction between $\frac{2}{6}$ and $\frac{3}{6}$.

4 What if you started with two unlike fractions such as $\frac{1}{5}$ and $\frac{1}{2}$? Is there a fraction between $\frac{1}{5}$ and $\frac{1}{2}$?

5 Can you always find a fraction between any two fractions? Explain.

223

Cumulative Review

Choose the correct letter for each answer.

Number Concepts	Operations

1. What is 32.965 rounded to the nearest tenth?

   A. 30

   B. 32.9

   C. 32.97

   D. 33.0

2. Which of the following statements is NOT true?

   A. $\frac{3}{4} > \frac{1}{2}$

   B. $\frac{5}{8} < \frac{3}{4}$

   C. $\frac{5}{8} > \frac{1}{2}$

   D. $\frac{7}{8} < \frac{3}{4}$

3. Which fraction is equivalent to $\frac{2}{3}$?

   A. $\frac{10}{12}$

   B. $\frac{10}{15}$

   C. $\frac{9}{15}$

   D. $\frac{4}{12}$

4. What is the least common multiple of 6 and 9?

   A. 3

   B. 18

   C. 36

   D. 54

5. What is the difference between 71.4 and 37.7?

   A. 43.7   **D.** 33.7

   B. 43.1   **E.** Not Here

   C. 37.3

6. Rose sorted buttons into a tray with 6 sections. She put skirt buttons in 2 sections, jacket buttons in 1 section, and blouse buttons in 3 sections. How much more of the tray held blouse buttons than jacket buttons?

   A. $\frac{1}{6}$ **C.** $\frac{1}{2}$

   B. $\frac{1}{3}$ **D.** $\frac{5}{6}$

7. What is the sum of $\frac{5}{6}$ and $\frac{2}{3}$?

   A. $1\frac{1}{2}$ **C.** $1\frac{1}{6}$

   B. $1\frac{1}{3}$ **D.** $\frac{7}{9}$

8. On Wednesday, Joe and Fred ate $\frac{1}{2}$ of a pizza. On Thursday, they ate $\frac{1}{3}$ of the pizza. Which picture shows how much was left?

A.   **C.**

B.   **D.**

Patterns, Relationships, and Algebraic Thinking	Measurement

9. Henry can solve 10 math problems in 3 minutes. He has 25 problems to solve. Which equivalent ratios can be used to find out how long this will take?

A. $\frac{10}{3} = \frac{25}{n}$

B. $\frac{3}{10} = \frac{25}{n}$

C. $\frac{n}{10} = \frac{25}{3}$

D. $\frac{3}{n} = \frac{25}{10}$

10. Which point best represents the ordered pair (4, 2)?

A. P
B. Q
C. R
D. S

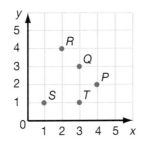

11. Maria is putting boxes on shelves. She put 4 boxes on the top shelf, 7 boxes on the next shelf down, 11 boxes on the next shelf, and 16 boxes on the fourth shelf. If she continues this pattern, how many boxes will be on the next shelf?

A. 16
B. 18
C. 20
D. 22

12. Which point best represents the number 3.25 on the number line?

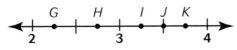

A. G **C.** I
B. H **D.** J

13. The perimeter of a rectangular patio is 72 feet. If the patio is 8 feet wide, how long is it?

A. 9 ft
B. 14 ft
C. 16 ft
D. 28 ft
E. 56 ft

14. Yolanda saw an alligator that was 96 inches long. How many feet long was the alligator?

A. 6.5 ft
B. 7 ft
C. 8.5 ft
D. 9 ft
E. Not Here

15. Mr. Diaz wants to plant a border of grass around the perimeter of a square patio. Each side of the patio is 4.5 yards long. Which equation can be used to find out how many yards long the border of grass, B, will be?

A. $4.5 + 4.5 = B$
B. $4 \times 4.5 = B$
C. $2 \times 4.5 = B$
D. $4(4.5 + 4.5) = B$
E. $(2 \times 4.5) \times (2 \times 4.5) = B$

16. Diane needs to supply the team with 23 quarts of a sports drink. If it is only sold in gallons, how many gallons does she need to buy? (4 qt = 1 gal)

A. 12 gal
B. 6 gal
C. 5 gal
D. 4 gal

Chapter 6

Multiplying and Dividing Fractions

Chapter Theme: BUSINESS

Real Facts

Many organizations help students get an education. Even small fund-raisers like the car wash at the right can help.

Donations made to the United Negro College Fund (UNCF) help thousands of African Americans get a college education. Funding goals in 1998 for the New Jersey Chapter are shown on the circle graph below.

United Negro College Fund
(New Jersey Chapter)
1998 Estimated Total Goal: $3,600,000

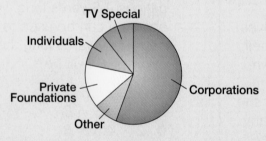

- About what fraction of the planned donations comes from individuals? About how many dollars is this?

- Why is a circle graph a good way to show this data?

Real People

Meet Donna Carter-Butler, the New Jersey Director of the United Negro College Fund. She has found that raising money for a good cause is a rewarding job that requires good math skills and good people skills, too. Each year she works with many volunteers, businesses, and private foundations to achieve the New Jersey goal.

COMMUNITY
FUND-RAISER

100%
90%
80%
70%
60%
50%
40%
30%
20%
10%

A Lot of Good

Sometimes it's necessary to find a fraction of a fraction.

Learning About It

The students from Crenshaw High School turned a vacant lot into a vegetable garden. Tomatoes were planted in $\frac{4}{5}$ of the garden space. Plum tomatoes took up $\frac{1}{6}$ of that space. What part of the garden was planted in plum tomatoes?

To find out, multiply $\frac{1}{6} \times \frac{4}{5}$.

Science Connection ➤
Soil can be improved for gardening by adding leaves, grass clippings, and even vegetable scraps from your kitchen.

THERE'S ALWAYS A WAY!

● **One way** is to use grid paper.

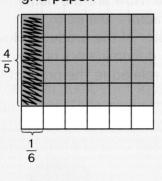

● **Another way** is to use paper and pencil.

Step 1 Multiply the numerators. Then multiply the denominators.

$$\frac{1}{6} \times \frac{4}{5} = \frac{1 \times 4}{6 \times 5} = \frac{4}{30}$$

Step 2 Simplify if possible.

$$\frac{1}{6} \times \frac{4}{5} = \frac{4}{30} = \frac{2}{15}$$

$\frac{2}{15}$ of the garden was planted in plum tomatoes.

More Examples

A. $\frac{2}{3} \times \frac{3}{5} = \frac{2 \times 3}{3 \times 5} = \frac{6}{15} = \frac{2}{5}$

B. $4 \times \frac{3}{5} = \frac{4}{1} \times \frac{3}{5} = \frac{4 \times 3}{1 \times 5} = \frac{12}{5} = 2\frac{2}{5}$

Connecting Ideas

Take another look at $\frac{1}{6} \times \frac{4}{5}$. Another way to solve this problem is by simplifying *before* you multiply.

Step 1 Find a common factor of any numerator and any denominator.

$4 \div 2 = 2$

$\frac{1}{6} \times \frac{4}{5}$

$6 \div 2 = 3$

Step 2 Divide the numerator and denominator by the common factor. Then multiply.

$$\frac{1}{_3\cancel{6}} \times \frac{\cancel{4}^2}{5} = \frac{1 \times 2}{3 \times 5} = \frac{2}{15}$$

More Examples

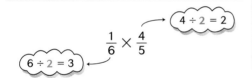

A.
$$\frac{1}{_1\cancel{4}} \times \frac{\cancel{8}^2}{9} = \frac{1 \times 2}{1 \times 9} = \frac{2}{9}$$

$8 \div 4 = 2$

$4 \div 4 = 1$

B.
$$\frac{^1\cancel{5}}{_2\cancel{6}} \times \frac{\cancel{9}^3}{\cancel{10}_2} = \frac{1 \times 3}{2 \times 2} = \frac{3}{4}$$

Think and Discuss If you multiply two fractions that are less than one, is the product less than one? Why or why not?

Try It Out

Write a multiplication expression for each.

1.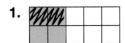

2.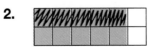

3.

Multiply. Write each answer in simplest form.

4. $\frac{3}{5} \times \frac{6}{15}$ **5.** $\frac{5}{8} \times \frac{4}{25}$ **6.** $4 \times \frac{3}{4}$ **7.** $\frac{3}{10} \times \frac{4}{15}$

Practice

Write a multiplication expression for each picture. Solve each expression and write your answers in simplest form.

8.

9.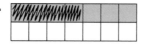

10.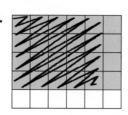

Name the common factors you can use to simplify each multiplication expression.

11. $\frac{4}{9} \times \frac{6}{11}$

12. $\frac{2}{3} \times \frac{3}{10}$

13. $\frac{8}{15} \times \frac{5}{12}$

14. $\frac{14}{25} \times \frac{5}{21}$

Multiply. Write each answer in simplest form.

15. $\frac{1}{2} \times \frac{1}{8}$

16. $\frac{2}{5} \times \frac{2}{3}$

17. $\frac{5}{6} \times \frac{2}{7}$

18. $\frac{4}{9} \times \frac{2}{5}$

19. $\frac{2}{3} \times \frac{9}{11}$

20. $8 \times \frac{3}{4}$

21. $\frac{3}{5} \times \frac{5}{7}$

22. $\frac{4}{7} \times \frac{3}{8}$

23. $4 \times \frac{3}{4}$

24. $\frac{5}{12} \times \frac{8}{15}$

25. $\frac{7}{10} \times \frac{5}{21}$

26. $\frac{3}{8} \times \frac{2}{9}$

27. $\frac{8}{35} \times \frac{7}{40}$

28. $6 \times \frac{15}{27}$

29. $\frac{11}{12} \times \frac{48}{55}$

30. $\frac{9}{14} \times \frac{7}{15}$

Using Mental Math Find each product using mental math.

31. $9 + \left(3 \times \frac{1}{3}\right)$

32. $\frac{5}{8} + \left(\frac{3}{4} \times \frac{1}{2}\right)$

33. $\frac{4}{5} \times \left(\frac{1}{4} \times 5\right)$

34. $3\frac{4}{9} - \left(\frac{2}{3} \times \frac{2}{3}\right)$

35. $6\frac{1}{4} + \left(3 \times \frac{1}{4}\right)$

36. $5 - \left(\frac{2}{3} \times \frac{3}{2}\right)$

Kid Connection ➤
These students from California turned a vacant lot into a moneymaking business. Part of the profits from selling natural food products were donated to homeless shelters.

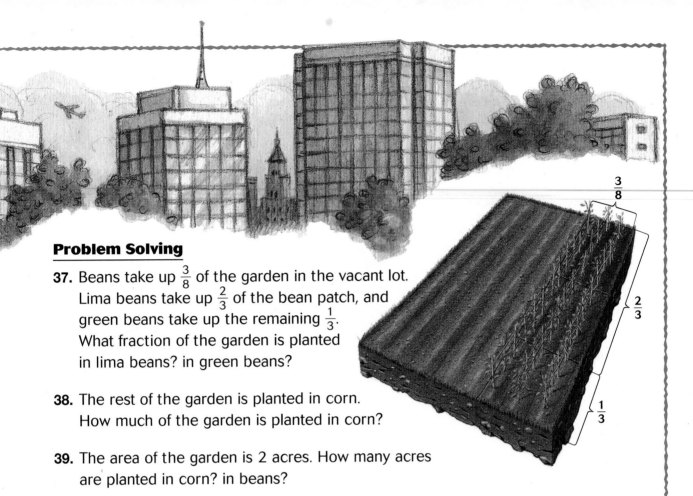

Problem Solving

37. Beans take up $\frac{3}{8}$ of the garden in the vacant lot. Lima beans take up $\frac{2}{3}$ of the bean patch, and green beans take up the remaining $\frac{1}{3}$. What fraction of the garden is planted in lima beans? in green beans?

38. The rest of the garden is planted in corn. How much of the garden is planted in corn?

39. The area of the garden is 2 acres. How many acres are planted in corn? in beans?

40. **What If?** Suppose the students decide to plant lettuce in $\frac{1}{3}$ of the area originally set aside for corn. What fraction of the garden would be planted in lettuce?

41. The garden is $\frac{3}{5}$ as wide as it is long. If the garden is 360 feet long, how wide is it?

42. Lima beans sold for $0.79 per pound. How much did the students earn if they sold 100 lb of lima beans?

43. Corn sells for $5.00 a bushel. How much would you pay for $\frac{4}{5}$ of a bushel of corn and 40 pounds of lima beans?

44. **Analyze** The students spent $25 for seeds and $\frac{3}{5}$ of that amount for fertilizer and mulch. If they made $75 selling vegetables in June, did they make a profit?

Review and Remember

Rename each mixed number as an improper fraction.

45. $2\frac{3}{4}$ **46.** $1\frac{1}{3}$ **47.** $9\frac{5}{6}$ **48.** $6\frac{1}{2}$ **49.** $3\frac{7}{12}$

50. $8\frac{5}{8}$ **51.** $6\frac{2}{3}$ **52.** $9\frac{7}{8}$ **53.** $10\frac{2}{5}$ **54.** $11\frac{1}{2}$

For Extra Practice, see Set A, page 256.

Button, Button . . .

You can use what you know about multiplying fractions to multiply mixed numbers.

Learning About It

Pat and Luna went into business making buttons. They received an order from a local store for $5\frac{1}{2}$ sets of large buttons. If it takes $1\frac{1}{3}$ sheets of paper to make a set of large buttons, how many sheets of paper will they need?

To find out, multiply $5\frac{1}{2} \times 1\frac{1}{3}$.

$1\frac{1}{3}$

Step 1 Write each mixed number as an improper fraction.	**Step 2** Look for common factors and simplify.	**Step 3** Multiply. Simplify the fraction.
$5\frac{1}{2} \times 1\frac{1}{3} = \frac{11}{2} \times \frac{4}{3}$	$\frac{11}{\underset{1}{2}} \times \frac{\overset{2}{4}}{3} = \frac{11}{1} \times \frac{2}{3}$	$\frac{11}{1} \times \frac{2}{3} = \frac{22}{3} = 7\frac{1}{3}$

They will need $7\frac{1}{3}$ sheets of paper.

More Examples

A. $4 \times 2\frac{1}{8} = \frac{\overset{1}{4}}{1} \times \frac{17}{\underset{2}{8}} = \frac{17}{2} = 8\frac{1}{2}$

B. $4\frac{2}{3} \times \frac{9}{16} = \frac{\overset{7}{14}}{\underset{1}{3}} \times \frac{\overset{3}{9}}{\underset{8}{16}} = \frac{7}{1} \times \frac{3}{8} = \frac{21}{8} = 2\frac{5}{8}$

Think and Discuss How is multiplying a fraction by a mixed number different from multiplying a fraction by a fraction? How is it the same?

Try It Out

Multiply. Write each answer in simplest form.

1. $5 \times 1\frac{2}{5}$

2. $\frac{1}{3} \times 4\frac{1}{2}$

3. $3\frac{1}{8} \times \frac{3}{5}$

4. $3\frac{1}{4} \times \frac{12}{13}$

5. $5\frac{5}{6} \times 2\frac{4}{7}$

6. $\frac{7}{8} \times 1\frac{5}{6} \times 3$

7. $10 - \left(3\frac{4}{7} \times 1\frac{2}{5}\right)$

8. $11 + \left(2\frac{1}{4} \times \frac{1}{3}\right)$

Practice

Multiply. Write each answer in simplest form.

9. $6 \times 2\frac{3}{4}$

10. $4 \times 3\frac{3}{8}$

11. $5 \times 2\frac{1}{5}$

12. $9\frac{1}{8} \times 16$

13. $5\frac{5}{8} \times \frac{1}{3}$

14. $2\frac{3}{10} \times \frac{9}{11}$

15. $2\frac{5}{8} \times \frac{9}{10}$

16. $1\frac{6}{7} \times \frac{7}{8}$

17. $3\frac{1}{3} \times \frac{9}{10}$

18. $2\frac{2}{5} \times \frac{5}{12}$

19. $5\frac{1}{5} \times 1\frac{5}{13}$

20. $2\frac{2}{5} \times \frac{5}{8}$

21. $2\frac{7}{8} \times 3\frac{1}{4}$

22. $3\frac{3}{4} \times 3\frac{3}{4}$

23. $4\frac{3}{5} \times 1\frac{1}{2}$

24. $5\frac{3}{7} \times 6\frac{1}{8}$

25. $3\frac{1}{3} \times 4\frac{1}{4}$

26. $2\frac{9}{10} \times 5\frac{10}{12}$

27. $4\frac{4}{5} \times 3\frac{5}{6}$

28. $6\frac{3}{10} \times 1\frac{5}{6}$

Using Mental Math   Use number sense to find each answer.

29. $3 - \left(\frac{3}{4} \times \frac{2}{3}\right)$

30. $\left(2\frac{1}{2} + \frac{1}{2}\right) \times \frac{2}{3}$

31. $\left(1\frac{1}{2} \times \frac{2}{3}\right) + \frac{3}{4}$

32. $\left(1 - \frac{1}{2}\right) \times 2$

Problem Solving

33. To advertise their business, Pat and Luna pinned buttons to their clothing. Luna wore a vest with $2\frac{2}{3}$ dozen buttons pinned to it. Pat pinned $2\frac{1}{4}$ times as many buttons to his jacket and cap. How many buttons did Pat wear?

34. Analyze   Pat took $3\frac{3}{4}$ hours to make 3 dozen buttons. Luna worked $2\frac{2}{5}$ times as long to make $1\frac{2}{3}$ times as many buttons. They sold the buttons for $0.75 each. How much did they earn?

Review and Remember

 Use a calculator to change each fraction to a decimal.

35. $\frac{1}{2}$

36. $\frac{3}{10}$

37. $\frac{1}{4}$

38. $\frac{2}{5}$

39. $\frac{5}{8}$

40. $\frac{7}{8}$

41. $\frac{2}{3}$

42. $\frac{3}{8}$

Guess Smart

You will know if your answer is reasonable if you estimate before finding an exact answer.

Learning About It

Liam and some friends have a delivery service. Stores pay them to deliver packages by bicycle to customers. Liam figures that the average distance he travels each hour is $4\frac{7}{8}$ miles.

Last week Liam worked $18\frac{1}{4}$ hours. About how far did he travel?

Use rounding to estimate the product $4\frac{7}{8} \times 18\frac{1}{4}$.

Step 1 Round each mixed number to the nearest whole number.	**Step 2** Multiply the whole numbers.
$4\frac{7}{8} \times 18\frac{1}{4}$ ⬇ ⬇ 5 18	$5 \times 18 = 90$

Liam traveled about 90 miles.

More Examples

A. $1\frac{5}{6} \times \frac{8}{15}$

⬇   ⬇

$2 \times \frac{1}{2} = 1$

B. $\frac{5}{9} \times \frac{11}{12}$

⬇   ⬇

$\frac{1}{2} \times 1 = \frac{1}{2}$

C. $2\frac{1}{2} \times \frac{3}{4}$

⬇   ⬇

$3 \times 1 = 3$

Connecting Ideas

Another way to estimate is to use compatible numbers.

Use compatible numbers to estimate the product $\frac{1}{6} \times 118$.

Step 1 Change the whole number to the nearest number compatible with the denominator of the fraction.

$$\frac{1}{6} \times 118$$

$$\downarrow \qquad \downarrow$$

$$\frac{1}{6} \times 120$$

Step 2 Simplify, then multiply.

$$\frac{1}{\overset{1}{\underset{1}{6}}} \times \overset{20}{\cancel{120}} = 1 \times 20 = 20$$

So $\frac{1}{6} \times 118$ is about 20.

Think and Discuss Is 100 a reasonable estimate for the product of $1\frac{2}{3}$ and 120? Explain.

Try It Out

Use rounding or compatible numbers to estimate.

1. $12\frac{7}{8} \times 4\frac{2}{7}$ 2. $\frac{1}{4} \times 122$ 3. $\frac{1}{6} \times 177$ 4. $49\frac{3}{4} \times 1\frac{5}{6}$ 5. $\frac{3}{5} \times 219$

Practice

Use rounding or compatible numbers to estimate.
Tell which method you used.

6. $1\frac{5}{8} \times 120$ 7. $3\frac{1}{8} \times 7\frac{5}{6}$ 8. $\frac{7}{8} \times \frac{7}{16}$ 9. $5\frac{1}{3} \times 19\frac{1}{7}$ 10. $\frac{3}{8} \times 162$

Problem Solving

11. Liam works an average of $5\frac{3}{4}$ hours a day. Last week he worked $4\frac{1}{4}$ days. About how many hours did he work?

12. Holly delivers 106 packages in 5 months. About how many is that per month?

13. **Journal Idea** If you were a delivery person, would you rather be paid $0.50 for each mile you travel or $2.00 per delivery? Describe the reasoning behind your choice.

Review and Remember

Estimate the sum or difference.

14. $0.32 + 0.78$ 15. $1.24 - 0.65$ 16. $0.99 + 86$ 17. $0.88 - 0.29$

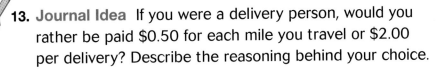

For Extra Practice, see Set C, page 257.

Developing Skills for
Problem Solving

*First read for understanding and then focus
on which operation to choose.*

READ FOR UNDERSTANDING

You and a friend have a dog-walking service. The sign at the right shows how much you charge for this service.

Ms. Glazer, one of your best customers, has two dogs, Rupert and Lucy. Each week you walk the dogs for $\frac{1}{2}$ hour on Monday and Wednesday and for $1\frac{1}{2}$ hours on Friday.

1 How much do you charge to walk 1 dog? to walk 2 dogs?

2 How many of Ms. Glazer's dogs do you walk?

WALK-A-DOG

1 DOG	2 DOGS
$4	**$6**
per hour	per hour

Ms Glazer

Week	S	M	T	W	Th	F	S
1		$\frac{1}{2}$		$\frac{1}{2}$		$1\frac{1}{2}$	
2		$\frac{1}{2}$		$\frac{1}{2}$		$1\frac{1}{2}$	
3							
4							

THINK AND DISCUSS

MATH FOCUS

Choose the Operation Clues in a problem can help you decide what operation to use. You add to combine groups, subtract to compare groups, multiply to combine equal groups, and divide to separate into equal groups.

Reread the paragraphs at the top of the page.

3 What operation or operations would you use to find the number of hours you spend walking the two dogs in one week?

4 Ms. Glazer pays for your service every four weeks. How much does she pay? What operations did you use to solve this problem?

5 Tell how you know when to use addition instead of multiplication to solve a problem.

Show What You Learned

Answer each question. Give a reason for your choice.

$\mathbf{M}$r. Ryder is going on vacation for 3 weeks. He hires your service to walk his dog Domino $\frac{1}{2}$ hour every day while he is away. You charge $4 per hour to walk 1 dog and $6 per hour to walk 2 dogs.

1 Which expression shows how many hours a week you will spend walking Domino?

   a. $7 + \frac{1}{2}$

   b. $7 - \frac{1}{2}$

   c. $7 \times \frac{1}{2}$

2 Which expression shows how much you will earn walking Domino?

   a. hours walked per week $\times$ $4 $\times$ 3 weeks

   b. hours walked per week $+$ $4 $\times$ 3 weeks

   c. hours walked per week $\times$ $4 $+$ 3 weeks

3 **What If?** Suppose a customer with 2 dogs goes on vacation for 4 weeks. Write an expression to show how much money you will earn walking the dogs.

$\mathbf{Y}$ou reward each dog with a biscuit at the end of every walk. On Monday you buy a box of dog biscuits. Each biscuit weighs $\frac{1}{8}$ lb. From Monday through Friday you walk 3 dogs a day and on Saturday you walk 5 dogs.

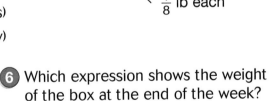

$\frac{1}{8}$ lb each

4 How would you decide how many biscuits were given away each week?

   a. (3 dogs + 5 days) $\times$ 6 days

   b. (3 dogs $\times$ 1 day) + (5 dogs $\times$ 5 days)

   c. (3 dogs $\times$ 5 days) + (5 dogs $\times$ 1 day)

5 Which expression shows the weight of the biscuits given away?

   a. number of biscuits $+ \frac{1}{8}$ lb

   b. number of biscuits $\div \frac{1}{8}$ lb

   c. number of biscuits $\times \frac{1}{8}$ lb

6 Which expression shows the weight of the box at the end of the week?

   a. 4 lb $+$ (number of biscuits $\times \frac{1}{8}$ lb)

   b. 4 lb $-$ (number of biscuits $\times \frac{1}{8}$ lb)

   c. 4 lb $\times$ (number of biscuits $\times \frac{1}{8}$ lb)

7 **Explain** If you start with a 10-lb box of dog biscuits, how much will the box of biscuits weigh after 2 weeks? What operations did you use to solve the problem?

✓ Checkpoint

Multiplying Fractions

Write the multiplication sentence for each model. (pages 228–229)

1.

2.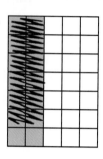

3.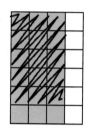

Multiply. Write each answer in simplest form. (pages 228–231)

4. $\frac{1}{4} \times \frac{5}{6}$

5. $\frac{2}{3} \times 5$

6. $\frac{6}{7} \times \frac{7}{12}$

7. $\frac{15}{16} \times \frac{8}{25}$

Multiply. Write each answer in simplest form. (pages 232–233)

8. $1\frac{1}{2} \times 2\frac{2}{3}$

9. $2\frac{7}{8} \times \frac{2}{3}$

10. $5\frac{1}{4} \times 2\frac{1}{7}$

11. $5\frac{1}{2} \times 8$

12. $1\frac{4}{5} \times \frac{1}{3}$

13. $1\frac{2}{3} \times 3\frac{1}{5}$

14. $3\frac{1}{5} \times 9$

15. $2\frac{2}{3} \times 1\frac{1}{4}$

Use rounding to estimate. (pages 234–235)

16. $3 \times 2\frac{1}{6}$

17. $5\frac{1}{5} \times 6\frac{7}{8}$

18. $\frac{1}{2} \times \frac{7}{8}$

19. $\frac{3}{8} \times \frac{7}{12}$

Use compatible numbers to estimate. (pages 234–235)

20. $27 \times \frac{3}{5}$

21. $\frac{7}{8} \times 30$

22. $\frac{5}{9} \times 17$

23. $13 \times \frac{5}{6}$

Mixed Practice

Multiply. Write each answer in simplest form.

24. $2\frac{3}{4} \times 6$

25. $\frac{3}{4} \times 40$

26. $\frac{1}{4} \times 1\frac{3}{5}$

27. $1\frac{5}{9} \times 3\frac{3}{8}$

28. $\frac{3}{4} \times \frac{2}{9}$

29. $\frac{2}{7} \times 1\frac{3}{4}$

30. $\frac{2}{3} \times \frac{15}{20}$

31. $1\frac{1}{11} \times \frac{3}{4}$

32. $4\frac{1}{5} \times 1\frac{1}{3}$

What do you think?

When you multiply a whole number by a fraction that is less than 1, will the product be greater than the whole number? Explain.

Problem Solving

33. Leslie and Harriet walked to the bake sale. Leslie walked $1\frac{3}{5}$ miles. Harriet walked $2\frac{1}{2}$ times farther than Leslie. How far did Harriet walk?

34. Fran sold $1\frac{1}{4}$ times as many muffins as Carol did. If Carol sold 4 dozen muffins, how many did Fran sell?

35. Martin sold $1\frac{1}{2}$ brownies in the first hour of the bake sale, 3 in the second hour, and 6 in the third hour. At this rate, during what hour will Martin sell 48 brownies? What strategy did you use to find out?

Journal Idea

Explain the steps you follow to multiply a mixed number by a whole number.

Critical Thinking Corner

Number Sense

Parts of the Whole

Pat and Luna made $60.00 selling buttons in one day at the county fair. After paying for materials, advertising, and rental space for their booth, they put the rest of the money, which was their profit, in the bank.

The circle graph shows how Pat and Luna used the $60.00.

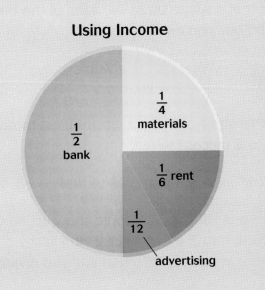

Using Income

1. How much money was spent on materials?

2. How much more was spent on rent than on advertising?

3. If Pat and Luna sell the same amount each day for two more days, how much profit will they make for the entire three-day period?

EXPLORE: Dividing Fractions

Going to Pieces

You can use fraction pieces to answer such questions as "How many pieces?" and "What part of a whole?"

Learning About It

You're helping to run a pizza stand for the summer. To attract customers, you've decided to pass out free samples.

Work with a partner.

Step 1 You cut 3 pizzas in half. How many pieces of pizza do you have now? To find out, you divide 3 by $\frac{1}{2}$.

How many halves are in 3?
$3 \div \frac{1}{2} = \blacksquare$

Now use fraction pieces to find $4 \div \frac{1}{2}$.

How many halves are in 4?

Step 2 More customers than you expected show up, so you cut each pizza half into two equal pieces. What part of a whole pizza will each of the pieces be? To find out, you divide $\frac{1}{2}$ by 2.

What part of a whole is $\frac{1}{2} \div 2$?
$\frac{1}{2} \div 2 = \blacksquare$

What size fraction pieces are used to divide one half into 2 pieces?

Now use fraction pieces to find $\frac{1}{2} \div 3$.

Step 3 Still more people show up, so you cut each fourth into 2 equal pieces. How many $\frac{1}{8}$ pieces are there in one half? To find out, you divide $\frac{1}{2}$ by $\frac{1}{8}$.

How many $\frac{1}{8}$ pieces are there in a $\frac{1}{2}$ piece?
$\frac{1}{2} \div \frac{1}{8} = \blacksquare$

Now use fraction pieces to model $\frac{1}{2} \div \frac{1}{10}$.

How many $\frac{1}{10}$ pieces are there in $\frac{1}{2}$?

What You Need

For each pair:
fraction pieces

240

Think and Discuss How could you use fraction pieces to solve $2\frac{1}{4} \div 3$?

Practice

Use fraction pieces to model each problem.

1. How many $\frac{1}{4}$ pieces are in 3?

   $3 \div \frac{1}{4}$

2. What part of a whole is $\frac{1}{4}$ divided by 3?

   $\frac{1}{4} \div 3$

Write a division sentence for each picture.

3. How many $\frac{1}{2}$ pieces?

4. What part of a whole?

5. How many $\frac{1}{6}$ in $\frac{1}{3}$?

Using Algebra Use fraction pieces to model *a* and *b*. Look for a pattern.

6. a. $2 \div \frac{1}{2}$

   b. $2 \times \frac{2}{1}$

7. a. $\frac{1}{2} \div 4$

   b. $\frac{1}{2} \times \frac{1}{4}$

8. a. $\frac{1}{2} \div \frac{1}{4}$

   b. $\frac{1}{2} \times \frac{4}{1}$

9. a. $1\frac{1}{2} \div \frac{1}{2}$

   b. $1\frac{1}{2} \times \frac{2}{1}$

10. **Journal Idea** Explain how you can use multiplication to solve a division problem.

Critical Thinking Corner

Number Sense

Multiplying and Dividing Fractions

Now that you've passed out samples, it's time to sell some pizza! But first, of course, you have to make it—with delicious crispy crust. Here's a recipe for pizza dough. The recipe will make crust for two small pizzas.

1. You want to make enough dough for 6 small pizza crusts. How would you change the recipe?

2. At home you want to make one small pizza for your family. How would you change the recipe?

CRISPY PIZZA CRUST

Mix (in the order shown)
1⅛ cups warm water
3 cups flour
2 tsp. sugar
1 tsp. salt
1½ tsp. yeast

Storytellers, Inc.

When dividing fractions, it is important to remember that multiplication and division are inverse operations.

Learning About It

Several students started a business called "Storytellers, Inc." They use salt dough to make storyteller dolls like those made by the Native American Pueblo people.

How many dolls can they make using the amounts in the recipe if one doll takes $\frac{3}{4}$ pound?

To find out, solve $3 \div \frac{3}{4}$.

SALT DOUGH RECIPE

(MAKES 3 POUNDS OF DOUGH)

Ingredients

4 cups flour (any kind except self-rising)
$1\frac{1}{2}$ cup warm water
1 cup salt

THERE'S ALWAYS A WAY!

● **One way** is to use fraction pieces to model the problem.

Divide into $\frac{1}{4}$ pieces and regroup into $\frac{3}{4}$ pieces.

You have 4 groups of $\frac{3}{4}$.

● **Another way** is to use paper and pencil.

Step 1 Find the reciprocal of the divisor. The reciprocal of $\frac{3}{4}$ is $\frac{4}{3}$. Rewrite as a multiplication exercise.

$$3 \div \frac{3}{4} = 3 \times \frac{4}{3}$$

Step 2 Multiply and then simplify if possible.

$$\frac{\overset{1}{\cancel{3}}}{1} \times \frac{4}{\underset{1}{\cancel{3}}} = \frac{1}{1} \times \frac{4}{1} = 4$$

They can make 4 dolls.

More Examples

A. $\frac{3}{4} \div 3 = \frac{\overset{1}{\cancel{3}}}{4} \times \frac{1}{\underset{1}{\cancel{3}}} = \frac{1}{4}$

B. $\frac{3}{8} \div \frac{5}{6} = \frac{3}{\underset{4}{\cancel{8}}} \times \frac{\overset{3}{\cancel{6}}}{5} = \frac{9}{20}$

Think and Discuss When a whole number is divided by a proper fraction, will the quotient always be greater than the whole number? Explain.

Try It Out

Using Algebra Write the reciprocal of each fraction.

1. $\frac{3}{8}$ **2.** $\frac{4}{9}$ **3.** 14 **4.** $\frac{1}{12}$

Divide. Write each answer in simplest form.

5. $3 \div \frac{1}{8}$ **6.** $\frac{1}{8} \div \frac{7}{8}$ **7.** $\frac{2}{3} \div 16$ **8.** $\frac{3}{7} \div \frac{9}{14}$

▲ **Social Studies Connection** The tradition of making storyteller dolls like the one shown here began in 1964. Helen Cordero made the first doll to honor her grandfather, who was a Pueblo storyteller.

Practice

Divide. Write each answer in simplest form.

9. $\frac{1}{4} \div \frac{2}{3}$ **10.** $\frac{3}{4} \div 4$ **11.** $\frac{5}{8} \div \frac{1}{2}$ **12.** $\frac{3}{7} \div \frac{3}{4}$ **13.** $12 \div \frac{12}{13}$

14. $\frac{5}{6} \div \frac{5}{8}$ **15.** $\frac{4}{5} \div \frac{5}{6}$ **16.** $\frac{3}{5} \div \frac{3}{10}$ **17.** $\frac{3}{4} \div \frac{5}{6}$ **18.** $\frac{1}{5} \div 3$

19. $9 \div \frac{36}{37}$ **20.** $\frac{3}{5} \div 2$ **21.** $\frac{7}{8} \div \frac{4}{7}$ **22.** $16 \div \frac{2}{3}$ **23.** $\frac{5}{8} \div \frac{5}{8}$

Problem Solving

Use the information below to solve Problems 24–25.

INTERNET ACTIVITY
www.sbgmath.com

Large storyteller dolls take $\frac{7}{8}$ pound of salt dough, and small dolls take $\frac{3}{8}$ pound of dough. The recipe makes 3 pounds of dough.

24. How many small dolls can be made from 3 pounds of salt dough? How many large dolls can be made?

25. **Analyze** The students double the recipe. How many large dolls can they make? How much dough is left?

26. **Create Your Own** Write a problem that requires dividing fractions. Exchange with a partner to solve.

Review and Remember

Multiply.

27. 305×400 **28.** 4.73×8.4 **29.** 72×597.6 **30.** 89×0.2047

Quite a Handful

Remember that mixed numbers can be renamed as fractions.

Learning About It

Amy and Jason make hand puppets, which they sell at street fairs and craft shows. They need $1\frac{1}{8}$ yards of cloth for each puppet. If they have $6\frac{3}{4}$ yards of cloth, how many puppets can they make?

To find the answer, solve $6\frac{3}{4} \div 1\frac{1}{8}$.

$1\frac{1}{8}$ yd

Step 1 Write each mixed number as an improper fraction.

$$6\frac{3}{4} \div 1\frac{1}{8} = \frac{27}{4} \div \frac{9}{8}$$

They can make 6 puppets.

Step 2 Multiply by the reciprocal of the divisor. Simplify if possible.

$$\frac{27}{4} \div \frac{9}{8} = \frac{\overset{3}{\cancel{27}}}{\underset{1}{\cancel{4}}} \times \frac{\overset{2}{\cancel{8}}}{\underset{1}{\cancel{9}}} = \frac{6}{1} = 6$$

More Examples

A. $4\frac{2}{5} \div \frac{2}{3} = \frac{22}{5} \div \frac{2}{3} = \frac{\overset{11}{\cancel{22}}}{5} \times \frac{3}{\underset{1}{\cancel{2}}} = \frac{33}{5} = 6\frac{3}{5}$

B. $5\frac{1}{3} \div 4 = \frac{16}{3} \div \frac{4}{1} = \frac{\overset{4}{\cancel{16}}}{3} \times \frac{1}{\underset{1}{\cancel{4}}} = \frac{4}{3} = 1\frac{1}{3}$

C. $8 \div 3\frac{1}{5} = \frac{8}{1} \div \frac{16}{5} = \frac{\overset{1}{\cancel{8}}}{1} \times \frac{5}{\underset{2}{\cancel{16}}} = \frac{5}{2} = 2\frac{1}{2}$

Think and Discuss How is dividing with mixed numbers different from dividing with fractions?

Try It Out

Divide. Write each answer in simplest form.

1. $1\frac{2}{3} \div 1\frac{1}{4}$

2. $1\frac{3}{8} \div 4\frac{1}{3}$

3. $\frac{3}{5} \div \frac{1}{2}$

4. $8\frac{1}{3} \div 2\frac{1}{2}$

5. $5\frac{1}{3} \div \frac{3}{4}$

6. $\frac{1}{2} \div 3\frac{1}{4}$

7. $2\frac{5}{8} \div 7$

8. $5 \div 1\frac{1}{4}$

Practice

Write each mixed number as an improper fraction.
Then write the reciprocal of that fraction.

9. $4\frac{2}{5}$ **10.** $3\frac{7}{8}$ **11.** $1\frac{9}{10}$ **12.** $8\frac{4}{5}$ **13.** $10\frac{1}{5}$ **14.** $7\frac{3}{4}$

Divide. Write each answer in simplest form.

15. $7 \div 3\frac{1}{2}$ **16.** $3\frac{2}{3} \div 1\frac{1}{3}$ **17.** $1\frac{1}{8} \div \frac{3}{4}$ **18.** $5\frac{3}{4} \div 2$

19. $4\frac{2}{5} \div 1\frac{1}{10}$ **20.** $4\frac{3}{8} \div 3\frac{3}{4}$ **21.** $2\frac{3}{8} \div 4$ **22.** $2\frac{1}{10} \div 1\frac{1}{5}$

23. $\frac{5}{8} \div 1\frac{2}{3}$ **24.** $44 \div 1\frac{5}{6}$ **25.** $\frac{3}{4} \div 1\frac{7}{8}$ **26.** $6\frac{3}{5} \div 2\frac{1}{2}$

27. $7\frac{1}{2} \div 4\frac{1}{6}$ **28.** $7\frac{1}{4} \div 3$ **29.** $4\frac{1}{2} \div 2\frac{7}{10}$ **30.** $3\frac{3}{8} \div 2\frac{1}{4}$

Problem Solving

Use the information below to solve Problems 31–33.

Amy and Jason decided to make some large puppets with red fronts and yellow backs. Each front takes $\frac{7}{8}$ yard of cloth, and each back takes $1\frac{1}{4}$ yards. They have $4\frac{2}{3}$ yards of red cloth and $5\frac{7}{8}$ yards of yellow cloth.

31. How many red puppet fronts can they make?

32. How many yellow backs can they make?

33. Analyze How many puppets can they make?

Kid Connection
Brandi Champion, a student from Maryland, makes and sells mop dolls. The money Brandi makes goes straight into the bank for her college education. ▼

Review and Remember

Using Algebra Follow or find the rule to complete each input/output table.

Rule: Subtract 11

	Input	Output
34.	91	■
35.	■	67
36.	119	■

37. Rule: _____?_____

	Input	Output
	24	40
38.	■	28
39.	309	■

For Extra Practice, see Set E, page 257.

Problem Solving
Solve a Simpler Problem

*Using simpler numbers can help
you solve more difficult problems.*

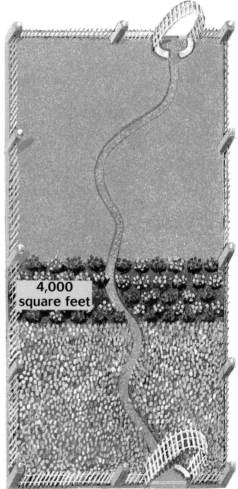

Erica's Lawn and Garden Service maintains the city park shown at the right. One half of the park is grass and one half is a flower garden. One fourth of the flower garden is roses. What is the area of the park?

 UNDERSTAND

What do you need to find?

You need to find the area of the park.

 PLAN

How can you solve the problem?

You can **solve a simpler problem**. Use simpler numbers to solve a similar problem.

 SOLVE

Roses take up 4,000 square feet. Since 4,000 is 4 × 1,000, use the simpler number 4 to represent the area covered by roses.

> 4,000
> square feet

One fourth of the flower garden is roses. So the total area of the flower garden is 4 times the area of the roses. The total flower-garden area can be represented by 4 × 4, or 16. Since the area of the flower garden is one half of the area of the park, the area of the park can be represented as 2 × 16, or 32.

The actual area of the park is 32 × 1,000, or 32,000 square feet.

 LOOK BACK

Why is it necessary to multiply 32 by 1,000 to find the actual area of the park?

Using the Strategy

Solve by using simpler numbers.

1. Erica is planting shrubs that will cover $\frac{1}{4}$ of each of three house lots. How many square feet of each lot will be covered with shrubs?

   Lot A: 28,000 square feet

   Lot B: 32,000 square feet

   Lot C: 36,000 square feet

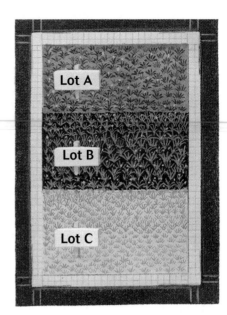

2. A roll of weed-blocking material was 480 square feet. If $\frac{1}{8}$ of the material was used on Mr. Jackson's landscaping, $\frac{1}{4}$ on Ms. Knight's landscaping, and $\frac{5}{8}$ on landscaping at the school, how many square feet of weed-blocking material was used at each location?

3. Erica had 3,600 tulip bulbs. She planted $\frac{2}{3}$ of the bulbs and donated $\frac{1}{2}$ of the remaining bulbs to the city. How many bulbs does she have left?

4. A parcel of land with an area of 24,000 square feet is to be divided into 3 lots. The first lot will take $\frac{2}{3}$ of the parcel. The area of the second lot will be equal to the area of the third lot. Find the area of each lot.

Mixed Strategy Review

Try these or other strategies to solve each problem.
Tell which strategy you used.

THERE'S ALWAYS A WAY!

Problem Solving Strategies

- Guess and Check
- Use Logical Reasoning
- Work Backwards
- Find a Pattern

5. **Predict** Ed used a pattern to plant six rows of mums. He made the first row 48 feet long, the second row 24 feet long, and the third row 12 feet long. What were the lengths of the fourth, fifth, and sixth rows?

6. One day Erica earned one half of her income weeding gardens, one fourth mowing lawns, and the rest planting shrubs. If she earned $30 planting shrubs, how much did she earn that day?

7. You have 75 daffodil and tulip bulbs. There are 23 more tulip than daffodil bulbs. How many tulip bulbs do you have?

Putting It All Together

*You can use more than
one method to multiply or divide fractions.*

Learning About It

You can use models, pencil and paper, or mental math to
multiply and divide fractions and mixed numbers. Sometimes
one way is easier to use than another.

THERE'S ALWAYS A WAY!

• **One way** to multiply or divide is to use models.

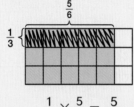

$$\frac{1}{3} \times \frac{5}{6} = \frac{5}{18}$$

$$2\frac{1}{2} \div \frac{1}{8} = 20$$

• **Another way** to multiply or divide is to use paper and pencil.

$$12\frac{1}{3} \times \frac{3}{4} = \frac{37}{\overset{1}{\cancel{3}}} \times \frac{\overset{1}{\cancel{3}}}{4} = \frac{37}{4} = 9\frac{1}{4}$$

$$\frac{2}{5} \div \frac{1}{6} = \frac{2}{5} \times \frac{6}{1} = \frac{12}{5} = 2\frac{2}{5}$$

• **Another way** is to use mental math.

$$\frac{5}{9} \times 27$$

$$27 \div 9 = 3$$
$$5 \times 3 = 15$$

So $\frac{5}{9} \times 27 = 15$.

$$9 \div \frac{1}{3}$$

$$9 \times 3 = 27$$

So $9 \div \frac{1}{3} = 27$.

Think and Discuss Which method would you choose for
$24\frac{1}{4} \div \frac{1}{4}$? for $5 \times 1\frac{1}{10}$?

Try It Out

Multiply or divide. Write each answer in simplest form.

1. $\frac{2}{3} \times 21$ **2.** $\frac{3}{4} \times 8 \times \frac{1}{16}$ **3.** $\frac{3}{20} \div \frac{3}{5}$ **4.** $4\frac{3}{4} \div 6\frac{1}{3}$

Practice

Multiply or divide. Write each answer in simplest form.

5. $\frac{2}{3} \times \frac{5}{6}$

6. $\frac{1}{8} \times 40$

7. $1\frac{1}{4} \times 3\frac{3}{5}$

8. $3\frac{1}{2} \times 2\frac{1}{3}$

9. $3 \div \frac{2}{3}$

10. $\frac{3}{8} \div \frac{1}{4}$

11. $8 \div 2\frac{1}{2}$

12. $3\frac{3}{4} \div 1\frac{1}{4}$

13. $19\frac{3}{4} \times 4\frac{2}{3}$

14. $4\frac{7}{8} \times 6\frac{4}{5}$

15. $6\frac{3}{4} \div 3$

16. $4\frac{4}{7} \times 3\frac{1}{8}$

17. $1\frac{2}{3} \div \frac{1}{6}$

18. $3\frac{3}{5} \times 5\frac{1}{2}$

19. $\frac{6}{7} \div 1\frac{1}{21}$

20. $8\frac{1}{2} \div 1\frac{1}{4}$

Problem Solving

**Use the graph to solve Problems 21–24.
Write each answer in simplest form.**

21. Jenny ran a pet-sitting service for two months during her school vacation. How many pets did she care for during the month of July? What fraction of that total was rabbits?

22. Jenny took care of 18 dogs over the two-month period. What fractional part of that number did she care for in July?

23. How many cats and rabbits did Jenny take care of in August? What fractional part of that total was rabbits?

24. **Analyze** How many animals did Jenny care for over the two-month period? What fractional part of that total was cats?

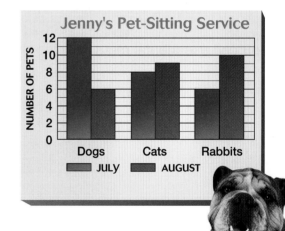

Jenny's Pet-Sitting Service

Review and Remember

Compute. Write each answer in simplest form.

25. $2\frac{1}{8} + 7\frac{5}{8}$

26. $12 - 4\frac{7}{9}$

27. $\frac{2}{3} + \frac{1}{2} + \frac{1}{4}$

28. $\frac{7}{8} \times \frac{1}{4}$

29. $18\frac{1}{8} + 5\frac{1}{6}$

30. $7\frac{5}{6} - 3\frac{5}{12}$

31. $3\frac{1}{4} \div 1\frac{1}{6}$

32. $3\frac{1}{4} \div \frac{5}{8}$

On the Shelf

Now that you can multiply and divide fractions,
you can use fractions to write and solve equations.

Learning About It

The Storytellers, Inc. dollmakers built display cases
for their figurines. Sue made the shelves for her
cases using 3 pieces of lumber. This was $\frac{3}{4}$ of the
lumber she had bought. How many pieces had
she bought?

You can write an equation to solve the problem.

$\frac{3}{4} \cdot x = 3$

> A centered dot can be used
> as a multiplication symbol.

You can use mental math to solve the equation.

$\frac{3}{4} \cdot x = 3$

$\frac{3}{4}$ times what number equals 3?

$\frac{3}{4} \cdot 4 = 3$

$x = 4$

Sue had bought
4 pieces of lumber.

$\frac{3}{4}$ of total
lumber bought

More Examples

Solve each equation.

A. $2 \cdot x = \frac{2}{3}$

$2 \cdot \text{?} = \frac{2}{3}$

$2 \cdot \frac{1}{3} = \frac{2}{3}$

$x = \frac{1}{3}$

B. $x \cdot \frac{1}{4} = 2$

$\text{?} \cdot \frac{1}{4} = 2$

$8 \cdot \frac{1}{4} = 2$

$x = 8$

C. $x \cdot 1\frac{1}{2} = 3$

$\text{?} \cdot 1\frac{1}{2} = 3$

$2 \cdot 1\frac{1}{2} = 3$

$x = 2$

Think and Discuss How could you check your solution to
an equation?

Try It Out

Solve. Write each answer in simplest form.

1. $\frac{2}{5} \cdot x = \frac{4}{5}$
2. $\frac{3}{4} \cdot x = \frac{3}{16}$
3. $\frac{6}{7} \cdot x = 6$
4. $\frac{3}{5} \cdot x = \frac{3}{10}$

Practice

Solve. Write each answer in simplest form.

5. $\frac{9}{14} \cdot x = 9$
6. $1\frac{1}{3} \cdot x = 4$
7. $\frac{4}{5} \cdot x = \frac{4}{25}$
8. $\frac{1}{6} \cdot x = \frac{1}{12}$

9. $\frac{2}{3} \cdot x = \frac{6}{9}$
10. $\frac{3}{5} \cdot x = \frac{3}{5}$
11. $\frac{5}{9} \cdot x = \frac{5}{27}$
12. $\frac{3}{16} \cdot x = \frac{3}{4}$

Problem Solving

13. It takes $\frac{3}{4}$ of an hour to bake a storyteller figurine. If only one figurine can be baked at a time, how many can be baked in 6 hours?

14. Karyn put 30 dolls on display. This was $1\frac{1}{2}$ times as many as she had last year. How many dolls did she have last year?

Review and Remember

Write each in words.

15. 11.54
16. 0.064
17. 14,700.01
18. 1.0005

Time for Technology
Using a Calculator

Multiplying Fractions and Decimals.

Joan sells apples for $1.24 a pound. Seth bought $5\frac{1}{2}$ pounds of apples. How much did Seth pay?

You can solve this problem by using a calculator.

Press: Display: 6.82

Solve, using a calculator.

1. $2\frac{4}{9} \times 3.79$

2. How much did Al pay for $9\frac{7}{8}$ pounds of turkey at $3.27 a pound?

For Extra Practice, see Set G, page 258.

Problem Solving
Using Fractions and Mixed Numbers

Fractions and mixed numbers can help you solve problems.

The Kid-Invest Company advises students on how to invest in the stock market. The company is recommending that you buy BP stock. How many shares can you buy for $247? How much will your stock be worth if the price goes up $\frac{1}{2}$ point ($0.50)?

STOCK TABLE		
Company	Price of One Share (in dollars)	Price Change From Yesterday (in dollars)
GSO	42 ¾	−1
TRP	25 ¼	+⅛
BP	9 ½	+½
CK	7 ¼	−¼
LGA	13	no change

▲ Stock prices are expressed with fractions instead of cents, so 42¾ means $42.75.

 UNDERSTAND

What do you need to know?

You need to know the price of one share of BP stock today.

INTERNET ACTIVITY
www.sbgmath.com

 PLAN

How can you solve the problem?

You can **write an equation** to find the number of shares you can buy. Then you can write another equation to find the value of those shares if the price goes up.

 SOLVE

First find out how many shares you can buy.	Then find the value of your shares if the price goes up.

$s = 247 \div 9\frac{1}{2}$

$s = 247 \div \frac{19}{2}$

$s = 247 \times \frac{2}{19} = 26$

You can buy 26 shares of BP stock.

$v = (9\frac{1}{2} + \frac{1}{2}) \times 26$

$v = 10 \times 26$

$v = 260$

Your stock will be worth $260.

LOOK BACK

What If? Suppose the stock dropped $\frac{1}{2}$ point instead of going up. What would your stock be worth?

Show What You Learned

Use the stock table on page 252 to solve Problems 1–8.

1 If you own 4 shares of GSO, what is it worth today?

2 **Using Estimation** About how many shares of CK stock could you buy for the cost of one share of GSO stock?

3 Which company had the greatest increase in the price of one share of stock from the previous day? Which company stock showed no change in price?

4 Lee bought $275 of stock today. He bought shares of LGA stock and CK stock. If he purchased 10 shares of LGA, how many shares of CK did he buy?

5 The Johnsons bought 30 shares of TRP stock last year at 29\frac{1}{2}$ per share. What is their stock worth now? How much money did they make or lose?

6 **Using Estimation** Kyle wants to buy 8 shares of GSO, 5 shares of BP, and 10 shares of LGA. Will $550 be enough to buy all the stock? Explain.

7 **Analyze** Yesterday the Kellers bought 18 shares of stock for $769.50. Which company's stock did they buy?

8 **You Decide** You sold 20 shares of GSO stock and will invest the money in two other companies. What stocks will you buy? Explain your choices.

▲ Tokyo, Japan

▲ London, England

▲ New York City, U.S.A.

Problem Solving

Practice What You Learned

Choose the correct letter for each answer.

1 Janine was cutting a 12-foot board into three-quarter-inch wide strips. How much of the board was left after she had cut 24 strips?

A. $9\frac{3}{4}$ ft

B. 10 ft

C. $10\frac{1}{2}$ ft

D. $11\frac{1}{4}$ ft

E. Not Here

Tip

Notice that the answer choices are in feet.

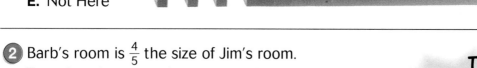

---

2 Barb's room is $\frac{4}{5}$ the size of Jim's room. Together the rooms have a combined area of 450 square feet. How large is the area of Jim's room?

A. 200 sq ft
B. 250 sq ft
C. 320 sq ft
D. 360 sq ft
E. Not Here

Tip

Try using the *Guess and Check* strategy to solve the problem.

---

3 To make a pattern for a quilt, Fred drew 3 lines on a rectangular piece of paper. One line divided the paper in half vertically, one line divided it in half horizontally, and one line was a diagonal. How many non-overlapping triangles did Fred get?

A. 2 triangles
B. 3 triangles
C. 6 triangles
D. 8 triangles
E. Not Here

Tip

Sketch a rectangle and draw the three lines to see what shapes result.

4 This graph shows how two groups of people spend their leisure time.

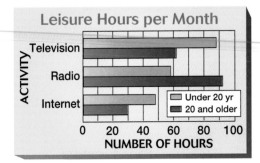

Leisure Hours per Month

ACTIVITY

Television
Radio
Internet

☐ Under 20 yr
■ 20 and older

0   20   40   60   80   100
NUMBER OF HOURS

About how many more hours per month do people aged 20 and older spend watching television than they spend on the Internet?

A. 25 h
B. 30 h
C. 35 h
D. 40 h
E. 60 h

5 Yolanda and Sid leave home at the same time. Yolanda drives at an average of 50 mph. Sid drives about 10 mph faster. Which is a reasonable distance for Yolanda to travel in $3\frac{1}{2}$ hours?

A. Less than 100 mi
B. About 125 mi
C. About 175 mi
D. About 200 mi
E. Not Here

6 Jim painted an ivy pattern on the kitchen wall. He put 3 leaves in the top row, 5 in the second row, and 7 in the third row. The next four rows had 11, 13, 15 and 19 leaves. If he continues this pattern, how many leaves will be in the **twelfth** row?

A. 23
B. 27
C. 31
D. 35
E. Not Here

7 An obtuse angle is greater than 90 degrees. On this street map, how many obtuse angles are there at the intersection of the 4 streets?

A. 2
B. 4
C. 5
D. 6
E. Not Here

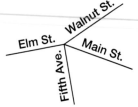

Elm St.
Walnut St.
Main St.
Fifth Ave.

8 Julie bought $10\frac{1}{2}$ lb of fruit. The apples weighed $4\frac{1}{8}$ lb. Which number sentence can be used to find the weight, w, of the other fruit?

A. $w = 10\frac{1}{2} + 4\frac{1}{8}$

B. $w = 10\frac{1}{2} \times 4\frac{1}{8}$

C. $w + 4\frac{1}{8} = 10\frac{1}{2}$

D. $w - 4\frac{1}{8} = 10\frac{1}{2}$

E. $w \times 4\frac{1}{8} = 10\frac{1}{2}$

9 Laura's, Gil's, and Matt's towns have these populations: 4,832; 3,397; 9,720. Which is the best estimate for the difference between the greatest and least populations?

A. 13,000   C. 7,000
B. 11,000   D. 5,000

10 John ran 1.6 miles in 12 minutes. Art ran twice as fast as John. Which expression shows how many minutes it took Art to run 1.6 miles?

A. 2×1.6 D. 12×2
B. $12 \div 1.6$ E. $12 \div 2$
C. $3.2 \div 12$

✓ Checkpoint
Dividing Fractions

Vocabulary

Fill in the blank with the correct word.

When dividing fractions, write each ___1.___ as an ___2.___ . Find the ___3.___ of the divisor and rewrite as a multiplication expression. Then look for ___4.___ and simplify.

Word Bank

denominators
common factors
improper fraction
numerators
mixed number
reciprocal

Concepts and Skills

Write the division sentence for each model. (pages 242-243)

5. How many $\frac{1}{4}$ pieces are shown?

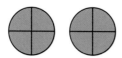

6. What part of the shaded piece is each section?

Write the reciprocal. (pages 242-243)

7. $\frac{4}{3}$ 8. $\frac{9}{10}$ 9. 3   10. $\frac{1}{21}$ 11. $\frac{8}{5}$ 12. 7

Write an equivalent multiplication expression and then multiply. (pages 242-243)

13. $\frac{2}{3} \div \frac{2}{3}$ 14. $8 \div \frac{6}{7}$ 15. $\frac{3}{4} \div \frac{1}{4}$ 16. $\frac{7}{10} \div \frac{14}{15}$

17. $\frac{3}{8} \div 9$ 18. $\frac{4}{5} \div \frac{2}{5}$ 19. $\frac{9}{10} \div \frac{3}{5}$ 20. $\frac{3}{8} \div 3$

Divide. Write each answer in simplest form. (pages 244-245)

21. $4\frac{4}{5} \div 6$ 22. $6\frac{1}{2} \div 3\frac{1}{4}$ 23. $12 \div 3\frac{3}{4}$ 24. $\frac{7}{8} \div 3\frac{3}{4}$

25. $1\frac{1}{8} \div 6\frac{3}{4}$ 26. $\frac{3}{5} \div 1\frac{1}{5}$ 27. $9\frac{3}{7} \div 4\frac{1}{2}$ 28. $3\frac{3}{4} \div 12$

Using Algebra Solve. Write each answer in simplest form. (pages 250-251)

29. $\frac{10}{7} \cdot x = 1$ 30. $x \cdot 1\frac{1}{5} = 6$ 31. $x \cdot \frac{4}{9} = \frac{2}{9}$ 32. $\frac{5}{8} \cdot x = \frac{1}{6}$

Problem Solving

33. Kevin uses $\frac{5}{8}$ yard of material to make one puppet. How many puppets can he make from 15 yards of material?

34. To make 11 puppets, Gloria used $5\frac{1}{2}$ yards of material. How much material did she use for each puppet?

35. Liam was paid $5\frac{1}{4}$ cents mileage pay for every mile he traveled over 25 miles. Last week he traveled $33\frac{4}{10}$ miles. How much mileage pay did he receive? Tell which strategy you used to solve the problem.

What do you think?

When you divide a whole number by a fraction less than 1, is the quotient greater than or less than the whole number? Explain.

Journal Idea

Write the steps you follow when dividing fractions. Include examples using fractions and mixed numbers.

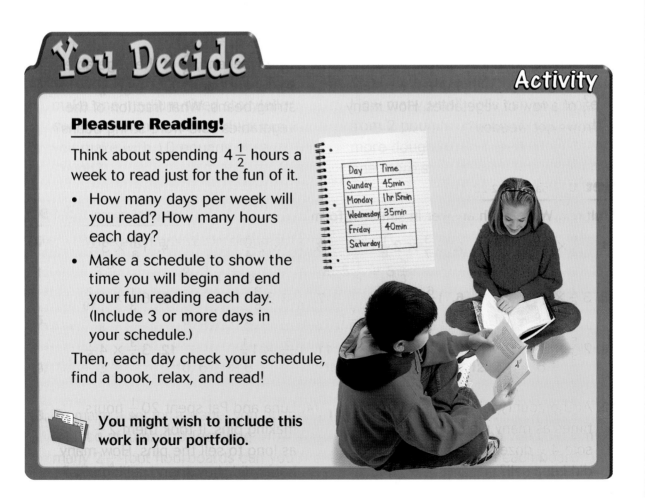

You Decide

Activity

Pleasure Reading!

Think about spending $4\frac{1}{2}$ hours a week to read just for the fun of it.

- How many days per week will you read? How many hours each day?

Day	Time
Sunday	45min
Monday	1hr 15min
Wednesday	35min
Friday	40min
Saturday	

- Make a schedule to show the time you will begin and end your fun reading each day. (Include 3 or more days in your schedule.)

Then, each day check your schedule, find a book, relax, and read!

You might wish to include this work in your portfolio.

Extra Practice

Set F (pages 248–249)

Multiply or divide. Write each answer in simplest form.

1. $\frac{6}{7} \times 9\frac{1}{3}$

2. $1\frac{5}{8} \times 4$

3. $9\frac{1}{5} \div 6$

4. $\frac{3}{4} \times 1\frac{3}{7}$

5. $8\frac{1}{2} \div 4$

6. $2\frac{2}{3} \div 6\frac{2}{5}$

7. $6\frac{3}{4} \div \frac{1}{8}$

8. $3\frac{1}{3} \times 6\frac{2}{7}$

9. $3\frac{3}{5} \times \frac{5}{9}$

10. $5\frac{3}{5} \div \frac{1}{5}$

11. $2\frac{1}{8} \times 3\frac{3}{7}$

12. $10 \div 2\frac{1}{4}$

13. $6\frac{2}{3} \times 2\frac{1}{5}$

14. $1\frac{1}{4} \div \frac{1}{8}$

15. $4 \div 1\frac{1}{9}$

16. $12 \times 2\frac{3}{4}$

17. Each puppet show was to run for $1\frac{1}{8}$ hours, which includes a rest period. How many shows could the students perform in $4\frac{1}{2}$ hours?

18. Kayla walks dogs to earn extra money. She walks $2\frac{1}{4}$ miles every day. How many miles did she walk altogether in 7 days?

Set G (pages 250-251)

Using Algebra **Solve each equation. Check your solution.**

1. $x \cdot \frac{1}{3} = \frac{4}{3}$

2. $2 \cdot x = \frac{2}{3}$

3. $\frac{1}{4} \cdot x = \frac{1}{8}$

4. $x \cdot \frac{1}{5} = \frac{2}{15}$

5. $\frac{2}{3} \cdot x = \frac{1}{9}$

6. $4 \cdot x = \frac{2}{3}$

7. $3 \cdot x = 1\frac{1}{5}$

8. $2\frac{1}{4} \cdot x = 1\frac{1}{8}$

9. $\frac{4}{7} \cdot x = \frac{1}{7}$

10. $\frac{3}{4} \cdot x = \frac{3}{20}$

11. $x \cdot \frac{3}{10} = \frac{3}{5}$

12. $x \cdot \frac{1}{6} = \frac{2}{9}$

13. $\frac{5}{9} \cdot x = 10$

14. $\frac{2}{7} \cdot x = 2$

15. $x \cdot 3 = \frac{1}{3}$

16. $x \cdot \frac{5}{8} = 40$

Using Algebra **Write an equation. Then solve.**

17. Steve wanted to make shelves for his room. If each shelf is to be $\frac{1}{2}$ foot long, how long a board does he need to make 10 shelves?

18. Colleen used 12 of her dolls in storytelling programs this week. This is $\frac{3}{4}$ of the total number of dolls she has. How many dolls does she have?

 **Chapter Test**

Complete each sentence.

1. Two fractions whose product is 1 are known as ___?___.

2. Numbers that are easy to compute mentally are ___?___ numbers.

Multiply. Write each answer in simplest form.

3. $\frac{2}{5} \times \frac{2}{3}$

4. $\frac{3}{4} \times \frac{4}{9}$

5. $\frac{3}{4} \times \frac{8}{9}$

6. $\frac{7}{8} \times \frac{5}{7}$

7. $\frac{2}{9} \times \frac{3}{4}$

8. $1\frac{1}{8} \times 2\frac{1}{3}$

9. $3\frac{3}{4} \times 2\frac{2}{5}$

10. $3\frac{4}{7} \times 4\frac{1}{5}$

Use rounding or compatible numbers to estimate.

11. $\frac{4}{7} \times 48$

12. $\frac{9}{10} \times 19$

13. $3\frac{6}{7} \times 2\frac{4}{5}$

14. $3\frac{1}{5} \times 7\frac{7}{8}$

Divide. Write each answer in simplest form.

15. $2 \div \frac{1}{8}$

16. $\frac{7}{8} \div \frac{5}{16}$

17. $2\frac{2}{9} \div 2\frac{4}{9}$

18. $\frac{3}{4} \div 1\frac{1}{2}$

19. $4\frac{1}{3} \div 6\frac{1}{2}$

20. $5 \div \frac{1}{5}$

21. $2\frac{2}{5} \div 3\frac{3}{5}$

22. $16\frac{2}{3} \div 2\frac{7}{9}$

Solve.

23. Yolanda made lemonade to sell at the county fair. On the first day she made 40 pitchers of lemonade. How many ounces of lemonade did she make?

24. How many glasses could Yolanda fill from one pitcher of lemonade?

$62\frac{1}{2}$ oz $8\frac{1}{3}$ oz

25. Rick sold peanuts at the lemonade stand. Each bag of peanuts weighed $\frac{1}{4}$ pound. How many bags could he fill from a 48-pound sack of peanuts?

 Self-Check

Which lesson in this chapter was the easiest for you? Which gave you the most trouble? Tell what you might do to improve in the areas that gave you trouble.

Performance Assessment

Show What You Know About Fractions

1 Study the grid on the right. Then answer each question.

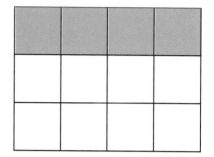

a. What part of the whole is $\frac{1}{2}$ of the shaded region?

b. Which region is bigger: $\frac{3}{4}$ of the shaded region or $\frac{1}{2}$ of the unshaded region?

c. Write a problem that could be solved using the grid.

d. Write a division sentence to show how many $\frac{1}{2}$ pieces are in $1\frac{1}{2}$.

Self-Check Did you recognize that the region is divided into 12 equal parts?

2 The Booster Club is planning to make school pennants and sell them at school sporting events. Each pennant will require $\frac{3}{8}$ of a yard of material. The club purchased 24 yards of material.

a. How many pennants can they make?

b. The material costs $3.50 a yard. What was the cost of the material?

c. If the club charges $1.75 for each pennant, how much profit, if any, will be earned?

Self-Check Does your answer to how many pennants can be made make sense?

 For Your Portfolio

You might wish to include this work in your portfolio.

Extension

A Range of Estimates

You can write an estimate as a single number or as a range. To find a range for your estimate, choose two compatible numbers—one that is less than the actual number and one that is greater.

In one month Liam made 21 deliveries from a grocery store to a lunch stand. On each delivery he traveled about $\frac{5}{6}$ mile. About how far did he travel to make the deliveries?

$$\frac{5}{6} \times 21 = \blacksquare$$

Use two compatible numbers to find a range.

$\frac{5}{6} \times 21$

$\frac{5}{6} \times 18 = 5 \times 3 = 15$

$\frac{5}{6} \times 21$

$\frac{5}{6} \times 24 = 5 \times 4 = 20$

Liam traveled between 15 and 20 miles on his deliveries.

Choose the best range of estimates. Write a, b, or c.

1. $\frac{2}{3} \times 77$

   a. 25 to 26

   b. 75 to 78

   c. 50 to 52

2. $\frac{5}{8} \times 236$

   a. 145 to 150

   b. 29 to 30

   c. 230 to 240

3. $\frac{1}{4} \times 39$

   a. 9 to 10

   b. 30 to 40

   c. 3 to 9

4. $\frac{1}{15} \times 459$

   a. 225 to 240

   b. 450 to 465

   c. 30 to 31

5. $\frac{3}{20} \times 711$

   a. 700 to 720

   b. 105 to 108

   c. 75 to 90

6. $\frac{6}{7} \times 50$

   a. 42 to 48

   b. 160 to 180

   c. 30 to 60

Using Math in Science

***Calculate** the volume
of regular and irregular solids.*

Getting in Shape

You are packing a wooden crate with objects for shipping. You have two objects left to pack. One is a rectangular prism made of marble. The other is a piece of pyrite, an irregularly shaped rock. You must find out which object has less volume. Volume is the amount of space an object takes up.

What You Need

For each group:
    small rock (or other irregularly
        shaped object)
    measuring cup, marked in
        metric units
    container of water
    paper towel

Explore

Step 1 Make a chart like the one below. You will record all your data in this chart.

Finding Volume of Solids	
Regular Solid	
$V = l \times w \times h = 4 \times 2 \times 6 =$ _____	
Irregular Solid	
Estimate	_____ cm^3
Volume of water	_____ mL
Water Level (water + rock)	_____ mL
Difference in Water Levels	_____ mL
Volume of Rock	_____ cm^3

Step 2 The regular solid at the right is a rectangular prism. You can find its volume by multiplying its length (*l*) by its width (*w*) by its height (*h*). Use the dimensions of this rectangular prism to find its volume. Record the volume in your chart in cubic centimeters (cm^3).

Step 3 A rock is an irregular solid. Notice that, unlike the regular prism, your rock has no easily measured dimensions. Compare the size of your rock to the size of the rectangular prism. Estimate the volume of your rock. Record this estimate in your chart.

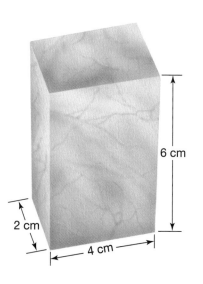

6 cm

2 cm

4 cm

Step 4 Pour about 300 mL of water into a measuring cup. Read the level of the water on the scale of the cup. This is the volume of the water. Record this volume in your chart.

Step 5 *Carefully* place the rock in the water in the measuring cup, as shown in the picture. Avoid splashing. As the rock sinks, it displaces, or pushes aside, some of the water. What effect does this have on the level of the water in the cup?

Step 6 Now record the level of the water with the rock at the bottom of the measuring cup. This is the combined volume of the water and the rock.

Step 7 You can determine the volume of an irregular solid by finding out how much water the object displaces. To find this number, calculate the difference between the measurements you recorded in Steps 4 and 6. Record this difference in the chart you just made.

Step 8 Using the fact that 1 cm^3 is equal to 1 mL, find the volume of your rock in cm^3. Record this information in the chart.

Analyze

1. How did the actual volume of your rock compare with your estimate?

2. Which has a greater volume—the rock or the rectangular prism?

3. If you used water displacement to calculate the volume of the rectangular prism, what would its volume be in mL?

For Your Portfolio

Write about your results. Explain in your own words what volume is and how it is calculated. Tell if the results of your experiment surprised you. Explain why or why not.

Explore Further!

Hypothesize Volume can also be used to express capacity—how much material something can hold. A 1-quart milk carton has a length of 7 cm, a width of 7 cm, and a height of 24 cm. What is its volume? Use what you know about volume to hypothesize how much milk the container can hold if it is filled to the top. Design an experiment to test your hypothesis.

Cumulative Review

★ ★ ★ ★ ★ **Preparing for Tests**

Choose the correct letter for each answer.

Number Concepts	Operations

Number Concepts

1. Which fraction is equivalent to $\frac{12}{40}$?

A. $\frac{3}{5}$

B. $\frac{4}{10}$

C. $\frac{1}{3}$

D. $\frac{3}{10}$

2. Which number is the least common multiple of 6 and 15?

A. 3
B. 21
C. 30
D. 60

3. What decimal number does this model represent?

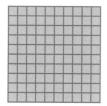 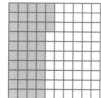

A. 0.143
B. 1.143
C. 1.43
D. 14.3

4. Which is the greatest common factor of 75 and 100?

A. 5   C. 25
B. 15   D. 50

Operations

5. Lee earns $15 per yard for mowing lawns and $5 per yard for trimming bushes. If Lee mows 3 yards and trims the bushes at 2 of them, how much money will she earn?

A. $45   D. $60
B. $50   E. $65
C. $55

6. Meg's family planted a vegetable garden. One fourth of the garden was planted in tomatoes. The rest of the garden was divided equally between peas and carrots. How much of the garden space was planted with peas?

A. $\frac{3}{8}$ C. $\frac{2}{3}$

B. $\frac{1}{2}$ D. $\frac{3}{4}$

7. What is the sum of 3.45, 0.678, and 0.091?

A. 42.190   D. 1.114
B. 11.140   E. 0.769
C. 4.219

8. Ralph can type about 48 words per minute. Which is the best estimate of how many words he can type in a half hour?

A. 120   D. 1,500
B. 150   E. 3,000
C. 1,200

Patterns, Relationships, and Algebraic Thinking	Measurement

9. The ratio of dogs to cats at a kennel is exactly 4 to 5. How many of each animal are at the kennel if the total number of animals is 36?

    A. 8 dogs, 10 cats
    B. 16 dogs, 20 cats
    C. 18 dogs, 18 cats
    D. 20 dogs, 16 cats

---

10. If $\frac{x}{y} = \frac{5}{6}$, what is y when $x = 30$?

    A. 25
    B. 36
    C. 150
    D. 180
    E. 300

---

11. Which number is missing from this pattern?

    . . . , 2, 7, 22, 67, ■, . . .

    A. 71
    B. 201
    C. 202
    D. 204
    E. 268

---

12. The following points are plotted on a coordinate plane.

    (0, 0), (1, 2), (2, 4), (3, 6)

    If the same pattern is continued, which would be the next point plotted?

    A. (3, 7)
    B. (4, 7)
    C. (4, 8)
    D. (4, 10)

13. Robert has a box 9 inches long by 5 inches wide by 3 inches deep. What is the *volume* of the box?

    A. 135 in.^{3}
    B. 60 in.^{3}
    C. 45 in.^{3}
    D. 27 in.^{3}
    E. 15 in.^{3}

---

14. What is the *area* in square yards of a platform that measures 9 feet by 30 feet? (1 yd = 3 ft)

    A. 300 yd^2
    B. 90 yd^2
    C. 30 yd^2
    D. 10 yd^2
    E. 3 yd^2

---

15. Carol's bedroom rug covers 48 square feet of her floor. The rug is 72 inches wide. How many *feet* long is the rug?

    A. 2 ft
    B. 4 ft
    C. 6 ft
    D. 8 ft
    E. 96 ft

---

16. A jar holds 5.50 L of water. How many milliliters is this? (1 L = 1,000 mL)

    A. 0.0055 mL
    B. 0.0550 mL
    C. 550 mL
    D. 5,500 mL

Chapter 7 Measurement

Chapter Theme: SPORTS

Real Facts

It's a home run! One of the most exciting events in baseball is when a player hits a ball out of the park. But the distance required for a home run varies depending on whether you hit the ball to left field, center field, or right field. The player on the right hopes for a home run at the Little League World Series in Williamsport, PA. The bar graph shows the distance required to hit a home run.

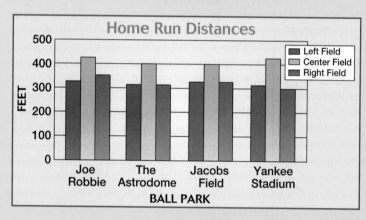

Home Run Distances

- Which field is probably the hardest to hit a home run to—left field, center field, or right field? Explain.

- About how much longer is the average center-field home run than the average left-field home run?

Real People

Meet Dave Fanucchi. He keeps the baseball statistics for the St. Louis Cardinals. Each time a player steals a base, makes a hit, scores a run, or makes an error, Dave writes down numbers that become part of baseball history.

Everybody's Racket

*Understanding how customary units of length are related
helps you change a measure from one unit to another.*

Learning About It

The drawing at the right shows the dimensions of a
regulation tennis court. The court measures 36 feet
by 78 feet or 12 yards by 26 yards.

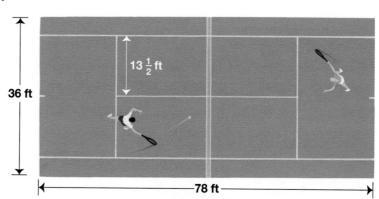

Customary Units of Length

1 foot (ft) = 12 inches (in.)
1 yard (yd) = 36 inches
1 yard = 3 feet
1 mile (mi) = 5,280 feet
1 mile = 1,760 yards

To change from a smaller to a larger unit of length, divide.

78 ft = ▓ yd
78 ÷ 3 = 26   (3 ft = 1 yd)
78 ft = 26 yd

To change from a larger to a smaller unit of length, multiply.

5 yd = ▓ in.
5 × 36 = 180   (1 yd = 36 in.)
5 yd = 180 in.

More Examples

A. 9 yd 2 ft = ▓ in.
(9 × 36) + (2 × 12) = 348   (1 yd = 36 in. / 1 ft = 12 in.)
9 yd 2 ft = 348 in.

B. 378 in. = ▓ ft
378 ÷ 12 = 31 R6
378 in. = 31 ft 6 in., or $31\frac{1}{2}$ ft

Think and Discuss Would it be reasonable to say that
$1\frac{1}{2}$ miles is about 8,000 feet? Explain your reasoning.

Try It Out

Complete.

1. 108 in. = ▓ ft

2. 96 ft = ▓ yd

3. 144 in. = ▓ yd

4. $4\frac{1}{3}$ yd = ▓ ft

5. 3 mi = ▓ yd

6. 10,560 ft = ▓ mi

Practice

Choose the most reasonable unit of measure for the length of each item. Write *in., ft, yd,* or *mi.*

7. pencil

8. tennis racket

9. distance the ball is hit

10. scoreboard

11. score card

12. distance from home to a park

Estimate. Then use a ruler to measure to the nearest inch.

13. width of a door

14. length of a shoe

15. thickness of a textbook

16. length of a pencil

17. height of a chair

18. length of your hand

Choose a Method **Use mental math, paper and pencil, or a calculator to complete. Tell which method you used.**

19. 60 in. = ▨ ft

20. 20 ft = ▨ yd

21. 144 in. = ▨ ft

22. 4,400 yd = ▨ mi

23. 15 ft = ▨ in.

24. 17 ft = ▨ yd

25. 2 yd = ▨ in.

26. 48 in. = ▨ yd ▨ ft

27. $2\frac{1}{3}$ yd = ▨ ft

28. $3\frac{1}{2}$ ft = ▨ in.

29. $\frac{3}{4}$ yd = ▨ in.

30. 5 yd 2 ft = ▨ in.

Problem Solving

31. A tennis ball bounces about 55 inches high when it is dropped from a height of 100 inches onto a hard surface. About how many feet high does it bounce?

32. The width of a tennis court for a doubles game is 36 ft. If the length of the back court is half this width, what is the length of the back court in yards?

33. Analyze The width of each of the two service courts is $13\frac{1}{2}$ feet. The entire tennis court is 36 ft wide. How many inches wider is this than the width of both service courts?

Russian tennis player
Anna Kournikova ▼

Review and Remember

Estimate first. Then use a calculator to find each answer.

34. 4,898 ÷ 62

35. 168 × $\frac{3}{4}$

36. 1,978 + 98

37. 4,529 − 888

38. $4\frac{5}{8} + 5\frac{1}{40}$

39. 5,000 × 0.078

Having a Ball

The ounce, pound, and ton are related measures of weight in the customary system.

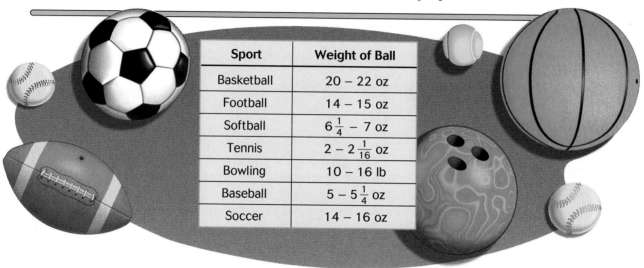

Sport	Weight of Ball
Basketball	20 – 22 oz
Football	14 – 15 oz
Softball	$6\frac{1}{4}$ – 7 oz
Tennis	$2 - 2\frac{1}{16}$ oz
Bowling	10 – 16 lb
Baseball	$5 - 5\frac{1}{4}$ oz
Soccer	14 – 16 oz

Learning About It

The design of a ball that is used in a sport depends on how the sport is played. The size and weight of a basketball make it easy to bounce, pass, and shoot. A 20-ounce basketball weighs $1\frac{1}{4}$ pounds.

> **Customary Units of Weight**
>
> 1 pound (lb) = 16 ounces (oz)
> 1 ton (T) = 2,000 pounds

To change from a smaller to a larger unit of weight, divide.

20 oz = ■ lb   (16 oz = 1 lb)
20 ÷ 16 = 1 R4
20 oz = 1 lb 4 oz, or $1\frac{1}{4}$ lb

To change from a larger to a smaller unit of weight, multiply.

$1\frac{1}{4}$ T = ■ lb   (1 T = 2,000 lb)
$1\frac{1}{4} \times 2,000 = \frac{5}{4} \times 2,000 = 2,500$

Think and Discuss How could you find the number of pounds in $\frac{1}{4}$ T?

Try It Out

Complete.

1. 48 oz = ■ lb

2. 2 lb = ■ oz

3. 6 T = ■ lb

4. 5,000 lb = ■ T

5. $10\frac{1}{2}$ lb = ■ oz

6. $\frac{1}{8}$ lb = ■ oz

Practice

Write oz, lb, or T for the most reasonable unit of measure.

7. football player

8. sand for the infield

9. table tennis ball

Complete.

10. 8 lb = ▨ oz

11. $1\frac{1}{2}$ lb = ▨ oz

12. 5 T = ▨ lb

13. 6,000 lb = ▨ T

14. 80 oz = ▨ lb

15. 4.5 lb = ▨ oz

Problem Solving

Use the chart on page 268 to solve Problems 16–17.

16. What is the maximum shipping charge for 20 softballs if the charge is $0.50 for each pound and $0.30 for any extra fraction of a pound?

17. Using Estimation About how many footballs equal the weight of the heaviest bowling ball? Describe your reasoning.

Review and Remember

List all the factors of each. Then write *prime* or *composite*.

18. 12

19. 19

20. 49

21. 40

22. 79

23. 13

Time for Technology

Using a Calculator

Using the Memory Keys

Find the total weight of a shipment of six 14-oz footballs and five 22-oz basketballs.

Step 1 Press: (6) (×) (1) (4) (=) (M+) to find and store the total weight of the footballs.

Step 2 Press: (5) (×) (2) (2) (=) (M+) to find the total weight of the basketballs and add it to the weight of the footballs in memory.

Step 3 Press: (MR) to display the weight of the shipment.

Now use the memory keys to find the weight of a shipment with half as many footballs and twice as many basketballs.

Race to the Finish

*You can use customary units of capacity
to describe how much a container can hold.*

Learning About It

During a marathon, volunteers passed out
21 quarts of water at one station. This is
the same as 42 pints, or 5 gallons 1 quart.

Customary Units of Capacity

1 cup (c) = 8 fluid ounces (fl oz)
1 pint (pt) = 2 cups
1 quart (qt) = 2 pints
1 gallon (gal) = 4 quarts

21 qts
42 pt
5 gal 1 qt

To change from a smaller to a larger unit of capacity, divide.	To change from a larger to a smaller unit of capacity, multiply.

21 qt = ■ gal   (4 qt = 1 gal)
21 ÷ 4 = 5 R1
21 qt = 5 gal 1 qt, or $5\frac{1}{4}$ gal

21 qt = ■ pt   (1 qt = 2 pt)
21 × 2 = 42
21 qt = 42 pt

More Examples

A. 56 fl oz = ■ pt   (8 fl oz = 1 c)
      (16 fl oz = 2 c = 1 pt)
56 ÷ 16 = 3 R8
56 fl oz = 3 pt 8 fl oz, or 3 pt 1 c,
      or $3\frac{1}{2}$ pt

B. 3 gal = ■ pt   (1 gal = 4 qt)
      (1 qt = 2 pt)
3 × 8 = 24   (1 gal = 8 pt)
3 gal = 24 pt

Think and Discuss Explain how you could change
6 gallons to fluid ounces.

Try It Out

Complete.

1. 24 fl oz = ■ c   **2.** 5 gal = ■ qt   **3.** 12 pt = ■ qt

4. 2 qt = ■ c   **5.** 32 pt = ■ gal   **6.** 9 qt = ■ gal

Practice

Choose the most reasonable unit of measure for each capacity. Write *fl oz, c, pt, qt,* or *gal.*

7. fish tank

8. drinking straw

9. bottle of juice

10. coffee mug

11. medicine dropper

12. swimming pool

Choose a Method Use paper and pencil, mental math, or a calculator to complete. Tell which method you used.

13. 7 gal = ▧ qt

14. 6 pt = ▧ c

15. 48 fl oz = ▧ c

16. 36 qt = ▧ gal

17. 16 c = ▧ pt

18. 9 c = ▧ fl oz

19. 7 c = ▧ qt

20. 5 qt = ▧ gal

21. 16 pt = ▧ gal

22. $2\frac{1}{2}$ gal = ▧ qt

23. $3\frac{1}{2}$ pt = ▧ fl oz

24. 16 c = ▧ gal

25. 16 qt = ▧ gal

26. 2 c = ▧ qt

27. 3 pt = ▧ fl oz

Problem Solving

28. How much is saved by buying one gallon of juice for $4.99 instead of four quarts of juice for $1.39 a quart?

29. What is the difference in price per fluid ounce between juice in a 1 pt 4 oz bottle at $0.78 and a 10 oz bottle at $0.49?

30. Name an object that could have each capacity.

    a. 6 fl oz   **b.** 15 gal   **c.** 2 qt

31. Create Your Own Write a problem about capacity that requires changing units of measure. Exchange problems with a partner and solve.

Review and Remember

Add, subtract, multiply, or divide.

32. $\frac{1}{2} + \frac{1}{3}$

33. $\frac{2}{5} - \frac{1}{6}$

34. $0.12 \div 0.3$

35. $\frac{9}{10} \times \frac{1}{5}$

36. $100 \div 2.5$

37. $4\frac{1}{3} \times \frac{1}{6}$

38. $4{,}003 - 403$

39. $9\frac{5}{7} + 3\frac{2}{21}$

40. 0.125×0.5

41. $3\frac{3}{4} \div \frac{1}{8}$

▼ Jean Driscoll participates in the 100th Boston Marathon.

For Extra Practice, see Set C, page 293.

Developing Skills for Problem Solving

Sometimes you need an exact answer.
Sometimes an estimate is enough.

READ FOR UNDERSTANDING

Jonah is at a baseball game when the notice at the right flashes on the stadium video screen. He knows that he can't count all the people in the stadium. Looking around, he sees that the stadium is about $\frac{2}{3}$ full. The seating capacity, or the number of seats in the stadium, is shown on the seating plan below.

GUESS TODAY'S
ATTENDANCE
PICK ONE:

24,189
33,619
11,822
17,010

1. How many seats are in the stadium?

2. About how full is the stadium?

THINK AND DISCUSS

MATH FOCUS

Exact or Estimated Data Exact data represents an amount that can be counted. Estimated data represents an amount that has been rounded or that cannot be counted or measured.

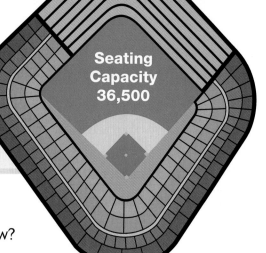

Seating Capacity 36,500

Reread the paragraph at the top of the page.

3. Is the stadium exactly $\frac{2}{3}$ full? How do you know?

4. Will the figure for today's attendance be exact or estimated? Explain your reasoning.

5. If Jonah uses the number of seats in the stadium and his estimate that the stadium is about $\frac{2}{3}$ full, is it likely that his answer will match one of the four choices? Why or why not?

6. When solving problems, why is it important to know if data is exact or estimated?

Show What You Learned

Use the prices shown at the right to answer Problems 1–6. Give a reason for your choice.

TICKET PRICES
Bleachers $5.50
Grandstand $7.50
Box seats $14.50

REFRESHMENTS
Hot dogs $3.00
Juice $1.50
Peanuts $2.00

SOUVENIRS
Pennants $5.00
Program $3.00
Baseball $5.00

Martha's mother is taking Martha and a friend to a baseball game. She plans to buy box seats and 3 programs. She knows that they will each have some refreshments. She also plans to buy each of the young people a souvenir. She is trying to decide how much money to take to the game.

1. Should Martha's mother use an estimated amount or an exact amount to decide?
   a. Exact; she knows the prices of the tickets and programs.
   b. Estimated; she does not know exactly how much she will spend.
   c. Exact; she knows exactly what she will buy.

2. Which best describes how many programs Martha's mother plans to buy?
   a. Less than 3
   b. Exactly 3
   c. More than 3

3. Which data in the paragraph and in the price information at the top of the page is exact? Which data is estimated? Tell how you know.

Ms. Gomez and the 23 students in her class will use their bake sale profits to go to a baseball game. Ms. Gomez has to order 24 grandstand tickets and rent a bus. The bus rental will be $88, and each student will have $4.00 for spending money.

4. Which of the following is exact information?
   a. 24 tickets must be ordered.
   b. The bus rental costs $88.
   c. Both of the above

5. **Explain** The expression 8.00×25 can be used to show that the cost of $200 for tickets is an estimate. Why?

6. **Describe** List the exact data that must be used to calculate the total cost of the trip. Then find the total cost of the trip.

A Long Jump

In this lesson you will learn to add, subtract, multiply, and divide with customary units.

Learning About It

In 1994, Jackie Joyner-Kersee set the U.S. national record with a jump of 24 feet 7 inches.

In 1995, Fiona May of Italy won the long-jump event in the Women's World Track and Field Championship with a jump of 22 feet 11 inches. Fiona May's jump was shorter than Jackie Joyner-Kersee's record jump by 1 foot 8 inches.

$$
\begin{array}{r}
24 \text{ ft} \quad 7 \text{ in.} \\
- \ 22 \text{ ft } 11 \text{ in.}
\end{array}
$$

Rename before subtracting.
24 ft = 23 ft 12 in.

$$
\begin{array}{r}
23 \text{ ft } 19 \text{ in.} \\
- \ 22 \text{ ft } 11 \text{ in.} \\
\hline
1 \text{ ft} \quad 8 \text{ in.}
\end{array}
$$

7 in. + 12 in. = 19 in.

More Examples

A.
$$
\begin{array}{r}
5 \text{ lb} \quad 9 \text{ oz} \\
+ \ 3 \text{ lb} \quad 8 \text{ oz} \\
\hline
8 \text{ lb } 17 \text{ oz} = 9 \text{ lb } 1 \text{ oz}
\end{array}
$$

B.
$$2\overline{)5 \text{ yd } 1 \text{ ft}}$$
5 yd 1 ft = 4 yd 4 ft
$$2\overline{)4 \text{ yd } 4 \text{ ft}} \ = 2 \text{ yd } 2 \text{ ft}$$

C.
$$
\begin{array}{r}
2 \text{ gal } 1 \text{ qt} \\
\times \qquad 5 \\
\hline
10 \text{ gal } 5 \text{ qt} = 11 \text{ gal } 1 \text{ qt}
\end{array}
$$

D.
$$
\begin{array}{r}
7 \text{ yd } 1\frac{1}{2} \text{ ft} \\
- \ 5 \text{ yd } 2\frac{1}{4} \text{ ft}
\end{array}
$$
7 yd = 6 yd 3 ft
$$
\begin{array}{r}
6 \text{ yd } 4\frac{1}{2} \text{ ft} \\
- \ 5 \text{ yd } 2\frac{1}{4} \text{ ft} \\
\hline
1 \text{ yd } 2\frac{1}{4} \text{ ft}
\end{array}
$$

Think and Discuss Suppose you want to divide a recipe in half. Show how you could find half of $6\frac{1}{4}$ c.

Try It Out

Compute.

1. 30 ft   9 in.
    − 26 ft 11 in.

2. 8 qt 1 pt
    + 2 qt 1 pt

3. 6 ft 3 in.
    ×   5

4. $3\overline{)15\text{ lb }9\text{ oz}}$

Practice

Add, subtract, multiply, or divide.

5. 20 lb 5 oz
    − 8 lb 9 oz

6. 9 yd 2 ft
    + 8 yd 2 ft

7. 6 ft
    − 4 ft 5 in.

8. 3 c 7 fl oz
    + 4 c 6 fl oz

9. $4\overline{)16\text{ lb }8\text{ oz}}$

10. $5\overline{)21\text{ yd }2\text{ ft}}$

11. 3 pt ÷ 2

12. 6 ft 3 in. ÷ 5

13. 3 × 6 ft 4 in.

14. $1\frac{1}{4}$ c ÷ 5

15. $2\frac{1}{2}$ ft ÷ 5

16. 5 × 2 c 4 fl oz

17. 5 ft 6 in.
    ×   2

18. 5 c 6 fl oz
    ×   2

19. 4 gal 1 qt
    + 5 gal 2 qt

20. 7 pt
    − 6 pt 1 c

21. 6 lb 4 oz
    ×   6

22. 11 lb 9 oz
    − 9 lb 4 oz

23. 1 mi
    − 500 yd

24. 2 gal 1 qt
    ×   4

Problem Solving

Use the table to solve Problems 25–28.

25. Which gold medalist jumped the greatest distance?

26. What is the difference between the greatest and the least distance jumped?

27. What is the difference between Carl Lewis's 1984 jump and his 1996 jump?

28. For which two consecutive Olympics did the long jump distance change the most?

Olympic Long Jump Champions

Year	Name	Distance
1968	Bob Beamon	29 ft $2\frac{1}{2}$ in.
1972	Randy Williams	27 ft $\frac{1}{2}$ in.
1976	Arnie Robinson	27 ft $4\frac{1}{2}$ in.
1980	Lutz Dombrowski	28 ft $\frac{1}{4}$ in.
1984	Carl Lewis	28 ft $\frac{1}{4}$ in.
1988	Carl Lewis	28 ft $7\frac{1}{4}$ in.
1992	Carl Lewis	28 ft $5\frac{1}{2}$ in.
1996	Carl Lewis	26 ft 3 in.

INTERNET ACTIVITY
www.sbgmath.com

Review and Remember

Order from least to greatest.

29. 1.07; 1.075; 1.105; 1.80

30. 0.04; 0.404; 0.014; 0.104

31. 1.113; 1.105; 1.101; 1.019

32. 0.13; 0.73; 0.37; 0.013

Problem Solving
Make a Table

Problem solving often becomes easier when you organize information in a table.

Tina works in the shipping department at a sporting goods factory. The shipping boxes that Tina is using can hold up to 5 pounds. Tina has to ship all the items listed on the clipboard at the right. Each box must contain only one kind of item. How many boxes will she need?

INVENTORY

tennis balls	24
baseballs	15
hockey pucks	22
golf balls	35

WEIGHT

tennis balls	2 oz.
golf balls	1 oz.
baseballs	5 oz.
hockey pucks	6 oz

 UNDERSTAND

What do you need to know?

You need to know the total weight of each kind of item to be shipped.

 PLAN

How can you solve the problem?

You can **make a table** to organize the information. Then find the total weight for each type of item in pounds and ounces. Finally, determine how many boxes are needed for each type of equipment.

 SOLVE

Tina's Packing Plan					
Equipment	Weight of 1(oz)	Quantity	Total Weight (oz)	Total Weight (lb and oz)	Number of Boxes Needed
Hockey pucks	6	22	132	8 lb 4 oz	2
Golf balls	1	35	35	2 lb 3 oz	1
Tennis balls	2	24	48	3 lb	1
Baseballs	5	15	75	4 lb 11 oz	1

Tina needs 5 boxes in all.

 LOOK BACK

What If? Suppose the shipping company accepted boxes up to 10 pounds. How many boxes would be needed?

Using the Strategy

Make a table to solve Problems 1–3. Use the information at the right for Problems 1–2.

SPORTS PALACE

hockey stick....$ 25.
baseball bat ....$ 40.
tennis racquet..$120.

SPORTS KING

hockey stick....$35.
baseball bat.....$40.
tennis racquet..$80.

SPORTSWAY

hockey stick....$40.
baseball bat ....$55.
tennis racquet..$95.

1 You want to buy one of each item, and you will visit all three stores. What is the least amount of money you will have to spend?

2 Analyze You need to buy one of each advertised item and you want to shop at only one store. Where would you shop to spend the least amount of money? How much would you spend?

3 Once a year Sportsway has a clearance sale. During the first hour of the sale, 5 people entered the store. The second hour, 3 times as many people entered, and none left. The third hour, twice as many people entered as entered the second hour and none left. If 60 more people entered during the fourth hour and none left, how many people were in the store at the end of the fourth hour?

Mixed Strategy Review

Try these or other strategies to solve each problem. Tell which strategy you used.

THERE'S ALWAYS A WAY!

Problem Solving Strategies

- Use Logical Reasoning
- Make a Table
- Guess and Check
- Find a Pattern
- Draw a Diagram
- Write an Equation

4 A soccer ball weighs more than a football. A basketball weighs more than a softball. A football weighs less than a basketball. The weight of a soccer ball is between that of a football and a basketball. Which ball weighs the most?

5 Analyze From the information given in Problem 4, can you tell which ball weighs the least? Explain.

6 There are 8 teams in a soccer tournament. Each team must play each of the other teams once. How many games must be played?

7 Analyze An ice hockey rink is 200 feet long. Suppose hockey sticks, each 4 ft 6 in. long, are placed end-to-end along the ice. How many hockey sticks are needed to create a line from one end of the rink to the other?

✓ Checkpoint

Customary Measurement

Complete. (pages 266–267)

1. 21 ft = ■ yd

2. 13 yd = ■ in.

3. 3 mi = ■ ft

4. $5\frac{1}{2}$ ft = ■ in.

5. 17 ft = ■ yd

6. $\frac{1}{2}$ mi = ■ yd

7. $3\frac{1}{4}$ yd = ■ in.

8. 66 in. = ■ ft

9. $2\frac{1}{2}$ mi = ■ ft

Complete. (pages 268–269)

10. 6 lb = ■ oz

11. 64 oz = ■ lb

12. 4 T = ■ lb

13. $\frac{1}{2}$ lb = ■ oz

14. 24 oz = ■ lb

15. $2\frac{1}{4}$ lb = ■ oz

16. 3,000 lb = ■ T

17. $1\frac{1}{4}$ T = ■ lb

18. 20 oz = ■ lb

Complete. (pages 270–271)

19. 32 c = ■ pt

20. 40 fl oz = ■ c

21. 10 pt = ■ c

22. 4 qt = ■ pt

23. 12 pt = ■ qt

24. 20 qt = ■ gal

25. 3 gal = ■ qt

26. 2 gal = ■ pt

27. 1 qt = ■ c

Compute. (pages 274–275)

28.
```
  12 ft 6 in.
+ 20 ft 3 in.
```

29.
```
  3 qt
− 2 qt 1 pt
```

30.
```
  1 ft 4 in.
×        2
```

31.
```
  18 lb 6 oz
− 14 lb 4 oz
```

Mixed Practice

Choose the most reasonable unit of measure for each.

32. A pen is about 7 __?__ long.

33. A soup bowl holds about 8 __?__ .

34. A bag of potatoes weighs about 5 __?__ .

35. A buffalo weighs about 1 __?__ .

36. A fish tank holds about 13 __?__ .

Problem Solving

37. One of the four Olympic gymnastic events for women is the balance beam. Gymnasts perform somersaults, cartwheels, and turns on a beam that is $16\frac{1}{2}$ feet long and 4 inches wide. How many inches long is the balance beam?

What do you think?

Are all measurements approximate? Why or why not?

38. Weight lifting is a sport that measures strength. A super heavyweight record was 1,014.1 lb. Approximately how many tons is this?

39. Al Oerter was the leading Olympic discus thrower from 1956 to 1968. His shortest throw was 184 ft $10\frac{1}{2}$ in. in 1956. His longest throw was 212 ft $6\frac{1}{2}$ in. in 1968. What is the difference between the two throws?

40. The Ethiopian runner Abebe Bikila won two consecutive Olympic marathons in 1960 and 1964. He ran the first race barefoot for the entire distance, about 26 miles. About how many yards is this?

Journal Idea

Explain your strategy for estimating distances. Give a specific example of how you would use your strategy to estimate the length of your classroom.

Critical Thinking Corner

Logical Thinking

Converting Units

Coach Connor needs 11 quarts of sports drink for his team. The drink is sold only in pints and gallons. How many pints and gallons would Coach Connor buy if he wanted the least number of containers?

Give two other ways Coach Connor could buy the sports drink if he was not concerned about the number of containers.

Measure Up!

In this lesson you will explore the relationship between customary and metric units of measure.

Learning About It

How do customary units of measure compare to the units of the metric system?

Work with your group. Record your results.

Step 1 Work with units of length.

Compare a yardstick to a meterstick. About how many inches equal 1 meter? About how many centimeters equal 1 inch?

Step 2 Work with units of weight and mass.

Use a balance scale. Place a 1-kilogram mass on one side. About how many pounds equal 1 kilogram?

Step 3 Work with units of capacity.

Pour water into a metric measuring container 1 cup at a time. About how many milliliters equal 1 cup? About how many cups equal 1 liter?

Pour 1 quart of water into the metric measuring container. About how many quarts equal 1 liter?

Think and Discuss What items can you think of that are often measured in customary units? in metric units?

What You Need

For each group:
  yardstick
  meterstick
  balance scale
  1-kilogram mass
  several items weighing
    1 pound each
  1-cup measure
  1-liter measure

Practice

Complete each statement.

1. 6 inches is about ■ centimeters.

2. 5 kilograms is about ■ pounds.

3. $\frac{1}{4}$ liter is about ■ cup.

4. $\frac{1}{3}$ meter is about ■ inches.

5. 4 cups is about ■ milliliters.

6. 4 quarts is about ■ liters.

7. $\frac{1}{10}$ meter is about ■ inches.

8. 1 pint is about ■ liter.

9. 1 pound is about ■ kilogram.

10. 1 meter is about ■ feet.

11. **Explain** Suppose you find the length of a room to be 4 yards. Estimate how many meters this is. Explain how you chose your estimate.

12. Rewrite the recipe on the right, using liters as the unit of measure for each ingredient.

13. **Journal Idea** There are 1,760 yards in a mile and 1,000 meters in a kilometer. Explain how the distance of a mile compares to that of a kilometer.

Fruity Surprise Punch

46 fluid ounces of pineapple juice

1 quart orange juice

32 fluid ounces cranberry juice

2 cups apple juice

Money $ense

Opening Day

It's opening day. You're at the ball park and you have $25.00 to spend any way you choose.

Where do you want to sit? What refreshments and souvenirs do you want? Use the price lists to decide how you will spend your money. Then find out how much change, if any, you'll take home.

TICKET PRICES

BLEACHERS $5.50
GRANDSTAND $7.50
BOX SEATS $12.00

REFRESHMENTS

HOTDOGS $3.00
PEANUTS $1.50
POPCORN $1.50
COLD DRINKS $2.00

SOUVENIRS

NY

PROGRAMS $3.50
PENNANTS $4.00
BASEBALL $6.00
TEAM PHOTO $3.50
T-SHIRTS $12.00

Run, Jump, Throw

You can change from one metric unit of length to another by multiplying or dividing by powers of 10.

Learning About It

The decathlon combines 4 track events, 3 throwing events, and 3 jumping events. One track event is the 1,500-meter run, a distance of 1.5 kilometers.

The chart below shows how metric units are related to the meter and how to change from one unit to another.

32 USA OOO Centennial Olympic Games 1996

$\times 10 \quad \times 10 \quad \times 10 \quad \times 10 \quad \times 10 \quad \times 10$

kilometer	hectometer	dekameter	meter	decimeter	centimeter	millimeter
km	hm	dam	m	dm	cm	mm
1 km = 1,000 m	1 hm = 100 m	1 dam = 10 m		1 dm = 0.1 m	1 cm = 0.01 m	1 mm = 0.001 m

$\div 10 \quad \div 10 \quad \div 10 \quad \div 10 \quad \div 10 \quad \div 10$

To change from a smaller to a larger unit of length, divide.	To change from a larger to a smaller unit of length, multiply.
1,500 m = ■ km (1,000 m = 1 km) 1,500 ÷ 1,000 = 1.5 1,500 m = 1.5 km	28 m = ■ cm (1 m = 100 cm) 28 × 100 = 2,800 28 m = 2,800 cm

More Examples

A. 0.34 hm = ■ dm
0.34 × 1,000 = 340
0.34 hm = 340 dm

B. ■ km = 7,000 m
7,000 ÷ 1,000 = 7
7 km = 7,000 m

Think and Discuss

The door to a room is about 1 meter wide. How could you use this information to estimate the length of the room?

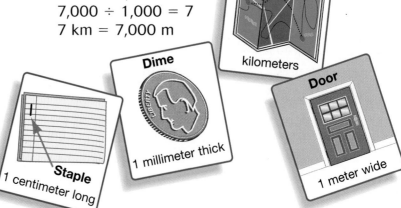

Map

kilometers

Dime

1 millimeter thick

Door

1 meter wide

Staple
1 centimeter long

Try It Out

Complete.

1. 150 mm = ▨ cm   **2.** 3 km = ▨ m   **3.** 2,500 mm = ▨ m

4. ▨ dm = 1 m   **5.** ▨ dam = 500 dm   **6.** 5.5 cm = ▨ mm

Practice

Choose the most reasonable unit of measure for each measurement. Write *km*, *m*, *cm*, or *mm*.

7. height of a bowling pin   **8.** thickness of a sports magazine

9. height of a basketball hoop   **10.** distance from New York to San Francisco

Using Estimation **Estimate each measure. Then measure to the nearest centimeter, using a meterstick.**

11. length of a pencil   **12.** length of a paper clip   **13.** height of a door

Using Mental Math **Complete.**

14. 1, m = ▨ cm   **15.** ▨ mm = 1 cm   **16.** 1,000 m = ▨ km

17. ▨ hm = 1,200 m   **18.** 35 cm = ▨ mm   **19.** ▨ cm = 7.6 dm

20. 6.7 km = ▨ m   **21.** 25 m = ▨ km   **22.** 12 dam = ▨ cm

Problem Solving

23. The 100-meter run, the 400-meter run, and the 110-meter hurdles along with the 1.5 kilometer run are the four track events in the decathlon. Find the total distance, in kilometers, for these four events.

24. Generalize Write *increase* or *decrease* to complete each sentence.

a. When changing from smaller to larger units, the number of units will __?__.

b. When changing from larger to smaller units, the number of units will __?__.

Review and Remember

Using Mental Math **Add, subtract, multiply, or divide.**

25. $\frac{2}{3} \times 6$ **26.** $9\frac{3}{10} + 1\frac{7}{10}$ **27.** $100 \div \frac{1}{2}$ **28.** $\frac{1}{2} - \frac{1}{6}$

29. 200×30 **30.** $80 + 70$ **31.** $30,000 \div 6$ **32.** $1,200 - 600$

33. $4.5 + 5.5$ **34.** 1.25×4 **35.** $11.75 - 7.5$ **36.** $2.5\overline{)100}$

Toss It

In the metric system, the gram is a basic unit of mass.

Learning About It

One of the oldest throwing events in track and field is the shot put. Athletes compete to see how far they can throw a heavy metal ball. The women's shot has a mass of 4 kilograms, or 4,000 grams.

Metric Units of Mass
1 gram (g) = 1,000 milligrams (mg)
1 kilogram (kg) = 1,000 grams
1 metric ton (t) = 1,000 kilograms

Tablet — 1 gram (g)

Stamp — 32¢ — 50 milligrams (mg)

Book — SPORTS — 1 kilogram (kg)

School Bus — 10 metric tons (t)

To change from a larger to a smaller unit of mass, multiply.	To change from a smaller to a larger unit of mass, divide.
4 kg = ■ g 4 × 1,000 = 4,000 4 kg = 4,000 g	1,500 kg = ■ t 1,500 ÷ 1,000 = 1.5 1,500 kg = 1.5 t

Think and Discuss Would it be reasonable to say that 6.35 grams is about 6,500 milligrams?

Try It Out

Complete.

1. 200 g = ■ mg

2. 3.5 kg = ■ g

3. 140 mg = ■ g

4. 30 mg = ■ g

5. ■ t = 2,000 kg

6. ■ g = 0.02 kg

Shot putter Ramona Pagel ▶ from the United States.

Practice

Write the missing unit. Choose *mg, g, kg,* or *t*.

7. A slice of bread has about 100 __?__ of salt in it.

8. A marble has a mass of about 20 __?__ .

9. A baseball bat has a mass of about 1 __?__ .

10. A car has a mass of about 2 __?__ .

Using Mental Math Complete.

11. 1 kg = ▧ g

12. ▧ g = 0.001 kg

13. 1,000 g = ▧ mg

14. 500 kg = ▧ t

15. ▧ t = 40,000 kg

16. 7.5 g = ▧ mg

17. 575 mg = ▧ g

18. 1.6 t = ▧ kg

19. ▧ g = 4,700,000 mg

Problem Solving

INTERNET ACTIVITY
www.sbgmath.com

Use the table to solve. Write *true* or *false* for Problems 20–22.

20. The mass of the women's javelin is $\frac{3}{5}$ the mass of the women's discus.

21. The mass of the men's discus is 4 times the mass of the men's javelin.

22. The mass of the women's shot put is more than 6 times the mass of the women's javelin.

23. There were 8 more 6th graders at the discus event than 7th graders. There were 136 sixth and seventh graders at the event. How many 6th graders were at the discus event? What strategy did you use to solve the problem?

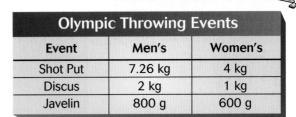

Olympic Throwing Events		
Event	Men's	Women's
Shot Put	7.26 kg	4 kg
Discus	2 kg	1 kg
Javelin	800 g	600 g

▲ Discus throwing is an event that tests strength and skill.

Review and Remember

Using Algebra Compare. Write >, <, or = for each ●.

24. 0.03 × 10 ● 0.3 × 1,000

25. 17.32 + 11.96 ● 13 + 16.28

26. $1\frac{1}{2} \times \frac{1}{3}$ ● $1\frac{2}{3} \times \frac{1}{5}$

27. $\frac{5}{12} \times \frac{3}{10}$ ● $\frac{6}{8} \times \frac{7}{16}$

28. 0.25 ÷ 0.5 ● 0.25 × 2

29. 3.24 × 100 ● 0.324 × 10

For Extra Practice, see Set F, page 294.

Icing the Rink

In the metric system, the liter is the basic unit of capacity.

Learning About It

Ice hockey is the fastest team sport in the world. An ice hockey rink may hold about 30,000 liters of water, or 30 kiloliters.

Metric Units of Capacity

1 kiloliter (kL) = 1,000 liters
1 liter (L) = 1,000 milliliters (mL)

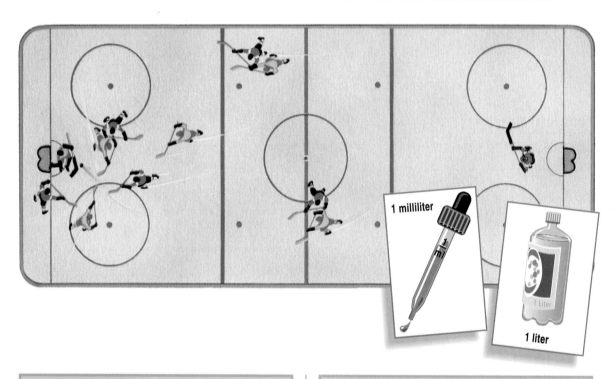

1 milliliter

1 liter

To change from a smaller to a larger unit of capacity, divide.	To change from a larger to a smaller unit of capacity, multiply.
30,000 liters = ■ kiloliters	3 liters = ■ milliliters
30,000 ÷ 1,000 = 30	3 × 1,000 = 3,000
30,000 liters = 30 kiloliters	3 liters = 3,000 milliliters

Think and Discuss What decimal part of a liter is 1 milliliter?

Try It Out

Complete.

1. 50 L = ■ mL

2. 650 mL = ■ L

3. ■ kL = 4,250 L

4. ■ L = 1,250 mL

5. 2 kL = ■ L

6. 1.5 L = ■ mL

Practice

Choose the most reasonable capacity for each item.

7. can of soup
  a. 450 mL
  b. 45 L
  c. 450 kL

8. bathtub
  a. 25 kL
  b. 250 mL
  c. 0.25 kL

9. milk carton
  a. 1 kL
  b. 1 L
  c. 100 mL

10. spoon
  a. 5 mL
  b. 50 mL
  c. 5 L

Using Mental Math Complete.

11. 1.25 kL = ▧ L

12. 15 L = ▧ kL

13. 6.5 L = ▧ mL

14. 4 kL = ▧ mL

15. 3 L = ▧ kL

16. 200 L = ▧ kL

17. 8,000 mL = ▧ L

18. 0.5 kL = ▧ L

19. 400 mL = ▧ L

Problem Solving

20. Using Estimation An adult male has about 4.7 L of blood in his body. During strenuous exercise the human heart may pump as much as 45 L a minute. About how many times does the entire blood supply circulate through the heart in one minute of exercise?

21. Science Connection Respiration is one way the body loses fluid. An adult needs at least 2.5 L of water a day to replace what is lost. Some fluid is replaced by eating. How many 250-mL glasses of water would be needed to replace lost fluids daily if no food was eaten?

Review and Remember

Using Algebra Find the next three terms in each pattern.

22. 0, 2, 6, 12, ▧, ▧, ▧

23. 1, $\frac{1}{2}$, $\frac{1}{4}$, $\frac{1}{8}$, ▧, ▧, ▧

24. 1, 3, 9, 27, ▧, ▧, ▧

25. 0.5, 1, 2, 4, ▧, ▧, ▧

Critical Thinking Corner

Logical Thinking

What's Wrong?

The clock in the tower chimes every hour on the hour. The number of chimes equals the hour. It takes $\frac{1}{2}$ second for each chime, and there are 2 seconds between chimes. At 4:00 it takes 8 seconds to complete the chiming. Jason reasons that it will take twice as long, or 16 seconds, to complete the chiming at 8:00. Why is Jason's reasoning incorrect?

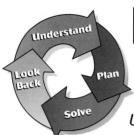

Problem Solving
Using Time Zones

Using a problem-solving strategy, such as logical reasoning, can help you understand time zones.

At 9:00 A.M. local time, skaters in the Ice Palace Tour leave Honolulu, Hawaii, for Chicago, Illinois. Their flight takes 8 hours. What will the time be in Chicago when they arrive?

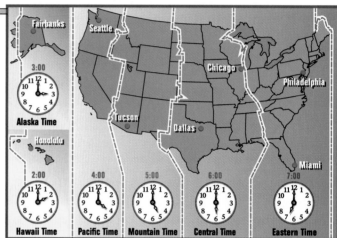

U.S. Time Zones

 UNDERSTAND

What do you know?

You know that it is 9:00 A.M. in Honolulu when the plane departs and that the flight takes 8 hours.

 PLAN

How can you solve the problem?

You can **use logical reasoning** to solve the problem. First use the map to find out what time it is in Chicago when it is 9:00 A.M. in Honolulu. Then use this information and the flying time to determine what time it will be in Chicago when the skaters arrive.

 SOLVE

You can tell from the map that if it is 2:00 in Honolulu, then it is 6:00 in Chicago. So the time in Chicago is 4 hours later than the time in Honolulu.

If it is 9:00 A.M. in Honolulu, then it is 1:00 P.M. in Chicago. If the plane leaves Honolulu at 1 P.M. Chicago time, then it arrives at 9:00 P.M. Chicago time.

 LOOK BACK

What If? Suppose the plane had left Honolulu at 12 noon local time. What time would it have been in Chicago when it landed?

Practice

Use the time zone map on page 288 and the program at the right to solve Problems 1–8.

ICE PALACE Show

Part 1 begins
8:00 p.m.

Intermission
9:30 p.m.

Part 2 begins
9:45 p.m.

Show Ends
11:00 p.m.

1 The Ice Palace Show starts at 8:00 P.M. in Seattle and will be broadcast live in Miami, Florida. What will the time be in Miami when the show begins?

2 The star skater plans to call home to Fairbanks, Alaska, during intermission in Seattle. What time will it be in Fairbanks when he makes his call?

3 **Explain** Members of a fan club are leaving Tucson, Arizona, at 6:15 P.M. Mountain Time for a 2-hour flight to Seattle. Will they arrive in time for the start of the show?

4 From Philadelphia, the skaters will travel to Seattle for their last performance of the tour. The flight is scheduled to leave Philadelphia at 11:00 P.M. Eastern Time. Arrival time in Seattle will be 1:50 A.M. Pacific Time. How long is the flight?

5 One skater has to catch a flight to Dallas 1 hour and 30 minutes after the show in Seattle ends. The flight takes 4 hours and 45 minutes. What time will it be in Dallas when her flight arrives?

6 **Journal Idea** Will travelers going from Chicago to Philadelphia arrive in time for an 8:00 P.M. show if their 3-hour flight leaves Chicago at 5:00 P.M.? Explain your thinking.

7 **Analyze** After the last show, the star of the show will take a 4-hour flight to Honolulu. The director of the show will take a 5-hour flight to Miami. Both flights take off from Seattle at midnight. What time will each person arrive at his or her destination?

8 **Create Your Own** Make up a problem that includes at least two different time zones. Exchange problems with a classmate and solve.

Practice What You Learned

Choose the correct letter for each answer.

1 Jules is numbering raffle tickets. The first 6 ticket numbers are 6135, 6118, 6101, 6084, 6067, and 6050. If he continues this pattern, what is the number of the *tenth* ticket?

A. 5067
B. 5982
C. 5999
D. 6001
E. Not Here

Tip

Try using the *Find a Pattern* strategy for this problem.

2 Small desk lamps are on sale at 2 for $12.97. Which is reasonable for the cost of 5 small desk lamps?

A. $3.25
B. $6.50
C. $32.50
D. $65.00
E. $120.00

Tip

When solving multiple-choice problems, you can sometimes eliminate one or more answer choices.

3 Eve made this drawing of a patio.

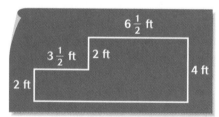

Later Eve decided to make the sides of the patio $1\frac{1}{2}$ times as long as those shown on the drawing. What was the length of the *longest* side of the new patio?

A. $9\frac{3}{4}$ ft   **D.** 15 ft

B. 10 ft   **E.** Not Here

C. $11\frac{1}{2}$ ft

Tip

In this problem, you'll first need to find the missing dimension on the drawing.

4 Paul bought a 10-lb turkey and a 12-lb ham. Sally bought an 8-lb ham and a 14-lb turkey. Did Paul and Sally together buy more turkey or more ham? How much more?

A. Turkey; 24 lb
B. Turkey; 4 lb
C. Ham; 4 lb
D. Ham; 8 lb
E. Not Here

5 While out bird watching, Pete estimated he saw 115 Canada geese, 60 different ducks, and 220 other birds. Which is reasonable for the total number of birds he saw?

A. Between 100 and 200
B. Less than 300
C. About 400
D. Exactly 400
E. More than 400

6 Mike and Angela jogged from their home to the mall and back home again. This graph shows their times and distances.

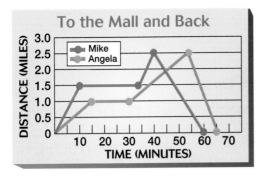

To the Mall and Back

Choose the best interpretation of the graph.

A. Angela stopped to rest for a longer time than Mike.
B. Angela got to the mall first.
C. Mike ran farther than Angela.
D. Angela got home first.
E. Mike got home first.

7 Kate is designing a square metal hot plate. She starts with a square 8.2 cm on each side. Then she increases each side by 0.5 cm. Which number sentence shows the area of the new square?

A. $A = (8.2)^2$
B. $A = (8.2 + 0.5)^2$
C. $A = (8.2)^2 + (0.5)^2$
D. $A = (8.2)^2 + (2 \cdot 0.5)$
E. $A = 8.2 \times 0.5^2$

8 One milliliter (mL) equals one thousandth of a liter (L). A scientist used about one-third of a 1.8 L solution. Which is the best estimate of how much she used?

A. 1,800 mL
B. 1,200 mL
C. 600 mL
D. 60 mL
E. 0.6 mL

9 A photograph is 8 in. by 10 in. The mat around the photo is 2 in. wide, and the frame is $1\frac{1}{4}$ in. wide. What are the dimensions of the framed photograph?

A. 10 inches by 12 inches
B. 11 inches by 14 inches
C. $11\frac{1}{4}$ inches by $14\frac{1}{4}$ inches
D. 16 inches by 20 inches
E. Not Here

10 Betty and Roger have numbered ticket stubs. The numbers each have four digits. Roger's number is 1,455. If the sum of the two numbers is 6,886, which of these must be Betty's number?

A. 5,431   D. 3,451
B. 5,413   E. Not Here
C. 4,135

✔ Checkpoint

Metric Measurement

Vocabulary

Write the missing word that completes each sentence.

1. The __?__ system of measurement measures length in meters, capacity in liters, weight in grams, and temperature in Celsius.

2. To change from a smaller to a larger unit of measure, __?__ .

3. To change from a larger to a smaller unit of measure, __?__ .

Word Bank

customary
divide
metric
multiply

Concepts and Skills

Using Mental Math Complete. (pages 282–283)

4. 2.2 km = ■ m

5. 350 mm = ■ m

6. 5,000 m = ■ km

7. 12 cm = ■ mm

8. 2.7 km = ■ m

9. 75 mm = ■ cm

Write the missing metric unit. (pages 284–285)

10. A book might have a mass of 2 __?__ .

11. An athlete might lift 150 __?__ a day.

12. A truck might carry 10 __?__ of cargo.

13. A potato might have a mass of 250 __?__ .

Choose the equivalent measure for each. (pages 286–287)

14. 1,000 liters
   a. 0.1 kL
   b. 1 kL
   c. 1,000 mL

15. 5,000 milliliters
   a. 50 L
   b. 5 kL
   c. 5 L

16. 10 kiloliters
   a. 0.1 mL
   b. 10,000 L
   c. 100 L

Mixed Practice

Using Mental Math Complete.

17. 7.5 m = ■ mm

18. 0.5 km = ■ m

19. 3.2 cm = ■ mm

20. 10 g = ■ kg

21. 100 L = ■ kL

22. 100 mL = ■ L

23. 10 kL = ■ L

24. 105 kg = ■ g

25. 110 mg = ■ g

Problem Solving

Use the chart on the right to solve Problems 26–30.

26. Who jumped 9 centimeters farther than Robert Emmiyan?

27. How many more centimeters did Mike Powell jump than Bob Beamon?

28. **What If?** Suppose Robert Emmiyan jumped 10 centimeters more than he did. How would that affect his standing?

29. What is the difference in centimeters between Carl Lewis's best jump and Mike Powell's jump?

30. What is the difference in millimeters between Mike Powell's jump and Robert Emmiyan's jump?

Long Jump Champions	
Jumper	Distance (m)
Mike Powell	8.95
Bob Beamon	8.90
Robert Emmiyan	8.86
Carl Lewis	8.79
Carl Lewis	8.76
Carl Lewis	8.75

Journal Idea

Explain how the metric system of measurement relates to the place value system we use. Tell how this relationship helps you change one unit of measure to another. Give an example.

What do you think?

With which system of measurement do you prefer to work, customary or metric? Explain.

You Decide

Activity

Thirst Quenching!

Your school is playing a soccer game today. You are in charge of buying a sports drink.

- The drink you want comes in 2 sizes: 1 qt 8 oz at $2.50 per container and 2 qt 6 oz at $3.75 per container.

- Plan to purchase at least 10 quarts, but no more than 15 quarts, of the sports drink. How many of each container will you buy? Why? How much will you spend?

You might wish to include this work in your portfolio.

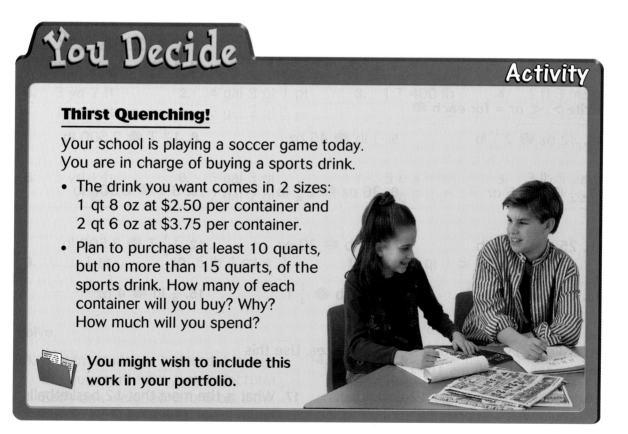

Extra Practice

Set E (pages 282–283)

Write **km, m, cm,** or **mm** for the most reasonable unit
of length.

1. thickness of a CD   **2.** length of a field   **3.** distance walked in 4 h

Using Mental Math Complete.

4. 3 m = ▓ cm   **5.** 12 cm = ▓ mm   **6.** 3,000 m = ▓ km

Solve.

7. Analyze If someone can run 100 meters in
10 seconds, should we assume that she can
run $\frac{1}{10}$ of a kilometer in $\frac{1}{6}$ of a minute? Explain.

Set F (pages 284–285)

Write **g, kg,** or **t** for the most reasonable unit of mass.

1. a bowling ball   **2.** an entire football team   **3.** an apple

Using Mental Math Complete.

4. 3 kg = ▓ g   **5.** ▓ kg = 2,500 g   **6.** 3,000 kg = ▓ t

Solve.

7. Thirty men have a mass of 105 kg each. Can they cross
a bridge together if the bridge holds no more than 3 t?

Set G (pages 286–287)

Write **kL, L,** or **mL** for the most reasonable unit of capacity.

1. pond   **2.** fuel tank of a car   **3.** soupspoon

Using Mental Math Complete.

4. 1.5 kL = ▓ L   **5.** 1,575 mL = ▓ L   **6.** 220 L = ▓ kL

Solve.

7. Jan drinks seven 250-mL glasses of water each day. If
she buys twenty-eight 1-L bottles of water, how long
will they last?

Chapter Test

Use a customary unit of measure to complete each sentence.

1. A cup holds 8 ___?___ of water.

2. A tennis ball weighs about 2 ___?___.

3. A new pencil is about 6 ___?___ long.

4. An athlete might run about 5 ___?___.

Complete.

5. 3 yd = ■ ft

6. 36 oz = ■ lb

7. 17 ft = ■ yd

8. 5,000 lb = ■ T

9. 7 qt = ■ gal

10. 3 gal = ■ pt

Compute.

11. 5 ft 7 in.
      +2 ft 8 in.

12. 3 gal 1 qt
      −1 gal 3 qt

13. 3 lb 6 oz
      ×   6

14. 3 ft 6 in. ÷ 6

Use a metric unit of measure to complete each sentence.

15. Every morning you might drink 200 ___?___ of juice.

16. A basketball player might be 210 ___?___ tall.

17. An automobile might have a mass of 2 ___?___.

Complete.

18. 7 m = ■ km

19. 85 L = ■ kL

20. 2.3 L = ■ mL

21. 3.2 kg = ■ g

22. 1,750 g = ■ kg

23. 250 cm = ■ m

Solve.

24. Bob trained 6 days for a race. The first day, he ran 0.5 km. Each day after that, he ran twice as far as he did the day before. After 6 days, how far had he run in all?

25. A car carrier is carrying 6 cars. Each one weighs $1\frac{3}{4}$ T. If the carrier weighs 5 tons when empty, can it cross a bridge with a 15-ton weight limit? Explain.

 Self-Check

Look back at Exercises 11−14. Did you remember to rename where necessary before or after computing?

Performance Assessment

Show What You Know About Measurement

1 Make an estimate in metric units for each of the following measurements. Then, choose an appropriate metric measuring instrument and determine the actual measurement in each case.

What You Need

large milk containers
meter stick or metric tape
balance with metric masses
liter measuring cup

   a. the length of your classroom

   b. the height of your desk

   c. the mass of a notebook

   d. the capacity of a milk container

Self-Check For Question 1c, did you remember to use grams to measure the mass of the notebook?

2 Linda wants to hang several posters up on her wall. The wall measures 4 meters long and 300 centimeters high. If she wants to hang up four posters which will cover her wall, what could be the dimensions of the posters? Draw a picture to help you find a reasonable answer.

Self-Check Could you have used four different-sized posters?

For Your Portfolio

You might wish to include this work in your portfolio.

Extension

Computer Spreadsheets

The Bay County Stadium hosts many different sports events. There are a variety of seating options and prices from which to choose. The accounting department at the stadium is responsible for keeping track of the number of different tickets sold for each sports event. They use a computer **spreadsheet** to organize and analyze this data.

This is data from the attendance at a baseball game.

	A	B	C	D	
1	SEATING	PRICE PER SEAT	NUMBER OF SEATS	AMOUNT COLLECTED	
2	bleachers	$4.00	80	= B2 * C2	
3	upper level	$6.50	125		
4	upper boxes	$9.00	65		
5	club boxes	$15.50	40		← cell D5
6	mail level	$11.50	60		
7	main boxes	$14.00	55		
8	field boxes	$19.50	25		
9	TOTAL				

A **cell** is the box where a row and a column meet. For example, the box where Column B and Row 5 meet is cell B5. The value in cell B5 is $15.50. To find the amount of money recorded for club boxes, you enter the formula =B5*C5 into cell D5. Then the computer calculates the amount of $620.00 automatically.

1. What is the value in cell C7? What does this number represent?

2. What formula would give you the amount of money recorded for upper box seats? What amount would be automatically calculated?

3. Which cell will show the total amount of money collected for the sale of tickets for this sports event? What will be the formula to calculate this?

Cumulative Review

★ ★ ★ ★ ★ **Preparing for Tests**

Choose the correct letter for each answer.

Operations	Geometry and Spatial Reasoning

Operations

1. A golden retriever weighs 3 times as much as a terrier. If the retriever weighs 75 lb, how much does the terrier weigh?

 A. 15 pounds
 B. 25 pounds
 C. 50 pounds
 D. 225 pounds
 E. Not Here

2. Gretchen read 130 pages of a book the first week and another 241 the next week. For 3 weeks after that, she read 124 pages each week. How many pages did she read in the 5 weeks?

 A. 459   **D.** 743
 B. 495   **E.** Not Here
 C. 502

3. An average of 680 people visit a local zoo each day. Which is the best estimate of how many people visit the zoo in a month?

 A. 15,000   **C.** 27,000
 B. 21,000   **D.** 210,000

4. What is the sum of $\frac{3}{8} + \frac{5}{6}$?

 A. $\frac{5}{16}$ **D.** $1\frac{5}{24}$

 B. $\frac{4}{7}$ **E.** $1\frac{1}{3}$

 C. $\frac{8}{14}$

Geometry and Spatial Reasoning

5. Which angle measurement represents an acute angle?

 A. 180°
 B. 120°
 C. 90°
 D. 60°

6. A circle has a radius of 24 cm. What is its diameter?

 A. 8 centimeters
 B. 12 centimeters
 C. 36 centimeters
 D. 48 centimeters

7. A figure has one right angle and two 45° angles. What figure is it?

 A. a square
 B. a rhombus
 C. an equilateral triangle
 D. a right triangle

8. Which best describes the triangles shown below?

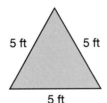

 A. The triangles are congruent.
 B. The triangles are similar.
 C. The triangles are isosceles.
 D. The triangles are scalene.

Measurement	Probability and Statistics

Measurement

9. How many feet are in $2\frac{1}{2}$ miles? (1 ft = 5,280 mi)

A. 1,320 ft
B. 4,400 ft
C. 10,560 ft
D. 13,200 ft

10. It costs $3.00 to ship a box weighing up to 2 lb and $0.48 for each additional ounce over 2 lb. How much would it cost to ship a box weighing 3 lb 3 oz? (1 lb = 16 oz)

A. $12.12
B. $9.12
C. $7.44
D. $6.48
E. Not Here

11. An Olympic-size swimming pool is 50 meters long. How many kilometers long is this? (1 km = 1,000 m)

A. 0.005 km
B. 0.05 km
C. 0.5 km
D. 5 km

12. A floor puzzle measures 12 ft long and 9 ft wide. Half of the puzzle is a design of many squares. What is the *area* of the puzzle in square yards? ($A = l \times w$)

A. 9 yd^2
B. 12 yd^2
C. 21 yd^2
D. 108 yd^2
E. 216 yd^2

Probability and Statistics

13. Samantha received the following scores on her math quizzes: 88, 85, 92, 89, 94, 92. What was her mean (average) score?

A. 89　　　C. 91
B. 90　　　D. 92

14. Tim studied for 45 minutes on Monday, 1 hour 30 minutes on Tuesday, and 1 hour on Wednesday. What was the average amount of time he spent studying?

A. 1 h 30 min　　C. 1 h
B. 1 h 5 min　　　D. 45 min

Use the graph for Questions 15–16.

This graph shows the number of students who chose different subjects as their favorites.

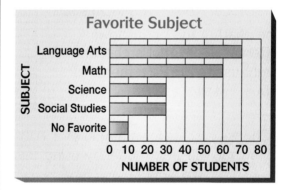

Favorite Subject

15. How many students did **NOT** choose a favorite subject?

A. 5　　　C. 15
B. 10　　　D. 30

16. How many more students prefer science or math to language arts as their favorite subject?

A. 90　　　C. 30
B. 70　　　D. 20

Chapter 8

Ratio, Proportion, and Probability

Chapter Theme: HOBBIES

Real-World Math

·················Real Facts···················

Architects use scale models when designing large buildings. The models are proportionally smaller than the actual buildings. Suppose a model was made to a scale of 1 inch to 20 feet. The following proportion tells how tall the model of a 100-foot tall building would be.

$$\frac{1 \text{ in.}}{20 \text{ ft}} = \frac{5 \text{ in.}}{100 \text{ ft}}$$ ← Model Size / ← Actual Size

The model would be 5 inches tall.

The chart at the right shows different scales that architects might use to create a model of a building site.

Architect's Scales
Model: Actual
1 in. = 10 ft
1 in. = 20 ft
1 in. = 30 ft
1 in. = 40 ft
1 in. = 50 ft
1 in. = 60 ft
1 in. = 80 ft

• Choose a scale for a model of a 100-foot building. How tall will your model be using this scale?

• Which model will be taller, a model built to a scale of 1 in. = 30 ft or a model built to a scale of 1 in. = 60 ft?

···········Real People···················

Meet Michael Kwartler, an urban planner. He started building models when he was ten years old. Now he builds models for parks, buildings, and other city structures. The children at the right are putting together a puzzle to create a model of the Capitol building in Washington, D.C.

Using Algebra

Patch It Up

You can use a ratio to compare two quantities.

Learning About It

Quilting is a hobby with a rich history and tradition. Many quilt patterns repeat colors and shapes. The photo at the right shows a piece of a quilt called a block. How many small turquoise squares are in the block? How many purple squares?

You can use a ratio to compare the number of turquoise squares to the number of purple squares.

A **ratio** is a comparison of two quantities.

number of turquoise squares ⟶ $\frac{12}{9}$
number of purple squares ⟶

The ratio of turquoise to purple squares is 12 to 9.

There are three ways to write a ratio.

12 to 9 $\frac{12}{9}$ 12:9

A ratio can also be used to compare the number of squares of a certain color to all the squares in the quilt block.

part ⟶ turquoise squares ⟶ $\frac{12}{25}$
whole ⟶ all squares ⟶

The ratio of turquoise squares to all the squares in the block is 12 to 25.

whole ⟶ all squares ⟶ $\frac{25}{9}$
part ⟶ purple squares ⟶

The ratio of all the squares in the block to purple squares is 25 to 9.

Word Bank

ratio
equivalent ratio

Fine Arts Connection ➤
Professor Faith Ringgold is one of many quilters involved in a strong tradition of African American quilting. Dr. Ringgold's quilts tell stories about families and historical events.

Connecting Ideas

You have just compared turquoise squares to purple squares to understand ratios. Now look at the squares in this quilt to understand equivalent ratios.

Find the number of turqouise squares on the quilt.

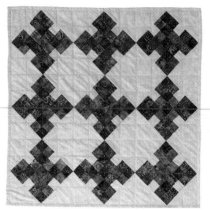

In one block ⟶ turquoise ⟶ 12
                        purple ⟶ 9

In the quilt ⟶ turquoise ⟶ ? 108
                      purple ⟶ 81

You can use equivalent ratios to find out. When both terms of a ratio are multiplied or divided by a number other than zero, the result is an **equivalent ratio**.

first term ⟶ $\dfrac{12}{9} = \dfrac{12 \times 9}{9 \times 9} = \dfrac{108}{81}$
second term ⟶

There are 108 turquoise squares in the quilt.

More Examples

Which ratios are equivalent?

A. $3{:}4 \stackrel{?}{=} 12{:}16$

$\dfrac{3 \times 4}{4 \times 4} = \dfrac{12}{16}$

So, $3{:}4 = 12{:}16$

B. $\dfrac{10}{35} \stackrel{?}{=} \dfrac{2}{5}$

$\dfrac{10 \div 5}{35 \div 5} = \dfrac{2}{7}$

So, $\dfrac{10}{35} \neq \dfrac{2}{5}$

C. 18 to 12 $\stackrel{?}{=}$ 24 to 16

Simplify each ratio.

$\dfrac{18}{12} = \dfrac{3}{2}$ $\dfrac{24}{16} = \dfrac{3}{2}$

So, 18 to 12 = 24 to 16

Think and Discuss If the ratio of yellow to turquoise is $\dfrac{4}{12}$, how many turquoise squares would there be in a quilt with 100 yellow squares?

Try It Out

Write each ratio in three ways as shown on page 300.

1. triangles to squares

2. green shapes to blue circles

Are the ratios equivalent? Write = or ≠ in place of ⬤.

3. 2 to 3 ⬤ 6 to 9

4. $\dfrac{15}{12}$ ⬤ $\dfrac{5}{4}$

5. 7:8 ⬤ 21:32

6. $\dfrac{6}{10}$ ⬤ $\dfrac{9}{15}$

Practice

Look at the quilt on the right. Write each ratio in three ways.

7.  to

8. to ⚘

9. ⚘ to ◣

10. 🍃 to ⚘

Tell whether the ratios are equivalent. Write = or ≠ in place of ●.

11. 3:4 ● 12:16

12. $\frac{3}{5}$ ● $\frac{12}{15}$

13. $\frac{12}{32}$ ● $\frac{3}{8}$

14. 25 to 15 ● 5 to 2

15. 4:7 ● 12:21

16. $\frac{8}{12}$ ● $\frac{6}{9}$

17. $\frac{15}{21}$ ● $\frac{5}{8}$

18. 7 to 6 ● 28:24

Find the number that makes the ratios equivalent.

19. ■:12 = 5:6

20. $\frac{4}{■} = \frac{2}{5}$

21. $\frac{12}{9} = \frac{4}{■}$

22. $\frac{3}{■} = \frac{12}{4}$

23. 14:7 = ■:14

24. $\frac{■}{7} = \frac{30}{42}$

25. 4:3 = ■:12

26. 5 to ■ = 25 to 35

For Exercises 27–30, refer to the table below. Each section of a quilt has the same ratio of yellow squares to blue squares.

Yellow Squares	2	4	6	8	
Blue Squares		6			15

27. If there are 2 yellow squares, how many blue squares are there?

28. If there are 8 yellow squares, how many blue squares are there?

29. If there are 15 blue squares, how many yellow squares are in the section?

30. **Analyze** If there are 50 yellow squares in the quilt, how many blue squares are there in the quilt?

Problem Solving

A quilter begins with a basic geometric pattern. Some quilts and their patterns are shown at the right.

31. Look at "Julie's Bird."

    a. What is the ratio of the number of blue triangles to all triangles?

    b. Suppose the pattern is repeated to make a larger quilt. If there are 32 triangles in all, how many are blue triangles?

32. Look at "Carl's Fish."

    a. What is the ratio of dark blue triangles to purple triangles?

    b. Suppose the pattern is repeated to make a larger quilt. If there are 24 white triangles in the larger quilt, what is the total number of triangles?

    c. Draw a picture of the large quilt.

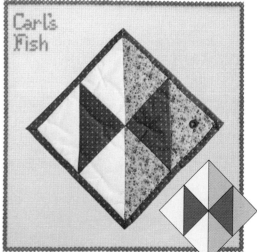

33. Look at "A Bunny's Dream."

    a. How many red triangles were used to form the red hexagon?

    b. What is the ratio of the red triangles to the white triangles?

    c. Which two colors form the ratio 1:1?

34. Create Your Own Trace the pattern below and create your own quilt pattern.

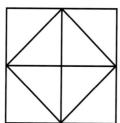

Review and Remember

Solve.

35. $7{,}000 - 599$ **36.** $800 \div 3{,}200$ **37.** 2.05×0.009

38. $5 - 0.23$ **39.** $1\frac{1}{8} + \frac{5}{8}$ **40.** $2\frac{6}{7} \div 1\frac{3}{7}$

Using Algebra

Count Me In!

You can use counters to help you understand proportions.

Learning About It

You can use counters to show equivalent ratios.

Work with a partner.

Step 1 Use your two-color counters to show the ratio 2 red to 5 yellow. Ask your partner to use counters to show a ratio that is equivalent to 2 red to 5 yellow.

Word Bank

proportion

What You Need

For each pair:
   two-color counters

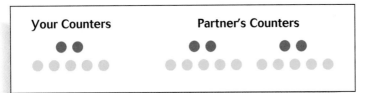

Your Counters	Partner's Counters

Step 2 Check to see if your ratio and your partner's ratio are equivalent. Write an equation to state that the ratios are equivalent. This equation is called a **proportion**.

Step 3 Use the counters to find another ratio that is equivalent to $\frac{2}{5}$. Compare your ratio with that of your partner. Write a proportion using your ratio.

Step 4 Use counters to show the ratio 3 yellow to 2 red. Have your partner show an equivalent ratio and form a proportion. Tell how the proportion was made.

Connecting Ideas

Knowing how to use counters to form a proportion can help you find a missing number in a proportion.

Step 1 Use counters to show the equation $\frac{3}{2} = \frac{6}{n}$.

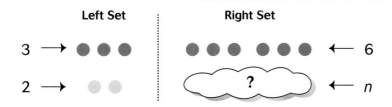

Step 2 Match 2 yellow counters for every 3 red counters on the right. What is the value of n?

Step 3 Place the value of n that you found in the equation $\frac{3}{2} = \frac{6}{n}$. What do you notice? Are the ratios equivalent? Did you form a proportion?

Think and Discuss Use counters to see how many proportions you can make with the numbers 2, 4, 5, and 10.

Practice

Write each proportion shown.

Find the missing counters in each proportion.

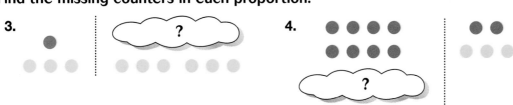

Use counters to find the missing number.

5. $\frac{2}{n} = \frac{8}{12}$ **6.** $\frac{4}{5} = \frac{n}{10}$ **7.** $\frac{3}{n} = \frac{6}{12}$ **8.** $\frac{n}{3} = \frac{6}{9}$ **8.** $\frac{5}{4} = \frac{n}{16}$

7. Create Your Own Use counters to create a proportion. Have your partner create a different proportion using one of your ratios.

Using
Algebra

Picture This!

If two ratios are equivalent, you can write a proportion.

105 mm

69 mm

Learning About It

The Photography Club makes prints from negatives for the yearbook. Are the sides of a print proportional to the sides of a negative?

To find out, write two ratios and test to see if they form a proportion. Remember, a proportion is an equation stating that two ratios are equivalent.

Order is important when you write the ratios to test for a proportion.

Negative		Print
length ⟶	$\dfrac{35 \text{ mm}}{23 \text{ mm}} = \dfrac{105 \text{ mm}}{69 \text{ mm}}$	⟵ length
width ⟶		⟵ width

23 mm

35 mm

Now see if you have formed a proportion.

THERE'S
ALWAYS
A WAY!

- **One way** to test for a proportion is to use equivalent ratios.

$$\frac{35}{23} = \frac{35 \times 3}{23 \times 3} = \frac{105}{69}$$

Equivalent Ratios

- **Another way** to test for a proportion is to use cross products.

$$\frac{35}{23} = \frac{105}{69}$$

$$35 \times 69 = 23 \times 105$$

$$2,415 = 2,415$$

Since the cross products are equal, the ratios are equivalent and form a proportion.

The sides of the print and the negative are in proportion.

Connecting Ideas

You used cross products to see if you have a proportion. Sometimes you know that you have a proportion, but one number is missing. You can use cross products to find the missing number.

Find the missing number in the proportion $\frac{4}{6} = \frac{n}{15}$.

Step 1 Write the cross products.

$$\frac{4}{6} = \frac{n}{15}$$

$6 \times n = 4 \times 15$ cross products

Step 2 Solve the equation.

$6 \times n = 4 \times 15$
$6 \times n = 60$
$n = 60 \div 6$
$n = 10$

The missing number in the proportion $\frac{4}{6} = \frac{n}{15}$ is $n = 10$.

More Examples

A. $\frac{4}{5} = \frac{12}{n}$

$4 \times n = 5 \times 12$
$4 \times n = 60$
$n = 60 \div 4$
$n = 15$

B. $\frac{1.5}{n} = \frac{6}{12}$

$6 \times n = 1.5 \times 12$
$6 \times n = 18$
$n = 18 \div 6$
$n = 3$

C. $\frac{n}{8} = \frac{25}{40}$

$40 \times n = 8 \times 25$
$40 \times n = 200$
$n = 200 \div 40$
$n = 5$

Think and Discuss How is the expression below the same or different from the photograph problem on page 306? Is it a proportion? How do you know?

Length		Width	
negative ⟶ print ⟶	$\frac{35 \text{ mm}}{105 \text{ mm}}$	$=$	$\frac{23 \text{ mm}}{69 \text{ mm}}$ ⟵ ⟵ negative print

Try It Out

Write the cross products for each proportion.

1. $\frac{2}{3} = \frac{8}{12}$

2. $\frac{3}{5} = \frac{15}{25}$

3. $\frac{6}{10} = \frac{9}{15}$

4. $\frac{9}{12} = \frac{12}{16}$

Find the missing number in each proportion.

5. $\frac{6}{n} = \frac{5}{10}$

6. $\frac{3}{7} = \frac{n}{70}$

7. $\frac{2}{6} = \frac{3}{n}$

8. $\frac{n}{2} = \frac{15}{5}$

Practice

Tell whether each pair of ratios can form a proportion.

9. $\frac{4}{5}, \frac{12}{15}$

10. $\frac{3}{8}, \frac{9}{21}$

11. $\frac{2}{3}, \frac{18}{27}$

12. $\frac{5}{8}, \frac{40}{64}$

13. $\frac{4}{10}, \frac{6}{15}$

14. $\frac{6}{9}, \frac{9}{12}$

15. $\frac{6}{8}, \frac{9}{12}$

16. $\frac{6}{10}, \frac{9}{15}$

Find the missing number in each proportion.

17. $\frac{2}{3} = \frac{n}{21}$

18. $\frac{n}{3} = \frac{3}{9}$

19. $\frac{3}{4} = \frac{21}{n}$

20. $\frac{n}{5} = \frac{8}{20}$

21. $\frac{2}{10} = \frac{n}{15}$

22. $\frac{8}{6} = \frac{12}{n}$

23. $\frac{1}{n} = \frac{4}{72}$

24. $\frac{5}{n} = \frac{15}{24}$

25. $\frac{n}{8} = \frac{9}{24}$

26. $\frac{4}{n} = \frac{12}{15}$

27. $\frac{n}{3} = \frac{9}{27}$

28. $\frac{2}{7} = \frac{n}{21}$

29. $\frac{6}{9} = \frac{8}{n}$

30. $\frac{9}{15} = \frac{n}{10}$

31. $\frac{4}{n} = \frac{6}{15}$

32. $\frac{n}{9} = \frac{4}{12}$

 Use a calculator to find the missing number in each proportion.

33. $\frac{20}{30} = \frac{n}{45}$

34. $\frac{n}{20} = \frac{24}{32}$

35. $\frac{10}{n} = \frac{14}{35}$

36. $\frac{14}{n} = \frac{24}{36}$

37. $\frac{n}{150} = \frac{90}{450}$

38. $\frac{144}{n} = \frac{720}{125}$

39. $\frac{64}{11} = \frac{n}{121}$

40. $\frac{125}{625} = \frac{500}{n}$

Choose two proportions that can be used to solve each problem.

41. Four rolls of film cost $18.00. How many rolls of the same film can you buy for $27.00?

    a. $\frac{4}{18} = \frac{n}{27}$ **b.** $\frac{4}{27} = \frac{18}{n}$

    c. $\frac{4}{n} = \frac{18}{27}$ **d.** $\frac{4}{n} = \frac{27}{18}$

42. Thirty-two prints fit on 4 pages of an album. How many prints of the same size fit on 3 pages?

    a. $\frac{32}{4} = \frac{n}{3}$ **b.** $\frac{4}{3} = \frac{n}{32}$

    c. $\frac{3}{4} = \frac{32}{n}$ **d.** $\frac{32}{n} = \frac{4}{3}$

Problem Solving

Use the photographs on the right for Problems 43 and 44.

43. You are enlarging a print that is 5 in. wide and 7 in. long. If the width of the enlargement is 15 in., what is the length?

44. You are reducing a print that is 10 in. wide and 12 in. long. If the length of the reduction is 6 inches, what is the width?

45. If 5 rolls of film cost $12.00, would it be reasonable to say that 8 rolls would cost $19.20? How do you know?

46. Three rolls of film cost $10.50. What does one roll of film cost?

47. **What If?** Suppose you could buy 12 rolls of film for $39.95 instead of buying the film at 3 rolls for $10.50. How much would you save?

48. **Explain** You can take 108 photos with 9 rolls of film. How many rolls of the same film will you need to take 84 photos? Tell how you found your answer.

49. **Analyze** The cost of film is $3.99. Developing the film cost $4.29. How many rolls did you buy and develop if the total cost was $24.84?

50. **Journal Idea** Explain how you would know when sides of a figure are proportional to sides of another figure?

Review and Remember

Using Algebra Complete the tables.

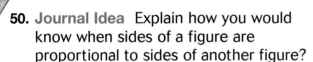

Input	Output
$\frac{1}{2}$	$\frac{1}{4}$
$\frac{1}{8}$	$\frac{1}{16}$
51. $\frac{2}{6}$	■
52. ■	$\frac{3}{8}$

Input	Output
1	$\frac{1}{4}$
$2\frac{1}{2}$	$1\frac{3}{4}$
53. ■	$\frac{1}{12}$
54. $\frac{6}{7}$	■

5 in.

4 in.

7 in.

5 in.

10 in.

8 in.

Developing Skills for Problem Solving

First read for understanding and then focus on identifying the information necessary to solve a problem.

READ FOR UNDERSTANDING

Lisa has 600 stamps in her collection as shown in the table. Her uncle plans to give her some more airplane stamps.

Lisa's Stamp Collection	
Type of Stamp	Number of Stamps
Flowers	83
Women	57
Airplanes	60
Presidents	120
Animals	114
Others	166

1 How many stamps does Lisa have?

2 How many flower stamps does she have?

THINK AND DISCUSS

MATH FOCUS

Too Much or Too Little Information If a problem contains too much information, you must decide what to use to solve the problem. You also need to know if there is too little information to solve the problem.

Reread the paragraph at the top of the page.

3 Is there enough information to find the ratio of airplane stamps to the total stamps Lisa has now? Explain.

4 Is there enough information to find the ratio of airplane stamps to total stamps after Lisa's uncle gives her the new stamps? Explain.

5 Why is it important to know when there is too much or too little information when solving a problem?

Show What You Learned

Answer each question. Give a reason for your choice.

Jenny has a $\frac{1}{2}$-cent Benjamin Franklin stamp printed in 1954. She also has a $10.75 American Eagle stamp. Jenny wants to compare the purchase price of the American Eagle stamp to the price of the Franklin stamp.

1 What information is needed to compare the prices?

   a. The names of both stamps

   b. The prices of both stamps

   c. The ages of both stamps

2 What information is not needed to compare the prices?

   a. The year that the Franklin stamp was printed

   b. The price of the American Eagle stamp

   c. The price of the Benjamin Franklin stamp

3 What ratio can be used to compare the price of the American Eagle stamp to the price of the Benjamin Franklin stamp?

   a. $\frac{1}{2}$

   b. $\frac{1954}{1895}$

   c. $\frac{10.75}{0.005}$

▲ **Social Studies Connection**

The Benjamin Franklin stamp is the smallest denomination of any U.S. stamp ever printed. The American Eagle stamp is the largest denomination of any U.S. stamp used for postage within the United States.

James, a stamp collector, read about a block of four 24-cent stamps issued in 1918 that has an inverted image of an airplane. The last time the block of stamps was sold, a collector paid $1.1 million for it. James wondered how much profit was made by the last person to sell the stamps.

4 What does James want to know?

   a. How much money it cost to buy the stamps in 1918

   b. How much money the last person to sell the stamps made on the sale

   c. How much money the last person to buy the stamps has

5 What information does James have that will help him?

   a. The cost of the stamps in 1918

   b. The number of stamps in the block

   c. The last price paid for the stamps

6 **Explain** What other information does James need to solve the problem?

Using Algebra

3, 2, 1, Blastoff!

You can use what you learned about ratios to help you with rates.

Word Bank

unit price
unit rate
rate

Learning About It

The model rocket club builds and launches rockets. Two stores have the Alpha model rocket on sale. Which store has the better buy?

To find out, you need to know the cost of one rocket in each store. You need to find the **unit price**.

ROCKY'S ROCKET SHOP

ALPHA ROCKETS ON SALE!

$60.00 for 12

FLYAWAY SHOP

ALPHA ROCKETS SALE

$79.95 for 15 Rockets

You can use a proportion.

ROCKY'S ROCKET SHOP	FLYAWAY SHOP
$\dfrac{\$60.00}{12 \text{ rockets}} = \dfrac{n}{1 \text{ rocket}}$	$\dfrac{\$79.95}{15 \text{ rockets}} = \dfrac{n}{1 \text{ rocket}}$
$12 \times n = 60.00 \times 1$	$15 \times n = 79.95 \times 1$
$n = 60 \div 12 \text{ or } 5$	$n = 79.95 \div 15 \text{ or } 5.33$
The unit price is $5.00.	The unit price is $5.33.

Rocky's Rocket Shop has the better buy.

A unit price is a **unit rate**. A **rate** is a ratio that compares two different quantities, such as miles per hour.

More Examples

A. 120 miles in 4 hours

$$\frac{120 \text{ miles}}{4 \text{ hours}} = \frac{n}{1 \text{ hour}}$$
$$4 \times n = 120 \times 1$$
$$n = 120 \div 4 \text{ or } 30$$

The unit rate is 30 miles per hour.

B. 240 calories in 6 servings

$$\frac{240 \text{ calories}}{6 \text{ servings}} = \frac{n}{1 \text{ serving}}$$
$$6 \times n = 240 \times 1$$
$$n = 240 \div 6 \text{ or } 40$$

There are 40 calories per serving.

Think and Discuss Is 35 miles per gallon a unit rate? Why or why not?

Try It Out

Find the unit rate. Round to the nearest hundredth.

1. $85 for 12 rockets

2. $36 for 24 engines

3. 1,800 feet for 5 seconds

4. 150 miles every 3 gallons

5. 150 calories in 8 servings

6. 18 cups for 4 people

Practice

Find the unit price. Round to the nearest cent.

7. $87.50 for 10 Alpha III rockets

8. $46.20 for 6 Tornadoes

9. 2 launch controllers for $75.00

10. $25.56 for 4 repair kits

11. 8 rocket kits for $71.12

12. $15.00 for 1 dozen engines

Use a calculator to determine the better buy.

13. $31.50 for 6 rockets
or $27.50 for 5 rockets

14. 3 rocket locators for $68.97
or 5 rocket locators for $109.30

INTERNET ACTIVITY
www.sbgmath.com

Problem Solving

Use the advertisements on the right for Problems 15–18.

15. Which store has the better buy on launch controllers?

16. Which store has the better buy on launch pads?

17. **Explain** Should you buy all your supplies from one store? Why or why not?

18. **You Decide** The club has $105 to spend. They need a launch pad and a controller. Decide where you will shop and exactly how much they will both cost.

HOBBY WORLD
Launch Controllers   Launch Pads
6 for $179.70   2 for $147.90

FLYAWAY SHOP
Launch Controllers $55 for 2
Launch Pads 5 for $329.80

ROCKY'S ROCKET SHOP
Launch Controllers 3 for $94
Launch Pads 3 for $206.97

Review and Remember

19. 500×6

20. $400 \div 80$

21. $1.06 + 3$

22. $7.01 - 6.9$

23. $1.5 \div 0.003$

24. $\frac{3}{8} \times \frac{16}{27}$

25. $1\frac{2}{5} - \frac{1}{2}$

26. $8\frac{5}{6} + 1\frac{1}{3}$

Model It!

You can use scale drawings, maps, and models to show an object larger or smaller than its actual size.

Learning About It

The Concord Middle School is building a new soccer field for the soccer club. What is the actual length of the field? To find out, use the scale drawing below.

A **scale drawing** is a reduction or enlargement of an actual object. The **scale** is a ratio that compares a measure on the drawing with the actual measure.

Follow the steps to find the actual length of the field.

Word Bank

scale drawing
scale

What You Need

ruler

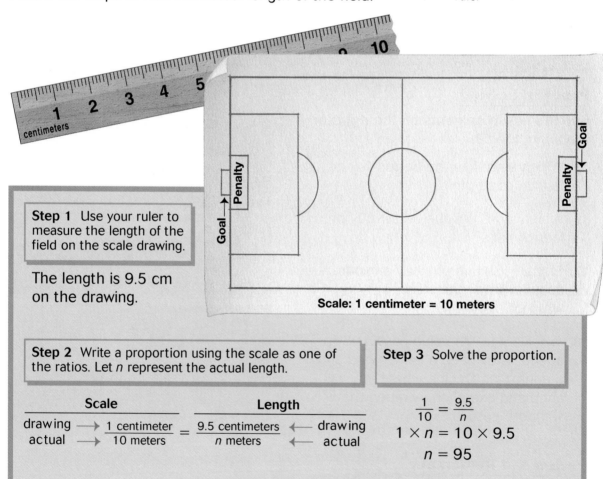

Step 1 Use your ruler to measure the length of the field on the scale drawing.

The length is 9.5 cm on the drawing.

Scale: 1 centimeter = 10 meters

Step 2 Write a proportion using the scale as one of the ratios. Let *n* represent the actual length.

$$\underbrace{\text{drawing} \longrightarrow \dfrac{1 \text{ centimeter}}{10 \text{ meters}}}_{\text{Scale}} \longleftarrow \text{actual} = \underbrace{\dfrac{9.5 \text{ centimeters}}{n \text{ meters}}}_{\text{Length}} \begin{array}{l}\longleftarrow \text{drawing} \\ \longleftarrow \text{actual}\end{array}$$

Step 3 Solve the proportion.

$$\frac{1}{10} = \frac{9.5}{n}$$
$$1 \times n = 10 \times 9.5$$
$$n = 95$$

The actual length of the field is 95 meters.

Connecting Ideas

Since maps are scale drawings, you can use what you learned about scale drawings to read maps.

The soccer club is traveling from Washington to Indianapolis for a tournament. About how many miles do they travel?

To find the distance, follow these steps.

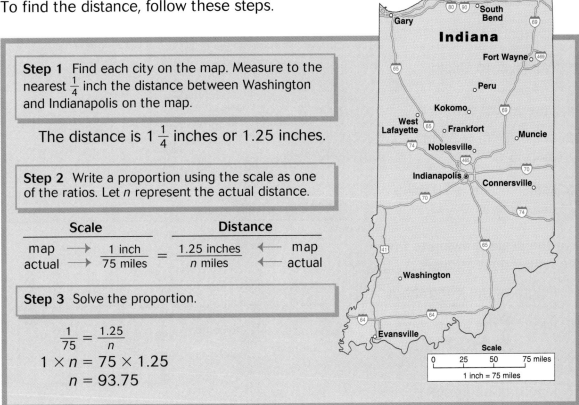

Step 1 Find each city on the map. Measure to the nearest $\frac{1}{4}$ inch the distance between Washington and Indianapolis on the map.

The distance is $1\frac{1}{4}$ inches or 1.25 inches.

Step 2 Write a proportion using the scale as one of the ratios. Let n represent the actual distance.

$$\underset{\text{actual}}{\overset{\text{map}}{}} \longrightarrow \frac{1 \text{ inch}}{75 \text{ miles}} = \frac{1.25 \text{ inches}}{n \text{ miles}} \longleftarrow \underset{\text{actual}}{\overset{\text{map}}{}}$$

Scale — **Distance**

Step 3 Solve the proportion.

$$\frac{1}{75} = \frac{1.25}{n}$$
$$1 \times n = 75 \times 1.25$$
$$n = 93.75$$

The distance the club travels is about 94 miles.

Think and Discuss Suppose 1 centimeter on a scale drawing is equal to 1 millimeter on the actual object. Is the actual object larger or smaller than the scale drawing? Explain.

INTERNET ACTIVITY
www.sbgmath.com

Try It Out

Use the scale drawing of the soccer field on page 314 to find the measures of the actual soccer field.

1. Length of the penalty box   **2.** Width of the field   **3.** Length of the goal

Use the map of Indiana to estimate the distance from

4. South Bend to Peru   **5.** Frankfort to Noblesville   **6.** Gary to Evansville

Practice

Use the map to find the approximate distance from

7. Boston to New Bedford

8. Newburyport to New Bedford

9. Providence to Boston

10. Lawrence to New Bedford

11. Fall River to Salem

Find the actual distance.

12. scale: 1 cm = 3 km
    map: 6 cm

13. scale: 1 inch = 10 miles
    map: $2\frac{1}{2}$ in.

Use the scale drawing to find the actual dimensions.

14. length of the living room

15. width of the living room

16. width of the balcony

17. length of bedroom 1

18. total length of the house

19. **Create Your Own** Make a scale drawing of a floor plan where you live.

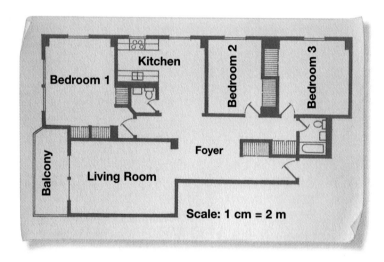

Find the actual measure. Use the scale $\frac{1}{4}$ in. = 1 ft.

20.

21.

22.

Problem Solving

Use the photo for Problems 23–26.
The scale for the model house is 1 in. = $2\frac{1}{2}$ ft.

23. Jon says that the room in the attic of the real house is 20 feet long. Do you agree? Why or why not?

24. How much did it cost to furnish this model bedroom? Use the chart below.

25. Can Sue put a 15-ft plant in this room in the real house? Why or why not?

26. You Decide Amy has $25 to spend on furniture for the kitchen. Which items might she choose to buy, and how much will she spend?

Doll House Furniture	
Refrigerator	$13.98
Sink	$9.98
Stove	$11.98
Chair	$6.98
Table	$14.98
Lamp	$5.98
Bed	$25.95
Dresser	$17.49
Crib	$12.75

Review and Remember

27. 8,045 ÷ 125   **28.** 16.5 ÷ 0.05   **29.** 7 ÷ 10   **30.** 20.8 ÷ 4   **31.** 90 ÷ 0.3

Ratios and Proportions

Choose a word from the Word Bank for each description.
(pages 300-317)

1. Comparison of two quantities

2. Ratio that compares two different quantities

3. Cost of one item

4. An equation stating that two ratios are equivalent

5. A drawing that is a reduction of an actual object

Word Bank

ratio
proportion
scale drawing
rate
unit price

Using Algebra **Find the missing number that makes the ratios equivalent.** (pages 300-303)

6. ■ : 6 = 40:60

7. $\frac{9}{■} = \frac{36}{44}$

8. 32 to 56 = ■ to 7

9. $\frac{14}{21} = \frac{■}{3}$

10. ■ : 45 = 5 to 9

11. $\frac{81}{63} = \frac{9}{■}$

12. 5 to 3 = 60 to ■

13. 15 to ■ = $\frac{60}{28}$

Using Algebra **Find the missing number.** (pages 304-309)

14. $\frac{n}{35} = \frac{6}{7}$

15. $\frac{15}{n} = \frac{1}{3}$

16. $\frac{12}{16} = \frac{3}{n}$

17. $\frac{77}{33} = \frac{n}{3}$

Find the unit rate. (pages 312-313)

18. $34.86 for 7 rockets

19. 146 miles in 4 hours

20. 16 cups for 4 people

21. 186 mi every 6 gal

22. $35.88 for 12 pounds

23. $4.50 for 30 pieces

Determine the better buy.

24. $46.50 for 6 airplanes or 8 airplanes for $61.04

25. 12 rockets for $119.40 or 6 rockets for $53.34

Use the scale drawing on the right. (pages 314-317)

26. Find the actual length of the room.

27. Find the actual width of the window.

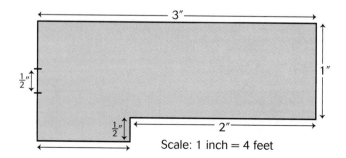

Scale: 1 inch = 4 feet

Problem Solving

28. Jenny reduced a print that was 9 in. wide and 15 in. long. If the width of the reduction is 3 in., what is the length?

29. For every 6 triangles on the quilt, there are 2 squares. What is the ratio of triangles to squares? Squares to triangles?

30. It costs 15¢ to develop a 4" × 6" photo and 30¢ to develop a panoramic photo. How many ways can you spend exactly $1.50 developing these types of photos? Which strategy did you use to solve the problem?

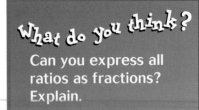

What do you think?

Can you express all ratios as fractions? Explain.

Journal Idea

In some ways, ratios are like fractions and in some ways they are different. Give examples to illustrate.

Critical Thinking Corner

Visual Thinking

The Golden Ratio

The rectangle the Greeks believed to be most pleasing to the eye is called the Golden Rectangle. Look at the rectangle in the photo. Find the ratio of the length to the width.

The ratio you found is an approximation of the **golden ratio.** Look for the golden ratio in architecture, works of art, and nature.

319

What Are My Chances?

Understanding probability can help you make predictions.

Learning About It

Suppose you play a game by tossing a number cube. You win if a 2 lands face up. What are the chances that a 2 will land face up when you toss the cube?

Work with a partner.

Conduct 3 experiments to see how often a 2 lands face up.

Step 1 Make a chart like the one below to record the result of each experiment. A trial is a toss of the number cube. The outcome is the number that appears face up when you toss the cube.

Step 2 Toss the number cube. Record the result in your chart. Look at the chart to see how many times to toss the number cube for each experiment.

What You Need

For each pair:
  number cube 1 to 6

Experiment 1	**10 Trials**	Outcome	1	2	3	4	5	6
		Tally						
Experiment 2	**25 Trials**	Outcome	1	2	3	4	5	6
		Tally						
Experiment 3	**50 Trials**	Outcome	1	2	3	4	5	6
		Tally						

Step 3 For each experiment, write a ratio comparing the number of times a 2 lands face up to the total number of trials. What happens as the number of trials increases?

Connecting Ideas

You have done experiments with one number cube. Now look at how your chances change when you toss two number cubes.

Step 1 Copy and complete the chart on the right. The chart shows all of the possible ways two number cubes can land. A (2, 2) means that a 2 lands face up on both cubes.

Step 2 Toss two number cubes 50 times. Keep a tally of the results. How many times did a 2 land face up on both cubes?

Think and Discuss What is more likely, tossing a 2 with one number cube or tossing two 2s with two number cubes?

Possible Outcomes

	2nd cube					
1st cube	**1**	**2**	**3**	**4**	**5**	**6**
1	1,1	1,2	1,3	1,4	1,5	1,6
2	2,1	2,2	2,3		2,5	2,6
3	3,1	3,2	3,3		3,5	
4				4,4	4,5	
5		5,2			5,5	
6	6,1		6,3			6,6

Practice

1. Toss a coin 50 times. Keep a tally of your results. Compare your results with the class.

   heads   tails

2. Make a spinner like the one on the right. Spin the spinner 50 times. Keep a tally of your results.

   red   yellow   blue

Time for Technology
Using the Math Processor™ CD-ROM

Explore Probability

Link a number cube space to a spreadsheet, and a bar graph.

- Click menu number cube. Drag to "2 cubes." Roll 100. Roll 400. Roll 500. Roll 1,000.

- Click menu number cube. Drag to "3 cubes." Roll 100. Roll 400. Roll 500. Roll 1,000.

Write about what you observed.

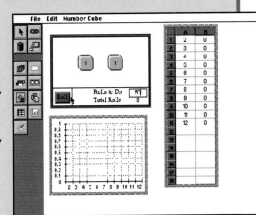

Tossing and Spinning

You can use a ratio to indicate a probability.

Learning About It

Some board games are based on chance. You do not know what number will be tossed or where the spinner will land. You can use probability to find out whether a specific event or outcome is likely to occur.

Word Bank

probability
impossible event
certain event

> The **probability** of an event is the ratio of the number of favorable outcomes to the number of all possible outcomes.
>
> $$P = \frac{\text{number of favorable outcomes}}{\text{number of possible outcomes}}$$

What is the probability of tossing a 5 on the number cube?

$P(5) = \frac{1}{6}$ ← one 5 on the cube
← six numbers on the cube

The probability of a 5 is $\frac{1}{6}$.

What is the probability of the spinner landing on green?

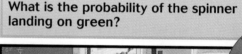

$P(\text{green}) = \frac{4}{8}$ ← four green sections
← eight sections in all

The probability of green is $\frac{4}{8}$ or $\frac{1}{2}$.

More Examples

A. Tossing an even number

$P(\text{even numbers}) = \frac{3}{6}$ or $\frac{1}{2}$

B. Landing on green or yellow

$P(\text{green or yellow}) = \frac{6}{8}$ or $\frac{3}{4}$

Connecting Ideas

You have learned how to find the probability that an event will happen. You can use what you know to find the probability that an event will not happen.

The probability that 5 will land face up on the number cube is $\frac{1}{6}$. What is the probability that 5 will not land face up on the cube? This means that any number can land face up but 5.

There are five such numbers: 1, 2, 3, 4, or 6.

$$P(\text{not }5) = \frac{5}{6} \quad \begin{array}{l} \leftarrow \text{ five possible numbers} \\ \leftarrow \text{ six numbers on the cube} \end{array}$$

Notice that $P(5) + (\text{not }5)$ is $\frac{1}{6} + \frac{5}{6} = \frac{6}{6}$ or 1.

The probability of an event can be any number from 0 to 1.

An event that has a probability of 0 is an **impossible event**.

$$P(7) = 0$$

An event that has a probability of 1 is a **certain event**.

$$P(1,2,3,4,5, \text{ or } 6) = 1$$

More Examples

Look at the spinner on page 322.

A. $P(\text{not yellow})$

$P(\text{yellow}) = \frac{1}{4}$

$P(\text{not yellow}) = 1 - \frac{1}{4} = \frac{3}{4}$

B. $P(\text{purple})$

There is no purple on the spinner.

$P(\text{purple}) = 0$

Think and Discuss Look at page 322. Tossing any number on the number cube is equally likely. Is spinning any color on the spinner equally likely? Why or why not?

INTERNET ACTIVITY
www.sbgmath.com

Try It Out

Look at the spinner on the right. Find the probability.

1. $P(1)$

2. $P(2)$

3. $P(\text{not }2)$

4. $P(1 \text{ or } 4)$

5. $P(\text{odd number})$

6. $P(6)$

7. $P(4 \text{ or not }4)$

8. $P(\text{even number})$

9. $P(4)$

Practice

Look at the spinner at the right to find each probability.

10. $P(B)$ **11.** $P(C)$ **12.** $P(\text{not } C)$

13. $P(B \text{ or } C)$ **14.** $P(\text{not } A)$ **15.** $P(D)$

16. Create Your Own   Write a probability question for the spinner on the right. Provide the answer.

Suppose you mix the marbles, then choose one from the box at the right without looking. Find each probability.

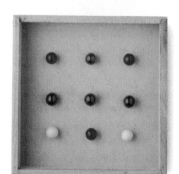

17. $P(\text{red})$ **18.** $P(\text{green})$

19. $P(\text{white})$ **20.** $P(\text{green or yellow})$

21. $P(\text{not yellow})$ **22.** $P(\text{marble})$

23. Analyze   A box has 10 marbles. If $P(\text{green}) = \frac{4}{5}$ and $P(\text{yellow}) = \frac{1}{5}$, how many of each color are in the box?

The letters at the right are put in a bag. Suppose you choose a letter without looking. Find each probability.

24. $P(N)$ **25.** $P(R)$ **26.** $P(O \text{ or } R)$ **27.** $P(\text{not } P)$

28. $P(\text{vowel})$ **29.** $P(A)$ **30.** $P(N \text{ or } O)$ **31.** $P(\text{not } O)$

Critical Thinking Corner

Logical Thinking

What's Wrong?

Tom wanted to make a number cube so that

$$P(2) = \frac{1}{2} \qquad P(4) = \frac{1}{3} \qquad P(6) = \frac{1}{6}$$

To make the number cube, Tom placed the numbers 2, 4, and 6 as shown on the pattern on the right. What did Tom do wrong?

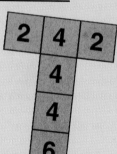

Problem Solving

Use the photo at the right for Problems 32–37.
Suppose a student picks a marble without looking,
and then puts the marble back.

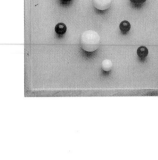

32. Mical's favorite color is green. What is the probability
that Mical will pick a green marble?

33. What is the probability that Alexis will pick a big
marble?

34. David likes yellow marbles. What is the probability
that David will not pick a yellow marble?

35. What is the probability that Dawn will pick a small
red marble?

36. Explain Cathy looked when she picked her marble.
What is the probability that she picked her favorite
marble?

37. Analyze Is the probability of picking a green marble
or a red marble greater than the probability of picking
a green marble? Why or why not?

Review and Remember

Using Algebra Solve for x.

38. $x + 8 = 17$

39. $12 - x = 8$

40. $9x = 900$

41. $7x = 707$

42. $x \div 5 = 100$

43. $900 \div x = 9$

Money $ense

Figure It Out

Margaret bought a pair of jeans, four
pairs of socks, a denim jacket, and a
sweat shirt. After figuring out an
estimated total, Margaret gave the clerk
$76.00. Was this a reasonable estimate?
How much change should she expect to
get back? If Margaret had $100.00 to
spend, could she buy another pair of
jeans and 2 more pairs of socks? Explain.

2 pair
$2.75

$32.95

$17.95

$19.95

Problem Solving
Use a Simulation

You can sometimes solve a problem by simulating the action, or acting it out.

*S*even identical boxes are arranged in a circle. The boxes are numbered 1 to 7 clockwise, and a prize has been placed in box number 7. To win the prize, a player must remove every box from the circle except for box number 7. The player removes a box and then, moving clockwise, removes every other box until only box number 7 remains. To be sure the box with the prize is the last one left, where should a player begin?

UNDERSTAND

What do you need to know?

You need to know where to begin so that the box with the prize is left.

PLAN

How can you solve the problem?

You can **use a simulation** to solve the problem. Number seven pieces of paper from 1 to 7 and arrange them in a circle, going clockwise from 1 to 7.

SOLVE

Choose any numbered paper as the starting point. Start by removing that number and continue removing pieces of paper, according to the rule, until there is only one numbered paper left. If necessary, choose a different starting point and try again. Repeat until only the piece of paper with the 7 is left.

   To win a player must start on the number 2.

LOOK BACK

What If? Suppose the rules require a player to remove every third box. Where should you begin, so that box number 7 will be left at the end?

Using the Strategy

Try using a simulation to solve Problems 1–4.

1 Carl has 9 baseball cards with 3 players from each of 3 teams. He wants to put 3 cards in a row and 3 rows on a page in his album. How can he arrange the cards so that each row and each column has one player from each team?

2 Katie is playing a board game with her sister. She moves her piece 8 spaces forward from START, then 2 spaces back, and 3 spaces forward. Her sister moves 12 spaces forward from START and then 3 spaces back. How far apart are their two pieces?

3 You want to cut a square piece of plastic into 9 equal squares to be used as a game. What is the fewest number of cuts you can use to make the squares?

4 Six friends formed a circle for a cheerleading routine. Karyn stood at Ellen's right. Ellen stood across from Sue. Tracy did not stand next to Sue, but she did stand next to Colleen. Marsha stood between Karyn and Sue. Who stood at Sue's right?

Mixed Strategy Review

Try these or other strategies to solve each problem.
Tell which strategy you used.

THERE'S ALWAYS A WAY!

Problem Solving Strategies

- Guess and Check
- Find a Pattern
- Work Backwards
- Make a Table

5 While playing Rocket Race, Gina recorded her scores in a table like the one at the right. If this pattern continues, what will her score be for the seventh game?

Rocket Race						
Game	1	2	3	4	5	6
Score	25	30	40	60	100	180

6 Sabrina had 20 points at the end of the Monster Maze game. During the game, she lost 10 points when she took a wrong turn. She lost twice as many points when she fell off the bridge. How many points did she have when she started to play?

7 Freddy and Eileen collect video games. Freddy has 8 more games than Eileen. Together they have a total of 44 games. How many games does each of them have?

Lots of Food

Sometimes you have a combination of events and you need to count all the possible outcomes.

Learning About It

The cooking club has a "Sandwich Luncheon." A sandwich consists of one choice of bread and one choice of filling. What kind of sandwiches can be made? How many different kinds of sandwiches are there?

Word Bank

tree diagram
counting principle

beef

chicken

vegetables

pita

tortilla

- **One way** to find the number of different kinds of sandwiches is to draw a **tree diagram**.

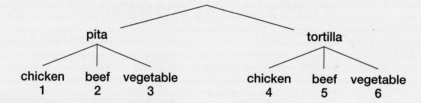

pita				tortilla		
chicken	beef	vegetable		chicken	beef	vegetable
1	2	3		4	5	6

There are 6 different kinds of sandwiches.

- **Another way** is to use the **counting principle**.

If there are *m* possible outcomes for the first event and *n* possible outcomes for the second event, then there are *m* x *n* total possible outcomes.

2 possible breads x 3 possible fillings = 6 kinds of sandwiches

There are 6 kinds of sandwiches that can be made.

Think and Discuss Explain how you would use a tree diagram to find the number of possible sandwiches if you had a choice of 2 breads, 3 fillings, and 2 toppings.

Try It Out

Sauces	Pasta
alfredo	spaghetti
tomato	fettuccini
carbonara	

1. Draw a tree diagram to show the possible combinations of sauce and pasta. How many possible outcomes are there?

2. How many possible outcomes do you have if you include another sauce?

3. Use the counting principle to find the number of possible outcomes for tossing a number cube and tossing a coin.

Practice

**For Exercises 4 and 5, draw a tree diagram.
Tell how many possible outcomes there are.**

4.

5.

Yogurt Flavor	Size
strawberry	small
orange	medium
chocolate	large
vanilla	

Use the counting principle to find the number of possible outcomes taking one from each category.

6. 5 vegetables, 7 fruits　　7. 12 colors, 4 cards　　8. 10 meals, 4 desserts

Problem Solving

9. Find the number of possible outcomes for a meat and vegetable.

10. Find the number of possible outcomes for a meat, a vegetable, and a sauce.

11. **Journal Idea** Does the order in which choices are made affect the number of possible outcomes? Explain why or why not.

meats: chicken, hamburger

vegetables: broccoli, peppers, carrots, onions

sauces: ketchup, mustard

Review and Remember

Compare. Use >, < or = for each ●.

12. $\frac{1}{4}$ ● $\frac{2}{3}$　　　13. 4 ● $3\frac{5}{5}$　　　14. $1\frac{1}{2}$ ● $1\frac{5}{8}$

Being Independent

Use the counting techniques you learned to find the probability of two or more events.

Learning About It

All year long everyone looks forward to the carnival sponsored by the Math Club.

Part of the carnival has games of chance. You can win a prize by spinning an A and then a yellow. What is the probability of winning a prize?

You need to find P(A, yellow).

THERE'S ALWAYS A WAY!

● **One way** is to count the outcomes and find the probability.

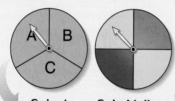

Spin A		Spin Yellow		
1	×	2	= 2	favorable outcomes

First Spinner		Second Spinner		
3	×	4	= 12	possible outcomes

$$P(\text{A, yellow}) = \frac{2}{12} \text{ or } \frac{1}{6}$$

● **Another way** is to find the probability of each event and multiply.

Step 1 Find the probability.	**Step 2** Multiply.
$P(\text{A}) = \frac{1}{3}$ $P(\text{yellow}) = \frac{1}{2}$	$P(\text{A, yellow}) = \frac{1}{3} \times \frac{1}{2} = \frac{1}{6}$

The probability of winning a prize is $\frac{1}{6}$ or 1 out of 6 tries.

Think and Discuss If you use a tree diagram to count the number of total outcomes, do you need to list the color yellow twice? Why or why not?

Try It Out

The duck pond is a game where players choose two ducks without looking. After picking the first duck, they replace it and pick the second duck. Use the information to find each probability.

1. P(red, red)   **2.** P(green, red)   **3.** P(yellow, green)   **4.** P(green green)

5. Analyze Is P(green, yellow) the same as P(yellow, green)? Why or why not?

Practice

Suppose that when you throw a dart without looking, you hit a balloon on the dartboard. Each time a balloon is burst, it is replaced with one of the same color. Use the information to find each probability.

6. P(red, green)   **7.** P(red, red)   **8.** P(blue, green)   **9.** P(red, blue)

10. P(red, white)   **11.** P(red, not red)   **12.** P(yellow, green)   **13.** P(red, not blue)

Players toss two cubes numbered 1 to 6. Find each probability.

14. P(1, 1)   **15.** P(3, 5)   **16.** P(1, even)

17. P(odd, even)   **18.** P(not 1, 6)   **19.** P(not 3, not 4)

Problem Solving

Players pick a letter from a bag without looking. They record it and put it back. They pick another letter in the same way.

20. What is the probability of picking the letter S twice?

21. What is the probability of not picking a vowel either time?

22. What is the probability of forming the word IS?

Review and Remember

23. 10,005 − 899   **24.** 23,455 + 459 + 7   **25.** 205 × 207

For Extra Practice, see Set G, page 338.

Problem Solving
Using Sampling

Sampling can help you predict about how many items in a large number will have certain characteristics.

In a sample of 25 miniature race cars, the quality control department at the Power Track Toy Factory rejected 2 cars for manufacturer's defects. About how many cars will be rejected in a production run of 10,000 cars?

 UNDERSTAND

What do you know?

You know 2 out of every 25 cars were rejected in the sample.

 PLAN

How can you solve the problem?

You can use the information to write a proportion. Then use the proportion to solve the problem.

 SOLVE

Let y represent the number of cars that will be rejected in a production run of 10,000 cars.

Sample		Production Run
$\frac{2}{25}$	$=$	$\frac{y}{10{,}000}$

$$25 \times y = 2 \times 10{,}000$$
$$y = 20{,}000 \div 25 = 800$$

About 800 cars will be rejected.

 LOOK BACK

Check your answer by comparing $\frac{2}{25}$ and $\frac{800}{10{,}000}$. Are $\frac{2}{25}$ and $\frac{800}{10{,}000}$ equivalent?

Show What You Learned

Employees at the Power Track Toy Factory came up with suggestions for improving the quality of the game pieces they manufacture. Use their suggestions and the concept of sampling to solve Problems 1–6.

Jesse—
"Why don't you give each of us a $25 bonus every time we complete a production run of 5,000?"

Bob—
"I could do my job better if I had a 10-minute break every 2 hours."

Dominique:
"I would like our goal to be no more than 800 defective game pieces in a production run of 20,000."

Colleen—
"I think someone should check 10 game pieces every 15 minutes."

Gina:
"Let's check 3 out of every 5 game pieces for defects."

Geraldo—
"We need to reduce the number of defective game pieces to only 1 out of 100."

1 **Describe** How many game pieces will be checked in a production run of 20,000 if Gina's suggestion is followed? Do you think this is reasonable? Why or why not?

2 If Geraldo's idea is accepted, about how many game pieces will be defective in a production run of 10,000 game pieces?

3 How many game pieces will be checked in an 8-hour shift if Colleen's suggestion is implemented?

4 If Bob's suggestion is approved, how much time will he spend on breaks in an 8-hour shift?

5 **Explain** About how many game pieces will be defective in a sample of 25, if Dominique's idea is used?

6 **Analyze** If Jesse's idea is accepted, how much will she make in bonus money if she completes seven production runs of 10,000 each?

7 **Create Your Own** Make up your own suggestion for the suggestion box. Write a problem that involves samples. Use a proportion to solve the problem.

Checkpoint

Probability and Counting Outcomes

Vocabulary

Choose a word from the word bank for each description.

1. An event that has a probability of zero

2. Ratio of the number of favorable outcomes to the number of all possible outcomes

3. A way to find the total possible outcomes for a combination of events

4. An event that has a probability of one

> **Word Bank**
>
> certain event
> counting principle
> impossible event
> probability

Concepts and Skills

Use the spinner at the right to find each probability.
(pages 322–325)

5. $P(8)$ **6.** $P(5)$ **7.** $P(5 \text{ or } 7)$

8. $P(2 \text{ or } 5)$ **9.** $P(\text{not } 1)$ **10.** $P(\text{not } 7)$

The letters of the word VACATION are put in a hat. Pick a letter without looking. Find each probability.
(pages 322–325)

11. $P(I)$ **12.** $P(V)$ **13.** $P(\text{not } A)$ **14.** $P(C)$ **15.** $P(\text{vowel})$

Using Algebra Draw a tree diagram. Find the number of possible outcomes taking one from each category.
(pages 328–329)

16.

Bread	Meat
rye	turkey
wheat	ham
	beef

17.

Vegetable	Dip
broccoli	onion
carrot	salsa
celery	cheese

18.

Ice Cream	Topping
vanilla	fudge
chocolate	butterscotch
strawberry	

19. 5 flavors, 2 sizes   **20.** 4 salads, 4 dressings   **21.** 7 colors, 3 styles

The letters of the word SCHOOL are put in a hat. Pick a letter from the hat and replace it. Find each probability.
(pages 330–331)

22. $P(S, C)$ **23.** $P(H, \text{not } L)$ **24.** $P(O, \text{not } O)$ **25.** $P(O, L)$

Problem Solving

Use the table below to solve Problems 26–29.

Cereals	Milks	Fruits
corn flakes	skim	strawberries
rice puffs	1%	raisins
oat puffs	2%	blueberries
corn puffs	whole	
wheat flakes		

What do you think?

How can you use tree diagrams to help you count?

26. Draw a tree diagram to show all the possible outcomes for choosing a cereal and fruit.

27. What is the number of possible outcomes for choosing a cereal, milk, and a fruit?

28. What is the number of possible outcomes for choosing a cereal and a milk?

29. What is the probability of choosing rice puffs and whole milk?

30. Mrs. Bernstein is giving a pop quiz next week. What is the probability that the quiz will be on Tuesday?

Journal Idea

The probability of picking a red marble from a bag is $\frac{3}{5}$. You add a green marble to the bag. Now what is the probability of picking a red marble? Explain.

You Decide

Activity

Tops and Bottoms

Tina, Tom, and Marc are planning a "tops and bottoms" shopping spree. Help them decide on the ratio of shirts to pants each should buy. Then, using that ratio, describe or cut out clothing ads for five to ten different shirts and pants for them to buy.

- Make a list of all the different outfits they can wear with the shirts and pants that they will buy.

You might wish to include this work in your portfolio.

Extra Practice

Set A (pages 300–303)

Look at the set to the right for Exercises 1–3.
Write each ratio in three ways.

1. blue triangles to green squares

2. red circles to green squares

3. blue shapes to red shapes

Tell whether the ratios are equivalent.

4. $\frac{3}{5}, \frac{5}{7}$

5. $\frac{10}{8}, \frac{15}{12}$

6. $\frac{12}{20}, \frac{3}{5}$

7. 6 to 5 , 12 to 10

Using Algebra **Find each missing number.**

8. $\frac{2}{7} = \frac{\blacksquare}{21}$

9. $\frac{12}{5} = \frac{36}{\blacksquare}$

10. $\frac{6}{\blacksquare} = \frac{30}{5}$

11. $\frac{\blacksquare}{6} = \frac{6}{18}$

12. $\frac{2}{3} = \frac{14}{\blacksquare}$

13. $\frac{\blacksquare}{27} = \frac{1}{9}$

Solve.

14. What is the ratio of red triangles to green triangles?

15. If this pattern is repeated so that there are 24 red triangles, how many green triangles will there be?

Set B (pages 306–309)

Tell whether the ratios can form a proportion.

1. $\frac{9}{8}, \frac{7}{8}$

2. $\frac{4}{3}, \frac{12}{9}$

3. $\frac{2}{11}, \frac{7}{77}$

4. $\frac{5}{8}, \frac{45}{70}$

Using Algebra **For each proportion, find n.**

5. $\frac{6}{10} = \frac{n}{15}$

6. $\frac{10}{12} = \frac{5}{n}$

7. $\frac{n}{20} = \frac{45}{60}$

8. $\frac{12}{n} = \frac{30}{5}$

9. $\frac{n}{9} = \frac{15}{27}$

10. $\frac{6}{n} = \frac{42}{49}$

11. $\frac{3}{8} = \frac{n}{56}$

12. $\frac{5}{8} = \frac{25}{n}$

Solve.

13. The Photography Club wants to enlarge a photograph that is 10 inches wide and 14 inches long. If the length of the enlargement is 28 inches, what is the width?

Extra Practice

Set C (pages 312–313)

Find the unit price. Round to the nearest cent.

1. $5.95 for 10 disks

2. $79.95 for 3 ink cartridges

3. $38.98 for 2 dust covers

4. $6.95 for 200 sheets

5. $379 for 5 keyboards

6. $179.97 for 3 CD's

 Use your calculator to determine the better buy.

7. $79 for 16 MB of memory
or $139 for 32 MB

8. $42.50 for 12 mousepads
or $35.20 for 8

Solve.

9. A catalog offered a surge protector for $27.95. A computer store will sell 6 of the same surge protectors for $156.59. Which offer should the Computer Club recommend?

10. A roll of film that takes 24 photographs costs $3.36. Another roll costs $3.78 for 27 photographs. Do the rolls cost the same amount for each photograph?

Set D (pages 314–317)

Use the scale drawing to find the actual dimensions.

1. length of the Picnic Bench area

2. width of the Picnic Bench area

3. width of the duck pond at its widest point

4. length of the footpath from the entrance to the exit

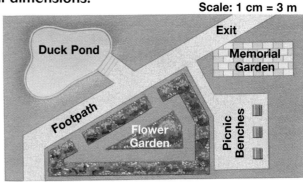

Solve.

5. The Gardening Club wants to buy 10 new picnic tables. If the tables are 1.5 m by 2 m, will they fit in the Picnic Bench area? Why or why not?

6. For Memorial Day, a small flag will be placed every 0.5 meters around Memorial Garden. About how many flags must be purchased?

Extra Practice

Set E (pages 322–325)

Use the spinner at the right to find each probability.

1. $P(X)$ **2.** $P(Z)$ **3.** $P(\text{not } Y)$

4. $P(\text{not } Z)$ **5.** $P(Y)$ **6.** $P(\text{not } X)$

The letters of the word BLINDFOLD are put in a hat. Suppose you choose a letter without looking. Find each probability.

7. $P(B)$ **8.** $P(I)$ **9.** $P(\text{not } F)$ **10.** $P(D)$ **11.** $P(B \text{ or } D)$

12. $P(\text{vowel})$ **13.** $P(L)$ **14.** $P(D \text{ or } L)$ **15.** $P(S)$ **16.** $P(F)$

Set F (pages 328–329)

Use the counting principle to find the number of possible outcomes taking one from each category.

1. 4 colors, 3 sizes   **2.** 5 pastas, 4 sauces   **3.** 3 sizes, 7 toppings

Use the table on the right to solve Problems 4–5.

4. Find the number of possible outcomes for an art and a sport.

5. Find the number of possible outcomes for a sport and a performing activity.

After School Activities		
Arts	**Sports**	**Performing Arts**
Pottery	Soccer	Band
Painting	Lacrosse	Orchestra
Sketching	Basketball	Chorus
	Softball	Drama
		Ballet

Set G (pages 330–331)

Suppose you toss two cubes labeled A–F. Find each probability.

1. $P(A, B)$ **2.** $P(C, F)$ **3.** $P(A, \text{not } A)$ **4.** $P(\text{not } C, \text{not } D)$

Use the bag on the right to solve Problems 5–6.

5. Suppose you pick 3 letters, one at a time, replacing the letter each time. What is the probability of spelling OUR?

6. Look back at 5. What is the probability of spelling FOR?

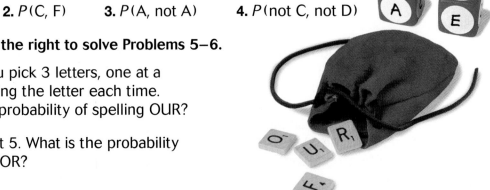

Look at the shapes on the right. Write each ratio in 3 ways.

1. all circles to all squares

2. red circles to green triangles

3. red shapes to blue squares

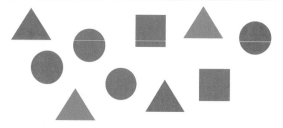

For each proportion, find *n*.

4. $\frac{9}{45} = \frac{3}{n}$

5. $\frac{7}{n} = \frac{49}{63}$

6. $\frac{11}{12} = \frac{n}{36}$

Find the unit price. Round to the nearest cent.

7. 9.2 lb bananas at $3.99

8. 6 oz tuna at $1.29

Use the scale drawing on the right to answer Problems 9–11.

9. What is the actual length of the store?

10. What is the actual width of the store?

11. What is the actual length of each aisle?

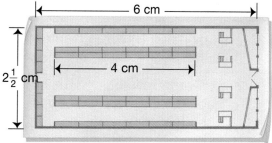

Scale: 1 cm = 4 m

Suppose you pick a marble without looking. Find each probability.

12. P(red)

13. P(green)

14. P(not red)

15. P(yellow)

Replace the first marble. Pick again. Find each probability.

16. P(red, green)

17. P(green, green)

18. P(green, yellow)

Solve.

19. Jen stopped for yogurt. There were 4 flavors and 3 toppings. Find the number of possible choices for a yogurt with a topping.

20. A copy machine reduced the size of a copy that was 12 inches wide and 16 inches long. If the width of the copy was 9 in., what was the length?

 Self-Check For Questions 4–6, did you use cross products to check your answers?

Performance Assessment

Show What You Know About Ratio, Proportion, and Probability

1 The table shows part of the inventory at a hobby shop.

    a. Write two equivalent ratios using different items. Write the ratios in as many ways as possible.

    b. Find the total number of items in the hobby store if the ratio of kites to the total number of items is 1:8.

    Self-Check For Question 1a, did you remember that ratios can be written in three different forms?

Hobby Shop	
Item	**Number**
Kites	25
Model cars	37
Model trains	40
Model ships	18
Model planes	15
Doll houses	24
Other items	?
Total number of items	?

2 Tommy made this tree diagram to show the outcomes for spinning a spinner and tossing a coin.

    a. Draw the spinner, assume that each color is equally likely. Then find the probability of spinning a red.

    b. How many possible outcomes are shown for his experiment of spinning a spinner and tossing a coin?

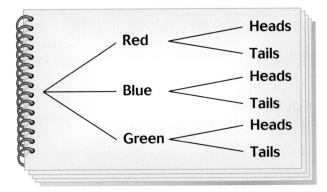

    c. Tell how you can use the tree diagram to find the probability of spinning a blue on the spinner and tossing a tail on the coin.

    d. Is P(red) the same as P(heads)? Explain your reasoning.

    Self-Check Did you remember that the probability is the number of favorable outcomes divided by the total number of outcomes?

For Your Portfolio

You might wish to include this work in your portfolio.

Extension

Dependent Events

Suppose Joe picks a sock from the laundry basket without looking. He picks a blue sock and puts it on. He then picks another sock from the same laundry basket without looking. What is the probability that Joe will pick a blue sock the second time?

Since Joe does not put the first sock back, the laundry basket now has 11 socks. The probability that Joe will pick a blue sock the second time depends on the color of the first sock he picked.

▶ If Joe picks a blue sock the first time, then there are only 2 blue socks left.

P(Joe picks blue the second time) $= \frac{2}{11}$

▶ What if Joe does not pick a blue sock the first time? There are still 3 blue socks in the laundry basket.

P(Joe picks blue the second time) $= \frac{3}{11}$

Suppose Joe puts the two socks back. Then his brother Al picks a sock from the same laundry basket.

1. If Al picks a white sock the first time, find the probability that the color of the sock he picks the second time will be

   a. blue   b. white   c. brown

2. If Al picks a brown sock the first time, find the probability that the color of the sock he picks the second time will be

   a. blue   b. white   c. brown

3. **Create Your Own** Create a probability problem where one event is dependent on another.

Cumulative Review

Preparing for Tests

Choose the correct letter for each answer.

Number Concepts	Operations

Number Concepts

1. Which fraction is greater than $\frac{5}{16}$?

   A. $\frac{1}{8}$

   B. $\frac{1}{5}$

   C. $\frac{1}{4}$

   D. $\frac{3}{8}$

2. What is 432.668 rounded to the nearest ten?

   A. 432.700
   B. 432.670
   C. 430
   D. 400

3. Which decimal is equivalent to $\frac{6}{8}$?

   A. 0.45
   B. 0.60
   C. 0.75
   D. 0.80

4. Which is the prime factorization of 100?

   A. $2^2 \times 5^2$
   B. $5^2 \times 3^2$
   C. 3×25
   D. 2×50

Operations

5. Monica is taping a television show that is 3 hours long. If she has taped $1\frac{3}{4}$ hours of the show, how much of the show is still left to be taped?

   A. $2\frac{3}{4}$ h   C. $1\frac{1}{4}$ h

   B. $2\frac{1}{4}$ h   D. $\frac{3}{4}$ h

6. If you can buy 12 batteries for $10.80, how much will 15 batteries cost?

   A. $10.80   D. $15.90
   B. $12.80   E. Not Here
   C. $13.50

7. Dave saved $124.45. Then he bought a boom box for $56.89 and 4 CDs for $9.99 each. How much did he have left?

   A. $27.60   D. $96.85
   B. $57.57   E. Not Here
   C. $67.56

8. Ruth rode her bike $5\frac{1}{8}$ miles on Friday, $2\frac{3}{4}$ miles on Saturday and $3\frac{3}{8}$ miles on Sunday. How many miles did she ride in all?

   A. $10\frac{1}{4}$ mi   C. $11\frac{1}{4}$ mi

   B. $10\frac{6}{8}$ mi   D. $11\frac{3}{8}$ mi

Patterns, Relationships, and Algebraic Thinking	Probability and Statistics

9. What is the ratio of triangles to squares in the picture below?

- **A.** 4:2
- **B.** 3:2
- **C.** 2:4
- **D.** 3:1

10. Which number makes the ratios equivalent?

$10:x = 5:6$

- **A.** 8
- **B.** 12
- **C.** 15
- **D.** 30

Use the coordinate grid below to answer Questions 11–12.

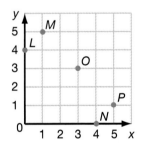

11. Which point is best named by the ordered pair (1,5)?

- **A.** L
- **B.** M
- **C.** N
- **D.** O
- **E.** P

12. Which ordered pair is best represented by Point N?

- **A.** (5, 1)
- **B.** (1, 5)
- **C.** (0, 4)
- **D.** (4, 0)

13. Frank is playing a game with his brother. He will win if he gets a 3 the next time he tosses a cube numbered from 1 to 6. What are his chances of winning?

- **A.** 1 out of 3
- **B.** 2 out of 6
- **C.** 3 out of 4
- **D.** 1 out of 6

14. There are 12 marbles in a box. If $P(\text{red}) = \frac{3}{6}$, $P(\text{blue}) = \frac{1}{6}$, and $P(\text{white}) = \frac{2}{6}$, how many red marbles are in the box?

- **A.** 2
- **C.** 4
- **B.** 3
- **D.** 6

Use the diagram below to answer Questions 15–16.

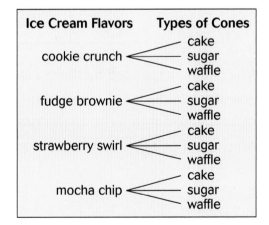

15. How many different combinations of ice cream cones can you buy?

- **A.** 3
- **C.** 7
- **B.** 4
- **D.** 12

16. If you only like sugar cones, how many choices do you have?

- **A.** 1
- **C.** 4
- **B.** 3
- **D.** 7

Understanding and Using Percent

Chapter Theme: SHOPPING

REAL-WORLD
Math

··················Real Facts···················

Store owners often use percent when they hold a sale. They select the items they want to put on sale. Then they decide by what percent to reduce prices.

Prices for Selected Items			
Item	Original Price	Percent Off	Sale Price
Backpack	$40	50%	$20
Pants	$48	25%	$36
Gloves	$22	50%	$11
Jacket	$105	40%	$63

• Which item is reduced by the greatest dollar amount?

• How does 50% of $22 differ from 50% of $40?

• Which items are reduced by the greatest percent?

• Which item or items do you think are the best buy? Explain why.

··················Real People···················

Meet Mohamed Ayad. He owns and operates **CAPS +**, where he sells personalized caps, shirts, and jackets. If you want something personalized, he is the one to see! The girl in the photograph at the right is about to order a special item from Mohamed.

Squares and Percents

You can use a hundreds grid to model percents.

Learning About It

A **percent** is a special ratio that compares a number with 100. *Percent* means "per hundred."

You can use a grid with 100 squares to model percents.

40% means "40 out of 100." The grid at the right has 100 squares and shows 40%. How many squares out of 100 are shaded?

Work with a partner.

Step 1 Look at the grids below. For each grid, count how many squares out of 100 are shaded. What percent does each grid represent?

What You Need

For each pair:
  grid paper
  ruler

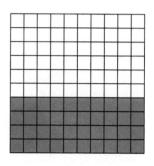

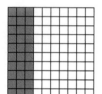 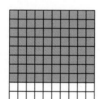

Step 2 Outline several hundreds grids and draw a model for each percent below. Compare your drawings with those of your partner.

  70%   15%   64%   8%

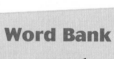
Word Bank

percent

Step 3 Look back at the grid that shows 40%. You can represent the shaded part by writing a percent, a decimal, or a fraction.

Percent	Decimal	Fraction
40%	0.40	$\frac{40}{100}$ or $\frac{2}{5}$

Look at the models you made for Step 2. Record the shaded part of each model as a percent, a decimal, and a fraction.

Think and Discuss Use the grid that shows 40%. Write a percent, a decimal, and a fraction that describes the part of the grid that is not shaded.

Practice

Write the percent shown by the shaded part of each grid.

1. 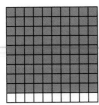 **2.** 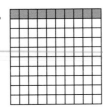 **3.** 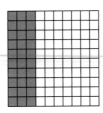 **4.**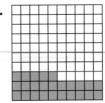

5. 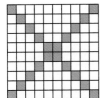 **6.**   **7.** 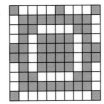 **8.**

Use grid paper to represent each percent.

9. 10% **10.** 45% **11.** 75% **12.** 90%

13. 32% **14.** 28% **15.** 2% **16.** 100%

Choose the correct percent.

17. 10 per hundred

   a. 1% **b.** 10% **c.** 100%

18. $\frac{3}{100}$

   a. 3% **b.** 30% **c.** 300%

19. Generalize Look back at each grid you made for Exercises 9–16. For each grid, how does the percent shaded and the percent unshaded compare with 100%?

20. How many squares would you shade to represent 100%? 150%?

21. Analyze If $\frac{1}{4}$ of the grid is shaded, what percent of the grid is shaded? What if you shade $\frac{3}{4}$ of the grid?

22. Journal Idea Suppose that 50% of the students in your school eat lunch at noon. Does that mean that 50 students eat lunch at your school at noon? Explain your reasoning.

23. Create Your Own Outline a hundred grid and shade some of the squares. Have your partner find the percent of the grid you have shaded.

Paint Shop

You can write a percent as a decimal or a decimal as a percent.

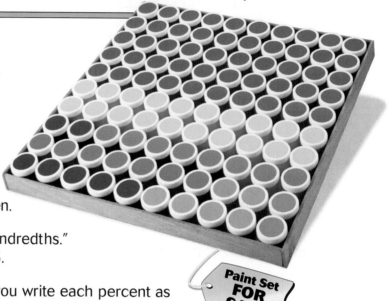

Paint Set
FOR
SALE

Learning About It

The paint shop sells a package of 100 paints. What percent of the paints are green? How could you write the percent of green paints as a decimal?

Look at the paint set. 5 out of 100, or 5%, of the paints are green.

5% means "5 out of 100, or 5 hundredths."
5 hundredths can be written 0.05.

You can use place value to help you write each percent as a decimal. Study the table below.

Color	Number/Total	Place Value	Percent	Decimal
Green	5 out of 100	5 hundredths	5%	0.05
Red	50 out of 100	50 hundredths	50%	0.50
Yellow	20 out of 100	20 hundredths	20%	0.20
Brown	2 out of 100	2 hundredths	2%	0.02

▶ Think about the position of the decimal point in the percent column. Then compare its position with that in the decimal column. How does the position of the decimal point change when writing a percent as a decimal?

▶ Write a rule that describes the movement of the decimal point to change a percent to a decimal. Use your rule to represent 45% as a decimal.

More Examples

Write each percent as a decimal.

A. 3%

3% means "3 out of 100, or 3 hundredths."
3 hundredths = 0.03

B. 65%

65% means "65 out of 100, or 65 hundredths."
65 hundredths = 0.65

C. 12.5%

12.5% means "12.5 hundredths, or 0.125."

Connecting Ideas

You now know how to write a percent as a decimal.
You can also write a decimal as a percent.

Write 0.75 as a percent.

Remember that 0.75 means
"75 hundredths, or 75 out of 100."

75 out of 100 is 75%.

Is there a rule that you can use to help you write a decimal
as a percent? To find out, look at the percent and decimal
column from the table on page 346.

▶ Look at the position of the decimal point in the
decimal column. Then compare its position with that in
the percent column. How does the position of the
decimal point change when writing a decimal as a
percent?

▶ Write a rule that describes the movement of the
decimal point to change a decimal to a percent. Use
your rule to represent 0.09 as a percent.

More Examples

Write each number as a percent.

A. $0.35 = 35.\% = 35\%$

B. $4. = 400.\% = 400\%$

Think and Discuss How is writing a decimal as a percent
similar to writing a percent as a decimal? How is it different?

Try It Out

Write each percent as a decimal or each decimal as a percent.

1. 15%	**2.** 99%	**3.** 0.08	**4.** 100%	**5.** 0.315
6. 0.120	**7.** 60%	**8.** 0.76	**9.** 44.4%	**10.** 1.2
11. 4.3%	**12.** 0.06	**13.** 33%	**14.** 0.125	**15.** 300%

	Percent	Decimal
16.	10%	
17.		0.54
18.	43.2%	

	Decimal	Percent
19.		15%
20.	0.70	
21.		1%

	Percent	Decimal
22.	3.5%	
23.		0.06
24.		0.37

▲ **Kid Connection** Wang Yani has been an artist since she was three. When she was ten, she had solo exhibitions in the United States, Europe, and Asia.

Practice

Write each percent as a decimal.

25. 60% **26.** 34% **27.** 20% **28.** 25%

29. 3% **30.** 4% **31.** 100% **32.** 10%

33. 17% **34.** 16% **35.** 2.7% **36.** 600%

Write each decimal as a percent.

37. 0.10 **38.** 0.25 **39.** 0.50 **40.** 1.75

41. 0.24 **42.** 0.09 **43.** 0.88 **44.** 0.07

45. 0.55 **46.** 0.04 **47.** 2 **48.** 0.87

Copy and complete.

	Percent	Decimal
49.	70%	
50.		0.85
51.	5%	

	Decimal	Percent
52.	0.405	
53.		30%
54.	0.99	

	Percent	Decimal
55.		1.43
56.		0.012
57.	748%	

Compare. Use >, <, or = for each ●.

58. 0.05 ● 50%

59. $\frac{1}{2}$ ● $\frac{1}{4}$

60. 3 ● 300%

61. 75% ● $\frac{75}{100}$

62. $12\frac{1}{2}$% ● 125%

63. 45% ● 4.5%

64. 0.25 ● 2.5%

65. 30% ● 0.3

66. $\frac{6}{100}$ ● 60%

Problem Solving

Use the graph on the right to answer Problems 67–69.

67. Write a ratio that describes the percent for paints.

68. Write the percent for pens and markers as a decimal.

69. Half of the paints are acrylic. What percent of the inventory is this?

70. Analyze Greg sketched 100 different drawings. Of these, 65% are of animals, 15% are of plants, and the rest are of sports figures. What percent of his drawings are sports figures?

71. Explain How can you use hundreds grids to show 200%? 250%?

Paint Shop Inventory

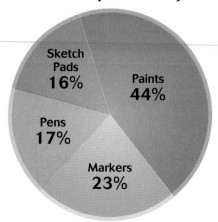

Review and Remember

Round each number to the nearest hundredth.

72. 8.987   **73.** 0.659   **74.** 0.1241   **75.** 6.428   **76.** 12.652

77. 0.287   **78.** 4.321   **79.** 9.299   **80.** 8.467   **81.** 7.832

Critical Thinking Corner

Visual Thinking

Estimating Percents

Sometimes you can visually estimate what percent of a figure is shaded. For example, about 50% of the square on the right is shaded orange.

Estimate what percent of each figure is shaded. Compare your estimates with a friend.

For Extra Practice, see Set A, page 376.

Wrap It Up!

You know that a percent can be written as a decimal. A percent can also be written as a fraction.

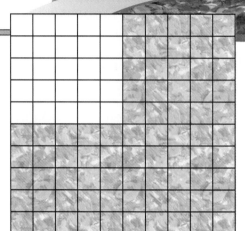

Learning About It

Beautiful wrapping paper is a lovely finishing touch for special presents. If you used $\frac{3}{4}$ of a sheet of wrapping paper to wrap some gifts, what percent of the wrapping paper did you use?

To find out, write $\frac{3}{4}$ as a percent.

THERE'S ALWAYS A WAY!

● **One way** is to use equivalent fractions.

Step 1 Since *percent* means "per hundred," write an equivalent fraction whose denominator is 100.

$$\frac{3}{4} = \frac{3 \times 25}{4 \times 25} = \frac{75}{100}$$

Step 2 Write the fraction as a percent.

$$\frac{3}{4} = \frac{75}{100} = 75\%$$

● **Another way** is to divide to find a decimal. Then write the decimal as a percent.

$\frac{3}{4}$ means "3 ÷ 4."

$$\frac{3}{4} = 4\overline{)3.00} \quad \begin{array}{r} 0.75 \\ \underline{2\ 8} \\ 20 \\ \underline{20} \\ 0 \end{array}$$

0.75 means "75 hundredths."

$$\frac{3}{4} = 0.75 = 75\%$$

You used 75% of the wrapping paper.

More Examples

Represent each fraction as a percent.

A. $\frac{1}{3}$

$$\frac{1}{3} = 3\overline{)1.00}^{\,0.33\frac{1}{3}} = 33\frac{1}{3}\%$$

B. $\frac{2}{3}$

$$\frac{2}{3} = 3\overline{)2.00}^{\,0.66\frac{2}{3}} = 66\frac{2}{3}\%$$

C. $\frac{3}{2}$

$$\frac{3}{2} = \frac{3 \times 50}{2 \times 50} = \frac{150}{100} = 150\%$$

Connecting Ideas

You could use equivalent fractions to write a fraction as a percent. You could also use equivalent fractions to write a percent as a fraction.

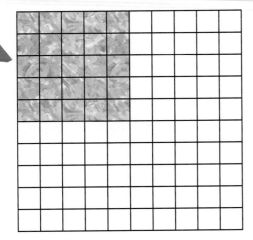

What percent of the wrapping paper is left? How could you write this number as a fraction?

If you used 75% of the wrapping paper, you have 25% of the paper left.

Write 25% as a fraction.

Step 1 Write the percent as a fraction with the denominator of 100.

$$25\% = \frac{25}{100}$$

Step 2 Simplify by writing the fraction in simplest form.

$$\frac{25}{100} = \frac{25 \div 25}{100 \div 25} = \frac{1}{4}$$

More Examples

Write each percent as a fraction.

A. 2%

$$2\% = \frac{2}{100} = \frac{1}{50}$$
$$2\% = \frac{1}{50}$$

B. 200%

$$200\% = \frac{200}{100} = \frac{2}{1}$$
$$200\% = \frac{2}{1}, \text{ or } 2$$

C. 54%

$$54\% = \frac{54}{100} = \frac{27}{50}$$
$$54\% = \frac{27}{50}$$

Think and Discuss How would you write 20% as a fraction? Compare this fraction to those in Examples A and B. Which fraction is the greatest? the least?

Try It Out

Write each fraction as a percent.

1. $\frac{40}{100}$

2. $\frac{40}{50}$

3. $\frac{9}{100}$

4. $\frac{2}{50}$

5. $\frac{3}{50}$

6. $\frac{1}{5}$

7. $\frac{2}{5}$

8. $\frac{4}{8}$

9. $\frac{2}{25}$

10. $\frac{1}{10}$

11. $\frac{3}{8}$

12. $\frac{1}{3}$

Write each percent as a fraction. Simplify if necessary.

13. 65%   14. 30%   15. 6%   16. 21%

17. 74%   18. 50%   19. 3%   20. 450%

Practice

Write each fraction as a percent or each percent as a fraction.

21. $\frac{1}{4}$ 22. $\frac{3}{25}$ 23. $\frac{1}{2}$ 24. $\frac{4}{5}$

25. $\frac{3}{50}$ 26. $\frac{7}{10}$ 27. $\frac{14}{20}$ 28. $\frac{15}{30}$

29. $\frac{3}{5}$ 30. $\frac{1}{20}$ 31. $\frac{2}{5}$ 32. $\frac{1}{8}$

33. 35%   34. 55%   35. 3%   36. 28%

37. 5%   38. 45%   39. 18%   40. 34%

41. 85%   42. 4%   43. 10%   44. 300%

Copy and complete.

	Fraction	Decimal	Percent
45.		0.80	80%
46.	$\frac{1}{5}$		
47.			65%
48.			2%
49.		0.16	
50.	$\frac{7}{8}$		

Compare. Use >, <, or = for each ●.

51. $\frac{2}{3}$ ● 66%   52. $\frac{1}{4}$ ● 25%   53. $\frac{1}{10}$ ● 1%

54. 0.40 ● 40%   55. $\frac{1}{20}$ ● 20%   56. 0.25 ● 24%

Complete each statement.

57. To write a fraction as a percent, you can use ___?___ fractions.

58. To write 55% as a fraction, you could write $\frac{55}{100}$ or ___?___.

59. ___?___% can be written as $\frac{3}{5}$.

Social Studies Connection ⋀
Around the world, gifts are given in different ways. Decorative cloth holds a gift in Kenya; a wooden shoe in the Netherlands has a candy surprise; red envelopes enclose a money gift in China.

Problem Solving

Using Estimation Use the circle graph to solve Problems 60–62.

Gift-Wrap Store

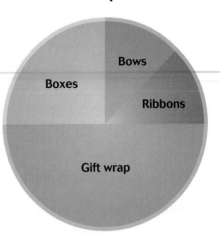

60. What percent of the store's inventory is boxes?

61. Write a fraction to show how much of the inventory is gift wrap.

62. What fraction of the inventory is bows and ribbons? Is this fraction the same as the fraction of inventory that is boxes?

63. Analyze Gale bought some wrapping paper. Some paper was yellow, 25% was green, and the remaining $\frac{3}{5}$ of the paper was blue. What percent of the paper was yellow?

Review and Remember

Using Algebra Give the next three terms for each sequence.

64. 1, 3, 6, 10, ▨, ▨, ▨

65. 2, 4, 8, 16, ▨, ▨, ▨

66. 1, 99, 2, 98, ▨, ▨, ▨

Time for Technology

Using a Calculator

Percents as Decimals and as Fractions

You can use the calculator to help you write a percent as a decimal or as a fraction.

- Write 5% as a decimal.

  Press: (5) (%)

  Display: (0.05)

- Write 5% as a fraction.

  Press: (5) (%) (F◯D) (Simp) (=)

  Display: (1/20)

Write each percent as a decimal, and then as a fraction.

1. 50%   **2.** 85%   **3.** 5%   **4.** 400%   **5.** 87.5%

Order from least to greatest. Use a calculator to help you.

6. 30%, $\frac{1}{3}$, 0.33   **7.** $\frac{1}{4}$, 20%, 0.24   **8.** $\frac{1}{5}$, 0.5, 5%

Dare to Wear Denims

To find the percent of a number, you can use proportions or solve an equation.

Learning About It

The Jeans Factory is having a sale. How much money will you save at this store if you buy a pair of jeans on sale that originally cost $60.00?

You can find out how much you will save by finding 30% of $60.00.

- **One way** is to write a proportion.

percent taken off price $\dfrac{30}{100} = \dfrac{n}{60}$ ← money saved ← original price

$$30 \times 60 = 100 \times n$$
$$n = 1,800 \div 100$$
$$n = 18$$

Use cross products to solve for n.

- **Another way** is to write an equation.

What number equals 30% of 60?

$$n = 0.30 \times 60$$

Solve the equation to find n.

$$n = 18$$

You will save $18.00.

More Examples

A. Write a proportion to find 40% of 50.

$$\dfrac{40}{100} = \dfrac{n}{50}$$

$$40 \times 50 = 100 \times n$$
$$n = 2,000 \div 100 = 20$$

20 is 40% of 50.

B. Write an equation to find 12.5% of 200.

What number equals 12.5% of 200?

$$n = 0.125 \times 200$$
$$n = 25$$

25 is 12.5% of 200.

Think and Discuss How could you use mental math to find 20% of 50? How could you use cross products? Which method is easier for you?

▲ Social Studies Connection
Jeans were originally developed in the United States in the mid-1800s for miners. A pair of jeans cost 22¢ in 1850. Today, some designer jeans cost hundreds of dollars!

Try It Out

Find the percent of each number.

1. 40% of 120 **2.** 25% of 245 **3.** 20% of 60 **4.** 6% of 25

5. 10% of 46 **6.** $33\frac{1}{3}$% of 90 **7.** 45% of 50 **8.** 100% of 7

Practice

Find the percent of each number.

9. 20% of 220 **10.** $66\frac{2}{3}$% of 300 **11.** 90% of 55

12. 60% of 70 **13.** 75% of 160 **14.** 6% of $800

15. 40% of 200 **16.** 9% of 50 **17.** 85% of 40

Choose a Method Use mental math, paper and pencil, or a calculator to find the percent of each number. Tell which method you use.

18. 10% of 50 **19.** 3% of 300 **20.** 18% of 16.50

21. 25% of 80 **22.** 100% of 500 **23.** 12.5% of 16

Problem Solving

24. Discount Denims sells a $60 pair of jeans at a 30% discount. Jeans Factory sells them for 20% off. How much more will you save at Discount Denims than at Jeans Factory?

25. Analyze Outdoor Outfits has socks on sale. The sale price for each pair of socks is $4.50. How many pairs of socks could you buy if you had $25.00?

INTERNET ACTIVITY
www.sbgmath.com

Review and Remember

Estimate. Then use a calculator to find the answer.

26. 4.67×2.51 **27.** $0.65 + 0.08$ **28.** $3.53 - 2.99$ **29.** $4.02 \div 2$

Catch a Dream

Estimating percents is very useful in solving real-world problems.

Learning About It

A crafts store is donating 9% of the price of each dream catcher to a school's scholarship fund. If you were to buy the dream catcher on the right, about how much money would you be contributing?

You can use rounding to estimate 9% of $19.99.

9% × $19.99

10% × $20.00 =

0.10 × 20 = 2

About $2.00 of your money will go to the scholarship fund.

Since you rounded 9% up to 10% and $19.99 up to $20.00, your estimate is an overestimate. The actual amount that you will donate will be slightly less than $2.00.

▲ By tradition, dream catchers are supposed to keep the good dreams with you and keep the bad dreams away.

More Examples

A. Estimate 28% of 71.

28% of 71 ⟶ rounds to ⟶ 30% of 70

30% of 70 = 0.30 × 70 = 21

28% of 70 is about 21.

B. Estimate 82% of 202.

82% of 202 ⟶ rounds to ⟶ 80% of 200

80% of 200 = $\frac{4}{5}$ × 200 = 160

82% of 202 is about 160.

Think and Discuss Suppose you estimated 17% of 199 to be 40. Did you overestimate or underestimate? Explain.

Try It Out

Estimate.

1. 49% of 49

2. 11% of 38

3. 9% of $59.97

4. 22% of 78

5. 71% of $17.89

6. 20% of 36

7. 18% of 22

8. 56% of 72.98

9. 14% of 23

Practice

Estimate.

10. 11% of 99

11. 22% of $31.00

12. 49% of 86

13. 5% of 199

14. 68% of $37.95

15. 30% of 298

16. 18% of $29.99

17. 77% of 40

18. 89% of 6

19. 26% of 30

20. 17% of 19

21. 63% of 102

22. 101% of 35

23. 48% of $17.99

24. 29% of 16

Tell whether each estimate is reasonable or unreasonable. Explain your thinking.

25. 27% of 28 is about 9.

26. 82% of 43 is about 32.

27. 48% of 16 is about 8.

28. 60% of 66 is about 23.

Problem Solving

Use this information to solve Problems 29–31.

A jewelry store sponsors a local sports team. The store donates 12% of every purchase to the team for equipment and uniforms.

29. You spent $29.95 on jewelry. About how much money is donated?

30. Analyze You spent $41.95 on gifts. Your friend bought 5 jewelry sets at $8.95 per set. About how much is donated for each purchase?

31. Journal Idea You want to find 19% of $29.95. Would it be easier to find an overestimate or an underestimate? Explain your reasoning.

▲ **Fine Arts Connection**
Silver and turquoise are often used by Navajo craftworkers to create world-famous jewelry.

Review and Remember

Simplify.

32. $\frac{15}{6}$

33. $3\frac{5}{15}$

34. $6\frac{17}{13}$

35. $\frac{9}{1}$

36. $\frac{14}{6}$

37. $9\frac{54}{36}$

38. $\frac{450}{200}$

39. $7\frac{3}{2}$

40. $\frac{21}{49}$

41. $\frac{81}{3}$

42. $4\frac{4}{4}$

43. $\frac{325}{100}$

44. $\frac{70}{5}$

45. $2\frac{10}{6}$

46. $6\frac{20}{5}$

Developing Skills for
Problem Solving

*First read for understanding and then focus on
whether an estimate is enough to solve a problem.*

READ FOR UNDERSTANDING

Jeremy went to the Western Shop, which
was having a sale on hats and boots. He
saw three different hat styles and was
trying to decide which style to buy.

1. Which hat costs $90 before any
   discount is given?

2. What is the discount on the
   Sidewinder?

3. On which hat is the 15% discount
   given?

The Wrangler
$90.00
Take 40% off

The Sidewinder
$75.00
Take 25% off

The Westerner
$65.00
Take 15% off

THINK AND DISCUSS

 MATH FOCUS

Is an Estimate Enough? Sometimes an
estimate is all you need to solve a problem.
Whether an estimate is enough or an exact
answer is needed depends on the situation.

**Reread the paragraph and look at the photographs at the
top of the page.**

4. Which hat costs the least before any discount is given?
   Which costs the most?

5. When a cashier calculates the amount of discount, does
   he find an estimate or an exact answer?

6. How might Jeremy estimate which hat style would save
   him the most money?

7. Which hat will be least expensive after the discount?
   Tell whether you found the exact cost of each hat or
   an estimate and why.

Show What You Learned

Use the price tags for three styles of shirts to help you answer Problems 1–3. Give a reason for your choice.

*E*lla went to the Western Shop to buy a new shirt. She has $45.00 to spend. There are three different shirt styles on sale.

Style A
$20.00
Take 25% off

1 How can Ella find the shirt style that offers the greatest savings?

    a. Estimate the savings on the styles that offer the same percent discount.

    b. Estimate the product of the regular price times the percent discount for each style.

    c. Find the greatest percent off.

Style B
$22.00
Take 25% off

2 How could Ella find the exact savings on shirt style C?

    a. Multiply $58 by 0.40

    b. Subtract $40 from $58.

    c. Divide $58 by 0.40.

Style C
$58.00
Take 40% off

3 **Explain** Is an estimate enough to determine whether style C is still the most expensive shirt after the discount? Tell why or why not?

*R*oger is planning to see a movie about the Old West starting at 1:00 P.M. The movie runs for 1 hour and 40 minutes. Roger tells his friends to meet him at the bookstore at 2:45 P.M. The bookstore is a 15-to-20 minute walk from the movie theater.

4 Which of the following is an estimate?

    a. The running time of the movie

    b. The time that the movie ends

    c. The time needed to walk from the theater to the bookstore

5 Which expression shows the earliest time Roger could arrive at the bookstore?

    a. 100 minutes + 15 minutes

    b. 1:00 P.M. + 20 minutes

    c. 2:40 P.M. + 15 minutes

6 **Explain** Will Roger arrive at the bookstore on time? Explain how you would estimate the meeting time.

✔ Checkpoint

Percents, Fractions, and Decimals

Write each percent as a decimal. (pages 346–349)

1. 58%   **2.** 60%   **3.** 75%   **4.** 20%

5. 45%   **6.** 88%   **7.** 9%   **8.** 200%

Write each decimal as a percent. (pages 346–349)

9. 0.35   **10.** 0.15   **11.** 0.72   **12.** 0.02

13. 0.362   **14.** 0.49   **15.** 0.06   **16.** 3

What do you think?

How do you find the percent of a number? Will your answer be greater or smaller than the number? Explain.

Write each fraction or whole number as a percent. (pages 350–353)

17. $\frac{25}{100}$ **18.** $\frac{5}{10}$ **19.** $\frac{4}{50}$ **20.** $\frac{3}{25}$

21. $\frac{1}{5}$ **22.** $\frac{20}{80}$ **23.** 2   **24.** $\frac{1}{3}$

Write each percent as a fraction or whole number. (pages 350–353)

25. 25%   **26.** 50%   **27.** 14%   **28.** 55%

29. 33%   **30.** 2%   **31.** 500%   **32.** $66\frac{2}{3}$%

Find the percent of each number. (pages 354–355)

33. 10% of 50   **34.** 25% of 12   **35.** 60% of 80   **36.** 7% of 620

37. 3% of 2   **38.** 75% of 160   **39.** 40% of 224   **40.** 55% of 100

Estimate to find the percent of each number. (pages 356–357)

41. 52% of 299   **42.** 22% of 38.98   **43.** 39% of 80   **44.** 7% of 60

Mixed Practice

Copy and complete.

	Percent	Fraction	Decimal
45.	39%		
46.		$\frac{2}{5}$	
47.			0.15
48.		$\frac{2}{3}$	
49.	2%		

	Percent	Fraction	Decimal
50.			0.32
51.		$\frac{1}{8}$	
52.	4%		
53.		$1\frac{1}{4}$	
54.			0.875

Problem Solving

Use the advertisements to the right to solve Problems 55–60.

55. Louise wants to buy a pair of jeans on sale. About how much less will she pay than the regular price of $49.98?

56. Joan bought three shirts on sale that had been $18.00 a shirt. How much did she save altogether?

57. **You Decide** Rose has $75 to spend. The regular prices of items are: shoes, $35; socks, $2.40; shirts, $15; and jeans, $38. What might Rose decide to buy? Remember to use the discounts.

58. **Analyze** If you had $20.00 to spend on a shirt, how much could the original price be?

59. Bruce buys 6 pairs of socks regularly priced at $2.45 a pair. He also buys 2 shirts regularly priced at $16.50 each. According to the receipt, he saved more than $5.00. Was his receipt correct? Explain.

60. Judy bought a pair of jeans originally priced at $42.00. She said she saved more than 50%. If she paid $28.00 for the jeans, was she correct? Explain how you know.

Journal Idea

Explain the steps you follow to express a percent as a fraction and as a decimal.

Critical Thinking Corner

Number Sense

What's Wrong?

Save-a-Lot Stores offer an additional 20% off their sale price. Tom bought some sneakers marked 30% off the original price of $50.00. He said that with the additional 20% off, he will actually save 50%. The receipt showed less than 50% off the original price. What is wrong with Tom's calculations?

Problem Solving
Write an Equation

Some problems can be solved by writing an equation.

For lunch Jenny had a small fruit cup, a large garden salad, and an orange juice. She left the waiter a 15% tip. What was the amount of the tip?

 ## UNDERSTAND

What do you need to know?

You need to know the total cost of Jenny's food.

 ## PLAN

How can you solve the problem?

You can **write an equation**. Find the total cost of the items Jenny ordered for lunch. Then multiply by 15% to determine the tip.

Salad Sensations

Small Garden Salad	$3.00
Large Garden Salad	$5.50
Small Fruit Cup	$2.25
Large Fruit Cup	$3.50
Small Pasta Salad	$4.00
Large Pasta Salad	$6.50
Milk	$1.00
Orange Juice	$1.25
Cranberry Juice	$1.50

 ## SOLVE

Let y represent the amount of the tip.

small fruit cup	large garden salad	orange juice		

$$(\$2.25 + \$5.50 + \$1.25) \times 15\% = y$$

$$\$9.00 \times 0.15 = y$$

$$\$1.35 = y$$

Jenny left a tip of $1.35.

 ## LOOK BACK

How can you use mental math to check your answer? Explain what you would do.

Using the Strategy

Using Algebra **Write an equation to solve each problem. Use the menu on page 364.**

1 Jake ordered a large garden salad and orange juice. He left a 15% tip for the waiter and a 5% tip for the busboy. What was the total amount of his tips?

2 Explain A group of friends ordered 3 small pasta salads. They left 7 quarters for a tip. Was the tip more or less than 15%?

3 Analyze Which is greater, a 15% tip for a small pasta salad or a 20% tip for a small fruit cup?

4 Hannah left the waitress a 20% tip for a large pasta salad and cranberry juice. How much did she spend in all?

Mixed Strategy Review

Try these or other strategies to solve each problem. Tell which strategy you used.

Problem Solving Strategies

- Find a Pattern
- Work Backwards
- Write an Equation
- Guess and Check
- Use Logical Reasoning
- Draw a Diagram

5 If a 15% tip is exactly $3.90, what is the total bill?

6 Murray paid half as much for lunch as he paid for dinner. The total cost of both meals was $18.75. What was the cost of each meal?

7 Edna made $20 in tips on Sunday, $15 on Monday, $25 on Tuesday, $20 on Wednesday, and $30 on Thursday. If this pattern continues, how much can she expect in tips on Friday?

8 Carol, Mae, Bill, and Rick sat at different sides of a square table. Rick was on Carol's left. Bill was on Mae's right but not next to Carol. Who sat across from Rick?

Sports Shop

Using Algebra

Understanding percents can help you find the sales tax.

Learning About It

Sports equipment is a popular item for many shoppers. Suppose you want to buy a soccer ball priced at $14.69. If the rate of the sales tax is 6.5%, what is the total cost of the ball?

Estimate first: 6.5% of $14.69 is about 7% of $15.00.
7% of $15.00 is $1.05.

The estimated total cost is $16.05.

THERE'S ALWAYS A WAY!

• **One way** is to use paper and pencil.

Step 1 Find the sales tax.	Step 2 Find the total cost.
= 6.5% × 14.69	= $14.69 + $0.96
= 0.065 × 14.69	= $15.65
= 0.95485	
Sales tax is always rounded up to the next cent.	
= 0.96, or $0.96	

• **Another way** is to use a calculator.
To find the sales tax,

Press: 6 . 5 % × 1 4 . 6 9 =   Display: 0.95485

To find the total cost,

Press: 1 4 . 6 9 + . 9 6 =   Display: 15.65

The total cost of the soccer ball is $15.65.

How do you know that the answer of $15.65 is reasonable?

Think and Discuss If you used the key sequence below to find the total cost of the ball, will the answer be correct? Explain. Press: 1 0 6 . 5 % × 1 4 . 6 9 =

Try It Out

Find the sales tax and the total cost. Round up the sales tax to the nearest cent.

1. cost: $2.25
rate of sales tax: 5%

2. cost: $12.20
rate of sales tax: 4.5%

3. cost: $34.99
rate of sales tax: 6.25%

Practice

Choose a Method Use paper and pencil, mental math, or a calculator. Find the sales tax and the total cost.

4. cost: $29.95
rate of sales tax: 7%

5. cost: $100
rate of sales tax: 6.9%

6. cost: $44.50
rate of sales tax: 3%

7. cost: $19
rate of sales tax: 8%

8. cost $412
rate of sales tax: 6%

9. cost: $62.50
rate of sales tax: 5.5%

Copy and complete the chart.

	Cost	Rate of Sales Tax	Sales Tax	Total Cost
10.	$25.00	5%		$26.25
11.	$100.00	8%		$108.00
12.	$20.00	5%		
13.	$15.50	10%		

Problem Solving

14. Jeff and Frank bought two pairs of swimming goggles for $26.50. If the rate of sales tax was 6%, what was the total cost of the goggles?

15. Using Estimation In Texas the rate of sales tax is 6.25%. If four footballs cost $95.00, estimate the total cost.

16. Joe orders a meal that costs $11.05. The sales tax is 4.5%. If Joe leaves a tip that is 15% of the bill after tax, what does he pay?

17. Analyze A basketball cost $30. With sales tax, the bill came to $31.50. Find the rate of sales tax. Explain how you solved the problem.

Review and Remember

Complete the following.

18. 48 oz = _____ lb

19. 5 qt = _____ pt

20. 6 gal = _____ qt

21. 3 mi = _____ ft

22. 10 yd = _____ ft

23. 3 yd = _____ ft

For Extra Practice, see Set F, page 378.

Kaleidoscope Craze

To find the sale price, subtract the discount from the regular price.

Learning About It

The Nature Shop had a 25% sale on kaleidoscopes. Mike bought one priced at $15.99. How much did he pay on sale?

Estimate first: 25% of $15.99 is about 25% of $16.
25% of $16 = $4.00

The estimated sale price is $12.00.

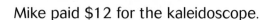

Step 1 Find the discount.

discount = regular price × rate of discount
= $15.99 × 25%
= $15.99 × 0.25
= $3.9975
discount = $3.99

Discounts are always rounded down.

Step 2 Find the sale price.

sale price = regular price − discount
= $15.99 − $3.99
sale price = $12

Mike paid $12 for the kaleidoscope.

How does the actual discount compare with the estimate?

Another Example

Find the discount and the sale price.

regular price = $99

rate of discount = $33\frac{1}{3}\% = \frac{1}{3}$

discount = $99 × \frac{1}{3} = 33

sale price = regular price − discount
sale price = $99 − $33 = $66

Think and Discuss If the discount is 25%, what percent of the regular price is the sale price?

25% OFF

▲ **Science Connection**
Kaleidoscopes were invented in 1817 by David Brewster, a Scottish scientist. A kaleidoscope usually contains two mirrors.

Try It Out

Find the discount and the sale price.

1. regular price: $200
rate of discount: 10%

2. regular price: $56
rate of discount: 25%

3. regular price: $66
rate of discount: $33\frac{1}{3}\%$

Practice

Choose a Method Use paper and pencil, mental math, or a calculator. Find the discount and the sale price.

4. regular price: $16
rate of discount: 25%

5. regular price: $50
rate of discount: 50%

6. regular price: $50.50
rate of discount: 15%

7. regular price: $650
rate of discount: 20%

8. regular price: $11.99
rate of discount: 10%

9. regular price: $36
rate of discount: 25%

10. regular price: $175
rate of discount: 20%

11. regular price: $300
rate of discount: 10%

12. regular price: $21.99
rate of discount: $33\frac{1}{3}$%

Copy and complete the chart below.

	Regular Price	Rate of Discount	Discount	Sale Price
13.	$40	12.5%	$5.00	
14.	$2,650	5.0%	$132.50	
15.		10.0%	$569.00	$5,121

Problem Solving

16. Tommy bought two kaleidoscopes on sale for 20% off. If each kaleidoscope cost $29 before the sale, what did Tommy pay for both on sale?

17. Linda bought some crystals for 15% off the regular price of $18. She bought rocks for 25% off the regular price of $22. How much did Linda spend altogether?

18. Using Mental Math A crystal-growing kit regularly priced at $40.00 is 20% off the regular price. What is the sale price?

19. What If? Look back at Problem 18. If a 6% sales tax is added onto the sale price, how much is the kit?

20. Analyze Shirley bought a telescope on sale for $37.50. What was the rate of discount? Guess and check your answer.

Review and Remember

Find the GCF for each pair of numbers.

21. 36, 48   **22.** 125, 90   **23.** 99, 27   **24.** 400, 350   **25.** 64, 126

Making Money

Earning interest is one way money can work for you.

Learning About It

You can make money by saving money! **Interest** is the amount the bank pays you when you put your money in a savings account. Interest is also the amount you pay to borrow money.

The **principal** is the money placed in a bank or borrowed. The **rate of interest** is the percent earned or charged. The time is how long the money is in the account or borrowed.

To find simple interest, multiply the principal, rate, and time.

interest = principal × rate × time

> Suppose you want to put $100.00 of your money in a savings account for 1 year, earning 5.5% interest. How much interest will you earn? What is the total you will have in your account?

Word Bank

interest
principal
rate of interest

BANK

interest	=	principal	×	rate	×	time
interest	=	$100.00	×	0.055	×	1
interest	=	$5.50				

After 1 year, your money will have earned $5.50 in interest. Now find the total amount in your account.

total amount = original amount + interest
= $100 + $5.50
= $105.50

You will have a total of $105.50 in your account after 1 year.

Another Example

If you want to borrow $500.00 for 6 months at 12% interest, how much money will you owe the bank?

interest = $500 × 0.12 × $\frac{1}{2}$ = $30   (6 months is $\frac{1}{2}$ of a year.)

total amount owed = loan amount + interest
= $500.00 + $30.00

After 6 months, you will owe the bank $530.00.

Think and Discuss Bank A pays 6% interest on $1,000 savings each year. Bank B pays 6% every 6 months and adds the interest to the principal. Which account pays more in one year? Explain.

Try It Out

Find the interest and the total with interest.

	Principal	Rate of Interest	Time
1.	$6,000	5.0%	5 months
2.	$4,500	18.0%	6 months
3.	$1,020	4.0%	7 months
4.	$500	7.5%	1 year

▲ **Kid Connection**
Young Americans Bank in Denver has over 18,000 accounts. The average age of an account holder is 9 years.

Practice

Choose a Method Use paper and pencil or a calculator. Tell which method you used to complete the chart.

INTERNET ACTIVITY
www.sbgmath.com

	Principal	Rate of Interest	Time	Interest	Total With Interest
5.	$500	7.00%	3 mo		
6.	$775	20.00%	1 yr		
7.	$18,000	5.25%	4 mo		
8.	$6,500	8.00%	1 yr		
9.	$8,800	12.00%	8 mo		
10.	$2,000	5.00%	6 mo		
11.	$1,500	10.00%	9 mo		

Problem Solving

Use the interest formula to solve Problems 12–13.

12. Alfred earned 5% on $100 in his savings account for 1 year. Rebecca earned 3% on $200. Who earned more interest on their account? Explain your answer.

13. **Analyze** Charlie puts $2,000 into an account earning 5% per year. Interest is paid at the end of each year and added to the principal. How much is the principal after 2 years?

Review and Remember

Estimate first. Then use a calculator to add or subtract.

14. $14.38 - 2.084$ 15. $0.073 + 2.817$ 16. $9.98 + 0.732$ 17. $7.896 - 4.32$

18. $406.2 + 3.4$ 19. $0.88 + 3.47$ 20. $798 - 61.3$ 21. $14.62 - 12.61$

Problem Solving
Using Percent

Understanding discounts and sales tax can help you solve some problems.

What is the price of a Hillsdale Hornets T-shirt purchased by a senior citizen?

 UNDERSTAND

What do you need to find?

You need to find the regular price of the T-shirt and the discount given to senior citizens.

 PLAN

How can you solve the problem?

First find the amount of the senior-citizen discount on the T-shirt. Then find the difference between the regular price and the discount.

 SOLVE

Step 1 Find the amount of discount.	**Step 2** Find the discounted price.
Let *d* represent the senior-citizen discount.	Let *p* represent the discounted price.
$d = 6\%$ of $\$12.50$	$p = \$12.50 - \$0.75$
$d = 0.06 \times 12.50$	$p = \$11.75$
$d = 0.75$	
The discount is $\$0.75$.	A senior citizen would pay $\$11.75$ for a Hillsdale Hornets T-shirt.

 LOOK BACK

What If? Suppose you find 94% of $12.50. Why is the result the same as your answer above?

Show What You Learned

Use the T-shirt prices and discounts shown on this page and the information on page 372 to solve Problems 1–7.

1. Kara used a coupon worth 15% off to purchase a Bach to Nature T-shirt. How much did she save?

2. What is the cost of a Bach to Nature T-shirt purchased by a senior citizen?

3. What is the sale price of a Save the Planet T-shirt?

4. **Analyze** What is the sale price of a Save the Planet T-shirt for a senior citizen?

5. Bill plans to buy two Save the Planet T-shirts and one Bear With Me T-shirt. How much will he pay for the three shirts?

6. Lance bought a Bear With Me T-shirt and a Save the Planet T-shirt. If he gave the clerk $30, how much change did he receive?

7. Joe bought three Bach to Nature T-shirts, some Bear With Me T-shirts, and two Save the Planet T-shirts. He spent $106. How many Bear With Me T-shirts did he buy? What strategy did you use to solve the problem?

Some states charge 5% sales tax on clothes. This amount is added to the price of the item after the discount is taken. Use a 5% sales tax for Problems 8–10.

8. What is the total cost of a Bach to Nature T-shirt and a Bear With Me T-shirt, including sales tax?

9. **Explain** Would $20 be enough to purchase a Bear With Me T-shirt, including sales tax? Explain.

10. **Create Your Own** Write a problem involving sales tax and using the information from the T-shirt prices.

Practice What You Learned

Choose the correct letter for each answer.

1 This graph shows Mark's progress on a bicycle trip. Which is reasonable for Mark's average speed (in mph) between 2:00 P.M. and 4:00 P.M.?

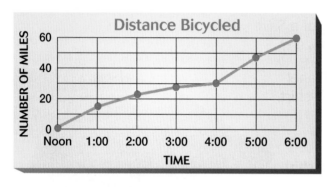

Distance Bicycled

NUMBER OF MILES / TIME

A. 5 mph   D. 20 mph

B. 10 mph   E. 30 mph

C. 15 mph

Tip

When solving multiple-choice problems, you can sometimes use the strategy *Use Logical Reasoning* to eliminate one or more choices.

---

2 Rick estimated that 36 out of 122 people at a movie were children. About half of the remaining people in the theater were senior citizens. Which is the best estimate for the percent of children at this movie?

A. 20%   D. 45%

B. 30%   E. 50%

C. 40%

Tip

Try using compatible numbers to find the estimate.

---

3 Jeannie paid 5% sales tax on a CD player that cost $180. Which equation could you use to find n, the amount of tax she paid?

A. $\$180 \div 0.05 = n$

B. $\$180 \times 0.05 = n$

C. $\$180 + \$5 = n$

D. $n = 5 \times \$180$

E. $0.05n = 180$

Tip

Choose one of the answers, solve for n, and see if you get a reasonable amount for the sales tax.

$180 PLUS TAX

4 On Sunday the temperature was 45.5°F. For the next three days, it went up 1.2°F, 2.4°F, and 3.6°F. If this pattern continues, what will the temperature be on *Friday*?

A. 57.5°F   C. 63.5°F
B. 62.3°F   D. 70.7°F

---

5 Rob is making a quilt from material that costs $1.35 per yard. These figures are part of the quilt design. Which figure is 75% *white*?

A.   C.

B.   D.

---

6 Molly needs 5.6 m of cord to make 4 pillows. The cord is sold only in 25-cm lengths. If each length costs $0.39, how much will Molly spend for the cord? (1m = 100 cm)

A. $2.18
B. $8.58
C. $8.97
D. $17.47
E. Not Here

---

7 The population of Westfall is 4,260. Easterly has only 1,730 people. Almost two thirds of the people in the two towns are registered to vote. More than half of the voters are women. Which is the best estimate for the number of registered voters?

A. 2,000
B. 3,000
C. 4,000
D. 5,000
E. 6,000

---

8 A scientist believes that the number of cells in an experiment will increase in this pattern.

Day	1	2	3	4	5
Number	7	15	31	63	127

If she is right, how many cells will there be on the *seventh* day?

A. 227 cells   C. 511 cells
B. 255 cells   D. 512 cells

---

9 The amount collected for tickets to a dance was $45,000. The tickets cost either $50 each or $70 each, depending on whether or not food was included in the price. Which is reasonable for the number of tickets sold?

A. Less than 500
B. Between 100 and 600
C. Between 300 and 600
D. Between 600 and 900
E. More than 1,000

---

10 The graph shows the results of a survey about vacations. Which are the best estimates for the numbers of employed people and retired people represented on this graph?

A. 700 employed; 750 retired
B. 700 employed; 800 retired
C. 750 employed; 700 retired
D. 750 employed; 775 retired
E. 800 employed; 800 retired

Checkpoint

Sales Tax, Discount, and Interest

Vocabulary

Match each word with its description.

1. A special ratio that compares a number to 100

2. This may be used to find the percent of a number

3. Amount subtracted from the regular price to find the sale price

4. Money earned on a savings account

Word Bank

discount
interest
percent
proportion
ratio

Concepts and Skills

Use mental math to find the percent of each number.
(pages 362–363)

5. 40% of 150

6. $33\frac{1}{3}\%$ of 150

7. 75% of 200

8. 60% of 300

9. 15% of 500

10. 250% of 10

What do you think?
How is calculating sales tax similar to calculating discount?

Using Algebra Find the sales tax and total cost.
(pages 362–363)

11. cost: $175
rate of sales tax: 5.5%

12. cost: $879.99
rate of sales tax: 4%

13. cost: $1,279
rate of sales tax: 8%

Using Algebra Find the discount and the sale price.
(pages 368–369)

14. regular price: $120
rate of discount: $33\frac{1}{3}\%$

15. regular price: $65
rate of discount: 20%

16. regular price: $29.99
rate of discount: 25%

Using Algebra Copy and complete the chart. (pages 370–371)

	Principal	Rate	Time	Interest
17.	$1,000	8.5%	9 months	
18.	$450	7%	1 year	
19.	$695	12.5%	6 months	

Problem Solving

Use the advertisement at the right to solve Problems 20–23.

SNORKEL SET 20% off

Regular price $39.95

5% sales tax on all items

20. How much will you save if you buy a snorkel set on sale?

21. What is the sale price without tax?

22. If you use the sale price to calculate tax, what is the total cost of a snorkel set including the sales tax?

23. Mrs. Kent bought 5 snorkel sets. How much did she save with the discount? How much sales tax did she pay?

24. The bill for your dinner is $30.00. If you want to leave a 15% tip, how much will you spend altogether?

25. What If? Look back at Problem 24. If the state tax on the meal was 8%, how much would you spend altogether?

Journal Idea

Explain two methods you can use to find the percent of a number.

You Decide

Activity

Eat for a Week

You have $35 for lunches this week. Use the menu below to answer the questions. Include a tip and tax when calculating your bill for each day.

- What will you order each day? How much will your bill be?

- What is the total amount you will spend for the week?

Food Frenzy

Pizza........................ $2.75 per slice
Chicken Sandwich.............. $4.75
Salad.............$.75 small $1.25 large
Fries............ $1.50 small $2.25 large
Noodle Soup... $2.75 cup $3.25 bowl
All Drinks..... $1.50 small $2.50 large

 You might wish to include this work in your portfolio.

Extra Practice

Set F (pages 366–367)

Using Algebra **Find the sales tax.**

1. cost: $5.50
   rate of sales tax: 5%

2. cost: $8.75
   rate of sales tax: 6%

3. cost: $23.60
   rate of sales tax: 4%

Use the guest check to the right for Problems 4–6.

4. If the sales tax is 6%, how much sales tax must be paid?

5. How much is a 15% tip if it is figured after the tax is added?

6. What is the total cost of the meal, including tax and tip?

Guest Check

| SERVER | TABLE | GUESTS | CHECK NUMBER |
| | | 2 | 80710 |

Dinner	$23.95
Beverage	$ 3.60
Dessert	$ 6.50
Subtotal	$34.05

Thank You   TAX
              TOTAL

Set G (pages 368–369)

Using Algebra **Copy and complete the chart below.**

	Cost	Rate of Sales Tax	Sales Tax	Total Cost
1.	$50.00	20%		
2.	$150.00	25%		
3.	$63.50	10%		

Solve.

4. Marissa bought three shirts on sale for 15% off. The original price was $19.99 for each shirt. How much did Marissa spend, not including tax?

5. **What If?** Look back at Problem 4. If Marissa had to pay 5% sales tax on the sale price, how much did Marissa pay in all for three shirts?

Set H (pages 370–371)

Using Algebra **Find the interest.**

1. principal: $500, rate: 5%, time: 2 years

2. principal: $850, rate: 8%, time: 3 years

Solve.

3. The mall borrowed $80,000 to make improvements in the parking lot. If the loan was for 3 months at 8.5%, how much interest was paid?

4. **What If?** Look back at Problem 3. If the interest rate was 7.75%, how much interest would be paid?

Chapter Test

Write each number as a percent.

1. 0.79

2. $\frac{7}{20}$

3. 0.625

Write each percent as a fraction and as a decimal.

4. 90%

5. 56%

6. 25%

Find the percent of each number.

7. 25% of 40

8. $33\frac{1}{3}$% of 24

9. 60% of 150

Find the sales tax and the total cost.

10. cost: $49
rate of sales tax: 5%

11. cost: $110
rate of sales tax: 6%

12. cost: $99
rate of sales tax: 3.5%

13. cost: $179.98
rate of sales tax: 4%

Find the discount and the sale price.

14. regular price: $250
rate of discount: 25%

15. regular price: $9.89
rate of discount: 10%

Find the interest.

16. principal: $400; rate: 8%; time: 1 year

17. principal: $1,250; rate: 5.7%; time: 4 years

18. principal: $3,725; rate: 9.2%; time: 9 months

Solve.

19. Rita bought a pair of sneakers on sale at 25% off the regular price. If the regular price was $69.97 and the sales tax was 5%, what was the total cost?

20. You get a $6.95 discount on a gift you buy for a friend. You pay $27.80 for the gift. If there is no sales tax, what was the original price?

 Self-Check

Look back at Exercises 7 through 9. How could you use estimation or mental math to check your work?

Performance Assessment

Show What You Know About Percents

1. Make a design on a hundreds grid using 4 different colored pencils. Describe how the number of squares for each color is related to the hundreds grid by using percents. Then show how the number of squares for each color is related to the hundreds grid by using decimals and fractions.

Self-Check Did you remember to compare the number of squares of each color to one hundred?

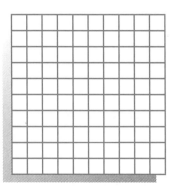

What You Need

hundreds grid
colored pencils

2. Michelle has $50.00 to spend on an outfit which consists of a pair of jeans and a shirt. Three stores have the outfit she wants.

Stores	Price of Jeans	Price of Shirt	Discount on Clothes
Denim World	$45.00	$16.00	20% off
Jeannie's Jeans	$48.00	$14.00	25% off
Discount Denims	$42.00	$12.00	10% off

Which store or stores would you tell Michelle to go to buy her outfit?

Self-Check Did you remember to subtract the discount from the original price to find the sale price?

 For Your Portfolio

You might wish to include this work in your portfolio.

Extension

More About Discounts

Using Algebra

Look at the table on the right. How much do you save by buying each book on sale? Which type of book is the best buy?

The sale price for each book is $2 less than the regular price. The savings, or discount, is $2.

To find the best buy, compare the savings to the regular price for each type of book. Find the rate of discount.

Lots of Books		
Type of Book	Regular Price	Sale Price
Romance	$20	$18
Mystery	$30	$28
Science fiction	$40	$38

Compare.

Romance

$2 to $20

$$\begin{array}{r} 0.10 = 10\% \\ 20\overline{)2.00} \\ -2.0 \\ \hline 0 \end{array}$$

Mystery

$2 to $30

$$\begin{array}{r} 0.06\frac{2}{3} = 6\frac{2}{3}\% \\ 30\overline{)2.00} \\ -1.80 \\ \hline 20 \end{array}$$

Science Fiction

$2 to $40

$$\begin{array}{r} 0.05 = 5\% \\ 40\overline{)2.00} \\ -2.00 \\ \hline 0 \end{array}$$

Romance books are the best buy because the rate of discount is the greatest. How can you use mental math to help you check your answers?

Use the table on the right.

1. What is the discount for cookbooks? What is the rate of discount?

2. What is the discount for reference books? What is the rate of discount?

3. What is the discount for nature books? What is the rate of discount?

4. Which type of book is the best buy?

5. **Create Your Own** Make a poster for book sales. Have a classmate find the best buy.

The Best Book Store		
Type of Book	Regular Price	Sale Price
Cookbook	$20	$15
Reference	$32	$24
Nature	$40	$30

381

Using Math in Science

*Use molecular formulas to **calculate** and **graph** the percent of certain elements in chemical compounds.*

Building Blocks of Matter

For a science fair project, you are using plastic foam balls to build models of different chemical compounds. The plastic foam balls represent different kinds of atoms forming the compounds. For your project you need to find the percent of each kind of atom in each compound.

Explore

Step 1 Make a chart like the one below.

What You Need

For each student:
  data table
  pencil
  calculator (optional)

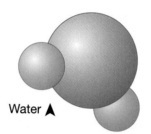

Water ▲

Name of Compound	Formula	Total Number of Atoms	Number of Each Type of Atom Compared to Total	Percent of Each Type of Atom in Compound
Glucose	$C_6H_{12}O_6$	24	$C = \dfrac{6}{24}$ $H = \dfrac{12}{24}$ $O = \dfrac{6}{24}$	$C = 25\%$ $H = 50\%$ $O = 25\%$
Water	H_2O			
Ammonia	NH_3			
Sodium chloride	NaCl			
Carbon dioxide	CO_2			
Methane	CH_4			

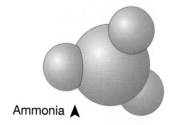

Ammonia ▲

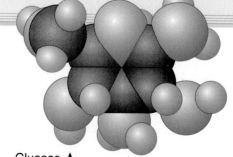

Glucose ▲

Step 2 Look at the information in the chart about the glucose compound. Notice that it has 24 atoms—6 carbon atoms, 12 hydrogen atoms, and 6 oxygen atoms. Now count the total number of atoms in water (H_2O). Record the number in the table. Repeat for the other compounds.

Step 3 For each compound, express as a fraction the number of each type of atom compared to the total number of atoms. Use the information for glucose as an example.

Step 4 Use the fractions you recorded in the fourth column to calculate the percent of each type of atom in the compounds listed. Use a calculator, if necessary.

Step 5 Use the data in your chart to make circle graphs that show the percent of each type of atom in each of the compounds listed.

Analyze

1. Which compound contains atoms in equal amounts? Write the percent of each atom.

2. Find the total number of atoms used in your project. Which type of atom represents the greatest percent of the total?

3. In which compound are the hydrogen atoms 75% of the total?

For Your Portfolio

Write about what you discovered. Explain how graphing helped you organize and understand your data. How could you use ratios to express the makeup of each compound?

Explore Further!

Analyze For glucose, the total number of each type of atom compared to the total is recorded as $C = \frac{6}{24}$; $H = \frac{12}{24}$; $O = \frac{6}{24}$. These fractions are not expressed in simplest terms. What effect, if any, do you think expressing the fractions in simplest terms will have on your finding the percents in Column 5? Do the calculations to find out.

Cumulative Review

★ ★ ★ ★ ★ **Preparing for Tests**

Choose the correct letter for each answer.

Number Concepts	Measurement

1. The length of Uncle Fred's fence is 437.54 meters. What is 437.54 rounded to the nearest *ten*?

  A. 437.0
  B. 437.5
  C. 438
  D. 440

2. Which set of numbers is in order from *greatest* to *least*?

  A. 0.344, 0.034, 0.434, 0.444
  B. 0.444, 0.434, 0.034, 0.344
  C. 0.444, 0.434, 0.344, 0.034
  D. 0.034, 0.344, 0.444, 0.434

3. On Monday Bart went to the library. Yesterday he read 20 pages of his 80-page book. What percent of his book did he read?

  A. 10%
  B. 25%
  C. 50%
  D. 66%

4. There are 44 students in the math club. One quarter of the students in the math club did not go to Math Field Day. What percent of the math club *did* attend Field Day?

  A. 25%
  B. 50%
  C. 70%
  D. 75%

5. The radius of a flying disc is 12 inches. What is the approximate *circumference* of the flying disc? (Use $\pi \approx 3.14$)

  A. 31.4 in.
  B. 37.68 in.
  C. 62.80 in.
  D. 75.36 in.

6. A ball weighs 450 grams. How many kilograms is this? (1 kg = 1,000 g)

  A. 0.45 kg
  B. 4.5 kg
  C. 45 kg
  D. 4,500 kg

7. A room is 12 feet by 15 feet. The ceiling is 8 feet high. If you wanted to carpet the whole room, how many *square yards* of carpeting would you need? (1 yd = 3 ft)

  A. 12 yd^2
  B. 20 yd^2
  C. 120 yd^2
  D. 180 yd^2

8. Jeff's fish tank is 2.5 feet long by 1.5 feet wide by 2 feet deep. The fish tank is on a stand that is 3 feet high. What is the *volume* of the tank?

  A. 6.0 ft^3 **D.** 11.25 ft^3
  B. 6.75 ft^3 **E.** 22.5 ft^3
  C. 7.5 ft^3

Geometry and Spatial Reasoning	Patterns, Relationships, and Algebraic Thinking

9. Triangle *HIJ* is inscribed in Triangle *DEF*. Which of the following pairs of line segments are parallel?

A. $\overline{DF}$ and $\overline{HJ}$
B. $\overline{DE}$ and $\overline{HI}$
C. $\overline{EF}$ and $\overline{HJ}$
D. $\overline{EF}$ and $\overline{IJ}$

10. Which statement is always true?

A. All angles in a triangle are acute angles.
B. The sum of the angles of a triangle is 180°.
C. All triangles have 2 right angles.
D. No two triangles can be congruent.

11. Which of the following shows a shows a *rotation* of the triangle?

A.   **C.**

B.   **D.**

12. Figure *JKLMN* is congruent to Figure *PQRST*. Which angle is congruent to ∠*L*?

A. ∠*P* **C.** ∠*R*
B. ∠*Q* **D.** ∠*S*

13. Karen made a paper chain. She first used 1 red loop, then she used 2 yellow, then 3 orange, then 2 brown, and finally, 1 purple loop. If she continues this pattern of loops in the chain, what color will the **twentieth** loop be?

A. Purple
B. Red
C. Yellow
D. Orange

14. If the ratio of girls to boys on the swim team is 3 to 4, then the team could have—

A. 21 girls and 28 boys
B. 28 girls and 21 boys
C. 20 girls and 15 boys
D. 24 girls and 16 boys

15. If $32 \div x = 8$, then $x =$

A. 3
B. 4
C. 6
D. 8

16. Which point best represents the number $3\frac{1}{3}$ on the number line?

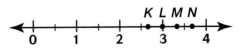

A. *K*
B. *L*
C. *M*
D. *N*

Chapter 10 Geometry

Chapter Theme: AMUSEMENT PARKS

.....................Real Facts....................

What can look real but is not real? People who work in the exciting field of virtual reality use math to create real-looking images that exist only in a computer. Many of the objects and characters they create begin as geometric shapes!

The computer-generated drawing below shows the geometry behind the virtual-reality scene pictured at right.

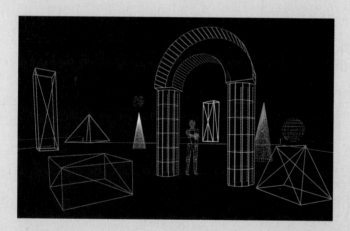

- Which shapes in the virtual-reality scene have an acute angle (angle less than 90°)?

- Which shapes have right (90°) angles?

- How many cones do you see? cylinders?

.............Real People...................

Meet Evelyn O'Shea. Using her artistic abilities and computer skills, she creates three-dimensional objects and characters for virtual-reality programs. Her creations come to life when you put on a computer headset!

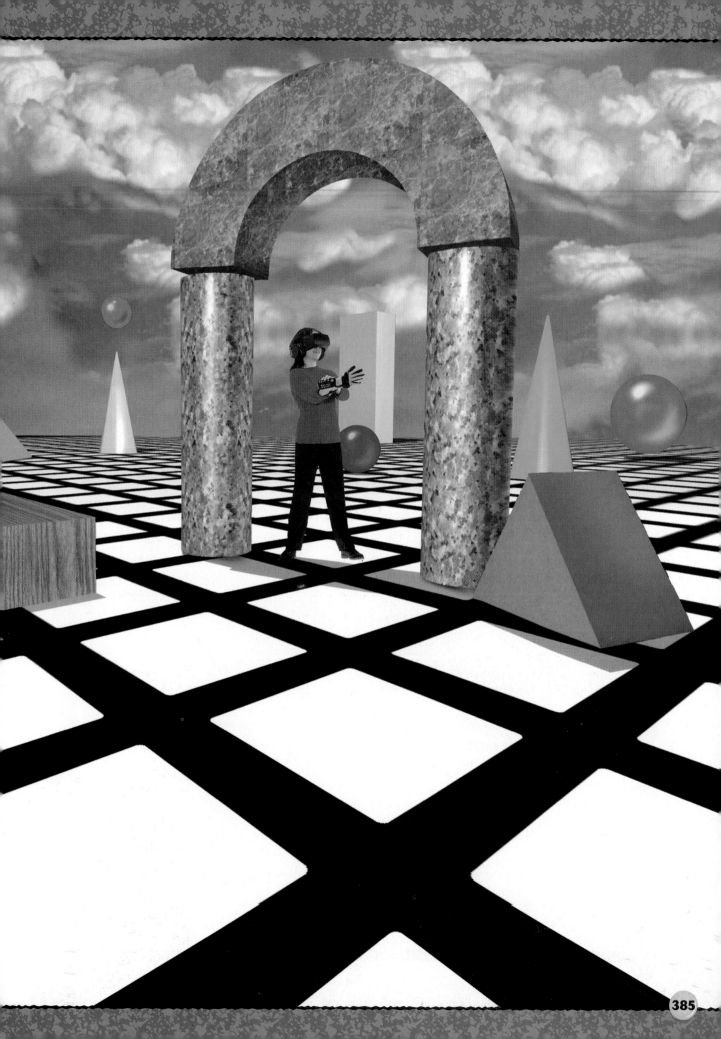

Learn the Basics

*You can see examples of basic geometric ideas
all around you, even at an amusement park.*

Learning About It

Did you know that geometry can be found in many different amusement parks? The table below gives you some geometric terms that you could use to describe geometric ideas in the photo.

Basic Geometric Ideas

Description	Example	Symbol/Read
A **point** marks an exact location in space. For example, look at the center of the Ferris wheel.	• *A*	point *A*
A **line** is a collection of points along a straight path extending endlessly in both directions.	*E*　*F*	line *EF*　$\overleftrightarrow{EF}$
A **line segment** is a part of a line between two endpoints. For example, look at the spokes of the Ferris wheel.	*A*　*D*	line segment *AD*　$\overline{AD}$
A **ray** is part of a line that has one endpoint and extends endlessly in one direction.	*A*　*C*	ray *AC*　$\overrightarrow{AC}$
An **angle** is formed by two rays with a common endpoint called a vertex. For example, look at the angle between two spokes.	*B*　*A*　*C*	angle *BAC*　∠*BAC*
A **plane** is a flat surface extending endlessly in all directions.	*J*　*K*　*L*	plane *LJK*

Think and Discuss Draw a picture of $\overrightarrow{XY}$ and $\overrightarrow{YX}$. How are they the same? How are they different?

Try It Out

Use the figure on the right to name an example of each term.

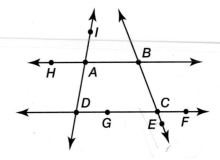

1. point
2. plane
3. ray
4. angle
5. line
6. line segment

Practice

Draw and label a figure for each symbol.

7. $\overrightarrow{EF}$ 8. $\angle DEB$ 9. $\overleftrightarrow{AB}$ 10. $\overline{JK}$ 11. $\overrightarrow{FE}$ 12. $\angle ABC$

Write the name and symbol for each figure.

13.

14.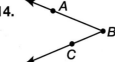

15.

16.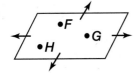

17.

18. •P

Problem Solving

19. Mark two points on a piece of paper. Label them A and B. How many different lines can you draw through points A and B?

20. Name at least two examples from your home or classroom that suggest a point, line, line segment, plane, and angle.

21. Imagine a line in space. How many different planes can pass through the line?

22. Mark one point on a piece of paper. How many different lines can you draw through the point?

23. Which geometric idea is suggested by a wall in a room? the height of a skyscraper?

24. **Explain** Which geometric idea is suggested by the hands of a clock?

Review and Remember

Change each decimal to a fraction or a mixed number.

25. 0.50   26. 0.25   27. 3.05   28. 1.8   29. 0.375

For Extra Practice, see Set A, page 426.

Scary Drops!

You can describe and classify angles by their measure.

Learning About It

Roller coasters are rated by the angles of depression, or drop. The Excaliber roller coaster in Shakopee, Minnesota, has a 60 degree drop. You can use a protractor to measure a 60° angle.

A **protractor** is an instrument used to measure angles. Follow the steps below to measure angles.

Word Bank

protractor
congruent
right angle
obtuse angle
acute angle
straight angle

Step 1 Place the center of the protractor on the vertex of the angle to be measured.

Step 2 Rotate the protractor so that one ray of the angle passes through 0° on one scale.

Step 3 Read the number of degrees on the protractor where the second ray crosses the scale. Be sure to read the scale that begins at 0° on the first ray.

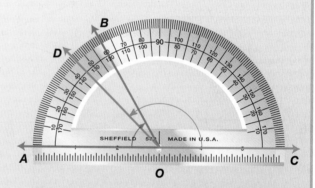

The measure of angle *AOB* is 60°.
The measure of angle *COD* is 135°.

Angles are classified according to their measures.

Right Angle
exactly 90°

Obtuse Angle
greater than 90° and less than 180°

Connecting Ideas

You used a protractor to measure an angle. You can also use a protractor to draw an angle.

Follow the steps below to draw an angle that measures 120°.

Step 1 Draw a ray. Label the ray.

Step 2 Place the center of the protractor on the endpoint of the ray. Then line up the ray with the 0° mark.

Step 3 Using the scale with the 0° mark, find the measure of the angle you wish to draw. Place a point on that mark. Then draw the other ray. Label one point on this ray.

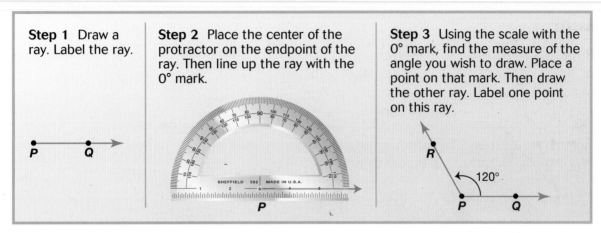

Angles that have the same measure are called **congruent** angles.

$\angle ABC \cong \angle DEF$ means "angle ABC is congruent to angle DEF."

Think and Discuss A protractor has two scales. How do you know which scale to read when you measure an angle?

Try It Out

Use the figure on the right for Exercises 1–4. Trace each angle. Then use a protractor to find the measure and classify the angle.

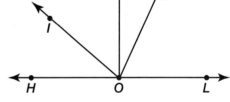

1. $\angle HOI$ **2.** $\angle HOL$ **3.** $\angle HOK$

4. Name two angles that are congruent.

Use a protractor to draw each angle.

5. 30° **6.** 120° **7.** 55° **8.** 145° **9.** 175°

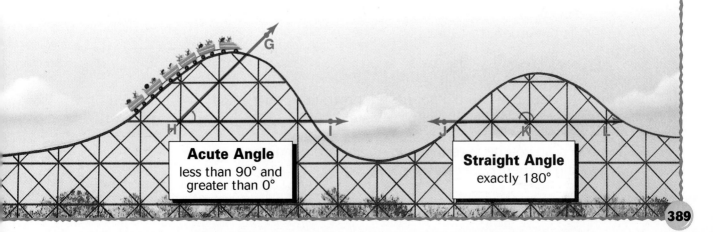

Acute Angle
less than 90° and greater than 0°

Straight Angle
exactly 180°

Practice

Trace each angle. Then use a protractor to find the measure and classify each angle.

10.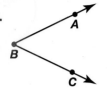

11.

12.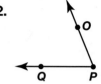

13.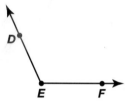

14.

15.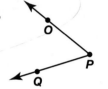

16.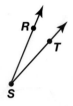

17.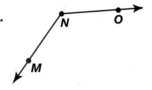

18.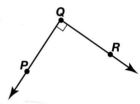

Use a protractor to draw and classify each angle.

19. 40°	**20.** 100°	**21.** 25°	**22.** 155°	**23.** 90°	**24.** 110°
25. 135°	**26.** 180°	**27.** 10°	**28.** 85°	**29.** 62°	**30.** 126°

For Exercises 31–36, estimate first. Then use a protractor to find the measure of each angle.

31. ∠BOA

32. ∠AOC

33. ∠COD

34. ∠EOF

35. ∠COE

36. ∠DOF

Use the figure to the right for Exercises 37 and 38.

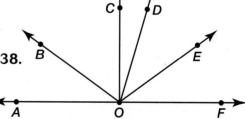

37. ∠AOB is congruent to ___?___.

38. ___?___ is a straight angle.

39. **What If?** Suppose you did not have a protractor, how could you draw an angle that was approximately 45°? 135°?

40. **Explain** Can you be sure that two angles are congruent by looking at them? Explain your thinking.

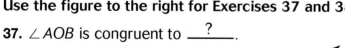

Problem Solving

Trace figure *KLMN* at the right for
Problems 41–44.

41. Name two angles that appear to be right.

42. Name two angles that appear to be acute.

43. Two angles are called supplementary
    angles if the sum of their measures is 180°.
    Name a pair of supplementary angles.

44. Two angles are called complementary
    angles if the sum of their measures is 90°.
    Is there a pair of complementary angles?
    Explain how you know.

45. At 3:00 P.M., what is the measure of the
    angle formed by the minute hand and the
    hour hand on an analog clock? Classify this
    angle. What strategy could you use to solve
    the problem?

46. Using Algebra   Rich divided an obtuse angle into three
    equal angles. If the sum of two angle measures is 80°,
    what was the measure of the obtuse angle?

47. Anna measured the angles formed by the corners of
    her room. What kind of angles can they be?

48. Create Your Own   Use a protractor to draw four angles
    on a piece of paper. Have a classmate measure and
    classify the angles you drew.

Review and Remember

Estimate first. Then find each sum or difference.

49. $3\frac{1}{2}$
    $+5\frac{3}{4}$

50. $4\frac{1}{5}$
    $-2\frac{1}{3}$

51. 6
    $-3\frac{3}{4}$

52. $6\frac{7}{8}$
    $+1\frac{1}{4}$

53. $5\frac{4}{9}$
    $+3\frac{1}{18}$

54. $4\frac{3}{8}$
    $+6\frac{2}{7}$

55. $9\frac{1}{6}$
    $-3\frac{2}{5}$

56. $7\frac{10}{11}$
    -2

57. $9\frac{11}{12} - 3\frac{1}{3}$

58. $48\frac{10}{15} - 9$

59. $\frac{3}{4} + \frac{7}{16}$

60. $8\frac{1}{3} + 2\frac{1}{6}$

Pathways to Fun

You can classify an angle by its measure. You can classify a line by its position relative to other lines.

Learning About It

Have you ever been lost in a maze like this one in St. Louis, Missouri? The pathways in a maze can be thought of as line segments. Look at the maze to the right. How do the segments intersect?

Lines

Description	Example	Read
Intersecting lines have one point in common.	C B M A D	$\overleftrightarrow{AB}$ intersects $\overleftrightarrow{CD}$ at point *M*.
Parallel lines are in the same plane but do not intersect.	J K H I	$\overleftrightarrow{HI} \parallel \overleftrightarrow{JK}$ $\overleftrightarrow{HI}$ is parallel to $\overleftrightarrow{JK}$.
Perpendicular lines are lines that intersect to form right angles.	N L O M	$\overleftrightarrow{NO} \perp \overleftrightarrow{LM}$ $\overleftrightarrow{NO}$ is perpendicular to $\overleftrightarrow{LM}$.
Skew lines lie in different planes. They do not intersect and are not parallel.	Q R P S	$\overleftrightarrow{PQ}$ and $\overleftrightarrow{RS}$ are skew lines.

Line segments can be intersecting, parallel, perpendicular, or skew.

Think and Discuss Look at the photo above. What colors represent parallel line segments? perpendicular line segments?

Try It Out

For each exercise, use the figure on the right. Write *true* or *false*. If the statement is false, write a correct statement.

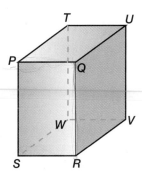

1. $\overline{PQ}$ intersects $\overline{QR}$.

2. $\overline{PQ}$ intersects $\overline{SR}$.

3. $\overline{PQ} \parallel \overline{UV}$

4. $\overline{PQ} \perp \overline{QU}$

5. $\overline{TU}$ and $\overline{SW}$ are skew segments.

Practice

Classify each pair of lines as intersecting, parallel, perpendicular, or skew.

6.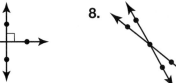

7.

8.

9.

Use the figure at the right to find two examples of each geometric idea.

10. right angle

11. acute angle

12. obtuse angle

13. intersecting lines that are not perpendicular

Use the cube at the right. Write ∥ or ⊥ for each ⬤.

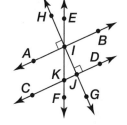

14. $\overline{AB}$ ⬤ $\overline{EF}$

15. $\overline{AB}$ ⬤ $\overline{AE}$

16. $\overline{AB}$ ⬤ $\overline{AD}$

17. $\overline{AD}$ ⬤ $\overline{BC}$

18. Name two pairs of skew segments.

Problem Solving

Look at the map to answer Problems 19–20.

19. Name a pair of streets that are parallel.

20. Name a pair of streets that are not parallel or perpendicular to each other.

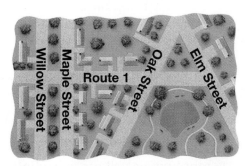

Review and Remember

Using Algebra Find the value of each *n*.

21. $n \times 2 = 28$

22. $n \div 6 = 4$

23. $20 + n = 35$

24. $63 - n = 13$

INTERNET ACTIVITY
www.sbgmath.com

Developing Skills for
Problem Solving

*First read for understanding and then use
spatial reasoning to solve problems.*

READ FOR UNDERSTANDING

Todd's pinwheel has 4 vanes that rotate around a point.
Shown below are three different views of his pinwheel turning.

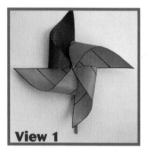
View 1

View 2

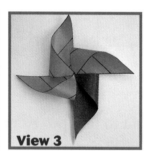
View 3

1 How many vanes does the pinwheel have?

2 How are the vanes similar? How are they different?

THINK AND DISCUSS

MATH FOCUS

Spatial Reasoning Spatial reasoning is
mentally picturing objects in different
positions and different ways. You can use
spatial reasoning when it is not practical
to use actual objects.

Look at the three views of the pinwheel again.

3 How does View 2 differ from View 1?

4 How does View 3 differ from View 2? from View 1?

5 **What If?** Suppose the pattern continues. How many
more views will there be before the pinwheel looks like
it does in View 1?

6 How does being able to turn the pinwheel mentally
help you answer Problem 5? Explain.

Show What You Learned

Answer each question. Give a reason for your choice.

Joan drew the shapes below on folded paper. Then she cut them out and unfolded them.

❶   **❷**   **❸**   **❹**

1 Which figure below shows Shape 2 unfolded?

a.   b.   c.

2 Which shape looks like this figure when unfolded?

a. Shape 1
b. Shape 2
c. Shape 3

3 Which shape might look like this figure if it was folded again horizontally?

a. Shape 1
b. Shape 2
c. Shape 3

Amaro made the design shown below. When he was finished, he noticed that the figure was made up of squares and triangles.

4 How many squares are in the design?

a. 3
b. 4
c. 7

5 How many triangles are in the design?

a. 8
b. 16
c. 32

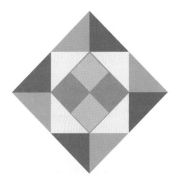

6 **Explain** Amaro wants to change his design to include more triangles. Explain how he could do this.

7 **Analyze** How many $\frac{1}{4}$ turns of Amaro's design are needed before the design looks like it does now?

Hold It Up

You can classify triangles in more than one way.

Learning About It

The triangle is often used to create structures that support a heavy load. Look at the picture at the right. How many different kinds of triangles do you see?

You can classify triangles by their side or angle measures.

Triangles

Classified by Side Measures		Classified by Angle Measures	
Description	**Example**	**Description**	**Example**
Three sides have the same length.	**Equilateral** 3 / 3 / 3	All angles are acute.	**Acute**
Two sides have the same length.	**Isosceles** 2, 5, 5	There is one right angle.	**Right**
No two sides have the same length.	**Scalene** 6, 4, 7	There is one obtuse angle.	**Obtuse**

An equilateral triangle has three congruent sides and angles.

More Examples

You can classify a triangle by using more than one name.

A. This triangle is isosceles and right.

You can use slashes to show equal sides. ↘
$\overline{FR} \cong \overline{RD}$

You can use arcs to show equal angle measures. ↙
$\angle F \cong \angle D$

F, 45°, R, 45°, D

B. This triangle is scalene and acute.

N, 80°, 5.2, 7, Y, 60°, 8, 40°, P

Connecting Ideas

You know that some triangles have different side and angle measures. However, the angles of every triangle are related.

You can show how the angles of any triangle are related by following the steps below. How do the steps show that the sum of the angles in any triangle is 180°?

Step 1 Cut out a triangle. Label each angle of the triangle.

Step 2 Tear the triangle so that there are 3 pieces. Each piece includes one angle.

Step 3 Rearrange the pieces so that the three angles form a straight line.

Think and Discuss Suppose the measure of angle E in triangle DEG is 90°. If the measure of angle G is half the measure of angle E, what is the measure of angle D?

Try It Out

Trace each triangle. Classify each triangle. Use as many classifications as possible.

1.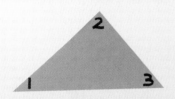

2.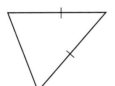

3.

4.

Using Algebra Find the value of each variable.

5. equilateral

6. isosceles

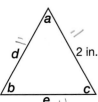

7. right scalene

8. right isosceles

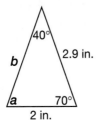

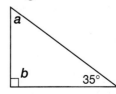

Practice

Classify each triangle. Use as many classifications as possible.

9.

4, 3, 5

10.

4, 4, 4

11.

100°

12.

4, 4

13.

2, $2\frac{1}{2}$, 3

14.

3, 3, 3

15.

$3\frac{1}{2}$, 2, 120°, 2

16.

2, 3

Using Algebra Use mental math, paper and pencil, or calculator. Find the value of each variable.

17.

8, 100°, c, a, 40°

18.

a, d, 7, c, e, b

19.

b, a, 30°

20.

a, 7, b, 7, 45°

Describe each triangle.

21.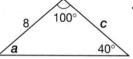

22.

F, 45°, 45°, R, D

23.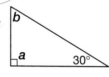

24.

25. Explain Can a triangle be classified as both equilateral and acute? equilateral and right? equilateral and obtuse?

Problem Solving

26. Using Algebra Look at the triangle on the right. Find the missing angle *n* and the missing height.

n, height, 45°, 5 ft

27. Explain Heather drew a triangle. The measure of the first angle has the same measure as the second angle. The third angle is 120 degrees. Find the measures of the first and second angles.

28. Journal Idea Can you have a triangle with two right angles? two obtuse angles? two acute angles? Explain how you know.

Use the figures below for Problems 29 and 30.

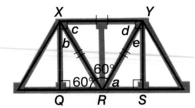

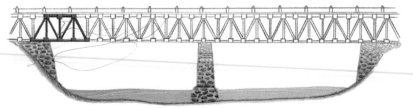

▲ Science Connection
Truss bridges are built over canyons, rivers, and gorges.

29. Some structural supports are called trusses. The above diagram shows a truss that might be used to support a bridge. Write the missing angle measures for the truss.

30. Classify each triangle according to its side and angle measures.

Review and Remember

Estimate first. Then find the answer. Write the answer in simplest form.

31. $2\frac{1}{3} + \frac{4}{5}$ **32.** $10\frac{2}{3} + 3\frac{5}{6}$ **33.** $19 - 1\frac{1}{4}$ **34.** $8 - \frac{8}{9}$

35. $5\frac{1}{4} \times 3$ **36.** $6\frac{1}{8} \times 2\frac{5}{6}$ **37.** $8\frac{1}{2} \div 2\frac{2}{3}$ **38.** $9\frac{1}{2} \div 2$

Time for Technology

Surfing the Net

Bridges on the Internet

You can use the Internet to find information about bridges.

There are many interesting sites on the Internet that provide information about bridges all around the world, such as the Golden Gate Bridge in California and the Akashi Kaikyo Bridge in Japan.

Explore the sites below. Search for other sites.

Keyword: bridges

www.pronet.co.jp/akashi/indexe.html

www.mcn.org/Goldengate/index.html

Sketch or describe the shapes you find in bridges. Share your findings with the class.

Off to Legoland!

You can identify quadrilaterals by their special properties.

Learning About It

It took several thousand Lego bricks to build this model. The face of each brick is shaped like a rectangle. A rectangle is a special kind of quadrilateral.

Quadrilaterals are polygons with four sides and four angles. Quadrilaterals are named according to the special properties of their sides and angles.

Quadrilaterals

Description	Example
A **trapezoid** has one pair of parallel sides.	Trapezoid $\overline{AB} \parallel \overline{DC}$
A **parallelogram** has two pairs of parallel sides. Opposite sides and opposite angles are congruent.	Parallelogram $\overline{EF} \parallel \overline{HG}$ $\overline{EH} \parallel \overline{FG}$
A **rhombus** is a parallelogram with all sides congruent.	Rhombus
A **rectangle** is a parallelogram with four right angles.	Rectangle
A **square** is a rectangle with four congruent sides.	Square

The sum of all the angles of any quadrilateral is 360°.

Think and Discuss Is every square a rhombus? Is every rhombus a square? Explain.

Social Studies Connection
This hippo can be found in Legoland, a park in Denmark. The park was created with 34 million bricks, covering an area of 19 football fields.

Try It Out

Using Algebra Find the measure of each missing angle *n*.
Then classify each polygon. Be as specific as possible.

1.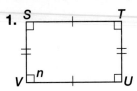

2.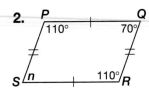

3.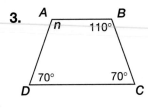

4.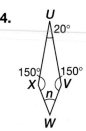

Practice

Classify each polygon. Use as many names as possible.

5.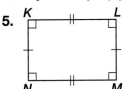

6.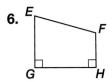

7.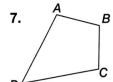

8.

Using Algebra Find the measure of each variable.

9.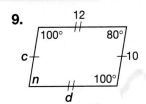

10.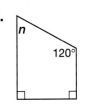

11.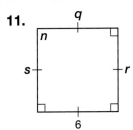

12.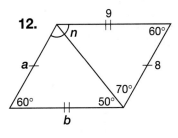

Problem Solving

Draw and classify each quadrilateral for Problems 13–15.

13. a figure that is both a rectangle and a rhombus

14. a quadrilateral that is not a rectangle, with two right angles

15. a parallelogram with all sides equal

16. Which quadrilateral describes the shape of a chalkboard? rooftop?

17. Journal Idea Barbara drew a quadrilateral. Three of the angles are right angles. What is the measure of the fourth angle? Explain how you know.

Review and Remember

Choose a Method Use paper and pencil or a calculator to find the answer.

18. $19.7 + 16.2$

19. $46.8 \div 2$

20. $9.86 - 3.7$

21. 14×5.5

22. 921×34

23. $43 + 59.8$

24. $16.4 \div 8.2$

25. $683 - 46$

Where Do You Go?

You can identify polygons by the number of their sides.

Learning About It

Amusement parks use signs to display information. Many signs have the shape of a polygon. Identify the polygons in the photos on the right. What kinds of polygons do you see?

A polygon is a closed plane figure with sides that are line segments. Polygons are classified according to the number of their sides.

Polygons

Description	Examples	Description	Examples
A **pentagon** has five sides.		An **octagon** has eight sides.	
A **hexagon** has six sides.		A **nonagon** has nine sides.	
A **heptagon** has seven sides.		A **decagon** has ten sides.	

- A **regular polygon** is a polygon with all sides congruent and all angles congruent.

- A **diagonal** is a line segment that connects two vertices of a polygon and is not a side.

Think and Discuss Are all triangles and quadrilaterals polygons? Are any triangles or quadrilaterals regular polygons? Name them.

Try It Out

Name each polygon below. Write *regular* for each regular polygon.

1.

2.

3.

4.

Practice

Name each polygon. If the figure is not a polygon, explain why it is not.

5.

6.

7.

8.

9.

10.

11.

12.

Problem Solving

Trace the pentagon on the right. Choose a vertex. Draw all the diagonals from this vertex. Use your figure for Problems 13–15.

13. How many triangles are there?

14. Analyze Find the sum of the angles in the pentagon.

> **Hint** Use the sum of the angles of the triangles.

15. What if you choose a different vertex as the endpoint of the diagonals? Will the number of triangles be the same?

Find the sum of the angle measures for each polygon.

16.

17.

18.

19.

Review and Remember

Write each percent as a decimal.

20. 25% **21.** 85% **22.** 400% **23.** 6% **24.** 15.5%

For Extra Practice, see Set F, page 427.

Checkpoint

Plane Figures

Choose the letter that best describes each term. (pages 386–403)

1. isosceles
2. plane
3. parallelogram
4. polygon
5. perpendicular lines
6. obtuse angle

a. quadrilateral that has two pairs of parallel sides
b. two lines that intersect to form right angles
c. angle greater than 90° and less than 180°
d. closed plane figure with line segments for sides
e. triangle with two equal sides
f. flat surface extending endlessly

Use the figure to name an example of each term.
(pages 386–393)

7. straight angle
8. right angle
9. ray
10. pair of parallel lines
11. line segment
12. acute angle

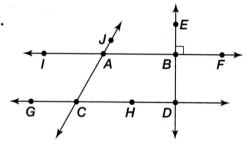

Classify each polygon. Use as many names as possible.
(pages 396–403)

13.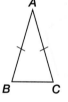

14.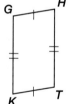

15.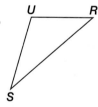

16.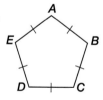

What do you think?

What kinds of figures are polygons? How do their sides or angles help describe them?

Using Algebra **Find the measure of each angle _n_.** (pages 396–403)

17.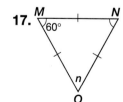

18.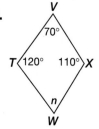

19.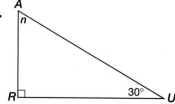

Problem Solving

20. Lynda drew a triangle with sides that are 2 inches, 5 inches, and 5 inches long. How would you classify her triangle?

21. The local park has a Do Not Litter sign in the shape of an octagon. Draw a sketch of how the sign might look.

22. How would you classify a rhombus with right angles?

23. Draw and label a pair of angles that together make an obtuse angle.

24. Al drew a polygon with four equal sides. What could his polygon be?

25. Give an example of perpendicular line segments from your classroom.

Journal Idea

Write a paragraph explaining the steps for drawing an angle with a protractor. Use examples to help you explain.

Critical Thinking Corner

Visual Thinking

Fun With Fractals

Using Algebra Fractal shapes, like the Sierpinski triangle on the right, can be made from repeating patterns.

Follow these steps to make your own fractal triangle.

Step 1 Draw an equilateral triangle.

Step 2 Measure each side of the triangle. Then mark the middle of each side with a point.

Step 3 Create 4 smaller equilateral triangles by connecting the 3 middle points.

Step 4 Repeat steps 2 and 3 for three of the smaller triangles. Each smaller triangle should look similar to the large triangle. Continue marking middle points to create smaller and smaller triangles.

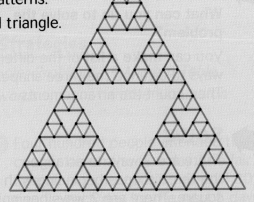

INTERNET ACTIVITY
www.sbgmath.com

On the Move

You can move a figure without changing its size or shape.

Learning About It

Rides at an amusement park can slide, flip, or turn. What happens to the ride as it moves from one position to another? Does the size change? Does the shape change?

For each example below, trace Figure I. Move the tracing paper to fit exactly on Figure II. Try not to lift the tracing paper from the page unless you have to. Tell how you had to move Figure I to change its position to Figure II.

Word Bank

translation
rotation
reflection

What You Need

tracing paper

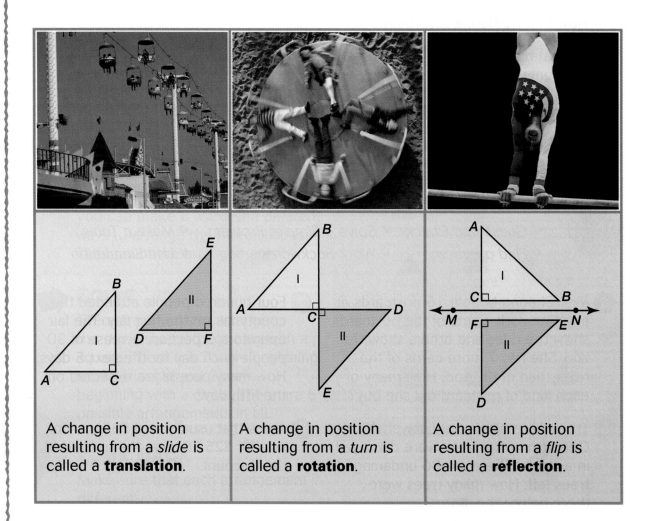

A change in position resulting from a *slide* is called a **translation**.

A change in position resulting from a *turn* is called a **rotation**.

A change in position resulting from a *flip* is called a **reflection**.

More Examples

A figure can change position by using one or more of the simple motions.

Describe the motions you can use to go from Figure I to Figure II.

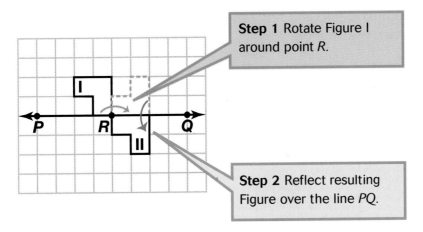

Step 1 Rotate Figure I around point *R*.

Step 2 Reflect resulting Figure over the line *PQ*.

Connecting Ideas

When you change a figure's position, the resulting figure is congruent to its original. You can tell if two figures are congruent by comparing their corresponding parts.

Two figures are congruent if their corresponding parts are congruent.

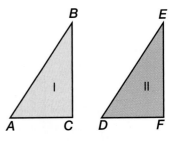

Congruent Triangles

△*ABC* ≅ △*DEF*

↑

is congruent to

Corresponding Angles

∠*A* ≅ ∠*D*

∠*B* ≅ ∠*E*

∠*C* ≅ ∠*F*

Corresponding Sides

$\overline{AB} \cong \overline{DE}$

$\overline{BC} \cong \overline{EF}$

$\overline{AC} \cong \overline{DF}$

Think and Discuss If the corresponding angles of two triangles are congruent, would it be reasonable to say the triangles will be congruent?

Try It Out

Trace Figure I. Move the tracing paper to fit exactly onto Figure II. Use translation, rotation, and reflection to describe the motions used.

1.

2.

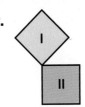

3.

Figure I is congruent to Figure II. Use the triangles on the right to complete each congruence statement.

4. $\triangle GHI \cong$ _____?_____

5. $\angle I \cong$ _____?_____

6. $\overline{GI} \cong$ _____?_____

7. $\overline{KL} \cong$ _____?_____

8. $\angle G \cong$ _____?_____

9. $\overline{HI} \cong$ _____?_____

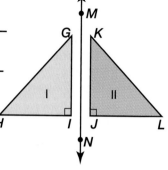

10. Describe If you flipped Figure II across a horizontal line, what would the resulting figure look like?

Practice

Figure I is congruent to Figure II. Trace Figure I. Move the tracing paper to fit exactly on Figure II. Describe the motions you use.

11.

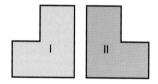

12.

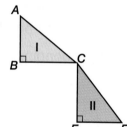

13.

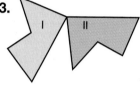

14.

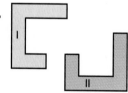

15.

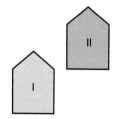

16.

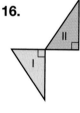

Use the triangles in Exercise 15 to complete each congruence statement.

17. $\triangle ABC \cong$ _____?_____

18. $\angle A \cong$ _____?_____

19. _____?_____ $\cong \overline{EF}$

20. $\angle B \cong$ _____?_____

Problem Solving

21. Which diagram shows a reflection along the dotted line?

a.

b.

c.

d.

22. Which of the following pairs of figures appears to be congruent?

a.

b.

c.

d.

23. Triangles *PQR* and *ZYX* are congruent. Which of these statements is true?

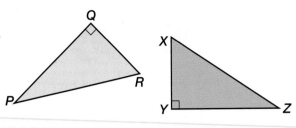

   a. $\overline{XY} \cong \overline{XZ}$ **b.** $\angle P \cong \angle Z$

   c. $\overline{PQ} \cong \overline{XZ}$ **d.** $\angle X \cong \angle P$

24. Analyze Look at Exercise 16. If you reversed the motions you used, would the result be the same? Explain how you know.

Review and Remember

List in order from least to greatest.

25. 1,245; 4,560; 991   **26.** 30.876; 40.98; 200.4   **27.** 60,950, 7,987; 24,540

28. 2.07; 2.009; 2.5; 2.15   **29.** 4.89; 48.9; 0.489   **30.** 1.045; 1.0988; 1.00786

Find the GCF for each pair of numbers.

31. 16 and 24   **32.** 36 and 48   **33.** 95 and 15   **34.** 42 and 72

Critical Thinking Corner

Visual Thinking

A Different View

The picture on the right shows two blocks. What if you looked at this picture from a different view?

A single picture cannot show all the views of a three-dimensional figure. However, you can show one view of the figure from either the front, back, side, or top.

The sketches to the right show the front and back views of the figure.

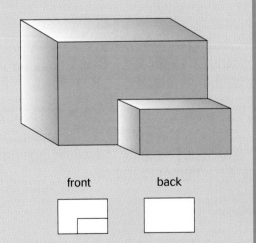

1. Draw the top, left, and right side views of the figure.

2. Look for a space figure in your classroom. Draw the top, front, side, and back views.

INTERNET ACTIVITY
www.sbgmath.com

Copy the Work

You can copy and bisect a line segment with a compass.

Learning About It

How can you construct congruent line segments without measuring? You can use a Triman compass to construct congruent line segments.

Work with a partner.

Follow the steps below to construct a line segment that is congruent to $\overline{AB}$.

A   B

What You Need

Triman compass

Step 1 Work with your partner and draw a ray. Label the endpoint C.

C ————————→

Step 2 Place the compass on point A as shown. Move the slider so that it lines up with point B. Tighten the knob.

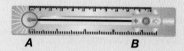
A   B

Step 3 Now place the compass on point C. Without changing the slider position, draw an arc that intersects the ray.

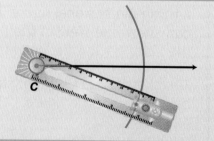
C

Step 4 Label point D where the arc intersects the ray. $\overline{CD} \cong \overline{AB}$

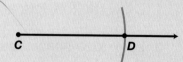
C   D

Connecting Ideas

If you can construct congruent line segments, you can bisect a line segment into two congruent parts.

Follow the steps below to bisect line segment EF.

Step 1 Place the compass on point E. Position the slider closer to point F than point E. Draw an arc above and below EF.	**Step 2** Without changing the position, place the compass on point F. Draw an arc above and below EF. Label the points where the arcs intersect G and H.	**Step 3** Draw line GH. Label point M where GH intersects EF. Point M is the midpoint of line segment EF. GH bisects EF at point M.
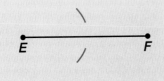	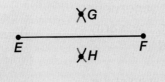	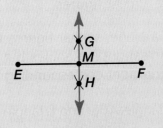

Use your compass to show that $\overline{EM} \cong \overline{MF}$.

Think and Discuss $\overleftrightarrow{GH}$ is a perpendicular bisector. How would you describe a perpendicular bisector?

Practice

Construct a line segment that is congruent to each given segment. Then bisect each line segment.

1.
   A   B

2. C————————D

3. E————————F

4. Construct a triangle using line segments congruent to the line segments on the right.

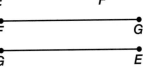

5. Classify the triangle from Exercise 4.

Pyramids of Giza

Similar figures have the same shape but not necessarily the same size.

Pyramid height: 450 ft

Model height: 18 ft

Learning About It

The pyramids of Giza, found near Cairo, Egypt, were built 4,500 years ago. The diagram shows the size relationship between the actual pyramid and its model. The model and the actual pyramid are similar figures.

In a plane, similar figures have congruent corresponding angles but not necessarily congruent corresponding sides.

Triangle *ABC* and triangle *DEF* are similar triangles. Use each pair of corresponding sides to form the following ratios: $\frac{AB}{DE}$, $\frac{BC}{EF}$, and $\frac{AC}{DF}$. What do you notice?

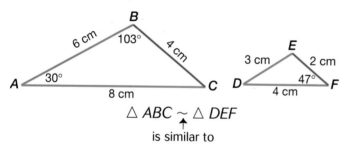

$$\triangle ABC \underset{\text{is similar to}}{\sim} \triangle DEF$$

▲ **Social Studies Connection**
The models of the pyramids can be found in Nikko, Japan. Each model is $\frac{1}{25}$ the actual size.

If two figures are **similar**, the corresponding angles are congruent and corresponding sides are proportional.

You can use these properties of similar figures to find the missing measures of △ *ABC* and △ *DEF*.

Word Bank

similar

Corresponding Angles

$\angle A \cong \angle D$ $m\angle D = 30°$

$\angle B \cong \angle E$ $m\angle E = 103°$

$\angle C \cong \angle F$ $m\angle C = 47°$

Corresponding Sides

$$\frac{AB}{DE} = \frac{6}{3} = \frac{BC}{EF} = \frac{4}{2} = \frac{AC}{DF} = \frac{8}{4}$$

Think and Discuss Are congruent triangles similar? Why or why not?

Try It Out

Quadrilateral *KLMN* is similar to quadrilateral *GHIJ*.

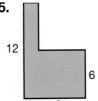
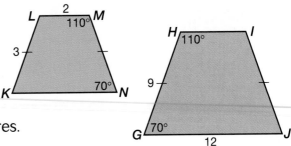

1. Name the corresponding parts.

2. Find the missing side and angle measures.

Practice

Each pair of figures is similar. Give the missing measure.

3.

4.

5.

Problem Solving

6. Denise has two squares. One side of the small square is 5 in. What is the measure of a side of the larger square if one side is three times that of the smaller square? What strategy did you use to solve the problem?

7. **Using Algebra** Louise drew two similar triangles. The sides of the smaller triangle are half the length of the bigger. Two of the angles in one triangle are 60° and 70°. What could the side and angle measures be for both triangles?

Review and Remember

Round each number to the nearest thousandth.

8. 0.00673   **9.** 4.8919   **10.** 63.4982   **11.** 7.7781   **12.** 4.3216

Money $ense

Riding the Rides

Don likes the roller coaster, Sue likes the Tilt-A-Whirl, and Amy likes the Whip. Don has $2.20, Sue has $1.30, and Amy has $1.90. If they combine their money, do they have enough so that each can go on their favorite ride twice?

Painting Your Face

You can use symmetry to help you draw figures.

Learning About It

Many artists in amusement parks use symmetry for face painting. Symmetry will be used to paint the other side of the butterfly on her face. The butterfly has one line of symmetry.

A figure has **line symmetry** if it can be folded along a line of symmetry so that both sides match.

Some figures have more than one line of symmetry.

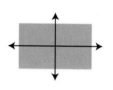   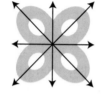   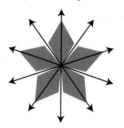

2 lines of symmetry   4 lines of symmetry   5 lines of symmetry

> **Word Bank**
> line symmetry

Find the lines of symmetry for the figure on the right. Trace over the picture and fold the figure so that both sides match. How many lines of symmetry does this figure have?

Think and Discuss Which capital letters in the alphabet have line symmetry?

Try It Out

Trace each figure and draw on the figure as many lines of symmetry as possible.

1.   2.   3.   4.   5.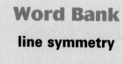

Draw each of the following figures. Use paper folding to check your work.

6. a figure with only 1 line of symmetry

7. a figure with more than 6 lines of symmetry

Practice

Is the black line a line of symmetry? Write *yes* or *no*.

8.

9.

10.

11.

Trace each figure and draw on the figure as many lines of symmetry as possible.

12.

13.

14.

15.

Trace each figure and its line of symmetry on grid paper. Then draw the other half of the figure.

16.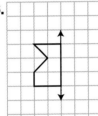

17.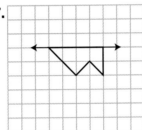

18.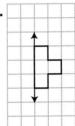

19.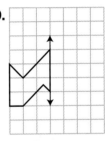

Problem Solving

A figure has rotational symmetry if it can be rotated less than a full turn to match the original. The figure on the right has rotational symmetry.

$\frac{1}{8}$ turn $\frac{1}{4}$ turn

Does each figure have rotational symmetry? Write *yes* or *no*.

20.

21.

22.

23.

Review and Remember

 Estimate first. Then use a calculator to find the answer.

24. 199×299

25. 14.02×20.7

26. $3.65 + 35.7$

27. $598.6 \div 20$

For Extra Practice, see Set I, page 428.

The Big Wheel

A circle has both line and rotational symmetry.

Learning About It

The Ferris wheel, one of the main attractions at many amusement parks, is in the shape of a circle. A circle is a closed plane figure. Every point on the circle is the same distance from a fixed point called the center.

The diagram below describes terms you can use to talk about circles. Find examples of as many terms as you can in the photo of the Ferris wheel at the right.

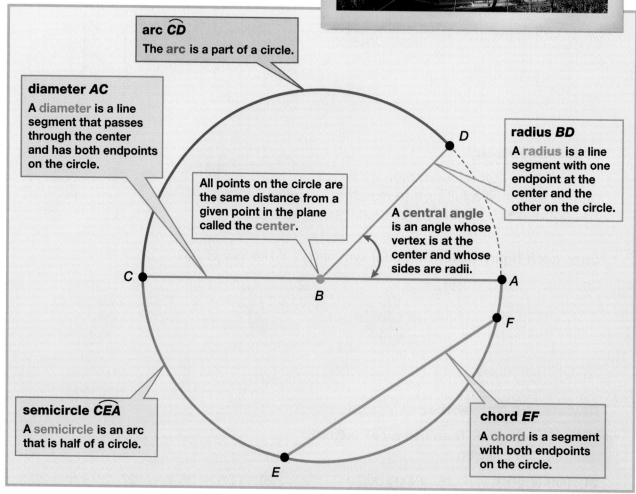

arc CD
The arc is a part of a circle.

diameter AC
A diameter is a line segment that passes through the center and has both endpoints on the circle.

All points on the circle are the same distance from a given point in the plane called the center.

radius BD
A radius is a line segment with one endpoint at the center and the other on the circle.

A central angle is an angle whose vertex is at the center and whose sides are radii.

semicircle CEA
A semicircle is an arc that is half of a circle.

chord EF
A chord is a segment with both endpoints on the circle.

Connecting Ideas

You know that central angles are angles formed by two radii. You can use central angles to help you make circle graphs.

What You Need

compass
protractor

There are 360 degrees in a circle. A circle graph uses central angles to display data that is part of a whole. Follow the steps below to understand how the data in the table is displayed in a circle graph.

Rides at the Amusement Park	
Water Rides	28%
Kiddie Rides	19%
Other Rides	53%

Step 1 Find the number of degrees represented by the percent. First write the percent in decimal form.

$$\text{Water Rides:} \quad 28\% = 0.28$$

Then multiply the decimal by 360° and round to the nearest degree.

$$0.28 \times 360° = 101°$$

101° will represent the 28% of rides that are water rides. Now repeat Step 1 for the kiddie and other rides.

Step 2 Use your compass to draw the circle. Then draw a radius.

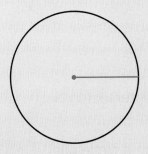

Step 3 Place the center of your protractor on the center of the circle and place the edge along the radius. Draw a second radius to form a central angle that represents the first item of data. Label the part inside.

Step 4 Move the protractor edge onto the second radius you drew. Continue drawing and labeling sections to represent all the data.

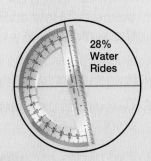

Step 5 Choose a title for your graph.

Think and Discuss How many degrees are there in half of a circle? one quarter of a circle?

Try It Out

Use the figure on the right. Identify an example of each term.

1. semicircle   2. diameter   3. arc

4. chord   5. radius   6. center

7. **Describe** Write a rule for finding the radius of a circle when you know the diameter. Write a rule for finding the diameter when you know the radius.

8. Make a circle graph for the following data.

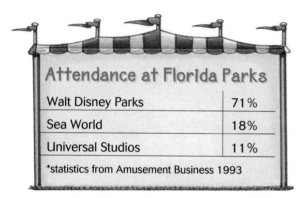

Attendance at Florida Parks

Walt Disney Parks	71%
Sea World	18%
Universal Studios	11%

*statistics from Amusement Business 1993

Practice

Use the circle on the right for Exercises 9–14.
Write the name for each symbol.

9. $\overline{QN}$ 10. $\overline{MO}$ 11. $\overset{\frown}{MN}$

12. $\overset{\frown}{PMN}$ 13. Q 14. $\overline{PO}$

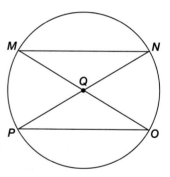

15. **Analyze** Can a circle have more than one diameter? How does your answer relate to the symmetry of a circle?

Write *true* or *false* for each statement.

16. Two circles can intersect in one point.

17. Two circles can intersect in two points.

18. Two circles can intersect in three points.

19. A central angle in a circle can measure 180°.

20. All circles have the same length radii.

21. All circles are polygons.

22. The measure of a chord must be less than or equal to the measure of the diameter.

Find the measure of the central angle on a circle graph represented by each percent. Round to the nearest degree.

23. 50%   **24.** 40%   **25.** 12%   **26.** 36%   **27.** 7%

Problem Solving

Use the table at the right to answer Problems 28–30.

28. Construct a circle graph with the data in the table on the right.

29. **Using Mental Math** If 100 people were at the park, about how many people would be from 19 to 59 years old?

30. **Using Estimation** If 2,995 people went to the park, would it be reasonable to say that about 2,000 of them would be older than 18?

Age Ranges of Park Visitors	
Under 13 years old	15%
13–18 years old	20%
19–59 years old	40%
over 59 years old	25%

Use the graph at the right to answer Problems 31 and 32.

31. If the total amount spent was $221, how much was spent on admission?

32. **Explain** Look at Problem 31. How much was spent on food? parking? transportation? How do the totals of each category compare with the total amount spent?

33. **Create Your Own** Keep a diary of how you spend your time one day. Make a circle graph to represent the data you record.

Spending at the Park

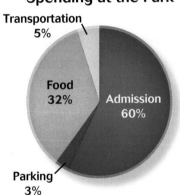

Review and Remember

Using Algebra Find the rule. Complete each table.

34. Rule:_____?_____

Input	Output
25	100
35. 40	▦
36. ▦	2,400

37. Rule:_____?_____

Input	Output
500	100
38. ▦	25
39. 45	▦

40. Rule:_____?_____

	Input	Output
41.	▦	150
	50	175
42.	125	▦

For Extra Practice, see Set J, page 428.

Problem Solving
Using Circle Graphs

Use data in circle graphs to help you solve problems.

The total cost for 25 students to go to Fun World Amusement Park and participate in everything is $1,050. The circle graph shows how each separate cost relates to the total cost. Fun World reduces the cost for those who do not wish to see the show or have lunch. How much will Linda pay if she does not go to the show?

Comparing Costs

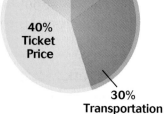

15% Show
15% Lunch
40% Ticket Price
30% Transportation

 ## UNDERSTAND

What do you need to know?

You need to know what it costs per person to go on the trip and to go to the show.

 ## PLAN

How can you solve the problem?

You can **write equations** to find what Linda will pay. First, find the cost of the trip for one student. Then find the cost of the show for one student. Finally, use this information to find the cost of a trip without the show.

 ## SOLVE

cost for the class		number of students		cost per student
$1,050	÷	25	=	$42.00

cost per student		% charged for show		cost of show
$42.00	×	15%	=	$6.30

cost per student		cost of show		cost without show
$42.00	−	$6.30	=	$35.70

Linda will pay $35.70.

 ## LOOK BACK

Check the answer by multiplying $42.00 × 85% to find the cost without the show.

Show What You Learned

Use the data in the circle graph on page 422 to help you solve Problems 1–3.

1. If you did not want to pay for lunch or the show, how much would the trip cost?

2. What is the cost of one admission ticket? Of transportation for one student?

3. Another park, Amazing Amusements, charges a total of $980.00 for 25 students. This price includes transportation and a ticket. Lunch costs an extra $5.90 per student. If you are going to pay for lunch but not the show, which park offers the better deal? Explain how you know.

The total amount of money raised at the school fair was $3,500.00. Use the circle graph at the right to help you solve Problems 4–6.

4. Which booths together raised one fourth of the total?

5. If the fair lasted 8 hours, how much money did the face-painting booth average per hour?

6. **Explain** Which booth made about $22.00 an hour? Explain how you know.

7. A local park expects a group of four visitors to spend $120.00. If 25% of the money is spent on food, and the rest of the money is spent on tickets, what is the price per ticket?

8. **Create Your Own** Use the circle graph on page 422. Make up a problem about how much you would spend at Fun World.

Money Raised At Each Booth

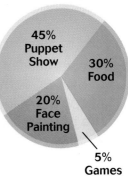

45% Puppet Show

30% Food

20% Face Painting

5% Games

Problem Solving

Practice What You Learned

Choose the correct letter for each answer.

1 Which expression can you use to find the average height, in inches, of 3 people who are 58 in. tall, 63 in. tall, and 49 in. tall?

A. $\frac{1}{3} \times 58 + 63 + 49$
B. $58 + 63 + 49 \div 3$
C. $(58 + 63 + 49) \div 3$
D. $(58 + 63 + 49) \times 3$
E. $(58 + 63) + (3 \times 49)$

Tip

Think about how you would compute the average of 3 numbers. Then look over the answer choices.

2 The vertices of a triangle are labeled *A*, *B*, and *C*. Side *BC* is the longest side. Point *D* is the midpoint of side *AC*. Which of these angles has the greatest measure?

A. ∠ABC   **D.** ∠DCB
B. ∠BAC   **E.** ∠CBA
C. ∠BCA

Tip

Using the *Draw a Diagram* strategy can help you solve this problem.

3 Which is reasonable for the percent of the total number of students that are members of the drama club *or* the dance club?

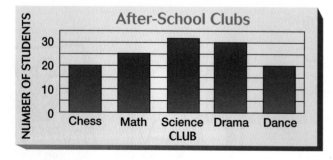

A. 15%   **D.** 40%
B. 20%   **E.** 60%
C. 30%

Tip

First decide what information from the graph you need to solve the problem.

4 Two years ago, a computer cost $1,950. Today, the cost of the same computer is 10% less than it was last year. If the price last year was $1,489, which is the best estimate for the price of the computer today?

A. $800
B. $1,000
C. $1,100
D. $1,350
E. $2,000

5 Bill made this drawing as part of a wall mural. Which statement best describes the relationship of the two triangles?

A. They are congruent.
B. They are similar.
C. They are both right triangles.
D. One is a reflection of the other.
E. One is a translation of the other.

6 Anne cut out a cardboard pattern of a polygon having two right angles. Which of these could **NOT** be the shape Anne cut out?

A. Pentagon
B. Triangle
C. Parallelogram
D. Trapezoid
E. Hexagon

7 Lyle collects rocks, and his sister collects shells. She has 64 shells in her collection. If Lyle gives one third of his rock collection to his sister, she will get 37 rocks. How many rocks are in Lyle's collection?

A. 37   D. 148
B. 74   E. Not Here
C. 111

8 Based on the information in the graph, who worked more hours from September through November? How many more hours did he work?

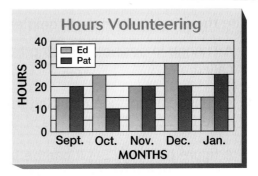

A. Pat; 50 more hours
B. Ed; 60 more hours
C. Pat; 10 more hours
D. Ed; 10 more hours
E. Not Here

9 The sum of two angles of a triangle is 80°. Which equation could you use to find the measure of the third angle, *n*, in this triangle?

A. $(2 \times 80) + 2n = 180$
B. $(2 \times 80) \div n = 180$
C. $80 + 2n = 180$
D. $180 - 80 = n$
E. $\frac{80}{2} + n = 180$

10 Maria is saving to buy a new computer. This chart shows Maria's savings over a 5-week period.

Week	1	2	3	4	5
Dollars	$55	$59	$68	$84	$109

If Maria's savings continue in this pattern, how much money will she have at the end of 8 weeks?

A. $115   D. $294
B. $194   E. $325
C. $258

Checkpoint

Motion Geometry and Similar Figures

Vocabulary

Write the missing word that completes each sentence.

1. A change in position resulting from a turn is called a __?__ .

2. A change in position resulting from a slide is called a __?__ .

3. A figure has __?__ if it can be folded along a line so that both sides match.

Word Bank

symmetry
reflection
rotation
translation

Concepts and Skills

Figure I is congruent to Figure II. Describe each change in position from Figure I to Figure II. (pages 408–411)

4.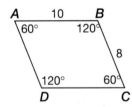

5.

6.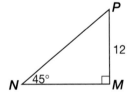

Use the triangles in Exercise 6 to complete Exercises 7–9.

7. ∠A ≅ ∠___

8. ∠B ≅ ∠___

9. ∠C ≅ ∠___

Using Algebra   Use the pairs of similar figures to find each measure in Exercises 10–13. (pages 414–415)

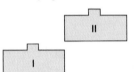

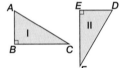

10. measure of ∠F

11. measure of ∠L

12. measure of $\overline{NM}$

13. measure of $\overline{EH}$

Is the green line a line of symmetry? Write *yes* or *no*. (pages 416–417)

14.

15.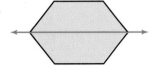

16.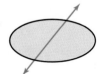

Problem Solving

Use the graph on the right to help you solve Problems 17–20.

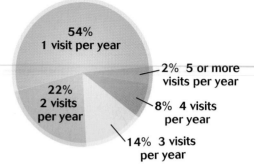

54% 1 visit per year

2% 5 or more visits per year

22% 2 visits per year

8% 4 visits per year

14% 3 visits per year

17. How often do most people visit the park each year?

    a. once   **b.** twice   **c.** more than twice

18. How many people visit the park more than twice a year?

    a. 540   **b.** 220   **c.** 480   **d.** 240

19. How many people visit the park less than three times a year?

    a. 900   **b.** 760   **c.** 540   **d.** 140

20. How many people visit the park five or more times a year?

    a. 20   **b.** 400   **c.** 960   **d.** 4

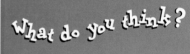

What do you think?

How can you make a circle graph given a table of values? Use examples to help you explain.

Journal Idea

Sketch two equilateral triangles that are similar but not congruent. Explain why they are similar. Then describe how you would change the sketch to show two congruent triangles.

You Decide

Activity

Robot-ometry

Pretend you are designing a robot for a new amusement park feature. Write a description of your robot. Be sure to use geometric terms.

- What shapes will you use? Will they be similar, congruent, symmetrical?
- How can you use slides, flips, turns, angles, and line segments?

 You might wish to include this work in your portfolio.

Extra Practice

Set A (pages 386–387)

Write the name and symbol for each figure.

1.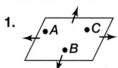

2.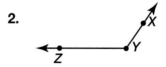

3.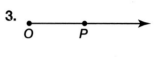

Solve.

4. Give an example of an angle and a line segment found in a park.

Set B (pages 388–391)

Trace each angle. Then use a protractor to find the measure.

1.

2.

3. L ●————————● S

Use a protractor to draw each angle.

4. 60°   5. 70°   6. 105°   7. 20°   8. 48°   9. 55°

Use the figure at the right for Exercises 10–12.

10. Name two straight angles.

11. Name two obtuse angles.

12. Name two acute angles.

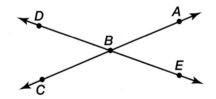

Set C (pages 392–393)

Draw a figure for each geometric idea.

1. parallel lines   2. skew lines   3. perpendicular lines

Copy the drawing on the right. Then add the streets that are described.

4. Second St. intersects Houston Ave. and Miami Ave. but is not parallel to First St.

5. Cross St. is parallel to Second St.

Extra Practice

Set D (pages 396–399)

Using Algebra **Classify each triangle. Use as many names as possible. Find the value of each variable.**

1.

2.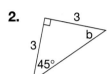

3.

4.

Copy the dots. Then connect them to draw each triangle.

5. equilateral acute triangle

6. obtuse scalene triangle

7. right scalene triangle

• • • • • •
A B C D E F

• • • • • •
G H I J K L

Set E (pages 400–401)

Using Algebra **Classify each quadrilateral. Be as specific as possible. Then find the value of each variable.**

1.

2.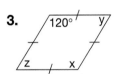

3.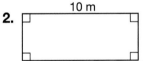

4.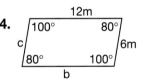

Solve.

5. Bob labeled a drawing as a rectangle and a rhombus. Ron called it a square. Could both be correct? Explain.

Set F (pages 402–403)

Name each polygon. If the figure is not a polygon, explain why it is not.

1.

2.

3.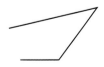

4.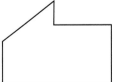

Solve.

5. Can a triangle have two right angles? Explain.

Extra Practice

Set G (pages 408–411)

Describe each change in position from Figure I to Figure II.
Use the terms reflection, rotation, and translation.

1.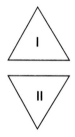

2.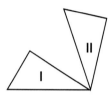

3.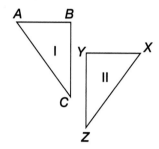

Complete each congruence statement from Exercise 3.

4. △ABC ≅ _____

5. ∠B ≅ _____

6. ∠C ≅ _____

Set H (pages 414–415)

Using Algebra Each pair of figures is similar. Give the
missing side measures and angle measures.

1.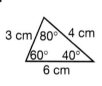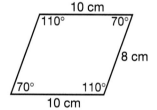

2.

Set I (pages 416–417)

Is the green line a line of symmetry? Write *yes* or *no*.

1.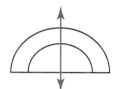

2.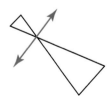

3.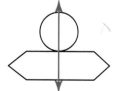

4.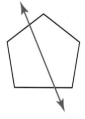

Set J (pages 418–421)

Draw a circle and label the following parts.

1. radius

2. central angle

3. chord

4. arc

Use a protractor to draw each angle. Classify each angle.

1. 90°   2. 115°   3. 180°   4. 45°

Use the figure at the right to answer 5–11.

5. Name two parallel lines.

6. Name two perpendicular lines.

7. Name intersecting lines that are not perpendicular.

8. The sum of the measures of ∠___ and ∠___ is 180°.

9. Classify *CHGD* and give the sum of its angle measures.

10. Classify △*BDG*, using as many names as possible.

11. Name two skew lines. If you cannot, explain why.

Use the triangles below to answer Exercises 12–16.

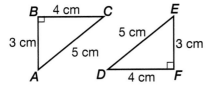

12. Name two congruent triangles.

13. Which triangles are similar?

14. What is the measure of ∠*GHI*?

15. What is the measure of $\overline{GI}$?

16. Name the corresponding sides and angles for △*ABC* and △*EFD*.

Use the figures at the right to answer Exercises 17–18.

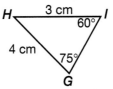

17. Tell whether the change in the position of Figure I to Figure II is a result of a translation, rotation, or reflection.

18. How many lines of symmetry does Figure I have?

19. Make a circle graph from the table.

20. Use your graph from Problem 19. How many people chose the Ferris wheel?

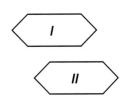

Favorite Rides of 160 People	
Ferris Wheel	25%
Roller Coaster	30%
Water Ride	45%

 Self-Check

How did learning about circles help you answer Problem 20?

Performance Assessment

Show What You Know About Geometry

1 Describe this figure. Use as many geometry words as you can.

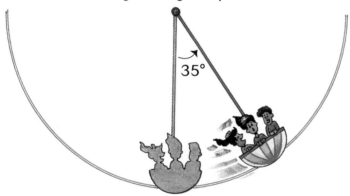

Self-Check Did you remember that the figure is made up of many smaller shapes?

2 This ride is moving 35 degrees per second.

35°

a. Draw and label an angle that represents the position of the cup with respect to the starting point after 2 seconds.

b. Draw and label an angle that represents the position of the cup after 3 seconds.

c. Between which two consecutive seconds will a straight angle be formed with respect to the starting point ?

Self-Check Did you remember that a straight angle measures 180°?

What You Need

protractor

For Your Portfolio

You might wish to include this work in your portfolio.

Extension

Cross Sections

Look at the cube at the right. All six faces are congruent.

By slicing a cube horizontally, you are cutting parallel to the base and creating a **cross section**. The new face resulting from the cut is congruent to every face of the original cube.

By slicing a cube vertically, you are making a cut perpendicular to the base. How does this face compare to the others?

Sometimes when cross sections are created by perpendicular or parallel cuts to a space figure, the resulting face is not congruent to any face of the original space figure.

Describe the face of the cross section which will result when each space figure below is cut as shown.

1.  **2.**  **3.**   **4.**

5. Describe How are the horizontal cross sections of a cylinder or a cone like the base or different from the base?

6. Explain How are the horizontal cross sections of a triangular pyramid and a triangular prism with horizontal bases alike or different?

Cumulative Review

★ ★ ★ ★ ★ **Preparing for Tests**

Choose the correct letter for each answer.

Number Concepts	Geometry and Spatial Reasoning

Number Concepts

1. Each of two different fifth grade classes will be divided into groups of the same size. The classes have 36 and 48 students. Which is the greatest common factor of 36 and 48?

   A. 4
   B. 8
   C. 12
   D. 24

2. Which expression shows 60 as a product of prime factors?

   A. 6×10
   B. $2 \times 6 \times 5$
   C. $2 \times 2 \times 3 \times 5$
   D. $2 \times 3 \times 10$

3. Which number sentence is **NOT** true?

   A. $\frac{3}{8} > \frac{1}{4}$ **C.** $\frac{3}{4} < \frac{7}{8}$

   B. $\frac{1}{2} = \frac{6}{12}$ **D.** $\frac{4}{5} > \frac{9}{10}$

4. Scott is a writer. He has completed $\frac{2}{5}$ of his latest book and sent it to his editor. What percent of the book does he still have left to complete?

   A. 20%   **C.** 40%
   B. 30%   **D.** 60%

Geometry and Spatial Reasoning

5. How many squares are in the figure shown?

   A. 4
   B. 6
   C. 8
   D. 10

6. Look at the triangle below. What is the measure of $\angle x$?

   A. 30°
   B. 45°
   C. 60°
   D. 90°

Use the triangles below to answer Questions 7 and 8.

Triangle *ABC* is **similar** to Triangle *DEF*.

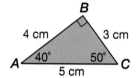

7. What is the length of side *DE*?

   A. 2 cm
   B. 3 cm
   C. 4 cm
   D. 8 cm

8. What is the measure of $\angle D$?

   A. 20°
   B. 40°
   C. 50°
   D. 80°

Measurement	Probability and Statistics

9. The Dallas Cowboys started a drive on their own 32-yard line. They went 68 yards to score a touchdown. How many **feet** did they go?

   A. 300 ft   **C.** 108 ft
   B. 204 ft   **D.** 96 ft

10. Debbie has 2 boxes that are each 40 inches long, 20 inches wide, and 2 inches high. What is the total volume of the 2 boxes?

   A. 124 in.^{3} **C.** 1,600 in.^{3}
   B. 800 in.^{3} **D.** 3,200 in.^{3}

11. Which would be the best way to find the **area** of the shaded region?

   A. Find the perimeter of the triangle and subtract the perimeter of the square.
   B. Find the area of the square and add the area of the triangle.
   C. Find the area of the triangle and subtract the area of the square.
   D. Find the perimeter of the square and add the area of the triangle.

12. A circle has a circumference of 310 meters. Which measure is the best estimate of the **radius** of the circle?

   A. 40 m
   B. 50 m
   C. 60 m
   D. 100 m

13. A combination for a lock is 3 single-digit numbers. The first number is 4, and the second is 5. How many numbers might Andy have to try before the lock opens?

   A. 7   **C.** 9
   B. 8   **D.** 10

14. There are 3 red pens, 2 blue pens, and 4 purple pens in a box. If 1 pen is chosen without looking, what is the probability that the pen will be green?

   A. 1   **C.** $\frac{1}{3}$
   B. $\frac{4}{9}$ **D.** 0

15. On a 5-day trip, Katie's family traveled the following distances: 154 miles, 203 miles, 61 miles, 0 miles, and 182 miles. What was the average number of miles traveled each day?

   A. 100 mi   **C.** 150 mi
   B. 120 mi   **D.** 170 mi

The graph shows the percent of types of shoes sold by Shoe City.

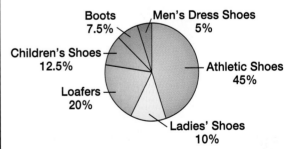

16. If Shoe City sold $200,000 worth of shoes last year, how much was from the sale of loafers?

   A. $40,000   **C.** $10,000
   B. $20,000   **D.** $5,000

Chapter 11

Perimeter, Area, and Volume

Chapter Theme: FIELD DAY

REAL-WORLD Math

..................Real Facts...................

People of all ages enjoy playing miniature golf. The challenge for players is to hit a golf ball as few times as possible, so it moves around and through obstacles and into a hole. Each hole has different obstacles.

When planning a miniature golf course, a designer needs to know the perimeter and area of each hole.

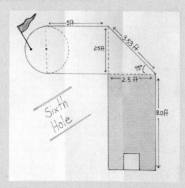

• How could you find the perimeter and area of the green rectangle in the design above?

• How could you find the perimeter of the figure formed by the triangle and the green rectangle together?

• How would you use perimeter and area to design a golf course?

..................Real People...................

Meet Al Tirrell, a designer of miniature golf courses. He shapes each green differently, so each hole is one of a kind. He designed his Jungle Golf course around a jungle theme, using life-size wild animals as props!

How Far Around?

Formulas can be used to find distances around objects.

Learning About It

You are roping off a rectangular section of a local park for your school's field day. How much rope do you need? You need to find the distance around the rectangle. The distance around any polygon is called the **perimeter** (*P*). You can find the perimeter of a polygon by adding the lengths of its sides.

You can use a formula to find the perimeter.

> l = length w = width

$$P = l + l + w + w$$
$$= 2l + 2w$$
$$= (2 \times 120) + (2 \times 50)$$
$$= 340$$

You need 340 yards of rope.

> **Word Bank**
>
> **perimeter**

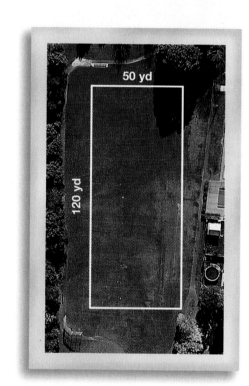

50 yd

120 yd

More Examples

A.

$$P = s + s + s + s = 4s$$

B.
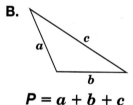

$$P = a + b + c$$

Think and Discuss What is the formula for the perimeter of a regular hexagon?

Try It Out

Estimate. Then find the perimeter of each polygon.

1.

9 in.   9 in.
9 in.

2.
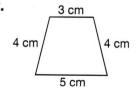
3 cm
4 cm   4 cm
5 cm

3.
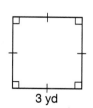
3 yd

4.
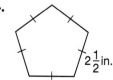
$2\frac{1}{2}$ in.

Practice

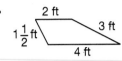
Find the perimeter of each polygon.

5.
16 in.

6.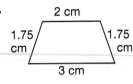
2 cm
1.75 cm
1.75 cm
3 cm

7.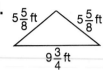
$5\frac{5}{8}$ ft $5\frac{5}{8}$ ft
$9\frac{3}{4}$ ft

8.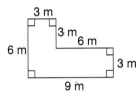
2 ft
$1\frac{1}{2}$ ft
3 ft
4 ft

9.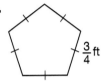
$\frac{3}{4}$ ft

10.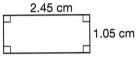
2.45 cm
1.05 cm

11.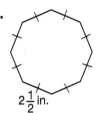
$2\frac{1}{2}$ in.

12.
3 m
3 m   6 m
6 m   3 m
9 m

Problem Solving

The drawings show the roof of a bandstand and a baseball diamond in the park.

13. What is the perimeter of the roof?

14. Analyze The base paths of the baseball diamond form a square. Suppose there are runners on first base and third base. If the batter hits a home run, how far do the players run altogether?

15. Several sections in the park are roped off for different activities. One rectangular section is twice as long as it is wide. What is the perimeter of this section if the width is 12 yards? What strategy did you use to solve this problem?

16. Analyze One of the sections is a square, and another is a regular pentagon. Each has a perimeter of 200 feet. Find the length of a side for each section.

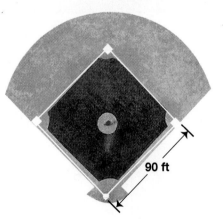
$3\frac{1}{2}$ yd

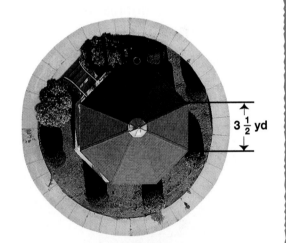
90 ft

Review and Remember

Complete the following exercises.

17. 45,206 + 3,176

18. 910 ÷ 130

19. 0.3 × 0.009

20. 24.96 + 5.7

21. 423.1 − 37.89

22. 7.2 ÷ 0.09

23. 6 × 10 − 3

24. 6 × (10 − 3)

25. 4 × (3 + 2) − 20

Mowing It Over

You can use the dimensions of a quadrilateral to find its area.

Learning About It

The section of the park you roped off needs to be mowed. Look at the drawing below. How many square yards of grass do you need to mow?

You need to find the **area** of the rectangular field. The number of square units needed to cover a region is the area *(A)* of the region.

You can use a formula to find the area of a rectangle.

$$A = lw$$

$$A = 120 \times 50 = 6{,}000 \text{ yd}^2$$

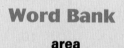

Word Bank

area

120 yd

50 yd

You need to mow 6,000 square yards of grass.

More Examples

A. Find the area of the square below.

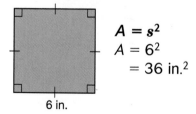

6 in.

$$A = s^2$$
$$A = 6^2$$
$$= 36 \text{ in.}^2$$

B. Find the area of the rectangle below.

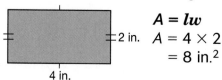

4 in.

2 in.

$$A = lw$$
$$A = 4 \times 2$$
$$= 8 \text{ in.}^2$$

◀ **Math Note**

The area of any figure is expressed in square units, such as square feet, or ft^2.

Connecting Ideas

You can use what you know about the area of a rectangle to find the area of a parallelogram.

Follow the steps below to write the formula for the area of a parallelogram.

What You Need

For each student:
tracing paper
scissors

Step 1 Trace the parallelogram at the right and cut the tracing out.

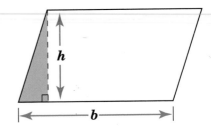

Step 2 Cut along the dotted line. Move the triangle to the opposite side of the parallelogram to form a rectangle.

Step 3 Now use the formula for the area of a rectangle to write the formula for the area of a parallelogram.

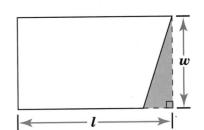

$A = lw$ The length of the rectangle is the base (*b*) of the parallelogram. The width of the rectangle
$A = bh$ is the height (*h*) of the parallelogram.

Now use the formula to find the area of a parallelogram with a base of 20 cm and a height of 4 cm.

$$A = bh$$
$$= 20 \times 4 = 80 \text{ cm}^2$$

Think and Discuss What kind of angle is formed by the height and the base of a parallelogram?

Try It Out

Estimate. Then find the area of each quadrilateral.

1.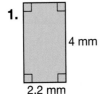
4 mm
2.2 mm

2.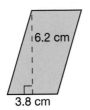
6.2 cm
3.8 cm

3.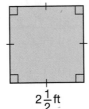
$2\frac{1}{2}$ ft

4.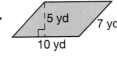
5 yd
7 yd
10 yd

5. rectangle
$l = 6$ in.
$w = 9$ in.

6. rectangle
$l = 12.7$ cm
$w = 4.3$ cm

7. parallelogram
$b = 23$ ft
$h = 10$ ft

8. parallelogram
$b = 5\frac{1}{2}$ ft
$h = 2\frac{1}{4}$ ft

9. **What If?** Suppose the base of a parallelogram is two times the height. If the base is 18 ft, what is the area?

Practice

Find the area of each quadrilateral.

10. 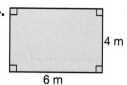 2 mm
8 mm

11. 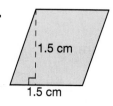 10 ft
30 ft

12. 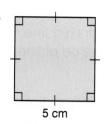 12 yd
24 yd

13. 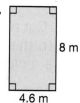 $1\frac{1}{2}$ in.
6 in.

14. 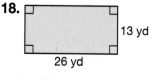 4 m
6 m

15. 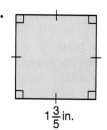 1.5 cm
1.5 cm

16.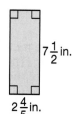
5 cm

17. 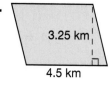 8 m
4.6 m

18. 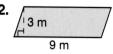 13 yd
26 yd

19.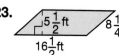
$1\frac{3}{5}$ in.

20. 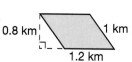 $7\frac{1}{2}$ in.
$2\frac{4}{5}$ in.

21. 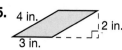 3.25 km
4.5 km

22. 3 m
9 m

23. $5\frac{1}{2}$ ft $8\frac{1}{4}$ ft
$16\frac{1}{2}$ ft

24. 0.8 km 1 km
1.2 km

25. 4 in. 2 in.
3 in.

26. rectangle

$l = 2.4$ cm

$w = 8.3$ cm

27. parallelogram

$b = 4$ in.

$h = 11$ in.

28. rectangle

$l = 4\frac{3}{5}$ in.

$w = 8\frac{2}{3}$ in.

29. parallelogram

$b = 38.2$ cm

$h = 41.7$ cm

30. The length of a rectangle is twice the width. If the width is $2\frac{1}{2}$ in., what is the area?

31. The height of a parallelogram is $\frac{1}{3}$ the base. If the height is 4 cm, what is the area?

32. Explain Look at the parallelogram at the right. Can you find the area with the dimensions given? Why or why not?

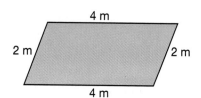
4 m
2 m 2 m
4 m

33. Generalize Look back at Exercise 16. Double the length of each side and find the new area. How does the area of a square change when you double the length of its sides?

438

Problem Solving

Use the diagram at the right to solve Problems 34–37.

34. A section of the field will be used for games. What is the area of this section?

35. What is the perimeter of the section roped off for games?

36. What are the dimensions of the section roped off for serving food? What is the area of that section?

37. What is the perimeter of the section for contests? What is the area of that section?

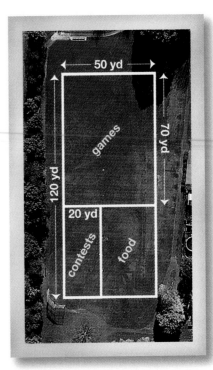

Review and Remember

Find the measure of each missing angle.

38.

47°
x   63°

39.

45°
x

40.

x
60°   x

41.

46°
x
58°

42.

128°
25°
x

43.

x
19°
26°

44.

x
10°
80°

45.

x
70° 61°

Time for Technology

Using a Calculator

Area of a Square

Suppose a large square park is 175 yd on each side. What is the area? There are two ways to use a calculator to find the area of a square.

Press: ⬛1⬛ ⬛7⬛ ⬛5⬛ ⬛×⬛ ⬛1⬛ ⬛7⬛ ⬛5⬛ ⬛=⬛   Display: **30625**

or

Press: ⬛1⬛ ⬛7⬛ ⬛5⬛ ⬛x^2⬛   Display: **30625**

The ⬛x^2⬛ button multiplies a number entered by that number.

Coverup

You can use what you know about parallelograms to find the area of a triangle.

Learning About It

In one section of the park, the grass is covered with plywood to make it easier for students to dance. How can you find the area of the covered section?

You need to find the area of the triangular section. You can use the formula for the area of a parallelogram to write the formula for the area of a triangle.

Step 1 Trace the parallelogram at the right and cut the tracing out.

Step 2 Cut the tracing in half along the red diagonal. Place one triangle on top of the other.

Notice that the area of each triangle is half the area of the parallelogram. You can use this relationship to write the formula for the area of a triangle.

Parallelogram	Triangle
$A = bh$	$A = \frac{1}{2} bh$

What You Need

For each student:
tracing paper
scissors

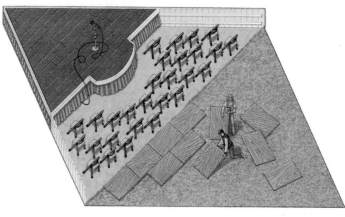

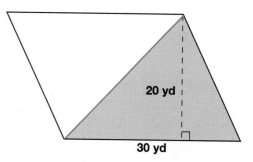

Now use the formula to find the area of the triangular section to be covered with plywood.

$$A = \frac{1}{2} bh$$

$$= \frac{1}{2} (30 \times 20) = \frac{1}{2} \times 600 = 300 \text{ yd}^2$$

The area of the covered section is 300 yd².

Think and Discuss Two triangles are formed when a square is cut along a diagonal. Are the triangles congruent? How do you know?

Try It Out

Use the formula $A = \frac{1}{2}bh$ to find the area of each triangle.

1.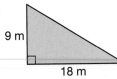
9 m
18 m

2.
18 ft
9 ft

3.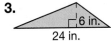
6 in.
24 in.

4.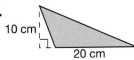
10 cm
20 cm

Practice

Find the area of each triangle.

5.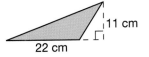
11 cm
22 cm

6.
3.6 ft
3.6 ft

7.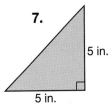
5 in.
5 in.

8.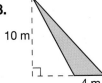
10 m
4 m

Find the area of each triangle. Each square of a grid is equal to 1 square unit.

9.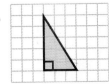

10.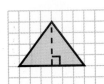

11.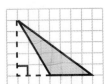

12.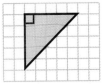

Problem Solving

These squares of colored paper will be cut in half to make triangular place mats for the picnic tables.

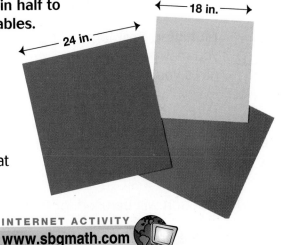
18 in.
24 in.

13. Find the area of a place mat made from a red paper square.

14. Find the area of a place mat made from a yellow paper square.

15. Analyze If the area of a green place mat is 200 in.², how long is each side of a green square?

INTERNET ACTIVITY
www.sbgmath.com

Review and Remember

Complete each exercise.

16. $\frac{5}{6} + \frac{2}{3} + \frac{1}{8}$

17. $21\frac{3}{8} - 14\frac{7}{12}$

18. 2.7×17.08

19. $7.8 \div 0.13$

Developing Skills for Problem Solving

First read for understanding and then focus on solving multistep problems.

READ FOR UNDERSTANDING

For the sixth-grade class picnic, parents will set up a table with lemonade, cider, grape juice, and fruit punch. The table is 8 ft long and 3 ft wide. They will use $\frac{1}{2}$ of the tabletop for lemonade and $\frac{1}{2}$ of the remaining tabletop for fruit punch. Then they will divide the remaining space equally and use it for cider and grape juice.

1 How long and wide is the table?

2 What fraction of the tabletop will be used for lemonade?

3 ft

8 ft

THINK AND DISCUSS

MATH FOCUS

Multistep Problems To solve some problems, you may need more than one step. Each step gives you some of the information you need.

Reread the paragraph at the top of the page. Think about what steps are needed to find the area that will be used for cider.

3 What is the area of the whole tabletop?

4 What fraction will be used for fruit punch? for cider?

5 What is the area of the part of the tabletop used for cider?

6 What steps were needed to find the area of the part of the tabletop that will be used for cider?

Show What You Learned

Answer each question. Give a reason for your choice.

At the picnic, food will be placed on one long table. The long table will be created by placing two smaller tables end-to-end as shown. A paper skirt will be wrapped around the long table and held in place by thumbtacks. If the thumbtacks are placed every 6 inches, how many thumbtacks are needed?

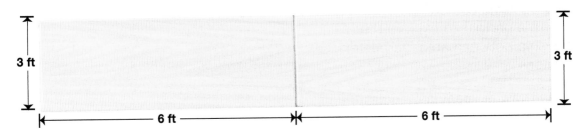

3 ft   6 ft   6 ft   3 ft

1 What do you need to do first to solve this problem?

   a. Find the perimeter of the long table.

   b. Find the area of the long table.

   c. Find the height of the long table.

2 Which of the following would you do to find the number of thumbtacks needed?

   a. Multiply the area of the long table by 2.

   b. Multiply the perimeter of the long table by 6.

   c. Multiply the perimeter of the long table by 12 and then divide by 6.

3 Which expression could you use to solve the problem?

   a. $(2l + 2w) \div 2$

   b. $[(2l + 2w) \times 12] \div 6$

   c. $(l \times w) \times 2$

There are 20 classes in the sixth grade with 25 students in each class. Frozen fruit bars are packaged in boxes of 12. All 20 teachers and every student will have a frozen fruit bar.

4 **Describe** Tell what steps you would use to find the total number of fruit bars needed for the teachers and students.

5 **Explain** How many boxes of fruit bars are needed? Tell what steps you used to find out.

Make the Most of It

Using Algebra

You can change the area of a figure without changing its perimeter.

Learning About It

You and your partner want to rope off part of the games field for an obstacle course. You only have 24 yards of rope. How can you and your partner find the greatest area for your obstacle course? Using grid paper, work with a partner to explore the relationship between area, perimeter, and shapes.

What You Need

For each pair:
grid paper

Step 1 Draw as many rectangles as you can that have a perimeter of 24 units. The length and width should be whole units. One rectangle is shown at the right.

Step 2 Find the area of each rectangle. The area of the rectangle at the right is 35 square units.

Step 3 Record your data in a chart like the one shown below.

Rectangle	Length	Width	Perimeter	Area
1	7	5	24 units	35 square units
2			24 units	
3			24 units	

- What do you notice about the width of the rectangle with the least area?

- What are the dimensions of the rectangle with the greatest area?

- What do you notice about the rectangle with the greatest area?

Connecting Ideas

You have seen that it is possible to change the area of a figure without changing the perimeter. You can also change the perimeter without changing the area.

How can you mark off an area of 48 square yards, using the least amount of rope possible? You need to find the rectangle with the shortest perimeter. You can use grid paper to solve the problem.

Step 1 Draw as many rectangles as you can with an area of 48 square units, using whole units for length and width.

Step 2 Find each perimeter.

Step 3 Record your data in a chart like the one shown below.

Rectangle	Length	Width	Area	Perimeter
1	1		48 square units	
2			48 square units	

Which rectangle has the shortest perimeter?

Think and Discuss The length of a rectangle is 3 ft and the width is 2 ft. What is the area? What happens to the area if the length is doubled? if both the length and width are doubled?

Practice

Using whole units and the perimeter given, find the dimensions of the rectangle with the greatest area.

1. $P = 20$

2. $P = 32$

3. $P = 60$

4. $P = 100$

Using whole units and the area given, find the dimensions of the rectangle with the shortest perimeter.

5. $A = 30$

6. $A = 36$

7. $A = 64$

8. $A = 80$

9. $A = 120$

10. $A = 84$

11. $A = 200$

12. $A = 400$

13. $A = 196$

14. $A = 342$

15. $A = 3,000$

16. $A = 104$

Putting Around

You can find the area of a figure by dividing it into shapes you know.

Learning About It

You have decided to have a miniature golf contest at your field day. Your contest will take place on a miniature golf course hole like the one shown at the right. How can you find the area of green carpet you need to cover the playing surface?

Step 1 Divide your golf course hole into recognizable figures whose areas you can find.

Step 2 Find the area of each figure.

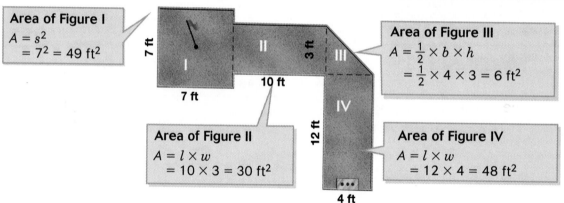

Area of Figure I
$A = s^2$
$= 7^2 = 49$ ft^2

Area of Figure II
$A = l \times w$
$= 10 \times 3 = 30$ ft^2

Area of Figure III
$A = \frac{1}{2} \times b \times h$
$= \frac{1}{2} \times 4 \times 3 = 6$ ft^2

Area of Figure IV
$A = l \times w$
$= 12 \times 4 = 48$ ft^2

Step 3 Add the areas to find the total area.

Total area = 49 + 30 + 6 + 48 = 133

The area of your golf course hole is 133 square feet.

Think and Discuss Find the area of the combined figure another way. Draw a diagram to show your thinking.

Try It Out

Find the area of each figure.

1.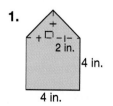
2 in.
4 in.
4 in.

2.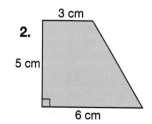
3 cm
5 cm
6 cm

3.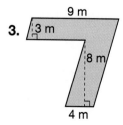
9 m
3 m
8 m
4 m

Practice

Find the area of each figure.

4.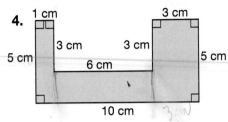
1 cm   3 cm
3 cm   3 cm
5 cm   5 cm
6 cm
10 cm

5.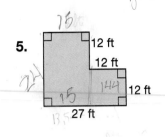
12 ft
12 ft
12 ft
27 ft

6.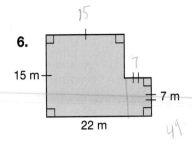
15 m
7 m
22 m

7.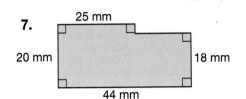
25 mm
20 mm   18 mm
44 mm

8.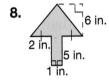
6 in.
2 in.
5 in.
1 in.

9.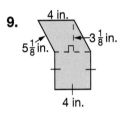
4 in.
$5\frac{1}{8}$ in. $3\frac{1}{8}$ in.
4 in.

Problem Solving

Use the diagram of the miniature golf course hole at the right to solve Problems 10–13.

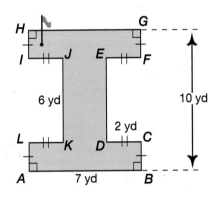
H   G
I   J   E   F
6 yd   10 yd
2 yd
L   K   D   C
A   7 yd   B

10. Describe how you can divide the diagram into recognizable figures.

11. Find the missing dimensions of the diagram.

12. What is the area shown?

13. What is the perimeter of the figure?

14. Look at the parallelogram at the right. Find the area of the shaded region to the nearest whole number. Explain how you solved the problem.

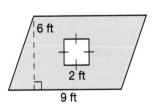
6 ft
2 ft
9 ft

15. Create Your Own Draw a figure, using more than one shape. Find its area and perimeter.

Review and Remember

Using Mental Math **Write each missing metric measure.**

16. 4 km = ▨ m

17. 940 cm = ▨ m

18. 12 cm = ▨ mm

19. 4.3 cm = ▨ mm

20. 7.25 g = ▨ kg

21. 0.6 L = ▨ kL

22. 89 m = ▨ mm

23. 680 mg = ▨ g

24. ▨ cm = 68.21 m

25. ▨ mg = 2.047 g

26. 275m = ▨ km

27. ▨ mL = 0.05L

For Extra Practice, see Set D, page 465.

Match the formula in Column A with the description in Column B. (pages 434–441)

Column A

1. $P = 4s$

2. $P = 2l + 2w$

3. $P = 8s$

4. $A = s^2$

5. $A = lw$

6. $A = bh$

7. $A = \frac{1}{2}bh$

Column B

a. Area of a square

b. Area of a triangle

c. Perimeter of a square

d. Area of a rectangle

e. Perimeter of a regular octagon

f. Perimeter of a rectangle

g. Area of a parallelogram

> **What do you think?**
> If you know the perimeter of a square, how can you find the area?

Mixed Practice

Using Algebra Find the perimeter of each polygon.
(pages 434–435)

8.
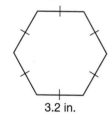
3.2 in.

9.
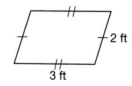
2 ft
3 ft

10.
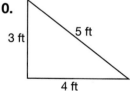
3 ft   5 ft
4 ft

Using Algebra Find the area of each polygon. (pages 436–444)

11.
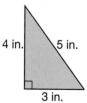
4 in.   5 in.
3 in.

12.
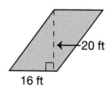
20 ft
16 ft

13.
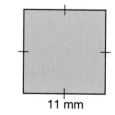
11 mm

14.
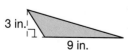
3 in.
9 in.

15.

11.2 ft
20.8 ft

16.
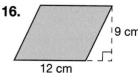
9 cm
12 cm

Problem Solving

Use the diagram at the right to solve Problems 17–20.

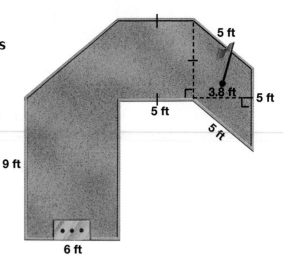

17. Into how many different polygons can you divide the figure? Name them.

18. What is the area of each polygon?

19. What is the total area of the figure?

20. **Analyze** Can you find the perimeter of the figure? Why or why not?

Journal Idea

If you know the area of a square, you can find its perimeter. Is the same true of a rectangle? Explain.

Critical Thinking Corner

Visual Thinking

Area of Irregular Figures

Suppose you wanted to find the approximate area of an irregular figure, such as the state of Texas. You could use a grid, as shown, to help you estimate. Each box equals 7,000 square miles.

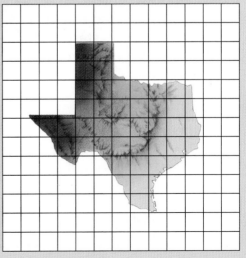

1. Count only squares that are completely covered by the figure. Estimate the area, using this method.

2. Now find partially-covered squares that equal one whole square. Revise your estimate in Question 1 to include the squares.

3. Was your first estimate an overestimate or an underestimate? Explain.

Problem Solving
Draw a Diagram

Drawing a diagram can help you understand and solve some kinds of problems.

Barry's kite for the kite-flying contest is made up of two triangles that share the same base. Two sides of one triangle are each 24 inches long. Two sides of the other triangle are each 30 inches long. Barry wants to attach two colored streamers to each corner of the kite and single streamers 6 inches apart around the rest of the kite. How many colored streamers does he need?

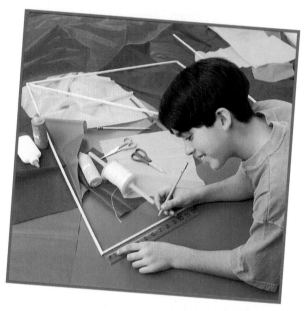

 ## UNDERSTAND

What do you need to know?

You need to know how many corners the kite has and at how many points streamers will be placed along the sides of the kite.

 ## PLAN

How can you solve the problem?

You can **draw a diagram** of the kite to solve the problem. On the diagram, label the length of each side. Then, starting at one corner, mark 6-inch intervals around the kite.

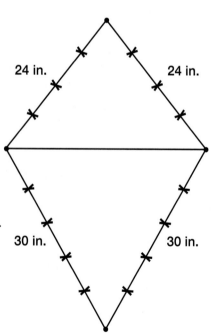

24 in. 24 in.

30 in. 30 in.

 ## SOLVE

Find the number of streamers for the corners (4 × 2 = 8). Count the number of streamers for the sides (14). Barry will need 22 streamers.

 ## LOOK BACK

How did using the diagram help you understand and solve the problem?

Using the Strategy

Try drawing a diagram to solve Problems 1–4.

1 Kim's kite is made up of six congruent equilateral triangles having 22-inch sides. Each triangle shares two of its sides with other triangles. What is the shape of Kim's kite? How many feet of tape will she need to trim the kite's edges?

2 Analyze The design for Emily's square kite has two congruent right isosceles triangles. The congruent sides of each isosceles triangle measure 3 feet. Will 8 square feet of fabric be enough to make the kite? Explain.

3 Barry is designing a second kite. This kite is made up of two congruent equilateral triangles, each having 36-inch sides. If he places streamers as he did on his first kite, how many streamers does he need?

4 Mia's rectangular kite is 22 inches long and 17 inches wide. She wants to decorate the surface of her kite with square stickers 3 inches on a side. If she places the stickers 2 inches apart and 2 inches away from each edge of the kite, how many stickers will she need?

Mixed Strategy Review

**Try these or other strategies to solve each problem.
Tell which strategy you used.**

THERE'S ALWAYS A WAY!

Problem Solving Strategies

- Make a List
- Make a Table
- Make a Graph
- Work Backwards

5 Barry's scores in the kite-flying contest were 8 for design, 6 for construction, and 5 for performance. In the same categories, Kim scored 9, 4, and 7; Emily scored 6, 8, and 3; and Mia scored 8, 4, and 7. Who came in first in each category? Who had the highest overall score?

6 Emily spent a total of $4.85. She spent $2.40 for fabric, $0.95 for string, and $0.69 for tape. The rest was spent on decals. How much did the decals cost?

7 In 1995, 12 boys and 4 girls competed in the kite-flying contest. In 1996 there were 7 girls and 10 boys. In 1997 there were 8 girls and 9 boys, and in 1998 there were 7 boys and 10 girls. Show the trend in the participation of boys and girls in the kite-flying contest from 1995 through 1998.

Using Algebra

Around and Across

Like a quadrilateral, a circle has dimensions that can be used to find the distance around the circle and its area.

Learning About It

One of the contests for field day is based on a Native American hoop-rolling game. How much plastic tubing do you need to make a hoop like the one in the picture?

You need to find the **circumference** *(C)*, the distance around a circle. The formula for circumference is:

d = diameter r = radius

$$C = \pi d \text{ or } C = 2\pi r$$

Work with a partner to explore the value of π.

Step 1 Use a compass to draw four different-size cardboard circles. Measure and record each diameter to the nearest tenth of a centimeter.

Step 2 Cut out each circle. Use string to measure each circumference. Record your results.

Step 3 Find the ratio $\frac{C}{d}$ for each circle.

The ratio is slightly more than 3. The Greek letter *pi* (π) represents the ratio. The value of π is approximately equal to ($\approx$) 3.14, or $\frac{22}{7}$.

Now find the circumference of the hoop.

What You Need

For each pair:
   Triman compass
   string
   posterboard
   scissors
   ruler

28 in

▲ Students are using the rolling hoop as a target for beanbags that they are throwing.

THERE'S ALWAYS A WAY!

● **One way** is to use paper and pencil.

$$C = \pi d$$
$$\approx \frac{22}{7} \times 28$$
$$\approx 88 \text{ in.}$$

● **Another way** is to use a calculator.

Press: $\boxed{\pi}$ $\boxed{\times}$ $\boxed{2}$ $\boxed{8}$ $\boxed{=}$

Display: $\boxed{87.964594}$

You need about 88 inches of plastic tubing.

Connecting Ideas

The value of π is used to find the circumference of a circle. It is also used to find the area of a circle.

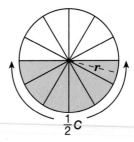

Divide a circle into sections as shown on the right. Rearrange the sections to approximate a parallelogram. Use the formula for the area of a parallelogram to write the formula for the area of a circle.

The height of the parallelogram is the radius of the circle.

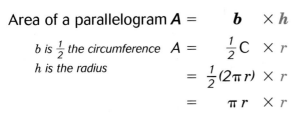

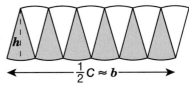

The base of the parallelogram is $\frac{1}{2}$ the circumference of the circle.

Area of a parallelogram $A = \quad \boldsymbol{b} \quad \times \boldsymbol{h}$

b is $\frac{1}{2}$ the circumference $\quad A = \quad \frac{1}{2}C \times r$

h is the radius

$\quad = \quad \frac{1}{2}(2\pi r) \times r$

$\quad = \quad \pi r \times r$

Area of a circle $\quad \boldsymbol{A = \pi r^2}$

Use this formula to find the area of a circle with a diameter of 8 cm.

Hint Remember that $r = \frac{d}{2}$, so $r = \frac{8}{2} = 4$.

THERE'S ALWAYS A WAY!

- **One way** is to use paper and pencil.

  $A = \pi r^2$

  $\approx 3.14 \times 4^2$

  ≈ 50.24

- **Another way** is to use a calculator.

  Press:

  Display:

The area of the circle, to the nearest whole number, is 50 cm².

Think and Discuss When might you use $\frac{22}{7}$ for π? When might you use 3.14?

Try It Out

Find the circumference of each circle to the nearest whole number.

1.
5 m

2.
3 in.

3.
4.5 cm

4.
7 ft

Find the area of each circle to the nearest whole number.

5.
1.4 cm

6.
2 cm

7.
6 yd

8.
19 ft

9. $r = 2.4$ yd

10. $d = 2.1$ km

11. $r = 56$ in.

12. $d = 19.9$ cm

Practice

Find the circumference to the nearest whole number.

13.
$3\frac{1}{2}$ ft

14.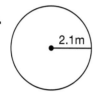
2.1m

15.
11 in.

16.
4.9 cm

17. $d = 15$ cm

18. $r = 5$ in.

19. $d = 8$ yd

20. $d = 1.1$ m

Choose a Method Use paper and pencil, mental math, or a calculator to find the area of each circle. Tell which method you used. Round to the nearest whole number.

21.
0.5 m

22.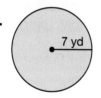
7 yd

23.
1.4 cm

24.
9 ft

25. $d = 4.2$ m

26. $r = 2.1$km

27. $d = 84$ in.

28. $d = 35$ yd

 Use a calculator to find the shaded area of each figure in square units. Round to the nearest whole number.

29.
4

30.
5 4 3

31.
10
18

32.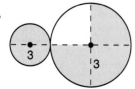
3 3

33.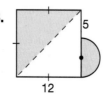
5
12

34.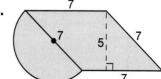
7 7 5 7

Problem Solving

A local store donated a target for field day. The target will be used for an archery contest with suction-cup safety arrows. Solve Problems 35–38.

35. What is the circumference of the yellow bull's-eye?

36. **What If?** Suppose the diameter of the yellow bull's-eye was 20 in. What would happen to the circumference?

37. What is the area of the bull's-eye?

38. **Analyze** Would it be reasonable to say that the circumferences of the yellow, red, blue, black, and white bull's-eyes create a pattern?

39. **Create Your Own** Use what you know about circles to write and solve your own problem about the target.

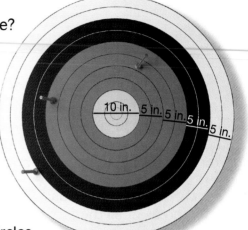

10 in. 5 in. 5 in. 5 in. 5 in.

Review and Remember

Use the graph to solve Problems 40–42.

40. Find the total hoop-rolling distance for each team.

41. Find the average distance the hoops were rolled by each team.

42. Which team rolled its hoops for the greater average distance? How much greater?

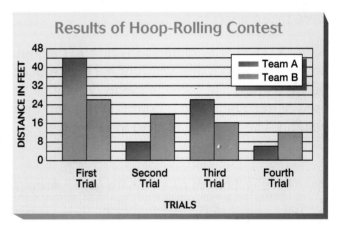

Results of Hoop-Rolling Contest

Team A
Team B

DISTANCE IN FEET

48
40
32
24
16
8
0

First Trial   Second Trial   Third Trial   Fourth Trial

TRIALS

Critical Thinking Corner

Visual Thinking

Optical Illusions

Sometimes things are not what they appear to be. Look at Figures A and B. Which line segment appears to be longer? Why did you pick that one? Now measure each one with a ruler.

Did you pick the right one? Why or why not?

A. >————————————<

B. <————————————>

On the Surface

You can use what you know about area to find the surface area of a space figure.

Learning About It

Equipment for your field day will be stored in a large box like the one shown. You have been asked to paint the box. To find out how much paint you will need, you have to find the surface area of the box.

The **surface area** of a space figure is the sum of the areas of all the faces of the figure.

Work with a partner.

Step 1 Study the diagram. It is a pattern that shows what the box would look like if it were taken apart to lie flat.

Step 2 Using the dimensions on the diagram, record the length and width of each face of the box in a chart like the one below. Then find the area of each face and record it in the appropriate column. The first row is filled in for you.

Word Bank

surface area

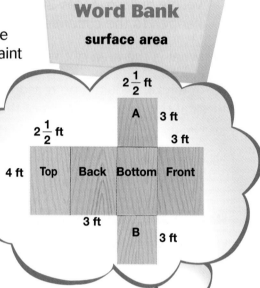

Face	Length (*l*)	Width (*w*)	Area (*l* x *w*)
Top	4 ft	$2\frac{1}{2}$ ft	10 ft²
Front			
Bottom			
Back			
End A			
End B			

Step 3 Find the surface area of the box by adding the area of each face.

Think and Discuss Suppose all the faces of the box were squares. What space figure would the box be?

Practice

Find the total area of each figure below.

1.

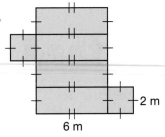

||
2 m
6 m

2.

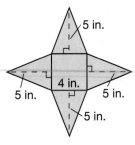

5 in.
5 in.
4 in.
5 in.
5 in.

3.

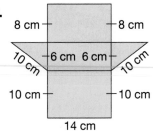

8 cm — 8 cm
10 cm — 6 cm 6 cm — 10 cm
10 cm — 10 cm
14 cm

 Find the surface area of each space figure.

4.

4 cm
6 cm
15 cm

5.

12 in.
16 in.
10 in.

6.

12 cm
10 cm
10 cm

Analyze Each space figure is made up of eight 1-cm cubes. Find the surface area of each figure.

7.

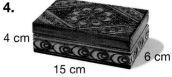

8.

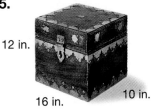

9.

Money $ense

Reels of Ribbon

Jan needs 12 feet of 1-inch wide ribbon. She can buy 1-inch ribbon, or she can buy wider ribbon and cut it into 1-inch widths. If ribbon is sold by the yard, what is the least amount Jan can pay for the ribbon that she needs? Explain.

3-in. ribbon
$1.45 a yd

1-in. ribbon
75¢ a yd

2-in. ribbon
$1.25 a yd

Problem Solving
Choose a
Computation Method

*Deciding which computation method to
use is essential to problem solving.*

The winners of the three-legged race receive their medals
in a winner's circle. You have been asked to rope off a
section of the field to create the winner's circle. The
distance from the center of the circle to the rope
barrier will be $9\frac{1}{2}$ feet. How much rope is
needed to make the barrier?

 ### UNDERSTAND

What do you need to find?

You need to find the circumference
of a circle, using the radius.

 ### PLAN

How can you solve the problem?

You can **write an equation** to find the
circumference. Use $C = 2\pi r$. Then decide which
computation method—mental math, paper and pencil,
or a calculator—you will use. Since the numbers may
not be easy to calculate mentally, you may wish to
use paper and pencil or a calculator.

 ### SOLVE

Use paper and pencil.	Use a calculator.
$C = 2\pi r$	$C = 2\pi r$
$= 2 \times 3.14 \times 9.5$	Press: (2)(×)(π)(×)(9)(.)(5)(=)
$= 59.66$	Display: 59.69026

About 60 feet of rope is needed.

 ### LOOK BACK

Compare the answers above. Why are they different?

Show What You Learned

**Use information from page 458 to solve Problems 1–3.
Tell what computation method you used.**

1 A photographer walked around the circle twice, taking pictures of the winning team and the crowd. About how many yards did he walk?

2 After the ceremony, the circular area was raked to get it ready for the next award. To the nearest square foot, what area was raked?

3 During a 50-meter three-legged race, a team fell down 15 meters from the finish line. How far had the team run? Tell why you chose your method of computation.

4 **You Decide** There are four race events: 25 meters, 50 meters, 100 meters, and the 200-meter four-person relay. You want to run in three events for a total of 200 meters. Which races will you choose? Explain your thinking.

5 **Journal Idea** A Field Day award certificate has a gold circle placed inside a white rectangle. The rectangle is 20 cm long and has an area of 520 cm^2. Explain how you can find the width of the rectangle. Include the method of computation you used.

6 **Create Your Own** Make up a problem about a relay race in which teams of four runners compete. Exchange problems with a classmate to solve. Explain why you chose your method of computation.

Problem Solving

Practice What You Learned

Choose the correct letter for each answer.

1 The pictograph shows the results of a survey of a local neighborhood. Which is the best estimate for the percent of people shown in this survey who live on Elm Street?

Registered Voters	
Street	**Number of People**
Pine	👤 👤 👤 👤 👤 👤 👤
Oak	👤 👤 👤 👤 👤
Elm	👤 👤 👤 👤 👤 👤 👤 👤

👤 = 100 people

A. 20%   **D.** 50%

B. 30%   **E.** 75%

C. 40%

Tip

Start by making sure you understand the key for the pictograph.

---

2 A large box holding food for a giraffe has a *volume* of 15.75 cubic feet. It has a rope handle 3 feet long that is used to hang it from a tree. The box is 2.5 feet long and 1.5 feet wide. How high is the box?

A. 7.5 ft

B. 5.5 ft

C. 4.2 ft

D. 2.5 ft

E. Not Here

Tip

Use one of the strategies to solve this problem.
* *Guess and Check*
* *Write an Equation*
* *Solve a Simpler Problem*

---

3 Paul jogged 3 times around a circular track having a radius of 100 meters. Which is reasonable for the distance Paul jogged?

A. 900 m

B. 1,200 m

C. 1,500 m

D. 1,900 m

E. 2,100 m

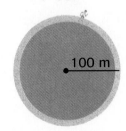

100 m

Tip

Remember, the circumference of a circle equals the diameter times π. To estimate, you can use 3 for π.

4 Sally bought 6 CDs. The least expensive was $6.45. The most expensive was $24.37. Which is reasonable for the total amount Sally spent?

   A. Less than $100
   B. Between $35 and $55
   C. Between $55 and $130
   D. Between $100 and $150
   E. More than $150

5 This figure is part of a scale drawing. What is the length of *one* curved side if each square represents 10 feet by 10 feet? (Use π ≈ 3.14)

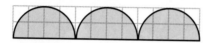

   A. 125.6 ft   **D.** 62.8 ft
   B. 1,256 ft   **E.** 6.28 ft
   C. 628.0 ft

6 Bert used a computer program to create a series of figures with areas that decreased in this pattern.

Figure	1	2	3	4	5
Area	122	101	82	65	50

What will be the *area* of Figure 8 in square units?

   A. 10 sq units   **D.** 25 sq units
   B. 16 sq units   **E.** Not Here
   C. 17 sq units

7 Vanna cut a circle 40 in. in diameter from some fabric measuring 45 in. by 54 in. Which equation could you use to find n, the approximate amount of fabric left over?

   A. $(3.14 \times 400) - (54 \times 45) = n$
   B. $(3.14 \times 1{,}600) - (54 \times 45) = n$
   C. $(54 \times 45) - (3.14 \times 400) = n$
   D. $(54 \times 45) - (3.14 \times 1{,}600) = n$
   E. $(54 \times 45) - (40 \times 40) = n$

8 This figure shows a design for a quilt. What is the *area* of the shaded part of the design?

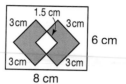

   A. 13.5 cm²   **D.** 50.25 cm²
   B. 30.0 cm²   **E.** Not Here
   C. 48.5 cm²

9 Five friends stood in line for tickets to a movie. Toni was between Jana and Fay. Jana was behind Toni and ahead of Cal. Fay was right behind Yuri. Which is a reasonable conclusion?

   A. Yuri was first in line.
   B. Jana was last in line.
   C. Cal was ahead of Toni.
   D. Yuri was between Jana and Cal.
   E. Fay was last in line.

10 The graph shows the amount of money raised for a hospital.

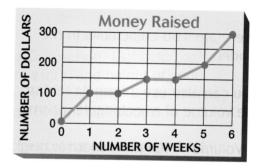

Which accurately compares the amount of money raised in the first 3 weeks to the amount raised in the last 3 weeks?

   A. $20 more in the first 3 weeks
   B. $50 more in the first 3 weeks
   C. $20 less in the first 3 weeks
   D. $50 less in the first 3 weeks
   E. The amounts were the same.

✓ Checkpoint

Circles and Prisms

Vocabulary

Match each term with its definition.

1. Sum of the areas of all the faces of a space figure

2. The number of cubic units needed to fill a space figure

3. The distance around any polygon

4. The distance around a circle

5. The number of square units needed to cover a region

Word Bank

area
circumference
diameter
perimeter
radius
surface area
volume

Concepts and Skills

Using Algebra Find the circumference and area of each circle.

6.

3.2 cm

7.

1 m

8.

11 ft

9.

$2\frac{1}{2}$ in.

10. $r = 2$ mi   11. $d = 9$ ft   12. $d = 0.5$ km   13. $r = \frac{3}{4}$ in.   14. $r = 7.5$ mm

Using Algebra Find the volume of each space figure.

15.

5.2 cm
2.1 cm   1.1 cm

16.
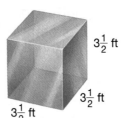
$3\frac{1}{2}$ ft
$3\frac{1}{2}$ ft
$3\frac{1}{2}$ ft

17.

4 ft
4 ft
4 ft

18.

10 ft
6 ft   2 ft

Problem Solving

Solve.

19. During a "dizzy race," students run around a circle with a 4-meter radius. For each trip around, how far does a runner run?

20. Look back at Problem 19. If 4 members of a team each travel around the circle 3 times, what is the total distance traveled by the team?

21. In the hoop-roll race, students have to roll a hoop 10 meters. If the hoop has a diameter of 63.7 cm, what is the least number of turns a hoop makes in one race?

22. **What If?** Look back at Problem 21. If the diameter of the hoop was doubled, how many turns would the hoop make in the same race?

23. In the water race, students carry a rectangular prism filled with water. The prism is 12 cm high. Its base is a square that measures 8 cm on a side. What is the volume of this prism?

24. **Analyze** A rectangular prism with a square base has a volume of 360 cm³. The sides of the base are 6 cm long. What is the height of the prism?

25. **Analyze** What would the radius of a circle be with a circumference of 37.68 cm?

Journal Idea

Design and describe a race that involves a circle.

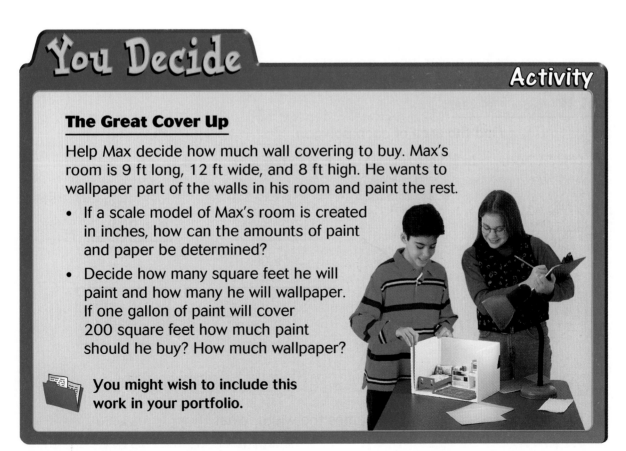

You Decide

Activity

The Great Cover Up

Help Max decide how much wall covering to buy. Max's room is 9 ft long, 12 ft wide, and 8 ft high. He wants to wallpaper part of the walls in his room and paint the rest.

- If a scale model of Max's room is created in inches, how can the amounts of paint and paper be determined?

- Decide how many square feet he will paint and how many he will wallpaper. If one gallon of paint will cover 200 square feet how much paint should he buy? How much wallpaper?

You might wish to include this work in your portfolio.

What do you think?

How would the circumference and area of a circle change if the radius is doubled?

Extra Practice

Set A (pages 434–435)

Using Algebra **Find the perimeter of each polygon.**

1.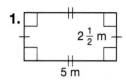
2 $\frac{1}{2}$ m
5 m

2.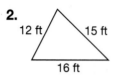
12 ft   15 ft
16 ft

3.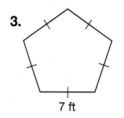
7 ft

4.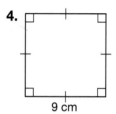
9 cm

5.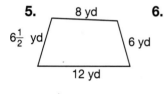
8 yd
6 $\frac{1}{2}$ yd   6 yd
12 yd

6.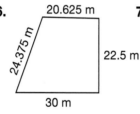
20.625 m
24.375 m   22.5 m
30 m

7.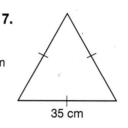
35 cm

8.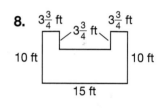
3 $\frac{3}{4}$ ft   3 $\frac{3}{4}$ ft
3 $\frac{3}{4}$ ft
10 ft   10 ft
15 ft

Solve.

9. Ron's yard is 4 times longer than it is wide. If his yard is 30 feet wide, what is the perimeter of Ron's yard?

10. Jessie's yard is 25 ft wide and 140 ft long. Whose yard has a greater perimeter, Ron's or Jessie's?

Set B (pages 436–439)

Using Algebra **Find the area of each polygon.**

1.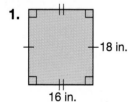
18 in.
16 in.

2.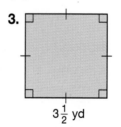
20 ft
44 ft

3.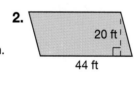
3 $\frac{1}{2}$ yd

4.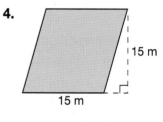
15 m
15 m

5.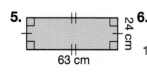
63 cm
24 cm

6.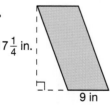
17 $\frac{1}{4}$ in.
9 in

7.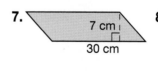
7 cm
30 cm

8.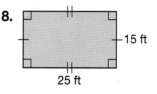
15 ft
25 ft

Solve.

9. The length of a rectangle is five times the width. What is the perimeter of the rectangle if the width is 3.75 m?

Extra Practice

Set C (pages 440–441)

Using Algebra Find the area of each triangle.

1.

20 in.
20 in.

2.
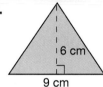
6 cm
9 cm

3.
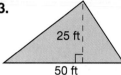
25 ft
50 ft

4.
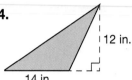
12 in.
14 in.

Use the grid to find the area of each triangle. Each square is equal to 1 square unit.

5.

6.

7.
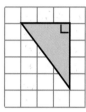

8.

Solve.

9. The napkins at Dana's Restaurant are squares, $6\frac{1}{2}$ inches on a side. What is the area of one side of each napkin?

10. When Dana sets tables she folds each napkin once, so that it has a triangular shape. What is the area of this triangle?

Set D (pages 446–447)

Using Algebra Find the area of each figure.

1.
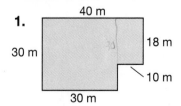
40 m
30 m
18 m
10 m
30 m

2.
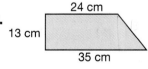
24 cm
13 cm
35 cm

3.
10 yd
8 yd
19 yd
22 yd
35 yd

Use the diagram of the swim club to answer Problems 4–6.

4. What is the area of the swim club?

5. What is the area of the pool?

6. What is the area of the lawn around the pool?

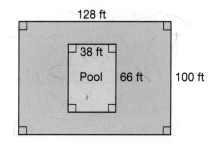
128 ft
38 ft
Pool 66 ft
100 ft

Extra Practice

Set E (pages 452–455)

Using Algebra Find the circumference and area of each circle.

1.
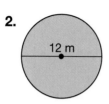
8 cm

2.
12 m

3.
2.5 in.

4.
5.8 m

5. $d = 2.5$ yd

6. $r = 6.5$ cm

7. $r = 6$ in.

8. $d = 5.5$ ft

Solve.

9. A tire has a diameter of 18 in. What is its circumference?

10. **Analyze** Look back at Problem 9. Imagine that the tire is rolling down a hill. About how many times will the tire go around if it travels 100 ft before stopping?

Set F (pages 460–461)

Using Algebra Find the volume of each space figure.

1.
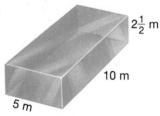
$2\frac{1}{2}$ m
10 m
5 m

2.
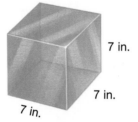
7 in.
7 in.
7 in.

3.

3 ft
7 ft
2 ft

4.
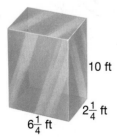
10 ft
$2\frac{1}{4}$ ft
$6\frac{1}{4}$ ft

5.
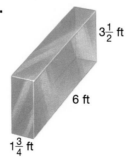
$3\frac{1}{2}$ ft
6 ft
$1\frac{3}{4}$ ft

6.

3 in.
3 in.
3 in.

Solve.

7. A cereal box is 3 in. wide, 10 in. long, and 18 in. high. What volume of cereal does it hold?

Chapter Test

Find the perimeter of each polygon.

1. 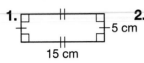 5 cm
15 cm

2. 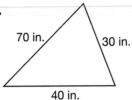 70 in. 30 in.
40 in.

3. 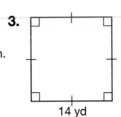 14 yd

4. 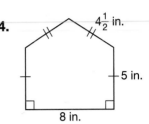 $4\frac{1}{2}$ in.
5 in.
8 in.

Find the area of each figure.

5. 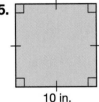 10 in.

6.  14 ft

7. 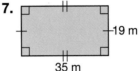 19 m
35 m

8. 13 ft
24 ft

Find the area of each polygon with the given dimensions.

9. square
$s = 25$ in.

10. rectangle
$l = 4.5$ m
$w = 6.7$ m

11. triangle
$b = 11$ in.
$h = 12$ in.

12. parallelogram
$b = 16$ yd
$h = 4$ yd

Find the area and circumference of each circle.

13. $d = 14$ ft

14. $r = 2.5$ m

15. $r = 5$ m

16. $d = 21$ in

Find the volume of each space figure.

17.  8 in.
8 in.
8 in.

18. 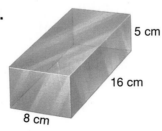 5 cm
16 cm
8 cm

19.  9.5 ft
7 ft
8.5 ft

Solve

20. Which has the larger area, a square 11 inches on a side or a circle with a 12-inch diameter? how much larger?

 Self-Check

How did learning formulas help you on this test?

Performance Assessment

Show What You Know About Perimeter, Area, and Volume

1 Measure and describe the empty box you were given in as many ways as you can. Then estimate how many base 10 blocks will fit inside the box.

Self-Check Did you remember to describe the box using as many geometry terms as you know?

What You Need

small empty box
base 10 blocks
ruler

2 A section of a playground that is $\frac{1}{4}$ of a circle is shown at the right. One section of the playground is grass. The other section is sand.

Which is greater, the area of the sand or the area of the grass? Explain the reason for your choice.

Self-Check Did you remember that the formula for the area of the circle is $A = \pi r^2$?

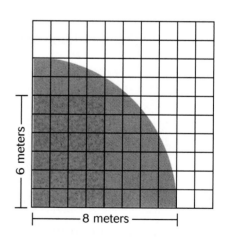

6 meters

8 meters

For Your Portfolio

You might wish to include this work in your portfolio.

Extension

Networks

Look at the two designs below. How can they be connected mathematically?

The snake wriggled out of its cage slithering among the bushes until at last it settled down to sleep. It uses every path only once. Can you find it?

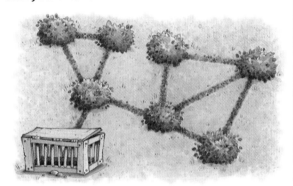

Can you trace over this line design without lifting your pencil or tracing over a line segment more than once?

The answers to the questions below will help you find the snake and decide if the line design can be traced without lifting your pencil or tracing over a line segment more than once.

1. Where did the snake go first? How do you know?

2. Did the snake visit some bushes twice? How do you know?

3. How many paths does each bush have? Did the snake always leave each bush? How do you know?

4. Where is the snake? How do you know?

5. **Generalize** Now look at the line design. Count the number of paths at each vertex. How do you know where you must start and finish? Why?

Which of the following line designs can be traced without lifting your pencil or tracing a line segment more than once? Tell how you know.

6.   7.   8.   9.   10.

Cumulative Review

★ ★ ★ ★ ★ **Preparing for Tests**

Choose the correct letter for each answer.

Operations	Measurement

Operations

1. It takes John about half as long to get home as it takes Kate. John left school at 4:30 P.M. If John got home today in 20 minutes, about how many minutes did it probably take Kate to get home?

   A. 5 min
   B. 10 min
   C. 30 min
   D. 40 min

2. What is the sum of 2.5, 1.23, and 2.75?

   A. 4.23
   B. 6.23
   C. 6.48
   D. 6.53

3. Kevin earns $2.55 a day feeding 2 cats for his neighbors. He earns $3.75 an hour walking 1 dog. If he spends 5 hours walking 2 dogs, how much will he make?

   A. $375.00
   B. $37.50
   C. $17.75
   D. $7.50

4. What is the quotient of $375.00 divided by 12?

   A. $37.50
   B. $31.25
   C. $31.00
   D. $25.00
   E. Not Here

Measurement

5. A playing field is 3 times as long as it is wide. If the length of the field is 150 yards, what is its *perimeter*?

   A. 1,200 yd
   B. 600 yd
   C. 400 yd
   D. 300 yd

6. What is the *area* of the right triangle shown? (1 yd = 3 ft)

   A. 162 yd^2
   B. 81 yd^2
   C. 27 yd^2
   D. 13.5 yd^2

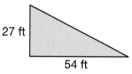

7. What are the dimensions of a rectangle that has a perimeter of 40 feet and the greatest area possible?

   A. 10 ft × 10 ft
   B. 12 ft × 8 ft
   C. 15 ft × 5 ft
   D. 16 ft × 2 ft

8. The picture shows a design for a playground. What is the *area* of the playground?

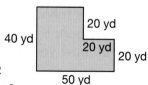

   A. 400 yd^2
   B. 1,200 yd^2
   C. 1,600 yd^2
   D. 2,400 yd^2

Patterns, Relationships, and Algebraic Thinking	Probability and Statistics

9. Which number is missing from this pattern?

. . . , ■, 37, 31, 25, 19, . . .

A. 39   **C.** 43
B. 40   **D.** 45

10. Garth can make 4 model wooden boats in 6 hours. He needs to make 8 model wooden boats for a project. Which proportion can be used to find out how long this will take?

A. $\frac{4}{?} = \frac{6}{8}$

B. $\frac{6}{4} = \frac{8}{?}$

C. $\frac{4}{6} = \frac{?}{8}$

D. $\frac{4}{6} = \frac{8}{?}$

11. A pool is 50 meters long. A lap is one length of the pool. If a swimmer can swim about 10 laps in 8 minutes, how many laps would she be able to swim in 16 minutes?

A. 14   **C.** 21
B. 20   **D.** 140

12. Which equation can be used to solve for ■?

x	3	15	37	x
y	8	20	42	■

A. $x + 5 = ■$
B. $5 + ■ = x$
C. $x + ■ = 5$
D. $x - 5 = ■$

13. Dana received these grades: 89%, 90%, 83%, 94%, 100%, 91%. What was her mean (average) grade, rounded to the nearest whole percent?

A. 90%   **C.** 92%
B. 91%   **D.** 93%

Use the graph below to answer Questions 14–16.

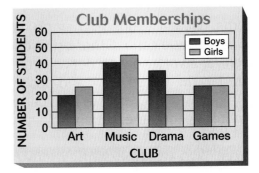

14. Which club was more popular with boys than with girls?

A. Art   **C.** Drama
B. Music **D.** Games

15. Which club was most popular with girls?

A. Art   **C.** Drama
B. Music **D.** Games

16. Which is a reasonable conclusion that can be drawn from the graph?

A. The Games Club was the most popular club overall.
B. The Art Club was more popular than the Drama Club.
C. The Music Club was the least popular club overall.
D. The Games Club was equally popular with boys and girls.

Chapter 12

Integers and Equations

Chapter Theme: FASCINATING FACTS

....................Real Facts....................

Some volcanic eruptions can rip hundreds of feet off the top of a volcano. Other eruptions can increase the height of a volcano with deposits of lava or solid rocky material. The negative (−) and positive (+) signs in the table below show whether a volcano lost or gained height in recorded eruptions.

Gain or Loss of Height From Volcanic Eruptions			
Volcano	Location	Eruption	Height Change
Heimaey	Iceland	1973	+735 ft
Mt. St. Helens	United States	1980	−1,200 ft
Paricutín	Mexico	1943–1952	+1,353 ft
Tower of Pelée	Nicaragua	1902–1903	+1,200 ft

- Which volcano lost the most height? How much did it lose?

- Which volcano gained the most height? How much did it gain?

- Which volcano gained about half as much height as Paricutín?

...............Real People...................

Meet Christina Heliker. As a volcanologist, she works atop Kilauea, an active volcano in Hawaii Volcanoes National Park. She studies the volcano by measuring lava flow. The students at the right watch steam erupt from Halemaumau, another active volcano in Hawaii.

Highs and Lows

In this lesson you will learn about numbers called integers.

Learning About It

From the frozen tundra of Antarctica to the deserts of Africa, our Earth is a land of diversity. Temperatures alone can vary from ⁻128°F to ⁺136°F.

The numbers ⁻128°F and ⁺136°F are integers. **Integers** consist of whole numbers and their opposites.

> **Word Bank**
>
> integers
> negative integers
> positive integers

Negative integers are less than 0. The symbol for negative five is ⁻5.

Zero is neither positive nor negative.

Positive integers are greater than 0. The symbol for positive four is ⁺4 or 4.

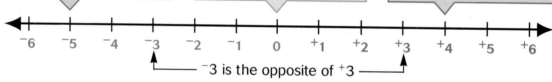

⁻6   ⁻5   ⁻4   ⁻3   ⁻2   ⁻1   0   ⁺1   ⁺2   ⁺3   ⁺4   ⁺5   ⁺6

⁻3 is the opposite of ⁺3

More Examples

Negative Integers	Positive Integers
• The temperature in Antarctica can drop to ⁻128°F. → ⁻128	• The temperature in Libya can go up to 136°F. → ⁺136
• 6 steps backward → ⁻6	• 10 steps forward → ⁺10
• 150 ft below sea level → ⁻150	• A gain of 15 yards → ⁺15

Think and Discuss Locate ⁻4 and ⁺4 on the number line above. Why do you think that they are called opposites?

Try It Out

Write an integer that describes each situation.

1. 75 degrees above 0   **2.** a deposit of $25   **3.** a loss of 10 yards

Use the number line for Exercises 4–7. Write the integer that represents each point.

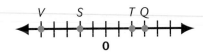

4. V   **5.** T   **6.** Q   **7.** S

Practice

Write an integer that describes each situation.

8. $19 profit   **9.** weight loss of 10 lb   **10.** 8 feet below ground

Use the number line for Exercises 11–18. Write the integer that represents each point.

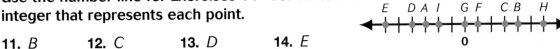

11. B   **12.** C   **13.** D   **14.** E

15. H   **16.** I   **17.** A   **18.** F

Place each integer on a number line.

19. $^-3$ **20.** $^+6$ **21.** $^-10$ **22.** $^+3$ **23.** $^+7$

24. $^-9$ **25.** $^+9$ **26.** $^-13$ **27.** $^+11$ **28.** $^+5$

29. the opposite of $^+7$ **30.** the opposite of $^-1$

Problem Solving

For each problem, start at 0 degrees on a thermometer and find the last temperature.

31. Up 3 degrees, down 7 degrees, up 2 degrees

32. Down 6 degrees, up 4 degrees, down 1 degree

33. Up 10 degrees, down 7 degrees, up 3 degrees

34. Analyze The temperature dropped from 21°F to $^-5$°F. By how many degrees did it change?

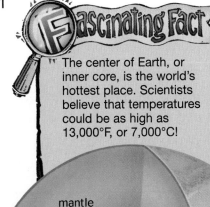

Fascinating Fact

The center of Earth, or inner core, is the world's hottest place. Scientists believe that temperatures could be as high as 13,000°F, or 7,000°C!

mantle

outer core

inner core

Review and Remember

Using Algebra   Evaluate.

35. 2^4 **36.** 9^2 **37.** 3^4 **38.** 5^2 **39.** 6^3

Using Algebra

Chilling Facts

Like whole numbers, integers can be compared and ordered.

Learning About It

Have you ever noticed that you feel much colder outside on a windy day than on a calm day with the same outdoor temperature? When the outdoor temperature is 0°F and the wind speed is 5 mph, the wind makes you feel as if the temperature were ⁻5°F.

Wind Chill Table					
Wind Speed (mph)	Outdoor Temperature (°F)				
0	0	10	20	30	40
5	⁻5	6	16	27	37
10	⁻22	⁻9	3	16	28
15	⁻31	⁻18	⁻5	9	23
20	⁻39	⁻24	⁻10	4	19
25	⁻44	⁻29	⁻15	1	16

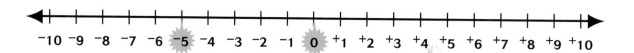

Look at the number line. Just as with whole numbers, integers increase in value as you move from left to right.
So, ⁻5 < 0

The wind chill makes the air feel 5 degrees colder than the actual outdoor temperature of 0 degrees.

Connecting Ideas

You used a number line to compare integers. You can also use a number line to order integers.

To order ⁻10, ⁻4, ⁺2, and ⁻5 from least to greatest, first locate the integers on the number line.

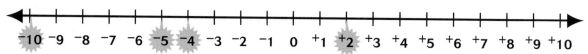

Then write the numbers from left to right.

⁻10, ⁻5, ⁻4, ⁺2

Think and Discuss Which is greater, ⁻3 or ⁻9? Tell how you can use a number line to find out.

Try It Out

Compare. Use >, <, or = for each ●.

1. $^+3$ ● $^-2$ 2. $^-7$ ● 0 3. $^-4$ ● $^-9$

Order from greatest to least.

4. $0, ^+5, ^-12, ^+15$ 5. $^+25, ^-17, 0, ^-22, ^+2$

6. $^+11, ^+9, ^-7, ^-9$ 7. $^+1, ^-1, ^+2, ^-2$

Practice

Compare. Use >, <, or = for each ●.

8. $^+12$ ● $^-13$ 9. $^-23$ ● $^-25$

10. $^+10$ ● $^+8$ 11. $^+25$ ● $^-25$

12. $^-70$ ● $^-52$ 13. $^+38$ ● $^-5$

14. $^-44$ ● 0 15. $^-16$ ● $^+31$

Write in order from least to greatest.

16. $0, ^-5, ^-2$ 17. $^-3, ^-4, ^-7$ 18. $^+3, ^-4, ^-2$ 19. $^+3, ^-3, ^-4$

20. $^+9, ^+6, ^-2$ 21. $^+5, ^+3, ^-1$ 22. $^-1, ^-2, ^-3, ^-4$ 23. $^+6, ^+8, 0, ^-3$

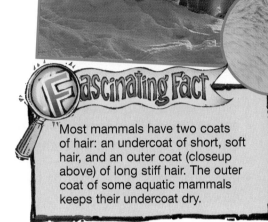

Fascinating Fact

Most mammals have two coats of hair: an undercoat of short, soft hair, and an outer coat (closeup above) of long stiff hair. The outer coat of some aquatic mammals keeps their undercoat dry.

Problem Solving

Use the Wind Chill Table for Problems 24–27.

INTERNET ACTIVITY
www.sbgmath.com

24. On Monday the temperature was 30°F and the wind speed was 20 mph. On Tuesday the temperature was 20°F and the wind speed was 5 mph. On which day did it feel colder?

25. On one day the temperature is 20°F and the wind speed is 25 mph. If the temperature drops to 0°F and the wind speed is 5 mph, will it feel colder or warmer?

26. **Analyze** What is the temperature and the wind speed when it feels like $^-5$°F?

27. **Create Your Own** Write a problem about wind chill temperatures. Ask a classmate to solve your problem.

Review and Remember

Using Algebra Use order of operations to evaluate each expression.

28. $28 - 4 \div 8 + 3.5$ 29. $52 - 12 + 10 \times 2$ 30. $2 \times 6 - 4 \div 2$ 31. $\frac{1}{4} + \frac{3}{4} \times \frac{1}{6}$

32. $3\frac{1}{3} - \frac{3}{4} \times \frac{8}{9} + \frac{5}{6}$ 33. $2\frac{1}{4} \times 1\frac{1}{3} + \frac{1}{2} \div \frac{1}{4}$ 34. $70 - 0.4 \times 50$ 35. $5 - \frac{1}{3} \div \frac{2}{3}$

For Extra Practice, see Set B, page 508.

Electrified

Counters can help you understand how to add integers.

Learning About It

The protons and electrons of an atom can be represented as positive and negative integers. The charge of an atom is the sum of its protons and its electrons.

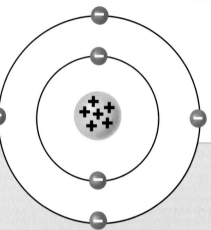

- When there is an equal number of electrons and protons, the positive and negative charges are balanced, producing a charge of 0.

- If an atom has more protons than electrons, its charge is positive.

- If an atom has more electrons than protons, its charge is negative.

Science Connection ▲
All life forms on Earth are based on carbon compounds. A single carbon atom has six protons and six electrons.

Work with a partner. Find the charge of another atom that has 6 protons and 4 electrons.

Step 1 Use yellow counters to represent the protons ($^+6$). Use red counters to represent the electrons ($^-4$).

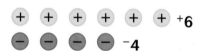

What You Need

For each pair:
   20 red counters
   20 yellow counters

Step 2 Pair a yellow counter with a red counter until you have only one color left. How many counters are left unpaired? What color are they?

Every pair of red and yellow counters is a zero pair.

Step 3 The number of unpaired counters is the sum.

- If they are yellow, the sum is positive.

- If they are red, the sum is negative.

What is the sum of $^+6$ and $^-4$?

Step 4 Record your result in a chart like the one below.

Counters			
Begin With	**Add**	**Sum**	**Number Sentence**
6 yellow	4 red	2 yellow	$^+6 + {}^-4 = {}^+2$

Step 5 Use counters to find each sum. Record your work in your chart.

a. $^+3 + {}^-4$ b. $0 + {}^-2$ c. $^+6 + {}^+1$ d. $^-3 + {}^+4$

e. $^-5 + {}^+3$ f. $^-7 + {}^-5$ g. $^-1 + {}^+6$ h. $^+3 + {}^-8$

Think and Discuss Without adding, tell whether the sum of $^-7 + {}^-8$ is positive or negative. How did you decide?

Practice

Write the number sentence for each model.

1. ⊖ ⊖ ⊖ ⊖ ⊖ ⊖
   ⊕ ⊕ ⊕ ⊕

2. ⊖ ⊖ ⊖
   ⊖ ⊖

3. ⊕ ⊕ ⊕ ⊕ ⊕ ⊕ ⊕
   ⊖ ⊖

4. ⊖ ⊖
   ⊕ ⊕ ⊕ ⊕ ⊕

5. ⊕ ⊕
   ⊖ ⊖ ⊖ ⊖

6. ⊖ ⊖ ⊖ ⊖ ⊖ ⊖
   ⊕ ⊕ ⊕ ⊕ ⊕

Use counters to model each addition. Then find the sum.

7. $^-7 + {}^+9$ 8. $^-8 + 0$ 9. $^+5 + {}^+9$

10. $^-5 + {}^-9$ 11. $0 + {}^+6$ 12. $^+3 + {}^+8$

13. $^-3 + {}^-8$ 14. $^+6 + {}^-10$ 15. $^-4 + {}^+2$

16. $^+1 + {}^+12$ 17. $^-1 + {}^-5$ 18. $^+2 + {}^-10$

19. **Explain** Look back at the answers to Exercises 6 and 7. How are they related?

20. **Predict** Will the sum of two negative integers always be a negative integer? Use counters to explain.

21. **Journal Idea** When adding integers, how can you tell if a sum will be positive, negative, or zero without actually adding? Use examples to explain.

Can You Make Par?

You can add integers in different ways.

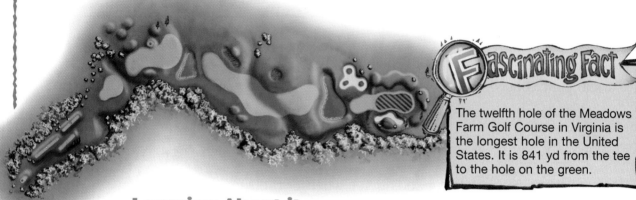

Fascinating Fact

The twelfth hole of the Meadows Farm Golf Course in Virginia is the longest hole in the United States. It is 841 yd from the tee to the hole on the green.

Learning About it

In golf, each hole has a par. Par is the number of strokes normally needed to get the golf ball into the hole. For example, if par is 5 and you sink the ball in 3 strokes, you are 2 strokes under par, or $^-2$. Suppose your score for the first two holes is $^+2$ and $^-3$. What is your score with respect to par so far?

$$^+2 + {}^-3 = n$$

THERE'S ALWAYS A WAY!

- **One way** to add integers is to use counters.

$$^+2 + {}^-3 = {}^-1$$

- **Another way** to add integers is to use a number line.

$$^+2 + {}^-3 = {}^-1$$

Your score so far is $^-1$, or 1 under par.

INTERNET ACTIVITY
www.sbgmath.com

More Examples

A. $^-4 + {}^+6 = {}^+2$

B. $^-2 + {}^-1 = {}^-3$

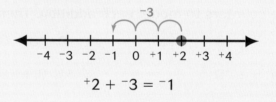

Think and Discuss How does adding $^-1$ differ from adding $^+1$ on the number line? Use an example.

Try It Out

Add. Use counters or a number line.

1. $^+2 + {}^-7$ **2.** $^+5 + {}^+3$ **3.** $^-4 + {}^-8$ **4.** $^+9 + {}^-5$

5. $^+4 + {}^-8$ **6.** $^-2 + {}^+2$ **7.** $^-3 + {}^-6$ **8.** $^+8 + {}^-7$

Practice

Add. Use counters or a number line.

9. $^-12 + {}^+5$ **10.** $^-7 + {}^-5$ **11.** $^+10 + {}^+6$ **12.** $^-15 + {}^+15$

13. $^+11 + {}^-13$ **14.** $^-10 + {}^+2$ **15.** $^+17 + {}^-19$ **16.** $^-20 + {}^+4$

17. $^+10 + {}^-11$ **18.** $^-4 + {}^+16$ **19.** $^+7 + {}^-14$ **20.** $^-14 + {}^+8$

21. $^+30 + {}^-8$ **22.** $^-12 + {}^+2$ **23.** $^+13 + {}^-7$ **24.** $^-21 + {}^+12$

Follow the rule to complete each table.

Rule: Add $^-4$

	Input	Output
25.	$^+6$	
26.	$^-9$	
27.	0	
28.	$^+1$	

Rule: Add $^+3$

	Input	Output
29.	$^-7$	
30.	$^-12$	
31.	$^+35$	
32.	$^-2$	

Rule: Add $^-5$

	Input	Output
33.	$^-19$	
34.	$^-50$	
35.	$^+28$	
36.	$^+3$	

37. Explain What is the sum of an integer and zero?

Problem Solving

38. James scores $^-2$, 0, $^+3$, and $^-1$ on the first four holes. What is his score so far with respect to par?

39. With respect to par, Cathy scored $^-2$, $^+5$, $^-1$ and Diane scored $^-1$, $^+3$, $^-2$. Who played better on these holes?

40. Analyze Tom and Sue played three holes of golf. Each had a total score of $^-2$ with respect to par. Yet for each hole, their score was different. What could they have scored on each hole?

Review and Remember

Using Algebra Find the value of the missing number.

41. $\frac{n}{5} = \frac{12}{20}$ **42.** $\frac{n}{8} = \frac{3}{4}$ **43.** $\frac{6}{n} = \frac{12}{4}$ **44.** $\frac{3}{n} = \frac{9}{15}$

45. $\frac{1}{7} = \frac{n}{28}$ **46.** $\frac{4}{9} = \frac{16}{n}$ **47.** $\frac{1.5}{n} = \frac{9}{2}$ **48.** $\frac{n}{3} = \frac{4.5}{27}$

For Extra Practice, see Set C, page 508.

Take It Away!

Counters can help you understand how to subtract integers.

Learning About It

There are many different ways to represent an integer with counters.

What You Need

For each pair:
    20 red counters
    20 yellow counters

The photo above shows 3 yellow counters. They represent ⁺3.

This photo shows 3 yellow counters and a zero pair. This photo shows ⁺3.

What number does this photo represent? Why?

Work with a partner. Model ⁺4 − ⁻3, using counters.

Step 1 Use yellow counters to represent ⁺4.

Step 2 You need to have at least 3 red counters to be able to subtract ⁻3, so add 3 red counters to your collection. To keep the value of the collection the same, add 3 yellow counters. How does this keep the value the same?

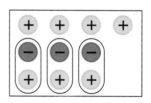

Step 3 Take 3 red counters away to show that you are subtracting ⁻3. How many counters are left? What color are they? What is ⁺4 − ⁻3?

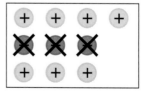

Step 4 Record your result in a chart like the one below.

Counters			Number Sentence
Begin With	**Subtract**	**Difference**	
4 yellow	3 red	7 yellow	$^+4 - {}^-3 = {}^+7$

Step 5 Use counters to find each difference. Record your work in your chart. You may have to add equal numbers of red and yellow counters before subtracting.

a. $^+6 - {}^+4$ **b.** $^+5 - {}^-3$ **c.** $^-4 - {}^+3$ **d.** $^-4 - {}^-3$

e. $^-3 - {}^+6$ **f.** $^+2 - {}^-4$ **g.** $^-5 - {}^-4$ **h.** $^+4 - {}^+6$

Think and Discuss Find $^-3 - {}^+5$ and $^-3 + {}^-5$. What do you notice?

Practice

Write the number sentence for each model.

1.

2.

3.

4.

5.

6.

Use counters to model each subtraction expression. Then find the difference.

7. $^+7 - {}^-3$ **8.** $^-7 - {}^+3$ **9.** $^-5 - {}^-3$ **10.** $^+4 - {}^-6$

11. $^-3 - {}^+7$ **12.** $^+1 - {}^-8$ **13.** $^-7 - {}^-7$ **14.** $^+5 - {}^-5$

15. $^+8 - {}^-4$ **16.** $^-4 - {}^+2$ **17.** $^+2 - {}^-4$ **18.** $^-4 - {}^-2$

19. Predict If you subtract a negative integer from a positive integer, will your answer always be positive? Use examples to explain.

20. What If? Suppose you subtract a negative integer from a negative integer. Will your answer always be positive or always be negative? Use examples to explain.

Making Changes

Using Algebra

You can use different ways to subtract integers.

Learning About It

Find the difference between ⁺5 and ⁻3.

$$^+5 - {}^-3 = n$$

THERE'S ALWAYS A WAY!

• **One way** to subtract an integer is to use counters.

Step 1 Line up the counters.	Step 2 Subtract.

$$^+5 - {}^-3 = {}^+8$$

• **Another way** to subtract an integer is to add its opposite.

Change subtraction to addition.

$$^+5 - {}^-3 = {}^+5 + {}^+3 = {}^+8$$

Write the opposite.

So, the difference between ⁺5 and ⁻3 is ⁺8.

Think and Discuss Before finding the difference for ⁻3 − ⁺5, how can you predict whether it will be positive or negative?

Try It Out

Subtract. Use counters to help.

1. ⁺5 − ⁻2   **2.** ⁻7 − ⁺3   **3.** ⁻6 − ⁻8   **4.** ⁺2 − ⁺4

5. ⁺10 − ⁻4   **6.** ⁻8 − 0   **7.** ⁻6 − ⁻9   **8.** ⁺5 − 0

9. Which two expressions have the same answer?

     a. ⁺10 − ⁻5   **b.** ⁻5 − ⁺10   **c.** ⁺10 − ⁺5   **d.** ⁺10 + ⁺5

Practice

Subtract. Use counters to help.

10. $^-10 - {}^-10$

11. $^+7 - {}^+3$

12. $^+6 - {}^-2$

13. $^-2 - {}^+8$

14. $^+12 - {}^-3$

15. $^-9 - {}^+5$

16. $^-15 - 0$

17. $^-14 - {}^-5$

18. $^+5 - {}^-4$

19. $^-6 - {}^+9$

20. $^+10 - {}^-1$

21. $^+9 - {}^+17$

22. $^+2 - {}^-4$

23. $^+1 - {}^+10$

24. $^+12 - {}^-7$

25. $^-3 - {}^+15$

26. $^+2 - {}^-5$

27. $^+8 - {}^+4$

28. $^-10 - {}^-1$

29. $^+5 - {}^-3$

30. $^+2 - {}^+9$

31. $^-2 - {}^+12$

32. $^-13 - {}^-4$

33. $^-5 - {}^+6$

Follow the rule.

Rule: Subtract $^-9$

	Input	Output
34.	$^+8$	
35.	$^-5$	
36.	$^+3$	

Rule: Subtract $^+4$

	Input	Output
37.	$^+3$	
38.	$^-9$	
39.	0	

Rule: Subtract $^-6$

	Input	Output
40.	$^-6$	
41.	$^+7$	
42.	$^-9$	

Problem Solving

For Problems 43–45, write an expression that represents each situation. Then solve.

43. Social Studies Connection Belukha, one of the Altai Mountains in Asia, is 14,783 ft high. Death Valley is 282 ft below sea level. How much higher is Belukha than Death Valley?

44. A scuba diver was 25 feet below the surface of the water. She went down 20 more feet. How far was she below the surface of the water?

45. Create Your Own Describe a situation that can be represented by the expression $^+35 - {}^-15$.

Fascinating Fact

The submersible *Trieste* reached the deepest part of the Pacific Ocean, almost 7 miles under the surface.

Review and Remember

Find the answer.

46. 75% of 20

47. $\frac{3}{8} \times 32$

48. 1% of 300

49. $\frac{1}{3} \times 120$

50. $\frac{2}{5} \times 15$

51. 40% of $82

52. $\frac{5}{6} \times 72$

53. 200% of 9

Using Algebra

Developing Skills for Problem Solving

*First read for understanding and then
focus on translating and using expressions.*

READ FOR UNDERSTANDING

Mei-Li enjoys scuba diving. Because diving can be dangerous, she has learned how water pressure and air pressure affect divers.

As a diver descends, the water pressure increases 0.445 pounds per square inch (psi) every foot below the water's surface. The total pressure a diver feels also includes an additional 14.7 psi, which is caused by the weight of the air pressing down on the water's surface.

1 How much does water pressure increase as a diver descends?

2 How much additional pressure is caused by the weight of the air on the surface?

3 What makes up the total pressure on a diver?

14.7 psi

5 ft

10 ft

15 ft

20 ft

25 ft

THINK AND DISCUSS

MATH FOCUS

Translating and Using Expressions
Mathematical expressions use variables and numbers. They are part of the language of symbols used in algebra. Writing and translating expressions can help you solve problems.

▲**Science Connection**
Water has weight, which creates pressure on a diver. The deeper you go, the greater the pressure becomes.

Reread the paragraphs at the top of the page.

4 How would you find the total pressure on a diver 10 feet below the water's surface? 20 feet?

5 What expression tells you how to find the total pressure at *d* feet below the surface?

6 Use your expression to find the total pressure on a diver at a depth of 67 feet.

Show What You Learned

Answer each question. Give a reason for your choice.

When Mei-Li returns to the surface after a dive, she must be careful not to come up too fast. If the depth of her dive is less than 30 feet, she must not come up more than 1 foot each second. To be safe, she came up from a 25-foot dive at a rate of 1 foot every 2 seconds.

1 What does Mei-Li do to come up safely?

   a. She returns to the surface faster than 1 foot per second.

   b. She returns to the surface at the rate of 1 foot per second.

   c. She returns to the surface more slowly than 1 foot per second.

2 To find out how long it will take her to reach the surface, what does Mei-Li need to know?

   a. The time at which she starts to come back to the surface

   b. The depth at which she starts to come back to the surface

   c. The pressure at which she starts to come back to the surface

3 Which expression tells how long it will take Mei-Li to resurface?

   a. 1×25

   b. 2×30

   c. 2×25

Mei-Li wants to explore some undersea caves. She spent $175 for a new wet suit for the trip. The rental fee for a boat with a driver is $65 an hour. The driver charges an additional fee of $75 for equipment. Mei-Li wants to know the cost of renting the boat.

BOAT RENTAL
$65.00 HOUR

FEE FOR EQUIPMENT
$75.00

4 What does Mei-Li know about the rental fee for the boat?

   a. It costs $65 for the whole day.

   b. It costs $65 for each hour.

   c. It costs $175 for the whole day.

5 What other cost does she have to consider when renting the boat?

   a. $175 for a wet suit

   b. $65 for equipment use

   c. $75 for equipment use

6 **Explain** Mei-Li uses the expression $65 \times h + 75$ to find the cost of renting a boat. Explain what each term of the expression represents.

Map It!

Using Algebra

In this lesson you will learn to name, locate, and graph ordered pairs on the coordinate grid.

Learning About It

Read the treasure map as you discover how to work with a coordinate grid. An **ordered pair** is used to describe a location. What ordered pair describes the location of the treasure on the grid below?

Word Bank

ordered pair
***x*-axis**
***y*-axis**
origin

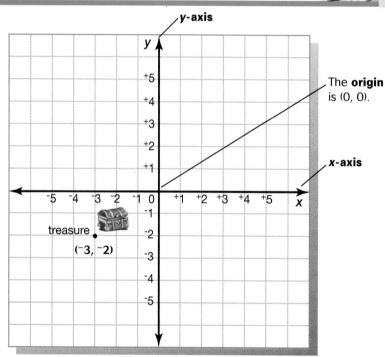

y-axis

The **origin** is (0, 0).

x-axis

treasure

(⁻3, ⁻2)

- The first number in an ordered pair is the number of units to the left or right of the origin. The treasure is 3 units to the left of the origin.

- The second number in an ordered pair is the number of units up or down from the origin. The treasure is 2 units down from the origin.

The ordered pair that locates the treasure is (⁻3, ⁻2).

Lines of latitude and longitude are used to locate places on Earth. The place where 0° latitude and 0° longitude meet is in the Atlantic Ocean off the coast of Africa.

You can also graph or plot a point. To graph the ordered pair ($^-$2, $^+$4):

- Begin at the origin.
- Move left on the *x*-axis, since $^-$2 is a negative integer.
- Then move up, since 4 is a positive integer.

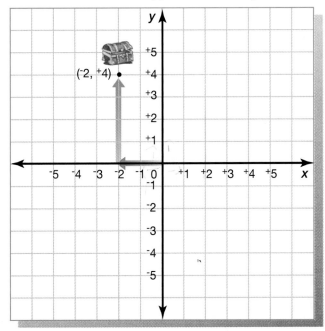

More Examples

Look at the grid on the right. The ordered pair for each point is shown below.

point *A* ($^+$5, $^+$2)   point *B* ($^-$4, $^+$5)

point *C* ($^-$3, $^-$4)   point *D* ($^+$4, $^-$5)

Think and Discuss Is the location of ($^-$3, $^+$5) the same as ($^+$5, $^-$3)? Why or why not?

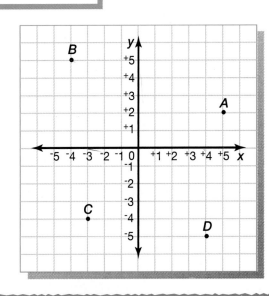

487

Try It Out

Write the ordered pair for each point.

1. A   **2.** B   **3.** C

4. D   **5.** E   **6.** F

7. G   **8.** H   **9.** I

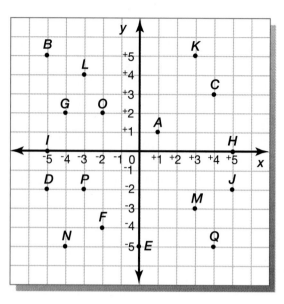

Name the point for each ordered pair.

10. ($^+$3, $^+$5)   **11.** ($^+$3, $^-$3)   **12.** ($^-$3, $^+$4)

13. ($^-$2, $^+$2)   **14.** ($^-$5, $^-$2)   **15.** ($^+$4, $^-$5)

16. ($^-$4, $^-$5)   **17.** ($^-$3, $^-$2)   **18.** ($^+$5, 0)

19. Use grid paper to plot each point. Connect the points in the order given and name the figure formed.

     ($^+$3, $^+$2), (0, $^+$4), ($^-$3, $^+$1), ($^-$2, $^-$3), ($^+$2, $^-$3)

Practice

Write the ordered pair for each point.

20. A   **21.** K   **22.** O

23. E   **24.** B   **25.** R

26. N   **27.** F   **28.** M

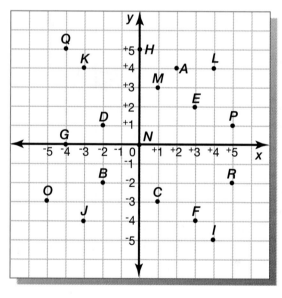

Name the point for each ordered pair.

29. ($^-$2, $^+$1)   **30.** ($^-$4, 0)   **31.** ($^+$5, $^+$1)

32. ($^+$4, $^+$4)   **33.** ($^-$4, $^+$5)   **34.** (0, $^+$5)

35. ($^+$1, $^-$3)   **36.** ($^+$4, $^-$5)   **37.** ($^-$3 , $^-$4)

Use grid paper to plot the points for Exercises 38 – 43. Connect the points and name the figure formed.

38. ($^-$1, $^+$3), ($^+$5, 0), ($^+$1 $^-$2), ($^-$5, $^+$1)   **39.** (0, 0), (0, $^+$5), ($^+$4, 0), (0, 0)

40. ($^+$4, $^-$3), ($^+$4, $^+$3), ($^-$4, $^+$3), ($^-$4, $^-$3)   **41.** ($^+$2, $^+$2), ($^-$2, $^+$2), ($^-$2, $^-$2), ($^+$2, $^-$2)

42. ($^-$2, $^+$4), ($^+$6, $^+$4), ($^+$2, $^-$3), ($^-$6, $^-$3)   **43.** ($^+$2, 0), ($^+$1, $^+$2), ($^-$1, $^+$2), ($^-$2, 0)

44. **Analyze** What is the *x*-coordinate for any point on the *y*-axis?

Problem Solving

Use the map at the right to answer Problems 45–47. Move through the city along the grid lines.

45. Start at Town Hall. Walk 2 blocks east and 3 blocks north. Where are you?

46. Start at Town Hall. Walk 2 blocks west and 3 blocks south. Where are you?

47. Create Your Own Design another landmark for the city. Write a problem about the route to your landmark, starting from Town Hall. Have a classmate solve it.

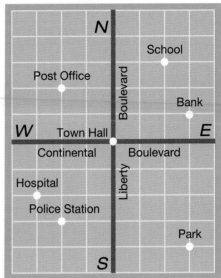

Dunnville

Review and Remember

Find the area of each figure. Use 3.14 for π.

48. 2 cm
8 cm

49. 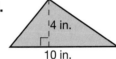 8 m

50. 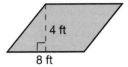 4 in.
10 in.

51. 4 ft
8 ft

Time for Technology
Using the Math Processor™ CD-ROM

Coordinate Graphing

You can link a coordinate graph and a spreadsheet to graph ordered pairs.

- Link a spreadsheet to a coordinate graph ⊞.

- In the spreadsheet enter the data for the ordered pairs from Exercises 10–18 on page 488.

- Click on a point in the graph and move it.

- Write about how the spreadsheet changes.

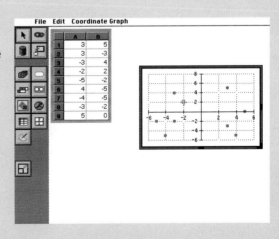

For Extra Practice, see Set E, page 509.

✓ Checkpoint

Adding and Subtracting Integers

Using Algebra **Order from least to greatest.** (pages 474–475)

1. $^+2, ^-6, ^-3, ^+5$
2. $^-1, 0, ^+4, ^-6$
3. $^-8, ^-10, ^-13, ^-5$

4. $^-3, ^+8, ^+11, ^-7$
5. $^-20, ^-27, ^+37, ^+13$
6. $^-43, ^-38, ^+25, ^+35$

Using Algebra **Find the sum.** (pages 478–479)

7. $^-7 + ^-8$
8. $^+19 + ^-3$
9. $^+20 + ^+12$
10. $^-16 + ^-12$

11. $^-29 + ^+17$
12. $^-12 + ^-28$
13. $^-32 + ^+6$
14. $^+39 + ^-49$

Using Algebra **Find the difference.** (pages 482–483)

15. $^+10 - ^+7$
16. $^-8 - ^-8$
17. $^-9 - ^+7$
18. $^+2 - ^+3$

19. $^-5 - ^+4$
20. $^+3 - ^-10$
21. $^+12 - ^+14$
22. $^+6 - ^-6$

Using Algebra **For Exercises 23–29, use the grid at the right.** (pages 486–489)

23. Write the ordered pair for point *A*.

24. Write the ordered pair for point *C*.

25. Write the ordered pair for point *F*.

26. Name the point at $(^-4, ^-2)$.

27. Name the point at $(^+1, ^-4)$.

28. Name the point at $(^-2, ^-4)$.

29. Write the ordered pair for the origin.

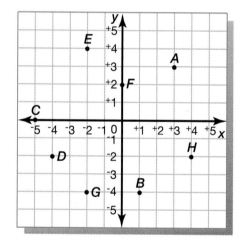

Mixed Practice

Using Algebra **Add or subtract.**

30. $^+1 - ^-10$
31. $^-5 + ^-6$
32. $^-2 + ^+8$
33. $^-3 + ^+10$

34. $^-4 - 0$
35. $^+6 - ^-4$
36. $^-9 + ^+5$
37. $^+7 - ^+9$

38. $0 - ^-5$
39. $^+9 + ^-3$
40. $^-8 + ^-2$
41. $^-4 + ^-7$

Problem Solving

42. The temperature at the top of a mountain was 30 degrees less than the temperature at the base of the mountain. If the temperature at the base is ⁻4°F, what is the temperature at the top?

43. The temperature on Saturday was ⁻4°F. On Tuesday, it was ⁻1°F. On which day was it warmer?

44. By evening, the temperature dropped 12° to a low of ⁻3°. What was the temperature before it dropped?

45. After playing five holes of golf together, Matthew's scores with respect to par were ⁻2, ⁺3, 0, and ⁺5. Rachel's scores were ⁻2, ⁺3, ⁻1, and ⁺6. Who has the lowest score so far?

Journal Idea

You earn $7 each time you walk a dog. Going to the movies costs you $5. How could you use integers to record your earnings and the money you spend on movies in a year?

What do you think?

How is subtracting integers and adding integers similar?

Critical Thinking Corner

Visual Thinking

Patterns and Relations

Using Algebra Solve each problem.

1. Joe's earnings depend on how long he works.

Hours Worked	1	2	3	4
Money Earned	$5	$10	$15	$20

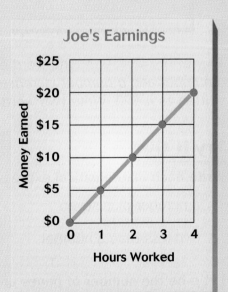

Joe's Earnings

a. How much will Joe earn after 8 hours?

b. If he earns $60, how long has he worked?

c. Write the ordered pair for the point on the graph that represents 3 hours of work.

d. How are the table and graph related?

2. Joe spent $50 for 5 tickets. Make a table and a graph to show how ticket cost relates to the number of tickets bought.

Talking Numbers

You can learn the language of algebra.

Learning About It

A mathematical expression written in words can be rewritten in symbols.

Mathematical Expressions	
In Words	**In Symbols**
Eight plus twelve	$8 + 12$
Nine subtracted from a number	$n - 9$
Twice a number	$2 \times n$ or $2n$
A number divided by six	$n \div 6$ or $\frac{n}{6}$
Three more than a number	$n + 3$
Five less than a number	$n - 5$

Think and Discuss The word expressions, *three added to a number* and *a number increased by three* can both be written as $n + 3$. Write two word expressions for $n - 3$.

Try It Out

Write each mathematical expression in symbols.

1. a number plus seven

2. eight times a number

3. two less than a number

4. a number decreased by four

Let p be the number of pages an author writes. Write each mathematical expression in symbols.

5. twice as many pages as p

6. forty pages more than p

Practice

Match each word expression with the symbolic expression.

7. a number minus 2

8. a number divided by 2

9. twice a number

10. two more than a number

11. one half a number

a. $n + 2$

b. $2n$

c. $n - 2$

d. $\frac{1}{2}n$

e. $n \div 2$

Write each mathematical expression in symbols.

12. a number increased by six

13. ten less than a number

14. a number divided by twenty

15. eight subtracted from a number

16. one third of a number

17. the product of nine and a number

Problem Solving

Let t be the number of telephone calls made last week. Write a symbolic expression for each problem. Then answer each question.

18. Marian made five more telephone calls this week than she made last week.

Question: If she made three calls last week, how many calls did she make this week?

19. Tom made six fewer telephone calls this week than he made last week.

Question: If he made ten calls last week, how many calls did he make this week?

20. Aaron made twice as many telephone calls this week as he made last week.

Question: If he made six calls last week, how many calls did he make this week?

Sign language is a way for hearing-impaired people to communicate. This girl is signing the word *mathematics*.

Review and Remember

Using Mental Math **Find each answer.**

21. $200 + 800$

22. 3×300

23. 0.5×5

24. $2.4 - 2$

25. $5\frac{3}{8} + 3\frac{7}{8}$

26. $15 \times \frac{3}{5}$

27. $1,200 \div 4$

28. $^-12 + {}^+12$

Problem Solving
Choose a Strategy

*Sometimes you can use more than one strategy
to solve a problem.*

Last week, the Acme Cycle Factory made twice as many tricycles as bicycles. If they used 320 wheels, how many of each kind of vehicle did they make?

 UNDERSTAND

What do you need to know?

You need to know that bicycles have two wheels and tricycles have three wheels.

 PLAN

How can you solve the problem?

Choose a strategy you can use to solve the problem.

 SOLVE

The number of bicycle wheels used plus the number of tricycle wheels used equals 320 wheels.

Guess and Check

Guess		Total Number of Wheels	
		Bicycle wheels ↓	Tricycle wheels ↓
Bicycles	**Tricycles**		
25	50	$2 \times 25 + 3 \times 50 = 200$ (too low)	
50	100	$2 \times 50 + 3 \times 100 = 400$ (too high)	
40	80	$2 \times 40 + 3 \times 80 = 320$	

Write an Equation

Let n be the number of bicycles. Then $2n$ is the number of tricycles, since there are twice as many.

$$(2 \times n) + (3 \times 2n) = 320$$
$$2n + 6n = 320$$
$$8n = 320$$
$$8 \times 40 = 320$$
$$n = 40, \text{ so } 2n = 80$$

The factory made 40 bicycles and 80 tricycles.

 LOOK BACK

How can knowing two strategies to use be helpful in checking your work?

Using Strategies

Try these or other strategies to solve each problem.
Tell which strategy you used.

Problem Solving Strategies

- Guess and Check
- Draw a Diagram
- Solve a Simpler Problem
- Find a Pattern
- Make a List
- Write an Equation

1 Acme makes wagons as well as bicycles and tricycles. Last week they made as many wagons as tricycles, and half as many bicycles as wagons. If they used 400 wheels, how many of each vehicle did they make?

2 George needs 40 apples for a science project. Each day he brings home 7 apples, but every night his sisters and brother eat 3 of them. On which day will he have 40 apples?

3 Anna, Ben, and Carol had a batting contest. Anna hit a ball 12 feet farther than Ben did. Carol hit a ball 180 feet, and the ball landed 6 feet short of where Ben's hit landed. How far did Anna hit the ball?

4 Jan goes to the swimming pool every third day. Gil goes to the same pool every fifth day. Both are at the pool on the same day. In how many days will they both be at the pool again?

5 The Miller family paid $90 for admission to the local aquarium. The aquarium charges $12 for adults and $9 for children under 16. They bought more tickets for children than adults. How many of each ticket did they buy?

6 Tom, Pat, and Sue decided to share expenses equally for a party. Tom spent $35 for food, Pat spent $26 for a gift, and Sue spent $20 for decorations. What should they do now to make sure each contributes the same amount?

7 Using Algebra Paula tracked the diving habits of a whale on a chart like the one shown at the right. If the pattern continues, at what time will the whale come up from its sixth dive?

Dive	Down	Up
1	8:00	8:05
2	8:06	8:11
3	8:12	8:17
4	8:18	8:23

Fascinating Fact

You can tell a whale by its tail! Whale watchers have learned to identify specific whales by telltale markings on their tails.

Balancing Act

A balance scale can help you understand and solve equations.

Learning About It

An equation is like a balanced scale. Each side of an equation represents the same value.

Work with a partner. Explore solving equations.

Step 1 Look at the balanced scale below. How many blocks are in the bag? How do you know?

$b + 3 = 8$

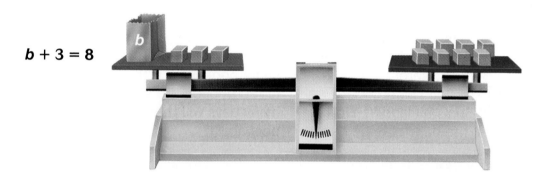

What You Need

For each pair:
  balance scale
  paper bag
  blocks

Step 2 Have your partner create an addition equation and represent it, on a pan balance. Do not look at how many blocks your partner puts into the bag.

Step 3 Without looking, find the number of blocks in the bag. Take an equal number of blocks from each side of the scale until the paper bag stands alone and the scale is balanced. How many blocks are in the paper bag? Explain.

Step 4 Record your work in a chart like the one below.

Equation	Blocks Removed From Each Side	Value of b	Check
$b + 3 = 8$	3	5	$5 + 3 ? 8$ $8 = 8$

Step 5 Now make up an addition equation for your partner to solve.

Connecting Ideas

When you use a scale to solve an equation, keep the scale balanced by taking the same number of blocks from each side.

Step 1 The scale below is balanced. The same number of blocks are in each bag. How many blocks are in each bag?

$3 \times b = 12$

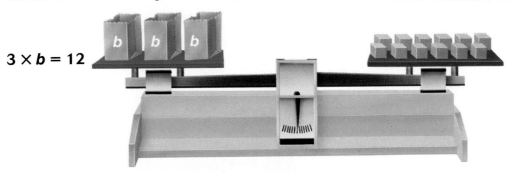

Step 2 Have your partner create a multiplication equation and represent it on a pan balance. Do not look at how many blocks are put into each bag.

Step 3 Without looking, find the number of blocks in each bag. Take all but one of the bags off the balance scale. Take blocks off the other side of the scale until the scale is balanced. How many blocks are on one side of the balance? How many blocks are in the bag?

Step 4 Record your work in a chart.

Step 5 Now make up a multiplication equation for your partner to solve.

Think and Discuss What number would you subtract from the expression $b + 15$ in order to have only b remaining? Explain.

Practice

Use a pan balance to solve each equation.

1. $y + 5 = 17$
2. $a + 9 = 23$
3. $3 \times b = 48$
4. $6 \times m = 72$
5. $z + 6 = 32$
6. $4 \times y = 68$
7. $35 + x = 103$
8. $d + 27 = 52$
9. $m \times 3 = 51$
10. $5 \times b = 60$
11. $t + 7 = 22$
12. $16 + v = 29$
13. $7 \times f = 56$
14. $8 + n = 19$
15. $3 \times m = 81$
16. $13 + j = 35$

17. **Journal Idea** By what numbers would you divide the expression $18n$ and the expression $25n$ so only n remains? Explain your reasoning.

Solving Addition and Subtraction Equations

Math on Parade!

You can solve an equation by using an inverse operation.

Learning About It

On Thanksgiving Day, there are parades in many cities around the country. The parade in New York City is famous for its giant balloons. At the seventieth annual parade, there were 58 entries that were not giant balloons. If there was a total of 77 entries, how many were giant balloons?

You can write an equation. Let x be the number of giant balloons.

$$x + 58 = 77$$

When equations are too difficult to solve mentally, you can use inverse operations.

$$x + 58 = 77$$
$$x + 58 - 58 = 77 - 58$$
$$x + 0 = 19$$
$$x = 19$$

The inverse of addition is subtraction. Subtract 58 from each side of the equation.

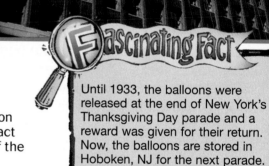

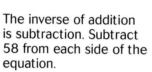

Until 1933, the balloons were released at the end of New York's Thanksgiving Day parade and a reward was given for their return. Now, the balloons are stored in Hoboken, NJ for the next parade.

To check the solution, replace x with 19 in the original equation. If the result is true, the solution is correct.

$$x + 58 = 77$$
$$19 + 58 \ ? \ 77$$
$$77 = 77$$

There were 19 giant balloons in the parade.

More Examples

A.
$$w - 15 = 37$$
$$w - 15 + 15 = 37 + 15$$
$$w = 52$$

B.
$$n + 12.5 = 20$$
$$n + 12.5 - 12.5 = 20 - 12.5$$
$$n = 7.5$$

Think and Discuss How can you show that the solution you found for an equation is correct?

Try It Out

Explain what you can do to both sides of each equation to find the value of the variable. Then solve.

1. $t - 17 = 35$ **2.** $r + 56 = 200$ **3.** $t + 2.9 = 7$ **4.** $z - 5 = 4.9$

Practice

Solve each equation. Then check your solution.

5. $s + 9 = 28$ **6.** $n - 15 = 9$ **7.** $p + 12 = 93$ **8.** $a - 70 = 55$

9. $m - 87 = 97$ **10.** $c + 19 = 78$ **11.** $x + 63 = 150$ **12.** $b - 110 = 235$

13. $a + 13 = 41$ **14.** $z - 38 = 102$ **15.** $t - 20 = 99$ **16.** $g + 79 = 300$

17. $d + 3 = 6.2$ **18.** $h - 4.6 = 5.4$ **19.** $r - 0.2 = 9.9$ **20.** $q + 9 = 12.1$

21. Predict Without solving, tell whether each variable is greater than, less than, or equal to 95.

    a. $k - 10 = 95$ **b.** $n + {}^-2 + 2 = 95$ **c.** $p + 40 = 95$

Problem Solving

Solve Problems 22 and 23 using equations.

22. Of the 77 entries in the parade, 13 were marching bands. How many entries were not marching bands?

23. The number of floats was 3 less than expected. There were 27 floats in the parade. How many floats were expected?

24. Analyze There were 8 more jugglers than acrobats in the parade. The total number of jugglers and acrobats was 26. How many jugglers were there? How many acrobats? Which strategy did you use?

Fascinating Fact

When inflated, the average height of a balloon in the Thanksgiving Day Parade is 5 stories high. A story is about 12 feet high.

Review and Remember

Using Estimation Estimate the answer.

25. $380 \div 9$ **26.** $4{,}968 - 2{,}792$

27. 5.1×0.08 **28.** $0.499 \div 5$ **29.** 23% of 16   **30.** $9\frac{1}{2}\%$ of 8,000

31. $3\frac{7}{8} + 2\frac{7}{16}$ **32.** $19 \times \frac{4}{9}$ **33.** $5\frac{1}{5} \times 8\frac{7}{8}$ **34.** 999×58

Solving Multiplication and Division Equations

Using Algebra

Divide the Gold

You can solve a multiplication equation by dividing.

Learning About It

Nathan helps out in the family pet shop on Saturdays. He separates a shipment of 108 fish equally into nine smaller bowls. How many fish will be in each bowl?

You can write an equation. Let m be the number of fish in each bowl.

$$9 \times m = 108$$

When equations are too difficult to solve mentally, you can use inverse operations.

$$9 \times m = 108$$
$$\frac{9}{9} \times m = \frac{108}{9}$$
$$1 \times m = 12$$
$$m = 12$$

The inverse of multiplication is division. Divide each side of the equation by 9.

There are 12 goldfish in each bowl.

More Examples

A. $2.8p = 14$

$p = \frac{14}{2.8}$

$p = 5$

B. $a \div 15 = 3$

$a = 3 \times 15$

$a = 45$

Think and Discuss Look at the two equations $a \times 10 = 40$ and $b \div 10 = 40$. Which variable is greater? Why?

Try It Out

Explain what you can do to both sides of each equation to find the value of the variable. Then solve.

1. $x \div 10 = 12$ **2.** $8 \times d = 104$ **3.** $9 \times t = 144$ **4.** $y \div 7 = 7$

Practice

Solve each equation. Then check your solution.

5. $3 \times c = 42$ **6.** $m \div 12 = 60$ **7.** $6 \times k = 48$ **8.** $w \div 6 = 1$

9. $h \div 8 = 12$ **10.** $15 \times r = 90$ **11.** $x \div 9 = 18$ **12.** $2 \times t = 36$

13. $4 \times d = 10$ **14.** $a \div 5 = 1.4$ **15.** $6 \times y = 9$ **16.** $n \div 3 = 16$

17. $z \div 4 = 5$ **18.** $p \div 21 = 7$ **19.** $25 \times j = 200$ **20.** $12 \times d = 144$

21. Predict Without solving, tell whether the variable is greater than, less than, or equal to 80.

   a. $5 \times m = 80$ **b.** $k \div 2 = 80$ **c.** $\frac{8}{8} \times b = 80$

Problem Solving

22. If Nathan puts 14 boxes of fish food on each shelf, how many boxes will 5 shelves hold? Write and solve an equation.

23. Analyze Carole had $50 to spend on fish supplies. She spent $\frac{1}{5}$ of the total for plants. Then she spent $\frac{1}{2}$ of what she had left on fish. How much did she spend on plants and fish?

Review and Remember

Add or subtract.

24. $^{+}8 + {}^{-}5$ **25.** $^{-}10 + {}^{+}6$

26. $^{-}7 + {}^{-}3$ **27.** $^{+}12 + {}^{-}4$

28. $^{+}9 - {}^{-}2$ **29.** $^{-}3 - {}^{+}4$

ascinating Fact

The large fish shown in the photo is a koi. The koi is related to the goldfish. It can grow to be 3 feet long.

Critical Thinking Corner

Logical Thinking

What's Wrong?

Tara wanted to arrange her 208 baseball cards into equal groups of 4. To determine how many cards would be in each group, she wrote the equation $4 \times g = 208$. Tara said there would be 832 cards in each group. What did she do wrong?

14 Integer Equations

Using Algebra

Go Fish

You can use what you know to solve integer equations.

Learning About It

In the picture on the right, a kingfisher hovers over his prey. How far above the water is the bird?

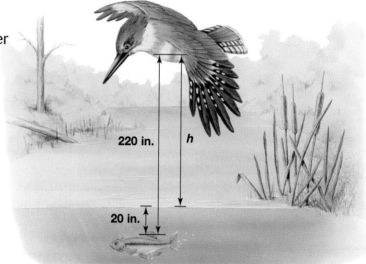

220 in.   *h*

20 in.

You can write a subtraction equation to represent the distance between the fish and the bird.

$$h - {}^{-}20 = 220$$

↑   ↑   ↑

bird above   fish below   total
water   water   distance

Now solve the equation.

Step 1 Rewrite the subtraction as addition.	**Step 2** Solve the addition equation.	
$h - {}^{-}20 = 220$ $h + {}^{+}20 = 220$	$h + 20 = 220$ $h + 20 - 20 = 220 - 20$ $h + 0 = 200$ $h = 200$	Subtract 20 from both sides of the equation.

The bird is 200 inches above the water.

More Examples

A. $y + {}^{-}3 = {}^{-}5$

$\boxed{?} + {}^{-}3 = {}^{-}5$ ← mental math

${}^{-}2 + {}^{-}3 = {}^{-}5$

$y = {}^{-}2$

B. $m - 9 = {}^{-}2$

$m - 9 + 9 = {}^{-}2 + 9$ ← inverse operation

$m + 0 = 7$

$m = 7$

Think and Discuss Tell how you would solve $b + {}^{-}2 = 1$.

Try It Out

Solve each equation. Then check your solution.

1. $r - {}^{-}8 = 10$ **2.** $a + {}^{-}1 = {}^{-}4$ **3.** $x - 5 = {}^{-}3$ **4.** $s + {}^{-}6 = 4$

Practice

Solve each equation. Then check your solution.

5. $a - 1 = {}^-5$ **6.** $k + 8 = {}^-2$ **7.** $w - {}^-3 = 9$ **8.** $c + {}^-7 = {}^-1$

9. $q + {}^-3 = 6$ **10.** $d - 5 = 1$ **11.** $z + 9 = 1$ **12.** $g - 8 = {}^-2$

13. $m - {}^-5 = {}^-3$ **14.** $t + 2 = {}^-7$ **15.** $f + {}^-6 = {}^-3$ **16.** $a - 4 = 0$

17. $j + {}^-8 = 5$ **18.** $x - 1 = {}^-6$ **19.** $h - {}^-4 = 20$ **20.** $y + {}^-1 = 11$

Problem Solving

21. A diver was 50 ft below the surface of the water. He rose 20 ft. How many feet below the surface of the water is he now?

22. A pelican sat on top of a 10-ft pole that was on a dock 3 ft above the water. The pelican dove to a depth of 5 ft. What was the total distance the pelican traveled? Which strategy did you use?

Review and Remember

Compare. Use >, <, or = for ⬤.

23. 1,254 ⬤ 1,524

24. 0.01 ⬤ 0.001

25. $\frac{4}{8}$ ⬤ $\frac{1}{2}$

26. $2\frac{7}{8}$ ⬤ $2\frac{3}{4}$

27. ${}^-5$ ⬤ ${}^-3$

28. ${}^+8$ ⬤ ${}^-8$

Fascinating Fact

The belted kingfisher dives after small fish that swim near the surface of the water. The birds build their nests using fish bones and scales.

 Money $ense

Give and Take

In a game called Give and Take, each player starts with $3. Players take turns picking 5 cards. Using the cards, each player finds a new total amount of money. How much money would you have after picking these five cards?

Pick up

Spend $1.35

Lose

Find 45¢

For Extra Practice, see Set I, page 510.

Problem Solving
Using Integers

Many real-world problems use integers.

On a football field the 50-yard line divides the field into two halves. The team with the ball gains yards (+) when it moves the ball toward the other team's goal line. It loses yards (−) when it is forced towards its own goal line by the other team.

In one quarter the Hawks gained 7 yards on the first play and then lost 10 yards. On the third play they gained 8 yards. How many yards had the Hawks gained or lost by the end of three plays?

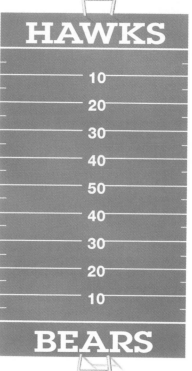

 ### UNDERSTAND

What do you need to find?

You need to find the total number of yards gained or lost by the end of the three plays.

 ### PLAN

How can you solve the problem?

You can **write an equation**. Add the yards gained (+) and the yards lost (−).

 ### SOLVE

Let y = number of yards gained or lost by the end of 3 plays.

$y = {}^+7 + {}^-10 + {}^+8$
$y = {}^+15 + {}^-10$
$y = {}^+5$

The Hawks gained 5 yards during the three plays.

 ### LOOK BACK

How could you draw a diagram to check if the answer is reasonable?

Show What You Learned

Using Algebra Use integers and the diagram of the football field on page 504 to solve Problems 1–4.

1 The Bears lost 12 yards on the first play, gained 5 yards on the second play, and lost 3 yards on the third play. How many yards had the Bears gained or lost by the end of the 3 plays?

2 The Hawks gained 9 yards on the first play. After the second play the Hawks had lost a total of 5 yards during the two plays. Did they they gain or lose yards on the second play? how many?

3 Analyze From their 35-yard line, the Hawks kicked the ball a distance of 40 yards toward the Bears' goal line. On what yard line did the Bears get the ball?

4 Create Your Own Make up a problem in which a team has the ball for 3 plays and loses a total of 12 yards.

Using Algebra Use the formula below and the table shown at the right for Problems 5–8. The R in the formula stands for rushing average, or average yards gained per run.

$$R = \frac{y}{n} \quad \begin{matrix}\leftarrow \text{ yards gained} \\ \leftarrow \text{ number of carries}\end{matrix}$$

Rushing Totals		
Player	Yards Gained	Number of Carries
C. Lee	95	15
B. Johnson	85	16
I. O'Brien	73	14
M. Gold	72	8

5 Chauncey Lee led all ball carriers with 95 yards gained. Find his rushing average to the nearest tenth of a yard.

6 In one game, Bill Johnson and Ian O'Brien led their teams in rushing. Which player had the greater rushing average?

7 Analyze In the first half of the game, Micah Gold ran with the ball 8 times for a total of 72 yards. If he were to run with the ball 12 times in the second half, how many yards will he have to gain to keep his rushing average from changing?

8 Analyze Rasheed Ewing's rushing average is 5 yards per run. If he rushed for a total of 50 yards, how many times did he carry the ball?

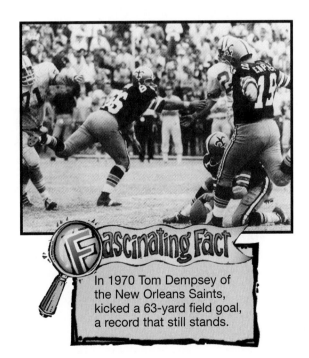

ascinating Fact

In 1970 Tom Dempsey of the New Orleans Saints, kicked a 63-yard field goal, a record that still stands.

Problem Solving

Practice What You Learned

Choose the correct letter for each answer.

1 Starting Monday, December 1, the temperature went down 0.5°F each day until Friday. What was the temperature on Saturday?

A. ⁻0.5°F
B. ⁻2.5°F
C. ⁻3°F
D. ⁻3.5°F
E. Not Here

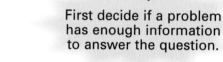

Tip

First decide if a problem has enough information to answer the question.

---

2 Pete is older than Joan, but younger than Vic. Sam is older than Pete. Which of these is a reasonable conclusion?

A. Sam is older than Joan.
B. Joan is older than Sam.
C. Vic is older than Sam.
D. Sam is older than Vic.
E. Pete is younger than Joan.

Tip

Use Logical Reasoning to help you solve this problem.

---

3 The table shows how the price of a stock changed over a five-day period.

Tip

Negative integers represent a decrease in the value of the stock.

Change in Stock Price					
Day	Mon.	Tues.	Wed.	Thurs.	Fri.
Price Change	0	⁻1	⁻3	+3	+2½

What was the range of the price changes?

A. 0 to ⁻3
B. ⁻3 to ⁺3
C. ⁻1 to ⁻3
D. 0 to ⁺3
E. ⁻1 to ⁺2$\frac{1}{2}$

▲ Traders keep track of stock prices on the floor of the American Stock Exchange.

4 Trudy's class is making 100 magnetic compasses. For each compass, they need a piece of metal wire $8\frac{7}{8}$ centimeters long. Which is a good estimate of the total amount of wire the class needs?

A. 600 cm   **D.** 900 cm
B. 750 cm   **E.** 1,000 cm
C. 800 cm

---

5 These triangles are part of a design for a room-size rug. Which statement describes the relationship between the two triangles?

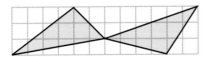

A. They are congruent.
B. They are similar.
C. One is a reflection of the other.
D. One is a rotation of the other.
E. They have the same area.

---

6 The price of a stock went down half a point a day for 5 days. In which equation does n equal the total change in the value of the stock?

A. $5(^-\frac{1}{2}) = n$ **D.** $5n = ^-\frac{1}{2}$

B. $^-5(^-\frac{1}{2}) = n$ **E.** $^-\frac{1}{2}n = 5$

C. $^-5n = ^-\frac{1}{2}$

---

7 At the start of the dog sled race, the temperature was $^-2°F$. By the end of the race, the temperature had increased 12°F. What was the temperature at the end of the race?

A. $^-14°F$ **D.** $^+18°F$
B. $^-10°F$ **E.** Not Here
C. $^+10°F$

---

8 The graph shows the hours worked in the school library by 4 students in 1 week. About what percent of the total number of hours did Bob work?

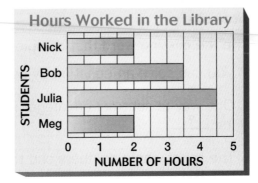

A. 10%   **D.** 30%
B. 15%   **E.** 50%
C. 20%

---

9 Mark planted a variety of flower bulbs over a period of 8 weeks. The chart shows how many bulbs he planted each week for the first 5 weeks.

Week	1	2	3	4	5
Number	15	30	20	35	25

If Mark continues in this pattern, how many bulbs will he plant in the *eighth* week?

A. 60   **D.** 45
B. 55   **E.** 40
C. 50

---

10 This figure is part of a drawing for a machine. The diameter of the circle is 10 in. Which expression could you use to find the approximate *area* of the shaded part of the figure?

A. $25\pi - 24$
B. $25\pi - 48$
C. $100\pi - 24$
D. $100\pi - 48$
E. $100\pi + 24$

8 in.   6 in.

Checkpoint

Expressions and Equations

Vocabulary

Write the missing word that completes each sentence.

1. You can solve an equation by using ___?___ .

2. One way to subtract an integer is to add its ___?___ .

3. The set of whole numbers and their opposites is called the set of ___?___ .

4. An ___?___ is used to describe a location.

Word Bank

equation
integers
inverse operations
opposite
ordered pair

Concepts and Skills

Using Algebra **Write a symbolic expression for each word expression.** (pages 492–493)

5. four less than a number

6. a number times four

7. one fourth of a number

8. four more than a number

9. a number divided by four

10. four divided by a number

Using Algebra **Find the value of the variable.** (pages 498–499)

11. $t + 20 = 36$

12. $a - 7 = 14$

13. $b + 1.7 = 9$

14. $r - 0.8 = 10.1$

15. $c - 70 = 120$

16. $y + 0.4 = 7.2$

17. $e - 12 = 73$

18. $28 + z = 72$

19. $m \times 8 = 96$

20. $p \div 7 = 9$

21. $n \times 8 = 32$

22. $z \div 5 = 7$

23. $9 \times w = 72$

24. $d \div 9 = 9$

25. $y \times 5 = 40$

26. $j \div 4 = 12$

Using Algebra **Solve each equation. Check your solution.** (pages 502–503)

27. $f + {}^-2 = 6$

28. $g - {}^-5 = 4$

29. $x + 8 = {}^-3$

30. $s - {}^-2 = 7$

31. $m - {}^-5 = {}^-9$

32. $h + 6 = 0$

33. $k + 6 = {}^-4$

34. $v + {}^-4 = 4$

What do you think?

If you add 3 to one side of an equation, what should you do to the other side of the equation?

Problem Solving

Use the table on the right to solve Problems 35–40.

Above and Below Sea Level	
Place	**Elevation (ft)**
Death Valley	−282
Salton Sea	−235
Foraker	17,400
Mt. St. Elias	18,008
Mt. McKinley	20,320

35. Which is closer to sea level, Death Valley or Salton Sea?

36. What is the difference between the elevation of Salton Sea and Death Valley?

37. What is the difference in elevation between Mt. St. Elias and Salton Sea?

38. Mt. McKinley is how much higher in elevation than Death Valley?

39. **Analyze** What is the elevation of a mountain that is 12,000 ft higher than Death Valley?

40. **What If?** Suppose the elevation of a mountain was 18,290 ft higher than Death Valley. Which mountain could this be?

Journal Idea

Make a list of places, activities, or situations in which integers can be used. Explain how integers would be helpful in each instance.

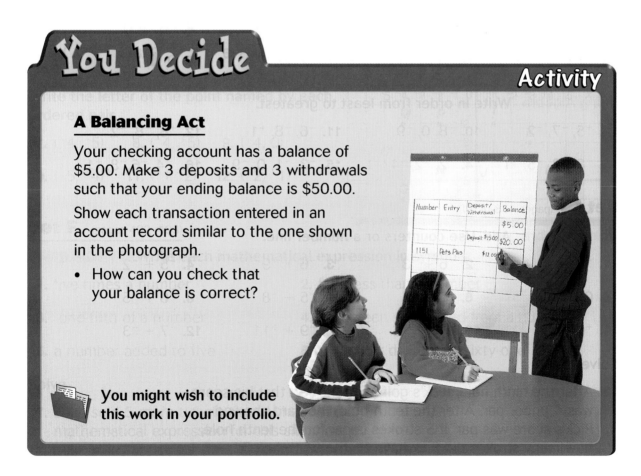

You Decide

Activity

A Balancing Act

Your checking account has a balance of $5.00. Make 3 deposits and 3 withdrawals such that your ending balance is $50.00.

Show each transaction entered in an account record similar to the one shown in the photograph.

- How can you check that your balance is correct?

You might wish to include this work in your portfolio.

Extra Practice

Set G (pages 498–499)

Using Algebra **Solve each equation. Then check your solution.**

1. $r - 7 = 15$ **2.** $t + 19 = 31$ **3.** $a + 23 = 41$ **4.** $c - 70 = 30$

5. $s - 12 = 4$ **6.** $u + 20 = 49$ **7.** $n + 71 = 85$ **8.** $p - 0.9 = 3.1$

Write and solve an equation for Problems 9–10.

9. A parade route was extended 1.8 miles so that more people could view it. If the new route is 7.9 miles, how long was the original route?

10. Thousands of people came to see the parade. When it began to rain, about 800 people left and 1,200 remained. About how many people were there to see the parade before it began to rain?

Set H (pages 500–501)

Using Algebra **Solve each equation. Then check your solution.**

1. $5 \times d = 30$ **2.** $m \div 4 = 24$ **3.** $8 \times u = 72$ **4.** $a \div 7 = 56$

5. $6 \times y = 48$ **6.** $v \div 4 = 8$ **7.** $p \div 15 = 25$ **8.** $7 \times u = 49$

Write and solve an equation for Problems 9–10.

9. A container of roses was used to make 7 displays, each with 48 roses. How many roses were in the container?

10. Six floral displays used an equal number of carnations. If 540 carnations were used in all, how many were in each display?

Set I (pages 502–503)

Using Algebra **Solve each equation.**

1. $r + {}^-1 = {}^+8$ **2.** $d - {}^-4 = {}^+8$ **3.** $a + {}^+4 = {}^-1$ **4.** $t - {}^+5 = {}^-7$

5. $z - {}^-3 = {}^+5$ **6.** $v + {}^-6 = {}^-5$ **7.** $e - 0 = {}^-5$ **8.** $x + {}^-5 = {}^-7$

Write and solve an equation for Problems 9–10.

9. A miner was 40 feet below the surface. He then descended 30 feet through a shaft. How many feet below the surface did he go?

10. Another miner descended 29 feet to 78 feet below the surface. Where was he before this move?

 Chapter Test

Compare. Use >, <, or = for each ⬤.

1. $^+3$ ⬤ $^-5$ **2.** $^-9$ ⬤ 0 **3.** $^-2$ ⬤ $^-1$

Write in order from least to greatest.

4. $^-5, 0, ^-3$ **5.** $^+5, ^+7, ^-6, ^-4$

Add or subtract.

6. $^+8 + ^-7$ **7.** $^-9 + ^-3$ **8.** $^-6 - ^+9$

9. $^-5 - ^-3$ **10.** $^-2 + ^+2$ **11.** $^-2 - ^+2$

Use the grid for Exercises 12–14.

12. Name the point located at $(^-4, ^+3)$.

13. Name the point located at $(^+5, ^-2)$.

14. Name the ordered pair for point D.

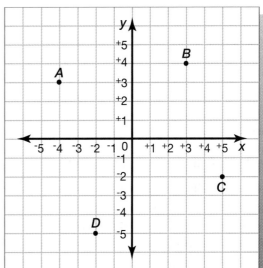

Solve each equation.

15. $n + 12 = 61$ **16.** $t - 8 = 23$

17. $6 \times d = 54$ **18.** $x - ^-5 = ^-13$

Write and solve an equation for Problems 19–20.

19. Death Valley is 282 ft below sea level. A hot-air balloon flying over this desert is 200 ft above sea level. How many feet above Death Valley is the balloon?

20. At 6:00 A.M. you check the thermometer. It reads $^-18°$F. At noon the thermometer shows that the temperature has risen to $23°$F. How many degrees did the temperature rise?

 Self-Check

Look back at Exercises 15–18. To check your work, did you replace the variable with your solution?

Performance Assessment

Show What You Know About Integers and Equations

1 Look at the balanced scales below. The same number of unit cubes are in each bag. How many unit cubes should you put on the right side of scale B to balance the scale? Tell why.

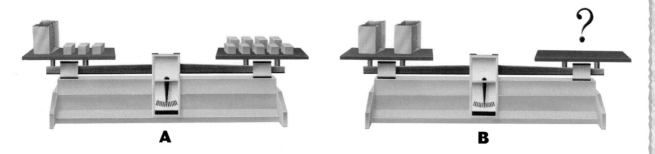

A   B

Self-Check Did you remember to have the same number of cubes for each bag?

2 Use the graph for these problems.

a. Which city has the highest temperature? Which has the lowest temperature?

b. Which city has a higher temperature, Kansas City or Indianapolis?

c. If the temperature in New York City went up 4 degrees, what would the temperature be?

d. If the temperature in Kansas City increased to 1°F, how many degrees did it increase?

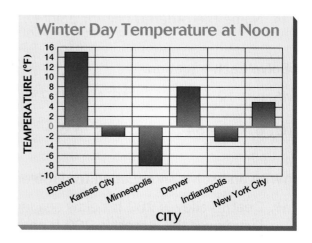

Self-Check Did you study and read the graph carefully?

 For Your Portfolio

You might wish to include this work in your portfolio.

Extension

Using Algebra

Inequalities

A balanced scale is like an equation. But scales are not always balanced. An inequality is like a scale that is not balanced.

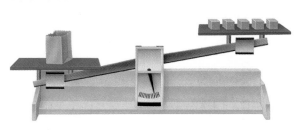

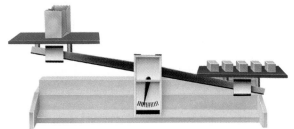

x is heavier than 5.

$x > 5$

x is greater than 5.

x is lighter than 5.

$x < 5$

x is less than 5.

You can use a number line to picture each inequality.

The open circle shows that 5 is not included.

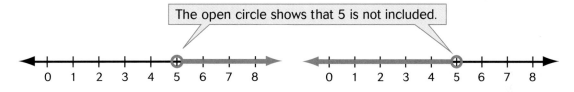

x can be any number greater than 5.

x can be any number less than 5.

Notice that inequalities have more than one solution.

List three possible solutions for each inequality.

1. $p < 10$ **2.** $t > 7$ **3.** $d > 0$ **4.** $k < 3\frac{1}{2}$

Write the inequality for each number line.

5.
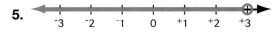

6.

7.
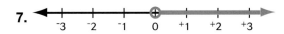

8.
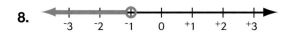

Show the solutions to each inequality on a number line.

9. $n > {}^-1$ **10.** $x < {}^+2$ **11.** $d > {}^+2$ **12.** $z < {}^+1$

Cumulative Review

★ ★ ★ ★ ★ **Preparing for Tests**

Choose the correct letter for each answer.

Number Concepts	Operations

Number Concepts

1. Which integer describes this situation?

Loss of 15 dollars

A. $^+1500$
B. $^+15$
C. $^-15$
D. $^-1,500$

2. Which number sentence is true?

A. $^-3 < ^-2$
B. $^+4 = ^-4$
C. $^-1 > 0$
D. $0 < ^-10$

3. Which set of integers is in order from *greatest* to *least*?

A. $^-1, ^+2, 0, ^-3$
B. $0, ^-1, ^+2, ^-3$
C. $^-3, ^+2, ^-1, 0$
D. $^+2, 0, ^-1, ^-3$

4. Nick helps out at a day-care center. There are 16 three-year-olds, 12 four-year-olds, and 8 five-year-olds at the center. Nick wants to divide the children into groups so that each group has the same number of children of each age. What is the greatest number of groups Nick can make?

A. 2
B. 4
C. 6
D. 8

Operations

5. What is the sum of $^+6$ and $^-8$?

A. $^-14$
B. $^-2$
C. $^+2$
D. $^+14$
E. Not Here

6. The temperature dropped 6 degrees and then rose 11 degrees. What was the total change in temperature?

A. $^-17$
B. $^-5$
C. $^+5$
D. $^+17$
E. Not Here

7. Lupe wants to leave a 15% tip on his bill at a restaurant. If his total bill was $13, how much tip should he leave?

A. $0.85   C. $1.70
B. $1.30   D. $1.95

8. An airplane flies at a speed of 330 mph. The distance between Boston, MA, and Houston, TX, is approximately 1,600 miles. If the plane flies a direct route nonstop, about how long does it take to get from Boston to Houston?

A. 3.5 hours   C. 5.0 hours
B. 4.0 hours   D. 7.0 hours

Patterns, Relationships, and Algebraic Thinking	Probability and Statistics

Patterns, Relationships, and Algebraic Thinking

9. Ronnie scored twice as many points in basketball games this week as he did last week. If the number of points he scored this week is *p*, which expression could be used to find how many points he scored last week?

A. $2 \times p$
B. $p + 2$
C. $p \div 2$
D. $p - 2$

10. Which point best represents ⁻1.5 on the number line?

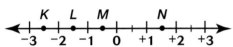

A. *K*   **C.** *M*
B. *L*   **D.** *N*

Use the graph below to answer Questions 11–12.

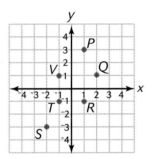

11. Which ordered pair is best represented by point *P*?

A. ($^+3$, $^+1$)   **C.** ($^+1$, $^+2$)
B. ($^-1$, $^-3$)   **D.** ($^+1$, $^+3$)

12. Which point on the graph best represents the ordered pair ($^-1$, $^+1$)?

A. *V*   **C.** *R*
B. *T*   **D.** *Q*

Probability and Statistics

13. What is the mode for the following set of data: 105, 100, 96, 100, 98, 101, 100, 103?

A. 105   **C.** 96
B. 100   **D.** 9

14. Three boys are 59 in., 58 in., and 61 in. tall. Which of the following is a reasonable average height of the 3 boys?

A. 55 inches
B. 58 inches
C. 60 inches
D. 62 inches

Use the graph to answer Questions 15 and 16.

15. Which 5-year period showed the smallest price increase?

A. 1975–1980
B. 1980–1985
C. 1985–1990
D. 1990–1995

16. How much more would you have paid for a movie ticket in 1985 than in 1980?

A. $1.25
B. $1.00
C. $0.50
D. $0.25

Additional Resources

Tables

MEASURES

Customary

Length	Weight	Capacity
1 foot (ft) = 12 inches (in.)	1 pound (lb) = 16 ounces (oz)	1 cup (c) = 8 fluid ounces (fl oz)
1 yard (yd) = 36 inches	1 ton (T) = 2,000 pounds	1 pint (pt) = 2 cups
1 yard = 3 feet		1 quart (qt) = 2 pints
1 mile = 5,280 feet		1 quart = 4 cups
1 mile = 1,760 yards		1 gallon = 4 quarts

Area

1 square foot (ft^2) = 144 square inches (in.^{2})

1 square yard (yd^2) = 9 square feet

1 acre = 43,560 square feet

1 square mile (mi^2) = 640 acres

Metric

Length	Mass/Weight	Capacity
1 millimeter (mm) = 0.001 meter (m)	1 milligram (mg) = 0.001 gram (g)	milliliter (mL) = 0.001 liter (L)
1 centimeter (cm) = 0.01 meter	1 centigram (cg) = 0.01 gram	1 centiliter (cL) = 0.01 liter
1 kilometer (km) = 1,000 meters	1 kilogram (kg) = 1,000 grams	1 kiloliter (kL) = 1,000 liters
	1 metric ton (t) = 1,000 kilograms	

Area

1 square centimeter (cm^2) = 100 square millimeters (mm^2)

1 square meter (m^2) = 10,000 square centimeters

1 hectare (ha) = 10,000 square meters

1 square kilometer (km^2) = 1,000,000 square meters

SYMBOLS

=	is equal to	%	percent	$\angle ABC$	angle ABC
≠	is not equal to	π	pi (approximately 3.14)	$\triangle ABC$	triangle ABC
>	is greater than	°	degree	∥	is parallel to
<	is less than	°C	degree Celsius	⊥	is perpendicular to
≥	is greater than or equal to	°F	degree Fahrenheit	2:5	ratio of 2 to 5
≤	is less than or equal to	$\overleftrightarrow{AB}$	line AB	10^2	ten to the second power
≈	is approximately equal to	$\overline{AB}$	line segment AB	$^+4$	positive 4
≅	is congruent to	$\overrightarrow{AB}$	ray AB	$^-4$	negative 4
~	is similar to			(3, 4)	ordered pair 3, 4
1.$\overline{3}$	repeating decimal 1.333 . . .			P(E)	probability of event E

FORMULAS

$P = 2l + 2w$	Perimeter of a rectangle	$C = \pi \times d$	Circumference of a circle
$A = l \times w$	Area of a rectangle	$A = \pi \times r^2$	Area of a circle
$A = b \times h$	Area of a parallelogram	$V = l \times w \times h$	Volume of a rectangular prism
$A = \frac{1}{2} \times b \times h$	Area of a triangle	$I = p \times r \times t$	Simple interest

Glossary

acute angle An angle with a measure less than 90°. (p. 389)

acute triangle A triangle with three acute angles. (p. 396)

addends Numbers that are added. (p. 27)

Example: 7 + 8 = 15
The addends are 7 and 8.

angle Two rays with a common endpoint called the vertex. (p. 386)

Example:

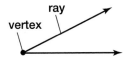

arc A part of a circle. (p. 418)

area The number of square units needed to cover a region. (p. 436)

associative (grouping) property of addition The way that addends are grouped does not change the sum. (p. 14)

Example: (2 + 3) + 4 = 2 + (3 + 4)

associative (grouping) property of multiplication The way that factors are grouped does not change the product. (p. 48)

Example: (2 × 3) × 4 = 2 × (3 × 4)

B

bar graph A graph that uses vertical or horizontal bars to represent numerical data. (p. 106)

base (in geometry) A particular side of a figure. (p. 437)

Example:

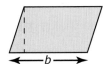

base (in numeration) The number that is multiplied by itself when raised to a power. (p. 150)

Example: In 5³, 5 is the base.

C

capacity The amount a container can hold. (p. 270)

center The point from which all points of a circle are equally distant. (p. 418)

centimeter (cm) A unit of length in the metric system equal to 0.01 meter. (p. 282)

central angle An angle that has its vertex at the center of a circle. (p. 418)

Example:

certain event An event that is sure to happen. A certain event has a probability of 1. (p. 322)

chord A line segment with both endpoints on the circle. (p. 418)

circle A closed plane figure with all of its points the same distance from a point called the center. (p. 418)

circle graph A graph that represents a total divided into parts. (p. 422)

circumference The distance around a circle. (p. 452)

common denominator A common multiple of two or more denominators. (p. 167)

Example: 24 is a common denominator of $\frac{1}{6}$ and $\frac{1}{8}$.

Glossary

common factor A number that is a factor of two or more given numbers. (p. 156)

Example: 1, 2, and 4 are common factors of 4 and 8.

common multiple A number that is a multiple of two or more given numbers. (p. 166)

Example: 6, 12, and 18 are common multiples of 2 and 3.

commutative (order) property of addition The order of the addends does not change the sum. (p. 14)

Example: $9 + 7 = 7 + 9$

commutative (order) property of multiplication The order of the factors does not change the product. (p. 48)

Example: $3 \times 6 = 6 \times 3$

compass An instrument used to construct angles. (p. 412)

Example:

compatible numbers Numbers that are easy to compute mentally. (p. 70)

Example: $5 + 15 = 20$

composite number A whole number greater than one that has more than two factors. (p. 152)

congruent figures Figures that have the same size and shape. (p. 388)

Example:

coordinate grid A plane with a horizontal number line, called the *x*-axis, and a vertical number line, called the *y*-axis, intersecting at a point called the origin. Each point of the grid corresponds to an ordered pair of numbers. (p. 486)

corresponding parts Matching parts of congruent and similar figures. (p. 409)

counting principle If one choice can be made in *m* ways and a second choice can be made in *n* ways, then the two choices can be made together in $m \times n$ ways. (p. 328)

cubic unit A cube used to measure volume. Each edge is equal to a unit of measure. (p. 460)

Example: a cubic meter, m^3

cup (c) A unit of capacity in the customary system equal to 8 fluid ounces (2 cups equals 1 pint). (p. 270)

cross products Products obtained by multiplying the numerator of one fraction by the denominator of a second fraction and the denominator of the first fraction by the numerator of the second fraction. (p. 306)

Example: $\frac{2}{3} = \frac{4}{6}$
$2 \times 6 = 3 \times 4$

customary system A system of weights and measure that measures length in inches, feet, yards, and miles; capacity in cups, pints, quarts, and gallons; weight in ounces, pounds, and tons; and temperature in degrees Fahrenheit. (pp. 266–270)

———————— ————————

data Information that is gathered. (p. 102)

decagon A polygon with ten sides. (p. 402)

decimal A number with one or more digits to the right of a decimal point. (p. 4)

Examples: 0.7, 1.8, 2.06, 0.175

decimal point The dot used to separate dollars from cents and ones from tenths. (p. 4)

decimeter (dm) A unit of length in the metric system equal to 0.1 meter. (p. 282)

dekameter (dam) A unit of length in the metric system equal to 10 meters. (p. 282)

degree (°) A unit for measuring angles. (p. 388)

denominator The number below the fraction bar in a fraction. (p. 144)

Example: $\frac{2}{5}$ The denominator is 5.

dependent events Two events in which the outcome of the second is affected by the outcome of the first. (p. 341)

diagonal A segment that joins two vertices of a polygon but is not a side. (p. 402)

Example:

diameter A line segment that passes through the center of a circle and has both endpoints on the circle. (p. 418)

digit Any of the symbols used to write numbers: 0, 1, 2, 3, 4, 5, 6, 7, 8, and 9. (p. 2)

distributive property Multiplying a sum by a number produces the same results as multiplying each addend by the number and adding the products. (p. 48)

Example: $2 \times (3 + 4) = (2 \times 3) + (2 \times 4)$

dividend The number to be divided. (p. 78)

Example: $6\overline{)36}$ or $36 \div 6$
The dividend is 36.

divisible A number is divisible by another number if the remainder is 0 after dividing. (p. 146)

division An operation on two numbers that results in a quotient. (p. 74)

divisor The number used to divide another number. (p. 68)

Example: $6\overline{)36}$ or $36 \div 6$
The divisor is 6.

double bar graph A graph that uses pairs of bars to compare information. (p. 106)

Example: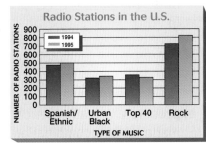

double line graph A graph that uses pairs of lines to compare information. (p. 113)

E

equation A number sentence stating that two expressions are equal. (p. 11)

equilateral triangle A triangle with all sides congruent. (p. 396)

Example:

equivalent fractions Fractions that name the same number. (p. 142)

Glossary

equivalent ratios Ratios that represent the same rate or make the same comparison. (p. 300)

estimate To give an approximate rather than an exact answer. (p. 20)

event One or more outcomes of an experiment. (p. 322)

expanded form A number written as the sum of the values of its digits. (p. 2)

Example: 500 + 50 + 5 is the expanded form for 555.

experiment To carry out a plan that tests a prediction. (p. 320)

exponent A number that tells how many times the base is used as a factor. (p. 150)

Example: $10^3 = 10 \times 10 \times 10$
The exponent is 3 and the base is 10.

expression A mathematical phrase made up of a combination of variables and/or numbers and operations. Expressions with variables are also called algebraic expressions. (p. 10)

Examples: $5n$, $4x - 7$, $(5 \times 2) - \frac{6}{3}$

———— ————

factor tree A diagram used to show the prime factors of a number. (p. 153)

Example:

```
        40
       /  \
      4  × 10
     / \   / \
    2 × 2 × 2 × 5
```

factors The numbers that are multiplied to give a product. (p. 150)

Example: $3 \times 5 = 15$
The factors are 3 and 5.

fair game A game in which all players have the same chance of winning. (p. 326)

fluid ounces (fl oz) A unit of capacity in the customary system equal to 2 tablespoons. (p. 270)

foot (ft) A unit of length in the customary system equal to 12 inches. *pl. feet.* (p. 266)

formula An equation that expresses a rule. (p. 434)

fractal A geometric figure in which each smaller figure is similar to the whole figure. (p. 405)

Example:

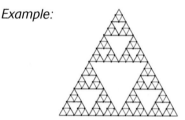

fraction A number that names part of a whole or part of a set. (p. 142)

Examples: $\frac{1}{2}$, $\frac{2}{3}$, $\frac{6}{6}$

frequency table A table used to record the number of times something occurs. (p. 124)

front digit The digit with the greatest place value, used in front-end estimation. (p. 21)

front-end estimation A method of estimating sums, differences, products, and quotients using front digits. (p. 21)

———— ————

gallon (gal) A unit of capacity in the customary system equal to 4 quarts. (p. 270)

golden ratio It is a common ratio found in art and nature. The approximate value for the ratio is 1.62 to 1. (p. 319)

gram (g) The basic unit of mass in the metric system. (p. 284)

graph A drawing used to show information. (p. 100)

greatest common factor (GCF) The greatest number that is a factor of each of two or more numbers. (p. 156)

Example: The greatest common factor of 36 and 48 is 12.

grid A set of uniformly spaced horizontal and vertical lines. (p. 58)

―――――――― H ――――――――

hectometer (hm) A unit of length in the metric system equal to 100 meters. (p. 282)

height (of a parallelogram) The length of a segment drawn perpendicular from the opposite side to the base. (p. 437)

Example:

height (of a triangle) The length of a segment drawn perpendicular to a side of a triangle from the opposite vertex. (p. 440)

Example:

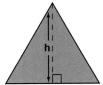

heptagon A polygon with seven sides. (p. 402)

hexagon A polygon with six sides. (p. 402)

histogram A bar graph that represents frequency data. (p. 125)

hundredth One of one hundred equal parts of a whole. (p. 4)

Examples: 0.01, $\frac{1}{100}$

―――――――― ――――――――

identity property of addition The sum of any number and 0 is that number. (p. 14)

identity property of multiplication The product of any number and 1 is that number. (p. 48)

impossible event An event that cannot happen. An impossible event has a probability of 0. (p. 323)

improper fraction A fraction in which the numerator is greater than or equal to the denominator. (p. 164)

Examples: $\frac{4}{3}, \frac{6}{6}$

inch (in.) The basic unit of length in the customary system. (p. 266)

independent events Two events in which the outcome of the second is not affected by the outcome of the first. (p. 330)

inequality Comparison of two expressions using one of the symbols $<$, or $>$. (p. 513)

integers The set of numbers . . . $^-3$, $^-2$, $^-1$, 0, $^+1$, $^+2$, $^+3$, . . . (p. 472)

interest The amount paid for the use of money. (p. 370)

intersecting lines Lines that have exactly one point in common. (p. 392)

Example:

Glossary

inverse operations Two operations with an opposite effect. Addition and subtraction are inverse operations. Multiplication and division are inverse operations. (pp. 242, 498)

isosceles triangle A triangle with two congruent sides. (p. 396)

─── **K** ───

kilogram (kg) A unit of mass in the metric system equal to 1,000 grams. (p. 284)

kiloliter (kL) A unit of capacity in the metric system equal to 1,000 liters. (p. 286)

kilometer (km) A unit of length in the metric system equal to 1,000 meters. (p. 282)

─── **L** ───

least common denominator (LCD) The least common multiple of the denominators of two or more fractions. (p. 166)

Example: 6 is the least common denominator of $\frac{1}{2}$ and $\frac{1}{3}$.

least common multiple (LCM) The least number, other than zero, that is a multiple of each of two or more numbers. (p. 166)

Example: 6 is the least common multiple of 2 and 3.

length The distance from one end of an object to the other. (p. 266)

like fractions Fractions that have the same denominator. (p. 167)

Example: $\frac{3}{4}$ and $\frac{1}{4}$ are like fractions.

line An endless collection of points along a straight path. A line has no endpoints. (p. 386)

Example:
E   F

line graph A graph used to show changes over a period of time. (p. 112)

line of symmetry A line that divides a figure in half into two congruent parts when folded. (p. 416)

Examples:

line plot A graphing method that shows each item of data on a number line. (p. 103)

line segment A part of a line having two endpoints. (p. 386)

Example:
A   D

liter (L) The basic unit of capacity in the metric system. (p. 286)

─── **M** ───

map Representation of part of the earth's surface on a plane often showing physical features, cities, etc. (p. 315)

mass The amount of matter an object contains that causes it to have weight. (p. 284)

mean The average of the numbers in a set of data. (p. 104)

median The middle number or average of the two middle numbers in a collection of data when the data are arranged in order from least to greatest. (p. 104)

mental math Performing a computation without the use of paper and pencil or a calculator. (p.14)

meter (m) The basic unit of length in the metric system. (p. 282)

metric system A measurement system that measures length in millimeters, centimeters, meters, and kilometers; capacity in liters and milliliters; mass in grams and kilograms; and temperature in degrees Celsius. (pp. 280–286)

metric ton (t) A unit of mass equal to 1,000 kilograms. (p. 284)

mile (mi) A unit of length in the customary system equal to 5,280 feet, or 1,760 yards. (p. 266)

milligram (mg) A unit of mass in the metric system equal to 0.001 gram. (p. 284)

milliliter (mL) A unit of capacity in the metric system equal to 0.001 liter. (p. 286)

millimeter (mm) A unit of length in the metric system equal to 0.001 meter. (p. 282)

mixed number A number written as a whole number and a fraction. (p. 164)
Example: $2\frac{5}{6}$

mode The number(s) that occur most often in a set of data. (p. 104)

multiple The product of a given number and another whole number. (p. 166)

Example: 2, 4, 6, . . .are multiples of 2.

negative integer An integer whose value is less than zero. (p. 472)
Examples: ⁻5, ⁻10, ⁻456

nonagon A polygon with nine sides. (p. 402)

Example:

numerator The number above the fraction bar in a fraction. (p. 144)
Example: $\frac{3}{4}$ The numerator is 3.

obtuse angle An angle with a measure greater than 90° but less than 180°. (p. 388)

obtuse triangle A triangle with one obtuse angle. (p. 396)

Example:

octagon A polygon with eight sides. (p. 402)
Example:

order of operations The order in which operations are done in calculations. Work inside parentheses is done first. Then multiplication and division from left to right, and finally addition and subtraction from left to right. (p. 46)

ordered pair A pair of numbers used to locate a point on a coordinate grid. (p. 486)

origin The point of intersection of the *x*- and *y*-axis on a coordinate grid. (p. 486)

outcome A result in a probability experiment. (p. 320)

ounce (oz) The basic unit of weight in the customary system. (p. 268)

Glossary

parallel lines Lines in the same plane that never intersect. (p. 392)

Example:

pattern A repeated sequence or design. (p. 52)

parallelogram A quadrilateral with each pair of opposite sides parallel and congruent. (p. 400)

Example: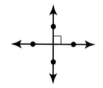

pentagon A polygon with five sides. (p. 402)

percent A special ratio that compares a number with 100. Percent means parts per hundred. (p. 344)

Example: 75% means 75 parts per hundred.

perimeter The distance around a polygon. (p. 434)

period In a large number, a group of three digits of a number, set off by commas. (p. 2)

Example: In 23,456,789; 456 is in the thousands period.

perpendicular lines Two lines that intersect to form right angles. (p. 392)

Example:

pi (π) The ratio of the circumference of a circle to its diameter. π is approximately 3.14 or $\frac{22}{7}$ (p. 452)

pictograph A graph that represents numerical data using pictures. (p. 109)

pint (pt) A unit of capacity in the customary system equal to 2 cups. (p. 270)

place value The value determined by the position of a digit in a number. (p. 2)

plane A flat surface extending endlessly in all directions. (p. 386)

point An exact location in space. (p. 386)

polygon A closed plane figure made up of line segments. (p. 402)

positive integer An integer greater than zero. (p. 472)

pound (lb) A unit of weight in the customary system equal to 16 ounces. (p. 268)

power The number of times a number is multiplied by itself, 4^2 is read "4 to the second power". Since 4^2 equals 16, the second power of 4 is 16. (p. 150) *See exponent.*

predict To declare in advance based on observation, experience, or reasoning. (p. 103)

prime factors Factors of a number that are prime. 2 and 3 are prime factors of 12. (p. 152)

prime factorization Writing a number as the product of its prime factors. (p. 153)

Example: $24 = 2 \times 2 \times 2 \times 3$

prime number A whole number greater than 1 with only two factors — itself and 1. (p. 152)

Example: 5, 7, and 11 are prime numbers.

principal An amount of money borrowed or loaned. (p. 370)

prism A space figure with two parallel and congruent bases that are polygons. (p. 431)

probability The ratio of the numbers of favorable outcomes to all outcomes of an experiment. (p. 322)

product The answer in multiplication. (p. 48)

property of zero The product of any number and zero is zero. (p. 48) See *zero property of multiplication.*

proper fraction A fraction in which the numerator is less than the denominator. (p. 199)

Examples: $\frac{3}{4}, \frac{5}{8}$

proportion A sentence that states that two ratios are equivalent. (p. 304)

Example: $\frac{7}{12} = \frac{14}{24}$

protractor An instrument used to measure or draw angles. (p. 388)

Example:

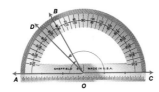

quadrilateral A polygon with four sides. (p. 400)

quart (qt) A unit of capacity in the customary system equal to 4 cups. (p. 270)

quotient The answer in division. (p. 76)

radius A line segment with one endpoint on the circle and the other endpoint at the center. (p. 418)

Example:

range The difference between the greatest and least numbers in a set of data. (p. 104)

rate A ratio that compares different kinds of units. (p. 312)

rate of interest A percent of the principal that determines how much interest is paid or owed. (p. 370)

ratio A comparison of two quantities. (p. 300)

Examples: 3 to 5, 3:5, $\frac{3}{5}$

ray A part of a line that has one endpoint and goes on and on in one direction. (p. 386)

reciprocals Two fractions whose product is 1. (p. 242)

Example: $\frac{3}{4} \times \frac{4}{3} = 1$

rectangle A parallelogram with four right angles. (p. 400)

rectangular prism A space figure whose faces are all rectangles. (p. 460)

Example:

Glossary

reflection The mirror image of a figure about a line of symmetry. (p. 408)

Example:

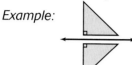

regular polygon A polygon with all sides congruent and all angles congruent. (p. 402)

Example:

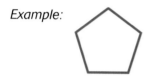

repeating decimal A decimal in which a digit or group of digits repeats endlessly. (p. 183)

rhombus A parallelogram with all sides congruent. (p. 400)

Example:

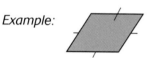

right angle An angle that measures 90°. (p. 388)

right triangle A triangle with one right angle. (p. 396)

rotation A transformation obtained by rotating a figure through a given angle about a point. (p. 408)

Example:

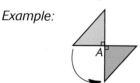

scale The ratio of the measurements in a drawing to the measurements of the actual objects. (p. 314)

scale drawing A drawing made so that actual measurements can be determined from the drawing by using the scale. (p. 314)

scalene triangle A triangle that has no congruent sides. (p. 396)

scatter plot A graph that represents two related sets of data as points on a coordinate grid. Also, scattergram. (p. 119)

scientific notation A number expessed as the product of two factors. The first factor is a number from 1 to 10. The second factor is a power of 10 in exponent form. (p. 99)

semicircle A half circle. (p. 418)

sequence A list of numbers that often follow a rule or a pattern. (p. 24)

set Any collection of things. (p. 198)

short division A method of dividing in which the multiplication and subtraction are performed mentally. (p. 74)

short word form A number written using both numerals and words. (p. 2)
Example: 2 thousand, 1 hundred, 36

side A segment used to form a polygon. A ray used to form an angle. (p. 386)

similar figures Figures that have the same shape but not necessarily the same size. (p. 414)

simplest form A fraction is in simplest form when the greatest common factor of the numerator and denominator is 1. Also, lowest terms. (p. 157)

simple interest The amount equal to principal × rate × time. (p. 370)

skew lines Lines that are not in the same plane and do not intersect . (p. 392)

Example:

simulation Representing the conditions of a problem using models, drawings, or a computer rather than actual objects or events. (p. 326)

space figure A geometric figure with points that are in more than one plane. (p. 461)

square A rectangle with all sides congruent. (p. 400)

square unit A square used to measure area. Each edge is equal to a unit of measure. (p. 436)

Example: a square centimeter, cm²

statistics Collecting, organizing, and analyzing data. (p. 100)

standard form A number written with commas separating groups of three digits. (p. 2)

stem-and-leaf plot A display that shows data in order of place value. The leaves are the last digits of the numbers. The stems are the digits to the left of the leaves. (p. 122)

straight angle An angle that measures 180°. (p. 389)

Example:

supplementary angles Two angles with a sum of 180°. (p. 391)

surface area The sum of the areas of all the faces of a space figure. (p. 456)

sum The answer in addition. (p. 20)

survey To collect data to study some characteristic of a group. (p. 101)

symmetry A figure has symmetry if it can be folded along a line so that the two resulting parts match exactly. (p. 416)

─────── **T** ───────

tally A mark made to keep score or to count. (p. 124)

tenth One of ten equal parts of a whole. (p. 4)

Example: $0.1, \frac{1}{10}$

thousandth One of one thousand equal parts of a whole. (p. 4)

Example: $0.001, \frac{1}{1,000}$

time zone A geographical region within which the same standard time is used. (p. 288)

ton (T) A unit of weight in the customary system equal to 2,000 pounds. (p. 268)

transformation Turning, sliding, or flipping a plane figure. (p. 408)

translation A change in position resulting from a slide without any turn or flip. (p. 408)

Example:

trapezoid A quadrilateral with only one pair of opposite sides parallel. (p. 400)

Example:

Glossary

tree diagram A diagram used to organize outcomes of an experiment to make them easier to count. (p. 328)

triangle A polygon with three sides. (p. 396)

U

unfair game A game in which not all players have an equal chance of winning. (p. 326)

unit fraction A fraction with a numerator of 1. (p. 197)

unit price The rate of price per unit of measure. (p. 312)

unit rate A ratio that compares a quantity to a unit of 1. (p. 312)

unlike fractions Fractions that have different denominators are unlike fractions. (p. 167)

Example: $\frac{1}{2}$ and $\frac{2}{3}$ are unlike fractions.

V

variable A letter used to stand for a number in an expression or equation. (p. 50)

Venn diagram A diagram that uses overlapping circles to show the relationships between groups of objects. (p. 158)

vertex The point of intersection of two sides of a polygon. The point of intersection of three edges of a space figure. (p. 386)

volume The number of cubic units that fit inside a space figure. (p. 460)

W

whole numbers The numbers in the set {0, 1, 2, 3, . . .}. (p. 2)

X

x- and y-axes The horizontal and vertical number lines that intersect to form a coordinate plane. (p. 486)

Example:

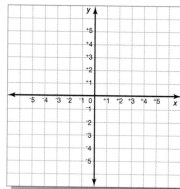

Y

yard (yd) A unit of length in the customary system equal to 36 inches, or 3 feet. (p. 266)

Z

zero property of multiplication The product of any number and zero is zero. (p. 48)
See *property of zero*.

Index

Index

Index

Index

Index

Credits

PHOTOGRAPHS

All photographs by Silver Burdett Ginn (SBG) unless otherwise noted.

Front cover: photo of LABYRINTH by Silver Burdett Ginn/courtesy, TOYS R US, Paramus, NJ.

ix: *l.* Jerry Jacka Photography; *m.l.* Artist: Meghan Welsh/Photo: Gail Dickel; *m.r.* Artist: Katie D'Agostino (grade 6)/Photo: Gail Dickel; *r.* Artist: Anna Zimmer (grade 6)/Photo: Gail Dickel. 0: Kevin Bennett for Silver Burdett Ginn. 0–1: Bob Daemmrich/Stock Boston. 2: Dan de Wilde for Silver Burdett Ginn; Richard Hutchings for Silver Burdett Ginn; Courtesy, Karyn Mueller, Doug Bates, Siok Tin Sodbinow, Alethia Carter, Sarah Carroll, Jennie Rakos, Helene Weintraub, Phyllis Hillwig, Alice Firgau, Gale Marx, Salita Mehta, & Marcin Rogalski. 4: *l.,m.l.,m.r.* Roger J. Cheng. 5: Dennis Kunkel/CNRI/Phototake. 6: Ray Mathis/The Stock Market. 7: *l.* Guido Alberto Rossi/The Image Bank; *r.* © Will & Deni McIntyre/Photo Researchers, Inc. 8: Corbis-Bettmann. 15: Steve Winter/© National Geographic Image Collection. 19: Runk/Schoenberger/Grant Heilman Photography, Inc. 20: *l.* © Calvin Larsen/Photo Researchers, Inc.; *m.* The Image Bank; *r.* Joe Baraban/The Stock Market. 22: Richard T. Nowitz Photography. 26: Kaku Kurita/The Gamma Liaison Network. 27: National Museum of American Art, Washington, DC/Hemphill Collection/Art Resource, NY. 28: *l.* Novovitch/The Gamma Liaison Network; *r.* Dennis Brack/Black Star. 31: © NASA/Science Photo Library/Photo Researchers, Inc. 32: Steve Winter/Black Star. 34: Tim Crosby/The Gamma Liaison Network. 34A: *t.,m.,b.* Tim Crosby/The Gamma Liaison Network. 42: Seth Resnik/Stock Boston. 43: © 1998 Michael Heron/Woodfin Camp & Associates. 49: Richard Hutchings for Silver Burdett Ginn. 50: *t.* Richard Hutchings for Silver Burdett Ginn. 53: © 1999 Paula Lerner/Woodfin Camp & Associates. 54: Paul Spinelli/NFL Photos. 55: Vernon Biever/NFL Photos. 57: Richard T. Nowitz Photography. 59: Runk/Schoenberger/Grant Heilman Photography. 61: NASA. 68: Leonard Lessin/Photography Alliance. 69: Breck Kent. 70: Southwest Museum, Los Angeles/Schenck & Schenck Photography. 71: *t.* Jerry Jacka Photography. 74: *l.* Paul Freed/Animals Animals; *r.* Joe McDonald/Animals Animals. 77: *t.* Grant Heilman Photography; *b.* Richard T. Nowitz Photography. 78: *r.* Richard Hutchings for Silver Burdett Ginn. 81: Richard Hutchings for Silver Burdett Ginn. 83: Lee Boltin/Boltin Picture Library. 84: Sao Paolo, Museo d'Arte/Art Resource, NY. 88: *m.t.* Alon Reininger/The Stock Market. 88A: *b.* Myrleen Ferguson/PhotoEdit. 88: *b.* Scott Gog/The Stock Market. 88A: *5th from top* William Waterfall/The Stock Market; *13th from top* David Pollack/The Stock Market. 100–101: Nickelodeon. 103: John Biever/Sports Illustrated. 104: Jack Vartoogian. 105: © Marbeth 1996/Students of Alvin Ailey American Dance Center. 108: Bob Daemmrich/Stock Boston. 112: Warner Brothers/Motion Picture & Television Photo Archive. 113: *l.* Sygma Photo News; *m.l.* Gabi Rona/ABC/Motion Picture & Television Photo Archive; *m.r.* Universal/Motion Picture & Television Photo Archive; *r.* Sygma Photo News. 117: Benno Friedman/Outline Press Syndicate, Inc. 122: *l.* John Biever/Sports Illustrated; *r.* Maco/Focus On Sports. 124: Courtesy, Ringling Bros. and Barnum & Bailey Combined Shows. 140: Martin Fox. 140–141: Martin Fox. 143: Charles Thatcher/Tony Stone Images. 145: John M. Roberts/The Stock Market. 147: Mary Kate Denny/PhotoEdit. 148: Larry E. Neibergall/Tony Stone Images. 149: *t.* Joan Iaconetti/Bruce Coleman Inc.; *b.* Stuart Westmorland/Tony Stone Images. 154: Gale Zucker/Stock Boston. 157: *l.* Patricia Bruno/Positive Images; *r.* © Blair Seitz/Photo Researchers, Inc. 165: *bkgd.* Arthur C. Smith III/Grant Heilman Photography. 168: Lionel Trains, Inc. 171: Michael Newman/PhotoEdit. 175: Kevin Syms/David R. Frazier Photolibrary. 184: Dennie Eagleson. 184–185: Stephen Frisch/Stock Boston. 188: *bkgd.* Terry Donnelly/Tom Stack & Associates. 194: Lawrence Migdale/Stock Boston. 197: British Museum/Michael Holford. 202: © Norris Taylor/Photo Researchers, Inc. 212: John N. Trager/Visuals Unlimited. 213: *l.* Kim Taylor/Bruce Coleman, Inc.; *m.l.,m.r.* Kim Taylor/Bruce Coleman, Inc.; *r.* Jane Burton/Bruce Coleman, Inc. 230: *l.* Ian Howarth; *r.* Ian Howarth. 236: *b.* David Young-Wolff/PhotoEdit. 242: *t.* Artist: Meghan Sodoro (grade 6)/Photo: Gail Dickel; *m.* Artist: Anna Zimmer (grade 6)/Photo: Gail Dickel. 243: *l.* Artist: Claire Bieker (grade 4)/Photo: Gail Dickel; *m.l.* Artist: Katie D'Agostino (grade 6)/Photo: Gail Dickel; *m.r.* Artist: Meghan Welsh/Photo: Gail Dickel; *r.* Jerry Jacka Photography. 245: Daniel R. Westergren/© National Geographic Image Collection. 249: © Renee Lynn/Photo Researchers, Inc. 252A: *l.* Dave Bartruff/Stock Boston; *m.* Janet Gill/Tony Stone Images; *r.* Kunio Owaki/The Stock Market. 264: Jim Herren Photography for Silver Burdett Ginn. 264–265: The Terry Wild Studio. 267: Focus On Sports. 271: Matthew Stockman/Allsport. 274: *l.* Tony Duffy/NBC/Allsport; *r.* Steven E. Sutton/

Duomo. 281: Susie Howard/The Stock Market. 284: David Madison. 285: David Madison/Tony Stone Images. 297: Robert Brenner/PhotoEdit. 300: *b.* Faith Ringgold. 302: *t.r.* American Quilter's Society. 303: *t.,m.,b.* Reprinted with permission from *Small Folk Quilters*, ©1989, by Ingrid Rogler, published by Chitra Publications. 309: © Lawrence Migdale/Photo Researchers, Inc. 311: *t.* The Granger Collection, New York. 319: Jessica Ehlers/Bruce Coleman, Inc. 348: *l.,r.* Cynthia Johnson/The Gamma Liaison Network. 357: © 1999 Adam Woolfitt/Woodfin Camp & Associates. 362: *b.* Aneal F. Vohra/Unicorn Stock Photos. 368: *t.* Dennis Degnan/Westlight. 371: Courtesy, Young Americans Bank, Denver, CO. 386: Bonnie Kamin/PhotoEdit. 391: Bill Aron/PhotoEdit. 392: David R. Frazier Photolibrary. 396: Color Box/FPG International. 400: Annie Griffiths Belt. 402: *m.,b.l.* Tony Freeman/PhotoEdit; *b.r.* Cindy Charles/PhotoEdit. 408: *l.* Thomas Braise/The Stock Market; *m.* Don Mason/The Stock Market; *r.* Doug Pensinger/Allsport. 414: Richard T. Nowitz/© National Geographic Image Collection. 418: Guy Marche/FPG International. 432: Bill Barley for Silver Burdett Ginn. 432–433: Bill Barley for Silver Burdett Ginn. 434: Alex S. MacLean/Landslides. 435: *t.,b.* Alex S. MacLean/Landslides. 439: Alex S. MacLean/Landslides. 451: Chris Luneski/Image Cascade. 457: *b.* Richard Hutchings for Silver Burdett Ginn. 458A: *l.* Mark C. Burnett/Stock Boston. 470: J.D. Griggs/US Geological Survey. 470–471: Philip Rosenberg Photography. 472: *l.* © David Vaughan/Science Photo Library/Photo Researchers, Inc.; *r.* © Tom Hollyman/Photo Researchers, Inc. 475: *t.* David E. Myers/Tony Stone Images; *b.* John Shaw/Bruce Coleman, Inc. 478: Courtesy, Meadows Farms Golf Course. 483: Thomas J. Abercrombie/© National Geographic Image Collection. 495: © Francois Gohier/Photo Researchers, Inc. 498: © Rafael Macia/Photo Researchers, Inc. 499: © Rafael Macia/Photo Researchers, Inc. 501: Tim Flach/Tony Stone Images. 503: *t.* Silvestris/Gross/Peter Arnold, Inc. 504A: AP/Wide World Photos. 505: Alan Schein/The Stock Market.

IlIUSTRATIONS

4: Larry Jost. 9: Frank Riccio. 10–11: Tate Nation. 14–15: Patrick Gnan. 26,30,: Tate Nation. 35: Gary Torrisi. 42: Tate Nation. 46–47: Rick Stromoski. 48–49: Skip Baker. 50–51: Eric Larson. 56,58: Patrick Gnan. 60,62–63: Carlyn Iverson. 66: Tim Blough. 74: Rick Stromoski. 88–89: Stuart Zastrow. 91: Eric Larson. 99: Jeff Seaver. 106,108: Susan Tolonen. 110: Roger Roth. 112,114: Tate Nation. 120–121: Eric Larson. 124: Susan Tolonen. 129: Andrew Shiff. 136–137: Tate Nation. 139: Gary Torrisi. 143,145,147: Olivia McElroy. 150: Jody Jobe. 154,157: Olivia McElroy. 159: Garry Colby. 162–163,165,168: Olivia McElroy. 170–171: Sarah Jane English. 171: Olivia McElroy. 172: Dan McGowan. 173: Dale Gustafson. 174: Sarah Jane English; Olivia McElroy. 175: Olivia McElroy. 182: Jody Jobe. 191: Eric Larson. 195: Tim Blough. 197: Frank Riccio. 200–202: Karen Minot. 204: Stuart Zastrow. 207: Stuart Zastrow. 211: Karen Minot. 214: David Uhl. 215: Dale Gustafson. 222: Jody Jobe. 223: David Goldin. 228–229: David Uhl, Roger Roth. 230: Jim Frazier. 230–231: Roger Roth. 231: David Uhl. 233: Jim Frazier. 234: Manuel King. 240: Jody Jobe. 242–243: Linda Montgomery. 245: Jim Frazier. 246–247: Dan McGowan. 253: Gary Torrisi. 261: David Goldin. 262: Gary Torrisi. 263: Stuart Zastrow. 266: Dale Gustafson. 267: Tim Blough. 272: Tim Blough. 272: Mary Anne Ganley. 273: Garry Colby. 277: Mary Anne Ganley. 281: Eric Larson. 282: M. Ganley. 284: Tim Blough, Mary Anne Ganley. 286: Dale Gustafson, Mary Anne Ganley 288: Geoffry McCormak. 289: Dale Gustafson. 296: Sam Ward. 300: Margaret Cusak. 302–303: Margaret Cusak. 306: Garry Colby. 312–313: Barbara Freidman. 314: Dale Gustafson. 316: Dale Gustafson. 329: Douglas Schneider. 331: Eric Larsen. 332: Tate Nation. 333: Gary Torrisi. 337: Dale Gustafson. 339: Dale Gustafson. 341: Rick Stromoski. 348: Dan McGowan. 355: Tate Nation. 357: Dan McGowan. 361: Tate Nation. 366: Tim Blough. 370: Tate Nation. 375: Babara Friedman. 377: Babara Friedman. 382–383: Nadine Sokol. 386: Don Baker. 388: Patrick Gnan. 392: Lehner and Whyte; Don Baker. 393: Patrick Gnan. 395: Bob Berry. 396: Don Baker. 399: Patrick Gnan; Rob Schuster. 400: Don Baker. 402: Don Baker. 412: Lehner and Whyte. 414: Patrick Gnan. 416: Lehner and Whyte. 419: Lehner and Whyte. 420: Jody Jobe. 423A: Michael Sloan. 430: Jody Jobe. 431,436: Dale Gustafson. 440: Randy Hamblin. 443: Patrick Gnan. 446: Dale Gustafson. 449: Dale Gustafson; Susan Johnston Carlson. 455: Stuart Zastrow. 457: Patrick Gnan. 458: Susan Spellman. 459: Patrick Gnan. 460–462,466–467: Dale Gustafson. 468: Randy Hamblin. 469: Dale Gustafson. 473: Carlyn Iverson; Tate Nation. 476,484: Carlyn Iverson. 485: Mary Anne Ganley. 486–487: Tate Nation. 487: Geo Systems. 492–493,495: Tate Nation. 496–497: Patrick Gnan. 501: Michael Sloan. 502: Carlyn Iverson. 504: Bernard Adnet. 504A: Tate Nation. 512–513: Patrick Gnan. 539: Andrew Shiff. 541: Garry Colby. 542: Partrick Gnan. 543: Garry Colby.

Becoming a Better Test Taker

You've learned a lot of math skills this year! These skills will help you with your school work and with everyday activities outside of school. How can you show what you've learned in math? One way is by taking tests.

Did you know you could do better on tests just by knowing how to take a test? The test-taking strategies on these pages can help you become a better test taker. They might also help you think of test questions as a fun challenge! When you take a test, try to use these strategies to show all you know.

Multiple Choice Questions
Know Your ABCs!

For multiple choice questions, you are given several answer choices for a problem. Once you have solved the problem, you need to choose the right answer from the choices that are given.

1 Ⓐ Ⓑ Ⓒ Ⓓ Ⓔ

2 Ⓐ Ⓑ Ⓒ Ⓓ Ⓔ

3 Ⓐ Ⓑ Ⓒ Ⓓ Ⓔ

Example

$13,266 \div 6 =$ ▦

A 221   **B** 2,120   **C** 2,200   **D** 2,211   **E** Not Here

Think It Through

Read   Did I read the problem carefully?
                I need to divide 13,266 by 6.

Cross Out   Are there any answers that are not reasonable?
                221 has no digit in the thousands place, so I can cross out answer A.

Solve   What is $13,266 \div 6$?
                $13,266 \div 6 = 2,211$

Check   Is there a way that I can check my answer?
                I can multiply: $2,211 \times 6 = 13,266$.

Choose   Which letter is next to my answer?
                D is next to the answer 2,211.

Try It!

1 $32 \times 87 =$ ▦

   A 278   **B** 2,414   **C** 2,784
   D 27,840   **E** Not Here

2 $56,000 \div 70 =$ ▦

   A 80   **B** 700   **C** 800
   D 900   **E** Not Here

3 $686 \times 12 =$ ▦

   A 823   **B** 6,162   **C** 6,860
   D 8,232   **E** Not Here

TESTING TIPS

▷ Estimate whenever you can before you solve a problem. You can use an estimate to check whether an answer is reasonable, or to identify answer choices that are not reasonable.

▷ Reread the question and check your work before choosing "Not Here."

▷ Make sure you fill in the letter on the answer sheet that matches your answer!

Multistep Questions
One Step at a Time

Sometimes you need to do more than one step to answer a multiple choice question.

▷ Always look at all of the answer choices that are listed.

▷ Even if you find your answer among the choices check your work. Answers that come from making common mistakes are usually included in the choices!

▷ If you are having trouble answering a question, go on to the next question and come back to the more difficult question later.

Example

> **There are 1,200 ants in an ant farm. Some escape and there are 828 left. Half of the escaped ants are found. How many still need to be found?**
>
> **A** 146   **B** 160   **C** 186   **D** 400   **E** Not Here

Think It Through

Read Did I read the problem carefully?
I need to find out how many ants still need to be found.

Cross Out Are there any answers that are not reasonable?
The number of ants that escaped is about 400, so I can cross out answer D.

Solve How many ants still need to be found?
1,200 − 828 = 372 and 372 ÷ 2 = 186.

Check Is there a way that I can check my answer?
I can work backwards:
186 × 2 = 372 and 372 + 828 = 1,200.

Choose Which letter is next to my answer?
D is next to the answer 186.

Try It!

1 **Sharon and her brother Jack baked 12 dozen cookies to sell at a food booth. If 5 dozen cookies were peanut butter and the rest were oatmeal, how many cookies were oatmeal?**

   A 144   **B** 84   **C** 72   **D** 60   **E** Not Here

2 **The club wants to buy a present for each of 2 members who are moving. Each present costs $17.93. How much should each of the remaining 22 members contribute to pay for the presents?**

   A $1.63   **B** $2.00   **C** $8.97

   D $16.32   **E** Not Here

Measurement Questions
Measure Up!

Sometimes you will need to use a ruler to help you solve a multiple choice question.

Example

You want to buy a frame for the picture shown at the right. Use a ruler to measure the size of the picture to the nearest eighth of an inch.

A 1 inch by 1 inch

B $1\frac{1}{4}$ inches by $1\frac{1}{2}$ inches

C $1\frac{1}{4}$ inches by $1\frac{7}{8}$ inches

D 2 inches by 2 inches

Think It Through

Read   Did I read the problem carefully?
I need to use the inch side of the ruler.

Cross Out   Are there any answers that are not reasonable?
I know that the picture is not a square so I can cross out answers A and D.

Solve   What can I do to solve the problem?
I will measure the width and the length of the picture. It measures $1\frac{1}{4}$ inches by $1\frac{7}{8}$ inches.

Check   Is there a way to check my answer?
I can measure again.

Choose   Which letter is next to my answer?
The letter C is next to $1\frac{1}{4}$ inches by $1\frac{7}{8}$ inches.

- Make sure you are using the correct side of the ruler when measuring.

- Make sure you line up the 0 mark on the ruler with one end of the object you are going to measure.

- Check to see how precisely you need to measure the object, such as to the nearest $\frac{1}{2}$ in. or the nearest $\frac{1}{4}$ in.

Try It!

Rose rode from her house to Sally's house, and from there to the gas station. Rose's house is 6 km from Sally's house. Use a ruler to find the distance from Sally's house to the station.

Rose's House   Sally's House   Gas Station

Scale: 1 cm = 2 km

A 5 km   **B** 6 km   **C** 8 km   **D** 10 km

Short Answer Questions
The Write Stuff

Sometimes a test question asks you not only to *solve* a problem but to show *how* you solved the problem. For questions like these, you need to be able to write your thoughts on paper.

Example

Each student invented one creature for a science class experiment that would take three weeks. David invented a "tribble," which tripled its size every week. If the tribble weighed 108 grams at the end of the experiment, how much did it weigh when the experiment started?

Think It Through

Read   What am I being asked to write about?
              I need to find how much a tribble weighed at the beginning of a science experiment.

Plan   What can I do to solve the problem?
              I can find out what the tribble weighed each week.

Solve   What is the answer to the problem?
              The tribble weighed 4 grams when the science experiment started.

Explain   How did I get my answer?
              First I multiplied $3 \times 3 \times 3 = 27$, since the experiment lasted for 3 weeks. Then I divided the total weight of the tribble, 108 grams, by 27 and got 4 grams as my answer.

Try It!

Answer Questions 1 and 2. Explain how you got your answer.

1. Camille picks oranges. Each day she picks twice as many as the day before. On the fifth day she picks 64 oranges. How many did she pick on the first day?

2. Vicky and Todd bowl together. The combined score of their first game was 280. Vicky's score was 40 more than Todd's. What was each of their scores?

> Be sure to follow the directions carefully. Sometimes you will be asked to write an explanation in words. Other times you will be asked to show your work in numbers or with drawings.

> Be prepared to take more time to answer short answer questions than to answer multiple choice questions.

> You can usually get partial credit for an answer. So, even if you can't solve the whole problem, write what you can!

Long Answer Questions
In Your Own Words

Long answer questions are like short answer questions, only they are longer and often have more than one step.

> Remember to explain *how* you got your answer.

> When you're finished writing, read the question again to be sure you've answered it completely.

> Keep trying! If your first strategy doesn't work, try another one. You might get partial credit even if you can't find an answer.

> Long answer questions take longer to answer! Be patient, and take your time.

Example

Archaeologists on a dig have excavated two sites in an ancient city. Each site has different depths and has been divided into levels. Site A has 35 levels. Each is 12 inches deep. Site B has 41 levels. Each is 12 inches deep. A tunnel that is 3 feet deep has been found at the bottom of Site A. Which excavated site is deeper, including the tunnel?

Think It Through

Read   What am I being asked to write about?
I need to compare the depths of two excavated sites.

Plan   What can I do to solve the problem?
I can find the total depth of each site and see which one is the deeper site.

Solve   What is the answer to the problem?
Site B is deeper than Site A.

Explain How did I get my answer?
I found the depth of Site A first:
35 × 12 inches = 420 inches. Then I changed the tunnel depth from 3 feet to 36 inches:
420 + 36 = 456 inches. To find the depth of Site B, I multiplied 41 times 12 inches and got 492 inches. Site B is deeper than Site A.

Try It!

Answer Questions 1 and 2. Explain how you got your answers.

1. While on a trip, Ellen sent letters and postcards to her friends. She spent $2.16 on stamps. If stamps for her letters cost $0.32 and stamps for postcards cost $0.20, how many postcards and letters did Ellen send?

2. Karen went horseback riding on a trail. She rode 5 miles east and then 7 miles north. After she rested, she rode 6 miles south. How far is Karen from where she started?